SPARKNOTES
STEP-BY-STEP GUIDE TO
THE
GED

SPARKNOTES®
STEP-BY-STEP GUIDE TO
THE
GED

SPARK
NOTES

A DIVISION OF BARNES & NOBLE PUBLISHING

Spark Publishing
A Division of Barnes & Noble
120 Fifth Avenue
New York, NY 10011

Please submit all comments and questions or report errors to www.sparknotes.com/errors.

Printed and bound in Canada.

ISBN-13: 978-1-4114-0246-1
ISBN-10: 1-4114-0246-4

CONTENTS

PART II

CONTENTS

PART III

CHAPTER 8

PRACTICE TESTS 401

INTRODUCTION

You are holding this book in your hands, so it seems safe to assume that you're thinking about taking the GED test and earning your high school equivalency. Congratulations! You've taken the first step toward achieving your goals. And you've picked the right book for the job.

The *Step-by-Step Guide to the GED* has been carefully organized and streamlined to provide the most effective GED preparation in the least amount of time. SparkNotes' *Step-by-Step Guide to the GED* focuses only on what the GED *really* tests. Our GED experts are not interested in giving you extra bulk and the illusion of extra preparation. Instead, we give you only what you need to know.

You are not alone in taking the GED. Each year, almost 1 million adults throughout the country take the GED. Passing the GED enables you to pursue better jobs, promotions, a college education, and other personal goals.

A QUICK LOOK AT THE GED

The GED (General Educational Development) tests measure the skills and knowledge that are usually gained during four years of high school. When you pass the GED tests, you earn a GED credential, which certifies that you have the knowledge and skills equivalent to a high school diploma.

The GED tests cover five core subject areas:

- Language Arts, Writing
- Social Studies
- Science
- Language Arts, Reading
- Mathematics

The chart below shows the number of questions and the time limits for each of the tests:

Test	Number of Questions	Time Limit
Language Arts, Writing (Part I)	50 questions	75 minutes
Language Arts, Writing (Part II)	1 essay	45 minutes
Social Studies	50 questions	70 minutes
Science	50 questions	80 minutes
Language Arts, Reading	40 questions	65 minutes
Mathematics (Part I)	25 questions with optional use of a calculator	45 minutes
Mathematics (Part II)	25 questions without use of a calculator	45 minutes

If you add all that time up, you'll realize that the tests take a little more than 7 hours to complete. That's a long time. The good news is that you usually won't have to take all the tests in one sitting. Contact your local GED testing center for more information on how many tests you can take at one time, as different states and territories have different rules about this.

Most of the questions you face on the GED are multiple-choice questions with five possible answers listed. You must select the best answers to these questions and darken the circles on a grid in the answer booklet. In addition, the Language Arts, Writing test requires you to write a timed essay on a topic of general interest.

The questions on each test cover a variety of skills. Some test your knowledge of a subject; others ask you to apply information to a real-life situation, analyze the relationships between ideas, form theories, or evaluate data. Let's look at exactly what each of the five tests covers.

LANGUAGE ARTS, WRITING

Grammar? Usage? Dangling participles? We're afraid so. The Language Arts, Writing test assesses your knowledge of grammar, including sentence structure, usage, and mechanics, as well as paragraph organization. Don't know your comma splices from your split infinitives? Fear not. You do not have to name the sentence error. You only need to recognize that it's wrong and correct it. This book will help ensure that you can. The Writing test is divided into two parts. The multiple-choice questions in Part I ask you to identify how to best correct, revise, and reorganize sentences. These questions are based on workplace, how-to, and informational documents.

In Part II, you write an essay stating your opinion on a topic of general interest. The essay does not require you to have particular knowledge of a subject; you simply draw on your experiences. Like the multiple-choice questions, the essay tests your grasp of basic grammar and your command of written English, including how well you develop and organize your ideas. You write the essay on the two pages of lined paper included in your answer booklet. Chapter 3 (Language Arts, Writing) provides you with a sure-fire plan of action to help you breeze through the essay worry-free.

SOCIAL STUDIES

Who is buried in Grant's Tomb? When was the Battle of 1812? Ah, if only all the questions were this easy. But the good news is that the Social Studies test does *not* quiz you on facts. Instead, you must understand and interpret information included in short passages, cartoons, charts, tables, graphs, maps, photographs, and/or figures. The test covers United States, Canadian, and world history, as well as geography, civics, government, and economics. If you understand what you read and can draw conclusions, then you'll ace the Social Studies test. We give you all the review you need, so no question can take you by surprise.

SCIENCE

While you may understand the chemistry between you and that beautiful creature you see walking to work every day, are you completely lost when it comes to atoms, molecules, and matter? Well, don't worry too much. The science section tests your ability to understand, interpret, and apply scientific information. All the information you need to answer the questions is provided in short passages, graphs, charts, tables, maps, and figures. In other words, you don't have to bring a ton of knowledge with you to the test; you only need to become comfortable working with the information you get. The questions cover the areas of physics, chemistry, life science, earth science, and space science.

LANGUAGE ARTS, READING

Finally, a test on something you already know how to do. In fact, you are doing it right now. The Language Arts, Reading test measures your ability to understand and interpret a variety of texts. You are presented with workplace and academic reading selections followed by questions. The questions require you to understand, apply, and analyze information in the selections. We give you plenty of practice so that you are completely comfortable on test day.

About 75 percent of the selections are literary. They include at least one selection from:

- Poetry
- Drama
- Prose fiction before 1920
- Prose fiction between 1920 and 1960
- Prose fiction after 1960

The test also includes two nonfiction selections, which may include essays, critical reviews of visual and performing arts, and workplace or community documents. Workplace and community documents include legal documents, letters, and excerpts from manuals.

MATHEMATICS

The Mathematics test is one of the longest. Not quite as confident as you want to be when it comes to variables and equations? No problem. Chapter 7 (Mathematics) guides you step by step through everything you need to know. The Mathematics test assesses your understanding of mathematical concepts and your ability to apply those concepts to real-world situations. The test covers four main areas: number operations and number sense; measurement and geometry; data analysis, statistics, and probability; and algebra, functions, and patterns.

You must interpret diagrams, charts, graphs, and drawings. A page of math formulas is provided for your reference. We go over this page of formulas to make sure you know how to get the most out of them.

**THE
GED**

On Part I of the Mathematics test, you have the option to use a Casio *fx*-260 calculator to compute answers. The calculator is provided at the testing center along with instructions on how to use it.

Part II tests your ability to estimate and use mental math. You may not use the calculator on Part II.

Twenty percent of the Mathematics test requires you to construct your own answers. With these questions, you must record answers on either a standard or coordinate plane grid. The test includes directions on how to fill in these answers, and we go over them in the Mathematics chapter.

REGISTERING FOR THE GED

Your first step in preparing for the GED should be to find out if you are eligible to take the tests. You are eligible if you meet the following requirements:

- You are not enrolled in high school.
- You have not graduated from high school.
- You are at least 16 years old.
- You meet your state, provincial, or territorial requirements regarding age, residency, and the length of time since leaving school.

To determine whether you may take the GED tests and to find your local GED testing center, call the GED Hotline: **1-800-62-MYGED** or **1-800-626-9433.** You may also call the GED office in Washington, D.C., at (202) 939-9490. There are about 3,400 official GED testing centers.

The center provides key state-by-state information, such as:

- Residency requirements.
- How much it costs to take the tests.
- When the tests are given.
- What identification is required.
- Where to find a GED instructional program.

Adult education centers, community colleges, and school boards run GED testing centers. You can also check your telephone listings under "GED," "Adult Education," or "Continuing Education" to find the nearest GED testing center.

Another way to get information about the GED is to ask a librarian at your local library. You can also check the official Web site for the GED testing service: http://www.acenet.edu/clll/ged.

This is the Web site of the American Council on Education, which is the group that writes the GED tests. This site provides lots of information about how and where to sign up for the tests. You can also download additional practice questions.

FREQUENTLY ASKED QUESTIONS

WHERE DO YOU TAKE THE TESTS?

There are 3,400 official GED testing centers in the United States and Canada. There are also more than 100 international sites where you can take the GED. If you live outside the United States or Canada and wish to take the GED tests, contact your regional registration center for information about testing locations and times.

HOW LONG DO THE TESTS TAKE?

It takes 7 hours and 5 minutes to complete all five tests. In some places, you must take all the tests in one or two sittings. In other places, you can take one test each time you go to the testing center. Call your local GED testing center to find out about the procedures in your area.

HOW MUCH DOES IT COST?

The cost of taking the GED tests varies from place to place. In some states, the tests are free, while in others they may cost up to $80. To find out about fees, call your local GED testing center.

HOW ARE THE TESTS SCORED?

Each of the five tests is scored separately on a scale ranging from 200 (the lowest) to 800 (the highest). You need a standard score of 410 or above to pass each of the GED tests. You must also earn an overall average score of 450 for all five tests to pass the GED.

Some states may set the passing scores higher than these minimums. Most places, however, use these passing scores. To find out what the passing scores are in your area, ask the local GED testing center.

To receive a passing score on each test, you generally need to answer 60 to 65 percent of the questions correctly. Each correct answer is worth one point. There are no deductions for incorrect answers. All points are then converted to a standard score for each individual subject test. For the Language Arts, Writing test, you receive a combined score for the multiple-choice and the essay portions. We discuss how the essay is scored in the Language Arts, Writing chapter on pages 96–108.

After you complete the GED tests, you receive a GED transcript. Your transcript shows your standard scores for each test and your percentile ranks. If your percentile rank is 75, that means that you have outperformed 75 out of 100 GED test-takers.

Your local GED testing center can tell you how to get your scores. If you don't pass all the GED tests the first time, you can take one or more of the tests again. Check with your local GED contact person to find out what the requirements are for retaking a test. In some cases, you must wait for a few months before retaking the test. In some areas, you also have to take a GED preparatory course before taking the test again.

THE
GED

THE
GED

WHAT IF THERE ARE SPECIAL CIRCUMSTANCES?

Special accommodations are available for candidates who have physical disabilities, learning disabilities, attention-deficit or hyperactivity disorder, psychological disabilities, chronic health issues, and other disabilities.

Tests can be taken in U.S. English-language Braille, U.S. and Canadian English-language audiocassette, and large-print editions. Candidates who have documented disabilities may also receive extended time, supervised breaks, use of scribes, or private rooms for testing. Candidates with disabilities should request forms for different accommodations from your GED testing center.

You may also be able to take the GED tests in Spanish or French. Contact the local GED testing center to find out if these versions are available in your area.

HOW TO USE THIS BOOK

The *Step-by-Step Guide to the GED* gives you exactly what you need to do your best on the GED—no more, no less. When you focus on exactly what you need to know, you get the most out of your study time and improve your score. To help you get the most out of our book, we've created a four-step study plan.

4 STEPS TO GED SUCCESS

STEP 1: UNCOVER YOUR STRENGTHS AND WEAKNESSES

The GED is long. More than 7 hours long, in fact. That's a lot of test-taking time and a lot of material to cover. Trying to study everything covered on the test is a tall order for anyone, especially someone as busy as you. Good test-takers focus on the subjects they need the most help with before reviewing other material.

To help you find out exactly where to focus your time, we have designed five pretests. Chapter 1 contains shortened versions of each GED subject test. After you complete each pretest, look at the scoring explanations that follow and you will see how much you need to study in each particular subject area.

The answers and explanations tell you why the correct answer is correct and how to eliminate incorrect choices. In addition, the explanations indicate which topic is being tested. For example, an explanation for a Language Arts, Writing question may indicate that the question tested punctuation and spelling. An explanation for a Social Studies question may test your understanding of visual materials. Therefore, after you take each pretest, you can tell not only which subjects you need to work on, but also which topics within each subject area need more work. You will see the topic being tested indicated at the end of the explanation, following the picture of a ladder rung, like this: 🟠.

Because Part II of the Language Arts, Writing test requires you to write an essay, there is no pretest for this section. To determine how prepared you are to write the essay, simply review pages 96–108 in Chapter 3 (Language Arts, Writing). These pages tell you what the essay questions look like and what the test-makers expect from an essay. If you need to learn more, the chapter tells you how to write a successful essay.

STEP 2: LEARN TEST-TAKING BASICS

In addition to studying all of the subjects that are covered on a test, good test-takers also know *how* to take a test.

Chapter 2 (Test-Taking Basics) helps you become an expert test-taker. This chapter offers the general strategies and tips you need to score high on the GED. It explains guessing strategies, including using "process of elimination" to increase your scores. Reading this chapter helps you face the GED with confidence in your test-taking skills.

STEP 3: MASTER EACH SUBJECT WITH THE LADDER METHOD

There's a lot of material to cover, but we help you stay on top of it. We created a ladder structure in each chapter that you can use as a study tool. Think of it as your personal guide.

This book contains one chapter for each GED subject test. Each subject chapter provides specific strategies you need in order to tackle the types of questions that appears on that subject test. Each subject is broken down into a certain number of steps, which we show you as rungs on a ladder. For example, here is the Language Arts, Writing ladder:

Rung 1: Introduction
Rung 2: Capitalization and Spelling
Rung 3: Punctuation
Rung 4: Verbs
Rung 5: Pronouns
Rung 6: Common Sentence Errors
Rung 7: Coordination and Subordination
Rung 8: Misplaced and Dangling Modifiers
Rung 9: Parallel Structure
Rung 10: Restructuring Paragraphs
Rung 11: The Essay

Each rung is designed to be a manageable chunk of information that you can work through in one study session (a little less than an hour). The first rung of every chapter is always an introduction to the test. On this rung, you review the basics for each test, including the types of questions it asks and key strategies to help you beat each test. For each rung after that, we give you:

- A subject review.
- Sample questions.
- A practice set of questions to assess whether you need further review or have mastered this topic and are ready to move on to the next step.

Most subject ladders move from the basics, such as Capitalization and Spelling in the ladder seen on the previous page, to more complicated skills, such as writing an essay. Because you assess yourself after every single step, you can be confident that by the time you reach the top rung, you have mastered all the skills you need to do your best on that GED subject test.

As you work through the material on a particular step, the corresponding rung of the ladder on that page is high-lighted. When you move to the next step, the next rung is highlighted. The ladder icon is printed on each page. With a quick glance, you can tell where you are in your study process.

Each rung on the ladder is a manageable chunk of information that you can work through in one study session (a little less than an hour).

STEP 4: MEASURE YOUR PROGRESS

After you have studied all the subject sections, it is time to take the GED practice test at the back of this book and see where you stand. You may take all the tests at once or one at a time as you finish your review of each subject. Use this book in the way that best suits your needs. After finishing the practice tests, review any subjects or topics that you feel you need to work on by using the answers and explanations provided.

The skill being tested is indicated at the end of each explanation and preceded by an icon. Therefore, you can return to the corresponding rung in this book and review any category that you still need help with.

Ready to get started? Then let's get right to the pretests.

THE
GED

PART

I

CHAPTER

1

DIAGNOSTICS PRETESTS

CHAPTER

1

DIAGNOSTIC
PRETESTS

THE

GED

GUIDELINES

DIAGNOSTIC PRETESTS

Before you study for the GED tests, you must evaluate your strengths and weaknesses so you know which subjects you most need to study. That's the purpose of the pretests in this chapter. If you find out your skills in some areas are sharper than you thought, don't waste time studying those subjects you already know. If you work through these diagnostic pretests, you'll know exactly what you have to do to pass all of the GED tests.

We have created one diagnostic pretest for each GED subject test, and each diagnostic has ten questions. That's just a fraction of the length of a real test, but it's enough to predict how well you would do on the real test. You do not have to prepare for these diagnostics. Just find a quiet spot where you can concentrate, and plan to spend one to two hours working through all the pretests.

Note the time you start and finish each test so you can estimate how many minutes you spend on each question. If you find that you got most of the questions on one test right, but it took you more than an hour to finish the ten questions, you probably need some review on that subject and some work on your time management. This book can help you with both.

After you finish taking the tests, turn to the Pretest Answers and Explanations, which start on page 21. A scoring guide at the end of each test explanation helps you evaluate how well you did. The explanations indicate which topic within the subject is tested by each question, so you can figure out where you need to focus.

PRETEST: LANGUAGE ARTS, WRITING, PART I

Directions: Choose the one best answer to each question.

Questions 1 through 6 refer to the following letter.

February 18, 2005

Fastball Computing
2000 Millennium Drive
New York, NY 10087

Dear Sir or Madam:

(A)
(1) I am writing to notify you that I am rejecting the goods described below, which were not delivered in an acceptable state. (2) The goods is enclosed in this package, and I am demanding a complete cash refund.

(B)
(3) On February 12, 2004, you agreed to deliver the enclosed laser printer according to the information outlined in the attached copies of the receipt and advertisement. (4) You will state that the printer would be free from defects and in proper working order. (5) Fortunately, when the merchandise was delivered on February 17, I discovered that the printer was missing the paper tray. (6) In addition, the printer's casing appears to be worn from previous use. (7) Upon discovering these defects. (8) I called your customer service department. (9) Magdalena schapiro, the customer service agent I spoke with, directed me to return the printer with this letter and the enclosed receipt. (10) I am disappointed by the poor quality of your merchandise, and I expect a full refund upon your receipt of this package. (11) If you have any questions, please call me at (718) 555-8722. (12) Thank you for your speedy attention to this matter.

Sincerely,

Jamal Hoffman

Jamal Hoffman
2525 Faraway Ave., #208
Brooklyn, NY 11215

1. Sentence 2: **The goods is enclosed in this package, and I am demanding a complete cash refund.**

   Which correction should be made to sentence 2?

   (1) Insert a comma after goods.
   (2) Change is to are.
   (3) Change am demanding to is demanding.
   (4) Remove the comma.
   (5) No correction is necessary.

2. Sentence 4: **You will state that the printer would be free from defects and in proper working order.**

   Which correction should be made to sentence 4?

   (1) Change will state to stated.
   (2) Insert a comma after printer.
   (3) Replace would with wood.
   (4) Replace defects with defect's.
   (5) No correction is necessary.

CHAPTER

1

DIAGNOSTIC
PRETESTS

THE
GED

LANGUAGE
ARTS,
WRITING
PART I

3. Sentence 5: **Fortunately, when the merchandise was delivered on February 17, I discovered that the printer was missing the paper tray.**

Which correction should be made to sentence 5?

(1) Replace <u>Fortunately</u> with <u>However</u>.
(2) Remove the first comma.
(3) Replace <u>February</u> with <u>february</u>.
(4) Change <u>discovered</u> to <u>will discover</u>.
(5) No correction is necessary.

4. Sentences 7 and 8: **Upon discovering these <u>defects. I called</u> your customer service department.**

Which is the best way to write the underlined portion of these sentences? If the original is the best way, choose answer (1).

(1) defects. I called
(2) defects, calling
(3) defects. A call was made
(4) defects, I called
(5) defects having called

5. Sentence 9: <u>**Magdalena schapiro, the customer service agent I spoke with,**</u> **directed me to return the printer with this letter and the enclosed receipt.**

Which is the best way to write the underlined portion of this sentence? If the original is the best way, choose answer (1).

(1) Magdalena schapiro, the customer service agent I spoke with,
(2) Magdalena schapiro the customer service agent I spoke with
(3) Magdalena Schapiro, the customer service agent I spoke with,
(4) Magdalena schapiro. The customer service agent I spoke with,
(5) Magdalena schapiro, the customer service Agent I spoke with

6. Which revision would improve the effectiveness of this letter?

Begin a new paragraph with

(1) sentence 4
(2) sentence 5
(3) sentence 6
(4) sentence 8
(5) sentence 10

Questions 7 through 10 refer to the following paragraph.

Sea Anemones

(1) Sea anemones are beautiful, flowerlike creatures that live in the worlds oceans. (2) There are more than a thousand different types of anemones. (3) Some anemones are brightly colored. (4) Many kinds of anemones live on the coasts of North America. (5) Sea anemones can be very tiny or up to five feet in length. (6) Using a suctioning disk, these creatures attach to surfaces such as rocks shells, or wharfs. (7) Sea anemones have soft, cylindrical bodies, and tentacles surround their mouths. (8) I once saw a sea anemone in a fish tank. (9) The tentacles contain a poison that the anemones use to capture prey. (10) Anemones sting prey such as shrimp, fish, and other small marine animals using these tentacles. (11) After the poison stuns the prey, the anemones eat the animals.

7. Sentence 1: **Sea anemones are beautiful, flowerlike creatures that live in the worlds oceans.**

   Which correction should be made to sentence 1?

   (1) Replace <u>Sea</u> with <u>See</u>.
   (2) Change <u>are</u> to <u>is</u>.
   (3) Replace <u>creatures</u> with <u>creatures'</u>.
   (4) Replace <u>worlds</u> with <u>world's</u>.
   (5) Replace <u>oceans</u> with <u>Oceans</u>.

8. Sentence 6: **Using a suctioning disk, these creatures attach to surfaces <u>such as rocks shells , or wharfs</u>.**

   Which is the best way to write the underlined portion of this sentence? If the original is the best way, choose answer (1).

   (1) such as rocks shells, or wharfs
   (2) such as; rocks shells, or wharfs
   (3) such as rocks, shells, or wharfs
   (4) such as rocks shells or wharfs
   (5) such as rocks. Shells or wharfs

9. Sentence 10: **Anemones sting prey such as shrimp, fish, and other small marine animals using these tentacles.**

   If you rewrote sentence 10 beginning with

   <u>Using these tentacles,</u>

   the next words should be

   (1) and prey anemones sting
   (2) anemones sting prey
   (3) shrimp, fish, and other
   (4) and other small marine
   (5) stinging prey such as

10. Which revision would improve the effectiveness of the paragraph?

    (1) Remove sentence 1.
    (2) Move sentence 2 to the end of the paragraph.
    (3) Move sentence 3 to the end of the paragraph.
    (4) Remove sentence 8.
    (5) No revision is necessary.

Check your answers to the Language Arts, Writing pretest on page 21.

PRETEST: SOCIAL STUDIES

CHAPTER

1

DIAGNOSTIC
PRETESTS

THE

GED

SOCIAL
STUDIES

Directions: Choose the <u>one best answer</u> to each question.

<u>Questions 1 through 3</u> are based on the following information.

The Federalist Papers

The 85 essays that make up *The Federalist Papers* were written in haste, with a singular purpose in mind: to persuade the public and delegates to state conventions to ratify the new U.S. Constitution. Following the Constitutional Convention in Philadelphia in May of 1787, a debate had arisen with George Washington, Benjamin Franklin, and other powerful leaders supporting the Constitution's ratification and other illustrious figures opposing its enactment. The proposed Constitution outlined a much stronger centralized government to supplant the existing Articles of Confederation, which had left political and economic power mostly in the hands of the states.

Critics of the Constitution, who were known as the Anti-Federalists, accused its supporters of making a federal government that would be too powerful. These Anti-Federalists were afraid that the freedoms that had been hard won during the American Revolution would be wiped out by a strong federal government. State legislators, who held the reins of power under the existing system, did not want to sacrifice their authority for the sake of a new form of government. These opponents of the Constitution were not passive. After the Philadelphia Convention, Anti-Federalist leaders began writing hundreds of pamphlets, speeches, articles, and letters to daily newspapers attacking the new plan. The creators of the Constitution had deemed that at least nine of the thirteen states would need to ratify the document in order for it to be enacted. Opposition to the Constitution was strong in many states, including New York. Two of New York's three delegates had withdrawn in protest from the Constitutional Convention. The governor of New York, George Clinton, was also known as an opponent of the plan.

Recognizing that a huge propaganda campaign was necessary to defend the proposed changes in government, Alexander Hamilton, then a delegate to the Convention from New York, launched *The Federalist Papers*. The essays were published in four of the five New York newspapers beginning in October of 1787. Enlisting the help of James Madison and John Jay, Hamilton continued to draft and publish the essays at a furious pace through the winter and spring of 1788. Whether or not the essays were successful in persuading New York's delegates to ratify the Constitution is open to debate. However, *The Federalist Papers* have functioned since the 1780s as the most important interpretation of the Constitution.

1. Based on the information, which is an opinion, rather than a fact, about *The Federalist Papers*?

   The Federalist Papers

   (1) were written speedily over a period of several months.
   (2) were drafted by three people, including John Jay.
   (3) were written to persuade the public and delegates.
   (4) supported the newly created U.S. Constitution.
   (5) convinced New York's delegates to ratify the Constitution.

2. According to the passage, what is one reason the Anti-Federalists opposed the Constitution?

   (1) Alexander Hamilton was not well liked as a military commander.
   (2) The Anti-Federalists feared a strong, centralized government.
   (3) The Federalists had begun a propaganda campaign in 1783.
   (4) The Constitution would abolish slavery in the South.
   (5) Nine out of thirteen states would have to ratify the Constitution.

3. The passage supports which of the following statements?

(1) *The Federalist Papers* were written after the American Revolution.
(2) *The Federalist Papers* were largely ignored in the eighteenth century.
(3) The Anti-Federalists were a disorganized group of people.
(4) Every nation should have a Constitution.
(5) State power is stronger today than it was at the time of *The Federalist Papers*.

Question 4 refers to the following map.

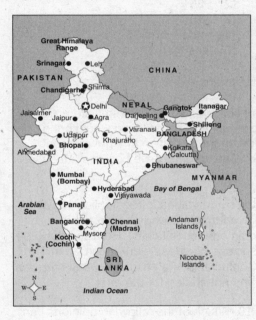

4. What conclusion about India does the map support?

(1) India's largest city is Mysore.
(2) India's highest mountains are in the South.
(3) Industry is more important than agriculture.
(4) The Arabian Sea attracts tourism.
(5) Delhi is the capital of India.

Questions 5 and 6 refer to the following poster.

Plummer, Ethel McClellan. "Vote for Woman Suffrage." Rpt. Literary Digest (Oct. 9, 1915).

5. What is the main idea represented by the artist of this poster?

(1) Only women should ask for suffrage.
(2) The right to vote is an international issue.
(3) Women should have the right to vote.
(4) Women are a powerful interest group.
(5) Congress will approve the Equal Rights Amendment.

6. Which political and economic assumption does the poster suggest is held by women suffragists?

(1) Women are entitled to the same rights of government as other citizens.
(2) Women contribute 60 percent of the economic productivity of the U.S.
(3) Women earn seventy-five cents to every dollar that men earn.
(4) Women should lobby at the state, not federal, level of government.
(5) Women's suffrage will be paid for by increased taxes on the wealthy.

CHAPTER

1

DIAGNOSTIC
PRETESTS

THE
GED

SOCIAL
STUDIES

Questions 7 and 8 refer to the following graph.

The Energy Crisis: Oil Prices, 1973–1981

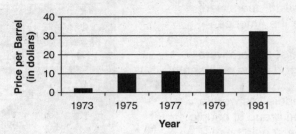

7. Soaring oil prices during the 1970s caused many problems for U.S. consumers. About how much did a barrel of oil cost in 1975?

   (1) $2
   (2) $10
   (3) $15
   (4) more than in 1977
   (5) less than in 1973

8. If the trend in the graph were to continue, what would you predict the price per barrel of oil would be in 1983?

   (1) $22
   (2) $25
   (3) $30
   (4) more than $35
   (5) less than $25

Questions 9 and 10 are based on the following information.

Kongzi, or Confucius, was the most influential philosopher in Chinese history. Born in 551 B.C., Confucius promoted a code of conduct that he believed would bring order to life in China. As a young man, he tried to get a position in a government office but failed in this quest. Instead of working as an official, he became a teacher and soon gained many followers.

Confucius stressed the need for a code of ethics and values to reestablish social harmony and political order in China. He believed that knowing one's place in society and acting according to one's role would enhance stability. He also promoted the structure of family as a model for larger society. His ideas were recorded in *The Analects.* The writings became the basis of Confucianism, a philosophy that stresses traditional values, respect for elders, family, and admiration for the past.

9. Based on the passage, how did Confucius influence Chinese society?

   (1) He became a high-ranking official in Chinese government.
   (2) He promoted a system of thought and behavior according to strict rules.
   (3) He wrote a series of articles persuading the public to adopt Taoism.
   (4) His writings reached missionaries from the United States who had traveled to China.
   (5) He introduced the idea that families should be matriarchal.

10. Which of the following opinions can be supported by the passage?

   Confucius can be characterized as a(n)

   (1) disruptive promoter of anarchy.
   (2) important but largely overlooked figure.
   (3) tolerant teacher of various ways of living.
   (4) conservative advocate of traditional values.
   (5) energetic writer of political treatises and policies.

Check your answers to the Social Studies pretest on page 23.

PRETEST: SCIENCE

Directions: Choose the <u>one best answer</u> to each question.

<u>Questions 1 and 2</u> are based on the following information and figure.

The pH scale shows the relative amount of hydrogen ion in a solution. The pH of most solutions falls between zero and fourteen. A solution with a pH of zero is highly acidic. A solution with a pH of 14 is highly basic. Neutral solutions such as water have pH levels of around 7. Bases have relatively low concentrations of hydrogen ions.

pH	Solution
0	concentrated hydrochloric acid
2	stomach acid, lemon juice
3	vinegar, cola
4	tomatoes
5	spinach
6	normal rainwater
7	saliva, blood
8	sea water
9	baking soda
11	cleaning ammonia
13	oven cleaner
14	sodium hydroxide

pH Values of Common Solutions

CHAPTER

1

DIAGNOSTIC
PRETESTS

THE
GED

SCIENCE

1. Which substance is more acidic than vinegar?

   (1) spinach
   (2) oven cleaner
   (3) saliva
   (4) sea water
   (5) lemon juice

2. Which of the following statements explains how an antacid works to relieve stomach pain?

   (1) Antacids contain basic substances that neutralize excess stomach acid.
   (2) Antacids have high concentrations of hydrogen ions.
   (3) Antacids probably fall somewhere between 0 and 7 on the pH scale.
   (4) The pH of any solution can be determined using a pH meter.
   (5) Stomach acid has a similar pH to lemon juice and hydrochloric acid.

CHAPTER

1

DIAGNOSTIC
PRETESTS

THE
GED

SCIENCE

3. Malte Andersson, a scientist at Oxford University, discovered that the female widowbird prefers mates with long tails. The longer the tail, the more attractive male widowbirds are likely to be to their potential mates. Andersson concluded that female widowbirds prefer to nest in areas where males whose tails had been artificially extended resided. Long ago, Charles Darwin theorized that such female preferences for extreme male traits could explain the evolution of elaborate male features that are harmful to the males' survival.

Which of the following statements best supports Darwin's theory?

(1) Migration causes gene flow or the movement of alleles out of a population.
(2) Mutations are the raw material for natural selection.
(3) Elaborate features may draw the attention of predators that reduce the population.
(4) Small populations that are isolated can differ greatly from one another.
(5) Male widowbirds with long tails are more likely to be better hunters than those with short tails.

4. Baking soda, or sodium hydrogen carbonate ($NaHCO_3$), is used in baking and to absorb odors in the refrigerator. Baking soda can also be used to put out a grease fire.

Which of the following statements explains how baking soda might work to put out a fire?

(1) Baking soda raises the level of hydronium ions concentrated in the materials.
(2) When dissolved in water, baking soda conducts electricity, becoming an electrolyte.
(3) When it is heated, baking soda crystallizes, which raises the temperature of the fire.
(4) When it is heated, baking soda releases CO_2, which deprives the fire of oxygen.
(5) Baking soda neutralizes the acid in the burning materials, restoring the pH to 7.

5. Saturn has a spectacular system of rings, which encircle the planet. These rings are bands of small pieces of dust, rock, and ice. The pieces range in size from millimeters to meters. Gravitational forces from Saturn and its satellites hold the pieces in place so that they stretch around Saturn. The material forming the rings may have come from a shattered satellite or moon.

Great Images in NASA, http://grin.hq.nasa.gov/

Which of the following statements best describes Saturn's rings?

The rings

(1) resemble a solid block, like a Frisbee or a compact disk.
(2) were formed when Saturn was formed.
(3) enable Saturn to rotate at high speeds around its axis.
(4) are 95 times the mass of the planet Earth.
(5) are made of separate particles of dust, rock, and ice.

6. Amphibians use their lungs to get oxygen from the air. The lungs of an amphibian are baglike organs that allow gas to be exchanged between blood and air. The internal surface area of a lung determines the amount of oxygen that the lung can absorb. The greater the surface area, the more readily oxygen can be absorbed. The lungs of amphibians are sacs with many internal folds. Air flows through a tube in the head into the lungs and back out again.

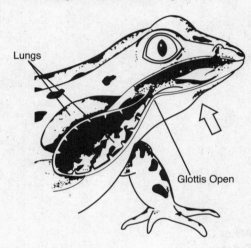

Lungs

Glottis Open

Based on the passage, why might the lungs of amphibians contain many internal folds?

(1) Amphibians can obtain oxygen through their skin.
(2) Air flow through the tube in the head may be restricted.
(3) Amphibian lungs are similar to those of reptiles and mammals.
(4) The thin skin of amphibians is easily damaged by the sun.
(5) Internal folds increase the surface area of the lung.

Questions 7 and 8 refer to the following map.

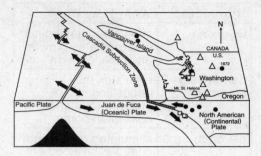

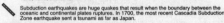

☐ Deep earthquakes (30 Miles below the Earth's surface) are within the subducting oceanic plate as it bends beneath the continental plate. The largest deep Northwest earthquakes known were in 1949 (M 7.1), 1965 (M 6.5), and 2001 (M 6.8).

● Shallow earthquakes (less than 15 miles deep) are caused by faults in the North American Continent. The Seattle fault produced a shallow magnitude 7+ earthquake 1,100 years ago. Other magnitude 7+ earthquakes occured in 1872, 1918, and 1946.

／ Subduction earthquakes are huge quakes that result when the boundary between the oceanic and continental plates ruptures. In 1700, the most recent Cascadia Subduction Zone earthquake sent a tsunami as far as Japan.

△/△ Mt. St. Helen / Other Cascade Volcanoes

7. Based on the map, which area had the least amount of shallow earthquake activity in the region?

(1) eastern Washington
(2) western Washington
(3) Canada
(4) Vancouver Island
(5) northern Oregon

8. Which of the following conclusions is supported by the information in the map?

(1) Earthquakes rarely occur in northern Oregon.
(2) Subduction earthquakes have little impact on the environment.
(3) The most recent deep earthquake in the area occurred in 2001.
(4) Shallow earthquakes occur most frequently in the summer months.
(5) Volcanic activity was last recorded in the region in 1918.

CHAPTER

1

DIAGNOSTIC
PRETESTS

THE
GED

SCIENCE

Questions 9 and 10 refer to the following chart.

Hormones	What They Do
thyroxine	stimulates metabolism and regulates growth and development
parathyroid hormone	regulates the depositing of phosphorous and calcium in bones
estrogen	stimulates estrus and controls development of secondary sex characteristics
testosterone	controls the development of secondary sex characteristics
adrenaline	raises blood pressure and acts as a neurotransmitter when the body is under stress

9. Which is the best title for the chart?

    (1) Hormones and Their Functions
    (2) How Hormones Are Released
    (3) How Testosterone and Estrogen Are Alike
    (4) How Adrenaline Affects the Nervous System
    (5) The Circulatory System and Hormones

10. Which hormone is most likely to be increased in the body when you are in an accident?

    (1) thyroxine
    (2) estrogen
    (3) testosterone
    (4) parathyroid hormone
    (5) adrenaline

Check your answers to the Science pretest on page 25.

PRETEST: LANGUAGE ARTS, READING

Directions: Choose the one best answer to each question.

Questions 1 through 5 refer to the following poem.

How Does the Speaker Feel About His Mistress?

Sonnet 130
by William Shakespeare

My mistress' eyes are nothing like the sun;
Coral is far more red than her lips' red;
If snow be white, why then her breasts are dun;
If hairs be wires, black wires grow on her head.
I have seen roses damasked,° red and white,   *variegated*
But no such roses see I in her cheeks;
And in some perfumes is there more delight
Than in the breath that from my mistress reeks.
I love to hear her speak, yet well I know
That music hath a far more pleasing sound;
I grant I never saw a goddess go;°   *walk*
My mistress, when she walks, treads on the ground.
    And yet, by heaven, I think my love as rare°   *admirable*
    As any she belied° with false compare.   *misrepresented*

1. Which of the following best describes the speaker's attitude toward his mistress?

    (1) He thinks she is beautiful and talented.
    (2) He believes her voice is like music.
    (3) He feels indifferently toward her.
    (4) He admires her in spite of her flaws.
    (5) He wishes she would leave the country.

2. To what does the speaker compare his mistress's hair?

    (1) the sun
    (2) wires
    (3) snow
    (4) roses
    (5) perfume

3. Which words best describe the speaker's tone?

    (1) sad and resigned
    (2) rueful and regretful
    (3) playful and humorous
    (4) tired and overwhelmed
    (5) bold and energetic

4. Which of the following sentences best states the theme of the poem?

    (1) You don't have to be beautiful to be beloved.
    (2) Nature will always triumph over humankind.
    (3) True love occurs after knowing someone for many years.
    (4) Art is truth, and truth is all that matters.
    (5) Roses are a powerful symbol of everlasting youth.

5. Based on the poem, what can be inferred about the speaker?

    (1) He is about to leave his mistress.
    (2) He prefers solitude to company.
    (3) He values luxury and material comforts.
    (4) He is realistic and appreciative of love.
    (5) He is a servant to the Queen of England.

CHAPTER

1

DIAGNOSTIC
PRETESTS

THE
GED

LANGUAGE
ARTS,
READING

Questions 6 through 10 refer to the following article.

IS *THE FLYING DUTCHMAN* WORTH SEEING?

'Dutchman' Leads Manage To Soar

Austin Lyric Opera's production of *The Flying Dutchman* was not successful in every department. The sets were ugly and dark (what do you expect when you rent from New Orleans Opera?) and Garnett Bruce's direction was static and clunky (what do you expect from the director of lasts season's theatrical disaster, *La Traviata*?).

The alternating performances in the two principal roles, however, were solid, even top-drawer. In Richard Wagner's early opera about a sailor doomed to wander until he finds eternal love, Donnie Ray Albert's Dutchman, heard at Thursday's final dress rehearsal, could have used more nuance, but his presence and the beauty and power of the voice were tremendous. His Senta, Mary Jane Johnson, had the vocal stamina for the part, but a wide vibrato hampered her character's credibility.

The Senta in Friday's opening, Elizabeth Byrne, had trouble with the top notes toward the end of this cruelly long role, yet her tone had the quality of a girl—something rare and valuable with this character—and every last pitch was sung fully and exactly in tune. Louis Otey's Dutchman had the look and movement of an imposing sea captain, but errors of tuning and text undercut the dramatic effect.

In the roles that are the most difficult to make convincing, Daniel Sumegi as Senta's father, Daland, and Richard Brunner as her boyfriend, Erik, were credible without achieving fully fleshed-out characterizations. The two smallest roles were beautifully sung, Rose Taylor as Mary and George Dyer as a youthful steersman. The ALO Chorus, augmented by male voices from Texas State University, still lacked a hearty sound, but the chorus, especially the women, did well with a challenging part. Conductor Guido Ajmon-Marsan scored a technical and stylistic bull's-eye. He controlled the heavy-handed brass writing in Wagner's earliest operatic masterpiece, with tempos motivated by the drama and an ear for the singers and for the story. The orchestra responded with musically refined playing.

David Mead, *Austin American-Statesman*, April 1, 2004 (available at http://www.austin360.com/xl/content/arts/xl/04-april/wkendreviews_04-01-04.html)

6. Which of the following <u>most</u> accurately states the main idea of the second paragraph?

   (1) The role of Daland was played by Daniel Sumegi.
   (2) The two leading singers in the opera performed well.
   (3) *The Flying Dutchman* is one of Wagner's greatest operas.
   (4) The supporting roles fleshed out the roles of the Dutchman and Senta.
   (5) People are doomed to wander the earth until they find eternal love.

7. Which of the following <u>best</u> expresses the reviewer's opinion of the opera performance?

   (1) It isn't perfect, but it is worth seeing.
   (2) It is the best production of Wagner ever made.
   (3) It features a young, untrained group of performers.
   (4) It involves many changes of set and lighting.
   (5) The roles are easy to sing and mostly humorous.

8. What is the overall tone of this article?

(1) harsh
(2) vengeful
(3) delighted
(4) indifferent
(5) descriptive

9. What does the reviewer mean when he states in the fourth paragraph that the conductor "scored a technical and stylistic bull's-eye"?

The conductor

(1) failed to understand the opera's story.
(2) delivered an impressive performance.
(3) emphasized style over substance.
(4) wrote an original set of songs for the opera.
(5) studied under one of Wagner's pupils.

10. Based on the article, with which of the following statements would the reviewer most likely agree?

(1) Good singing is key to the success of an opera performance.
(2) An opera is not worth seeing if the set is unappealing.
(3) It's easy to create a successful opera performance.
(4) The Flying Dutchman is one of the worst operas of all time.
(5) The best operas can no longer be performed, because singers lack training.

Check your answers to the Language Arts, Reading pretest on page 27.

CHAPTER

1

DIAGNOSTIC
PRETESTS

THE
GED

MATHEMATICS

PRETEST: MATHEMATICS

FORMULAS

AREA of a:

square	Area = side^2
rectangle	Area = length × width
parallelogram	Area = base × height
triangle	Area = $\frac{1}{2}$ × base × height
trapezoid	Area = $\frac{1}{2}$ × (base$_1$ + base$_2$) × height
circle	Area = π × radius^2; π is approximately equal to 3.14

PERIMETER of a:

square	Perimeter = 4 × side
rectangle	Perimeter = 2 × length + 2 × width
triangle	Perimeter = side$_1$ + side$_2$ + side$_3$

CIRCUMFERENCE of a circle   Circumference = π × diameter; π is approximately equal to 3.14

VOLUME of a:

cube	Volume = edge^3
rectangular container	Volume = length × width × height
square pyramid	Volume = $\frac{1}{3}$ × (base edge)^2 × height
cylinder	Volume = π × radius^2 × height; π is approximately equal to 3.14
cone	Volume = $\frac{1}{3}$ × π × radius^2 × height; π is approximately equal to 3.14

COORDINATE GEOMETRY   distance between points = $\sqrt{(x_2 - x_1)^2 + (y_2 - y_1)^2}$; (x_1, y_1) and (x_2, y_2) are two points in a plane

slope of a line = $\frac{y_2 - y_1}{x_2 - x_1}$; (x_1, y_1) and (x_2, y_2) are two points on a line

PYTHAGOREAN RELATIONSHIP $a^2 + b^2 + c^2$; a and b are legs and c is the hypotenuse of a right triangle

MEASURES OF CENTRAL TENDENCY   **mean** = $\frac{x_1 + x_2 + \ldots + x_n}{n}$; where x's are the values for which a mean is desired, and n is the total number of values for x

SIMPLE INTEREST   interest = principal × rate × time

DISTANCE   distance = rate × time

TOTAL COST   total cost = (number of units) × (price per unit)

Directions: Choose the <u>one best answer</u> to each question.

1. Last month, the balance in Carla's checkbook was $2,334.10. Since then, she has deposited her last paycheck of $2,343.00 and written checks for $800.00 (rent), $85.34 (utilities), and $34.99 (phone).

   What is the current balance in Carla's checking account?

   (1) $933.40
   (2) $2,133.55
   (3) $3,756.77
   (4) $3,929.57
   (5) $5,249.90

2. Duong purchased a $3,000 certificate of deposit (CD) at his local bank. The CD will pay him 8% simple interest annually at the end of the two years.

   How much INTEREST, in dollars, will Duong have earned from his CD at the end of the two-year period?

   Mark your answer in the circles in the grid below.

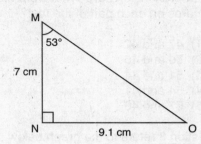

Question 3 refers to the following diagram.

M

53°

.7 cm

N   9.1 cm   O

3. If ΔMNO is a right triangle, what is the measure of ∠O?

   (1) 25°
   (2) 37°
   (3) 53°
   (4) 90°
   (5) 127°

4. A moving box measures 5 feet long, 2 feet wide, and 3 feet high. What is the volume of the box in cubic inches?

   (1) 3,900
   (2) 10,230
   (3) 39,200
   (4) 51,840
   (5) 92,730

5. Which of the following expressions is equal to the expression

   $-r(3r + 2t) + 4tr + 3r^2$?

   (1) $2tr$
   (2) $4tr$
   (3) $-3r^2 + tr$
   (4) $3r^2 + tr$
   (5) $3r^2 + 4tr$

6. What is the tenth term in the sequence below?

   0, 2, 2, 4, 6, 10, 16, 26, . . .

   (1) 32
   (2) 42
   (3) 68
   (4) 70
   (5) 112

CHAPTER

1

DIAGNOSTIC
PRETESTS

THE
GED

MATHEMATICS

CHAPTER

1

DIAGNOSTIC
PRETESTS

THE
GED

MATHEMATICS

7. Jose scored a total of 95 points on his Language Arts test. He scored five points more on the essay part of the test than on the reading comprehension part. What were his scores on each part of the test?

(1) 47 and 42
(2) 50 and 45
(3) 51 and 44
(4) 54 and 41
(5) 57 and 40

Question 8 refers to the graph below.

Coffee Drinks Sold in June
Total: $70,000

8. What was the total amount in dollars spent on lattes, espressos, and mochas in June?

(1) $46,900
(2) $50,500
(3) $52,700
(4) $68,900
(5) $90,700

9. Five students in Ms. Retman's class earned the following grades on a test:

80, 82, 82, 90, 97

What is the median grade of the students?

(1) 80
(2) 81
(3) 82
(4) 83
(5) 97

10. A bag contains 12 marbles. Five marbles are red, two are blue, three are yellow, and two are purple.

If a ball is chosen at random from the bag, what is the probability that it is yellow?

(1) $\frac{1}{2}$
(2) $\frac{1}{4}$
(3) $\frac{1}{6}$
(4) $\frac{3}{10}$
(5) $\frac{5}{12}$

Check your answers to the Mathematics pretest on page 29.

PRETEST ANSWERS AND EXPLANATIONS

Each pretest answer is explained in this section, and the specific skill on the corresponding subject ladder is indicated at the end of the explanation. You may notice that you have trouble with one subject in particular, or even one particular rung in one of the subjects. You can then spend more time on that rung to make the most of your study time.

LANGUAGE ARTS, WRITING, PART I

1.   (2)   Change <u>is</u> to <u>are</u>.
The plural noun *goods* takes the plural verb *are*. You can eliminate answer (1), since no comma is needed after <u>goods</u>. The original verb form *am demanding* is correct, so eliminate answer (3). Answer (4) is incorrect because the comma is necessary before the coordinating conjunction. (H) **Verbs**

2.   (1)   Change <u>will state</u> to <u>stated</u>.
The past tense is required in this sentence, since the action described took place in the past. Eliminate answer (2), since no comma is needed after *printer*. Answer (3) replaces the correct word *would* with an incorrect homonym. Answer (4) is wrong because the plural form *defects* is correct. (H) **Verbs**

3.   (1)   Replace <u>Fortunately</u> with <u>However</u>
The transition word *Fortunately* is incorrect, because it implies that the writer is pleased with the situation he describes. The transition word *However* makes more sense, because it implies contrast. Eliminate answer (2), because the comma is needed after an introductory phrase. Answer (3) is incorrect because months are capitalized. Answer (4) incorrectly changes the verb *discovered* from past tense to future tense (*will discover*). (H) **Coordination and Subordination**

4.   (4)   defects, I called
Sentence 7 is a sentence fragment, and answer (4) corrects it by combining the fragment with the sentence that follows it. Answers (2) and (5) create sentences that lack subjects. Answer (3) is incorrect because it maintains the fragment.
(H) **Common Sentence Errors**

5.   (3)   Magdalena Schapiro, the customer service agent I spoke with,
Proper names must be capitalized. Answer (2) is wrong because the comma is needed before the subordinate clause. Answer (4) creates a sentence fragment. Answer (5) unnecessarily capitalizes *agent*: professional titles do not need to be capitalized unless they precede a name. (H) **Capitalization and Spelling**

CHAPTER

1

DIAGNOSTIC
PRETESTS

THE
GED

LANGUAGE
ARTS,
WRITING
PART I

6.   (5)   sentence 10

Sentence 10 effectively begins a new paragraph focusing on the actions the writer wants to see happen. Answers (1), (2), and (3) can be eliminated, because sentences 4, 5, and 6 belong in paragraph B, which focuses on why the merchandise is being returned. Answer (4) is incorrect, because sentence 8 must be combined with the sentence fragment (sentence 7) that precedes it. 🅗 **Restructuring Paragraphs**

7.   (4)   Replace worlds with world's

The possessive form of *world's* is correct because the sentence refers to one world and the oceans that "belong" to it. You can rule out answer (1), because it replaces the correct word, *Sea*, with an incorrect homonym, *See*. Answer (2) changes the plural verb *are* to the incorrect singular verb *is*. Eliminate answer (3), because the form should remain plural. Eliminate answer (5), because there is no need to capitalize *oceans*. 🅗 **Capitalization and Spelling**

8.   (3)   such as rocks, shells, or wharfs

Commas are required between items in a series. Eliminate answers (2) and (4), because neither answer contains commas between the items. Answer (5) creates a sentence fragment. 🅗 **Punctuation**

9.   (2)   anemones sting prey

In the original sentence, the modifying phrase *using these tentacles* comes after *animals* and is thus misplaced. The phrase should be next to the word it modifies, *anemones*, because it is the anemones, not the other small marine animals, that are using the tentacles. Answer (2) is the only answer that provides this solution. The other answers do not place the modifying phrase close to the word that should be modified. 🅗 **Misplaced and Dangling Modifiers**

10.   (4)   Remove sentence 8

Sentence 8 should be removed because it contains information that is irrelevant to the paragraph. Answer (1) is incorrect, because sentence 1 is essential to the main idea of the paragraph. Answers (2) and (3) are incorrect because moving sentences 2 and 3 to the end of the paragraph would create confusion and disrupt the logical progression of ideas. 🅗 **Restructuring Paragraphs**

Evaluation

If you answered five or fewer questions correctly, you need to study the Language Arts, Writing chapter. You are not yet prepared to take the test.

If you answered six to eight questions correctly, you are in pretty good shape, but need to review some areas. You can match the categories you got wrong to their corresponding rungs, but it is probably a good idea to go through the entire chapter so you are fully prepared on test day.

If you answered nine to ten questions correctly, you are probably ready to take the Writing test. Take the full-length practice tests, starting on page 403, to familiarize yourself with the test. If you have some trouble on this full-length test, or if you go over the time limit, return to the Language Arts, Writing chapter for some extra practice. It is a good idea to review the final rung, "The Essay," regardless of how well you do on the full-length test.

CHAPTER

1

DIAGNOSTIC
PRETESTS

THE
GED

SOCIAL
STUDIES

SOCIAL STUDIES

1. **(5)   convinced New York's delegates to ratify the Constitution.**
The passage states that whether *The Federalist Papers* persuaded the delegates is open to debate and is thus an opinion. You can eliminate answers (1), (2), (3), and (4), because each of these facts is stated in the passage. **H Identifying Implications**

2. **(2)   The Anti-Federalists feared a strong, centralized government.**
This reason is stated in the second paragraph. You can rule out answers (1), (3), and (4), because these statements are not supported by the passage. While answer (5) is a statement in the passage, this fact is not given as a reason for the Anti-Federalists' opposition to the Constitution. **H Understanding What You Read**

3. **(1)   *The Federalist Papers* were written after the American Revolution.**
This question requires you to synthesize the information in the first and second paragraphs to determine that the *Federalist* was written several years after the American Revolution. Your knowledge of American history would also enable you to answer this question correctly. The statements in answers (2), (3), and (5) are directly contradicted by information in the passage. Answer (4) is an opinion, which is not necessarily supported by the passage. **H Analyzing Relationships**

4. **(5)   Delhi is the capital of India.**
The star on the map indicates that Delhi is the capital. Eliminate answer (1), because the map does not show the relative size of cities. Answer (2) is incorrect, because the only mountains on the map are in the north. The map does not give any information about industry or agriculture, so eliminate answer (3). Answer (4) can also be ruled

CHAPTER

1

DIAGNOSTIC
PRETESTS

THE
GED

SOCIAL
STUDIES

out, because the map does not give any evidence to support the statement about the Arabian Sea. 🔘 **Understanding Visual Material**

5. (3) Women should have the right to vote.

The text and drawing convey the idea that women should have the right to vote. Answers (1), (2), and (3) are not supported by the poster. Answer (5) is not supported by the poster, either. In addition, the Equal Rights Amendment, a constitutional amendment barring discrimination on the basis of sex, was not proposed until the 1970s. 🔘 **Understanding Visual Material**

6. (1) Women are entitled to the same rights of government as other citizens.

The question requires you to understand that women suffragists fought for women's right to vote based on the idea that women are entitled to the rights of citizenship. The other answers can be deleted, because the poster does not refer to them, nor do they necessarily support the idea that women should have the right to vote. 🔘 **Understanding Visual Material**

7. (2) $10

The question requires you to analyze the graph to determine that the cost was $10 in 1975. Answer (4) is wrong, because the bar for 1975 is smaller and thus represents a lower price than in 1977. The bar for 1975 is taller than the one for 1973, showing an increase in price, so answer (5) is incorrect. 🔘 **Understanding Visual Material**

8. (4) more than $35

The question requires you to look at the trend in the graph as a whole and make a prediction based on that information. From 1973 to 1981, the price of oil steadily increased, taking a large leap from 1979 to 1981. In 1981, the price per barrel was $32. If the trend were to continue, the price in 1983 would be higher than $32 dollars. Answer (4) is the only one that fulfills this prediction. 🔘 **Understanding Visual Material**

9. (2) He promoted a system of thought and behavior according to strict rules.

The passage states that Confucius is known as a philosopher and promoter of codes of behavior. Answer (1) is directly contradicted by the first paragraph. Answers (3), (4), and (5) all contain information that is not mentioned in the passage. 🔘 **Understanding What You Read**

10. (4) conservative advocate of traditional values.

The question requires you to use your knowledge of certain terms to determine which opinion is supported by the passage. *Anarchy* is the opposite of order, which Confucius valued, so eliminate answer (1). Answer (2) is incorrect, because there is no evidence to suggest that Confucius has been overlooked. Answer (3) is directly contradicted by the information in the passage. Answer (5) is wrong, because the passage emphasizes Confucius's philosophical writings and doesn't mention political writings. 🔘 **Identifying Implications**

Evaluation

If you answered five or fewer questions correctly, you need to study the Social Studies chapter. You are not yet prepared to take the test.

If you answered six to eight questions correctly, you are in pretty good shape but need to review some areas. You can match the topics you missed to their corresponding rungs, but it is probably a good idea to go through the entire chapter so you are fully prepared on test day.

If you answered nine to ten questions correctly, you are probably ready to take the Social Studies test. Take the full-length practice test, starting on page 429, to familiarize yourself with the test. If you have some trouble on this full-length test, or if you go over the time limit, return to the Social Studies chapter for some extra practice.

SCIENCE

1. (5) lemon juice

The question requires you to understand the information in the paragraph and the scale. On the pH scale, only lemon juice is more acidic and has a lower pH value than vinegar. The other answers all have higher pH values and thus are more basic. ⊕ **Physical Science**

2. (1) Antacids contain basic substances that neutralize excess stomach acid.

This question requires you to apply your knowledge of acids and bases to the information in the scale and paragraph to arrive at the answer. The figure tells you that stomach acid is highly acidic. You can guess that excess stomach acid causes upset stomach. To neutralize an acidic substance, you must add a basic substance. Only answer (1) offers this explanation of how antacids work. Answers (2) and (3) are directly contradicted by the information in the paragraph. Answers (4) and (5) are true statements, but they do not explain how antacids might work. ⊕ **Physical Science**

3. (3) Elaborate features may draw the attention of predators that reduce the population.

Only answer (3) explains why having elaborate features could be harmful to the survival of male widowbirds. Answers (1), (2), and (4) are true statements, but they are not relevant to the question. Answer (5) would not support Darwin's statement. ⊕ **Life Science I: Life on Our Planet**

4. (4) When it is heated, baking soda releases CO_2, depriving the fire of oxygen.

The question requires you to know that fire or combustion requires three elements to occur: a fuel, an ignition source, and oxygen. If fire is deprived of any of these elements, it stops burning. Answer (4) offers an explanation for how baking soda

CHAPTER

1

DIAGNOSTIC
PRETESTS

THE
GED

SCIENCE

stops fires. Answers (1), (2), and (5) are irrelevant to the question of how to put out a fire. Answer (3) is illogical, since raising the temperature of a fire would not put it out.  **Physical Science**

5.   (5)   are made of separate particles of dust, rock, and ice.
Answer (5) is the only answer supported by information in the passage. Answer (1) is directly contradicted by the information. Eliminate answers (2), (3), and (4), because the passage does not contain any information that supports those statements. **Earth and Space Science**

6.   (5)   Internal folds increase the surface area of the lung.
Answer (5) explains why having many internal folds is advantageous. The other statements may or may not be true, but they can be eliminated because none explains why the lungs contain many folds. **Life Science II: Human Body Systems**

7.   (3)   Canada
The map shows no shallow earthquake activity north of the Canadian border, so answer (3) is correct. Eastern Washington isn't shown on the map, so answer (1) is wrong. Western Washington shows some shallow earthquake activity, and both Vancouver Island and northern Oregon show a relatively high concentration of shallow earthquake activity, so answers (2), (4), and (5) are incorrect. **Physical Science**

8.   (3)   The most recent deep earthquake in the area occurred in 2001.
The key states that the most recent deep earthquake occurred in 2001. The map shows that earthquakes occur with some frequency in northern Oregon, so rule out answer (1). Answer (2) is incorrect, because the key states that subduction earthquakes are enormous earthquakes with large impacts. In answers (4) and (5), neither statement is supported by the information in the map or key. **Physical Science**

9.   (1)   Hormones and Their Functions
The chart lists hormones and what they do. Answer (2) is incorrect, because the chart does not explain how hormones are released in the body. The topics in answers (3), (4), and (5) are not covered by the information in the chart. **Life Science II: Human Body Systems**

10.   (5)   adrenaline
The chart states that adrenaline is released when the body is under stress. In an accident, you are likely to be under stress, and adrenaline is the hormone that will be released in quantity. The other answers should be eliminated, since the release of the other hormones is not tied to stressful situations so directly. **Life Science II: Human Body Systems**

Evaluation

If you answered five or fewer questions correctly, you need to study the Science chapter. You are not yet prepared to take the test.

If you answered six to eight questions correctly, you are in pretty good shape but need to review some areas. You can match the categories you missed to their corresponding rungs, but it is probably a good idea to go through the entire chapter so you are fully prepared on test day.

If you answered nine to ten questions correctly, you are probably ready to take the Science test. Take the full-length practice test, starting on page 457, to familiarize yourself with the test. If you have some trouble on this full-length test, or if you go over the time limit, return to the Science chapter for some extra practice.

LANGUAGE ARTS, READING

1.   **(4)   He admires her in spite of her flaws.**
The speaker elaborates on the mistress's unloveliness throughout the poem. However, the last two lines of the poem indicate that the speaker admires and cherishes his mistress. The speaker's statements directly contradict the other answers.
Theme and Point of View

2.   **(2)   wires**
In line 4, the speaker compares his mistress's hair to "black wires." Eliminate answer (1), because the sun is used to make a comparison with the mistress's eyes. Similarly, eliminate answers (3), (4), and (5), because snow, roses, and perfume are compared with the mistress's other qualities. **Figurative Language and Other Poetic Elements**

3.   **(3)   playful and humorous**
The speaker's tone is humorous and affectionate toward the subject. He invokes clichés about beauty, then pokes fun at these clichés immediately by saying his mistress is nothing like a conventional beauty. Eliminate answers (1), (2), and (4), because the tone of the poem is positive: the speaker is not sad, regretful, or tired. Answer (5) is a possibility, but answer (3) provides the more precise answer.
Mood, Tone, and Style

4.   **(1)   You don't have to be beautiful to be beloved.**
This is the central theme of the poem. The speaker states repeatedly that his mistress does not fit the conventions of beauty, but he also emphasizes that he finds her enticing. For the speaker, conventional beauty is not a requirement for love. Answers (2) and (4) are irrelevant to the poem. There is no evidence to support answer (3), because we do not know how long the speaker has known his mistress. Although roses are

mentioned, they do not symbolize youth in the poem, so answer (5) is incorrect.

 **Theme and Point of View**

5.   (4)   He is realistic and appreciative of love.

The speaker shows admiration and appreciation for his mistress, yet he is realistic about love. The descriptions of his love show that he is not a dreamer or someone who idealizes the person he loves. The evidence in the poem contradicts the statement in answer (1). The speaker clearly enjoys his mistress's company, so answer (2) is incorrect. Nothing in the poem supports the statements in answers (3) and (4).

 **Plot, Predictions, and Inferences**

6.   (2)   The two leading singers in the opera performed well.

The paragraph describes the performances of the two leading singers in the opera. Answer (1) is a statement from paragraph 4 and has nothing to do with paragraph 2. The opinion in answer (3) does not appear anywhere in the article. The information in answer (4) is also irrelevant to paragraph 2. Answer (5) contains a statement that is central to the opera, but not to paragraph 2 in the review.

 **Main Ideas and Supporting Details**

7.   (1)   It isn't perfect, but it is worth seeing.

The reviewer makes it clear in the first paragraph that not everything about the performance is successful. However, in the rest of the review, he praises particular performances, the conducting, and the orchestra. Eliminate answer (2), because the review does not support that opinion. Eliminate answers (3) and (4), because those statements are not found in the review. Answer (5) is directly contradicted by the review, which discusses the difficulty of several singing roles.  **Summarizing**

8.   (5)   descriptive

The reviewer describes various aspects of the opera in a thorough manner, so the tone is descriptive. The review is largely positive or neutral, not harsh or vengeful, so answers (1) and (2) are wrong. The reviewer is not completely delighted by the performance, either, so rule out answer (3). Answer (4) is incorrect, because the reviewer states his opinion of various aspects of the opera.  **Mood, Tone, and Style**

9.   (2)   delivered an impressive performance.

To "score a bull's-eye" means to do very well, even perfectly well. The sentences following this one also support the idea that the conductor performed admirably. Answer (1) is wrong because the review states that the conductor "had an ear . . . for the story," so obviously he did not fail to understand the opera's story. Style and substance are not compared in the review—substance is not mentioned at all—so answer (3) is wrong. The statements in answers (4) and (5) are not supported by evidence from the review.  **Main Ideas and Supporting Details**

10.   (1)   Good singing is key to the success of an opera performance.

The reviewer discusses the quality of the singing several times during the review, so you can conclude that he thinks singing is important to the success of the performance.

The reviewer mentions that the set is ugly, but he still conveys that the opera is worth seeing, so rule out answer (2). Answer (3) is incorrect because the review makes it clear that creating a successful opera is no easy task. Answer (4) is contradicted by the sentence in the last paragraph that calls the opera a "masterpiece." There is no evidence to support that the reviewer believes the statement in answer (5).

⊕ Drawing Conclusions and Making Interpretations

Evaluation

If you answered five or fewer questions correctly, you need to study the Language Arts, Reading chapter. You are not yet prepared to take the test.

If you answered six to eight questions correctly, you are in pretty good shape but need to review some areas. You can match the topics you missed to their corresponding rung, but it is probably a good idea to go through the entire chapter so you are fully prepared on test day.

If you answered nine to ten questions correctly, you are probably ready to take the Language Arts, Reading test. Take the full-length practice test, starting on page 479, to familiarize yourself with the test. If you have some trouble on this full-length test, or if you go over the time limit, return to the Language Arts, Reading chapter for some extra practice.

MATHEMATICS

1.   (3)   **$3,756.77**

To arrive at the answer, you need to add the amount of the paycheck to the existing balance and subt ract the amounts of the checks written. The values can be added and subtracted on the calculator in succession. You can also use rounding to eliminate answers (1) and (2) as too small and answer (5) as too large.

$$\$2,334.10 + \$2,343.00 - \$800.00 - \$85.34 - \$34.99 = \$3,756.77$$

⊕ The Basics: Whole Numbers and Basic Operations

CHAPTER

1

DIAGNOSTIC
PRETESTS

THE
GED

MATHEMATICS

2.

The formula for simple interest is found on the formulas page, which appears at the front of the Mathematics Test.

simple interest = principle × rate × time = $3,000.00 × 0.08 × 2 = $480.00

Beyond Counting Numbers: Fractions, Decimals, and Percent

3. (2) 37°

The sum of angles in a triangle equals 180°. To find the missing measure, subtract.

$180° - 90° - 53° = 37°$

You can eliminate answer (4), because the angle is clearly not a right angle. You can also eliminate answer (5), because the angle in question is not larger than 90°.

Geometry

4. (4) 51,840

You need to convert the measurements to inches.

5 feet = 60 inches; 2 feet = 24 inches; 3 feet = 36 inches

volume = length × width × height = 60 × 24 × 36 = 51,840 inches

You can eliminate answer (1) as too small after converting the measurements.

Geometry

5. (1) 2tr

This question requires you to simplify the expression by grouping like terms and combining them.

$-r(3r + 2t) + 4tr + 3r^2 = -3r^2 - 2tr + 4tr + 3r^2 = 2tr$

Algebra

6. (3) 68

The question requires you to identify the pattern. Each number in the sequence is formed by adding the previous two numbers. To get the tenth term, you need to calculate the next two numbers in the sequence, which are 42 (the ninth term) and 68, which is the tenth term. You can eliminate answer (1) as too small. **Algebra**

7. (2) 50 and 45

The scores must total 95 and show a difference of 5. Only answer (2) satisfies these criteria. Eliminate answers (1) and (5), because neither pair of numbers adds up to 95.

The difference between the numbers in answer (3) is 7, and the difference in answer (4) is 13, so both answers can also be eliminated.  **Algebra**

8.   **(1) $46,900**

To arrive at the answer, add the three percentages spent on lattes, espressos, and mochas:

$$40\% + 19\% + 8\% = 67\%$$

Then, multiply the resulting percentage by the total amount spent:

$$.67 \times \$70,000 = \$46,900$$

You can eliminate answer (4), since $68,900 is nearly the total amount of $70,000, and the total of lattes, espressos, and mochas does not come close to being the entire amount of the graph. You can also eliminate answer (5), since $90,700 is higher than the total amount spent. **Data Analysis**

9.   **(3)   82**

The median is the middle term in a series. The numbers in the list are in order, so the middle term is 82. Eliminate answer (1), because 80 is too low a number to be the median. You can also eliminate answer (5), because 97 is too high a number to be the median. **Data Analysis**

10.   **(2) $\frac{1}{4}$**

The total number of possible outcomes is 12. The total number of positive outcomes in which the ball is yellow is 3. To arrive at the answer, write the fraction with the positive outcomes over the total outcomes: $\frac{3}{12}$. Then, reduce the fraction to its lowest terms: $\frac{3}{12} = \frac{1}{4}$. **Data Analysis**

Evaluation

If you answered five or fewer questions correctly, you need to study the Mathematics chapter. You are not yet prepared to take the test.

If you answered six to eight questions correctly, you are in pretty good shape, but need to review some areas. You can match the topics you missed to their corresponding rungs, but it is probably a good idea to go through the entire chapter so you are fully prepared on test day.

If you answered nine to ten questions correctly, you are probably ready to take the Mathematics test. Take the full-length practice test, starting on page 501, to familiarize yourself with the test. If you have some trouble on this full-length test, or if you go over the time limit, return to the Mathematics chapter for some extra practice.

CHAPTER

1

DIAGNOSTIC
PRETESTS

THE
GED

MATHEMATICS

CHAPTER 2

TEST-TAKING BASICS

CHAPTER

2

TEST-
TAKING
BASICS

**THE
GED**

TEST-TAKING BASICS

Taking the GED is not what many people would call a fun thing to do on a Saturday afternoon. However, it doesn't have to be the brutal experience many people anticipate. Knowing how to take a test is a skill, and it is not difficult to learn how. In fact, the main secrets of test taking are quite simple. If you are equipped with all the basic test-taking skills and strategies, you will find it easier to perform your best on the tests. This chapter tells you all you need to know about how to take the GED tests.

GED ESSENTIALS

First things first: the GED is timed, so you should be aware of how much time you have left during the test. Bring a watch with you to the testing center. When you begin each test, write down the time you started on a piece of scratch paper. Also write down the time the test will end. When you check your watch, you'll know exactly how much time you have left.

Don't spend too much time on any one question. All the questions—both the easy and the hard ones—are worth one point. If you find yourself dwelling on a question, skip it and move on to another. You may find that the next questions are much easier to answer. After you have completed the other questions, you can go back and answer the more challenging ones. Remember that you don't have to be perfect. You just have to pass. We discuss pacing in more detail on pages 36–37.

Keep in mind that the GED does not punish you for wrong answers: it only gives you credit for correct answers, so don't leave any questions blank. Random guessing isn't a good idea, but if you're running out of time and have narrowed the answers down to two or three possibilities, guess away. You just might be correct.

APPROACHING THE QUESTIONS

Most of the questions on the test are multiple choice with five possible answers. When answering these questions, do the following:

- Read all directions carefully and listen to the directions the GED examiner gives at the start of the test.

- Some questions require you to read a passage. Be sure to read the whole passage or document before you start to answer questions.
- Read each question and the possible answers carefully.
- Make sure the answer you choose is supported by the passage.
- Pick only one answer for each question.
- Mark your answer sheet carefully, making sure you have filled in the right space next to the right number. Don't make any stray marks on your answer sheet.

MARKING THE ANSWER BOOKLET

When you take the GED test, you record your answers in an answer booklet. You cannot write on the tests themselves (the test-makers reuse the test booklets).

The testing center provides scratch paper so you can work out your problems. When you do the questions in this book, practice using scratch paper to figure out your answers. You can put the paper underneath the question you are working on. It's a good idea to make a note of any question you skip so you can go back to it if time allows.

Sample answer sheets like the ones used for the GED are on pages 525–536. Use these answer sheets to complete the practice tests at the end of this book. For most questions, you must "bubble in" or darken the ovals of the correct choices with a Number 2 pencil. Be careful that you do not make any stray marks on the answer sheets. The machine scoring your answer booklet may misinterpret stray marks as incorrect answers.

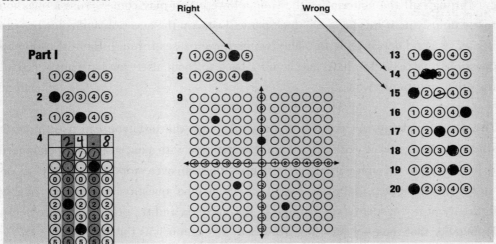

When you skip a question on the tests, be sure you also skip that line of bubbles on the answer sheet. When you skip a question, make a light mark next to it on the answer sheet. After you have completed the test, you can erase any light marks you have made.

To answer Part II of the Language Arts, Writing test, you must write your essay on the two sheets of lined paper in the answer booklet. Again, use scratch paper to make any notes or outlines before recording your final essay in the booklet.

The Mathematics test differs slightly from the other tests. It usually has about ten questions that aren't multiple-choice. These questions, called "alternate format questions," require you to come up with your own answer just as you would on a

CHAPTER

2

TEST-
TAKING
BASICS

THE
GED

regular math test. You enter your answer by filling in circles on a grid or a coordinate plane. The Mathematics chapter of this book explains in detail how to fill in these grids.

Remember that, with the exception of the essay portion of the Language Arts, Writing test, a machine, not a person, grades your test. Machines don't care about how you arrived at your answer or all the thinking you did to get there. It cares only about the bubble you have filled in. Give the machine only what it wants to see.

Now that you know some test-taking basics and how to work with the answer sheet, let's think about your own personal strategy for tackling these tests. The following strategies work for all five GED tests. Each chapter in the book provides subject-strategies, but let's focus on these general ones first.

You can always go back and erase an answer if you change your mind. Just make sure to erase the old answer completely. Then fill in the correct answer.

PACING

The GED tests are timed. To do your best, make the most of the time you have for each test. You should keep a steady pace when answering the questions. That means you should move slowly enough to avoid careless mistakes, but quickly enough to get through all the material in the time allowed. You may come across a question that stumps you. If this happens, don't panic. Just skip the question and come back to it later. A good approach is to make two or three passes through the test, skipping questions that seem too hard and coming back to them after you have answered all the other questions.

The X-O Strategy. As you make passes through the test, you can use the X-O strategy. Here's how it works: if you start to struggle with a question and spend more than a few minutes on it without coming up with an answer, stop and mark an "X" on the answer sheet next to the question. This is a "maybe" question. You could probably figure it out if you spent more time on it, but move on and try other easier problems. Remember that the easy questions are worth just as much as the hard ones.

If you come to a question that makes no sense at all, mark an "O" next to it on the answer sheet. These are guessing questions. Smart guessing strategies can improve your chances of selecting the right answer on these.

After you answer all the questions you can, return to the X questions and try them again. If they still give you trouble, apply a strategic guessing technique, such as process of elimination (we discuss strategic guessing shortly).

You may want to use a bookmark or ruler to track where you are in the test. It is easy to get confused with all the lines of blank bubbles.

Remember, you don't need a perfect score to pass the GED. While passing scores differ from state to state, generally, you need to score only around 65 percent to pass each test. That doesn't mean you should skip every third question, but don't sweat it if you miss one here and there.

After answering all the X questions, use a strategic guessing technique to answer the O questions.

The X-O strategy keeps you from getting stuck when you face a tough question. It ensures that you move on and get to the questions you *can* answer and thereby get all the points you can. Another thing to keep in mind when pacing yourself is the power of a quick break. Taking time out to stretch your arms or do some deep breathing can help you refocus and concentrate.

CHAPTER

2

TEST-
TAKING
BASICS

THE
GED

PROCESS OF ELIMINATION

There is no guessing penalty for the GED tests. In other words, no points are deducted for wrong answers. You should answer all the questions on the tests, even if you don't know what the right answers are. Strategic guessing techniques can help you guess correctly.

In many cases, you can use your common sense and experience to rule out incorrect answers. Ruling out wrong answers to find the right one is called the **process of elimination**. Process of elimination is one of the most powerful strategies you can use on any multiple-choice test.

On every multiple-choice test, the correct answers are always provided. You just have to identify which answer is right. If you guess blindly on the GED, you have a one in five chance of picking the right answer.

However, you can increase your odds of picking the right answer. Often, some of the choices seem obviously wrong or unreasonable, so you can eliminate them without even knowing what the correct answer is. Take a look at this question, for example:

When did the first astronaut land on the moon?

You may not know the answer to this question right away. Take a look at the answers and see if you can narrow it down:

When did the first astronaut land on the moon?

(1)   1776
(2)   1869
(3)   1901
(4)   1969
(5)   2004

If you eliminate only one answer as incorrect, you increase your chances of getting the right answer to one in four. If you eliminate three answers, your chances increase to fifty-fifty.

CHAPTER

2

TEST-
TAKING
BASICS

THE
GED

Answering this question should be easier now. Using your common sense and some previous knowledge, you can eliminate wrong answers. You know that the technology needed to send people into space wasn't developed until the late twentieth century. Look at answers (1), (2), and (3). All of those dates are too early to be right. You can eliminate those three options.

Now look at answer (5). The year 2004 is too recent. There were many moon landings prior to 2004. You can eliminate answer (5). That leaves answer (4), which is the correct answer.

You just used process of elimination to identify the right answer. The subject chapters in this book guide you in using this strategy for each of the subject tests. On many questions, you can eliminate answer choices because they seem illogical. Even if you eliminate only one or two choices and then guess, you have greatly improved your chances of guessing correctly.

Remember to use the process of elimination on the questions that stump you. Also remember to answer every question on the test. There is no penalty for guessing.

RELAXING DURING THE TEST

Being nervous before and during a test is normal. Most people experience test anxiety. The important thing is not to let stress overwhelm you. You will perform your best on the GED test when you are calm and relaxed. Here are a couple of techniques you can use to stay calm during the tests.

A FEW DEEP BREATHS

You may find yourself breathing too quickly during the tests. This can be a sign of test anxiety. If you feel like it's hard to catch your breath, take a couple of minutes to use the following deep-breathing technique:

Close your eyes and take a slow, deep breath through your nose while you count to four silently. Then slowly release the breath through your mouth for four counts. This activity should restore your breathing to normal and help you relax. It doesn't take very long, so you can do it whenever you need to.

You can also try to clear your mind by looking up and away from the test itself. Try focusing your eyes on a blank wall or out the window for a minute to relax and clear your head. When you feel calmer, go back to the test.

STRETCHING

All together, the GED tests are more than seven hours long. You may be taking the test in one or two sittings. It can be difficult and uncomfortable to remain in the same position for such a long time. The testing center gives you short breaks, and you should use these opportunities to get up and walk around. Sometimes just getting a drink of water is enough to restore your sense of comfort.

To stay alert, you can also do stretches while sitting. Try the following exercises:

NECK STRETCHES

Hold each of the following positions for five counts:

- Sit straight in your chair and tilt your head forward toward your chest.
- Tilt your head backward and look up at the ceiling. Keep your shoulders relaxed.
- Tilt your head to the right side so that your ear is close to your right shoulder.
- Tilt your head to the left side, bringing your left ear toward your left shoulder.
- Repeat as necessary.

SHOULDER ROLLS

- While seated at your desk, roll both shoulders forward in circular motions for a count of five. Keep your neck relaxed while you roll. Focus on moving your shoulders around in circles rather than just lifting them up and down.
- Roll your shoulders backward for a count of five.
- Clasp your hands together and extend your arms out from your chest. Concentrate on separating your shoulder blades and pulling the muscles in your upper back out toward your hands. Hold for five counts.

THE DAY BEFORE THE TEST

You've been preparing for test day for a long time. The last thing you want to do now is screw everything up by missing the test for a bad reason. Go to the testing center and familiarize yourself with the environment. Make sure you know how to get there, how long it takes, and where to park if you are driving. Also, try to see the room in which you will be taking the test. You don't want any surprises on test day.

Pack a bag or knapsack with all the things you will need on test day. Here is a list of things to bring to the testing center:

- Your GED registration or admission ticket, if necessary. You may have received the registration in the mail. If you haven't, don't worry. Just call the testing center to make sure you are registered.
- Several sharpened Number 2 pencils with erasers.
- A couple of pens with blue or black ink for the essay.
- Two forms of identification, such as a driver's license, passport, Social Security card, birth certificate, or green card. If you don't have two pieces of ID, call the testing center before the testing date.
- Snacks such as fruit, energy bars, and nuts.
- Bottled water.
- A sweater or light jacket in case it is cold.
- A watch.
- Lunch, if you will be at the testing center all day.

Pack your bag in a convenient place so it's ready to go the next day. You may not be able to take your entire bag to your desk on test day, but you will be able to store your items in a safe and convenient place at the center.

By the night before the test, you will be well prepared to take it. Instead of cramming at the last minute, be confident that you know what you need to know to pass

CHAPTER

2

TEST-
TAKING
BASICS

THE
GED

CHAPTER

2

TEST-
TAKING
BASICS

THE
GED

the GED. Try to relax, and do not stay up all night studying. The best thing you can do is eat a good meal and get a good night's sleep. The more rested you are, the better you will perform on the tests.

TEST DAY

It's the day you've been preparing for, and time to put all your hard work to good use. On the day of the test, try to stay calm and make yourself as comfortable as you can. Here are a few tips:

- Eat a good meal before going to the center. Most people concentrate better when they are not distracted by hunger. If you are taking the test in the morning, make sure that you get up early enough to eat breakfast and still get to the testing center on time.
- Wear comfortable clothing, such as a T-shirt and sweatpants. Wear layers in case it is too cold or too hot.
- Arrive at the testing center 20 minutes early so you have time to set up and settle down.
- Remember to bring the materials that you packed the night before.

If you can, find a good seat away from other people. You want to be in a place with as few distractions as possible. Once the test starts, take a deep breath and begin. When you complete one subject test, don't think about it anymore. Just move on to the next one. Be confident that you did your best and know that the next subject is an entirely new test.

Your test results will be mailed to you in the weeks following the test. The report includes individual test scores and your overall score. The score report also tells you whether you passed the test. You may request that the state GED office send your scores to your employer or a college. Ask the testing center about this.

Here are a few last tips about taking the GED:

- Be confident. You know that you are well prepared to take the test. Now you can prove how much you know.
- Review the test before starting. You may want to spend a few minutes familiarizing yourself with the test. Then, decide how to pace yourself.
- Stay focused and relaxed. Use the test-taking and relaxation strategies you've learned.
- Look over the test when you're finished. Make sure you have answered all the questions. Check your answer booklet to make sure the bubbles are filled in neatly and correctly. Erase any stray marks. Also, double-check to make sure the answer sheet choices correctly correspond to the questions.

As with any major goal, your hard work will pay off. Passing the GED takes effort on your part, but that effort will translate into accomplishment.

PART

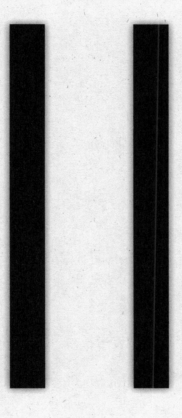

CHAPTER 3

LANGUAGE ARTS, WRITING

LANGUAGE ARTS, WRITING

Welcome to the Language Arts, Writing Chapter. This test is by far the longest of the five GED tests, with 120 minutes divided into two parts, one of which asks you to write an essay. Let's get started by reviewing the ladder for the Language Arts, Writing test.

Rung 1: Introduction
Rung 2: Capitalization and Spelling
Rung 3: Punctuation
Rung 4: Verbs
Rung 5: Pronouns
Rung 6: Common Sentence Errors
Rung 7: Coordination and Subordination
Rung 8: Misplaced and Dangling Modifiers
Rung 9: Parallel Structure
Rung 10: Restructuring Paragraphs
Rung 11: The Essay

By using the step-by-step ladder in this chapter, you can master all the skills you need to know to succeed on the Writing test. The ladder has eleven rungs. Each rung is designed as a single lesson and should take you just about an hour to complete. The essay rung may take a little longer. It's important to work through each rung, one at a time, to prepare yourself for the various kinds of questions you will see on the Language Arts, Writing test.

Each rung concludes with a set of practice questions. Answering these questions helps you to assess how prepared you are in each topic. If you answer most of the practice set questions correctly, you should move on the next rung. Answers and explanations to each practice set appear at the end of the chapter. The icon at the end of the explanation indicates which skill is being tested on that test question. Each rung builds on the rung before it. You can go back and review previous lessons if you feel you need to improve in a particular area.

By the time you reach the final rung, you will have the skills you need to handle the most challenging problems on the Writing test, including questions on usage, sentence structure, paragraph structure, and essay writing.

INTRODUCTION

The Language Arts, Writing test is given in two parts. Part I contains fifty multiple-choice questions assessing your knowledge of grammar and paragraph organization. Part II requires you to write an essay expressing an opinion on a familiar topic. The scores earned on both parts are combined and reported as a single score for the Writing test.

QUICK OVERVIEW

Test	Items	Time Limit
Language Arts, Writing, (Part I)	50 multiple-choice questions	75 minutes
Language Arts, Writing, (Part II)	Essay	45 minutes

The multiple-choice questions cover four content areas:
- **Mechanics (25%):** correcting errors in capitalization, punctuation, and spelling (limited to errors using possessives, contractions, and homonyms).
- **Usage (30%):** correcting errors in subject-verb agreement, verb tense, and pronoun usage.
- **Sentence structure (30%):** correcting sentence fragments, run-on sentences, comma splices, improper coordination and subordination, misplaced phrases and modifiers, and lack of parallel structure.
- **Organization (15%):** restructuring paragraphs or ideas within paragraphs, identifying topic sentences, creating unity and coherence.

THE THREE TYPES OF QUESTIONS

Each of the fifty questions on Part I of the Writing test is a multiple-choice question with five possible answers. You must choose the best answer among the five choices.

Part I of the Writing test has three types of multiple-choice questions:
- Correction
- Revision
- Construction shift

Each set of questions follows a short passage. The passages include workplace documents, how-to texts, and informational essays. Workplace documents may be application letters, memorandums, notices to employees, and other

Most passages on the Language Arts, Writing test are twelve to eighteen sentences long, in two or three paragraphs.

work-related documents. The how-to passages, of course, describe how to do something, such as how to fix a flat tire. The informational essays concern a wide range of topics.

The sentences in each passage are numbered. The paragraphs are lettered, beginning with (A). The questions following each passage ask you to correct and improve sentences in the passages or to improve the organization of the passage.

Refer to the passage below as we review each of the three types of questions.

Directions: Choose the one best answer to each question.

Questions 1 through 3 refer to the following paragraphs.

Angel Falls

(A)

(1) Angel Falls is the highest waterfall in the world. (2) The waterfall lies in a national park in the heart of Venezuela. (3) This remarkable waterfall plunges nearly 1,000 meters or 3,212 feet into the Devil's Canyon. (4) Angel Falls is 19 times higher than Niagara Falls on the U.S. and Canadian border.

(B)

(5) The name may make you think that the waterfall was named for falling angels. (6) The falls are named for an American pilot and adventurer. (7) Jimmie Angel, who accidentally came across it. (8) However, it was not named for heavenly, winged creatures.

CORRECTION QUESTIONS

On correction questions, you will be asked to identify grammatical errors in particular sentences and choose which options provide the best corrections to the errors. Each question will provide the sentence number and the sentence itself again. Here is a sample question:

1. Sentence 2: **The waterfall lies in a national park in the heart of venezuela.**

Which correction should be made to sentence 2?

    (1)   Insert a comma after waterfall.
    (2)   Insert and after heart.
    (3)   Change lies to lie.
    (4)   Change venezuela to Venezuela.
    (5)   No correction is necessary.

①②③●⑤

This question is typical of the correction questions on the GED test. You are asked to identify where the error lies in the sentence and which answer choice corrects the error. In this question, the answer is (4), since *venezuela* is a proper noun and should be capitalized. You would darken the oval for answer (4).

Notice that you do not have to provide the correction. If there is an error in the sentence, the right correction lies among the answer choices. Notice also that some questions give you the option of marking "No correction is necessary." Do not be afraid to choose this answer. In some cases, there is no error in the sentence.

 You don't need to know grammatical terms for the Language Arts, Writing test. You are not asked to say what type of error occurs. You simply have to identify which correction (if any) improves the sentence.

TEST-TAKING TIP

To answer correction questions, follow these steps:

1. Read the sentence. Trust your ear to identify the error. If it sounds wrong, it probably is.

2. Read each option, looking for a possible correction to the error.

3. Eliminate answer choices that are obviously incorrect.

4. Choose answer (5), "No correction is necessary," if there are no mistakes.

You can often pick out the error easily. After learning the rules of grammar in this chapter, you will know exactly what kinds of errors to look for.

REVISION QUESTIONS

Now let's look at the second type of question you'll face on the Writing test. Here's an example of a revision question based on the same passage given earlier:

2. Sentences 6 and 7: The falls are named for an American pilot <u>and adventurer. Jimmie Angel, who</u> accidentally came across it.

Which is the best way to write the underlined portion of these sentences? If the original is the best way, choose answer (1).

(1)   and adventurer. Jimmie Angel, who
(2)   and adventurer. Jimmie Angel that
(3)   and adventurer, Jimmie Angel, who
(4)   yet adventurer. Jimmie Angel, who
(5)   and adventurer; Jimmie Angel who

① ② ● ④ ⑤

In revision questions, you are asked to revise an underlined part of a sentence or sentences. You should assume that the other parts of the sentence are correct. The underlined part may or may not contain an error. You must choose the answer that

CHAPTER

3

LANGUAGE
ARTS,
WRITING

THE
GED

corrects the error, if there is one. If there is no error, mark answer (1), which indicates that there is no error in the underlined part.

In this question, the correct answer is answer (3), since it corrects the sentence fragment in the original sentence 7. We discuss sentence fragments and other common sentence errors on pages 72–75.

TEST-TAKING TIP
To answer revision questions, follow these steps:

1. Read the sentence(s), focusing on the underlined part. Trust your ear to identify the error.
2. Read each option, looking for a possible correction to the error.
3. Eliminate answer choices that are obviously incorrect.
4. Choose answer (1) if there are no mistakes.

Often, you can identify the error and the correct revision right away. The grammatical rules presented later in this chapter show you exactly what kinds of errors to look for.

CONSTRUCTION-SHIFT QUESTIONS
The third type of question asks you how to move sentences around in a passage or to identify topic sentences. These questions test organization, or how to structure sentences to present ideas clearly. Here's an example of a construction-shift question based on the same passage given earlier:

3. Which revision would improve the effectiveness of paragraph B?

    (1)   Move sentence 7 to the beginning of the paragraph.
    (2)   Move sentence 5 to the end of the paragraph.
    (3)   Remove sentence 6.
    (4)   Move sentence 8 to follow sentence 5.
    (5)   No revision is necessary.

In this question, you must figure out which sentence should be moved or removed to improve the flow of ideas in the passage. To do that, first read the entire passage. Then move on to the answers. Let's look at each of the options. If you move sentence 7 to the beginning of the paragraph as answer (1) suggests, the paragraph starts strangely. Sentence 7 is also a sentence fragment, which should not stand alone as a sentence. Therefore, eliminate answer (1).

Answer (2), moving sentence 5 to the end of the paragraph, also doesn't make sense. Sentence 5 serves as the topic sentence. It belongs where it is: at the paragraph's beginning. Eliminate answer (2). Rule out answer (3), as well, since sentence 6 contains ideas that are important to the paragraph. Removing sentence 6 would not improve the paragraph.

Answer (4) is the correct answer. Moving sentence 8 to follow sentence 5 improves the flow of ideas. The ideas in sentence 8 provide a clear transition to the ideas in sentences 6 and 7.

Most construction-shift questions are similar to this one. You must look at the paragraph or passage as a whole.

Construction-shift or organizational questions ask you to

- Identify where a paragraph break should occur.
- Identify which sentence makes the best topic sentence.
- Identify sentences irrelevant to the passage.
- Move sentences to create clear transitions between ideas.
- Move sentences to create logical order of ideas.

We look at more construction-shift questions when we discuss topic sentences, transitions, and restructuring paragraphs later in this chapter.

TEST-TAKING TIP

To answer construction-shift questions, follow these steps:
1. Read the paragraph or passage in question.
2. Read each answer choice, looking for a possible improvement in sentence order or paragraph organization.
3. Eliminate answer choices that are obviously incorrect or that make the paragraph more confusing.

Good work. You now know what kinds of questions you'll encounter and how to tackle them. Let's move on to the second ladder rung: Capitalization and Spelling.

CAPITALIZATION AND SPELLING

About 25 percent of the multiple-choice questions test "mechanics", which includes capitalization and spelling. This second rung of the ladder will bring you up to speed on these basic skills.

CAPITALIZATION

Obviously, we capitalize the first letter at the beginning of a sentence, but there are some other rules of capitalization that you may have forgotten.

- **Capitalize proper nouns:** A proper noun is a word that names a specific person, place, or thing, such as Jonathan Edwards, Martha, Wall Street, Mercer Island, Paraguay, Guild Movie Theater, Roasted Bean Coffee House

- **Capitalize proper adjectives:** A proper adjective is a descriptive word that is formed from a proper noun, such as Gregorian chant, Hellenistic period, Confucian philosophy

- **Capitalize titles before names:** President Washington, Ms. Lee, Governor Jackson

- **Capitalize titles and family appellations (aunt, father, etc.) when they are used to address someone directly:**

  Mr. Tully said, "Good morning, Mother."

  "How are you, Mayor?" asked the assistant.

  "Well, Madam, I would like to apply to be a baker in your restaurant."

- **Capitalize the names of all holidays, days of the week, and months of the year:** Tuesday, New Year's Day, Independence Day, January, October, March, Labor Day

You should also know when not to capitalize words.

- **Do NOT capitalize titles or family appellations that follow *a*, *the*, or a possessive pronoun such as *my*, *your*, *his*, *her*, or *their*:**

  Yi went to the play with his aunt. (but Yi went to play with Aunt Valerie.)

  Candyce met with the mayor to discuss the city budget.

  Pilar made an appointment with the president of the board.

- **Do NOT capitalize the names of the seasons:**

  spring, summer, winter, fall, autumn

  Sasha will take her exams in the fall.

- **Do NOT capitalize a school subject unless it is the name of a specific course or language:** Both of the following sentences are correct.

  Othello will take a biology course in the spring.

  Desdemona will take Iberian History 101 and Chinese.

- **Do NOT capitalize a direction word unless it refers to a specific place, such as the region of a country:** Both of the following sentences are correct.

  Jeremy and Joon drove north to the border.

  Joon grew up in this city, but Jeremy was born in the Northeast.

- **Do NOT capitalize a geographic place unless it is part of a specific place (or proper noun).** The following sentences are correct.

  Farrah lives near the pond.

  The twins wanted to go skating at Crane's Pond.

  The mountain is covered with snow.

  Mandy wants to go hiking at Mount Shasta.

Capitalize	Do Not Capitalize
proper nouns	titles or family appellations preceded by articles or possessive pronouns
proper adjectives	
titles and family names in direct address	seasons

Capitalize	Do Not Capitalize
holidays, days of the week, months	school subjects unless they are the names of specific courses or languages
	direction words unless they refer to specific places and are thus part of a proper noun

Capitalization errors occur mostly in correction questions. Here's an example of a typical question involving capitalization, following a very short passage:

EXAMPLE

MEMORANDUM

TO: All Employees at Hook, Line, and Sinker

FROM: Carmela Fuentes, Human Resources Director

RE: Casual Dress on Fridays

(1) Beginning next Friday, June 3, we will reinstate our summer policy regarding the dress code. (2) Following memorial Day, feel free to dress casually every Friday. (3) Casual dress includes polo shirts, khaki pants, and neatly pressed T-shirts. (4) Please do not wear cut-off pants or baseball caps. (5) The casual dress policy will be in effect through Labor Day weekend.

1. Sentence 2: **Following memorial Day, feel free to dress casually every Friday.**

   Which correction should be made to sentence 2?

   (1)   Change <u>memorial</u> to <u>Memorial</u>.
   (2)   Remove the comma.
   (3)   Change <u>Day</u> to <u>day</u>.
   (4)   Change <u>feel</u> to <u>felt</u>.
   (5)   No correction is necessary.

   ●②③④⑤

The answer is (1). *Memorial* should be capitalized because it is the name of a holiday. You can eliminate answer (3), since *Day* is also part of the holiday name and should remain capitalized.

SPELLING

The Language Arts, Writing test includes only three kinds of spelling errors, involving

- Possessives
- Contractions
- Homonyms

Once you know how to identify these types of errors, you'll be prepared for any spelling question.

CHAPTER

3

LANGUAGE
ARTS,
WRITING

INTRODUCTION

**CAPITALIZATION
AND SPELLING**

PUNCTUATION

VERBS

PRONOUNS

COMMON
SENTENCE ERRORS

COORDINATION
AND
SUBORDINATION

MISPLACED AND
DANGLING
MODIFIERS

PARALLEL
STRUCTURE

RESTRUCTURING
PARAGRAPHS

THE ESSAY

52

POSSESSIVES

Possessives are words that show possession or ownership. You need to know the following rules for possessives:

- **Add an apostrophe s (*'s*) to show the possessive for a singular noun and for a plural noun not ending in –*s*:**

    Erica's sister will go fishing with her.

    My boss's husband sent her a bouquet of roses.

    The children's toys are in the attic.

- **Add only an apostrophe to show the possessive for a plural noun ending in –*s*:**

    The dogs' leashes are in the garage.

    Natasha carefully lifted the wipers' blades.

- **Do NOT use an apostrophe with the possessive pronouns *hers*, *his*, *its*, *ours*, *theirs*, *yours*, and *whose*. These pronouns already indicate possession without the apostrophe:**

    Whose letter is this?

    The box of ribbons is his.

    My heart is yours.

Those are all the rules you need to know regarding possessives. Now let's go over contractions.

CONTRACTIONS

A **contraction** is a shortened form of a word or phrase. To create a contraction, you combine words and omit one or more letters. The letters are replaced by an apostrophe. Here are some rules to keep in mind:

- **Use an apostrophe to take the place of missing letters. Make sure the apostrophe is in the right place. The apostrophe should be where the missing letters would be.** Here are some examples of common contractions:

aren't	haven't	it's	wasn't	you're
can't	he'd	she'd	we're	you've
didn't	I'm	shouldn't	weren't	
don't	I've	they'll	wouldn't	

Notice that many contractions combine a verb and the word *not*, as in *don't*, *won't*, *can't*.

Other contractions combine a pronoun such as *I*, *you*, *he*, *she*, or *they* and a verb, as in *I'm*, *you've*, *he'd*, *she'll*, *they'd*.

- **Do NOT confuse contractions with possessives that sound the same:** Confusing contractions with possessives is a common error on the

Writing test. Look out particularly for errors in the use of *its* and *it's*. *Its* is a possessive form. *It's* is a contraction standing for *it is*. To determine whether the word should be a contraction or a possessive, substitute the words that stand for the contraction. If the sentence makes sense, the word is a contraction. For example, look at the next sentence:

Its going to rain later today.

If you substitute the two words *It is* in the sentence, you get

It is going to rain later today.

The sentence makes sense, so the word should be a contraction: *It's*. You've identified the error in this sentence.

HOMONYMS

The third type of spelling error involves **homonyms**, or words that sound alike but have different meanings, such as

brake/break	pedal/peddle	to/two/too
here/hear	shore/sure	weak/week
knew/new	their/there/they're	your/you're

You've already encountered homonyms involving contractions and possessives, such as *it's/its*. Sometimes, the test-makers present words that are not exactly homonyms but sound similar enough to be confused, such as

accept/except

than/then

Be prepared to find a couple of correction questions that contain errors such as the following:

EXAMPLE

Sentence 7: **Max was under the allusion that Minnie was obsessed with him.**

Which correction should be made to sentence 7?

    (1)   Change <u>was</u> to <u>were</u>.
    (2)   Replace <u>allusion</u> with <u>illusion</u>.
    (3)   Insert a comma after <u>under</u>.
    (4)   Change <u>that</u> to <u>which</u>.
    (5)   No correction is necessary.

① ● ③ ④ ⑤

An allusion is a reference to something. The sentence requires the word *illusion*, which is a false idea or conception. The correct answer is (2). Be on the lookout for similar pairs of easily confused words, such as set/sit, emigrate/immigrate, accept/except.

You've almost completed the second rung of the ladder. Take the following practice set to test your grasp of capitalization and spelling.

THE
GED

CHAPTER

3

LANGUAGE
ARTS,
WRITING

THE
GED

PRACTICE SET: CAPITALIZATION AND SPELLING

Directions: Choose the one best answer to each question.

Questions 1 through 5 refer to the following letter.

October 9, 2004
Mr. Peter Ali
70 Apple Lane
New York, NY 10029
Dear Mr. Ali:

(A)

(1) Thank you for allowing us to assist you with your balance transfer. (2) Your balance transfer request has been initiated. (3) Once the transaction is complete, the amount you requested will be transferred to your Greater Bank account. (4) Your annual percentage rate of 0% will be in force through december 2005.

(B)

(5) We are also sending you three access checks. (6) They are easy to use and are excepted everywhere that personal checks are used. (7) These checks are yours' to use whenever you need to access your credit line. (8) You can use these checks to transfer balances from other credit cards. (9) You may also want to use them to make home improvements this Spring. (10) When you use an access check, you'll benefit from the same low annual percentage rate of 0% through the end of 2005. (11) When this promotional rate ends, your annual percentage rate will be 12.99%.

(C)

(12) If you have questions regarding your Greater Bank account, please call me at 1-800-555-7890. (13) Its been a pleasure to serve you, and I look forward to assisting you in the future.

Sincerely,

Rosa Kammel

Rosa Kammel
Marketing Director

---

1. Sentence 4: **Your annual percentage rate of 0% will be in force through december 2005.**

   Which correction should be made to sentence 4?
   (1)   Insert a comma after <u>rate</u>.
   (2)   Replace <u>Your</u> with <u>You're</u>.
   (3)   Change <u>will be</u> to <u>had been</u>.
   (4)   Replace <u>december</u> with <u>December</u>.
   (5)   No correction is necessary.

2. Sentence 6: **They are easy to use and are excepted everywhere that personal checks are used.**

Which correction should be made to sentence 6?

(1) Change the first <u>are</u> to <u>is</u>.
(2) Replace <u>excepted</u> with <u>accepted</u>.
(3) Change <u>that</u> to <u>whose</u>.
(4) Replace <u>checks</u> with <u>check's</u>.
(5) No correction is necessary.

3. Sentence 7: **These checks are yours' to use whenever you need to access your credit line.**

Which correction should be made to sentence 7?

(1) Replace <u>checks</u> with <u>checks'</u>.
(2) Replace <u>yours'</u> with <u>yours</u>.
(3) Replace <u>need</u> with <u>knead</u>.
(4) Replace <u>access</u> with <u>excess</u>.
(5) Replace <u>your</u> with <u>you're</u>.

4. Sentence 9: **You may also want to use them to make home improvements this Spring.**

Which correction should be made to sentence 9?

(1) Replace <u>may</u> with <u>May</u>.
(2) Replace the first <u>to</u> with <u>two</u>.
(3) Change <u>make</u> to <u>making</u>.
(4) Replace <u>Spring</u> with <u>spring</u>.
(5) No correction is necessary.

5. Sentence 13: **Its been a pleasure to serve you, and I look forward to assisting you in the future.**

Which correction should be made to sentence 13?

(1) Replace <u>Its</u> with <u>It's</u>.
(2) Remove the comma.
(3) Replace <u>I</u> with <u>eye</u>.
(4) Replace the second <u>to</u> with <u>too</u>.
(5) No correction is necessary.

Check your answers on page 109. How did you do? If you missed most of the questions, review this rung once more. If you got most of the answers right, you're going to do just fine on this part of the test. Let's look at the next rung: Punctuation.

THE
GED

PUNCTUATION

Punctuation refers to using punctuation marks such as periods, question marks, commas, colons, etc. Here's the good news: **the GED is only concerned with commas!**

Punctuation Mark	Symbol
period	.
question mark	?
exclamation point	!
comma	,
semicolon	;
colon	:

A **comma** indicates a pause. Learn the following rules about how to use commas.

- **Use commas to separate items in a series:** Whenever there are two or more items in a list or series, you should use commas. Make sure there is a comma before "and" when it precedes the last item in a series.

  All my brothers, aunts, and grandparents came to the softball game.

  Frances plays golf, runs marathons, and sings country songs.

- **Do NOT use commas if each item in the series is joined by *and* or *or*. Also, do NOT use commas between two items that are separated by *and* or *or*.**

  I need a toothpick and a nail and a bottle of glue.

  José or Tanya or Beck will bring a hammer.

  Andrew and Margo are not eating lunch today.

- **Use commas to separate two or more adjectives before a noun.**

  Sherman said he's going to the hot, balmy tropics.

  Carlos is going to make a delicious, buttery cake for the party.

- **Use commas before *and*, *but*, *or*, *nor*, *for*, *so*, and *yet* when they join independent clauses. An *independent clause* contains a complete and separate thought.**

  Kara Osato changed the oil in her car, so the car should run smoothly.

  Kostya flew to Spain, and Tomasz flew to Croatia.

  Rachel sold four boxes of cookies, but Liam only sold one.

- **Use commas to set off nonessential clauses and phrases:**

  A *nonessential clause* or *phrase* is a group of words that adds information that is not needed to understand the main idea of the sentence. A good way of spotting a nonessential clause is to see if it could be put into parentheses. If so, it is not essential to the sentence.

Texas, which is a large state, lies in the southern portion of the country.

Shyam, studying for his exams, read 100 pages every day.

Erika, my coworker, lives in the suburbs.

- **Do NOT use commas with essential clauses and phrases:**
An essential clause or phrase is a group of words that adds information that is necessary to understand the main idea of the sentence.
All students <u>whose names begin with the letter Z</u> must attend the class.

Anyone <u>missing more than one meeting</u> will be replaced.

Mimi wanted to go to the shore to watch the birds <u>that live on the water</u>.

In the sentences above, you can't omit the underlined clause or phrase without changing the meaning of the sentence.

The word **which** is used to indicate a nonessential clause or phrase and should be preceded by a comma.

The word **that** is not preceded by a comma, since what follows it is usually essential to the sentence.

Example: Matt is using blue paint, which he bought at the hardware store.

Example: Emily always uses the paint that her mother recommends.

- **Use commas to set off introductory elements:** Introductory words such as *next, no, yes, therefore, well,* and *oh* should be set off by a comma.
Well, I hesitate to answer that question.

Yes, she's going to send a memo on that topic.

Next, move the chair to the right of Herman.

You should also use commas after introductory clauses and phrases, as in the following sentences:
After Bharati opened the window, she enjoyed the warm breeze.

Alarmed by the high prices, we went to another store to buy fruit.

By the end of the plane ride, the pilot was ready for a nap.

CHAPTER

3

LANGUAGE
ARTS,
WRITING

THE
GED

- **Use commas to set off parenthetical phrases:** Parenthetical phrases are side remarks that add minor information or that relate ideas to each other. Use a comma before and after these phrases when they appear in the middle of a sentence.

  Rhode Island, however, is a small state.

  The Mariners, for example, are having a very good season.

  In fact, the entire industry has experienced a setback since 2000.

Common Parenthetical Phrases
after all
at any rate
consequently
for example
for instance
however
in fact
meanwhile
moreover
nevertheless
of course
therefore

Questions about punctuation appear as correction or revision questions. Be prepared to find a couple of questions that contain errors such as the following:

EXAMPLE

Sentence 9: **No the post office will be open next Monday.**

Which correction should be made to sentence 9?

(1)   Insert a comma after <u>No</u>.
(2)   Replace <u>post</u> with <u>Post</u>.
(3)   Insert a comma after <u>office</u>.
(4)   Replace <u>Monday</u> with <u>monday</u>.
(5)   No correction is necessary.

●②③④⑤

The correct answer is (1). The introductory word *No* should be followed by a comma. You can eliminate answer (2), because there is no reason to capitalize *post*. Similarly, rule out answer (4), since *Monday*, a day of the week, should be capitalized. No comma is needed after *office*, so answer (3) is also wrong.

Sentence 3: **The students in Mr. Kim's class <u>will study violin piano, and guitar.</u>**

Which is the best way to write the underlined portion of this sentence? If the original is the best way, choose answer (1).

(1)   will study violin piano, and guitar.
(2)   will study violin, piano, and guitar.
(3)   will study violin piano and guitar.
(4)   will study violin piano, and, guitar.
(5)   No correction is necessary.

①●③④⑤

The correct answer is (2). *Violin* should be followed by a comma, because items in a series should be separated by commas. Eliminate answers (1) and (3), since commas are required. Eliminate answer (4), since no comma is needed after *and*.

You've almost finished the punctuation section. Next, answer the following practice set to test your grasp of punctuation.

PRACTICE SET: PUNCTUATION

Directions: Choose the <u>one best answer</u> to each question.

<u>Questions 1 through 5</u> refer to the following article.

How to Fix a Hole in a Wall

(A)

(1) Like many people, you may live in a place whose walls have a few holes in them. (2) Holes formed by nails are quite common. (3) Fortunately these nail holes are easy to fix. (4) The entire process should take about 30 minutes. (5) All you need are a few materials and tools that you can get at any hardware store.

(B)

(6) The first thing you should do is gather the materials you need. (7) You will need spackling paste, a putty knife a sponge, sandpaper, and painting supplies. (8) After you have gathered these materials apply spackling paste to the hole using the putty knife. (9) Push the spackling paste in as far as it will go. (10) Next, wipe the area clean with a damp sponge and let the area dry. (11) Once the area is dry, lightly sand it to smooth the edges around the hole. (12) Then, use primer to prepare the area and repaint it. (13) You may be tired after expending a bit of effort. (14) Your wall, however will look better than ever.

1. Sentence 3: **Fortunately these nail holes are easy to fix.**

   Which is the best way to write the underlined portion of this sentence? If the original is the best way, choose answer (1).

   (1)   Fortunately these nail holes
   (2)   Fortunately, these nail holes
   (3)   Fortunately this nail holes
   (4)   Fortunately these nail hole's
   (5)   Fortunately these nail, holes

2. Sentence 5: **All you need are a few materials and tools that you can get at any hardware store.**

   Which correction should be made to sentence 5?

   (1)   Replace <u>materials</u> with <u>material's</u>.
   (2)   Insert a comma after <u>materials</u>.
   (3)   Replace <u>tools</u> with <u>Tools</u>.
   (4)   Insert a comma after <u>tools</u>.
   (5)   No correction is necessary.

THE
GED

3. Sentence 7: **You will need spackling paste, a putty knife a sponge, sandpaper, and painting supplies.**

Which correction should be made to sentence 7?

(1)   Change <u>need</u> to <u>needed</u>.
(2)   Remove the comma after <u>paste</u>.
(3)   Insert a comma after <u>knife</u>.
(4)   Replace <u>supplies</u> with <u>supply's</u>.
(5)   No correction is necessary.

4. Sentence 8: **After you have gathered these materials apply spackling paste to the hole using the putty knife.**

Which correction should be made to sentence 8?

(1)   Change <u>have gathered</u> to <u>has gathered</u>.
(2)   Insert a comma after <u>materials</u>.
(3)   Replace <u>to</u> with <u>two</u>.
(4)   Insert a comma after <u>paste</u>.
(5)   No correction is necessary.

5. Sentence 14: <u>**Your wall, however will look**</u> **better than ever.**

Which is the best way to write the underlined portion of this sentence? If the original is the best way, choose answer (1).

(1)   Your wall, however will look
(2)   You're wall, however will look
(3)   Your wall however will look
(4)   Your wall, however, will look
(5)   Your wall, however would look

Check your answers on page 110. How did you do? If you missed most of these questions, review the Punctuation ladder rung again. If you got most of the answers right, you're ready to step up to the next rung: Verbs.

VERBS

Congratulations. You have finished studying all the mechanics content you need to know. If you understood the last sections, you'll do well with any mechanics questions you encounter on the test. Now let's look at the first type of "usage" problem: verbs.

   A **verb** is a word used to express an action or a state of being. Verb questions on the Writing test fall into two categories: subject-verb agreement and verb tense. We look at both types of questions in this section.

SUBJECT-VERB AGREEMENT

Subjects and verbs need to *agree* in number. Singular subjects need singular verbs, which generally end in *s*. Plural subjects need plural verbs, which generally don't end in *s*. In a regular, everyday sentence, you will probably recognize when there is subject-verb disagreement. Look at the following sentence:

Delia like to bicycle around the park.

The word *like* probably strikes you as incorrect. The singular subject *Delia* requires the singular verb form *likes*.

   However, errors in subject-verb agreement are not always so obvious. For example, in some questions, the order of the subject and verb are reversed or inverted. Try to identify the error in the following question:

EXAMPLE

Sentence 16: **Although some people prefer to eat pizza, there is others who would rather eat salad.**

Which correction should be made to sentence 16?

   (1)   Replace <u>some</u> with <u>sum</u>.
   (2)   Remove the comma after <u>pizza</u>.
   (3)   Change <u>is</u> to <u>are</u>.
   (4)   Replace <u>would</u> with <u>wood</u>.
   (5)   No correction is necessary.

①②●④⑤

The correct answer is (3). The plural subject *others* requires the plural verb *are* rather than the singular *is*. Notice how the verb follows the subject in the above sentence. Be on the lookout for errors in subject-verb agreement when the subject follows the verb. Remember that all you have to do is identify the subject and determine whether it takes a singular or plural verb.

THE

GED

The test-makers also like to separate the subject and the verb with a phrase. That's a GED trap. Look for the error in subject-verb agreement in the next question:

EXAMPLE

Sentence 1: **The sign near the entrance explain what to do in case of an emergency.**

Which correction should be made to sentence 1?

(1)   Insert a comma after <u>sign</u>.
(2)   Change <u>explain</u> to <u>explains</u>.
(3)   Replace <u>to</u> with <u>too</u>.
(4)   Insert a comma after <u>case</u>.
(5)   No correction is necessary.

①●③④⑤

The answer is (2). The singular subject *sign* should take the singular verb *explains* rather than the plural *explain*. The phrase that comes between the subject and the verb, *near the entrance*, has no effect on the number of the verb. Answers (1) and (4) are incorrect, since no commas are required in this sentence. Answer (3) would introduce an incorrect homonym.

You should also keep in mind the following rules regarding subject-verb agreement.

- **Subjects joined by *and* usually take a plural verb:**
  Elizabeth Bishop and Wallace Stevens were poets.

- **The following words are always singular subjects: *each, either, neither, one, everyone, everybody, everything, no one, nobody, nothing, anyone, anybody, anything, someone, somebody, something*.**
  Each of the parents runs a carpool.
  Nobody tells Gracie what to do.

- **The following words are always plural subjects: *several, few, both, many*.**
  Several of the cooks decide to take Tuesday off.
  Few of the candidates stay in the race.
  Were both of the candidates late?

- **The following words may be either singular or plural: *some, all, most, any, none*:**
  Some of the comedians were very entertaining.
  Some of the exhibit is educational.
  Most of his collection comes from Nevada.
  Most of his paintings are by one artist.

- **When subjects are joined by *or, nor, either . . . or*, or *neither . . . nor*, the verb agrees with the subject nearer the verb:**

  Neither Juan nor his brothers enjoy fishing.

  Either the teachers or Ms. Silverstein has the key.

  Anya or Gil is swimming in the competition.

- **Collective nouns can be either singular or plural.**

  A **collective noun** is singular in form but names a group of persons or things. Examples of collective nouns are *group, audience, class, committee, family, team*, and *majority*. When the group is acting as a unit, use a singular verb. When the individuals in the group are acting separately, use a plural verb.

  The group came to a decision.

  The class have finished their assignments.

Not Plural

When you see the following constructions, be on the lookout for subjects that look plural but are not:

either _____ or _____

neither _____ nor_____

_____ along with _____

_____ as well as _____

_____ in addition to _____

together with _____

Knowing these rules of subject–verb agreement will help you excel on the Writing test. Now, let's take a look at verb tenses.

VERB TENSES

The **tense** of a verb indicates the time of the action or state of being expressed by the verb. Verbs have six tenses in English: present, past, future, present perfect, past perfect, and future perfect. Look at the following chart:

The Six Tenses

Tense	Definition	Example
Present	existing or happening now	Jim **has** enough money.
Present Perfect	existing or happening sometime before now	Jim **has worked** all summer, and now he feels wealthy.
Past	existing or happening in the past	He **saved** nickels in his piggybank.
Past Perfect	existing or happening before a specific time in the past	Before he counted his bills, Jim **had taken** them out of his wallet.
Future	existing or happening in the future	He **will decide** how much to spend on a new notebook.
Future Perfect	existing or happening before a specific time in the future	Jim **will have considered** many options, and he will make an informed decision.

CHAPTER

3

LANGUAGE
ARTS,
WRITING

THE

GED

Keep in mind the following rules:

- **Use the (simple) present tense, past tense, and future tense when the condition described is usually true:**

  Ms. Marcus belongs to the union. [present tense]

  We looked for clothes to wear to work. [past tense]

  Oliver and Daisy will arrive soon. [future tense]

- **Use the perfect tenses to show more complex time relationships.**

  The perfect tenses use a helping verb. The helping verb is the verb *have*: *have, has, had, will have,* and *shall have.*

  The DiMeolas have invited us over for dinner. [present perfect tense]

  We had been raking leaves for hours when you called. [past perfect tense]

  By the time the mayor returns, I will have adjourned the meeting. [future perfect tense]

- **Do NOT change needlessly from one tense to another:** Tenses within a sentence or paragraph should be consistent unless the meaning requires a change.

  Ichiro fielded the ball and threw the runner out.

  He stands behind the plate and stares at the bleachers.

  When I greeted Josh, he waved to me.

  In some sentences, the meaning requires a shift in tense:

  If he forgets his appointment again, I will become impatient with him.

  In the sentence above, the action in the first part is in the present tense. However, the action in the second part of the sentence occurs after the action in the first part. Therefore, the future tense should be used in the second part.

Questions involving verb tense appear as correction or revision questions. Be prepared to find a couple of questions such as the following:

EXAMPLE

Sentence 3: **If you want to contact customer service, please have called the number above.**

Which correction should be made to sentence 3?

  (1)   Change <u>want</u> to <u>will want</u>.
  (2)   Remove the comma.
  (3)   Change <u>have called</u> to <u>call</u>.
  (4)   Insert a comma after <u>number</u>.
  (5)   No correction is necessary.

①②●④⑤

The correct answer is (3). The verb should be changed to the present tense to be consistent with the verb in the first part of the sentence (*want*). You can eliminate answer (1), because changing the tense from present to future does not make the tenses consistent in the sentence. Rule out answer (2), since the comma is necessary after the introductory subordinate clause. No comma is needed after *number*, so answer (4) is also wrong.

EXAMPLE

Sentences 7 and 8: **Yesterday, Hannah looked in the <u>newspaper for job listings. She sees</u> a few listings that look promising.**

Which is the best way to write the underlined portion of these sentences? If the original is the best way, choose answer (1).

    (1)   newspaper for job listings. She sees
    (2)   newspaper for job listings, she sees
    (3)   newspaper for job listing's. She sees
    (4)   newspaper for job listings. She saw
    (5)   newspaper for job listings. She will see

①②③●⑤

The correct answer is (4). The verb in the second sentence should be in the past tense to be consistent. Answer (2) creates a comma splice (we discuss comma splices in the section "Common Sentence Errors: Sentence Fragments, Run-Ons, and Comma Splices"). Eliminate answer (3), since the possessive form of *listing's* is incorrect. Answer (5) is wrong, because *will see* is in the future tense and is an incorrect verb tense.

THE
GED

PRACTICE SET: VERBS

Directions: Choose the <u>one best answer</u> to each question.

<u>Questions 1 through 5</u> refer to the following article.

The Salvation Army

(A)

(1) The Salvation Army is a religious organization. (2) It focuses on spreading the Christian faith, and it help people in need. (3) It offers shelter, food, and other types of aid to people throughout the world.

(B)

(4) An English minister named William Booth and his wife Catherine Booth founded the organization. (5) In 1865, William Booth started a mission in a poor section of London. (6) He assists people who were starving or without homes. (7) He also persuaded people to become Christian, beginning by setting up a tent in a graveyard and preaching from there. (8) Everyone were welcome to join the mission. (9) His services were an instant success, and the mission grew quickly. (10) In 1878, the mission took the name of The Salvation Army.

(C)

(11) Today, the group operate in more than 80 countries. (12) Its members preach in about 112 languages. (13) The Army has 16,000 religious centers, and it runs thousands of hospitals, schools, homeless shelters, and other centers to help people. (14) Today, there is about two million members of the organization.

1. Sentence 2: **It focuses on spreading the Christian faith, and it help people in need.**

   Which correction should be made to sentence 2?

   (1)   Change <u>focuses</u> to <u>focus</u>.
   (2)   Remove the comma.
   (3)   Change <u>help</u> to <u>helps</u>.
   (4)   Insert a comma after <u>people</u>.
   (5)   No correction is necessary.

2. Sentences 5 and 6: **In 1865, William Booth started a mission in a poor <u>section of London. He assists people who were</u> starving or without homes.**

   Which is the best way to write the underlined portion of these sentences? If the original is the best way, choose answer (1).

   (1)   section of London. He assists people who were
   (2)   section of london. He assists people who were
   (3)   section of London, he assists people who were
   (4)   section of London. He assisted people who were
   (5)   section of London. He assists people who was

3. Sentence 8: **Everyone were welcome to join the mission.**

Which correction should be made to sentence 8?

(1)   Change <u>were</u> to <u>was</u>.
(2)   Insert a comma after <u>welcome</u>.
(3)   Replace <u>to</u> with <u>two</u>.
(4)   Change <u>join</u> to <u>joins</u>.
(5)   No correction is necessary.

4. Sentence 11: **Today, the group operate in more than 80 countries.**

Which correction should be made to sentence 11?

(1)   Remove the comma.
(2)   Change <u>operate</u> to <u>operates</u>.
(3)   Change <u>operate</u> to <u>will operate</u>.
(4)   Replace <u>than</u> with <u>then</u>.
(5)   No correction is necessary.

5. Sentence 14: <u>**Today, there is about two million members**</u> of the organization.

Which is the best way to write the underlined portion of this sentence? If the original is the best way, choose answer (1).

(1)   Today, there is about two million members
(2)   Today there is about two million members
(3)   Today, there are about two million members
(4)   Today, there were about two million members
(5)   Today, there will have been about two million members

Check your answers on page 110. If you answered most of the questions correctly, go on to the next rung. If you missed a few questions, review the Verbs ladder rung again.

You're making good progress. Verbs make up a big portion of the usage questions on the test, and you've just proved your knowledge of that subject. Now let's look at the next rung, Pronouns—another big part of the test.

CHAPTER
3

LANGUAGE
ARTS,
WRITING

THE
GED

INTRODUCTION
CAPITALIZATION
AND SPELLING
PUNCTUATION
VERBS
PRONOUNS
COMMON
SENTENCE ERRORS
COORDINATION
AND
SUBORDINATION
MISPLACED AND
DANGLING
MODIFIERS
PARALLEL
STRUCTURE
RESTRUCTURING
PARAGRAPHS
THE ESSAY

PRONOUNS

A **pronoun** is a word used in place of a noun or nouns. When you see a pronoun on the test, be on the alert for an error. You will likely encounter a sentence in which the pronoun disagrees in number with the noun it refers to. Pronouns must agree in number with the nouns they refer to. See if you can spot the error in pronoun number in the sentence below:

EXAMPLE

Sentence 1: **The smartly dressed woman walked their dog in the rain.**

Which correction should be made to sentence 1?

    (1)   Insert a comma after <u>dressed</u>.
    (2)   Change <u>dressed</u> to <u>dress</u>.
    (3)   Change <u>walked</u> to <u>walking</u>.
    (4)   Change <u>their</u> to <u>her</u>.
    (5)   No correction is necessary.

①②③●⑤

Answer (4) is correct, since the pronoun *their* is plural while the noun it refers to (*woman*) is singular. The correct pronoun is *her*. Notice that you can use the process of elimination to get rid of the other options. Answer (1) is incorrect because no comma is needed after *dressed*. Answers (2) and (3) are wrong because they change the verbs to the wrong tenses.

Another pronoun error to watch for is pronouns in the wrong case. **Case** is the form of a pronoun that shows how the word is used. Pronouns may be in the nominative, objective, and possessive cases. In the next sentence, *I* is in the nominative case; *me* is in the objective case; and *my* is in the possessive case:

I forgot to bring **my** notes with **me** to the meeting.

Don't worry—it's not important for you to name pronoun cases on the test. You just have to be able to recognize when a pronoun is in the wrong case. Errors in pronoun case occur most often in *compound noun phrases*. A compound noun phrase occurs when the pronoun is linked with a noun or another pronoun. Look at the following sentence:

Him and Quincy traveled for ten days and nights on a leaky boat.

The compound noun phrase is *Him and Quincy*. In this phrase, the pronoun *Him* is in the wrong case, because the pronoun should be acting as a subject. Who traveled? *He* did. *Him* can't travel, because *him* is in the objective, not subjective, case. The trick with these questions is to isolate the pronoun and make sure that it is in the right case. To check the pronoun's case, try reading the phrase without the other part of the compound noun phrase.

A third pronoun error is in **pronoun shifts**. Pronoun shifts occur when the author begins a sentence or paragraph using one pronoun and then switches to another pronoun at some point in the text. See if you can identify the pronoun shift in the next sentence:

Whenever one attends a meeting, you should be prepared.

Pronoun Checklist

When you see a pronoun, check to see if there is an error in one of the following:

Number—Does it match the number of the noun it refers to?

Case—Is it in the right form?

Shift—Are the pronouns consistent in the sentence?

Reference—Does it refer clearly to something in the sentence?

If you identified the pronoun *you* as incorrect, you are right. The pronouns in the above sentence refer to the same performer, so they need to be consistent. *You* should be replaced by the pronoun that was originally used, which is *one*. The test-makers create pronoun shifts with words such as *you*, *one*, and *they* that are often used interchangeably in everyday speech. These pronouns should be consistent in standard written English.

The final area of pronoun problems is **reference**. A pronoun should always refer clearly to its *antecedent*. The **antecedent** is the noun the pronoun refers to. Be prepared to see sentences in which the pronoun can refer to more than one noun, as in the next sentence:

When the dog chased the cat, it was excited.

Who was excited—the dog or the cat? It is not clear what the pronoun *it* refers to, since the pronoun can refer to either the dog or the cat. When you see a pronoun, make sure that the pronoun refers clearly to a noun in the sentence. A better way to write this sentenced so you are sure who was excited is as follows:

The dog was excited when it chasd the cat.

Sometimes, you will find a sentence in which the pronoun has no clear antecedent, as in the next sentence:

On the radio show, **they** announced the date of Simon's next concert.

Who does *they* refer to? We don't know, since *they* does not have an antecedent. When you see sentences such as the one above, look for the option that corrects the vague pronoun reference.

Pronoun errors appear in correction and revision questions. Expect to see several errors involving pronouns on the test.

You are now almost finished reviewing usage issues. Try the next practice set to test your knowledge of pronouns.

CHAPTER

3

LANGUAGE
ARTS,
WRITING

THE
GED

PRACTICE SET: PRONOUNS

Directions: Choose the <u>one best answer</u> to each question.

<u>Questions 1 through 5</u> refer to the following memo.

MEMORANDUM

To: Teachers in Training

From: Michael Bendy, Director, Open Heart Yoga Center

Re: Teacher Training Retreat

(A)

(1) As you know, the Teacher Training Retreat will take place next week-end from Friday, October 8, through Sunday, October 10. (2) The retreat will take place at the Phoenicia Community Center on Jupiter Road. (3) Please see the attached map for directions to the center. (4) You can call Ruth or I if you need further explanation of how to get to the retreat.

(B)

(5) Plan to arrive at the center between 4 p.m. and 5 p.m. on Friday to check in. (6) Two instructors will lead a yoga class at 6 p.m. in the grand hall, and she will conclude the class at 6:45 p.m. (7) Dinner will begin promptly at 7:00 p.m. (8) All meals will be provided. (9) Shared housing is also available. (10) They will announce which cabin you are assigned to at dinner. (11) You can also provide his own shelter, as tents are welcome on the grounds.

(C)

(12) Remember to bring a blanket, mat, or pillow for meditation classes. (13) You should also bring a notebook and a pen for taking notes. (14) No alcohol, smoking, or pets are permitted on the premises. (15) If you have any questions before the retreat, one should call the center at 555-7832. (16) Thank you, and I look forward to seeing you next weekend.

---

1. Sentence 4: **You can call Ruth or I if you need further explanation of how to get to the retreat.**

   Which correction should be made to sentence 4?

   (1) Change <u>You</u> to <u>Your</u>.
   (2) Change <u>I</u> to <u>me</u>.
   (3) Replace <u>need</u> with <u>knead</u>.
   (4) Add a comma after <u>I</u>.
   (5) No correction is necessary.

2. Sentence 6: **Two instructors will lead a yoga class at 6 p.m. <u>in the grand hall, and she will conclude</u> the class at 6:45 p.m.**

Which is the best way to write the underlined portion of this sentence? If the original is the best way, choose answer (1).

(1)   in the grand hall, and she will conclude
(2)   in the grand hall and she will conclude
(3)   in the grand hall, and her will conclude
(4)   in the grand hall, and they will conclude
(5)   in the grand hall, and she has concluded

3. Sentence 10: **<u>They will announce which cabin you</u> are assigned to at dinner.**

Which is the best way to write the underlined portion of this sentence? If the original is the best way, choose answer (1).

(1)   They will announce which cabin you
(2)   They will announce which cabin your
(3)   The leaders will announce which cabin you
(4)   They will have announced which cabin you
(5)   They will announce which cabin they have

4. Sentence 11: **You can also provide his own shelter, as tents are welcome on the grounds.**

Which correction should be made to sentence 11?

(1)   Change <u>You</u> to <u>One</u>.
(2)   Remove the comma.
(3)   Change <u>his</u> to <u>your</u>.
(4)   Change <u>are</u> to <u>is</u>.
(5)   No correction is necessary.

5. Sentence 15: **If you have any questions before the retreat, one should call the center at 555-7832.**

Which correction should be made to sentence 15?

(1)   Remove the comma.
(2)   Change <u>have</u> to <u>will have</u>.
(3)   Replace <u>questions</u> with <u>questions'</u>.
(4)   Replace <u>one</u> with <u>won</u>.
(5)   Change <u>one</u> to <u>you</u>.

Check your answers on page 111. How did you do? Review this section if you missed a lot of questions. If you got most of them right, you're well prepared to answer the pronoun questions on the Writing test.

THE
GED

CHAPTER

3

LANGUAGE
ARTS,
WRITING

THE
GED

COMMON SENTENCE ERRORS

You have already mastered mechanics and usage problems. You are now ready to tackle questions involving "sentence structure." Sentence structure refers to how sentences are organized. Let's look at three common sentence errors that that are on the test.

SENTENCE FRAGMENTS

A **sentence fragment** is a group of words that looks like a sentence and is punctuated like a sentence but isn't a sentence. Sentences must express complete thoughts. Sentence fragments fail to express a complete thought.

Sometimes, a sentence fragment consists of only a subordinate clause, as in the following sentence, which does not express a complete thought:

Whenever Mr. Mian opens the store.

Sometimes, you find long sentence fragments posing as sentences, as in the following example.

A **subordinate clause** is a group of words that contains a verb and its subject but does not express a complete thought and cannot stand alone as a sentence. These clauses begin with subordinating conjunctions, such as **whenever**.

EXAMPLE

Sentences 3 and 4: **In May, I graduated from Queen Anne Community <u>College.</u> <u>Graduating with a degree</u> in graphic design.**

Which is the best way to write the underlined portion of these sentences? If the original is the best way, choose answer (1).

    (1)   College. Graduating with a degree
    (2)   College, I graduated with a degree
    (3)   College. A graduation with a degree
    (4)   College. Having graduated with a degree
    (5)   College with a degree

① ② ③ ④ ●

The original sentence 4 is a sentence fragment, since it lacks a subject. To answer the question, you should find the option that combines the two sentences effectively. Answer (5) provides a solution. Answers (3) and (4) both maintain sentence fragments. Answer (2) creates a different kind of sentence error called a comma splice, discussed later in this section.

Is it a fragment?
1. Does the sentence have a subject?
2. Does it have a verb?
3. Does it express a complete thought?
If the answer to any of these is "no," the sentence is a fragment.

Now, let's look at a different sentence structure problem: the run-on sentence.

RUN-ON SENTENCES

Read the next sentence:

In the movie *Adaptation*, a journalist interviews an orchid collector he shows her how to find rare orchids in the swamps.

This sentence is a **run-on sentence**. It includes independent clauses that are joined incorrectly. Independent clauses can stand alone as sentences in themselves. In the above sentence, there are two independent clauses: *In the movie* Adaptation, *a journalist interviews an orchid collector* and *he shows her how to find rare orchids in the swamps.* These two clauses are joined incorrectly, because there is no punctuation in between them.

There are four different ways to correct a run-on sentence:

1. Replace the lack of punctuation with a period, creating two sentences.

   In the movie *Adaptation*, a journalist interviews an orchid collector. He shows her how to find rare orchids in the swamps.

2. Use a semicolon to separate the clauses. The semicolon (;) is used to join two sentences that are closely related.

   In the movie *Adaptation*, a journalist interviews an orchid collector; he shows her how to find rare orchids in the swamps.

3. Revise the run-on sentence using a comma and a coordinating conjunction such as *and, but, yet, so,* or *or.*

   In the movie *Adaptation*, a journalist interviews an orchid collector, and he shows her how to find rare orchids in the swamps.

4. Make one of the independent clauses subordinate. Subordinate clauses contain a subject and a verb but do not express a complete thought. These clauses begin with subordinating conjunctions such as *after, before, when, until, so that, because, if,* and *as.*

CHAPTER

3

LANGUAGE
ARTS,
WRITING

THE
GED

Read the next run-on sentence:

Wesley was running late again Gina was getting frustrated.

A good way to revise this run-on sentence would be to make the first clause subordinate:

Because Wesley was running late again, Gina was getting frustrated.

Notice that a comma separates the two clauses. We discuss subordinate clauses and subordinating conjunctions more in the section "Coordination and Subordination" on pages 76–80.

Let's look at an example question. Choose the answer to the next revision question:

EXAMPLE

Sentence 2: **You're sure <u>to find people swimming there are</u> beautiful beaches.**

Which is the best way to write the underlined portion of this sentence? If the original is the best way, choose answer (1).

- (1)   to find people swimming there are
- (2)   to find people swimming their are
- (3)   to find people swimming wherever there are
- (4)   to find people swimming, yet there are
- (5)   to find people swimming there; are

①②●④⑤

Since each clause in the sentence is independent, the sentence is a run-on. Answer (3) offers a sentence in which the second clause is subordinate, so (3) is the correct answer. Answer (2) doesn't correct the run-on sentence. Answer (4) provides a grammatically correct option, but it doesn't make logical sense. Answer (5) is incorrectly punctuated, since what follows the semicolon is not an independent clause—the phrase lacks a subject.

You should also bear in mind that some run-ons consist of independent clauses joined by the conjunction *and*. Here's an example:

There are many types of résumés and you should choose the form that suits your needs and you will convey your purpose effectively.

Again, use any of the methods for fixing run-ons to correct these sentences:

There are many types of résumés. You should choose the form that suits your needs, so that you will convey your purpose effectively.

WAYS TO FIX A RUN-ON

You can fix a run-on sentence in any of the following ways:

1. Use a period to create two sentences.
2. Use a semicolon to join the clauses.
3. Use a comma and a coordinating conjunction.
4. Make one clause a subordinate clause.

COMMA SPLICES

A **comma splice** is a type of run-on sentence. In a comma splice, independent clauses are joined only by commas and are thus incorrect. Look at the next sentence:

The conference is set for next April, most of the speakers have accepted their invitations.

To fix this comma splice, you can use any of the methods for correcting run-ons. All of the following sentences are correct:

The conference is set for next April. Most of the speakers have accepted their invitations.

The conference is set for next April; most of the speakers have accepted their invitations.

The conference is set for next April, and most of the speakers have accepted their invitations.

You're ready to test your knowledge of common sentence errors. Try the following practice set.

THE
GED

CHAPTER

3

LANGUAGE
ARTS,
WRITING

THE
GED

PRACTICE SET: COMMON SENTENCE ERRORS

Directions: Choose the <u>one best answer</u> to each question.

<u>Questions 1 through 5</u> refer to the following article.

Maya Art

(A)

(1) The art of the Maya is a record of gods, kings, and everyday people. (2) Complex and beautiful artworks. (3) Revealing the lives and beliefs of a sophisticated and bloody civilization. (4) This civilization existed for millennia, before Columbus ever left the ports of Spain.

(B)

(5) For more than 2,000 years, Maya civilization thrived in southern Mexico, Belize, Guatemala, Honduras, and El Salvador. (6) The civilization reached its height of power and artistic achievement from about A.D. 250 to A.D. 900 this period is known as the classic period. (7) Experts estimate that at its peak, two million Maya lived, worked, and waged war in the forests and in their cities made of stone.

(C)

(8) Art was an important part of Maya life, it was everywhere. (9) Rulers and wealthy people hired artists to carve their faces in stone, make their portraits in plaster, and paint their likenesses on stone walls and this art decorated palaces, temples, and tombs. (10) Because their work was valued. (11) Artists enjoyed a respected place in Maya society. (12) Maya civilization started to decline after about A.D. 900. (13) Without the amazing works of art they left behind, we would know little about the Maya leaders, their beliefs, and their rituals.

1. Sentences 2 and 3: **Complex and beautiful <u>artworks. Revealing the lives</u> and beliefs of a sophisticated and bloody civilization.**

   Which is the best way to write the underlined portion of these sentences? If the original is the best way, choose answer (1).

   (1)   artworks. Revealing the lives
   (2)   artworks revealing the lives
   (3)   artworks'. Revealing the lives
   (4)   artworks. I reveal the lives
   (5)   artworks reveal the lives

2. Sentence 6: **The civilization reached its height of power and artistic achievement from about A.D. 250 to A.D. <u>900 this period is known</u> as the classic period.**

   Which is the best way to write the underlined portion of this sentence? If the original is the best way, choose answer (1).

   (1)   900 this period is known
   (2)   900. This period is known
   (3)   900, this period is known
   (4)   900, but this period is known
   (5)   900. Is known

3. Sentence 8: **Art was an important part of Maya life, it was everywhere.**

Which correction should be made to sentence 8?

(1) Remove the comma.
(2) Replace <u>Maya</u> with <u>maya</u>.
(3) Replace the comma with a semicolon.
(4) Change the second <u>was</u> to <u>is</u>.
(5) Replace <u>everywhere</u> with <u>everywheres</u>.

4. Sentence 9: **Rulers and wealthy people hired artists to carve their faces in stone, make their portraits in plaster, and paint their likenesses on stone <u>walls and this art decorated</u> palaces, temples, and tombs.**

Which is the best way to write the underlined portion of this sentence? If the original is the best way, choose answer (1).

(1) walls and this art decorated
(2) walls, because this art decorating
(3) walls. Having decorated this art
(4) walls. And this art decoration
(5) walls. This art decorated

5. Sentences 10 and 11: **Because their work was valued. Artists enjoyed a respected place in Maya society.**

The most effective revision of sentences 10 and 11 would include which group of words?

(1) Because of their working
(2) valued, artists enjoyed
(3) valuable to artists
(4) with respect to artists
(5) to enjoy their work

Check your answers on pages 112–113. If you need to review some of these topics, go back over this rung. If you got most of the Practice Set questions right, go on to the next topic.

COORDINATION AND SUBORDINATION

You've already mastered many of the key concepts on the Writing test. With the knowledge you have, you should be able to eliminate many incorrect answer choices on any test. Now, let's look at another area of sentence structure: coordination and subordination.

COORDINATION

Sentences containing two or more clauses need to be connected logically and grammatically. Coordinating conjunctions, such as *and, if, but, or,* and *yet,* connect independent clauses. You may recall that an independent clause has a subject and verb and can stand alone as a sentence.

Errors in coordination occur when the coordinating conjunction that is used does not connect the ideas in a logical manner. See if you can pick the correct answer to the next revision question:

EXAMPLE

Sentence 3: **Jen likes to do adventurous <u>sports, yet she started taking</u> ice-climbing lessons.**

Which is the best way to write the underlined portion of this sentence? If the original is the best way, choose answer (1).

(1)   sports, yet she started taking
(2)   sports, so she started taking
(3)   sports. Yet she started taking
(4)   sports, but she started taking
(5)   sports, yet she started to take

Does the sentence sound correct to you? Jen likes to do adventurous sports, yet she started doing an adventurous sport—that doesn't make logical sense. The problem lies with the coordinating conjunction. *Yet* does not logically express the relationship between the two clauses in the sentence, so you should look for an answer that contains a conjunction that does.

Answer (2) provides the right coordinating conjunction *so,* which means "therefore." Answer (3) can be eliminated, since it creates a sentence fragment. Answer (4) doesn't provide a logical coordinating conjunction, and answer (5) maintains the wrong coordinating conjunction.

Common Coordinating Conjunctions

Coordinating Conjunction	Shows Relationship
and	connects related ideas
but, yet	contrasts two ideas
for	shows a cause
so	shows an effect
or	gives different options
nor	gives negative options

When you use coordinating conjunctions to connect clauses, always use a comma before the conjunction. You may recall that you can also use semicolons to join two independent clauses. Both of the following sentences are correct:

Pollution has risen to unacceptable levels, and the committee has failed to curb polluters.

Pollution has risen to unacceptable levels; the committee has failed to curb polluters.

You can also use semicolons and conjunctive adverbs to join independent clauses. **Conjunctive adverbs** are connecting words such as *therefore*, *instead*, *meanwhile*, *still*, *furthermore*, *nevertheless*, and *however*. Follow a conjunctive adverb with a comma, as in the next sentence:

Pollution is on the rise; however, some companies have taken measures to lessen pollution.

Notice that you use a semicolon before the conjunctive adverb and a comma after it.

That's it for coordination. Now, let's look at subordination.

SUBORDINATION

Subordinating conjunctions, such as the ones in the chart below, introduce subordinate clauses.

Common Subordinating Conjunctions

after	before	so that	where
although	even though	than	wherever
as	if	unless	whether
as if	in order that	until	while
as long as	once	when	
because	since	whenever	

Be alert to faulty subordination in which the clauses in a sentence are both **subordinate clauses**, as in the following:

Whenever Elisabeta calls a meeting, while Paolo takes notes.

THE
GED

CHAPTER

3

LANGUAGE
ARTS,
WRITING

THE
GED

When you see subordinating conjunctions at the beginning of each clause, you know that one of them must become an independent clause. Look for the option that creates an independent clause, as in this revision:

Whenever Elisabeta calls a meeting, Paolo takes notes.

You should use a comma after a subordinate clause that begins a sentence.

One final point to keep in mind when joining sentences or clauses is to always choose the shortest, most concise option. Sometimes, the test asks you to combine ideas to make the writing smoother. Try to answer the next question:

EXAMPLE

Sentence 9: **Niko wrote his third play <u>and he was forty-five years old then</u>.**

Which is the best way to write the underlined portion of this sentence? If the original is the best way, choose answer (1).

(1)   and he was forty-five years old then.
(2)   upon reaching the age of forty-five years.
(3)   after becoming forty-five years old.
(4)   when he was forty-five.
(5)   at the time when he was forty-five.

① ② ③ ● ⑤

You may notice that the coordinating conjunction *and* does not provide the most logical connection between the two clauses. In addition, the sentence is not punctuated correctly. There should be a comma preceding the *and*.

Answers (2), (3), and (5) present logical alternatives, but the resulting sentences are wordy. The ideas can be expressed more succinctly. Given the options, you should choose the one that is most concise and clear. In this case, you would choose answer (4).

Coordination and subordination are key concepts for understanding sentence structure. You're ready to take the practice set to test your knowledge.

PRACTICE SET: COORDINATION AND SUBORDINATION

Directions: Choose the one best answer to each question.

Questions 1 through 5 refer to the following article.

How to Choose a Mover

(A)

(1) Most people move to a new home at some point in their lives. (2) If you are about to relocate and need help with the move consider the following points to help you choose a mover. (3) Begin by asking your friends, family, or colleagues if they can recommend a mover. (4) You should note their recommendations by writing them down in a notebook. (5) Then, you should call the companies to ask for an estimate, or you should take notes while getting the estimate. (6) The estimate should be free. (7) You should not be obligated to use the company when you ask for an estimate.

(B)

(8) You should also see if the companies offer the services you need. (9) Different people will require different things for example, some people need to ship a car or boat across the country. (10) Other people will need special handling of delicate items. (11) Before you should make sure that the company you hire can provide the services you need when you make your decision. (12) To be on the safe side, do some research into the company you hire. (13) You should ask the company to show you its operating license and call the Better Business Bureau to ask about complaints that have been made against the company.

1. Sentence 2: **If you are about to relocate and need help with the move consider the following points to help you choose a mover.**

   Which correction should be made to sentence 2?

   (1)   Change are to is.
   (2)   Change relocate to relocation.
   (3)   Insert a comma after move.
   (4)   Replace points with points'.
   (5)   No correction is necessary.

2. Sentence 5: **Then, you should call the companies to ask for an estimate, or you should take notes while getting the estimate.**

   Which correction should be made to sentence 5?

   (1)   Remove the first comma.
   (2)   Remove the second comma.
   (3)   Replace companies with company's.
   (4)   Replace for with four.
   (5)   Change or to and.

THE
GED

CHAPTER

3

LANGUAGE
ARTS,
WRITING

THE
GED

INTRODUCTION

CAPITALIZATION
AND SPELLING

PUNCTUATION

VERBS

PRONOUNS

COMMON
SENTENCE ERRORS

COORDINATION
AND
SUBORDINATION

MISPLACED AND
DANGLING
MODIFIERS

PARALLEL
STRUCTURE

RESTRUCTURING
PARAGRAPHS

THE ESSAY

3. Sentences 6 and 7: **The estimate should be free. You should not be obligated to use the company when you ask for an estimate.**

The most effective combination of sentences 6 and 7 would include which group of words?

(1)   free, you should
(2)   free and without obligation
(3)   in addition, the estimate you are obligated
(4)   under obligation to use
(5)   Free estimates and estimates from the companies

4. Sentence 9: **Different people will require different <u>things for example, some</u> people need to ship a car or boat across the country.**

Which is the best way to write the underlined portion of this sentence? If the original is the best way, choose answer (1).

(1)   things for example, some
(2)   things for example some
(3)   things, but for example, some
(4)   things; whenever, some
(5)   things; for example, some

5. Sentence 11: **<u>Before you should make sure that</u> the company you hire can provide the services you need when you make your decision.**

Which is the best way to write the underlined portion of this sentence? If the original is the best way, choose answer (1).

(1)   Before you should make sure that
(2)   Before making sure that
(3)   You should make sure that
(4)   Before, you should, make sure that
(5)   Before you should make sure which

Check your answers on page 113. If you feel that you need to review coordination and subordination, reread pages 78–79. If you feel that you have a good understanding of these topics, go to the next rung.

MISPLACED AND DANGLING MODIFIERS

A **modifier** is a word or a phrase that describes another word in the sentence. Modifiers need to be placed correctly within a sentence so that it is clear which word is being modified. Funny things happen when you place a modifier too far away from what it should modify, as in the next sentence:

Born last month, we adopted the tiny kitten.

The modifying phrase, *Born last month*, is misplaced. As the sentence now reads, the modifier appears to describe the people (*we*), which would mean "we were born last month." Logically, you know that the phrase should modify the kitten. The sentence should be changed to:

When you see an entire sentence underlined on the test, you should be on the alert for a modification error.

We adopted the tiny kitten, born last month.

Remember to always place the modifier close to the word it modifies.

Dangling modifiers may also appear on the test. Look at the next sentence:

Listening to voice mail, the knock at the door went unheard.

Who was listening to voice mail? The knock? Of course not, but since the dangling modifier (*listening to voice mail*) is closer to "the knock," that is the meaning of the sentence. To correct a dangling modifier, you need to add information:

Listening to voice mail, I failed to hear the knock at the door.

Sometimes, a revision question asks you to identify which option best rearranges words when there is a misplaced phrase. Try answering the next question.

EXAMPLE

Sentence 9: **I will be, as a project manager at your company, able to keep the team I supervise on track.**

If you rewrote sentence 9 beginning with

<u>As a project manager at your company,</u>

the next words should be

    (1)   I will be able
    (2)   and able I will be
    (3)   keeping and supervising with ability
    (4)   supervising those on track
    (5)   able to keep the team, I will

● ② ③ ④ ⑤

The original sentence is incorrect, because the modifying phrase *as a project manager at your company* interrupts the flow of ideas. When the phrase is placed at the beginning of the sentence, it should be followed by the word it modifies, which is *I*. Answer (1) is the only one that provides this solution. Answer (2) creates an awkward clause, so it should be eliminated. Answers (3), (4), and (5) are wordy and not entirely logical. Remember to choose the option that provides the shortest and smoothest sentence. Remember also to take a guess, after eliminating obviously wrong choices, if you're not sure of the answer.

You're likely to see at least one revision question involving misplaced or dangling modifiers. Test your knowledge of this topic by doing the following practice set.

PRACTICE SET: MISPLACED AND DANGLING MODIFIERS

Directions: Choose the one best answer to each question.

Questions 1 through 5 refer to the following letter.

March 31, 2005
Ms. Angela Kim
P.O. Box 9999
New Haven, CT 06533
Dear Ms. Kim:

(A)

(1) Our records show that your car is overdue for service. (2) According to our records, your vehicle should receive a 97,000-mile recommended maintenance check. (3) We will, during the maintenance check, inspect and rotate the tires, inspect the wiper blades, check and adjust fluid levels, inspect the front brake pads, replace the engine oil, and give your car a road test.

(B)

(4) Following the recommended maintenance schedule is the best way to ensure your vehicle's peak performance. (5) By keeping your car properly maintained, your car's resale value will increase. (6) As you know, the award-winning mechanics at Deluxe Auto are dedicated to providing quality service. (7) As local professionals in a competitive business, our clients' needs come first.

(C)

(12) Please call us at 203-555-7878 to schedule a service appointment. (13) If you bring this letter to your appointment with the coupon below, you will receive a 10% discount on the maintenance check. (14) Thank you for your time.
Sincerely,

Lyall Mole

Lyall Mole
Service Manager

---

1. Sentence 3: **We will, during the maintenance check, inspect and rotate the tires, inspect the wiper blades, check and adjust fluid levels, inspect the front brake pads, replace the engine oil, and give your car a road test.**

   If you rewrote sentence 3 beginning with

   <u>During the maintenance check,</u>

   the next words should be

   (1)   and we will inspect
   (2)   inspecting and rotating
   (3)   we will inspect
   (4)   to check and adjust
   (5)   will we inspect and rotate

CHAPTER

3

LANGUAGE
ARTS,
WRITING

THE
GED

INTRODUCTION

CAPITALIZATION
AND SPELLING

PUNCTUATION

VERBS

PRONOUNS

COMMON
SENTENCE ERRORS

COORDINATION
AND
SUBORDINATION

MISPLACED AND
DANGLING
MODIFIERS

PARALLEL
STRUCTURE

RESTRUCTURING
PARAGRAPHS

THE ESSAY

2. Sentence 5: **By keeping your car properly maintained, your car's resale value will increase.**

Which correction should be made to sentence 5?

(1)   Replace <u>By keeping</u> with <u>If you keep</u>.
(2)   Remove the comma.
(3)   Insert <u>but</u> after the comma.
(4)   Change <u>will increase</u> to <u>increases</u>.
(5)   No correction is necessary.

3. Sentence 6: **As you know, the award-winning mechanics at Deluxe Auto are dedicated to providing quality service.**

Which correction should be made to sentence 6?

(1)   Remove the comma.
(2)   Insert <u>and</u> after <u>Auto</u>.
(3)   Change <u>are dedicated</u> to <u>dedicating</u>.
(4)   Replace <u>to</u> with <u>too</u>.
(5)   No correction is necessary.

4. Sentence 7: **As local professionals in a competitive <u>business, our clients' needs come first.</u>**

Which is the best way to write the underlined portion of this sentence? If the original is the best way, choose answer (1).

(1)   business, our clients' needs come first.
(2)   business, our clients needs come first.
(3)   business, needing our clients comes first.
(4)   business, we put our clients' needs first.
(5)   business. Our clients' who need us come first.

5. Sentence 13: **<u>If you bring this letter to your appointment with the coupon below,</u> you will receive a 10% discount on the maintenance check.**

Which is the best way to write the underlined portion of this sentence? If the original is the best way, choose answer (1).

(1)   If you bring this letter to your appointment with the coupon below,
(2)   If you bring to your appointment this letter. With the coupon below,
(3)   If you, to your appointment, bring this letter with the coupon below,
(4)   To your appointment, the letter with the coupon below bring
(5)   If you bring this letter with the coupon below to your appointment,

Check your answers on page 114. How did you do? If you missed many of the questions, go back and review misplaced and dangling modifiers. If you have a good grasp of the topics, move on to the next rung: Parallel Structure.

PARALLEL STRUCTURE

Parallel structure is the last area of sentence structure we review. You've covered eight rungs so far, and have just three more to go.

Whenever items are compared, they must be expressed in the same grammatical forms. They should use the same verb tenses and the same types of modifiers. That is what is meant by *parallel structure*.

Look out for errors in parallel structure in sentences that use pairs of connective words. Notice the connective words in the following sentence:

The more Moraga complained about the heat, **the more** Burgos whined about the cold.

The connective words, *the more . . . the more*, require you to use parallel structure with what follows them, since the connective words imply comparison. The above sentence uses parallel structure effectively. In both parts of the sentence, there is a noun (Moraga/Burgos) followed by a past tense verb (complained/whined) followed by a preposition (about/about).

Connective Words Requiring Parallel Structure

neither/nor	whether/or	not only/but also
either/or	the better/the better	the more/the more
both/and		

You should also look for questions that test parallelism in lists of items. Lists require that all the items be in the same form, as in the following:

Ha plays the flute, writes novels, and bakes cookies.

Notice that all three items in the list are in the same form. They all employ verbs in the same tense (present tense). Correction and revision questions include errors in parallel structure. See if you can answer the next question.

EXAMPLE

Sentence 17: **On the weekends, Ann likes to play tennis, swim laps, and watching movies.**

Which correction should be made to sentence 17?

(1)   Change <u>likes</u> to <u>liking</u>.
(2)   Remove the second comma.
(3)   Change <u>swim</u> to <u>swum</u>.
(4)   Change <u>and</u> to <u>yet</u>.
(5)   Change <u>watching</u> to <u>watch</u>.

① ② ③ ④ ●

CHAPTER

3

LANGUAGE
ARTS,
WRITING

THE
GED

INTRODUCTION

CAPITALIZATION
AND SPELLING

PUNCTUATION

VERBS

PRONOUNS

COMMON
SENTENCE ERRORS

COORDINATION
AND
SUBORDINATION

MISPLACED AND
DANGLING
MODIFIERS

PARALLEL
STRUCTURE

RESTRUCTURING
PARAGRAPHS

THE ESSAY

You may have recognized that the third item in the list, *watching movies,* is not parallel to the other two items in the list. The other two items are in the present tense. Scanning the answer choices, you can look for the one that changes *watching* to *watch.* Answer (5) provides that correction.

Answer (1) is wrong, since it would change the correct verb tense to an incorrect one. Answer (2) can be eliminated, since commas are needed between items in a series. Answer (3) would also change the verb to an incorrect tense. Answer (4) would introduce an incorrect conjunction.

With the knowledge you've gained, you can successfully choose the correct answers to many questions and eliminate incorrect options. Try the next practice set to test your knowledge of parallel structure.

PRACTICE SET: PARALLEL STRUCTURE

Directions: Choose the one best answer to each question.

Questions 1 through 5 refer to the following article.

Comets

(A)

(1) Today, people look forward to seeing comets, but for many centuries comets were thought to be signs of disaster. (2) Not only were comets feared, but they have also been the object of misunderstanding. (3) In particular, people believed that comets foretold of plagues, to wage war, and death. (4) Comets were misunderstood until the astronomer Edmond Halley began observing them during the seventeenth century.

(B)

(5) Halley studied the written accounts of comets that had been observed since 1337, and he was calculating their orbits. (6) By realizing that certain comets moved in the same path or orbit, he figured out that these comets were really the same comet traveling in a circular path. (7) His observation helped scientists understand that comets can be seen at regular intervals and the times that are predictable.

(C)

(8) The center of a comet looks like a big, dirty snowball. (9) The center or core is dusty, rocky, metallic, and like ice. (10) About 30 new comets are discovered each year. (11) Most comets are faint and can only be seen through a telescope. (12) A handful of very bright comets have been seen from the Earth without a telescope, including the one named after Halley.

1. Sentence 2: **Not only were comets feared, but they <u>have also been the object of misunderstanding.</u>**

   Which is the best way to write the underlined portion of this sentence? If the original is the best way, choose answer (1).

   (1)   have also been the object of misunderstanding
   (2)   have also been; the object of misunderstanding
   (3)   were also misunderstood
   (4)   as objects of misunderstanding, have been
   (5)   have also been; however, the object of misunderstanding

2. Sentence 3: **In particular, people believed that comets foretold of plagues, to wage war, and death.**

   Which correction should be made to sentence 3?

   (1)   Change <u>believed</u> to <u>were believing</u>.
   (2)   Remove <u>to wage</u>.
   (3)   Change <u>plagues</u> to <u>plagues'</u>.
   (4)   Remove the second comma.
   (5)   No correction is necessary.

3. Sentence 5: **Halley studied the written accounts of comets that had been observed since 1337, and he was calculating their orbits.**

   Which correction should be made to sentence 5?

   (1)   Remove the comma.
   (2)   Replace <u>been</u> with <u>bean</u>.
   (3)   Change <u>was calculating</u> to <u>calculated</u>.
   (4)   Replace <u>their</u> with <u>there</u>.
   (5)   No correction is necessary.

4. Sentence 7: **His observation helped scientists understand that comets can be seen at regular intervals and <u>the times that are predictable.</u>**

   Which is the best way to write the underlined portion of this sentence? If the original is the best way, choose answer (1).

   (1)   the times that are predictable.
   (2)   the times, which are predictable.
   (3)   the times that may be predictable.
   (4)   the times as it was predicted.
   (5)   at predictable times.

5. Sentence 9: **The center or core is dusty, rocky, metallic, and like ice.**

   Which correction should be made to sentence 9?

   (1)   Change <u>is</u> to <u>are</u>.
   (2)   Remove the first comma.
   (3)   Remove the second comma.
   (4)   Change <u>like ice</u> to <u>icy</u>.
   (5)   No correction is necessary.

Check your answers on page 115. If you missed many of the questions, review this section again. Otherwise, you're ready for the next ladder rung, Restructuring Paragraphs, which deals with "organization" topics.

RESTRUCTURING PARAGRAPHS

You've completed the lion's share of the work preparing for the Writing test. Mechanics, usage, and sentence structure questions make up most of the Writing test. The final types of questions concern organization, or how a paragraph or essay is structured.

Like sentences, paragraphs also need effective structure. The ideas must flow smoothly from sentence to sentence. In addition, paragraphs must have topic sentences, which state the main idea.

Many organization questions ask you to restructure a paragraph to make it more effective. An effective paragraph does the following:

- Develops an idea by presenting information in a logical manner
- Contains a topic sentence, which states the main idea
- Contains details that support the main idea

An effective paragraph also has unity. **Unity** occurs when all the sentences in the paragraph support the main idea. In other words, none of the sentences are off-topic. A paragraph should also have coherence. **Coherence** occurs when all the sentences are presented in logical order.

With organization questions, you may be asked to

- Identify which option would best begin a paragraph—that is, which sentence would make an appropriate topic sentence
- Identify which option doesn't belong in a paragraph
- Identify which option would best conclude a paragraph
- Move sentences within a paragraph or essay
- Identify where an effective paragraph break should occur

Let's look at a few typical organizational questions based on the following paragraph:

EXAMPLE

(1) One of the things that makes sea kayaking a great sport is its accessibility. (2) Almost anyone can sea kayak. (3) The sport does not require amazing athletic ability. (4) Nor does it require lots of money or expensive equipment. (5) You do not have to be young to sea kayak. (6) Many people learn how to kayak for the first time late in life. (7) My aunt taught herself many activities when she was in her eighties. (8) The sport is highly adaptable, and it can be as relaxing or as vigorous as you need it to be.

1. Which revision would improve the effectiveness of this paragraph?

   (1)   Move sentence 1 to the end of the paragraph.
   (2)   Move sentence 4 to the beginning of the paragraph.
   (3)   Move sentence 5 to the end of the paragraph.
   (4)   Remove sentence 7.
   (5)   No revision is necessary.

   ① ② ③ ● ⑤

You should first determine what the paragraph is about. Reading it through once, you can determine that the paragraph describes why sea kayaking is a great sport.

Then consider the options for revision. Answer (1) would move sentence 1 to the end of the paragraph. Sentence 1 is a topic sentence—it states the main idea. Usually, the topic sentence comes at the beginning of the paragraph. In this case, moving the sentence to the end would not improve the paragraph. Answer (2) would move sentence 4 to the beginning of the paragraph, which would create a confusing beginning. Sentence 4 should logically follow sentence 3. Eliminate answer (2).

Answer (3) would move sentence 5 to the end of the paragraph. Sentence 5 logically precedes sentence 6, which also discusses age factors. Sentence 5 should remain where it is, so rule out answer (3). Answer (4) would have you remove sentence 7. Sentence 7 expresses an idea that is not necessary to the paragraph. The other sentences in the paragraph all relate to sea kayaking. Sentence 7 disrupts the unity of the paragraph, so it should be removed. Answer (4) is correct.

As you can see, organization questions ask you to consider a number of ways to restructure the paragraph. Some questions give you similar options to improve the effectiveness of the essay as a whole. When you see those questions, reread the whole essay and use the same skills to answer the question. We discuss the essay more in depth in the final section of this chapter.

Before doing a practice set, let's look at a few more areas of organization: topic sentences, transitions, and paragraph breaks.

TOPIC SENTENCES

A **topic sentence** expresses the main idea of a paragraph. The topic sentence often appears as the first or second sentence. When the topic sentence is at the beginning of a paragraph, the sentence helps the reader know what to expect in the rest of the paragraph. However, a topic sentence can appear anywhere. Sometimes, writers may place the topic sentence at the end of a paragraph to summarize the main idea.

You may encounter questions on the Writing test that ask you to identify topic sentences. These questions use the following forms:

- Which sentence would be most effective if inserted at the beginning of the paragraph?
- Which sentence would be most effective if inserted at the end of the paragraph?

EXAMPLE

Answer the question based on the following paragraph.

(1) For centuries, soy has been consumed as both a food and a drink in Asia. (2) Soy is also used to make a remarkable range of products, including paint enamel. (3) The plant is used in moisturizers. (4) Soy can also be found in many foods, including breads, burgers, desserts, and salad dressings.

Which sentence would be most effective if inserted at the beginning of the paragraph?

(1)   Soy is a type of plant protein.
(2)   Soy contains nutrients such as iron and zinc.
(3)   Soy has many uses, ranging from cosmetics to food.
(4)   Edamame is the name for young soybeans.
(5)   Soy may help prevent common diseases.

① ② ● ④ ⑤

The answer is (3), which provides a good topic sentence that states the main idea of the paragraph. Answers (1), (2), (4), and (5) provide more details about soy, but none of them effectively states the main idea of the paragraph, which is what the paragraph needs.

When you come across a question such as this one, reread the whole paragraph to figure out what the main idea might be. Then, look at the options for a similar statement.

TRANSITIONS

Transitions connect ideas to each other. Transitional words show how ideas are connected. Here is a list of some common transitions:

as a result	in addition	on the other hand
consequently	in fact	otherwise
eventually	meanwhile	similarly
finally	moreover	therefore
however	next	unfortunately

Transitions help make writing smooth. Transitions should be used to show relationships between ideas in different sentences. Transitions are also often used at the beginning of paragraphs to show how ideas in one paragraph relate to another.

When you use a transition at the beginning of a sentence, use a comma after it. Joshua was reluctant to leave the building. Eventually, he became weary, put on his coat, and left.

Okay, you're almost finished reviewing all the organization topics. Let's look at the final topic before the essay: paragraph breaks.

PARAGRAPH BREAKS

Each paragraph should develop only one main idea. Whenever a new main idea is introduced, a new paragraph should begin.

You may find questions on the test that ask you where a new paragraph should begin. When that happens, look for a sentence that initiates a new set of ideas. Try to answer the next question:

EXAMPLE

Ms. Leslie Mora
Editorial Director
ABC Books
20 High Ave.
Glenview, NY 10577
Dear Ms. Mora:
(A)
(1) Thank you for calling me yesterday about the Research Assistant position with ABC Books. (2) I would be very interested in working at your company and have attached my résumé for your perusal. (3) I am also enclosing a list of references. (4) In 2003, I graduated from the University of New York with a B.A. in history. (5) As a student, I gained extensive experience researching a variety of historical subjects. (6) From 2001 to 2003, I also assisted Dr. Lara Montana in her research on the milling industry during the 1930s. (7) I would greatly appreciate the opportunity to use my skills as a researcher at your company.
(B)
(8) Please let me know if I can provide any further information. (9) I can be reached at my home number at (914) 555-2348, at omarrubens@fastmail. com, or at the address below. (10) Thank you so much for contacting me. (11) I look forward to speaking with you soon.

Sincerely,

Omar Rubens

Omar Rubens
52 Center Lane
Glenview, NY 10577

Which revision would improve the effectiveness of this letter?

Begin a new paragraph with

(1)   sentence 3
(2)   sentence 4
(3)   sentence 6
(4)   sentence 7
(5)   sentence 9

This question requires you to study the entire letter to determine where an effective paragraph break should occur. A paragraph starting with sentence 4 would clearly outline the writer's educational experience, so answer (2) is the correct answer.

THE
GED

CHAPTER

3

LANGUAGE
ARTS,
WRITING

THE
GED

INTRODUCTION

CAPITALIZATION
AND SPELLING

PUNCTUATION

VERBS

PRONOUNS

COMMON
SENTENCE ERRORS

COORDINATION
AND
SUBORDINATION

MISPLACED AND
DANGLING
MODIFIERS

PARALLEL
STRUCTURE

RESTRUCTURING
PARAGRAPHS

THE ESSAY

Sentence 3 belongs with the first paragraph, so answer (1) is incorrect. Sentences 6 and 7 belong in the same paragraph as the sentences that precede them, so eliminate answers (3) and (4). Similarly, sentence 9 belongs in the paragraph with the other sentences about how the writer may be contacted to provide further information, so answer (5) is not the right answer.

Be prepared to find similar questions involving paragraph breaks on the test. Remember to look for which sentences belong together in the same paragraph.

You're ready to take the final practice set. This set includes a variety of organizational questions.

PRACTICE SET: RESTRUCTURING PARAGRAPHS

Directions: Choose the one best answer to each question.

Questions 1 through 5 refer to the following memorandum.

TO: All GIF Employees
FROM: Mavis Ming, Human Resources Director
DATE: June 13, 2005
RE: July Employee of the Month Award Nominations

(A)

(1) I am writing to remind you to submit nominations for the July Employee of the Month Award. (2) Nominations are due in the Human Resources office by Friday June 21. (3) Simply address your e-mail message to me, and I will take care of the rest. (4) Please fill out the attached nomination form and drop it off by next Friday. (5) Instead of using the attached form, you can also submit your nomination by e-mail.

(B)

(6) The Employee of the Month is someone who has exhibited a positive service attitude toward internal and external customers. (7) This individual has also made outstanding contributions to productivity and team-building. (8) The quality of this employee's work should be excellent. (9) Last month, I received three nominations. (10) Unfortunately, the Employee of the Month is someone who exemplifies professionalism. (11) When making your nomination, describe your reasons for doing so. (12) Be specific and provide examples of the individual's accomplishments. (13) The new Employee of the Month will be announced on Monday, July 1, in the employee cafeteria at 10:00 a.m. (14) Please attend the announcement meeting. (15) We will be serving coffee and cake to honor this person's achievements.

---

1. Which revision would improve the effectiveness of paragraph A?

(1)   Remove sentence 1.
(2)   Remove sentence 2.
(3)   Move sentence 3 to the end of the paragraph.
(4)   Move sentence 4 to the beginning of the paragraph.
(5)   No revision is necessary.

2. Which sentence would be most effective if inserted at the beginning of paragraph B?

(1) When making your nomination, please consider several criteria.
(2) The Employee of the Month for June is Margo Maggio.
(3) You can also find the form on the GIF Web site.
(4) To keep on top of the monthly news.
(5) The Employee of the Month form takes little time to complete.

3. Which revision would improve the effectiveness of paragraph B?

(1) Remove sentence 6.
(2) Remove sentence 7.
(3) Move sentence 7 to the end of the paragraph.
(4) Remove sentence 9.
(5) No revision is necessary.

4. Sentence 10: **Unfortunately, the Employee of the Month is someone who exemplifies professionalism.**

Which correction should be made to sentence 10?

(1) Change <u>Unfortunately</u> to <u>In addition</u>
(2) Remove the comma.
(3) Change <u>is</u> to <u>are</u>.
(4) Change <u>who</u> to <u>where</u>.
(5) No correction is necessary.

5. Which revision would improve the effectiveness of this memo?

Begin a new paragraph with

(1) sentence 2.
(2) sentence 7.
(3) sentence 8.
(4) sentence 12.
(5) sentence 13.

Check your answers on pages 115–116. How did you do? If you feel you need to review any aspect of restructuring paragraphs, please do so. If you feel confident about this skill, go to the final rung: The Essay.

THE ESSAY

You have reached the last rung of the Language Arts, Writing ladder and have learned how to handle every type of multiple-choice question on the Writing test. Now you can use this knowledge to write an effective GED essay.

An effective GED essay is not the same thing as a *great* essay. Truly great essays take hours or even days to plan, research, and write. The GED essay can't take more than 45 minutes. Your task is to write a standard essay that satisfies the requirements of the test-graders. To do that, you need to have an essay-writing strategy in place before you sit down to take the test. You then need to apply that strategy to whatever question the GED essay poses. On this rung, we teach you a strategy for writing a GED essay that works every time and on any topic.

THE FAST-FOOD ESSAY

One of the best things about fast food is not just that it's quick, it's *consistent*. If you walk into a McDonald's anywhere in the world and order a Big Mac, you know exactly what you are going to get. The Big Mac is the same no matter what. That is because restaurants like McDonald's use the same ingredients and preparation methods at every location.

In this section, we show you how to apply the concept behind fast food to the process of writing the GED essay. That way, you can write a top-notch GED essay every time. To make it happen, you need to know three key things that all the fast-food chains know:

- Your customers
- Your ingredients
- How to put the ingredients together

KNOW YOUR CUSTOMERS

The essay-graders are your *customers*. After you finish taking the GED, two essay-graders score your essay. Each reader gives your essay a score from 1 to 4, with 4 being the highest possible score. The scores are then averaged to find your final score. You must score a 2 or above on the essay to pass the Writing test. If you score less than a 2, you will have to take both parts of the Writing test again.

To understand exactly what your customers—the GED-graders—want, you must understand the GED directions.

THE GED ESSAY DIRECTIONS

Below are the directions as they appear on the GED:

Look at the box on the next page. In the box are your assigned topic and the letter of that topic.

You must write on the assigned topic ONLY.

You will have 45 minutes to write on your assigned essay topic. You may return to the multiple-choice section after you complete your essay if you have time remaining in this test period. Do not return the Language Arts, Writing booklet until you finish both Parts I and II of the Language Arts, Writing test.

Two evaluators will score your essay according to its overall effectiveness. Their evaluation will be based on the following features:

- Well-focused main points
- Clear organization
- Specific development of your ideas
- Control of sentence structure, punctuation, grammar, word choice, and spelling.

REMEMBER, YOU MUST COMLETE BOTH THE MULTIPLE-CHOICE QUESTIONS IN PART I AND THE ESSAY IN PART II TO RECEIVE A SCORE ON THE LANGUAGE ARTS, WRITING TEST. To avoid having to repeat both parts of the test, be sure to do the following:

- Do not leave the pages blank.
- Write legibly <u>in ink</u> so that the readers who evaluate your test will be able to read your writing.
- Write on the assigned topic. If you write on a topic other than the one assigned, you will not receive a score for the Language Arts, Writing test.
- Write your essay on the lined pages of the separate answer sheet booklet. Only the writing on these pages will be scored.

To save time, memorize the directions for the essay section. On test day, you won't have to waste valuable time.

THE

GED

We've expanded upon these directions and created a list of Dos and Don'ts in order to make the rules of effective GED writing easy to grasp:

DO	DON'T
Write only on the given topic.	Write on a topic that relates vaguely to the one given.
Take a clear position on the topic.	Take a wishy-washy position or try to argue two sides.
Write persuasively to convince the grader.	Try to be creative or funny.
Include reasons and examples that support your position.	Include examples not directly related to your position.
Write with correct grammar and spelling.	Forget to proofread your work for spelling and grammar mistakes.
Write as clearly as possible.	Use too many fancy vocabulary words or overly long sentences.
Write specifically and concretely.	Be vague or use generalizations.
Write about five paragraphs.	Put more importance on length than on quality.
Write only on the given lined paper.	Make your handwriting too large (or you'll sacrifice space).
Write as neatly as possible in print.	Write in cursive. Print is much easier to read.

THE GRADER'S INSTRUCTIONS

The GED essay-graders must refer to a set-in-stone list of grading standards when evaluating each essay and deciding what score (1 through 4) it deserves.

Here are guidelines, as well as what each level means:

GED Official Scoring Guide

1 Inadequate	2 Marginal	3 Adequate	4 Effective
Reader has difficulty identifying or following the writer's ideas.	Reader occasionally has difficulty understanding or following the writer's ideas.	Reader understands writer's ideas.	Reader understands and easily follows the writer's expression of ideas.

The essay is scored using a "holistic" approach, meaning that readers consider the essay **as a whole** and judge it based on the **overall impression** it makes. Errors in punctuation and spelling are not as important. Even with a few spelling and punctuation errors, you can still score high on the essay.

Now you know your customers, and you know what they want. The rest of this chapter teaches you precisely how to give it to them.

KNOW YOUR INGREDIENTS

To write a tasty GED essay, you have to line up the necessary ingredients. The different grades of 1 through 4 are based on the quality of your essay in four fundamental categories:

- **Positioning:** The strength and clarity of your stance on the given topic
- **Development:** The strength of the examples you use to support your argument
- **Organization:** The organization of each of your paragraphs and of your essay overall
- **Language Conventions:** Sentence construction, grammar, and word choice

POSITIONING

The Language Arts, Writing test requires you to write an essay about an issue or topic of general interest. You are asked to present your opinion or explain your views about the assigned topic. The broadness of the topics means that with a little thought you can come up with plenty of examples to support your position on the topic.

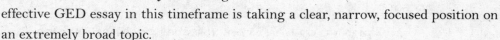
Remember to address only the assigned topic. You may want to write the question at the top of your piece of scratch paper before writing down ideas about the topic.

On the GED, you have 45 minutes to show what you can do. Forty-five minutes is not a lot of time. The key to writing an effective GED essay in this timeframe is taking a clear, narrow, focused position on an extremely broad topic.

Here is a sample prompt with the directions you will find on the test:

What is one important habit that you think everyone should have?

In your essay, identify that habit and explain why you think it is important. Use your personal observations, experience, and knowledge to support your view.

Simply choose a position and get to work supporting it. On the 45-minute, fast-food essay, there is no need to strain yourself to look for something original or creative. You simply need to decide on the "one important habit everyone should have." In our sample essay, we support the habit of being on time. Don't choose both sides or try to look at the pros and cons of each argument. Pick one and stick with it.

CHAPTER

3

LANGUAGE
ARTS,
WRITING

THE
GED

DEVELOPMENT

Support your position with strong examples. There are two things that make excellent GED examples stand out from the crowd:

- Variety of examples
- Specific examples

VARIETY OF EXAMPLES

In planning your essay, you may want to first brainstorm as many supporting ideas and examples as you can. Jot the ideas down on scratch paper. First, write down your topic statement. Then, list every idea about the subject that comes to your mind. For our sample topic question, your brainstorming notes might look like this:

In your examples, draw on your knowledge and experience to support your viewpoint.

One important habit everyone should have is to be on time.

we live in a busy culture

    – everybody is pressed for time

    – when people are late, it causes problems for other people

    – it's important to be on time in personal and work life

    work life

        – meeting deadlines

        – being on time for meetings with customers

        – being on time for work

    personal life

        – picking up kids from volleyball practice, making

         dinner, even going to sleep

being on time leads to other good habits

important to be respectful of others

SPECIFIC EXAMPLES

You do not have to have expert knowledge on a topic to come up with strong examples to answer the essay question. You just need to provide details from the experience and knowledge you already have. However, you must write *in detail* about your examples.

    A broad array of examples like those above provides a more solid and defensible position than three examples drawn from just one or two areas. Add any details that occur to you as you brainstorm. Cross out ideas that are too weak or vague or complicated to develop quickly. Feel free to move your ideas around using arrows or whatever method works for you. Once you jot down all your ideas, you are ready to outline the essay.

ORGANIZATION

No matter what topic you end up writing about, the organization of your essay should be the same. Whether you're asked to answer, "What is one important habit that you think everyone should have?" "What is the role of a grandparent?" or "Why are the Knicks the best team in the NBA?" the structure of your essay should be almost identical. The GED essay-graders are looking for standard ingredients, and the structure we're about to explain, using our Universal GED Essay Template, makes sure those ingredients stand out in your essay.

So, what's this magical essay structure? Well, back to the trusty fast-food analogy: a good GED essay is a lot like a triple-decker burger.

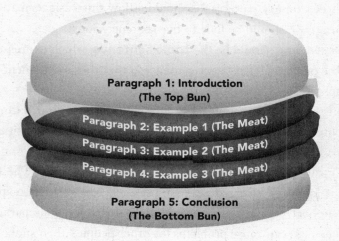

Paragraph 1: Introduction
(The Top Bun)

Paragraph 2: Example 1 (The Meat)

Paragraph 3: Example 2 (The Meat)

Paragraph 4: Example 3 (The Meat)

Paragraph 5: Conclusion
(The Bottom Bun)

No matter what the topic is, how you feel about it, or which examples you choose, you should always follow this five-paragraph structure on your GED essay. The first and last paragraphs are your essay's introduction and conclusion. The middle three paragraphs each discuss an example that supports and illustrates your argument. That's it.

Just as important as the organization of your entire essay is the organization within each of the five paragraphs. Let's take a closer look at each paragraph.

THE TOP BUN: INTRODUCTION

The introduction to a GED essay has to do three things:

- Grab the reader's attention
- Explain your position on the topic clearly and concisely
- Provide a smooth transition into your three examples

To accomplish these three goals, you need three to four sentences in your introduction. These three to four sentences must make your position clear and give the GED essay-grader a sense of the direction you take in the essay.

The Thesis Statement: The thesis statement is the first sentence of your essay. It identifies where you stand on the topic and should pull the GED essay-grader into the essay. A good thesis statement is strong, clear, and definitive. For example, a good thesis statement for the essay prompt, "What is one important habit that you think everyone should have?" is the following:

One important habit that everyone should have is to be on time.

The Essay Summary: After the thesis statement, the rest of the first paragraph should serve as a kind of preview of the examples you use to support your position on the topic. Explain and describe your three examples to make it clear how they fit into your argument. It's usually best to give each example its own sentence. Then the grader knows exactly what to expect from your essay.

THE MEAT: THREE EXAMPLE PARAGRAPHS

Each of your three example paragraphs should follow this basic format:

- Each paragraph should be four to five sentences long.
- The first sentence should be the **topic sentence**, which expresses the main idea of the paragraph (the topic sentence is the "thesis statement" of your paragraph).
- The next three to four sentences are for **developing your example**. In these sentences, use specific, concrete discussion of facts and situations to show just how your example supports your position.

The best "meat" paragraphs on the GED essay are specific. The GED's essay directions say it loud and clear: "Use your personal observations, experience, and knowledge to support your essay." If the topic sentence for your paragraph states, "Being late in business can cause problems for other people," then support that statement with specific examples of how your coworkers and customers are affected if you are late.

Transitions Between Meat Paragraphs: Your first meat paragraph dives right into its topic sentence, but the second and third meat paragraphs need **transitions**. Transitions are little bridges between one paragraph and another. They keep the flow of information smooth. The simplest way to build transitions is to use words like *also*, *another*, and *finally*. That means your second and third meat paragraphs should start with a transitional "bridge," such as "*Another* reason to be on time is . . ." or "Being on time *also* shows. . . ."

THE BOTTOM BUN: CONCLUSION

After developing your ideas in the body paragraphs, you should sum up your ideas in the concluding paragraph. The concluding paragraph should give your essay a sense of completeness. It must accomplish two main goals:

- Recap your argument.
- Expand on your position.

The Recap: The recap is a one-sentence summary of what you've already argued. Like the thesis statement, the recap should be strong, clear, and definitive. It may come at either the beginning or the end of the paragraph.

Expand on Your Position: The last paragraph of the essay should take your position a little further. One way to push your argument further is to provide examples of what would happen if everyone felt the same way as you do about your argument. The Bottom Bun wraps up the entire GED essay.

 Indent each paragraph. Write on every other line, so that you have room to make corrections neatly when you revise.

And there you have it! If you follow the fast-food template and break down the essay into its core ingredients, your GED essay will be strong, clear, and easy to write. Now let's look at the final step before examining a sample essay.

LANGUAGE CONVENTIONS

Language conventions are just rules about writing. If you take a clear position and defend it with solid, detailed examples, you will have made a strong start to a successful GED essay. But the GED-graders also want to see that you can write strong, grammatically correct sentences that are generally free of spelling errors. To satisfy the graders' expectations, keep these points in mind:

- **Vary your sentence structure.** Don't write an entire essay full of sentences that sound and look alike.
- **Create smooth transitions.** Just as there should be transitions between paragraphs in your essay, there should also be transitions between sentences. Keep thinking of transitions as bridges, and remember to use words and phrases such as *however, although, another,* and *on the other hand* to link one sentence to the next.
- **Avoid overly complex sentences.** Keep your sentences short and simple. Complex sentences are difficult to understand, and your GED essays should be as clear and easy to read as possible.
- **Choose the clearest words.** Word choice doesn't mean that you have to go for the big word every time. It means you should go for the *proper* word, the best word, the word that makes your essay as clear as possible. For example, instead of writing "One thing everyone should have is punctuality," try "One *habit* everyone should *cultivate* is punctuality."
- **Check your grammar and spelling.** A few grammar or spelling mistakes throughout your essay will not destroy your score, however you must be able to write solid grammatical sentences to score well on the essay. As for learning the grammar, well, you're in luck. This chapter covers all the rules of basic grammar and usage that you'll find on the Language Arts, Writing test.

THE GED

INTRODUCTION

CAPITALIZATION AND SPELLING

PUNCTUATION

VERBS

PRONOUNS

COMMON SENTENCE ERRORS

COORDINATION AND SUBORDINATION

MISPLACED AND DANGLING MODIFIERS

PARALLEL STRUCTURE

RESTRUCTURING PARAGRAPHS

THE ESSAY

KNOW HOW TO PUT THE INGREDIENTS TOGETHER

So, now you know your customers and all of the ingredients you should use to write an effective GED essay. Next, you must learn the writing process. Follow the five steps we describe below and you'll be on your way to a "4."

Five Steps to a "4" Essay

STEP 1:	Understand the prompt and take a position.	2 minutes
STEP 2:	Brainstorm examples.	4–6 minutes
STEP 3:	Create an outline.	5–7 minutes
STEP 4:	Write the essay.	25 minutes
STEP 5:	Proof the essay.	5 minutes

STEP 1. UNDERSTAND THE PROMPT AND TAKE A POSITION. (2 MIN.)

Before you even start to think about your essay, read the prompt very carefully. Make sure you understand the topic thoroughly by making it your own. To do that, choose a clear, simple position, as we discussed in the Ingredients section.

One important habit that everyone should have is to be on time.

That's it. One step down, four to go.

STEP 2. BRAINSTORM EXAMPLES. (4–6 MIN.)

Brainstorm to come up with examples to support your position. Don't skip this step, or you may find yourself halfway through the essay without enough examples to get yourself to the end. Don't try to edit yourself at this stage. Just jot down any ideas and examples that come to mind at first, then go back and choose your strongest concepts. Once you have picked your strongest brainstorming concepts, it's time to move on.

General Problems: Work, Personal Life, Many Benefits.

Work: Coworkers, Customers, Boss

Personal: Kids, Dinner, Home

Bonus: Respect, Positive Feelings, etc.

STEP 3. CREATE AN OUTLINE. (5–7 MIN.)

Organizing your ideas in outline form and then sticking to that outline is crucial. Though you may feel that you are wasting time that could be used for writing, the 5 or 6 minutes that you invest in creating an outline will pay off when you write the essay.

Since your outline is a kind of bare-bones "map" of your essay, the outline should follow our Universal GED Essay Template (Top Bun-Meat-Meat-Meat-Bottom Bun; see page 99). Here's a sample of an outline for an excellent GED essay response:

Sample Outline

I. Introduction: One important habit everyone should have is to be on time.
    a. Lateness causes problems at work
    B. Lateness causes problems in personal life
    C. Many benefits of punctuality

II. Lateness in business
    a. What happens when I'm late to my job
    B. Effect on coworkers
    C. Effect on customers

III. Lateness in personal life
    a. What happens if I don't pick kids up from volleyball on time
    B. Kids left in cold
    C. Dinner's not on time
    D. Bad home environment

IV. Bonuses of punctuality
    a. Show respect to others
    B. Doctor example: she's on time, so I'm more relaxed
    C. On time makes for positive feelings all around

V. Conclusion
    a. Being on time shows you have respect
    B. Shows you can organize and stick to goals
    C. Makes you a better coworker, parent, friend

Remember, your outline is your own personal roadmap. It doesn't need to make sense to anyone but you, but it does need to be clear enough to keep you pointed in the right direction. Once you have the outline down on paper, writing the essay is just a matter of creating transitions and adding a little polish to your sentences.

STEP 4. WRITE THE ESSAY. (25 MINUTES)

Writing the essay consists of following your outline and plugging in what's missing. Your outline should already contain a basic version of your thesis statement, one topic sentence for each of your three examples, and a conclusion statement that ties everything together. The final product will be about ten more sentences than what you've jotted down in your outline. So, all together, your essay should be about fifteen to twenty sentences long.

THE
GED

CHAPTER

3

LANGUAGE
ARTS,
WRITING

THE
GED

Do not break from your outline. Do not get sidetracked or start adding information that isn't related to your topic. Remember, you're serving a "fast-food" essay, and fast-food essays always stick to the core ingredients and the universal recipe.

If You Run Out of Time: If you're running out of time, drop one of your example paragraphs. You can still get a decent score. It is more important that you provide two well-written examples than three poorly written examples. Just be sure to include an introduction and a conclusion in every GED essay.

STEP 5. PROOFREAD YOUR ESSAY. (5 MINUTES)

Proofreading your essay means reading through your finished essay to correct mistakes or to clear up words that are difficult to read. If you don't have 5 minutes after you've finished writing the essay (step 4), spend whatever time you do have left proofreading. Search for rough writing, bad transitions, grammatical errors, repetitive sentence structure, and bad handwriting.

If you're running out of time and you have to skip a step, proofing is the step to drop. Proofing is important, but it's the only one of the Five Steps to a "4" that isn't absolutely crucial.

A SAMPLE GED ESSAY—UP CLOSE

Here's the sample prompt again:

What is one important habit that you think everyone should have?

In your essay, identify that habit and explain why you think it is important. Use your personal observations, experience, and knowledge to support your view.

Below is our example of the "4" essay. As you read, note that we have marked certain sentences and paragraphs to illustrate where and how the essay abides by our Universal GED Essay Template.

A "4" ESSAY

One important habit that everyone should have is to be on time. **(THESIS STATEMENT)** We live in a busy culture. People depend upon one another to get things done. Being late can cause problems for others at work and at home. Being on time has many benefits, including fostering other good habits.

Being late in business can cause problems for other people. **(TOPIC SENTENCE FOR EXAMPLE 1)** I work as a retail specialist in a large department store. If I'm late for work, my coworkers have to take on my responsibilities in addition to theirs. Having to cover for me may mean that our customers are not receiving the best service. If I'm late for an appointment with a customer,

that customer's whole schedule for the day may be ruined.
(FOUR DEVELOPMENT SENTENCES TO SUPPORT EXAMPLE 1)

Being late can also cause problems in people's personal lives.
(TOPIC SENTENCE FOR EXAMPLE 2) If I'm late picking up my children from volleyball practice, they have to wait outside in the cold. If I can't prepare dinner on time, my family is hungrier longer than they have to be. Being late sends a message of disrespect, which is not the atmosphere I want to create in my home. **(THREE DEVELOPMENT SENTENCES TO SUPPORT EXAMPLE 2)**

On the other hand, being punctual sends a message of respect.
(TOPIC SENTENCE FOR EXAMPLE 3) When you are on time, you show that you value another person's time as much as your own. I used to think that all doctors' appointments meant sitting in the waiting room for hours, but now I have a doctor who always sees me on time. I am more relaxed when I see her, because right away she has shown that she respects my needs. When you're on time, you set the tone for positive meetings by putting another person at ease.
(FOUR DEVELOPMENT SENTENCES TO SUPPORT EXAMPLE 3)

Being punctual says to everyone, including myself, that I am respectful and I deserve respect. Being on time also fosters other good habits. It's easier to keep a regular schedule and get tasks accomplished when you're on time. The habit of being on time helps me honor all my commitments, even the ones I make to improve myself. Punctual people are better coworkers, professionals, parents, friends, students, and selves, and everyone should develop this habit. **(THESIS STATEMENT REPHRASED)**

WHY THIS ESSAY DESERVES A "4"

This essay serves up all four GED essay ingredients. It takes a strong, clear stance on the topic in the first sentence and sticks to it from start to finish. It uses three examples from different areas and it never strays from using these examples to support the thesis statement's position. The organization of the essay follows our Universal GED Essay Template perfectly, both at the paragraph level (topic sentences and development sentences) and at the overall essay level (introduction, three meaty example paragraphs, a strong conclusion). The command of language remains solid throughout. The writer does not take risks with unfamiliar vocabulary but instead chooses a few out-of-the-ordinary words like *fosters*, *atmosphere*, and *punctual* that spread just the right amount of special sauce throughout the essay. Sentence structure varies often, making the entire essay more interesting and engaging to the grader. Finally, no significant grammar errors disrupt the overall excellence of this GED essay.

CHAPTER

3

LANGUAGE
ARTS,
WRITING

THE
GED

INTRODUCTION

CAPITALIZATION
AND SPELLING

PUNCTUATION

VERBS

PRONOUNS

COMMON
SENTENCE ERRORS

COORDINATION
AND
SUBORDINATION

MISPLACED AND
DANGLING
MODIFIERS

PARALLEL
STRUCTURE

RESTRUCTURING
PARAGRAPHS

THE ESSAY

CHAPTER

3

LANGUAGE ARTS, WRITING

THE GED

LAST WORDS ABOUT THE ESSAY

You have all the skills you need to write the essay. Here are a few final things to keep in mind while writing and revising your essay:

- Be as concise as possible. When revising your essay, look for ways to restate what you've said in the shortest, clearest way possible.
- Eliminate redundant sentences or phrases. Don't include extra sentences just to make your essay appear longer. Make sure that every sentence adds something to your essay.
- Make sure that the voice you use is consistent. It's fine to use the first-person *I*, as in the sample essay, but make sure that whatever voice you use is used throughout the essay. In other words, if you start out using *I* or *one*, don't switch to *you* halfway through the essay.
- Avoid using slang or informal language. Imagine you are writing this for a teacher.
- Check for grammatical errors. Using your knowledge of grammar, usage, and mechanics, you can effectively revise your essay, fixing mistakes as you go.

That's all there is to preparing for the Writing test.

You have completed the GED Language Arts, Writing ladder, and you are now well prepared to tackle Parts I and II of this subject test. If you feel you need to strengthen certain skills, such as punctuation or restructuring paragraphs, review those sections. You are the best judge of what you do and do not know. Your hard work has paid off, and you can face the Writing test with confidence.

ANSWERS AND LANGUAGE ARTS, WRITING EXPLANATIONS

CHAPTER

3

LANGUAGE
ARTS,
WRITING

THE
GED

ANSWERS
AND
EXPLANATIONS

PRACTICE SET: CAPITALIZATION AND SPELLING

1. (4) Replace <u>december</u> with <u>December</u>.
The word *December* should be capitalized, since it refers to a month. Eliminate answer (1), since no comma is needed after *rate*. The possessive *Your* is correct and should not be changed to the contraction *You're*, as in answer (2). Since the verb *will be* is already in the correct tense (future tense), rule out answer 3. **Capitalization**

2. (2) Replace <u>excepted</u> with <u>accepted</u>.
The word *excepted* means "with the exception of." That word should be replaced with *accepted*, which means "widely used or recognized." Answer (2) is the correct answer. Answer (1) creates the wrong form of the verb. Answer (3) introduces the possessive *whose*, which makes no sense. Answer (4) is incorrect, because the plural form *checks* is correct in the original sentence. **Spelling/homonyms**

3. (2) Replace <u>yours'</u> with <u>yours</u>.
Answer (2) is correct, because you should not use an apostrophe with possessive pronouns such as *yours*. Answer (1) is incorrect, because the original word is in the plural form and is correct. Since *knead* means "to fold or press a soft substance such as dough" and is thus the wrong word, eliminate answer (3). Similarly, the original word in answer (4), *access*, is correct. Answer (5) is incorrect, since the possessive *your* is the correct form in the sentence. **Spelling/possessives**

4. (4) Replace <u>Spring</u> with <u>spring</u>.
The names of seasons are not capitalized, so answer (4) is correct. Rule out answer (1), since the verb *may* is correct. Answer (2) replaces the correct word *to* with the incorrect word *two*. Answer (3) is incorrect, because the verb is already in the correct tense. **Capitalization**

5. (1) Replace <u>Its</u> with <u>It's</u>.
Answer (1) is correct, because the possessive pronoun *Its* should be replaced by the contraction *It's*, which stands for *It is*. The comma is necessary between two independent clauses, so answer (2) is wrong. Answer (3) introduces the incorrect homonym *eye*. Answer (4) is incorrect, since the original word *to* is correct as is.
 Spelling/homonyms

CHAPTER

3

LANGUAGE
ARTS,
WRITING

THE
GED

ANSWERS
AND
EXPLANATIONS

PRACTICE SET: PUNCTUATION

1.   (2)   Fortunately, these nail holes
The introductory element *Fortunately* needs to be followed by a comma. The singular *this* does not agree in number with the plural *holes*, so answer (3) is wrong. Eliminate answer (4), since the original plural form of *holes* is correct. Answer (5) is incorrect, since no comma is needed after *nail*. **Punctuation**

2.   (5)   No correction is necessary.
The original sentence is correct as is. You do not need a comma before *that*, so rule out answer (4). Eliminate answer (1), because the plural form of *materials* is correct. Answer (2) is wrong, since no comma is needed after *materials*. In answer (3), *tools* should remain uncapitalized, since the word is not a proper noun. **Punctuation**

3.   (3)   Insert a comma after knife.
Commas must separate items in a series. Answer (1) changes the verb to the wrong tense. Answer (2) is incorrect, since all the items must be separated by commas. Answer (4) replaces the correct plural form of *supplies* with an illogical possessive, *supply's*. **Punctuation**

4.   (2)   Insert a comma after materials.
The introductory phrase needs to be set off by a comma. Eliminate answer (1), since the verb is correct as is. Answer (3) can be eliminated, since *to* is the correct word. Answer (4) is wrong, because there should be no comma after *paste*. **Punctuation**

5.   (4)   Your wall, however, will look
The parenthetical expression *however* needs commas before and after it, so answer (4) is correct. Answer (3) takes the commas out altogether. The possessive *Your* in the original sentence is correct, so rule out answer (2). Answer (5) creates a sentence in which the verb is in the wrong tense. **Punctuation**

PRACTICE SET: VERBS

1.   (3)   Change help to helps.
The verb *help* must be changed to *helps* to agree in number with the singular subject *it*. Answer (1) can be eliminated, since *focuses* already agrees in number with *It*. The comma between clauses is necessary, so answer (2) is wrong. Answer (4) is incorrect, since no comma is needed after *people*. **Subject-verb agreement**

2.   (4)   section of London. He assisted people who were
The verb *assists* must be changed to the past tense *assisted* to be consistent with the verb *started*. Eliminate answer (2), since *London* is a proper noun and should be capitalized. Answer (3) creates a comma splice. Answer (5) is wrong, since *was* is singular and thus does not agree in number with *people*. **Verb tense**

3. **(1)   Change <u>were</u> to <u>was</u>.**
The word *everyone* is always singular and should take the singular form of the verb *was*. A comma isn't needed after *welcome*, so answer (2) is wrong. Answer (3) replaces the correct word *to* with its incorrect homonym *two*. Answer (4) changes the correct form of *join* to the incorrect form *joins*. ⊖ **Subject-verb agreement**

4. **(2)   Change <u>operate</u> to <u>operates</u>.**
The collective noun *group* acts as a singular subject, so the verb should be in the singular form: *operates*. Eliminate answer (1), because a comma should follow the introductory word. In answer (3), the suggested future verb tense of *will operate* is incorrect. Answer (4) can be eliminated, because the original word *than* is correct as is. ⊖ **Subject-verb agreement**

5. **(3)   Today, there are about two million members**
Although the subject and the verb are inverted, they still need to agree in number. The subject *members* is plural, so the verb form must be the plural *are*. Rule out answer (2), since the comma is needed after the introductory element. You can also rule out answers (4) and (5), because they change the verb to the wrong tenses. ⊖ **Subject-verb agreement**

PRACTICE SET: PRONOUNS

1. **(2)   Change <u>I</u> to <u>me</u>.**
The case of the pronoun *I* needs to be changed. *I* is in the nominative case, which is used when the pronoun acts as a subject. The pronoun should be in the objective case, since the word is being used as an object of the verb *call*. Who is being called? The answer is *me*. Eliminate answer (1), since *You* is the correct pronoun—it functions as a subject. The verb *need* is also correct, so eliminate answer (3). A restrictive clause starting with *if* needs no comma, so answer (4) is incorrect. ⊖ **Pronoun case**

2. **(4)   in the grand hall, and they will conclude**
In the original sentence, *she* is an incorrect pronoun, because the antecedent is the plural *Two instructors*. The pronoun should also be plural: *they*. You can eliminate answer (2), since the comma is needed to separate two independent clauses. Eliminate answer (3), since *her* is in the wrong case and number. The verb in the original sentence is in the correct tense, so answer (5) is wrong. ⊖ **Pronoun reference**

3. **(3)   The leaders will announce which cabin you**
They is a vague pronoun reference, since it does not refer to any clear antecedent. The subject should be specified to make it clear who is doing the announcing. Answer (2) changes the correct pronoun to an incorrect one. Answer (3) changes the verb tense to an incorrect one, and answer (5) introduces an incorrect pronoun and verb. ⊖ **Vague pronoun reference**

CHAPTER
3

LANGUAGE
ARTS,
WRITING

THE
GED

ANSWERS
AND
EXPLANATIONS

CHAPTER

3

LANGUAGE
ARTS,
WRITING

THE
GED

ANSWERS
AND
EXPLANATIONS

4.   (3)   Change <u>his</u> to <u>your</u>.

The pronoun *his* should be changed to *your* to be consistent with the subject *You*. Answer (1) creates a pronoun shift from the previous sentences in which *you* is consistent. Eliminate answer (2), because the comma is necessary before the independent clause. The original verb is in the correct plural form, so rule out answer (4).
H **Pronoun shift**

5.   (5)   Change <u>one</u> to <u>you</u>.

The pronouns should be consistent, so *one* should be changed to *you* to match the first pronoun. You can eliminate answer (1), since the comma is needed after an introductory subordinate clause. You can also eliminate answer (2), since the original verb tense is correct. The plural form of *questions* is correct, so eliminate answer (3). Answer (4) replaces the word with a nonsensical homonym.   **H** **Pronoun shift**

PRACTICE SET: COMMON SENTENCE ERRORS

1.   (5)   artworks reveal the lives

The original sentences are fragments. Answer (5) offers a way to combine the fragments to create a sentence that expresses a complete thought. Answers (1), (3), and (4) maintain the sentence fragments and should be eliminated. Answer (2) appears to combine the fragments, but the resulting group of words still lacks a verb, since *revealing* is in the wrong tense.   **H** **Sentence fragments**

2.   (2)   900. This period is known

The original sentence is a run-on sentence, because it contains two independent clauses that are improperly joined without punctuation. Answer (2) creates two sentences that are correctly punctuated. Answer (3) creates a comma splice. Answer (4) illogically uses the conjunction *but*. Answer (5) creates a sentence fragment.
H **Run-ons**

3.   (3)   Replace the comma with a semicolon.

The original sentence is a comma splice. Answer (3) fixes the comma splice, since you can correctly join two independent clauses with a semicolon. Rule out answer (2), since *Maya* is a proper noun and should remain capitalized. Answer (4) changes the verb to the wrong tense. Answer (5) replaces a correct word with an incorrect one.
H **Comma splices**

4.   (5)   walls. This art decorated

The original sentence is a run-on. Eliminate answer (2), since the subordinating conjunction *because* does not make sense. Answers (3) and (4) create sentence fragments. Answer (5) correctly divides the run-on into two sentences.   **H** **Run-ons**

5.   (2)   valued, artists enjoyed

(sentence fragments) Sentence 10 is a fragment. To correct the fragment, you should choose answer (2), which correctly joins the subordinate clause with an independent clause. The other options fail to combine the sentences in a way that maintains the original ideas in the sentences and corrects the fragment.

🌓 **Sentence fragments**

PRACTICE SET: COORDINATION AND SUBORDINATION

1.   (3)   Insert a comma after <u>move</u>.

You need to use a comma after an introductory subordinating clause. Answer (1) changes the verb to the wrong form. Answer (2) changes a correct verb form to an incorrect noun. Answer (4) replaces the correct plural form of *points* with an incorrect possessive form. 🌓 **Subordination**

2.   (5)   Change <u>or</u> to <u>and</u>.

The coordinating conjunction *or* must be changed to *and* in order for the sentence to make sense. Eliminate answer (1), since the comma is necessary after an introductory element. Eliminate answer (2), because the comma is necessary between independent clauses joined by a coordinating conjunction. Answer (3) replaces the correct plural form *companies* with the incorrect possessive form *company's*. Answer (4) introduces an incorrect homonym. 🌓 **Coordination**

3.   (2)   free and without obligation

You may occasionally see a question such as this one in which you are asked to combine sentences. Answer (2) offers the most succinct way to combine the ideas in both sentences. Answer (1) creates a comma splice. Answers (3) and (4) combine the ideas in ways that are not true to the original ideas. Answer (5) is wordy and does not make sense. 🌓 **Coordination**

4.   (5)   things; for example, some

The conjunctive adverb *for example* must be preceded by a semicolon and followed by a comma. Eliminate answer (2), since it lacks both types of punctuation. Eliminate answer (3), since you should not use both the coordinating conjunction *but* and the conjunctive adverb. Answer (4) is punctuated correctly, but the conjunctive adverb *whenever* doesn't make logical sense. 🌓 **Coordination**

5.   (3)   You should make sure that

In the original sentence, both clauses are subordinate, so one of them must be changed to an independent clause. Answer (3) effectively changes the first clause to an independent clause. None of the other options change the subordinate clauses.

🌓 **Subordination**

CHAPTER

3

LANGUAGE
ARTS,
WRITING

THE
GED

ANSWERS
AND
EXPLANATIONS

PRACTICE SET: MISPLACED AND DANGLING MODIFIERS

1. **(3) we will inspect**

In the original sentence, the phrase *during the maintenance check* interrupts the flow of ideas. When the phrase is placed at the beginning of the sentence, it should be followed by the word it modifies, which is the subject *we*. Answer (3) provides this solution. Eliminate answer (1), since the coordinating conjunction *and* should not start the clause. Answers (2) and (4) can be ruled out, since the resulting sentences would lack subjects. Answer (5) creates a sentence in which the subject and verb are inverted for no apparent reason.  **Misplaced phrase**

2. **(1) Replace <u>By keeping</u> with <u>If you keep</u>.**

In the original sentence, the phrase *By keeping your car properly maintained* is dangling, because it lacks a word to modify. Who is keeping the car maintained? By changing the phrase to *If you keep your car properly maintained*, you provide a subject for the sentence. Eliminate answer (2), since the comma is necessary after an introductory subordinate clause. Answer (3) adds an unnecessary coordinating conjunction after the comma. The verb tense is fine in the original sentence, so eliminate answer (4). **Dangling modifier**

3. **(5) No correction is necessary.**

The sentence is fine as is. The modifiers are all close to the words they modify. Answer (1) can be eliminated, since the comma is needed after an introductory element. Answer (2) is wrong, since no conjunction is needed after *Auto*. The verb form in the original sentence is fine, so answer (3) is wrong. Answer (4) replaces *to* with a nonsensical homonym. **Misplaced and dangling modifiers**

4. **(4) business, we put our clients' needs**

The phrase *As local professionals in a competitive business* is dangling, because it lacks a word to modify. Answer (4) provides the subject *we*, which is the word the phrase should modify. Answer (2) is incorrect, because *clients'* should be in the possessive form. Answer (3) is illogical. Answer (5) creates a sentence fragment. **Dangling modifier**

5. **(5) If you bring this letter with the coupon below to your appointment,**

The phrase *with the coupon below* modifies *letter*, so it should be placed near that word. Answer (5) provides that correction. The other options either leave the modifier misplaced or create sentence fragments. **Misplaced modifier**

PRACTICE SET: PARALLEL STRUCTURE

1.   (3)   were also misunderstood

The original sentence is not parallel, since the second verb is in a different form than the first one. Answer (3) makes both verbs parallel. It is also the most concise option. Answer (2) creates two incomplete clauses. Answer (4) creates an interrupting phrase and doesn't correct the faulty parallelism. Answer (5) introduces a nonsensical conjunctive adverb, *however*. 🖊 **Parallel structure**

2.   (2)   Remove <u>to wage</u>.

Items in a series must be parallel. The second item in the series should be a noun like the other two items, *plagues* and *death*. Answer (2) makes the second item a noun: *war*. Answer (1) changes the verb to an incorrect tense. Eliminate answer (3), since the noun should not be in possessive form. Answer (4) is wrong, since commas are needed between items in a series. 🖊 **Parallel structure**

3.   (3)   Change <u>was calculating</u> to <u>calculated</u>.

The verb should be in the past tense to be parallel with the tense of *studied*. Answer (1) is wrong, since the comma is needed between the clauses. Answers (2) and (4) replace correct words with incorrect homonyms. 🖊 **Parallel structure**

4.   (5)   at predictable times.

To be parallel with *at regular intervals*, the second phrase should begin with a preposition, such as *at*. Answer (5) provides a phrase that is parallel to the first one in the sentence—both phrases consist of a preposition followed by an adjective followed by a noun. The other options maintain faulty parallelism. 🖊 **Parallel structure**

5.   (4)   Change <u>like ice</u> to <u>icy</u>.

To be parallel, the phrase *like ice* must be changed to an adjective, *icy*. The singular verb *is* agrees with the singular subject *center*, so eliminate answer (1). Answers (2) and (3) can be eliminated, since commas must be used between items in a series. 🖊 **Parallel structure**

PRACTICE SET: RESTRUCTURING PARAGRAPHS

1.   (3)   Move sentence 3 to the end of the paragraph.

Sentence 3 elaborates on information in sentence 5, so sentence 3 should be moved to the end of the paragraph. Answers (1) and (2) are wrong, since sentences 1 and 2 are needed in the paragraph. Moving sentence 4 to the beginning would create confusion, so eliminate answer (4). 🖊 **Coherence**

2.   (1)   When making your nomination, please consider several criteria.

This question requires that you identify a correct topic sentence. Since the first half of the paragraph is about what criteria the Employee of the Month has, answer (1) provides an effective topic sentence. Answer (2) is incorrect, because the sentence is

CHAPTER

3

LANGUAGE
ARTS,
WRITING

THE
GED

ANSWERS
AND
EXPLANATIONS

CHAPTER

3

LANGUAGE
ARTS,
WRITING

THE
GED

ANSWERS
AND
EXPLANATIONS

irrelevant to the ideas in the paragraph. Eliminate answers (3) and (5), since their ideas belong more readily in paragraph A. Answer (4) is a sentence fragment.
🄷 Topic sentences

3.   (4)   Remove sentence 9.
Sentence 9 should be removed, since it involves extraneous or irrelevant ideas and disrupts the flow of ideas. Sentences 6 and 7 are important to the paragraph, so answers (1) and (2) are wrong. Moving sentence 7 to the end of the paragraph, as in answer (3), would create confusion. **🄷 Unity**

4.   (1)   Change Unfortunately to In addition.
The transition word should be changed to *In addition. Unfortunately* does not provide the correct transition, since it implies regret. The comma is needed after the transition word, so rule out answer (2). Answer (3) incorrectly changes the number of the verb.
🄷 Transitions

5.   (5)   sentence 13
Sentence 13 should start a new paragraph, since it introduces a new main idea about when and how the Employee of the Month will be announced. Sentence 2 belongs with the sentences in paragraph A, so eliminate answer (1). Answers (2) and (3) are incorrect, since sentences 7 and 8 belong in paragraph B. Sentence 12 does not make a suitable first sentence for a paragraph, so eliminate answer (4).
🄷 Paragraph breaks

CHAPTER

4

SOCIAL STUDIES

SOCIAL STUDIES

Many people are afraid they'll be asked questions like "Who was the twelfth president of the United States?" or "How does a bill become law?" on the GED test. Well, rest easy: you won't find any such questions. The Social Studies test doesn't require you to have huge amounts of history or civics or geography stored in your brain. It asks questions only about information that is provided to you in reading passages, maps, charts, and graphs.

However, that doesn't mean you don't have any work to do. To score high on the Social Studies test, you must be able to understand charts, graphs, and reading passages; interpret and evaluate that information; and then draw conclusions. But we've got you covered.

What follows in this chapter isn't a history lesson. It's a review of how to use the material given on the test to answer the questions correctly.

Here is your ladder for the Social Studies test.

Rung 1: Introduction
Rung 2: Understanding What You Read
Rung 3: Understanding Visual Materials
Rung 4: Identifying Implications
Rung 5: Applying Ideas
Rung 6: Interpreting Political Cartoons
Rung 7: Analyzing Relationships
Rung 8: Evaluating Information
Rung 9: Social Studies Concepts

By using the step-by-step ladder in this chapter, you can master all the skills you need to know to succeed on the Social Studies test. There are nine rungs in the ladder. Each rung is designed as a single lesson and should take you just about an hour to complete. It is important to work through each rung, one at a time, to prepare yourself for all of the kinds of questions you will see on the Social Studies test. Each rung builds on the rung before it.

Each section concludes with a set of questions. Aswering these questions helps you to assess how prepared you are in each topic. If you answer most of the practice set questions correctly, you should move on to the next rung. Explanations to each practice set appear at the end of the chapter and indicate which topic (rung) is being tested. You can go back and review previous lessons if you feel you need to improve in a particular area.

As you can see, the ladder begins with the simplest thought processes involving understanding presented and implied ideas. As you move down the ladder, you develop more complex skills like applying, analyzing, and evaluating information.

The last rung is Social Studies Concepts. Although the test does not require you to recall any specific fact, person, date, or event, you must be familiar with general social studies information in the areas of history, civics and government, economics, and geography so you are not confused or taken by surprise on test day. This last rung offers an overview of common topics that you are probably already comfortable with.

By the time you reach the final rung, you will have the skills you need to score high on the Social Studies test.

INTRODUCTION

As we discussed, the Social Studies test is not meant to measure your existing knowledge of social studies facts. Instead, it is an assessment of your reasoning skills. You use reasoning skills all the time, such as when you are driving, taking a bus, or picking out food on a menu. Success on this test depends on your thought process, not your memory.

The Social Studies test is designed to make sure you can keep up with the constantly changing world around you—no matter how the information is presented. Just like in your everyday life, the test presents newspaper articles, ads, magazine stories, government pamphlets, product inserts, maps, charts, pictures, diagrams, and tables for you to read, understand, describe, and use.

QUICK OVERVIEW

Test	Items	Time Limit
Social Studies	50 multiple-choice questions	70 minutes

As you can see, there are fifty questions on the Social Studies test. Each is a multiple-choice question with five possible answers. You must choose the best answer among the five choices. You have 70 minutes to complete the section, which gives you an average of almost a minute and a half for each question.

THE
GED

CHAPTER

4

SOCIAL
STUDIES

THE

INTRODUCTION

UNDERSTANDING
WHAT YOU READ

UNDERSTANDING
VISUAL MATERIALS

IDENTIFYING
IMPLICATIONS

APPLYING IDEAS

INTERPRETING
POLITICAL
CARTOONS

ANALYZING
RELATIONSHIPS

EVALUATING
INFORMATION

SOCIAL STUDIES
CONCEPTS

The multiple-choice questions cover four content areas:

- **History (40%: 25% U.S. history and 15% world history)**
  —past events concerning human civilization, including social and political developments in the United States and other parts of the world.
- **Civics and government (25%)**—systems of government, particularly characteristics, documents, and institutions of American democracy.
- **Economics (20%)**—ideas and implications of approaches to supply and demand of goods.
- **Geography (15%)**—the world's physical characteristics, including land and sea, plants and animals, weather, environment, and natural resources, and their impact on humankind.

TEST-TAKING TIPS

If there is one word that you could associate with the Social Studies test, it's *information.* You get a lot of it on this test. Information comes in the form of a single short statement, a paragraph, or a longer passage of several paragraphs. Graphs, tables, and maps include many data points. So, here are two big tips:

Big Tip Number 1: Don't try to remember or memorize anything on a chart, table, or map, or in a reading passage. You can return to the passage or graphic as often as you want to find your answer, so there is no need to spend time trying to memorize every fact. As a first step with every question, simply familiarize yourself with the material in the selection as you read through it the first time. Then read the answers and return to the passage, map, or diagram to find what you are looking for. Return to the selection as many times as you need to until you are sure of your answers, but remember, you are under a time limit. Which brings us to our next tip.

Big Tip Number 2: Use the X-O strategy that we discussed in Chapter 2, "Test-Taking Basics," to make sure that you answer all of the questions you know, thereby getting the easy points first. Easy questions are worth the same number of points as harder ones, so don't spend too much time struggling with an item you find very difficult. It is better to find and answer more of the questions that you are sure about.

Your score is a measure of the number of questions you answer correctly; it does not represent the number correct in terms of the number of questions you attempt. This means you are not penalized for guessing. You should indicate an answer for every question, even if it is a random choice. Your odds of picking the right answer improve if you use process of elimination before making your selection.

You should now have a pretty good idea of how the test shapes up and what you'll see on test day. Let's move on to the next rung.

UNDERSTANDING WHAT YOU READ

Comprehension is the key to success on the Social Studies test. If you understand what you read, you can likely answer questions at every rung of the ladder. But without understanding first, there is not much chance of applying, analyzing, and evaluating later.

Comprehension is not memorization. Luckily, it is much more interesting than that. When you read for comprehension, the goal is to get a good idea of what the author is trying to tell you. You do not have to remember everything the author wrote down, so relax and enjoy what you read, and practice reading for comprehension.

COMPREHENSION

There are two basic steps to understanding what you read. If you can answer the following questions for any written passage, you are on your way to mastering the art of reading comprehension:

- **What Is the Main Idea?** The main idea is the point of a message. It is the general idea that the author wants you to understand when you finish reading a passage or reviewing a visual communication.
- **What Are the Supporting Details?** The details of a passage demonstrate, justify, or enhance the main idea.

Reading Comprehension Workshop
Find a short article or story that interests both you and a friend. Ask the friend to read it and discuss it with you. You might choose a topic such as why downloading music from the Internet is against the law. Read up on it and think about what it means to you, how it affects the price of CDs, and what it means for new artists without record deals. If you practice thinking about and discussing what you read, your reading comprehension is sure to improve.

FINDING THE MAIN IDEA

The most important part of comprehending what you read is to get the writer's big point. Understanding a written passage does not require that you memorize every detail it presents, just that you come away from it with a sense of what the writer was trying to get across. The main idea of a paragraph is the author's message about the topic. It is often expressed directly, but it may also be implied.

There are several ways to identify the main idea of a written passage or a visual communication. Here are two different approaches. Try both, then select the method that makes the most sense to you.

1. **Examine the Parts:** Read the paragraph or passage and identify the subject and verb of each sentence. Most of the time, the main idea concerns the most frequent subject in the passage. The important idea about that subject is likely be found in the verbs.

   Try this example:

   The United States of America is located on the continent of North America. There are 50 states in the United States. Forty-eight of the states form the contiguous United States. The United States borders on Canada to the north, and Mexico and the Gulf of Mexico to the south. On the east coast, the United States is bordered by the Atlantic Ocean, and on the west coast it is bordered by the Pacific Ocean. To the northwest of Canada is the state of Alaska. The state of Hawaii is located in the Pacific Ocean, southwest of California. In addition to the 50 states, the United States has several territories and possessions, located in the Caribbean Sea and the Pacific Ocean. (Source: http://bensguide.gpo.gov/9-12/nation/index.html)

   Here is the same paragraph with the subject of each sentence in **bold** and the verbs underlined.

   The United States of America is located on the continent of North America. There are **50 states** in the United States. **Forty-eight of the states** form the contiguous United States. **The United States** borders on Canada to the north, and Mexico and the Gulf of Mexico to the south. On the east coast, **the United States** is bordered by the Atlantic Ocean, and on the west coast **it** is bordered by the Pacific Ocean. To the northwest of Canada is **the state of Alaska**. **The state of Hawaii** is located in the Pacific Ocean, southwest of California. In addition to the 50 states, **the United States** has several territories and possessions, located in the Caribbean Sea and the Pacific Ocean.

   Do you notice a theme? All the sentences are about one, some, or all of the fifty states in the United States. After considering each sentence separately, you can see that together they make up a paragraph about the geographical makeup of the United States. That's the main idea.

2. **Examine the Sentences:** Another way to find the main idea is to examine the sentences. It is easy to identify the main idea of a passage when it is directly expressed in the text. Directly expressed main ideas are often located at the beginning of a paragraph, usually in the first sentence. This type of sentence is called the *topic sentence*. Any time the first sentence explains the subject being discussed in the passage, you have probably found the "main idea."

   If it is not the first sentence in a paragraph, the main idea is often summed up in the last sentence. Some authors prefer to lead up to the main idea. They provide information that builds on a main idea in the last sentence. The main idea can be expressed as a summary of the information in the paragraph and may also serve as a transition, or link, to the next paragraph.

Read the following passage to find the main idea of each paragraph:

Duties and Responsibilities of Citizens

The right to vote is a duty as well as a privilege. It is important for all citizens to vote in every election to make sure that the democratic, representative system of government is maintained. Persons who do not vote lose their voice in the government.

Before voting in an election, each citizen should be well informed about the issues and candidates. Resources such as *GPO Access* can help citizens keep current on issues facing the Congress and how members of Congress vote on these issues. The political parties distribute brochures, pamphlets, and newsletters about their candidates, the party platform, and the party view on important issues. Citizens can read this information to learn about the differences among the parties. Some candidates are independent and do not belong to a political party. These candidates distribute their own information. Radio, television, newspapers, and magazines provide information, also. Each citizen needs to make his/her own decision about who would be the best representatives by considering all sides of the issues.

State and local elections involve voting on issues that are of concern to the citizens, such as businesses, schools, neighborhoods, transportation, safety, or health. In many states, the voters have a direct part in the lawmaking process. For example, a law that has been passed in the state legislature may be sent back to the voters to accept or reject. The voters decide directly if a new law should be put into effect. This is known as the power of referendum. Another form of direct lawmaking by the voters in some states is the initiative. In this process, a group of voters signs a petition asking for a specific law. If enough people have signed the petition, the qualified voters must be given a chance to vote for or against the proposed law. The law will go into effect if more than half (a majority) of the votes are in favor of the law. These two processes, referendum and initiative, show the authority of the people in the U.S. system of government and the importance of being a well-informed citizen. To keep the laws responsive to the needs of state and community, it is important to vote and be represented. (Source: http://bensguide.gpo.gov/9-12/citizenship/responsibilities.html)

To find the topic sentence, read the first sentence, then look at it again after you read each following sentence. Do the later sentences illustrate or emphasize the point made in the first sentence? If so, it is probably the topic. If not, try reading the last sentence, then looking back to see if it summarizes points illustrated in earlier sentences.

Here is the passage again, with the topic sentence of each paragraph in **bold**.

The right to vote is a duty as well as a privilege. It is important for all citizens to vote in every election to make sure that the democratic, representative system of government is maintained. Persons who do not vote lose their voice in the government.

The first sentence of the first paragraph is the topic, because the second and third sentences illustrate its point that voting is a duty (because that is how government is maintained) and a privilege (because to not vote is to lose your voice in government).

CHAPTER

4

SOCIAL
STUDIES

THE
GED

INTRODUCTION

**UNDERSTANDING
WHAT YOU READ**

UNDERSTANDING
VISUAL MATERIALS

IDENTIFYING
IMPLICATIONS

APPLYING IDEAS

INTERPRETING
POLITICAL
CARTOONS

ANALYZING
RELATIONSHIPS

EVALUATING
INFORMATION

SOCIAL STUDIES
CONCEPTS

Before voting in an election, each citizen should be well informed about the issues and candidates. Resources such as *GPO Access* can help citizens keep current on issues facing the Congress and how members of Congress vote on these issues. The political parties distribute brochures, pamphlets, and newsletters about their candidates, the party platform, and the party view on important issues. Citizens can read this information to learn about the differences among the parties. Some candidates are independent and do not belong to a political party. These candidates distribute their own information. Radio, television, newspapers, and magazines provide information, also. **Each citizen needs to make his/her own decision about who would be the best representatives by considering all sides of the issues.**

The topic of the second paragraph is summarized in the last sentence. The paragraph lists many places for voters to find information about an issue, then plainly states why so much information is needed.

State and local elections involve voting on issues that are of concern to the citizens, such as businesses, schools, neighborhoods, transportation, safety, or health. In many states, the voters have a direct part in the lawmaking process. For example, a law that has been passed in the state legislature may be sent back to the voters to accept or reject. The voters decide directly if a new law should be put into effect. This is known as the power of referendum. Another form of direct lawmaking by the voters in some states is the initiative. In this process, a group of voters signs a petition asking for a specific law. If enough people have signed the petition, the qualified voters must be given a chance to vote for or against the proposed law. The law will go into effect if more than half (a majority) of the votes are in favor of the law. These two processes, referendum and initiative, show the authority of the people in the U.S. system of government and the importance of being a well-informed citizen. **To keep the laws responsive to the needs of state and community, it is important to vote and be represented.**

The point of the last paragraph is summed up in the last sentence. The paragraph shows how voters influence the laws that govern their lives and that it is important for voters to be represented in the matters that affect them.

Now consider the three topic sentences together to get a sense of the main idea of the entire passage:

The right to vote is a duty as well as a privilege.

Each citizen needs to make his/her own decision about who would be the best representatives by considering all sides of the issues.

To keep the laws responsive to the needs of state and community, it is important to vote and be represented.

Is one supported by the others? Just as each sentence points to the main idea of a paragraph, each paragraph points to the main idea of a passage. In this case, the second and third topic sentences illustrate the first. So, the main idea of the passage is that voting is a duty and a privilege.

Finding the main idea is the first step to understanding what you read. The second step is to look at the details.

FINDING THE SUPPORTING DETAILS

Finding the main idea will give you a good idea of what the passage is about. But the second step solidifies things. Details are used to provide support to the main idea of a written passage. They may help you understand, accept, or apply the author's main idea. The details of a passage demonstrate, justify, or enhance the main idea. Details usually address *who*, *what*, *when*, *where*, *why*, and *how*. To identify the support in a paragraph, first find the main idea and then look for the elements that illustrate or prove that point.

Look again at the earlier passage about voting. Which details support the conclusion that voters should be well informed? How many different sources of information are listed?

Before voting in an election, each citizen should be well informed about the issues and candidates. Resources such as **GPO Access** can help citizens keep current on issues facing the Congress and how members of Congress vote on these issues. The **political parties** distribute brochures, pamphlets, and newsletters about their candidates, the party platform, and the party view on important issues. Citizens can read this information to learn about the differences among the parties. Some candidates are independent and do not belong to a political party. These **candidates** distribute their own information. **Radio, television, newspapers, and magazines** provide information, also. Each citizen needs to make his/her own decision about who would be the best representatives by considering all sides of the issues.

Being able to identify details is an important part of understanding what you read and an essential skill when it is time for you to apply, analyze, and judge the information in other questions.

Now that you've got down the two steps to understanding what you read, we've got two handy strategies to make both steps easier:

- **Identifying and Using Context Clues**
- **Active Reading**

IDENTIFYING AND USING CONTEXT CLUES

If a paragraph or passage includes unfamiliar words, you can still get the writer's meaning by using context clues to extend your understanding. Comprehending what you read relies heavily on your vocabulary. But don't lose heart if you haven't spent all your life reading the dictionary. You can use your life experience to help you understand words or ideas that might not be part of your existing vocabulary. For example, there is a big difference between recognizing a word that you have seen before and knowing what it means because you have some experience that is related. For instance, someone who has been fishing will understand the word *bait* differently than someone who has never held a fishing pole. Vocabulary and experience are both important contributions to reading comprehension.

Here again is the paragraph about the importance of voting. If a word such as *referendum* is unfamiliar, you can probably still understand the paragraph by

THE

GED

substituting another word or phrase that fits with the overall meaning. What could you say instead of *referendum* to make the passage clearer?

State and local elections involve voting on issues that are of concern to the citizens, such as businesses, schools, neighborhoods, transportation, safety, or health. In many states, the voters have a direct part in the lawmaking process. For example, a law that has been passed in the state legislature may be sent back to the voters to accept or reject. The voters decide directly if a new law should be put into effect. This is known as the power of **referendum**. Another form of direct lawmaking by the voters in some states is the initiative. In this process, a group of voters signs a petition asking for a specific law. If enough people have signed the petition, the qualified voters must be given a chance to vote for or against the proposed law.

You could substitute many different things for *referendum* and still have a logical sentence—blackmail, positive attitude, guilt trips, money—although we need to make sure the passage makes sense, too. But something like *popular vote* or *majority rule* is much closer to the meaning of *referendum,* because you can make that change and not change the meaning of the passage.

ACTIVE READING

Active reading is a tool that can help you understand what you read. By engaging your hand along with your brain, more of your senses are involved in actively reading. It may sound odd, but it works!

Active reading is a three-step process:

- Skim through the text and related graphics or visuals, and glance through the questions before trying to understand exactly what is written.
- Underline or circle the headline as well as keywords that describe the main idea or the important details.
- Finally, pay attention to keywords that describe the author's conclusions or summarize the purpose of the passage.

By following these three steps when you read, you are much more likely to both understand and remember what you've read. You may not be able to do this with every passage, as it takes some time to make active reading a habit, but even if you practice it once, it will help a lot.

You've learned the two steps to understanding what you read as well as two strategies to use if you get into trouble. Ready to try them out on a practice set?

PRACTICE SET: UNDERSTANDING WHAT YOU READ

The following passage and questions test your reading comprehension skills. Read carefully, then select the best answer to each question.

The United States Supreme Court outlawed racial segregation in public schools with the historic *Brown v. Board of Education of Topeka, Kansas*, in 1954. That year, Medgar Evers was a 29-year-old graduate of Alcorn College and veteran of World War II. He applied to law school at the University of Mississippi seeking the same education his home state offered its white citizens. After his application for admission was turned down, he went to work for the National Association for the Advancement of Colored People (NAACP) in Mississippi to end the state's racist policies. His boycotts of segregated businesses drew national attention to the injustices endured by southern minorities. In 1962, his efforts to help James Meredith become the first African American admitted to the University of Mississippi succeeded.

Not all Mississippians appreciated his accomplishments, however. Evers was shot in the back one night in 1963 and died in front of his wife and children. Even though the weapon that killed him was found nearby bearing the fingerprints of a known white supremacist named Byron De La Beckwith, justice did not come quickly. De La Beckwith was tried twice for Evers' murder, but both times the all-white juries could not reach a verdict. He remained free for more than 30 years until a multiracial jury found him guilty of the murder in 1994. De La Beckwith was 80 years old when he was convicted and sentenced to life in prison.

Even though Evers was assassinated in front of his family at home in 1963, his influence did not end there. Outrage over the senseless and violent death of the thoughtful and peaceful man contributed to the Civil Rights Act, signed by President Johnson in 1964. The influence of Medgar Evers stretches far beyond 1960s Mississippi, embodying the rights of racial equality for all Americans for all time.

1. What is the main idea of this passage?

   (1) The United States Supreme Court outlawed racial segregation in public schools with the historic *Brown v. Board of Education of Topeka* in 1954.
   (2) Medgar Evers was entitled to attend the University of Mississippi.
   (3) James Meredith was the first African American to attend the University of Mississippi.
   (4) President Johnson signed the Civil Rights Act into law in 1964.
   (5) The influence of Medgar Evers stretches far beyond 1960s Mississippi, embodying the rights of racial equality for all Americans for all time.

2. How did Medgar Evers work to end the racist policies in Mississippi?

   (1) He fought in World War II.
   (2) He went to college at the University of Mississippi.
   (3) He organized boycotts of segregated businesses.
   (4) He was killed by an assassin.
   (5) He supported the Civil Rights Act of 1964.

3. As used in the first sentence of the passage, what does "racial segregation" mean?

   (1) making members of one race less important than another race
   (2) not allowing members of a certain race to get an education
   (3) ignoring racial subjects in education
   (4) offering different opportunities to different races
   (5) teaching racist policies in public schools

4. Which is the best title for the passage?

   (1)   The Legacy of Medgar Evers
   (2)   Triumph in a Mississippi Court
   (3)   The Civil Rights Act of 1964
   (4)   De La Beckwith's Crime
   (5)   Civil Rights Martyrs

5. As used in the second paragraph of the passage, what does "white supremacist" refer to?

   (1)   one who welcomes progress
   (2)   a hired killer
   (3)   one who hates minorities
   (4)   one who preaches tolerance
   (5)   a sporting man

Check your answers on pages 189–190. How did you do? If you got most of the answers right, pat yourself on the back! You are ready to advance from understanding written passages to understanding visual material, the third rung of the ladder.

UNDERSTANDING VISUAL MATERIALS

The Social Studies test is full of pictures, graphs, charts, tables, maps, and even cartoons. You won't find lines and lines of writing in every question as you do on the Reading test. Visuals may stand alone with no explanations, or they may contribute information to a writer's larger point. However, these graphics can be tricky. It is important that you understand information represented in these visual forms in order to get the most out of information all around you.

Just as you must understand what you read before you can apply, analyze, or evaluate it, you must understand graphic representations of information before you can draw conclusions or form opinions about it. Let's continue down the ladder by exploring how to understand information in visual forms.

TABLES

Tables are used to show facts and figures so you can quickly grasp their relationships —if you know how to look at them.

A table is a presentation of figures or numbers, usually in two or more columns with several rows. The column title describes the most important categories; the rows usually contain the information related to each category for a particular unit, timeframe, or other item of interest.

More than half of the questions on the Social Studies test involve interpreting some visual material— maps, charts, graphs, tables, advertisements, political cartoons, and photographs— sometimes along with a written passage.

Tables can give you valuable information in all areas of social studies. In government, a table may summarize the positions of all the candidates running for city council. In geography, a table may help you see climate patterns in an area over a year. In economics, a table can help you compare the cost of living from one city to another. A table can also show you trends in history, such as how state population changes affect representation in Congress.

The following table illustrates the number of people currently living with HIV or AIDS in different regions of the world. The title tells you what information is contained in the table. The column headings tell you that the table contains details about what region is described, how many thousands of people in that region are living with HIV/AIDS, and what percentage of the total population of that region is affected.

People Living with HIV/AIDS		
Region	Thousands of People	Percentage of Region's Population
Sub-Saharan Africa	28,200	4.10%
North Africa & Middle East	730	0.22%
Asia	9,500	0.27%
Latin America & Caribbean	2,490	0.46%
Eastern Europe & Central Asia	1,800	0.44%
Western Europe	680	0.17%
North America	1,200	0.38%
Australia & New Zealand	18	0.06%
TOTAL	44,618	0.72%

The following question relates to the table above. Take a moment to see if you can find the information required to answer it.

According to the table, which is true of Latin America and the Caribbean?

(1)   It has the most people living with HIV/AIDS.
(2)   It has the second-highest number of people living with HIV/AIDS.
(3)   It has more people with HIV/AIDS than North America.
(4)   It has fewer people with HIV/AIDS than North America.
(5)   It has the fewest people living with HIV/AIDS.

To answer this question, first find out how many people in Latin America and the Caribbean are living with HIV/AIDS. The fourth row down has the heading "Latin America & Caribbean," and the second column has the heading "Thousands of People." Follow the fourth row over and the second column down until they meet: 2,490 thousand (2.49 million) in the region are living with HIV/AIDS. Now you are ready to evaluate the answer choices.

(1)   Does it have the most people living with HIV/AIDS?

This answer is incorrect, because a quick glance down the column shows that two other regions have higher numbers in the category.

(2)   Does it have the second-highest number of people living with HIV/AIDS?

This answer is incorrect, because two other regions, Sub-Saharan Africa and Asia, have higher numbers; Latin America and the Caribbean has the third-highest number of people living with HIV/AIDS.

(3)   Does it have more people with HIV/AIDS than North America?

We already know that 2.49 million people in Latin America and the Caribbean are living with HIV/AIDS. The table tells us that North America has 1.2 million infected people. So, Latin America and the Caribbean have more—this is the correct answer.

(4)   Does it have fewer people with HIV/AIDS than North America?

No. We have just found that it has more infected people than North America.

(5)   Does it have the fewest people living with HIV/AIDS?

No. A quick glance over the table shows that the region with the smallest number of people living with HIV/AIDS is Australia and New Zealand.

Tables are just one example of the graphics used on the test. Let's look at another.

GRAPHS

We have just looked at how writers use tables to present figures in an easily understandable arrangement. The graph is another tool used to highlight the relationships between figures. Graphs are more like pictures than tables, but once you know what to look for, you can see the trends and draw conclusions with ease. Let's look at a few different types of graphs.

THE CIRCLE (PIE) GRAPH

When dealing with parts that make up a whole, it can be tricky to understand how the numbers relate to each other when they are given in columns and rows. But when presented as different size slivers of a complete circle, the relationships are easy to see. People often think of the components of circle graphs as pieces of a pie.

Circle graphs show the relationship between all the elements being discussed in the form of a circle. The circle represents each part of the total as a wedge whose size corresponds to that part's portion of the total. The larger the slice, the higher the percentage one item represents. The largest slices typically indicate the most important or most descriptive groups in relation to everything being considered.

Here is the information from the second column of the table above represented as a pie chart. The entire circle represents everybody in the world living with HIV/AIDS, and the different sections show what portion of that total lives in which region.

Concentration of World HIV/AIDS Cases

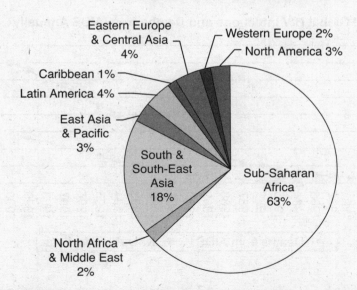

According to the circle graph, which region has the second-highest number of people living with HIV/AIDS?

This question requires you to take a quick look at the chart. Which piece of the pie is the second-biggest? It is clear that the vast majority of cases occur in Sub-Saharan Africa, but it is also easy to see that the second-biggest slice corresponds to South and Southeast Asia.

(1)   Sub-Saharan Africa
(2)   Western Europe
(3)   Caribbean
(4)   Latin America
(5)   South and Southeast Asia

Answer (5), South and Southeast Asia, is the correct answer.

THE LINE GRAPH

Line graphs are useful for illustrating how something changes from one category or group to another. Flat lines indicate that the groups titled across the baseline of the graph do not change very much, while lines that zig and zag suggest a great deal of change from one group to another. You usually see this type of graph when the author wants to show a trend.

Line graphs convert information into points on a grid. Each point represents the figure that corresponds to the categories on the vertical and horizontal edges, or axes, of the chart. Each fact is pinpointed, and these points are connected by a line to illustrate the trend.

This chart shows the trends over time in the numbers of deaths from AIDS, as well as the number of new HIV infections every year. The number of people affected is shown at the left on the vertical axis, and the years are shown at the bottom on the horizontal axis. By showing the two lines together, it also illustrates the relationship between the two trends.

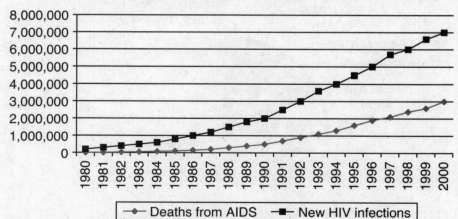

Estimated Global HIV Infections and Deaths from AIDS Annually

According to the line chart, which is **not** true?

    (1)   Deaths from AIDS are increasing.
    (2)   New HIV infections are increasing.
    (3)   More people contract HIV every year than die from AIDS every year.
    (4)   The relationship between new HIV infections and deaths from AIDS is constant.
    (5)   World population of people living with HIV/AIDS is growing.

To answer the question, first look at the chart. What do the lines tell you? Are any trends obvious? Both lines are rising, but at different rates. The line indicating new HIV infections is rising more sharply than the line indicating deaths from AIDS, so you can see that more people become infected every year than die from the disease. Be sure to notice that the question is asking you to find the answer that is **not** true. Now look at the answer choices.

    (1)   Deaths from AIDS are increasing.

This is true, so this answer is incorrect.

    (2)   New HIV infections are increasing.

This is true, so this answer is incorrect.

    (3)   More people contract HIV every year than die from AIDS every year.

This is true, so this answer is incorrect.

    (4)   The relationship between new HIV infections and deaths from AIDS is constant.

This is not true, because the graph shows the two lines growing farther apart every year. This is the correct answer.

    (5)   World population of people living with HIV/AIDS is growing.

The graph indicates that people are becoming infected with HIV faster than people are dying from AIDS, so we know that the number of people living with HIV/AIDS must increase every year. This is true, so this answer is incorrect.

THE BAR GRAPH

A bar graph, also called a bar *chart*, is very much like a line graph, and they are often used interchangeably. A bar graph is another way to visually present at least one set of facts in relation to another set. Instead of points and lines to describe the relationships between the categories, a bar graph represents amounts in terms of taller or shorter bars. Like a pie graph, you can instantly get a sense of the relative amounts of things by noticing what the biggest or smallest bars represent.

    Like a line graph, the top of the bar shows a piece of information as a point relative to the horizontal and vertical axes. But instead of connecting each point, each stands alone, connected to the horizontal axis with a bar that indicates its size relative to the others.

INTRODUCTION
UNDERSTANDING
WHAT YOU READ
**UNDERSTANDING
VISUAL MATERIALS**
IDENTIFYING
IMPLICATIONS
APPLYING IDEAS
INTERPRETING
POLITICAL
CARTOONS
ANALYZING
RELATIONSHIPS
EVALUATING
INFORMATION
SOCIAL STUDIES
CONCEPTS

The following bar chart has the same information as the table on page 128, but presented in a different way. Again, you notice immediately that there are far more people in Sub-Saharan Africa living with HIV/AIDS than in any other region. But what else does the bar chart reveal?

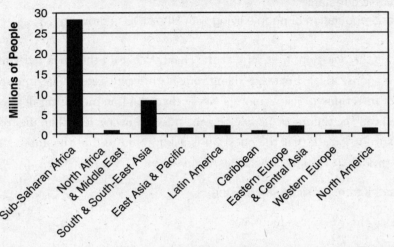

Millions of People Living with HIV/AIDS by Region

According to the bar chart, most world regions have how many people living with HIV/AIDS?

(1)   less than 5 million
(2)   between 10 million and 15 million
(3)   between 15 million and 20 million
(4)   between 20 million and 25 million
(5)   more than 25 million

To answer this question, look at the chart to see which level of the chart contains most of the bars that represent the regions of the world. While the two tallest bars are the most obvious at first glance, you should also notice that all the others fall under the 5 million level. So, answer (1), less than 5 million, is correct.

The key to understanding line and bar graphs is to identify what category the author has selected to represent on the horizontal axis (base) and what unit of measurement is used for the vertical axis.

MAPS

Like tables, charts, and graphs, maps are a visual way to present information. If you have a meeting in a new city, would you rather have written directions or a map to follow? Just as different people would rather have the information in different ways, writers may also prefer to present it in different ways. It is important to be able to read maps, so no matter how the facts are shown, you can understand them.

Maps illustrate divisions, locations, distances, and other characteristics of physical places. A map might show the political boundaries of countries, the natural

The title of a map and the information in its key often provide clues about the map's purpose or main idea. Labels and highlighted information on the map also point to the main idea. Before using a map, read its title and pay attention to the legend. This helps you know what you can expect from the map.

geography (topography) of a terrain, or the roads in your hometown. Information such as the way land is shaped; the location, direction, and distance of objects; regional weather patterns; and even the history of a place, is often easier to understand when it is illustrated in a map. To accurately restate information from maps, you must be able to read them.

The main tools for reading a map are the *title* and the *legend*. The legend is a key provided by the author to tell you what different symbols or colors on the map represent. If the map uses symbols, it always includes a legend (or key) to explain what the symbols mean. When a map is intended to show terrain, it may be presented as a "relief" map with the differences in height of land shown by lines. A map also includes a guide called a *compass rose* to indicate North, East, South, and West. Distance measurements are given in the map scale.

Reading a Map: To find out what subject a map presents, first look at the title. Then study the legend and notice how the information it represents is shown on the map. The map below shows the concentration of people living with HIV/AIDS. The legend at the bottom left of the map tells us what the different colors on the map mean.

People Living With HIV/AIDS by Country

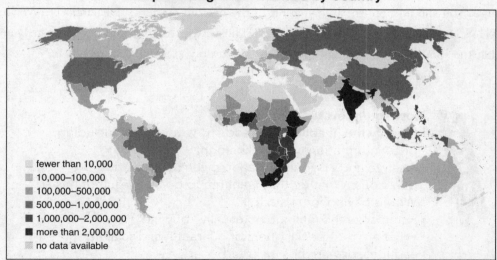

fewer than 10,000
10,000–100,000
100,000–500,000
500,000–1,000,000
1,000,000–2,000,000
more than 2,000,000
no data available

According to the map, which of the following is true of the countries represented in lighter colors?

To answer this question, find the map's legend. It is in the bottom left-hand corner of the map. It tells us that countries with the fewest cases of HIV/AIDS are represented by the lightest colors. The darker a color is, the higher the occurrence of HIV/AIDS in that area.

(1)   They are isolated from other countries.
(2)   They have small populations.
(3)   They have advanced medicine.
(4)   They have a low number of people living with HIV/AIDS.
(5)   They have a high number of people living with HIV/AIDS.

Answer (4) summarizes the information in the legend, so it is the correct answer.

Political maps show information relating to government, politics, and political parties. State and country boundaries are usually included. Physical maps show information relating to the earth's surface, climate, and currents. Rivers, deserts, and jungles are often included. Relief maps show the shape of the land and may use lines to show the height of mountains or other physical features.

ADVERTISEMENTS

Advertising is all around us. Some people have estimated that we see more than 3,000 ads a day. Reading and comprehending the selling intent of an ad requires you to ask and answer three main questions: *What do they want me to believe as a result of looking at this ad?*, *Who is paying for the ad?*, and *What can they gain?* Answering these questions can assist you in evaluating the ad, its truthfulness, and its meaning to you.

You must first find and read the headline, note the brand name or picture, and read the fine print (usually placed at the bottom of a print or television ad). Once you've identified and read the individual points, ask yourself, "What do they want me to think after seeing this ad?"

At first glance, the following advertisement may remind you of the earlier map. On closer inspection, though, you can see that it is meant to convey a persuasive message. You should note the information in the bottom corners: "December 1, World AIDS Day" and "www.knowhivaids.org." Those two things should indicate to you that the sponsor of this ad has an agenda. What do you think that agenda is?

How to understand an ad:
- Identify the headline and read any written text, including price information and the fine print.
- Analyze and apply information given by answering two questions: What do they want me to do as a result of this ad? Who is paying for this ad?
- Summarize the main point (usually "buy me").
- What are the special offers or guarantees, disclaimers, cautions, or warnings included?
- Judge whether you believe the claims of the advertisement to be trustworthy.

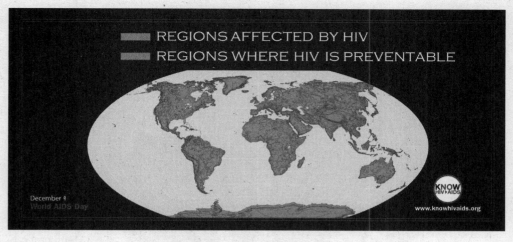

REGIONS AFFECTED BY HIV
REGIONS WHERE HIV IS PREVENTABLE

December 4
World AIDS Day

KNOW
HIV▶AIDS

www.knowhivaids.org

Source: http://www.knowhivaids.org/PSA/PDF/wadmap.pdf

What is the point of the advertisement?

Just as with the maps, look at the legend to learn what information is contained in the map. "Regions affected by HIV" and "Regions where HIV is preventable" are the same color—and the entire map is that color, too.

(1) Not every country should be worried about HIV.
(2) Only countries strongly affected by HIV should try to prevent it.
(3) HIV can be prevented.
(4) HIV will take over the world.
(5) The South Pole is safe from HIV.

Of the five choices, answer (3) is the message of the ad.

Tables, graphs, maps, and advertisements: we've covered them all. Ready to test your knowledge of this rung with a practice set?

PRACTICE SET: UNDERSTANDING VISUAL MATERIALS

The following passage, visual materials, and questions test your ability to understand visual materials. Read carefully, then select the best answer to each question.

Question 1 refers to the following paragraph, presidency scholar and Georgetown University professor Dr. Stephen J. Wayne's description of the electoral process, and to the map that follows it.

After each political party selects a presidential candidate, the candidates then run against each other in the general election. The population votes for the electors that represent the candidates and not the candidates themselves—in spite of the fact that the electors' names often don't appear on the ballots. The electors then vote for the candidates approximately one month after the ballots are cast by the general population. The candidates receive all the electoral votes of the states where they have the majority. For example, if candidate Smith receives 51% and candidate Brown receives 49% of the popular vote in a state, and the state has 12 electoral votes (the total number of senators and representatives), then candidate Smith wins all 12 of the electoral votes of that state. This policy is highly controversial because the electoral college is disproportionately represented by smaller states, which may result in election of the candidate who has received fewer votes. (Source: http://www.iwa.org/Publications/lectures/wayne.htm)

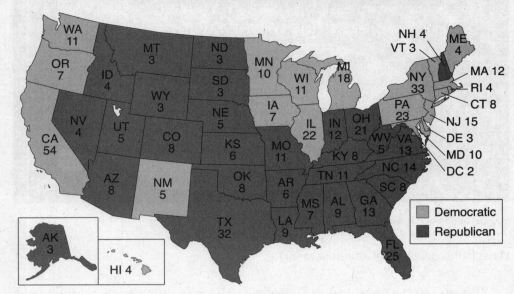

2000 Presidential Election Electoral College Results

1. Based on the passage and the map, what can you say about voters in Alabama in the 2000 presidential election?

   (1)   Only nine people voted.
   (2)   All Alabamians voted for the Republican candidate.
   (3)   They were less interested in the election than voters in Pennsylvania.
   (4)   Most of them voted for the Republican candidate.
   (5)   They tend to vote for Democrats.

Question 2 refers to the following line chart.

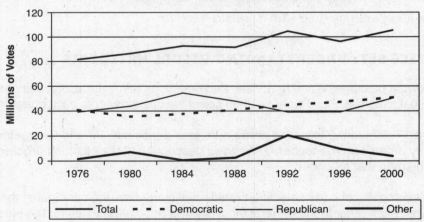

Presidential Voter Turnout, 1976–2000

2. Based on the line chart, which party has had the steadiest level of support since 1976?

   (1)   All parties have steady support.
   (2)   Democrats enjoy the steadiest support.
   (3)   Republicans enjoy the steadiest support.
   (4)   Parties other than Democrats or Republicans have steady support.
   (5)   No party has steady support.

Question 3 refers to the following paragraph, presidency scholar and Georgetown University professor Dr. Stephen J. Wayne's description of the electoral process, and to the bar chart that follows it.

    After each political party selects a presidential candidate, the candidates then run against each other in the general election. The population votes for the electors that represent the candidates and not the candidates themselves—in spite of the fact that the electors' names often don't appear on the ballots. The electors then vote for the candidates approximately one month after the ballots are cast by the general population. The candidates receive all the electoral votes of the states where they have the majority. For example, if candidate Smith receives 51% and candidate Brown receives 49% of the popular vote in a state, and the state has 12 electoral votes (the total number of senators and representatives), then candidate Smith wins all 12 of the electoral votes of that state. This policy is highly controversial because the electoral college is disproportionately represented by smaller states, which may result in election of the candidate who has received fewer votes. (Source: http://www.iwa.org/Publications/lectures/wayne.htm)

Presidential Electoral College Results, 1976–2000

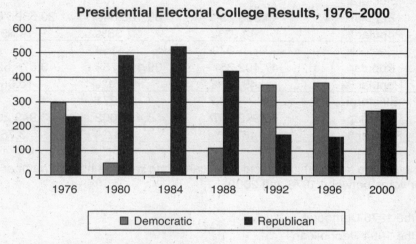

3. Based on the passage and the bar chart, which of the following was true about the 1984 presidential election?

(1)   The voters overwhelmingly favored the Republican candidate.
(2)   The voters overwhelmingly favored the Democratic candidate.
(3)   More people voted than in any other election between 1976 and 2000.
(4)   The Republican candidate won at least half of the votes in most of the states.
(5)   The Democratic candidate won at least half of the votes in most of the states.

Question 4 refers to the following table.

Presidential Election Results, 1976–2000

		Democratic	Republican	Other
1976	Electoral	297	240	1
	Popular	40,825,839	39,147,770	1,577,333
	Popular %	50.00%	48.00%	2.00%
1980	Electoral	49	489	0
	Popular	35,483,820	43,901,812	7,129,589
	Popular %	41.10%	50.90%	8.00%
1984	Electoral	13	525	0
	Popular	37,577,000	54,455,000	620,842
	Popular %	40.50%	58.80%	0.70%
1988	Electoral	111	426	1
	Popular	41,016,000	47,946,000	2,629,486
	Popular %	45.60%	53.40%	1.00%
1992	Electoral	370	168	0
	Popular	44,908,254	39,102,343	20,589,769
	Popular %	42.93%	37.38%	19.69%
1996	Electoral	379	159	0
	Popular	47,402,357	39,198,755	9,676,522
	Popular %	49.24%	40.71%	10.05%
2000	Electoral	266	271	1
	Popular	50,999,897	50,456,002	3,949,201
	Popular %	48.38%	47.87%	3.75%

4. According to the table, which presidential candidate won the highest number of popular votes between 1976 and 2000?

(1) the 1976 Democrat
(2) the 1984 Republican
(3) the 1992 "other" candidate
(4) the 1996 Democrat
(5) the 2000 Republican

Question 5 refers to the following pie charts.

Presidential Election Results, 1992–2000

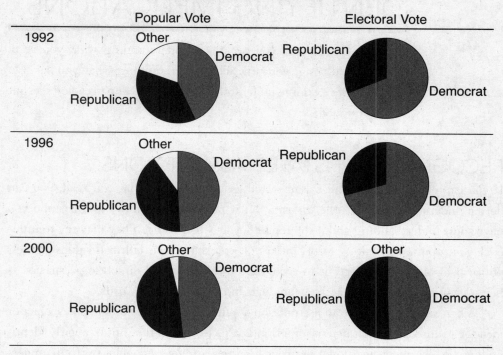

5. According to the pie charts, which is true of "other" candidates?

   (1)   Voting for the "other" candidate has the same effect as voting for a Democrat.

   (2)   Voting for the "other" candidate has the same effect as voting for a Republican.

   (3)   "Other" candidates are gaining support over time.

   (4)   The more votes the "other" candidate gets, the closer the outcome of the electoral vote.

   (5)   The fewer votes the "other" candidate gets, the closer the outcome of the electoral vote.

Check your answers on pages 190–192. How did you do? If you got most of the answers right, you should be proud of yourself! You are comfortable with understanding material that is clearly presented, and you are ready to move to the fourth rung of the ladder, Identifying Implications, to explore material whose meaning may not be so clear.

IDENTIFYING IMPLICATIONS

On the second rung, you practiced understanding what you read. On the third rung, you practiced understanding what you see. On this rung, we examine understanding what you don't read or see, but what is implied.

RECOGNIZING UNSTATED ASSUMPTIONS

If you can clearly understand the unstated assumptions in what you read, you can better understand and use the information it provides. Authors often assume you have some understanding about the topic they are discussing. They may try to influence your opinion by taking for granted that you share their cultural values or their political ideals. It is important to recognize when this kind of subtle persuasion is being used so that you can actively analyze and evaluate their words.

When an author makes an assumption about something, he or she takes a fact or idea for granted. An unstated assumption is a fact or condition not explicitly identified, but which must be known in order for the argument's conclusion to be understood and considered.

Identifying unstated assumptions is a bit of a detective job. Stay on guard when you read and consider everything with skepticism. Search for clues as you read by asking yourself, "What does the author assume I believe?"

Let's look for assumptions in the following excerpt from President John F. Kennedy's Inaugural Address on January 20, 1961. As you read, ask yourself, "What does he assume I know in order to understand his point?"

And if a beachhead of cooperation may push back the jungle of suspicion, let both sides join in creating a new endeavor, not a new balance of power, but a new world of law, where the strong are just and the weak secure and the peace preserved.

All this will not be finished in the first 100 days. Nor will it be finished in the first 1,000 days, nor in the life of this Administration, nor even perhaps in our lifetime on this planet. But let us begin.

In your hands, my fellow citizens, more than in mine, will rest the final success or failure of our course. Since this country was founded, each generation of Americans has been summoned to give testimony to its national loyalty. The graves of young Americans who answered the call to service surround the globe.

Now the trumpet summons us again—not as a call to bear arms, though arms we need; not as a call to battle, though embattled we are—but a call to bear the burden of a long twilight struggle, year in and year out, "rejoicing in hope, patient in tribulation"—a struggle against the common enemies of man: tyranny, poverty, disease, and war itself.

What does President Kennedy assume his audience knows in order to understand his reference in the phrase, "not as a call to bear arms, though arms we need; not as a call to battle, though embattled we are"?

(1)   We are trying to protect ourselves from attack by sea.
(2)   We are fighting a war with combat in an Asian jungle.
(3)   We plan to invade weaker nations before the USSR does.
(4)   We are racing to build more nuclear weapons than our rivals.
(5)   We need to establish colonies in major oil-producing countries.

In 1961, the year of the speech, Americans were very worried about the possibility of nuclear war with the Soviet Union. His reference to needing arms and being embattled does not suggest an upcoming or ongoing war, but our need to protect ourselves and prevent that war from happening. So, answer (4) is the condition that Kennedy assumes his listeners are aware of.

IDENTIFYING IMPLICATIONS

Once you know what the writers or speakers assume you agree with them about, you can take the unspoken aspects of the argument one step further. A conclusion is sometimes stronger when it is left unsaid for the readers and listeners to detect on their own. These unspoken conclusions are *implied* conclusions.

Implications are the conclusions that writers, artists, and speakers hint at but do not express outright. They are used a lot in persuasive communication, like campaign speeches, newspaper editorials, and political cartoons.

Just as with identifying unstated assumptions, you must read actively and question what you read in order to recognize implications. Search for clues as you read by asking yourself, "What does the author seem to be suggesting?"

Let's look at President Kennedy's Inaugural Address again to find what his speech implies.

And if a beachhead of cooperation may push back the jungle of suspicion, let both sides join in creating a new endeavor, not a new balance of power, but a new world of law, where the strong are just and the weak secure and the peace preserved.

All this will not be finished in the first 100 days. Nor will it be finished in the first 1,000 days, nor in the life of this Administration, nor even perhaps in our lifetime on this planet. But let us begin.

In your hands, my fellow citizens, more than in mine, will rest the final success or failure of our course. Since this country was founded, each generation of Americans has been summoned to give testimony to its national loyalty. The graves of young Americans who answered the call to service surround the globe.

Now the trumpet summons us again—not as a call to bear arms, though arms we need; not as a call to battle, though embattled we are—but a call to bear the burden of a long twilight struggle, year in and year out, "rejoicing in hope, patient in tribulation"—a struggle against the common enemies of man: tyranny, poverty, disease, and war itself.

What does President Kennedy imply by calling tyranny, poverty, disease, and war "the common enemies of man"?

(1) Each country is responsible for protecting its own people from disease.
(2) Tyranny is not a legitimate form of government.
(3) War is necessary to maintain the balance of power in the world.
(4) Rich nations have no responsibility to help poor nations.
(5) Peace is impossible without war.

He suggests that tyranny, poverty, disease, and war are things that all people are against. But tyrants are people, so the implication is that we will fight tyrants and we will be on the right moral side of that struggle. Answer (2) is therefore the correct answer.

Visual materials like cartoons can make implications too. When you see a picture on a magazine cover or in a cartoon on the editorial page, view it carefully and ask the same questions you would if it were a printed article or speech: What does the artist seem to be suggesting?

Look at this cover of *Time Magazine* from October 1960. It is from the same era as Kennedy's speech. What is the artist's implied comment?

Nikita Khrushchev, Satellite Leaders

Source: Time Magazine, October 3, 1960

Wearing matching jackets with the logo "East Side Rockets" and moving in a close pack, the artist assumes you understand that these are the leaders of Eastern Bloc countries.

What does the artist imply by portraying leaders of Eastern Bloc countries as a street gang?

(1) They are petty thugs.
(2) Their political philosophy is valid.
(3) They are harmless.
(4) They are above the law.
(5) Their leader deserves admiration.

His implication is that, like street gangs formed by teenagers, they deserve no respect and are no better than juvenile delinquents. Answer (1), that they are petty thugs, is correct.

You may not think that something as objective as facts and figures can make implications, but they can. Charts and graphs are designed by people who may just as easily have an unstated conclusion as writers and artists. Try looking for the implication in the following chart, accompanied with a passage about the Cold War for background information:

Real Military Purchases in Billions of 1982 Dollars, 1948–1987

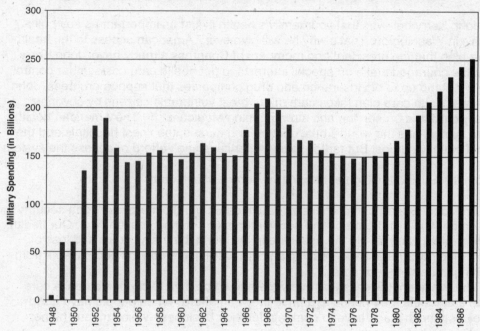

Source: Cato Policy Analysis no. 114, http://www.cato.org/pubs/pas/pa114.html

The Cold War was the period between the end of World War II in 1945 and the fall of the Berlin Wall in 1989. During the Cold War, distrust and suspicion between the United States and the Soviet Union (USSR) led the two nations to build impressive and threatening militaries and weapons stockpiles. The threat of mutual destruction kept the rivals balanced, neither wishing to unleash its full fury against the other.

What does the bar chart imply about tensions during the Cold War?

(1)   Rivalry between the United States and the USSR was strongest right after World War II.
(2)   Relations between the United States and the USSR were better in the 1960s than in the 1980s.
(3)   Tensions eased at the beginning of the 1970s.
(4)   Anxiety was at its strongest right before the end of the Cold War.
(5)   The Cold War gradually lost momentum and importance in the 1980s.

The bars in the chart steadily grow taller toward the end, so the implication is that anxiety was at its highest right before the end, when both the American and Soviet governments spent furiously trying to force the other to give in. Therefore answer (4) is the implication in the chart.

CHAPTER

4

SOCIAL
STUDIES

THE
GED

INTRODUCTION

UNDERSTANDING
WHAT YOU READ

UNDERSTANDING
VISUAL MATERIALS

IDENTIFYING
IMPLICATIONS

APPLYING IDEAS

INTERPRETING
POLITICAL
CARTOONS

ANALYZING
RELATIONSHIPS

EVALUATING
INFORMATION

SOCIAL STUDIES
CONCEPTS

PRACTICE SET: IDENTIFYING IMPLICATIONS

The following passages, graph, and questions test your ability to identify implications and unstated assumptions. Read carefully, then select the best answer to
each question.

The candidates in the 2004 presidential election believed health care was on the
minds of American voters. The Democratic candidate, Senator John Kerry, and the
Republican incumbent, President George W. Bush, agreed that it was an important
problem but disagreed about both the cause and solution. What follows is each
candidate's views on the health care issue from his own campaign materials.

From the Kerry campaign at *http://www.johnkerry.com*:

John Kerry believes that your family's health is just as important as any politician's in Washington. That's why he will give every American access to the health
care plan that the president and members of Congress already have. John Kerry
has the courage to take on special interests to get health care costs under control.
He will stand up to big insurance and drug companies that impede progress. John
Kerry's health care plan takes care of our most vulnerable citizens by covering
every child and preserving and strengthening Medicare. . . . The American health
care system has the world's best doctors and nurses, the finest hospitals and the
most effective drugs. But far too many Americans can't afford or access the system.

From the Bush campaign at *http://www.georgewbush.com*:

President Bush's comprehensive health care agenda improves health security for
all Americans by building on the best features of American health care. Our health
care system can provide the best care in the world, but rising costs and loss of
control to government and health plan bureaucrats threaten to keep patients from
getting state-of-the-art care.
The President believes that everyone should be able to choose a health care
plan that meets their needs at a price they can afford. When people have good
choices, health plans have to compete for their business—which means higher
quality and better care.
Before the American Medical Association, President Bush announced his bold
new proposal for modernizing and strengthening America's health care system by
giving Medicare recipients more health care choices. The President's plan gives
seniors more health care choices and helps them with the high costs of health care
and prescription drugs.

1. What does Senator Kerry imply by saying that "your family's health is just as
   important as any politician's in Washington"?

   (1)   Politicians have access to very good health care.
   (2)   All Americans have access to very good health care.
   (3)   Politicians have better access than private citizens have to health care.
   (4)   Politicians have the same access as private citizens have to health care.
   (5)   Politicians have worse access than private citizens have to health care.

2. What does Senator Kerry assume is the cause of the problem with American
   health care?

   (1)   Special interest groups are too involved.
   (2)   Special interest groups are not involved enough.
   (3)   Insurance companies are dishonest.
   (4)   Insurance companies are charitable.
   (5)   American lawmakers are controlled by greed.

3. What does President Bush assume is the cause of the problem with American health care?

(1) Our health care system can provide the best care in the world.
(2) Government and health plan bureaucrats want to prevent good health care.
(3) People do not have good choices in health care.
(4) The American health care system is primitive and weak.
(5) Prescription drugs are expensive.

4. What does President Bush imply is to blame for the high cost of health care in the United States?

(1) disease
(2) ignorance
(3) terrorism
(4) greed
(5) bureaucracy

National Health Expenditures Per Capita, 1986–2010

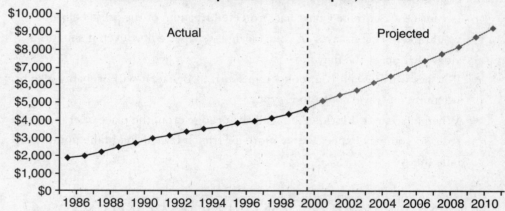

Centers for Medicare and Medicaid Services

5. What does the graph imply about health care for Americans?

(1) It is no more urgent than it has ever been.
(2) It is becoming more affordable.
(3) It is becoming less affordable.
(4) It is becoming more effective.
(5) It is becoming less effective.

Check your answers on pages 191–192. How did you do? If you got most of the answers right, way to go! You are ready to move up to more advanced skills.

INTRODUCTION

UNDERSTANDING WHAT YOU READ

UNDERSTANDING VISUAL MATERIALS

IDENTIFYING IMPLICATIONS

APPLYING IDEAS

INTERPRETING POLITICAL CARTOONS

ANALYZING RELATIONSHIPS

EVALUATING INFORMATION

SOCIAL STUDIES CONCEPTS

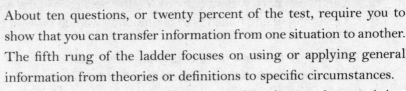

APPLYING IDEAS

About ten questions, or twenty percent of the test, require you to show that you can transfer information from one situation to another. The fifth rung of the ladder focuses on using or applying general information from theories or definitions to specific circumstances.

This is a major section on the Social Studies test because it is a major skill in life. Can you imagine if learning how to unscrew the lid from a jar of jelly, learning how to unscrew the cap from a bottle of soda, and learning how to unscrew the lid from a bottle of laundry detergent were all separate lessons in life? It would take forever to learn everything you need to know! If something unexpected came up, like a bottle of iced tea, you wouldn't be able to figure out what to do until somebody showed you. The key to intelligence is the ability to take knowledge from one circumstance and apply it to another.

In Social Studies, your application skills may help you draw conclusions such as the following:

- Because the Supreme Court has protected freedom of the press before, it would likely rule in favor of your local newspaper editor even if she ran a story that upset the mayor.
- If it was warm when you took a trip south to Belize, it will probably also be warm if you travel south to Egypt.
- When a freeze in Florida damaged the orange crop, the price of orange juice rose, so you may expect to pay more for french fries if the Idaho potato crop fails this year.

APPLYING INFORMATION IN NEW CONTEXTS

You've heard it before: Learn from your mistakes. That is all applying information in new contexts means. You must be able to apply ideas in new contexts in order to expand your knowledge and cut down on the time it takes you to react to a new situation. You do this all the time. If last Thanksgiving was a disaster because the oven broke and everything was undercooked, you know you have to fix it before your next party. If you felt run down for a few days before you got the flu last winter, this year you'll know to take it easy if you start to feel that way again. Being able to apply old lessons means you don't have to learn those lessons over and over. It's true when picking a doctor, a weatherman, a mayor—even a spouse!

To apply knowledge, first you have to have something to apply. Observe how something works, then think about what you've observed in general terms. Or study a theory and practice applying it to a practical situation. Let's take a principle of economics: supply and demand.

The theory of supply and demand states that price is determined by the amount of goods that are available (supply) and the amount of the product that consumers want (demand). In general, the harder it is to find a product, the more valuable it is, and the easier it is to find, the less valuable it is. Products that are scarce, like steak, cost more than products that are abundant, like peanuts. The market (sellers and buyers) settles on the price that results when the supply and demand curves cross.

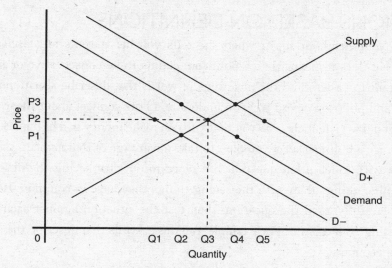

In the above chart, at a medium level of supply and a medium level of demand, the price the market will accept for a product is P2, and the quantity produced and bought is Q3. If supply remains constant but demand rises, the market would buy more (Q5) than is made (Q3) at the price P2. The goods become scarce, or harder to find, so the market adjusts to the price of P3 to bring supply and demand back into balance, or equilibrium. On the other hand, if demand for a product drops, the market wants less (Q1) of the product that the market will supply at P2. The product becomes abundant, therefore less valuable, so the price drops to P1.

Consider beef, for example. Usually, buyers and sellers are happy with the price P2. But what if market conditions change? If there is fear about the safety of the beef supply because of reports of an outbreak of mad cow disease, the supply level doesn't change immediately, but demand may fall. What happens to price? As you can see on the chart, at demand D– and the regular supply level, the price falls from P2 to P1. What do you expect to happen to the price of beef if consumers suddenly decide to eat more protein on a low-carbohydrate diet?

If the graph represents the market for ice cream, the price of which is currently P2 at quantity Q3, what will happen if scientists suddenly prove that ice cream prevents heart attacks?

(1)   Price will fall to P1, and quantity consumed will fall to Q2.
(2)   Price will remain at P2, and quantity consumed will rise to Q5.
(3)   Price will remain at P2, and quantity consumed will fall to Q2.
(4)   Price will rise to P3, and quantity consumed will fall to Q2.
(5)   Price will rise to P3, and quantity consumed will rise to Q4.

If we learned that ice cream prevented heart attacks, we would probably all go right out and get a scoop. We would expect demand for ice cream to rise, making it scarcer at its current price of P2. In response, people would be willing to pay more for the desired product that is now in short supply, prompting the ice cream makers to make more. If we learn that ice cream prevents heart attacks, we should expect both the price and the quantity demanded to rise, so answer (5) is correct.

QUESTIONS BASED ON DEFINITIONS

What does your neighbor mean when she tells you her parents are fascists? Or hippies? What does it mean when a politician claims to be conservative or liberal? It is important to understand the meanings of words that describe situations, characteristics, and philosophies so you can understand how you feel about those things that affect you. If a rich uncle tells you that you can make money in a bull market, you must recognize a bull market if you plan to take advantage of that advice.

Success with a definition question has more to do with seeing the differences between similar things than with the seeing things they have in common. Read the definitions carefully, read the question, then test the situation against each option before choosing your answer. For example, try these words that describe the state of the national economy.

growth: an increase in a nation's productivity. Growth offers more goods, services, and buying power to a nation's people.

stagnation: a period of many years of slow or no productivity growth.

inflation: an increase in prices that reduces the purchasing power of money. It happens when there is more money in the economy than there are things to spend it on.

recession: an extended decline in general business activity. It happens when people have less money to spend than they are used to, and it comes with a rise in the level of unemployment.

stagflation: a combination of low productivity with high unemployment with rising prices.

What are Americans likely to do in a period of growth?

(1)   take a vacation
(2)   lose their jobs
(3)   balance their budgets
(4)   increase their debt
(5)   spend at a constant level

Return to the definition of *growth*: an increase in a nation's productivity. Growth offers more goods, services, and buying power to a nation's people. What does that mean? It means that in a period of growth, people are enjoying an increase in wealth. What are you more likely to do when you find yourself with more money? The correct answer is 1, take a vacation. The other options are things people are more likely to do when they find their buying power is constant or decreasing.

What are Americans likely to do in a period of stagnation?

(1)   take a vacation
(2)   lose their jobs
(3)   balance their budgets
(4)   increase their debt
(5)   spend at a constant level

Return to the definition of *stagnation*: a period of many years of slow or no productivity growth. What does that mean? It means that people's financial situations are not getting better or worse. What are you more likely to do when you find your situation is not changing? The correct answer is (5), spend at a constant level. The other options are things people are more likely to do when they find their buying power is rising or falling.

What are Americans likely to do in a period of recession?

(1)   take a vacation
(2)   lose their jobs
(3)   balance their budgets
(4)   increase their debt
(5)   spend at a constant level

Return to the definition of *recession*: an extended decline in general business activity. It happens when people have less money to spend than they are used to, and it comes with a rise in the level of unemployment. What does that mean? It means that people's financial situations are getting worse. What are you more likely to do when you find your situation is not changing? The correct answer is (2): because recession causes more unemployment, in a period of recession, you are more likely to find yourself out of work.

Let's try a practice set now.

CHAPTER

4

SOCIAL
STUDIES

THE
GED

INTRODUCTION

UNDERSTANDING
WHAT YOU READ

UNDERSTANDING
VISUAL MATERIALS

IDENTIFYING
IMPLICATIONS

APPLYING IDEAS

INTERPRETING
POLITICAL
CARTOONS

ANALYZING
RELATIONSHIPS

EVALUATING
INFORMATION

SOCIAL STUDIES
CONCEPTS

PRACTICE SET: APPLYING IDEAS

The following map, definitions, passage, and questions test your ability to apply general ideas to specific situations. Read carefully, then select the best answer to each question.

World Climate Zones: Definitions

Tropical: a climate known for year-round high temperatures and a large amount of year-round rain.
Dry: a climate characterized by little rain and a huge daily temperature range.
Temperate: a climate characterized by warm, dry summers and cool, wet winters.
Cold: a climate typical of the interior regions of large land masses. Total precipitation is not very high, and seasonal temperatures vary widely.
Polar: climates in which ice and frozen ground are always present.

Global Warming and Global Reaction

Certain gasses in the Earth's atmosphere act like the glass in a greenhouse—trapping the heat of the sun and causing the temperature to rise. This phenomenon is known as the "greenhouse effect." Most scientists agree that it is a real problem, caused by pollution created by humans, and it could have devastating effects for the planet. Global warming is more than just warmer days. A heat wave in the Midwest killed nearly 700 people in the summer of 1995. Since warm air holds more moisture, global warming is also leading to higher rainfall, faster snowmelt, and more flooding. Ice melting at the North and South Poles is making sea levels rise and threatening habitats along coastlines. In addition to problems caused by too much water, higher temperatures lead to problems from not enough water at the same time. Heat causes water on the ground to evaporate more quickly, scorching crops and fueling brush fires.

To fight the effects of global warming, representatives from 161 countries met in Kyoto, Japan, in 1997 and negotiated a plan to reduce greenhouse gasses. The agreement was known as the Kyoto Protocol and will become legally binding 90 days after 55 percent of the countries representing at least 55 percent of the gas emissions agree to be bound by the plan. By 2002, 104 of the countries, representing 44 percent of the greenhouse gasses, had ratified the agreement.
The United States, the single largest producer of greenhouse gasses, does not intend to participate in the protocol. By early 2004, about 55 percent of the countries representing about 45 percent of the pollution had ratified the agreement.

World Climate Zones

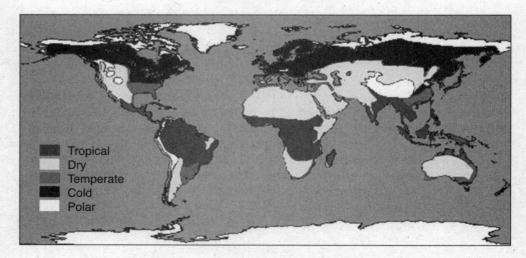

Tropical
Dry
Temperate
Cold
Polar

1. According to the map and the definitions, which continent is likely to have the lowest population?

   (1) North America, which is cold, temperate, and dry
   (2) South America, which is tropical, dry, and temperate
   (3) Europe, which is mostly cold
   (4) Africa, which is dry and tropical
   (5) Antarctica, which is entirely polar

2. A cactus is a "succulent" plant, meaning that its leaves retain most of the water it needs to survive. A cactus is best adapted to live in which climate zone?

   (1) tropical
   (2) dry
   (3) temperate
   (4) cold
   (5) polar

3. Some animals, like mice and snakes, get through a cold winter by hibernating. They eat to store fat when the weather is mild, then sleep through the cold months until food is abundant again in the spring. In which zone are these animals most likely to live?

   (1) tropical
   (2) dry
   (3) temperate
   (4) cold
   (5) polar

4. If global warming continues to increase, what would you expect to happen?

   (1) The tropical zone will expand.
   (2) The dry zone will become tropical.
   (3) The temperate zone will become dry.
   (4) The cold zone will grow.
   (5) The polar zone will shrink.

5. Participants in the Kyoto Protocol are most like which individuals?

   (1) members of a neighborhood association
   (2) inmates in a prison
   (3) a one-man band
   (4) soldiers in the army
   (5) family members at a reunion

Check your answers on pages 192–193. How did you do? If you got most of the answers right, you are doing a great job! Let's keep climbing, comprehending, understanding, and applying ideas with the next ladder rung: Political Cartoons.

INTERPRETING POLITICAL CARTOONS

Yes, there are cartoons on your GED test. However, you probably won't encounter *Peanuts* or *Garfield*. There will be only political cartoons, those that make a statement about something, usually in addition to making you laugh.

Political cartoonists provide people with enjoyable, approachable political insights. But it is important to understand that even though they are presented as entertainment, political cartoons are not objective: they carry the artist's agenda, or specific purpose. As a reader, you have to be aware of that bias and make up your own mind about a cartoon's message.

The first step in interpreting political cartoons is to recognize the characters portrayed. Public figures are shown with their distinctive physical features exaggerated: bushy eyebrows, big ears, unusual hairstyles. For added help to the reader, the artist often includes a nametag or nickname to let us know exactly who the butt of the joke is.

Once you recognize the characters, notice the way they are presented. Do they appear very ugly or small? Smiling? Serious? Childish? The artist's presentation of a situation tells you a lot about his or her feelings.

In addition to people in the national spotlight for a short time, there are several standard symbols that appear over and over in political cartoons. Here are the major ones:

Hawks and Doves: In international conflict, those in the administration who prefer military solutions and do not hesitate to use force are often characterized as hawks—birds of prey. Those who prefer diplomacy and consider military force as a last resort are characterized as doves—the bird of peace.

Mike Lane, Cagle Cartoons, Inc.

What is represented by the fighting birds in the cartoon?

(1) officials who disagree about whether to go to war
(2) officials who both want war, but disagree about the details
(3) officials trying to negotiate a way to avoid war
(4) enemies in a war
(5) officials fighting to decide who gets to fight the dove

The fighting birds are both hawks, showing that they are among the members of the administration that favor war. They are holding "Plan A" and "Plan B," suggesting that they both want a war but do not agree about the details. The correct answer is (2).

Bulls and Bears: In American economic slang, a bull market describes the situation when the prices of stocks in the financial market are generally increasing. When the stock market is rising, it is said to be charging like a bull. The opposite is a bear market, when stock prices are generally declining, or retreating like a hibernating bear.

Daryl Cagle, Cagle Cartoons, Inc.

What situation does the artist portray in the above cartoon?

(1) Executive greed is driving the bull market forward.
(2) Executive greed is sucking the blood out of a charging market.
(3) Executive greed wants to slow down a charging market.
(4) The market is strong enough to tolerate pests.
(5) Bull markets are spurred by executive greed.

Executive Greed is shown as a mosquito, a pest that feeds on the blood of its victims. Greed is not riding the market forward or spurring it on, but slowing it down. It is not slowing it on purpose, since the charging market is a good situation for the greedy to benefit. The correct answer is (2), that greed is sucking the blood out of the bull market.

CHAPTER

4

SOCIAL
STUDIES

THE
GED

INTRODUCTION

UNDERSTANDING
WHAT YOU READ

UNDERSTANDING
VISUAL MATERIALS

IDENTIFYING
IMPLICATIONS

APPLYING IDEAS

INTERPRETING
POLITICAL
CARTOONS

ANALYZING
RELATIONSHIPS

EVALUATING
INFORMATION

SOCIAL STUDIES
CONCEPTS

Jeff Parker, Cagle Cartoons, Inc.

What situation does the artist portray in the above cartoon?

(1)   A declining market is destroying personal wealth.
(2)   A declining market is enhancing personal wealth.
(3)   A rising market is destroying personal wealth.
(4)   A rising market is enhancing wealth.
(5)   Investors will be safe as soon as the market goes into hibernation.

The bear represents a stock market in decline, when the value of money invested in stocks shrinks. The correct answer is (1), the declining market is destroying personal wealth.

Donkeys and Elephants: The two major American political parties use animals as their symbols: donkeys for Democrats and elephants for Republicans. These animals often appear in political cartoons as shorthand for the respective parties.

Daryl Cagle, Cagle Cartoons, Inc.

What is the artist saying about the relationship between Democrats and Republicans?

(1)   The more aggressive party deserves the public's support.
(2)   The more timid party deserves the public's support.
(3)   They should take turns entertaining the voters.
(4)   They are rivals for the affection of the fickle voters.
(5)   They are partners in acting in the voters' best interests.

Showing both parties rivals for the attention of the same girl, the artist doesn't seem to suggest anything about one party being better than the other, just that they are rivals. Answer (4) is the correct answer.

Uncle Sam: First introduced as a character to boost military recruiting in World War I, Uncle Sam has come to represent the United States government. He is presented as an old man with white hair and a white beard, wearing a top hat decorated with stars and stripes.

Best of Latin America, Cagle Cartoons, Inc.

How does the artist portray the relationship of the United States with the rest of the world?

(1)   The United States is a nurse giving medicine to the world.
(2)   The United States is parent who knows what's best for a reluctant child.
(3)   The United States is a friend who wants to share a treat with a peer.
(4)   The United States is a restaurant eager to let the world taste democracy.
(5)   The United States is trying to get rid of a surplus of democracy.

Spoon-feeding is a gesture we associate with parents and children. The "world" character is wearing tennis shoes and a reluctant but obedient expression. The artist is saying that the United States is behaving like a parent, thinking that it knows what is best for the rest of the world even if the world disagrees. Answer (2) is the correct answer.

THE

GED

Lady Liberty: The Statue of Liberty was a gift to the United States from France to mark the nation's one-hundredth birthday. It stands on an island in New York Harbor and was the first glimpse of America for more than a million immigrants to the country between the 1890s and the 1950s. She wears a robe, sandals, and a spiked crown. The torch in her right hand represents the enlightenment of the world, and the tablet in her left hand bears the date the Declaration of Independence was signed: July 4, 1776. In political cartoons, Lady Liberty generally represents the personal liberties enjoyed by Americans.

Best of Latin America, Cagle Cartoons, Inc.

The above cartoon originally appeared in 2003. What does the artist suggest about American freedoms?

(1)   Liberty is safe from threats.
(2)   Liberty ignores threats.
(3)   Liberty is aggressive toward threats.
(4)   Liberty is nervous about threats.
(5)   Liberty is under attack.

The cartoon shows Liberty ducking to avoid a harmless fly, showing that she is nervous. The cartoon appeared after the attacks of 9/11 and represents the struggle to balance our personal freedoms and national security. Answer (4) is the correct answer.

Justice: Blind Justice, wearing a blindfold and carrying scales, represents the fair and equal administration of the law. She embodies the phrase "justice is blind," which means that no prejudice or favors will influence a legal outcome—that cases are decided strictly on the facts.

Sandy Huffaker, Cagle Cartoons, Inc.

What should the reader understand about Justice based on her surroundings in the cartoon?

(1)   She is in jail.
(2)   She is on vacation.
(3)   She is in her office.
(4)   She is relaxing at home.
(5)   She is sick in the hospital.

The lock on the door, the commode on the wall, and the chains on the bench indicate that Justice is in jail. The caption tells us that if the Supreme Court approved secret arrests, Justice would lose her power—that secret arrests are not just. The correct answer is (1).

Getting the hang of it? Let's move on to a practice set.

PRACTICE SET: INTERPRETING POLITICAL CARTOONS

The following cartoons and questions test your ability to interpret political cartoons. Read carefully, then select the best answer to each question.

Gary Jarvel, Creators Syndicate

1. What does the artist assume the reader knows about the term *pork* in federal legislation?

    (1)   It refers to necessary public works.
    (2)   It refers to wasteful spending.
    (3)   It refers to technical innovation.
    (4)   It refers to responsible lawmaking.
    (5)   It refers to politicians' sense of humor.

Mike Lukovich, Creators Syndicate

2. What comment is the artist making about people who conduct polls?

    (1)   They must observe events closely.
    (2)   Their constant observations are meaningless.
    (3)   Their dedicated reporting is critical.
    (4)   They are very serious people.
    (5)   They keep people informed with valuable information.

© Etta Hulme, reprinted by permission of Newspaper Enterprise Association, Inc.

3. What should the reader understand about the "hat-in-hand" gesture to best understand the cartoon?

    (1)   It indicates begging.
    (2)   It indicates lying.
    (3)   It indicates humility.
    (4)   It indicates respect.
    (5)   It indicates honor.

"NO, THEY LEFT THE MONEY, BUT, THEY SIPHONED ALL OUR GAS..."

© Bill Schodd, reprinted by permission of United Feature Syndicate, Inc.

4. What is the point the artist is making in the cartoon?

    (1)   Police are ineffective.
    (2)   Money is worthless.
    (3)   Roads are dangerous.
    (4)   Thieves are vicious.
    (5)   Gas is expensive.

THE

GED

© Etta Hulme, reprinted by permission of Newspaper Enterprise Association, Inc.

5. What does the artist assume the reader knows about deficits?

    (1)   Deficits are scary.
    (2)   Deficits are harmless.
    (3)   Deficits are desirable.
    (4)   Deficits are fictional.
    (5)   Deficits are uncommon.

Check your answers on pages 193–194. How did you do? If you got most of the answers right, you have successfully moved more than halfway down the ladder. You are experienced with comprehension and application questions and ready to move on to the next skill: Analyzing Relationships.

ANALYZING RELATIONSHIPS

When the GED test asks you to analyze relationships, it wants you to look at the way two different things interact. This skill is required in 40 percent of the test, or about twenty questions. You must be able to explore and understand the relationships between different kinds of information and to distinguish between conclusions and supporting details, facts, and opinions; cause and effect; and similarities and differences.

Just as application skills are a way to help you know more, analysis skills are a way to help you think more. Analyzing the relationships between ideas, facts, details, and opinions does not need to be any more intimidating than the chicken and the egg. We'll go step by step:

Step 1: Examine the relationship between conclusions and supporting details ("that chicken laid it, so it must be an egg").

Step 2: Differentiate facts from opinions ("chickens and eggs both provide protein, but eggs are yummier").

Step 3: Recognize cause and effect ("this chicken is so old, she can't lay any more eggs").

Step 4: Compare and contrast information ("neither chickens nor eggs can fly, but only chickens can walk").

Analysis is a necessary skill that helps you clarify your understanding of the author's message. Very often, news reporters, political analysts, stock market analysts, historians, economists, sociologists, and activists present only one side of an event or issue. There is always another side. The one-sided presentation of information might slant your opinion toward one point of view if you cannot analyze the content of a message for yourself.

You have to take things apart if you want to see how they work. It is just as true for arguments as it is for machines. If it makes sense to you, you can put it back together as good as new. Analysis is the process of taking apart assertions, persuasions, and conclusions to see what's inside. Read as if you doubt the writer—as if you need to be convinced. After every point or sentence, try saying, "Oh, really?" or "Says who?" or even "Prove it."

Certain words in the phrasing of a question should announce to you, loudly and clearly, that you are being asked to analyze. Watch for words such as **distinguish**, **compare**, **contrast**, **relate**, and **classify**.

STEP 1: EXAMINE THE RELATIONSHIP BETWEEN CONCLUSIONS AND SUPPORTING DETAILS

Recognizing conclusions as different from supporting details is a crucial part of deciding whether you will accept what you read. You have to decide if the details are valid support for the conclusion. You have to decide if the conclusion is reasonable based on the support. You have to know when an author tries to force you to accept a conclusion without good support.

Supporting details are the pieces of evidence that lead to the conclusion. A conclusion is a judgment or decision based on facts and details.

To identify a conclusion, first identify facts that offer information that stands on its own, independent from anything else in the passage. The conclusion is the author's assessment, or opinion, about what those facts mean.

Authors may indicate that they are drawing a conclusion by using words that link ideas to a statement about what those ideas mean. These words may include **consequently**, **thus**, **accordingly**, **hence**, and **therefore**.

Like main ideas, conclusions often appear as either the first or the last sentence of a paragraph. When the first sentence is a conclusion, all of the following details and facts contribute to the idea that the conclusion is true. It is sometimes difficult to identify when the conclusion occurs at the end, because the supporting details all lead you to believe it. When you are analyzing a passage, try to make sure that the details, whether they come before or after the conclusion, actually support the idea as the author has stated it.

For example, consider the following excerpt from President Franklin D. Roosevelt's address to Congress on December 8, 1941:

Yesterday, December 7, 1941—a date which will live in infamy—the United States of America was suddenly and deliberately attacked by naval and air forces of the Empire of Japan.

The United States was at peace with that nation and, at the solicitation of Japan, was still in conversation with the government and its emperor looking toward the maintenance of peace in the Pacific.

It will be recorded that the distance of Hawaii from Japan makes it obvious that the attack was deliberately planned many days or even weeks ago. During the intervening time, the Japanese government has deliberately sought to deceive the United States by false statements and expressions of hope for continued peace.

Yesterday, the Japanese government also launched an attack against Malaya.

Last night, Japanese forces attacked Hong Kong.

Last night, Japanese forces attacked Guam.

Last night, Japanese forces attacked the Philippine Islands.

Last night, the Japanese attacked Wake Island.

This morning, the Japanese attacked Midway Island.

Japan has, therefore, undertaken a surprise offensive extending throughout the Pacific area. The facts of yesterday speak for themselves. The people of the United States have already formed their opinions and well understand the implications to the very life and safety of our nation.

As commander in chief of the Army and Navy, I have directed that all measures be taken for our defense.

Always will we remember the character of the onslaught against us.

No matter how long it may take us to overcome this premeditated invasion, the

American people in their righteous might will win through to absolute victory.

I ask that the Congress declare that since the unprovoked and dastardly attack by Japan on Sunday, December 7, a state of war has existed between the United States and the Japanese empire.

Which is **not** a detail that supports President Roosevelt's conclusion that "since the unprovoked and dastardly attack by Japan on Sunday, December 7, a state of war has existed between the United States and the Japanese empire"?

(1)   The United States of America was suddenly and deliberately attacked by naval and air forces of the Empire of Japan.

(2)   The distance of Hawaii from Japan makes it obvious that the attack was deliberately planned many days or even weeks ago.

(3)   The Japanese government has deliberately sought to deceive the United States by false statements and expressions of hope for continued peace.

(4)   Japan has undertaken a surprise offensive extending throughout the Pacific area.

(5)   The American people in their righteous might will win through to absolute victory.

President Roosevelt laid out his case for war very carefully. The details give clear support to the conclusion that we were at war with Japan: we had been attacked, the attack was carefully planned, we had been deceived, Japan was on the offensive. That "the American people in their righteous might will win through to absolute victory" might make it easier to accept the prospect of war, but his argument that we were already at war had been established. Answer (5) is the detail that does not support the conclusion, because it is not an absolute statement of objective fact. Unlike the other supporting facts, "absolute victory" is the only one he could not prove at the time.

STEP 2: DIFFERENTIATE FACTS FROM OPINIONS

It is important to distinguish fact from opinion to ensure that your decisions are not based on someone else's biased view of the world. It is perfectly fine to take other people's opinions into consideration when you are making up your mind about issues, as long as you realize that those opinions are not objective truths.

Facts are statements that can be proved to be true; opinions are statements about how a person thinks or feels about things that cannot be proven. Facts exist outside of any individual's feelings about them. Humans need water to live. That is a fact and not influenced by anyone's feelings. Opinions are statements that are influenced by a person's background, values, life experience, and even life stage. For example, when we are young, we might refuse to drink any liquid unless it is bright orange and overly sweet. But as adults, we may decide we prefer the more bitter waters that come from mineral springs underground.

A fact can be proven to be true. An opinion is a judgment that may or may not be true.

Here's a quick look at the differences between facts and opinions:

• A fact is information about something that actually happened or actually exists. For example, when a reporter covers a political debate and writes about what participants said and how the audience reacted, she is reporting on things that exist and events that took place.

- An opinion is an interpretation of the facts. Opinions are influenced by people's interests, by what they know about a subject. If the reporter at the political debate describes the event as "shocking," "courageous," "visionary," or "misguided," her own feelings about the debate show through her choice of words. It is up to you to decide whether the statements are logical and based on truthful, valid, reliable information.

Identify a statement of fact by questioning the source of the information. A fact can be proven true by observation (rain clouds are thicker than clouds that do not cause rain) or may come from a reliable source, such as an encyclopedia, almanac, academic article, or official document.

To identify a statement of opinion, look for the source of the statement. An opinion will not attribute a reliable source. To decide if a source is reliable, ask yourself if that source has something to gain from your acceptance of its opinion.

Certain words and phrases provide clues that a statement is actually an opinion. The most important words for identifying an author's opinion are **should** and **ought**. Watch also for words that suggest values:

best	necessary
better	obviously
claim	people think
consider	possibly
desirable	probably
feel	undesirable
greatest	unnecessary
likely	we believe
might	worse

For an example of facts and opinions, read (and question) this excerpt from British Prime Minister Winston Churchill's address when he received an honorary degree from Westminster College in Foulton, Missouri, on March 5, 1946.

From Stettin in the Baltic to Trieste in the Adriatic an iron curtain has descended across the Continent. Behind that line lie all the capitals of the ancient states of Central and Eastern Europe. Warsaw, Berlin, Prague, Vienna, Budapest, Belgrade, Bucharest, and Sofia, all these famous cities and the populations around them lie in what I must call the Soviet sphere, and all are subject in one form or another, not only to Soviet influence but to a very high and, in some cases, increasing measure of control from Moscow.

The safety of the world, ladies and gentlemen, requires a new unity in Europe, from which no nation should be permanently outcast. It is from the quarrels of the strong parent races in Europe that the world wars we have witnessed, or which occurred in former times, have sprung. Twice in our own lifetime we have seen the United States, against their wishes and their traditions, against arguments, the force of which it is impossible not to comprehend, twice we have seen them drawn by irresistible forces, into these wars in time to secure the victory of the good cause, but only after frightful slaughter and devastation have occurred. Twice the United States has had to send several millions of its young men across the Atlantic to find the war; but now war can find any nation, wherever it may dwell between dusk and dawn. Surely we should work with conscious purpose for a grand pacification of Europe, within the structure of the United Nations and in accordance with our Charter. That I feel opens a course of policy of very great importance.

Which of the following is a fact, not an opinion, expressed by Churchill in the above speech?

(1) From Stettin in the Baltic to Trieste in the Adriatic an iron curtain has descended across the Continent.

(2) All these famous cities . . . are subject in one form or another, not only to Soviet influence but to a very high and, in some cases, increasing measure of control from Moscow.

(3) The safety of the world, ladies and gentlemen, requires a new unity in Europe, from which no nation should be permanently outcast.

(4) We should work with conscious purpose for a grand pacification of Europe.

(5) That I feel opens a course of policy of very great importance.

Answer (1) cannot be a fact unless we believe that an actual curtain made of iron has been drawn across Europe. "Iron curtain" is a figure of speech, and it is Churchill's opinion. Answer (2) describes something that we can verify: that a list of cities now falls within the area of Soviet influence and control. Answer (2) is indeed a fact. Answer (3) is Churchill's opinion about what the safety of the world requires. He is talking about things that may happen in the future, so it cannot possibly be a fact. Answer (4) features the word *should*, which is a clear indication of his opinion. Churchill identifies answer (5) as an opinion by using the phrase "I feel."

The speech is an outline of his vision and his fears, and based on his experience, should be given serious consideration. But he offers very few facts in his argument, so we should feel free to question them and draw our own conclusions.

STEP 3: RECOGNIZE CAUSE AND EFFECT

Events rarely occur in isolation. They are generally the result of outside influences or earlier events. Social studies topics, particularly history and economics, are often described in terms of the causes for different effects. Japan launched an unprovoked attack on Hawaii; therefore, the United States entered World War II. Scientists prove that ice cream prevents heart attacks; therefore, demand for ice cream increases. If a clear relationship between cause and effect cannot be shown, experts may develop hypotheses about the relationships. Hypotheses are ideas that have not been proven or disproven.

A cause is an event or circumstance that brings about an effect, result, or outcome. An effect is the outcome that results from a particular cause. Causes lead to effects; effects happen in response to causes. There is not necessarily a simple one-to-one relationship, though. A single cause may bring about several effects, just as a single effect may be the result of several causes.

To decide if a cause-and-effect relationship exists in material you are considering, ask yourself if the second event would have happened if the first event had not taken place. The words and phrases *because*, *since*, and *therefore* are clues that indicate a cause-and-effect relationship.

To explore cause-and-effect relationships, consider the following passage and map about the Iron Curtain:

CHAPTER

4

SOCIAL
STUDIES

THE
GED

INTRODUCTION

UNDERSTANDING
WHAT YOU READ

UNDERSTANDING
VISUAL MATERIALS

IDENTIFYING
IMPLICATIONS

APPLYING IDEAS

INTERPRETING
POLITICAL
CARTOONS

ANALYZING
RELATIONSHIPS

EVALUATING
INFORMATION

SOCIAL STUDIES
CONCEPTS

Lowering the Iron Curtain

As the end of World War II drew near, the leaders of the three main allies against Hitler met in Yalta in the Crimea on the Black Sea to plan for peace. British Prime Minister Winston Churchill, United States President Franklin Delano Roosevelt, and Soviet Union Premier Josef Stalin signed the agreement on February 11, 1945. The main purpose of the conference was to restore nations conquered by Germany. Although the fate of most European countries was on the table, no other nations were represented or even notified about what was decided by the "Big Three." Germany was divided into four zones, each under British, U.S., French or Soviet control. The treaty promised democratic elections in all the liberated territories. To the surprise of Roosevelt and Churchill, Stalin failed to keep his promises. He quickly prevented popular elections in Poland, Czechoslovakia, Hungary, Romania, and Bulgaria by assigning permanent Communist governments to each and suppressing all democratic supporters. By the next year, friends in the Second World War had become foes in the Cold War. In a speech in March 1946, Churchill declared that an "iron curtain" had descended across the Continent.

The "Iron Curtain," March 1946

Which was an effect of the Yalta agreement?

(1)   The Soviet Union adopted a communist ideology.
(2)   Democratic elections were held in Poland, Czechoslovakia, Hungary, Romania, and Bulgaria.
(3)   Germany was granted the same independent status it held before the war.
(4)   Germany was split by occupying forces at odds with each other.
(5)   Great Britain took control of Western Europe.

The question identifies the cause—the Yalta treaty—and asks you to identify the effect. Answer (1) is incorrect, because even though it is true that the Soviet Union embraced communism, the Soviets were already communists before the Yalta conference. Answer (2) is incorrect, because even though democratic elections were a priority of the treaty, Stalin prevented them from happening. Answer (3) is incorrect, because the countries that won the war were not interested in restoring the country that started the war. Answer (4) is the true effect of Yalta: Germany was divided among France, the United Kingdom, the United States (all of which shared western ideals of freedom and democracy), and the Soviet Union, which held a different point of view. Answer (5) is not an effect of the Yalta treaty because it is not true.

STEP 4: COMPARE AND CONTRAST INFORMATION

Comparing and contrasting things can help you identify facts and opinions and causes and effects. Looking at the similarities and differences between components of an argument or event can enhance your understanding. "What do I believe in?" Comparing and contrasting such concepts as Republican and Democrat or Liberal and Conservative will give you plenty to think about. "Whom should I vote for?" You can better understand candidates by examining the ways they are like each other and the ways they are different. "Whose fault was the war?" For starters, look at rival nations and their leaders. You may find that nations at war with each other have as much in common as they have differences.

To compare is to look for the ways things are similar. To contrast is to look for the ways things are different. In World War II, the Allied forces of the Soviet Union and the United States had enough in common to join together to defeat the Nazis. Within a couple of years, it would be hard to imagine that the two nations ever had anything in common at all.

You can compare and contrast items by trying to find the same facts or the answers to the same questions for both: Who is their leader? What is their culture? What is their style of government? What do they value? How do they deal with weaker nations? How do they respond to disaster? All are good questions to start to compare and contrast nations.

Let's go back to the Cold War example to see what the United States and Soviet Union had in common:

After World War II, European countries devastated by the war were unstable and vulnerable to outside influence. President Truman felt that the failure to rebuild Europe after the First World War contributed to the Second World War. He also feared that countries exhausted by war were targets for the Soviet Union's expanding communist control. By 1946, Truman had established a policy to contain the Soviet influence with aid to rebuild non-communist countries. Named for George Marshall, the U.S. Secretary of State, the Marshall Plan granted or lent more than $13 billion in aid to 15 Western European countries between 1948 and 1952.

The Soviet Union denounced the Marshall Plan as a plot to interfere "in the domestic affairs of other countries," and responded by establishing the Council for Mutual Economic Assistance, or COMECON. Bulgaria, Romania, Hungary, and East Germany received aid from COMECON, and Albania, Czechoslovakia, and Poland were at least pressured to refuse aid from the Marshall Plan. Beyond simple short-term aid, COMECON became an organization to protect and promote the economies of member countries. By the late 1970s, Mongolia, Cuba, and Vietnam had joined the communist organization.

The Marshall Plan and COMECOM were similar because each one

  (1)   provided economic assistance to struggling European economies.
  (2)   used financial aid to exert central control over member nations.
  (3)   guaranteed that member nations would work for their mutual benefit.
  (4)   embraced members beyond those affected by World War II.
  (5)   dissolved soon after accomplishing its short-term task.

CHAPTER

4

SOCIAL
STUDIES

THE
GED

INTRODUCTION

UNDERSTANDING
WHAT YOU READ

UNDERSTANDING
VISUAL MATERIALS

IDENTIFYING
IMPLICATIONS

APPLYING IDEAS

INTERPRETING
POLITICAL
CARTOONS

ANALYZING
RELATIONSHIPS

EVALUATING
INFORMATION

SOCIAL STUDIES
CONCEPTS

The Marshall Plan and COMECOM were different in the way they approached and accomplished their tasks, but each began as a way to protect its own ideology by helping fragile nations reestablish themselves after World War II. Answer (1) is the correct answer. Answers (2), (3), and (4) only describe COMECOM, while answer (5) only refers to the Marshall Plan.

Ready for a practice set? If not, return to the beginning of this rung and skim through it once more. It is a long section and a big part of the test. You want to be confident!

PRACTICE SET: ANALYZING RELATIONSHIPS

The following questions based on passages and graphs test your ability to analyze relationships in social studies. Read carefully, then select the best answer to each question.

Investing in Hope

In its simplest sense, investing in stocks is giving a company some of your money in exchange for a share of the company's worth. The company's worth includes all its assets as well as whatever profit it makes. Companies pay dividends to its stockholders according to their share of ownership. Of course, the company may choose to reinvest some of its profit in order to grow the scope or scale of the company. Shareholders are entitled to profit from dividends, as well as from future growth, which increases the value of their share of ownership.

Another way investors can make money by investing in stocks is by speculating that a company will grow quickly. Rather than owning a stock because of its real current worth in terms of profit and assets, speculators hope to make money by buying cheap stock before a company starts making profits and then selling it for a huge gain once the company takes off. Even if a company is deep in debt with no actual product and not a single dollar in sales, its stock price can skyrocket based on nothing more than the expectation that someday it will do well.

In the late 1990s, companies known as "dot-coms" were the target of heavy speculation and giddy investors expecting to find riches in the Internet. These technical companies traded largely on the NASDAQ exchange, which attracts smaller businesses and technical companies more than the New York Stock Exchange. Speculation in new technology companies led to an enormously over-valued market known as the "dot-com boom." The boom was soon followed by a "dot-com bust" when stock values dropped to levels more in line with the companies' actual worth.

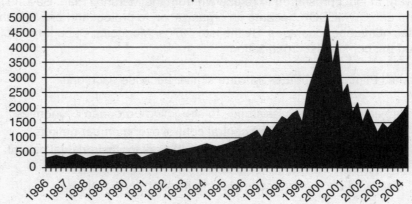

NASDAQ Composite Index, 1988–2004

1. Which was a cause of the "dot-com boom"?

   (1) Unproven companies were popular with investors who hoped to make a fast profit.
   (2) Careful investors favored companies with realistic business plans.
   (3) The NASDAQ lost almost 80 percent of its value between 2001 and 2003.
   (4) Investors foolishly got involved in a new industry they did not truly understand.
   (5) Dot-com companies enjoyed huge successes selling a whole new kind of product.

2. Which was a likely effect of the "dot-com bust"?

   (1) Investors refused to buy stock in a company that is not profitable.
   (2) Investors sued the dot-coms to recover the money they had lost.
   (3) Most investors sold their dot-com stocks and made big profits.
   (4) Investors became more cautious about investing in unproven businesses.
   (5) The NASDAQ bounced back as soon as investors got excited about the next "get-rich-quick" industry.

The following is an excerpt from an article called "Why Worry?" by financial historian Robert Sobel, which appeared in the March 30, 1998, issue of *Barron's*.

Although the past can't be used to predict the future, there have been some striking similarities—at least in terms of market volatility—between the present and the fateful year leading up to the Great Crash of 1929. Now, as then, it remains difficult to tell whether the latest correction is merely the latest buying opportunity . . . or the end of the bull market.

Hindsight, of course, is a wonderful thing. In December 1996, Fed Chairman Greenspan wondered aloud whether "irrational exuberance" was causing a "bubble." The next day, the market declined sharply, but then recovered. . . .

Any analysis of a past event is made with the knowledge of what happened, information unavailable to the participants as the drama unfolded. That's important in examining the year prior to the Great Crash, which was filled with drama.

There had been several . . . corrections in the 1920s. Investors and speculators were accustomed to volatility and had begun to take it in stride. Why not? Didn't stocks always come back? . . . By early 1929, volatility was so commonplace that some investors were more lulled than alarmed whenever it appeared. . . . In less than two years the market, as measured by the Dow, had come close to doubling, with most of the action coming toward the end of that stretch. . . .

Consider what might have gone through the minds of those who sold their stocks anywhere along the way, especially during the corrections. How would you have felt? Stupid, probably, and determined not to repeat your mistake. The Crash came the next month.

The Dow Jones Industrial Average is a measure of the general performance of the stock market. The following charts show the Dow's behavior in the first half and in the second half of the Twentieth Century.

Dow Jones Industrial Average, 1900–1950 and 1950–2000

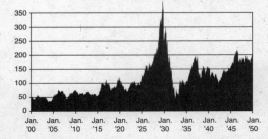

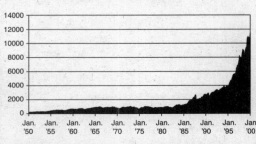

CHAPTER
4

SOCIAL
STUDIES

THE
GED

INTRODUCTION
UNDERSTANDING WHAT YOU READ
UNDERSTANDING VISUAL MATERIALS
IDENTIFYING IMPLICATIONS
APPLYING IDEAS
INTERPRETING POLITICAL CARTOONS
ANALYZING RELATIONSHIPS
EVALUATING INFORMATION
SOCIAL STUDIES CONCEPTS

3. What conclusion is supported by the details in Sobel's article?

(1)   The stock market may be heading for another crash like the one in 1929.
(2)   The latest correction is the end of the bull market.
(3)   Investors should be nervous when the market becomes volatile.
(4)   Investors who get out of the market before a crash are stupid.
(5)   There will never be another major crash like the one in 1929.

4. According to the graphs of the Dow Jones, what was similar about the two halves of the twentieth century in the stock market?

(1)   The Dow Jones rose and fell and rose in the first half, but climbed steadily in the second half.
(2)   The Dow spiked right before a sharp fall in both halves.
(3)   The Dow followed a general upward trend in both halves.
(4)   Relative to the beginning, the Dow had skyrocketed by the end of both periods.
(5)   The Dow recovered quickly from sudden sharp drops in value in both halves.

5. Which is an opinion Sobel expresses in his article?

(1)   There are similarities between the present and the past.
(2)   The market declined but recovered after Greenspan's "irrational exuberance" remark.
(3)   Investors in the 1920s were accustomed to volatility.
(4)   The Dow had nearly doubled in the two tears before the 1929 crash.
(5)   You would feel stupid if you sold your stocks during a market correction.

Check your answers on pages 194–195. How did you do? If you got most of the answers right, you have the skills that account for 80 percent of the questions on the GED Social Studies test. The next skill to master is Evaluating Information.

EVALUATING INFORMATION

You've been evaluated before. Back in the classroom, out on the job, even at home when doing the dishes, people always seem to be evaluating and judging you. Well, here's your chance to turn the tables.

Evaluation questions make up about 20 percent of the test, or about ten of the fifty questions. Evaluation questions ask you to make judgments about the value or usefulness of some pieces of information. They also require you to identify the values that influenced the decisions of other people.

WHAT IS EVALUATION?

Evaluation is a skill that requires you to judge the trustworthiness and appropriateness of information. No matter the source of the information—an article, a speech, a newscast, an advertisement—you must also consider what material might have been left out and what questions are left unanswered. In addition to helping you make good decisions, strong evaluation skills help you understand how and why other people have made certain choices. Understanding decisions and actions helps people from all backgrounds and circumstances cooperate and achieve goals.

To evaluate written, spoken, and visual material, you must decide several things:

- Is there is enough supporting data for the material or conclusion?
- Is that support suitable to the argument and conclusions being drawn? Is the information truthful? Is the information emotional?
- What are the speaker's values, thought processes, and intent? Is the speaker credible? Will the source benefit if I agree?

The more of these questions you consider, the more you can trust your judgment about the information.

SUPPORTING DATA

Supporting data is adequate when enough support for a conclusion is provided. The more support offered, the easier it is to accept a conclusion. One detail is rarely enough support a conclusion: you must weigh the details together to decide if they tip the balance toward agreement with the writer or artist.

To evaluate the adequacy of supporting information, you must review the material with several questions in mind:

- Is the information that supports the main idea and conclusion relevant to the topic?
- How current or recent is the information?
- Does the information provide details that help me understand the main idea completely?
- What else do I want to know about the topic?

THE
GED

- What might be left out?
- Does the supporting information identify who was, is, or may be affected?
- Does the supporting information identify why the event occurred? When? Where?

Let's return to Franklin D. Roosevelt's "Date Which Will Live in Infamy" speech to test the adequacy of support for his conclusion:

Yesterday, December 7, 1941—a date which will live in infamy—the United States of America was suddenly and deliberately attacked by naval and air forces of the Empire of Japan.

The United States was at peace with that nation and, at the solicitation of Japan, was still in conversation with the government and its emperor looking toward the maintenance of peace in the Pacific.

It will be recorded that the distance of Hawaii from Japan makes it obvious that the attack was deliberately planned many days or even weeks ago. During the intervening time, the Japanese government has deliberately sought to deceive the United States by false statements and expressions of hope for continued peace.

Yesterday, the Japanese government also launched an attack against Malaya.

Last night, Japanese forces attacked Hong Kong.

Last night, Japanese forces attacked Guam.

Last night, Japanese forces attacked the Philippine Islands.

Last night, the Japanese attacked Wake Island.

This morning, the Japanese attacked Midway Island.

Japan has, therefore, undertaken a surprise offensive extending throughout the Pacific area. The facts of yesterday speak for themselves. The people of the United States have already formed their opinions and well understand the implications to the very life and safety of our nation.

As commander in chief of the Army and Navy, I have directed that all measures be taken for our defense.

Always will we remember the character of the onslaught against us.

No matter how long it may take us to overcome this premeditated invasion, the American people in their righteous might will win through to absolute victory.

I ask that the Congress declare that since the unprovoked and dastardly attack by Japan on Sunday, December 7, a state of war has existed between the United States and the Japanese empire.

Now, let's look at his address to evaluate the adequacy of Roosevelt's supporting information:

Is the information that supports the main idea and conclusion relevant to the topic? The main idea is that Congress should declare war on Japan. The support is all focused on the ways Japan is already engaged in war throughout the Pacific. So, *yes*, the supporting information is relevant to the topic.

How current or recent is the information? The attacks described happened the day before and on the morning of his speech, so the information is extremely current.

Does the information provide details that help me understand the main idea completely? *Yes*, actual details about Japan's aggressions are provided to illustrate that a declaration of war is appropriate and necessary.

What else do I want to know about the topic? War is a major undertaking, and details about goals, strategies, and tactics might make the idea easier to accept. But in this case, the "why" of war is so clear that it can stand without the "how."

What might be left out? Is there any reason for Japan to strike at us in such hostility? Was the attack truly unprovoked? What's the bad news? How long will this take, and how much will it cost?

Does the supporting information identify who was, is, or may be effected? *Yes*, the support includes all the places currently under attack by Japan.

Does the supporting information identify why the event occurred? When? Where? *No*, the reason for the attacks is unclear. The attacks happened in the Pacific the day before the speech, but it is not clear why they occurred.

Does President Roosevelt give adequate support to his claim that Congress should declare war on Japan? *Yes*, he has provided strong and clear support. The fact that he doesn't mention why Japan launched the massive, coordinated, surprise attack does not weaken his argument for war.

IS THE SUPPORTING DATA APPROPRIATE?

Information that is appropriate is directly and clearly related to the main idea. Inappropriate details may include quotes or figures from people who are not experts. Misleading facts might be drawn from sources that are not related to the topic but could appear, at first glance, important or meaningful. For example, using information about how people feel about advertising is not appropriate in a discussion about the usefulness of television programs to teach social studies.

Identifying and understanding the appropriateness of information used to support a main idea or topic requires that you actively evaluate the relationships between facts and the main idea. It is a good idea to take notes as you read the original material, then reexamine the facts as you evaluate the information. See if you can draw direct links between the facts and supporting details. If not, the information might be irrelevant.

Ask yourself several questions about the appropriateness of the facts and supporting information:

- Are these facts clearly related to the topic?
- Did these events take place at the same time? If not, is the time sequence clearly defined?
- Are the facts or supporting details meaningful? Do they contribute unique information to my understanding of the topic, or are they repetitive?

Let's reexamine Churchill's "Iron Curtain" speech to evaluate the appropriateness of his supporting arguments:

From Stettin in the Baltic to Trieste in the Adriatic an iron curtain has descended across the Continent. Behind that line lie all the capitals of the ancient states of Central and Eastern Europe. Warsaw, Berlin, Prague, Vienna, Budapest, Belgrade, Bucharest, and Sofia, all these famous cities and the populations around them lie in what I must call the Soviet sphere, and all are subject in one form or another, not only to Soviet influence but to a very high and, in some cases, increasing measure of control from Moscow.

The safety of the world, ladies and gentlemen, requires a new unity in Europe, from which no nation should be permanently outcast. It is from the quarrels of the strong parent races in Europe that the world wars we have witnessed, or which occurred in former times, have sprung. Twice in our own lifetime we have seen the United States, against their wishes and their traditions, against arguments, the force of which it is impossible not to comprehend, twice we have seen them drawn by ir-resistible forces, into these wars in time to secure the victory of the good cause, but only after frightful slaughter and devastation have occurred. Twice the United States has had to send several millions of its young men across the Atlantic to find the war; but now war can find any nation, wherever it may dwell between dusk and dawn. Surely we should work with conscious purpose for a grand pacification of Europe, within the structure of the United Nations and in accordance with our Charter. That I feel opens a course of policy of very great importance.

Now, let's examine the appropriateness of the facts and supporting information in his address:

Are these facts clearly related to the topic? The topic is the need for cooperation among western nations to maintain peace. Churchill's support lists occasions when peace was threatened and when allies have defended each other. *Yes*, the facts are clearly related to the topic.

Did these events take place at the same time? If not, is the time sequence clearly defined? *No*, the events did not take place at the same time, but the events are recent and familiar enough to people in 1946 that leaving out that detail probably should not be taken as intent to deceive.

Are the facts or supporting details meaningful? Do they contribute unique information to my understanding of the topic or are they repetitive? *Yes*, the facts meaningfully show that European countries may be threatened and are stronger if they work together.

Does Winston Churchill provide appropriate support to his claim that nations should work together? *Yes*. By describing the threats and benefits that can be shared and not confusing the issue with irrelevant facts, Churchill makes a compelling case for cooperation.

Common American Values

can-do spirit	independence
change is good	justice
charity	materialism
democracy	patriotism
equality	pluralism
fairness	self-determination
freedom	social
hard work	responsibility
human rights	tolerance

WHAT ARE THE SPEAKER'S VALUES?

Values are the principles and qualities that are important and desirable to someone. People from similar backgrounds often have similar values. People who were alive during the Great Depression may share the value of thrift, just as people who had to fight to win the right to vote may share the value of civic responsibility. Your values are defined by the ideas and truths embraced by your culture and your family. Typically, values are moral standards that have been adopted to maintain a civilized society.

For example, Americans value education because we, as a nation, believe if the country is going to be run by its citizens, its citizens must be up to the task. Whether a quality is a desirable one depends on attitudes in different cultures. One group may value individuality, innovation, and art, while another could just as easily do without those things.

Authors may try to impose their values to persuade you about the validity and truthfulness of their claims. They use words that suggest *good* and *bad* to encourage you to reach the same conclusions that they are presenting. Other words that indicate an author is using value statements to gain your agreement or trust are *should, ought, clearly,* and *obviously.*

It's helpful to recognize other people's values even when they aren't trying to influence yours. To detect a writer's or speaker's values, ask yourself, "What is this person telling me is important?" Read the following famous quotes to see if you can identify the value that the speaker conveys.

The right to swing my fist ends where the other man's nose begins.

—Oliver Wendell Holmes

What does Oliver Wendell Holmes say is important? Our right to get into fights? No, he implies that both people have the right to do whatever they want as long as it doesn't affect the other. The value expressed by this quote is **personal freedom**.

The unforgivable crime is soft hitting. Do not hit at all if it can be avoided; but never hit softly.

—Theodore Roosevelt

What does Roosevelt want us to understand about his values? To "not hit at all if it can be avoided" seems to value diplomacy. But if a fight cannot be avoided, to "never hit softly" tells us that he will fight to win. The value expressed by this quote is **commitment**.

The tree of liberty must be refreshed from time to time with the blood of patriots and tyrants. It is its natural manure.

—Thomas Jefferson

What does Thomas Jefferson indicate is most important to him? It should come as no surprise that the man who wrote the *Declaration of Independence* would consider **liberty** a value worth dying or killing for.

If we practice an eye for an eye and a tooth for a tooth, soon the whole world will be blind and toothless.

—Mahatma Gandhi

THE
GED

What is Gandhi's point about retribution? "An eye for an eye" means that people should be harmed to the same degree that they cause harm. Gandhi does not agree. Instead of holding grudges and getting even, he tells us that **forgiveness** is an important value to him.

Evaluating information is one of the hardest rungs in the ladder. Ready to see how you're doing? Let's try a practice set.

PRACTICE SET: EVALUATING INFORMATION

Question 1 refers to the following passage.

The Life and Legacy of Medgar Evers

The United States Supreme Court outlawed racial segregation in public schools with the historic *Brown v. Board of Education of Topeka, Kansas*, in 1954. That year, Medgar Evers was a 29-year-old graduate of Alcorn College and veteran of World War II. He applied to law school at the University of Mississippi seeking the same education his home state offered its white citizens. After his application for admission was turned down, he went to work for the National Association for the Advancement of Colored People (NAACP) in Mississippi to end the state's racist policies. His boycotts of segregated businesses drew national attention to the injustices endured by southern minorities. In 1962, his efforts to help James Meredith become the first African American admitted to the University of Mississippi succeeded.

Even though Evers was assassinated in front of his family at home in 1963, his influence did not end there. Outrage over the senseless and violent death of the thoughtful and peaceful man contributed to the Civil Rights Act, signed by President Johnson in 1964. The influence of Medgar Evers stretches far beyond 1960s Mississippi, embodying the rights of racial equality for all Americans for all time.

1. Which value does this passage suggest was most important to Medgar Evers?

   (1)   equality
   (2)   individualism
   (3)   tradition
   (4)   responsibility
   (5)   education

Question 2 refers to the following paragraph, presidency scholar and Georgetown University professor Dr. Stephen J. Wayne's description of the electoral process, and the chart that follows it.

After each political party selects a presidential candidate, the candidates then run against each other in the general election. The population votes for the electors that represent the candidates and not the candidates themselves—in spite of the fact that the electors' names often don't appear on the ballots. The electors then vote for the candidates approximately one month after the ballots are cast by the general population. The candidates receive all the electoral votes of the states where they have the majority. For example, if candidate Smith receives 51% and candidate Brown receives 49% of the popular vote in a state, and the state has 12 electoral votes (the total number of senators and representatives), then candidate Smith wins all 12 of the electoral votes of that state. This policy is highly controversial because the Electoral College is disproportionately represented by smaller states, which may result in election of the candidate who has received fewer votes. (Source: http://www.iwa.org/Publications/lectures/wayne.htm)

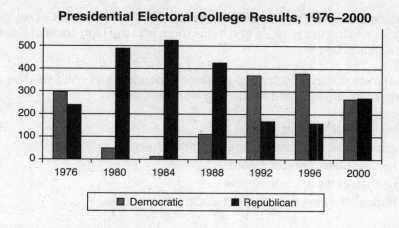

Presidential Electoral College Results, 1976–2000

Democratic / Republican

2. In the jargon of politics, a "landslide" is a victory in an election by an overwhelming majority of the votes. Which of the following details could lend the most support to the idea that the Republican victory in 1984 was a landslide?

(1) the number of total votes cast
(2) who the Democratic candidate was
(3) what portion of the popular vote was won by the Republican candidate
(4) how many electoral votes each state could cast
(5) what portion of the electoral vote was won by the Democratic candidate

Question 3 refers to the following information about the 2004 presidential candidates' views on health care.

The candidates in the 2004 presidential election believed health care was on the minds of American voters. The Democratic candidate, Senator John Kerry, and the Republican incumbent, President George W. Bush, agreed that it was an important problem but disagreed about the both the cause and solution. What follows is each candidate's views on the health care issue, from their own campaign materials.

From the Kerry campaign at *www.johnkerry.com*:

John Kerry believes that your family's health is just as important as any politician's in Washington. That's why he will give every American access to the health care plan that the President and Members of Congress already have. John Kerry has the courage to take on special interests to get health care costs under control. He will stand up to big insurance and drug companies that impede progress. John Kerry's health care plan takes care of our most vulnerable citizens by covering every child and preserving and strengthening Medicare. . . . The American health care system has the world's best doctors and nurses, the finest hospitals and the most effective drugs. But far too many Americans can't afford or access the system.

From the Bush campaign at *www.georgewbush.com*:

President Bush's comprehensive health care agenda improves health security for all Americans by building on the best features of American health care. Our health care system can provide the best care in the world, but rising costs and loss of control to government and health plan bureaucrats threaten to keep patients from getting state-of-the-art care.

The President believes that everyone should be able to choose a health care plan that meets their needs at a price they can afford. When people have good choices, health plans have to compete for their business—which means higher quality and better care.

Before the American Medical Association, President Bush announced his bold new proposal for modernizing and strengthening America's health care system by

CHAPTER
4

SOCIAL
STUDIES

THE
GED

INTRODUCTION

UNDERSTANDING
WHAT YOU READ

UNDERSTANDING
VISUAL MATERIALS

IDENTIFYING
IMPLICATIONS

APPLYING IDEAS

INTERPRETING
POLITICAL
CARTOONS

ANALYZING
RELATIONSHIPS

EVALUATING
INFORMATION

SOCIAL STUDIES
CONCEPTS

giving Medicare recipients more health care choices. The President's plan gives seniors more health care choices and helps them with the high costs of health care and prescription drugs.

3. Which of the following, if added to either candidate's argument, would be an appropriate piece of additional supporting information?

    (1)   testimonial from his mother
    (2)   endorsements from the Screen Actors Guild
    (3)   his complete medical record
    (4)   images of his military service
    (5)   budget showing how his plan would reduce costs

Question 4 refers to the following passage about global warming.

Global Warming and Global Reaction

Certain gasses in the Earth's atmosphere act like the glass in a greenhouse—trapping the heat of the sun and causing the temperature to rise. This phenomenon is known as the "greenhouse effect." Most scientists agree that it is a real problem, caused by pollution created by humans, and it could have devastating effects for the planet. Global warming is more than just warmer days. A heat wave in the Midwest killed nearly 700 people in the summer of 1995. Since warm air holds more moisture, global warming is also leading to higher rainfall, faster snowmelt, and more flooding. Ice melting at the North and South Pole is making sea levels rise and threatening habitat along coastlines. In addition to problems caused by too much water, higher temperatures lead to problems from not enough water at the same time. Heat causes water on the ground to evaporate more quickly, creating scorching crops and fueling brush fires.

To fight the effects of global warming, representatives from 161 countries met in Kyoto, Japan in 1997 and negotiated a plan to reduce greenhouse gasses. The agreement was known as the Kyoto Protocol, and will become legally binding 90 days after 55 percent of the countries representing at least 55 percent of the gas emissions agree to be bound by the plan. By 2002, 104 of the countries, representing 44 percent of the greenhouse gasses, had ratified the agreement. The United States, the single largest producer of greenhouse gasses, does not intend to participate in the protocol. By early 2004, about 55 percent of the countries representing about 45 percent of the pollution had ratified the agreement.

4. What does the United States' decision not to participate in the Kyoto protocol suggest about its values?

    (1)   that cooperation is important
    (2)   that reputation is important
    (3)   that the environment is not important
    (4)   that capitalism is not important
    (5)   that compromise is important

Question 5 refers to the following information about the Dow Jones Industrial Average.

The Dow Jones Industrial Average is a measure of the general performance of the stock market. The following charts show the Dow's behavior in the first half and in the second half of the twentieth century.

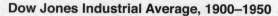

Dow Jones Industrial Average, 1900–1950

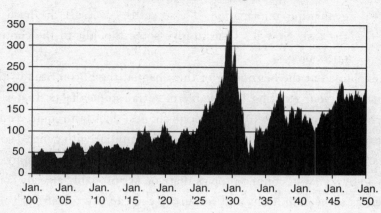

Dow Jones Industrial Average, 1950–2000

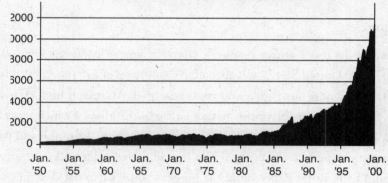

5. Some people say that the stock market crash of 1929 was the worst ever, while others claim that the crash in 1987 was worse. What information would **not** help you judge which crash was worse?

   (1)   the percentage of the market's value that was lost
   (2)   how many people went bankrupt as a result of the crash
   (3)   what the value of the Dow Jones Industrial Average is today
   (4)   how long it took the market to reach bottom
   (5)   how long it took for the market to recover

Check your answers on pages 195. How did you do? If you got most of the answers right, you have most of the skills you need to succeed on the GED Social Studies test. Whatever facts you need to answer the questions on the test are provided in the passage or visual material, but there are some general social studies concepts that you should be familiar with. We'll brush up on those ideas on the next rung—the ninth and last rung.

THE
GED

SOCIAL STUDIES CONCEPTS

You have reached the final rung. Look back and consider all the things that brought you to this point: understanding what you read, understanding visual materials, identifying implications, applying ideas, interpreting political cartoons, analyzing relationships, and evaluating information. Those skills cover all the hard work for the test. Now it's time to give some thought to the content of the questions.

As we explained at the beginning of this chapter, the Social Studies test is not meant to measure your existing knowledge of social studies facts. Instead, it is an assessment of your reasoning skills. Although the test does not require you to recall any specific fact, person, date, or event, you must be familiar with general social studies concepts in history, civics and government, economics, and geography. This last rung offers an overview of common topics that you are probably already comfortable with, as well as some definitions and resources you can use to refresh your understanding in these areas.

HISTORY

Forty percent of the test features readings, charts, maps, or cartoons focused on past events, both in the United States and abroad. As members of a democracy, it is important for us to know how our rights and roles emerged. American history is rich and fascinating. From the pre-European native cultures, English, French, and Spanish settlements, and a war for independence to expansion, civil war, and industrialization, our country experienced plenty by its one-hundredth birthday. The twentieth century brought the worst depression, the biggest wars, the most destructive weapons, and the loudest outcry for human rights.

To get a general idea of the topics encountered on the Social Studies test, review the following glossaries. They include the basic facts that will help you as you read and interpret the reading passages, maps, charts, and graphs on the test. Remember, you don't have to know these definitions and events. Just read them so you will be familiar with the concepts you will read about on test day.

GLOSSARY

abolitionists: people who favored making the practice of slavery illegal in the United States before the Civil War.

B.C.E. and C.E.: "before the common era" and "common era"—what used to be known as B.C. and A.D.

civil rights: personal liberties granted to U.S. citizens and protected in the Bill of Rights.

Civil War: War between the southern and northern states in America from 1861 to 1865. The Union won. The southern states were called the Confederacy, the president was Jefferson Davis, and the military leader was General Robert E. Lee. The northern states were the Union, the president was Abraham Lincoln, and the military leader was General Ulysses S. Grant. The war resulted in the end of slavery in the United States.

cold war: a period of diplomatic conflict, suspicion, and anxiety between the United States and the Soviet Union between 1945 and 1990. It did not involve actual warfare, but a massive buildup of militaries and weapons stockpiles to intimidate the other side. It ended with the fall of the Soviet Union.

colony: a settlement in a new land that remains under the control of the settler's home country.

communism: form of government based on the economic philosophy that the sources of enterprise are owned collectively by all citizens.

Confederacy: the southern states that tried to separate from the Union to form a new country, leading to the American Civil War.

discrimination: the practice of treating one group of people differently because of their race, background, religion, or other personal factor.

culture: the learned behavior of people, such as language, customs, beliefs, and artifacts.

emigration: people leaving one country to live in another.

empire: a group of political states collectively under the power of one dominant nation or power.

imperialism: strategy of powerful nations to maintain or increase their influence over weaker nations.

Industrial Revolution: a period of shift from an economy based on agriculture to one based on industry. It took place in Europe and the United States primarily during the 1800s and caused dramatic changes in society.

Nazism: the government in Germany under Adolf Hitler that believed Germans were the master race and attempted to establish Germany as the dominant world power. It ended with Germany's defeat at the end of World War II.

New Deal: President Franklin D. Roosevelt's economic plan for ending the Great Depression. The Federal Deposit Insurance Corporation and the Social Security Administration were both formed as a result.

revolution: a drastic change of government or society. Revolutionary wars led to securing national independence in the United States, overthrowing the monarchy in France, and establishing the Soviet Union.

segregation: keeping things separate. Overturning laws to support racial segregation was the aim of the Civil Rights movement in the 1950s and 1960s in the United States.

socialism: form of government based on government control over the distribution of assets and income.

suffrage: the right to vote. The Fifteenth Amendment to the U.S. Constitution guarantees that male citizens of all races may vote, and the Nineteenth Amendment extends that right to American women.

INTRODUCTION

UNDERSTANDING WHAT YOU READ

UNDERSTANDING VISUAL MATERIALS

IDENTIFYING IMPLICATIONS

APPLYING IDEAS

INTERPRETING POLITICAL CARTOONS

ANALYZING RELATIONSHIPS

EVALUATING INFORMATION

SOCIAL STUDIES CONCEPTS

values: goals and ideals; what people think is important, good, beautiful, worthwhile, or sacred.

World Wars: the first and second world wars took place in the first half of the twentieth century and pitted Germany against most of Europe and the United States. Germany was defeated both times. In World War II, the United States also fought Japan in the Pacific. The war with Japan ended when the United States used atom bombs in the Japanese cities of Hiroshima and Nagasaki.

CIVICS AND GOVERNMENT

Twenty-five percent of the test calls on you to show your understanding of systems of government, particularly characteristics, documents, and institutions of American democracy.

In the United States, we, the people, are in charge. Citizens of a democracy have rights and power, as well as serious responsibilities. We must recognize the importance of understanding the issues that we face as a nation, pay attention to both sides of an argument, and make careful decisions.

The structure of the government and the rights and responsibilities of its citizens are laid out in documents. The Declaration of Independence, the Constitution, and the Bill of Rights in particular outlined our current form of government more than 200 years ago. They are no less relevant today.

The U.S. government divides power between three branches: the legislative, made up of senators and congressional representatives; the executive, headed by the president; and the judicial, made up of judges. The Constitution provides each branch powers to balance the actions of the others, known as checks and balances. The Constitution also provides for its own survival through its power to adapt.

Of the people, by the people, and for the people, the United States of America is run by its citizens, who guide it with their votes. The two most prevalent schools of political thought are organized into parties known as Democrats and Republicans. The two-party system dates back to the 1800s and emerged as a mechanism to have primary elections—to elect a candidate before electing a governor, senator, or president.

GLOSSARY

administration: the period of time when a certain president is in office.

constitutional amendment: changes in or additions to the Constitution. In the United States, an amendment must be approved first by two-thirds of both houses of congress, then ratified (accepted) by three-quarters of the states.

bicameral: a legislative body made up of two houses. The federal legislature in the United States has two houses: the House of Representatives and the Senate.

Bill of Rights: the first ten amendments to the constitution. They limit governmental power and protect personal freedoms.

bureaucracy: government operations carried out by different administrative offices.

cabinet: heads of the major departments of the federal government. The cabinet secretaries are appointed by the president and approved by the senate. The serve at the president's pleasure and are his advisors on policy matters.

checks and balances: a system of protections built into the U.S. government that gives each of the three branches of government means to influence the actions of the other two.

conservatism: a general preference for keeping things the way they are and resisting major change through government agencies.

Constitution: the document that lays out the system of laws and principles that make up a government.

democracy: government based on the principle of equal rights and run by elected officials.

dictatorship: government where one person has absolute authority and citizens have no basic rights.

executive branch: the branch of government that carries out the laws of the land. In the United States, the president is in charge of the executive branch.

federal system: organization of government that divides power between a central government and regional governments, such as the U.S. national government and state governments.

impeachment: an official accusation of wrongdoing against a public official.

judicial branch: the branch of government that interprets the laws of the land. In the United States, the Supreme Court is the highest level of the judicial branch.

judicial review: the power of the Supreme Court to declare laws to be unconstitutional.

legislative branch: the branch of government that makes laws. In the United States, it includes the Senate and the House of Representatives.

liberalism: an outlook that favors progress by means of government action and change.

lobbyists: representatives of an issue or industry who try to convince members of Congress to support their cause in the legislature.

monarchy: government in which a single ruler holds political power through a claim of hereditary rights. The monarch, usually a king or queen, may have absolute power or power limited by a constitution.

ratification: to formally confirm or accept a judgment, decision, or treaty.

THE
GED

ECONOMICS

Twenty percent of the test requires you to understand economics, particularly the supply and demand of goods. Economics is an important aspect of social studies. In your personal life, it helps you to be a good consumer, plan for your future, and get the most out of your money. It also helps you understand the world around you, since a great deal of global politics are driven by issues with money. As a voter, you because a say in the country's budgeting, taxes, and expenditures, and you need to analyze and evaluate different options and courses of action to make the best choices for yourself and your country.

Different countries take different approaches to their economies. Different ideas about deciding how much people earn, how much things cost, who owns the resources, and how business is conducted define capitalist, socialist, communist, and fascist governments. The United States is a capitalist society.

Governments get involved in economic concerns when they feel that it is in the public's best interest to do so. Sometimes that involvement comes in the form of regulations, such as concerning monopolies. Sometimes the involvement has to do with encouraging spending or saving by adjusting the interest rate.

One of the basic concepts in economics is that of supply and demand. How much product producers are willing to make, and how much consumers want to buy, explains the price and quantity of that product in the marketplace. It also explains a lot about the behavior of consumers and industries.

In personal finance, investing is an important way to grow wealth and drive the economy. Companies raise money to operate by selling small pieces of ownership called stocks or shares. Investors buy them to get a share of current profits and future worth. Trading stocks on the New York Stock Exchange or NASDAQ has as many risks as potential rewards. It can affect you personally and affect national and global economies.

GLOSSARY

arbitration: a method of settling disputes between labor and management.

budget: a plan and estimate of earning and spending for an upcoming time period.

capitalism: an economic system based on private ownership of resources and little interference from government.

competition: rivalry between two or more businesses for a consumer's business.

Consumer Price Index: a statistic that describes prices for consumer goods and their spending trends over time.

deficit: the situation when a business's or government's spending is greater than its income.

depression: an economic condition of low productivity, high unemployment, and decreasing prices.

demand: The amount of a product that a buyer will buy at different prices.

entrepreneur: a person who enters into business in the hopes of making a profit.

exchange rate: the price of one currency relative to another, for example, euros per dollar.

Federal Reserve System: an organization of twelve district banks, national and state member banks, and a seven-member Board of Governors that regulates financial institutions and controls the flow of money and credit in the United States.

fiscal: describes government finances, including taxes and public spending. A country influences productivity, employment, and prices by adjusting taxes according to a *fiscal* policy.

gross domestic product: a measurement of the value of a country's output of goods and services in a year.

inflation: a general rise in prices that reduces buying power.

interest: the amount charged to borrow money.

market: a location or situation where buying and selling occurs.

monetary policy: management of the money supply through adjusting interest rates. A low interest rate motivates people to spend more, while a high interest rate prompts people to save more.

monopoly: control by one organization of the resources or means to produce a product.

profit: the difference between the cost of producing a product or service and the price for which it can be sold.

resources: the things used to make goods and services, like land, labor, and money.

scab: a worker who continues to work during a strike.

strike: a technique for workers to gain bargaining power with management by refusing to work until an agreement is reached.

supply: The amount of a product that a producer will offer to sell at different prices.

tax: the amount of money that individuals and organizations pay to support the operations of government.

wealth: an accumulation of goods with economic value.

GEOGRAPHY

Fifteen percent of the test questions relate to material about the world's physical characteristics, including land and sea, plants and animals, weather, environment, and natural resources, and the impact on humankind.

Geography refers not only to the shape of the land but to all the Earth's physical characteristics. You may think of physical features such as mountains, lakes, rivers, canyons, jungles, and ice caps when you hear the word *geography*. Or places and borders and government may leap to mind—this area is known as political geography. Other physical characteristics include climate patterns, population density and migration,

CHAPTER

4

SOCIAL
STUDIES

THE
GED

INTRODUCTION

UNDERSTANDING
WHAT YOU READ

UNDERSTANDING
VISUAL MATERIALS

IDENTIFYING
IMPLICATIONS

APPLYING IDEAS

INTERPRETING
POLITICAL
CARTOONS

ANALYZING
RELATIONSHIPS

EVALUATING
INFORMATION

SOCIAL STUDIES
CONCEPTS

188

and distribution of natural resources. Physical characteristics may also be elements created by humans, including railroads, canals, and pollution.

When thinking about geography topics, remember that they all change over time. If the ice caps are melting and sea level is rising, land at the coast may be lost, but oceanic volcanoes create new land. People move, boundaries change, and resources are used up and discovered. Geography is more than just the study of how the world is now, but also how it was and how it will be.

GLOSSARY

altitude: the elevation, or height, above sea level of a physical location.

climate: the average or typical weather conditions of a certain locale.

compass rose: the map tool that indicates the four cardinal directions—north, south, east, and west—on a map.

conservation: attempts to preserve natural resources and protect them from the impact of human activities.

continent: one of the seven great masses of land on earth: Africa, Antarctica, Asia, Australia, Europe, North America, and South America.

desert: an area that is too dry to support typical plant and animal life.

drought: a long period without enough rainfall.

demographics: statistics about a population, like age, income, and education.

ecosystem: the relationship between living organisms and the physical environment.

environment: the conditions on the surface of the earth.

equator: the imaginary line around the center of the earth, the same distance from the North and South Poles. Climate tends to get warmer the closer a place is to the equator.

hemisphere: half the globe. The equator divides the northern hemisphere from the southern, and east and west are divided by a meridian.

latitude: distance north or south, shown in parallel rings around the globe that start small at the poles and grow to the largest point, around the equator.

legend: the map tool that explains the meaning of a map's symbols.

longitude: distance east or west, shown in equal-sized circles that intersect at the poles and are farthest apart at the equator.

migration: people, individually or in groups, relocating from one place to another.

natural resources: forms of wealth found in nature, like oil, water, minerals, and gems.

ocean: one of the five great bodies of saltwater on earth: Atlantic, Pacific, Indian, Arctic, and Antarctic.

poles: the opposite ends of the earth's axis. The North Pole and the South Pole are the planet's coldest places.

precipitation: moisture in the form of rain, snow, and sleet that falls to the earth's surface.

prime meridian: the 0° meridian that runs through Greenwich, England. The other meridians are numbered from and described in relation to the prime meridian.

season: one of the four divisions of a year characterized by temperature and amount of daylight: winter, spring, summer, and fall (or autumn).

topography: the physical features of the Earth's surface in a region, including natural and man-made features.

CHAPTER

4

SOCIAL
STUDIES

THE
GED

ANSWERS AND
EXPLANATIONS

We're done. You should be confident that you are now ready to succeed on the Social Studies part of the test.

SOCIAL STUDIES ANSWERS AND EXPLANATIONS

PRACTICE SET: UNDERSTANDING WHAT YOU READ

1. (5) The influence of Medgar Evers stretches far beyond 1960s Mississippi, embodying the rights of racial equality for all Americans for all time.

Answer (5), the last sentence in the passage, is correct, because it sums up the writer's point. Answers (1), (3), and (4) are incorrect because they are details in the passage that support the main idea, but are not enough to be the main idea on their own. Answer (2) is incorrect because the question of Evers's entitlement is not addressed in the passage. 〇 **Main idea**

2. (3) He organized boycotts of segregated businesses.

Answer (3) is correct, because only "organized boycotts" answers the question, "How did he work?" Answers (1) and (4) are true, but they do not answer the question, "How did he work?" Answer (2) is incorrect, because it is not true, and answer (5) is incorrect because his support of the Civil Rights Act is not discussed in the passage. 〇 **Supporting details**

3. (4) offering different opportunities to different races

Answer (4) is correct, because the paragraph makes it clear that minorities like Medgar Evers were able to go to college, just not the same colleges as whites. Answer (1) is incorrect, because the importance of one race relative to another is not addressed in the passage. Answer (2) is incorrect, since Evers did graduate from college; it is not true that he was denied an education. Answers (3) and (5) are incorrect, because the passage does not talk about whether topics of race were taught in schools. 〇 **Context clues**

CHAPTER

4

SOCIAL
STUDIES

THE
GED

ANSWERS AND
EXPLANATIONS

4. **(1) The Legacy of Medgar Evers**

Answer (1) is the best title for the passage, because it is the best summary of the main idea. Answers (2), (3), and (4) all describe details of the passage, but none captures the broad idea. Answer (5), "Civil Rights Martyrs," is a broader idea than the passage presents, because it focuses on only one man. **Main idea**

5. **(3) one who hates minorities**

Answers (3) is the best answer, because it follows the clue that "Not all Mississippians appreciated his accomplishments." Answer (1) is incorrect, because someone who welcomes progress would have no reason to kill someone dedicated to progress. Answer (2) is incorrect because there was no indication that De La Beckwith was hired to do what he did. Answer (4) is incorrect, because a tolerant person would not kill someone with a different point of view. Answer (5) is incorrect, because deliberate murder is not a game. **Context clues**

PRACTICE SET: UNDERSTANDING VISUAL MATERIALS

1. **(4) Most of them voted for the Republican candidate.**

The passage explained that the candidate who wins the most votes in a state gets all the electoral votes for that state. The map indicates that the Republican candidate won all of Alabama's nine electoral votes; therefore, he won most, but not necessarily all, of the votes cast by Alabamians. The map and passage do not support any of those conclusions in answers (1), (2), (3), and (5). **Maps**

2. **(2) Democrats enjoy the steadiest support.**

Answer (2) is correct, because the line that represents Democratic voter turnout is straightest, or steadiest, of all the groups represented. Republican turnout and "other" turnout rises and falls from year to year, so answers (1), (3), (4), and (5) cannot be correct. **Line graphs**

3. **(4) The Republican candidate won at least half of the votes in most of the states.**

The passage tells us that to win all of a state's electoral votes, the candidate only has to win most, as little as 51 percent, of the popular vote. Answer (4) is correct, because it shows that he won the vast majority of the electoral votes, so he must have won at least half the popular vote in most of the states. Answers (1) and (2) are incorrect, because winning a strong electoral majority does not necessarily indicate a strong popular majority. Answer (3) is incorrect because the electoral results do not show the level of voter turnout. Answer (5) is incorrect because it is not true. **Bar charts**

4. **(2) the 1984 Republican**

Answer (2) is correct, because with more than 54 million votes, the Republican candidate in 1984 won more votes than any other candidate detailed in the table.

Answer (1) is wrong, because the 1976 Democrat won just 40.8 million votes. Answer (3) is incorrect, because the "other" candidates in 1992 won just 20.6 million votes. Answer (4) is incorrect, because the Democrat in 1996 won just 47.4 million votes. Answer (5) is incorrect, because the Republican in 2000 won just 50.5 million votes. **Ⓗ Tables**

5. (5) The fewer votes the "other" candidate gets, the closer the outcome of the electoral vote

Answer (5) is correct. The graphs show that in years when "other" candidates receive very little of the popular vote, the electoral vote is closer than in years when the "other" candidate wins a bigger portion of the popular vote. Answers (1) and (2) are incorrect, because the graphs show occasions when the "other" vote seems to have contributed to both Democratic and Republican victories. Answer (3) is in incorrect, because "other" candidates have gotten smaller and smaller portions of the popular vote since 1992. Answer (4) is incorrect, because the charts show that in years that "other" candidates win bigger portions of the popular vote, the electoral vote is won by a wider margin. **Ⓗ Circle graphs**

PRACTICE SET: IDENTIFYING IMPLICATIONS

1. (3) Politicians have better access to health care than private citizens.

By pointing out that your family's health is just as important as any politician's when talking about the health care problem, Kerry implies that even though everyone's health is equally important, not everybody is receiving equal care. Answer (3) is correct, because it represents how the current system is unfair to private citizens—the people whose votes he is trying to win. Answer (1) may be true, but it does not suggest that anything is unfair. If all Americans had access to very good health care, it would not be an important campaign issue, so answer (2) is wrong. Answers (4) and (5) are incorrect, because if private citizens had access to the same or better health care as politicians, it would not be an important campaign issue. **Ⓗ Implications**

2. (1) Special interest groups are too involved.

Answer (1) is the correct answer, because in the passage, the sentence "John Kerry has the courage to take on special interests to get health care costs under control" is the key to what Kerry assumes is the problem: someone needs to have the courage to take on special interests in order to get costs under control. Answer (2) is incorrect, because "taking on special interests" does not suggest that special interest groups need to be more involved. Answers (3) and (4) are incorrect; while the passage assumes that insurance companies impede progress, it does not suggest that they are dishonest or charitable. Answer (5) is incorrect, because the passage does not suggest anything about politicians' greed. **Ⓗ Assumptions**

CHAPTER

4

SOCIAL
STUDIES

THE
GED

ANSWERS AND
EXPLANATIONS

3.   (3)   People do not have good choices in health care.

Answer (3) is correct. Bush's plan focuses on giving people more choices, so he assumes that we agree with him that lack of choices is the problem. Answer (1) is incorrect, because being able to provide the best care in the world is not a problem. Answer (2) is incorrect, because he does not suggest anything about bureaucrats' bad intentions. Even though Bush has a proposal for "modernizing and strengthening" the system, he already said that ours can provide the best care in the world, so answer (4) is incorrect. Answer (5) is incorrect, because the high costs of prescription drugs is presented more as an effect of the problem, not the cause. **Assumptions**

4.   (5)   bureaucracy

With the statement, "rising costs and loss of control to government and health plan bureaucrats threaten to keep patients from getting state-of-the-art care," Bush implies that bureaucrats are to blame. Answers (1), (2), (3), and (4) are incorrect, because they are not mentioned in the passage. **Implications**

5.   (3)   It is becoming less affordable.

Answer (3) is correct, because the steady upward slope of the line suggests that health care becomes more expensive every year. If answer (1) were true, the line would be flat. If answer (2) were true, the line would slope downward. Answers (4) and (5) are incorrect, because the graph does not imply anything about the quality of health care. **Implications**

PRACTICE SET: APPLYING IDEAS

1.   (5)   Antarctica, which is entirely polar

Answer (5) is correct, because it is very difficult for humans to inhabit a region that is permanently frozen. Answers (1), (2), (3), and (4) are incorrect, because all of those regions have climates that humans are able to inhabit easily. **Application**

2.   (2)   dry

The correct answer is (2), because a cactus is adapted to live in areas with very little water, or dry regions. Answers (1), (3), (4), and (5) are incorrect, because they represent climates other than where it is very dry, which is what a cactus is best suited for. **Application**

3.   (4)   cold

The correct answer is (4), because animals that hibernate are adapted to areas with a wide variation in seasonal temperature. Answers (1), (2), and (3) are incorrect, because it won't get cold enough in tropical, dry, or temperate regions to make it necessary to sleep through the cold months. Answer (5) is incorrect, because in a polar region, all the months are cold, and a hibernating animal would never have the chance to take advantage of spring, summer, or fall to fatten up for the next winter. **Application**

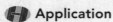

4.   (5)   The polar zone will shrink.

Answer (5) is correct, because increasing global temperatures will cause the ice and frozen ground to thaw. Answers (1), (2), and (3) are incorrect, because global warming may cause increases or decreases in rainfall, so it is impossible to guess if a particular area will become wetter or drier. Answer (4) is incorrect, because the cold zone is more likely to shrink as global temperatures rise. ⊞ **Application**

5.   (1)   members of a neighborhood association

Answer (1) is the correct, because participants in the Kyoto Protocol have no authority to force each other to do anything, but are trying to work together on common goals that will benefit all of them. Answers (2) and (4) suggest that members are subject to the authority of one central control, which is not the case. Answer (3) incorrectly suggests total independence from external influence or obligations. Answer (5) is incorrect, because a family reunion suggests more socializing and games than the serious business of promoting the common good. ⊞ **Application**

PRACTICE SET: INTERPRETING POLITICAL CARTOONS

1.   (2)   It refers to wasteful spending.

The most efficient and least expensive way to build a road between the two points in the cartoon would be to build it in a straight line. Spelling the word "Pork" in a highway would serve no purpose but to increase the cost of the project. Answer (2) is correct. Answer (1) is incorrect, because it is not necessary. Answer (3) is incorrect, because it is not innovative if it is pointless. Answers (4) and (5) are incorrect, because it is neither responsible nor funny to waste the taxpayers' money that way. ⊞ **Assumptions**

2.   (2)   Their constant observations are meaningless.

Answer (2) is the correct answer, because the boy reporting the details of the happenings on the see-saw is pointless. One is up when the other is down, then the other is up while the first is down—that's the way it works. Answer (1) is incorrect, because the artist does not hint that he believes it is important to pay such close attention. Answer (3) is incorrect, because he does not suggest that their reports are important. The artist seems to think that pollsters are silly and that the information we get from them is useless, so answers (4) and (5) are wrong. ⊞ **Implications**

3.   (1)   It indicates begging.

The gesture suggests that the congressman wants donations from the drug (Rx) company, so answer (1) is correct. It implies that if they donate to his campaign, he will protect their interests in Congress. Answers (2), (3), (4), and (5) are incorrect, because the gesture does not hint that the congressman is deceitful, humble, respectful, or honorable. ⊞ **Assumptions**

CHAPTER

4

SOCIAL
STUDIES

THE
GED

ANSWERS AND
EXPLANATIONS

4.   (5)   Gas is expensive.

Answer (5) is correct, because it shows that the gasoline was more valuable to the robbers than the cash being carried by the truck. Answer (1) is incorrect, because no judgment about the police is expressed. Answers (2), (3), and (4) are incorrect, because the main idea of the cartoon is about the price of gas. 🔘 Implications

5.   (1)   Deficits are scary.

Answer (1) is correct, because "deficits" is portrayed as a big, bad wolf, coming to get W. in his bed at night. It suggest a childhood fear of monsters. Answers (2), (3), (4), and (5) are incorrect, because the cartoon suggests the opposite: that deficits are dangerous, unwelcome, real, and common. 🔘 Assumptions

PRACTICE SET: ANALYZING RELATIONSHIPS

1.   (1)   Unproven companies were popular with investors who hoped to make a fast profit.

The dot-com boom was caused when investors were motivated by what they thought a company might be worth someday rather than what it was actually worth. Answer (1) is correct, because it is the circumstance that led to the overvalued market, or "boom." Answer (2) is incorrect because it is not true. Answer (3) is incorrect, because although the information is true, it did not contribute to the boom. Answer (4) is incorrect, because the passage did not discuss whether investors understood the technical businesses. Answer (5) is incorrect, because it is not true. 🔘 Cause and effect

2.   (4)   Investors became more cautious about investing in unproven businesses.

After the "dot-com bust," investors would most likely try to prevent the same disappointment from happening again. Answer (4) is correct, because after losing money by being swept up in a speculative frenzy, investors will probably be more careful. Answer (1) is incorrect, because investors may still find new companies attractive if their plans are realistic. Answer (2) is incorrect, because the companies themselves were not to blame for the bust. Answer (3) is incorrect, because the stocks had lost most of their value so could not be sold for a profit. Answer (5) is incorrect, because the graph does not represent the NASDAQ "bouncing back" to anything like the levels of the boom. 🔘 Cause and effect

3.   (1)   The stock market may be heading for another crash like the one in 1929.

Answer (1) is correct, because Sobel's main idea is that the current situation is like the situation before the 1929 crash, and so investors should be aware of that possibility. Answer (2) is incorrect, because it is not a conclusion, but something Sobel wondered about in his article. Answer (3) is incorrect, because investors' feelings about volatility is a detail, rather than a conclusion. Answer (4) is not true—is the opposite of Sobel's point. Answer (5) is incorrect, because Sobel's main point is that such a crash could very well happen again. 🔘 Conclusions

4.   (2)   The Dow spiked right before a sharp fall in both halves.

The question asks for similarities, so answer (2) is correct. It accurately describes a trend that is clear on both graphs. Answer (1) describes a difference, not similarity, between the graphs. Answers (3), (4), and (5) are not true: the Dow followed only an upward path and recovered quickly in the second chart. (H) **Compare and contrast**

5.   (5)   You would feel stupid if you sold your stocks during a market correction.

Answer (5) is the only option that cannot be known or proven by the writer. Answers (1), (2), (3), and (4) are incorrect, because they are all provable facts.
(H) **Fact or opinion**

PRACTICE SET: EVALUATING INFORMATION

1.   (1)   equality

Medgar Evers died trying to bring racial equality to his home state, so answer (1) is correct. Answers (2), (3), (4), and (5) are incorrect, because none is the value at the center of his life's work. (H) **Values**

2.   (3)   what portion of the popular vote was won by the Republican candidate

The passage explains that a candidate can win all of a state's electoral votes just by winning over half of the popular vote. To distinguish between a true popular landslide and winning 51 percent in most of the states, you would need to know the popular results. Answers (1), (2), (4), and (5) are irrelevant in deciding whether the 1984 race was truly a landslide. (H) **Adequacy**

3.   (5)   budget showing how his plan would reduce costs

Answer (5) is correct, because it is the only choice that relates directly to the candidates' plans for health care. Answers (1), (2), (3), and (4) would all confuse the issue with irrelevant information. (H) **Appropriateness**

4.   (3)   that the environment is not important

Regardless of whether it is the case, refusal to participate in an international attempt to reduce greenhouse gases suggests that the environment is not a priority for the United States, so answer (3) is correct. Answer (1) is incorrect, because by not taking part in the agreement, the United States hints that cooperation is not important. Answer (2) is incorrect, because if the United States were worried about its reputation in the world, it would not have been able to walk away from the treaty. Answer (4) is incorrect, because nothing is suggested about capitalism. Answer (5) is incorrect, because if compromise were important to the United States, it would have tried to reach one. (H) **Values**

5.   (3)   what the value of the Dow Jones Industrial Average is today

Answer (3) is the only option that does not help you understand the impact of the two crashes. Answers (1), (2), (4), and (5) are incorrect, because each would give you common measurements to help compare the two events. (H) **Appropriateness**

CHAPTER
4

SOCIAL
STUDIES

THE
GED

ANSWERS AND
EXPLANATIONS

CHAPTER

5

SCIENCE

SCIENCE

Welcome to the Science test. Let's get right to the good news. The Social Studies test didn't require you to posses an abundance of knowledge about history, economics, and which president came first. It asked you to only work with material given in the question on the test. The Science test is very similar. It doesn't measure your existing scientific knowledge. It asks you only to interpret and apply information given in charts, graphs, and reading selections. The skills you learned in preparing for the Social Studies test will serve you well on this test, too.

What follows in this chapter isn't a science lesson. It's a review of how to use the material on the test to answer the questions correctly. Let's get started.

Here is your ladder for the Science test.

Rung 1: Introduction
Rung 2: Review of Comprehension Strategies
    (See Social Studies Rungs 2 to 5)
Rung 3: Physical Science
Rung 4: Life Science I: Life on Our Planet
Rung 5: Life Science II: Human Body Systems
Rung 6: Earth and Space Science

The six rungs on the Science ladder focus on how to interpret scientific information on all the topics you need to know. The same key skills we covered in depth in the Social Studies chapter are reviewed in the second rung. Therefore, if you are preparing for the Science test before studying the Social Studies test, you will need to go back to Chapter 4, pages 118–182.

Each rung concludes with a set of practice questions. Answering these questions helps you to assess how prepared you are in each topic. If you answer most of the practice set questions correctly, you should move on to the next rung. Explanations to each practice set appear at the end of the chapter.

By using the step-by-step ladder in this chapter, you can master all the skills you need to succeed on the Science test. Each rung is designed as a single lesson and should take you about an hour to complete. It's important to work through each rung, one at a time, to prepare for all types of questions on the Science test. Each rung builds on the rung before it. You can go back and review previous lessons if you feel you need to improve in a particular area.

INTRODUCTION

The Science test consists of fifty multiple-choice questions about physical science, life science, and earth and space science. Each question refers to a passage and/or graphic of some sort. Success on the Science test depends on your ability to interpret graphs and charts, understand short passages about scientific topics, and draw logical conclusions. You will *not* have to memorize vast amounts of science.

QUICK OVERVIEW

Test	Items	Time Limit
Science	50 multiple-choice questions	80 minutes

The questions on the Science test cover three content areas:

- **Physical Science (35%)**—atoms, elements, molecules, radioactivity, matter, energy, and magnetism. Chemistry and physics are closely related in practice and on the GED test. These fields study *matter*, anything that has mass and volume, and *energy*, which exists in many forms, from heat to electricity. The GED test refers to physics and chemistry as physical science.

- **Life Science (45%)**—cells, heredity and health, and functions such as photosynthesis, respiration, body systems, and the behavior and interdependence of organisms. Biology is also an important area on the GED test. Biology is the study of life, from cells to individual organisms to the biosphere itself. The biosphere includes all living beings and their environment. These environments change, and species evolve over time. Most material related to the study of biology is referred to as life science on the GED test.

- **Earth and Space Science (20%)**—Earth's structure, rocks and minerals, earthquakes and volcanoes, weather and climate, and topics related to our solar system and beyond. Earth science includes the disciplines of geology, which covers the history of the earth, and meteorology, the study of weather and climate. Astronomy, or space science, involves the study of anything beyond the earth's atmosphere—from the solar system to the origin of the universe.

Remember that most of the information you need to answer the questions is provided on the test. However, you must be familiar with the basic concepts and terms of science. Do not worry about memorizing every law of physics or every part of the human body. Simply familiarize yourself with the vocabulary and concepts you can expect to see on test day so that nothing takes you by surprise.

THE
GED

TEST-TAKING TIPS

The best way to prepare for the Science test is to master strategies that will help you understand and draw conclusions based on the charts, graphics, and reading passages on the Science test. **Mastering these strategies is the most important part of your preparation for the test.**

That's exactly what this chapter provides for you.

On test day, remember the test-taking strategy that you learned in the Social Studies chapter:

- Don't try to memorize anything given to you on a chart, table, map, or reading passage. You can return to the passage or graphic as often as you want.
- Use the X-O strategy to make sure that you answer all of the questions that you know, picking up the easy points first. To review this strategy, turn back to the page 37 for a quick reminder.

Now, let's move on to the next step in the ladder and review reading comprehension strategies.

REVIEW OF COMPREHENSION STRATEGIES (SEE SOCIAL STUDIES RUNGS 2 TO 5)

Are you ready for a break? Well, you've got one. There's a reason the Science ladder is so short: the skills and strategies covered in the first four rungs of the Social Studies ladder work for Science, as well. The four rungs of the Social Studies ladder are:

- Understanding What You Read
- Understanding Visual Materials
- Identifying Implications
- Applying Ideas

If you already covered that chapter, just review the additional information below, tackle the practice set to make sure your reading comprehension skills are still in good working order, then move on to the next rung. It's like moving up four rungs at once. If you have not read the Social Studies chapter yet, review pages 119–182 carefully before starting the Science ladder.

WAIT! If you have not already worked through the first four rungs of the Social Studies ladder, you need to do so before beginning work on the Science ladder.

UNDERSTANDING WHAT YOU READ

Many questions on the Science test assess whether you can understand a short passage. You won't be asked to interpret anything, make any calculations, or explain the make-up of DNA. You simply have to demonstrate that you understand what you read. For example, take a look at this question:

1. Coastal erosion is the removal and redistribution of sand from a particular beach to another area. Forces such as wind, waves, currents, sea level, seasonal climate changes, and human activity cause coastal erosion. Residents of beach communities are challenged to find ways to protect valuable homes from the effects of erosion. While poor land-use methods can make erosion worse, careful development of the land near coasts can minimize both the damage to the beach and potential damage to residents' homes.

   Which of the following is <u>not</u> a force that contributes to coastal erosion?

   (1) wind
   (2) poor land use methods
   (3) sand
   (4) tides
   (5) changing seasons

First, make sure you read the question carefully. You are being asked to select the answer choice that is *not* a force of coastal erosion. You can rule out anything that the passage says *is* a force contributing to coastal erosion. The second sentence lists several factors that contribute to erosion. Look for those among the answer choices, and you will find that answers (1), (4), and (5) appear right there. The only answer choices you are left with are (2) and (3). If you read a little further into the paragraph, you see that the fourth sentence uses the exact phrase "poor land use methods" and then says that they "can make erosion worse." So (2) is a force contributing to coastal erosion. Answer (3), sand, is what coastal erosion removes. It isn't a force contributing to coastal erosion. This is the correct answer.

Beware of Science-Speak! Don't let the science-speak cause you to fumble a basic comprehension question. By test day, most of the words you see in the Science test passages will be familiar to you. Remember: most science terms will be defined for you in the passage in which they appear.

THE GED

UNDERSTANDING VISUAL MATERIAL

Many of the questions on the Science test involve interpreting graphics, such as charts, tables, graphs, maps, or figures. Review pages 129–141 of the Social Studies chapter for key strategies to help you interpret various types of charts, tables, and graphs. The only type of graphic that doesn't appear on the Social Studies test that sometimes appears on the Science test is the scattergram.

SCATTERGRAMS

Scattergrams can help reveal correlations, or connections, between things or events that may not seem obviously connected. It is a lot like a line graph, except that it has a bunch of scattered points instead of a line.

Understanding or interpreting a scattergram involves finding a pattern in the points. Do they seem to move up and to the right? Down and to the left? Are they level in the middle, bottom, or top? The points plotted do not usually fit exactly on the line, but you can often spot a general trend. The more closely the points resemble a line, the stronger the connection between the two events or things represented. The more loosely scattered or random the points appear, the weaker the connection.

Take a look at this example:

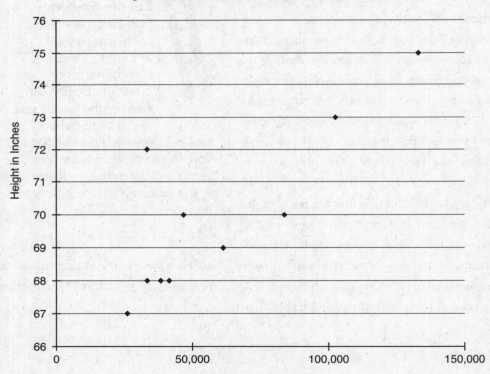

This scattergram correlates the annual income and height of a group of fictional forty-year-olds. Take a glance at the general shape of the points on the chart. Do you notice any pattern? There is no exact connection between height and income, but it does seem that, in general, the taller the man, the higher his income.

IDENTIFYING IMPLICATIONS

Identifying the implications of a passage or graphic involves somewhat more sophisticated reasoning than just understanding what you read. You have to look at a set of facts and draw conclusions for yourself.

On the Science test, you may encounter a question like this:

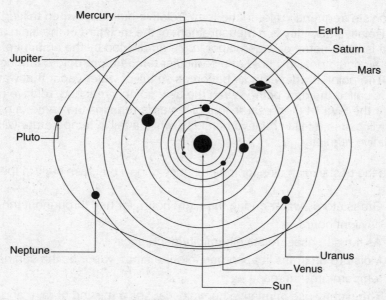

Astronomers have long referred to Venus as Earth's "sister planet." The two planets are very close to each other and are similar in size. They also share some geological features, such as volcanoes. However, conditions on Venus are nothing like those on Earth. Even though Mercury is closer to the sun than Venus, the surface temperature on Venus is slightly higher. Venus's atmosphere, composed mainly of carbon dioxide, traps the sun's heat and raises the planet's surface temperature to nearly 900 degrees Fahrenheit.

1. Which planet has the lowest surface temperature?

    (1)   Earth
    (2)   Venus
    (3)   Mercury
    (4)   Saturn
    (5)   Pluto

For a question like this, you may have to read between the lines. The passage is mostly about Venus, and it mentions Earth and Mercury, but there is no mention of Saturn or Pluto. How are you supposed to answer this question? Notice that the question asks you about surface temperature. The passage also talks about surface temperature. Venus, the passage tells us, is hotter than Mercury even though it is farther from the sun. What information can we find hidden in this statement? Well, first it seems unusual that a planet farther from the sun is hotter than a planet closer to the sun. The implication is that, usually, the closer a planet is to the sun, the hotter it is. If we take that knowledge and look at the diagram of the solar system, it seems clear that answer (5), Pluto, is our best answer choice. Pluto is the planet farthest from the sun.

THE
GED

APPLYING IDEAS

The hardest questions on the Science test ask you to take ideas learned in one context and apply them to a different situation. Review the strategies on pages 148–153 of the Social Studies chapter if you need to. On the Science test, an application question might look like this:

Meteorologists frequently refer to the term "relative humidity" when talking about the weather. Relative humidity is a measurement of the moisture of the air in a particular area. It is the amount of water vapor in the air divided by the amount of water vapor the air could possibly hold at a particular temperature before turning water to droplets. The point at which the air becomes so full of water vapor that water droplets form is called the dew point. When the dew point is reached, relative humidity is at 100%. If the level of air pressure in a given area remains the same, a rise in temperature will cause a fall in relative humidity, while a fall in temperature will cause a rise in relative humidity.

1. What is the <u>best</u> explanation for the presence of dew on grass early in the morning?

(1)   Grass stores water during the night hours for use throughout the warmer daylight hours.
(2)   As the sun rises, relative humidity decreases.
(3)   Moisture on grass is absorbed into the air as vapor as the sun rises and temperatures increase.
(4)   The nightly rise in relative humidity causes a misting of rain, and drops of rain are still present on the grass.
(5)   As the temperature falls during the night, the relative humidity in the air increases until the dew point is reached and water droplets form on the ground and in the grass.

First, make sure you know what the question is asking. In this case, we need to know why little drops of water are present on grass first thing in the morning. The passage explains the relationship between dew point, relative humidity, and temperature. You need to figure out what relative humidity, dew point, and temperature have to do with little drops of water on grass.

If you sort through the information in the passage step by step, you see that air can hold water vapor up to a certain point. When the air is holding all the water vapor it can, the relative humidity is 100%. After that, water droplets form. This is the dew point. If the temperature goes up, the relative humidity goes down, which means the air can hold more water vapor and droplets won't form. If the temperature goes down, the relative humidity goes up, which means you're moving toward the dew point and the appearance of water droplets. So, it seems that cooling down the air is likely to produce water droplets, or dew.

Now, let's take a look at our answer choices. Answer (1) isn't supported by the passage and has nothing to do with relative humidity. Answer (2) looks attractive. It is stated directly in the passage, so you know the statement is true, but is it the answer to the question? There is nothing in the statement about dew or grass, so it doesn't seem right. Skip it for now and come back to it if necessary. Answer (3) also seems accurate. It makes sense that as the temperature goes up, water droplets will become water vapor. But that still doesn't answer the question about how the dew got on the grass in the first place. Answer (4) is inaccurate. You probably know from personal experience that it doesn't have to rain for dew to appear on grass. Answer (5) looks good. Night makes the air cooler, relative humidity increases, and water vapor turns to dew on the grass. Bingo. Even though answers (2) and (3) were possible, the best answer is (5).

PRACTICE SET: REVIEW OF COMPREHENSION STRATEGIES

The following questions help you make sure that your reading comprehension skills are in top shape. Read the following questions carefully, then select the best option.

Question 1 is based on the following scattergram:

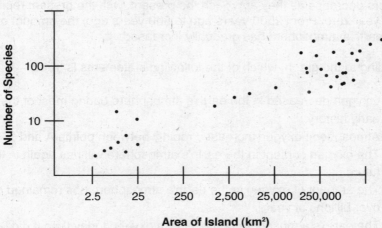

1. There are at least seven species of organisms on islands between two square kilometers and 250,000 square kilometers in size. Which of the following statements is supported by the scattergram?

   (1) There are more islands greater than 25,000 square kilometers in size than those less than 25,000 square kilometers in size.
   (2) There are more islands greater than 25 square kilometers in size than those less than 25,000 square kilometers in size.
   (3) There are more species of organisms on smaller islands than on larger islands.
   (4) There are more species of organisms on larger islands than on smaller islands.
   (5) The number of species of organisms decreases as the island size increases.

Question 2 is based on the following line graph:

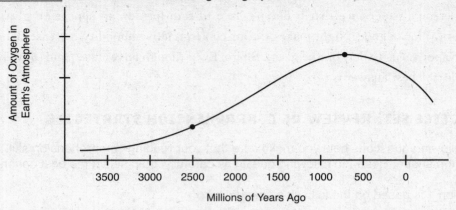

2. In this line graph, the numbers become smaller, as you move left to right. The numbers decrease as they approach the present, with the present represented by the year zero. From 2500 years ago to 500 years ago, the amount of oxygen in the earth's atmosphere has gradually increased.

According to the graph, which of the following statements is true?

(1)   Oxygen decreased in the earth's atmosphere during most of the planet's early history.

(2)   Atmospheric oxygen increased rapidly between points A and B.

(3)   The oxygen content in the earth's atmosphere will rise again in the near future.

(4)   The amount of oxygen in the earth's atmosphere has remained constant over billions of years.

(5)   The earth's atmosphere contains less oxygen today than it did 500 million years ago.

Question 3 is based on the following chart:

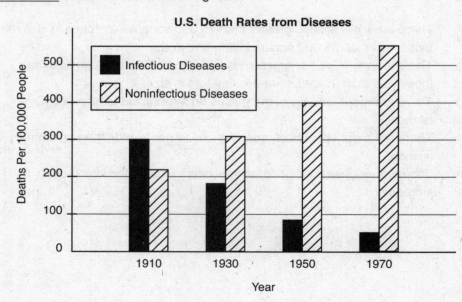

3. There were many more infectious diseases in 1910 than in 1990. By 1990, most infectious diseases were eradicated, but overall diseases were on the increase after 1950.

According to the graph, what is the reason for the rise in U.S. deaths due to non-infectious diseases between 1910 and 1970?

(1) Noninfectious diseases are easier to spread than infectious diseases.
(2) Infectious diseases are easier to spread than noninfectious diseases.
(3) Both types of disease spread at equal rates.
(4) There are more types of infectious diseases than noninfectious diseases.
(5) This graph does not address the reason for the rise in deaths.

Questions 4 and 5 refer to the following passage:

Gravity is the force of attraction between two objects. The reason objects on earth do not fly off the ground is that gravity, or attraction, exists between each object and the earth itself. The greater the mass of a particular object, the stronger the force of attraction it exerts. The sun, for example, exerts an enormous gravitational pull on all the planets of our solar system, which keeps them all in orbit.

4. Without the force of gravity, what would happen to the planets in our solar system?

(1) They would explode.
(2) They would stop orbiting the sun.
(3) They would collide.
(4) Their surface temperatures would rise.
(5) Their orbit of the sun would increase in speed.

5. Imagine Earth's mass was reduced by 50 percent. Which of the following would be a likely result?

(1) People and animals would be crushed by the force of gravity.
(2) Every object on Earth would fly off the ground.
(3) It would be much harder to throw a ball.
(4) People would be able to jump much higher.
(5) The oceans would become deeper.

Check your answers on pages 231–233. Are you comfortable applying your reading comprehension skills to scientific material? Did you get most of the questions right? If not, review pages 121–128 of the Social Studies chapter. If you did get most of the questions right, way to go! Let's move on to some specific content areas that are on the test.

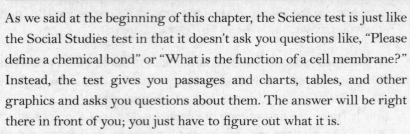

PHYSICAL SCIENCE

As we said at the beginning of this chapter, the Science test is just like the Social Studies test in that it doesn't ask you questions like, "Please define a chemical bond" or "What is the function of a cell membrane?" Instead, the test gives you passages and charts, tables, and other graphics and asks you questions about them. The answer will be right there in front of you; you just have to figure out what it is.

It is best to become familiar with the topics of these passages and graphics. That's where the next rungs of the ladder come in. Don't try to memorize the information included here. Just familiarize yourself so that the concepts and vocabulary aren't a surprise on test day. The first topic is physical science.

Physical science refers to chemistry and physics. Chemistry is the study of matter, and physics is the study of matter and energy. Although much of the research in these fields is done in the laboratory, every aspect of science and technology—and our everyday lives—is affected by the results. For example, engineers who design cars use physics principles to help them increase speed. Chemists create materials for air bags, seat belts, and bumpers to increase safety in a collision. Nine physical science topics are commonly covered on the GED:

1. ATOMS AND ELEMENTS

Atoms are made up of three primary components: **protons**, **electrons**, and **neutrons**. Protons have a positive charge, and electrons have a negative charge. Neutrons have no charge. Both protons and neutrons are found in the **nucleus** or core of the atom. Electrons are found outside of the nucleus. Electrons in the outer shells of an atom can help make it **reactive** (more on atomic reactions in a moment).

An **element** is a chemical that cannot be broken down into smaller substances. All known elements are arranged in the **periodic table**.

1 IA																	18 VIIIA
1 H	2 IIA											13 IIIA	14 IVA	15 VA	16 VIA	17 VIIA	2 He
3 Li	4 Be											5 B	6 C	7 N	8 O	9 F	10 Ne
11 Na	12 Mg	3	4	5	6	transition metals 7	8	9	10	11	12	13 Al	14 Si	15 P	16 S	17 Cl	18 Ar
19 K	20 Ca	21 Sc	22 Ti	23 V	24 Cr	25 Mn	26 Fe	27 Co	28 Ni	29 Cu	30 Zn	31 Ga	32 Ge	33 As	34 Se	35 Br	36 Kr
37 Rb	38 Sr	39 Y	40 Zr	41 Nb	42 Mo	43 Tc	44 Ru	45 Rh	46 Pd	47 Ag	48 Cd	49 In	50 Sn	51 Sb	52 Te	53 I	54 Xe
55 Cs	56 Ba	57 La	72 Hf	73 Ta	74 W	75 Re	76 Os	77 Ir	78 Pt	79 Au	80 Hg	81 Tl	82 Pb	83 Bi	84 Po	85 At	86 Rn
87 Fr	88 Ra	89 Ac	104 Rf	105 Db	106 Sg	107 Bh	108 Hs	109 Mt	110 Uun	111 Uuu	112 Uub					halogens	noble gases

alkali metals   alkaline earth metals

lanthanides	58 Ce	59 Pr	60 Nd	61 Pm	62 Sm	63 Eu	64 Gd	65 Tb	66 Dy	67 Ho	68 Er	69 Tm	70 Yb	71 Lu
actinides	90 Th	91 Pa	92 U	93 Np	94 Pu	95 Am	96 Cm	97 Bk	98 Cf	99 Es	100 Fm	101 Md	102 No	103 Lr

The lightest elements are at the top of the table, and the most reactive—meaning most likely to react with other elements—are generally on the left. Each element has a unique **atomic number**, defined by the number of protons it contains. For example, the atomic number of hydrogen (H) is 1, and oxygen (O) is 8, because hydrogen atoms have one proton and oxygen atoms have eight protons.

2. CHEMICAL REACTIONS

Most elements form **molecules**, which are chemically bonded by attractive forces. A **chemical bond** is the relationship between atoms in a molecule. These bonds are formed through the interaction of electrons.

Elements that are at the top of each column, or group, are generally more reactive than those below, which have higher atomic numbers. Elements in the first group are called **alkali metals**. Because they have only one electron in their outer valence shells, they are highly reactive, combining with other atoms to form compounds. The **inert gases**, such as helium, form the last column in the periodic table. These elements have complete outer shells of electrons and do not tend to react, or join, with other elements.

There are two types of bonds that occur between atoms. **Ionic bonds** occur when electrons are transferred from one atom to another. This transfer produces an electric charge, and these charged atoms are **ions**. When atoms share electrons, the bond between them is a **covalent bond**. Each atom contributes an electron to form the bond. Atoms that are joined by covalent bonds are called **molecules**.

Chemical compounds are represented by **chemical formulas** and **structural formulas**. For example, the hydrocarbon ethane has the chemical formula C_2H_6. The chemical formula is sort of like a recipe: "take two carbons and mix them with six hydrogens."

3. HYDROCARBONS

All living things contain **carbon**, which is one of the most important elements on Earth. Molecules made up of only hydrogen and carbon are called **hydrocarbons**. These include fossil fuels such as oil and gas.

There are two types of hydrocarbons: **saturated** and **unsaturated**. A saturated hydrocarbon, also known as an **alkane**, has the maximum number of hydrogen molecules. All the carbon atoms of alkanes are connected by single bonds. Because of these single bonds, alkanes are very stable molecules. Unsaturated **hydrocarbons**, such as alkenes, are more reactive than saturated hydrocarbons.

When hydrogen is added to an unsaturated hydrocarbon, it is called an **addition reaction**.

4. THE IDEAL GAS LAW

According to the **ideal gas law**, or kinetic-molecular theory, gases are affected by **temperature**, **volume**, and **pressure**. The particles of an ideal gas move randomly, and no energy is lost when they collide with each other. The ideal gas law states:

- If volume is held constant, pressure will increase as temperature increases. (The pressure of an ideal gas is exerted by the number of collisions that the gas particles make with the walls of a container.)
- If temperature is held constant, pressure will increase as volume decreases.
- If pressure is held constant, volume will increase if temperature increases.

5. DENSITY

Density is the mass of a substance per unit volume. When combined with other properties, it can help distinguish one substance from another. For example, an ounce of gold is much smaller than an once of iron because it is denser. A pound of sugar is smaller than a pound of cotton because it is denser.

For most substances, solids are denser than the liquid form. When you freeze something, it generally becomes smaller. There is one important exception. *Ice, the solid form of water, is less dense than the liquid water.* That is why ice freezes on top of the surface of a lake and ice cubes float. If you melt ice, its density increases.

6. WAVES

Waves are invisible electric force fields that transfer energy across space. Light, microwaves, x-rays, and radio transmissions are all examples of waves. They are classified in the **electromagnetic spectrum**, which ranges from the shortest waves, known as **cosmic waves**, to **radio waves**, the longest. In a vacuum, waves travel at the **speed of light** (approximately 186,281 miles per second), but most waves slow down in the atmosphere, in liquids, and when traveling through objects.

Our eyes can see only a small range of the electromagnetic spectrum. Visible light ranges from red, which is 700 nanometers (nm), to 400 nanometers, the color violet. Visible light is often measured in angstroms, represented by the symbol Å. An angstrom is equal to ten nanometers. The energy of light occurs in units called **photons**. Physicist Albert Einstein introduced the concept of protons as packets of light in the twentieth century.

7. NEWTON'S LAWS

English physicist Sir Isaac Newton summarized his findings on the motion of objects in three laws:

THE FIRST LAW OF MOTION

Objects that aren't moving tend to stay still, and objects that are moving tend to keep moving unless these objects are acted on by some outside force. For example, a ball resting on the floor won't move by itself. Someone or something—a child's foot, an earthquake, or whatever—must apply force to move it. If you drop a brick out of an airplane, it is going to keep falling and falling until something stops it (hopefully the ground and not someone's head). This is the concept of **inertia**. The greater the mass of an object, the more inertia it has. In other words, it's harder to stop a speeding freight train than to stop a floating feather, and harder to push a stalled car down the street than it is to push a child on swing.

Seat belts are designed to moderate the effects of this law in a car accident. If a car hits a wall, it will stop abruptly. Without a seat belt, the passenger would continue moving forward, perhaps hitting the dashboard or steering wheel with high impact. Seat belts reduce injuries by reducing the force of the impact on the driver.

THE SECOND LAW OF MOTION

The acceleration of an object is proportional to the magnitude of the force applied to the object and inversely proportional to the mass of an object. That's a scientific way of saying that the harder you push something, the faster it goes, and the heavier something is, the harder it is to get it to move quickly.

The relationship between force and acceleration makes sense. The harder you throw a baseball, the more force you apply to it and the faster it goes. You can throw a softball much faster than a cannon ball. If you apply the same force, a heavy object will move more slowly than a light one.

THE THIRD LAW OF MOTION

The third law is one of the most important principles of physics: If one object exerts force on another object, the second object exerts an equal and opposite force on the first object. We see the consequences of this law every day:

- When we walk, we exert force against the earth with every step. We push backward against the earth, and the earth pushes us forward.
- When you throw a ball at a wall, it recoils and bounces back. The wall is exerting an equal and opposite effect on the ball.

8. WORK AND ENERGY

In physics, **work** is defined as "a force that acts upon an object to cause displacement." In order for a force to be considered work, it must displace or move another object. Moving a pencil across a piece of paper is work, as is lifting a barbell.

Energy comes in various forms. **Mechanical energy** can be **kinetic energy**, if an object is in motion. A moving baseball has kinetic energy. An object can also have **potential energy**, when the mechanical energy is stored. A good example of stored potential energy is a barbell held above a weightlifter's head. Because of its position above the ground, the barbell has potential energy. It will become kinetic energy if the lifter drops the weight.

9. ELECTRICITY AND MAGNETISM

One of the many practical applications of physics is the study of **electricity** and **magnetism**. Electricity is a fundamental property of all matter. Every atom has a

THE
GED

positive electrical charge, from the protons, and a negative electrical charge, from the electrons. Charges can be transferred when electrons are gained or lost in an atom.

The electrical charges in matter can create potential energy, which can be stored in devices known as **capacitors**. Electric currents flow though materials. Physicists use the word **resistance** to describe how freely different kinds of matter allow electricity to flow. Water, for instance, doesn't have much resistance, and electricity flows freely through it. That's why lifeguards always make people get out of swimming pools when there is lightning. Rubber, on the other hand, has good resistance to electric current flow. Materials with high resistance are often used as insulators.

PRACTICE SET: PHYSICAL SCIENCE

Directions: Choose the <u>one best answer</u> to each question.

<u>Question 1</u> refers to the following passage and the Periodic Table of the Elements.

An element is a chemical that cannot be broken down into smaller substances. All known elements are arranged in the periodic table. The lightest elements are at the top of the table, and the most reactive—meaning most likely to react to other elements—are generally on the left. Each element has a unique atomic number, defined by the number of protons it contains. For example, the atomic number of hydrogen (H) is one, and oxygen (O) is eight because hydrogen atoms have one proton and oxygen atoms have eight.

1. Which of the following element pairs will most readily combine with each other?

    (1)   lithium (Li) and sodium (Na)

    (2)   potassium (K) and barium (Ba)

    (3)   sodium (Na) and chlorine (Cl)

    (4)   potassium (K) and krypton (Kr)

    (5)   hydrogen (H) and lithium (Li)

The electromagnetic spectrum covers the energies of waves from the longest waves (radio waves) to the shortest waves (cosmic waves). In a vacuum, electromagnetic spectrum waves travel at the speed of light (186,000 miles per second). The speed at which waves travel varies as the wave passes through objects. The denser an object, the more slowly a wave travels through it. Long waves are powerful and pass easily through solids, liquids, and gasses. Shorter waves cannot pass as well through solids.

Human eyes are able to detect only a small portion of the electromagnetic spectrum. We are able to see wavelengths between 700 nanometers (nm)—the wavelength of the color red—to 400 nm or the wavelength of the color violet. We cannot see infrared, which is longer than 700nm, or ultraviolet, which is shorter than 400nm. Sometimes, the unit called the Angstrom is used when discussing wavelengths of visible light. An Angstrom, Å, is ten nanometers, so 7,000 Angstroms equals 700 nanometers.

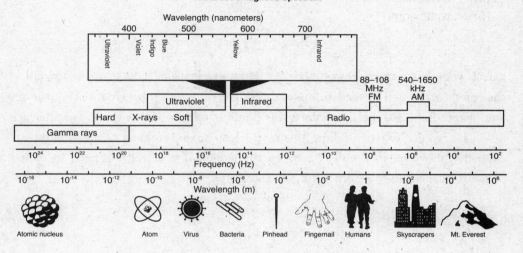

The Electromagnetic Spectrum

2. The frequency of a wave is measured in cycles per second (cps), or Hertz (Hz). According to the figure, what happens to the wavelength as the frequency of a wave increases?

   (1) The wavelength decreases.
   (2) The wavelength increases.
   (3) The wavelength does not change.
   (4) The wave becomes shorter.
   (5) The wave becomes taller.

3. According to the figure, how tall could a skyscraper be?

   (1) 1,000 centimeters
   (2) 1,000 Hz
   (3) 1,000 meters
   (4) 10,000 meters
   (5) 100 centimeters

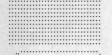
4. According to the figure, which of the following statements about the relative sizes of bacteria, viruses, and the wavelengths of visible light is accurate?

(1)   Viruses and visible light are about the same size.
(2)   Viruses must be larger than visible light, or they could not be seen.
(3)   Visible light wavelengths are the smallest waves that can be detected.
(4)   Bacteria are larger than viruses and visible light waves.
(5)   Bacteria and visible light waves are about the same size.

5. If the frequency of the highest frequency infrared wave is increased, which of the following will happen next? The highest frequency infrared wave will become

(1)   an ultraviolet wave.
(2)   the visible light wave red.
(3)   a powerful radio wave.
(4)   a television signal.
(5)   white light.

Check your answers on pages 232–233. How did you do? Did you see how all of the information you needed to answer the questions was provided in the passage and chart? Even so, the vocabulary was familiar to you, which gives you a big leg up on everyone else when taking this test. If you answered most of this practice set correctly, move on to the next rung in the ladder. If you feel you need to review physical science, do so before taking the next step.

THE
GED

LIFE SCIENCE I:
LIFE ON OUR PLANET

This rung of the Science ladder and the next present all of the biology you should be familiar with to score high on the test. The life sciences are concerned with all the living organisms on our planet, from tiny cells to entire ecosystems. This section of the GED test includes topics such as cell structures and functions, genetics, evolution, energy flow in ecosystems, and cycles in ecosystems.

Life science helps us understand plant and animal life, human life, and the systems that affect us. In this section, we explore plant and animal life, as well as genetics and evolution. Seven topics are commonly covered on the GED:

1. CELL STRUCTURES

The **cell**, the basic unit of life, has a number of special structures:

- **Cell membrane.** The plasma or cell membrane is the outer membrane of the cell. It regulates the transport of materials into and out of the cell.
- **Nucleus.** Animal and plant cells have a nucleus, typically located at the center of a cell, which contains the cell's genetic information.
- **Mitochondrion.** Animal and plant cells also have mitochondria, the organelles responsible for cellular respiration.
- **Ribosome.** Ribosomes are small organelles that manufacture protein molecules.
- **Golgi apparatus.** The Golgi apparatus is a stack of flattened sacs that play an active role in the synthesis, storage, and secretion of chemical products in the cell.

Almost half of the questions on the GED Science test have to do with life science.

There are two structures that differentiate plant cells from animal cells. Plants have **chloroplasts** and **cell walls**. Chloroplasts contain the green pigment **chlorophyll**, which helps plants convert light energy into chemical energy. This energy is stored as glucose and other sugars. This process of converting light energy into chemical energy is called **photosynthesis**.

Both animals and plant cells have mitochondria. Cellular respiration and photosynthesis are opposite processes. During cellular respiration, oxygen is consumed and carbon dioxide is expelled as a waste gas. During photosynthesis, carbon dioxide is consumed and oxygen is expelled as a waste gas. That's why animals and plants get along so well together. We breathe in what the plants breathe out, and the plants breathe in what we breathe out.

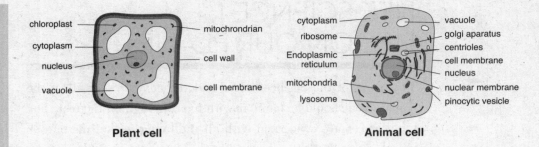

chloroplast	mitochrondrian
cytoplasm	
nucleus	cell wall
vacuole	cell membrane

Plant cell

cytoplasm	vacuole
ribosome	golgi aparatus
	centrioles
Endoplasmic reticulum	cell membrane
mitochondria	nucleus
lysosome	nuclear membrane
	pinocytic vesicle

Animal cell

2. CELL CYCLE

The **life cycle of the cell** involves growth and division. There are five stages in the cell cycle:

    a. interphase

    b. prophase

    c. metaphase

    d. anaphase

    e. telophase

    Interphase is the longest part of a cell's life during which it grows and carries out the processes essential for survival.

    Mitosis, which includes prophase, metaphase, anaphase, and telophase, is the process of cell division. At the end of interphase, the cell grows and the genetic material, its **chromosomes**, are copied. During the stages of mitosis, the chromosomes line up along the middle of the cell nucleus. After aligning, the paired chromosomes move to opposite sides of the cell, and the cell divides in a process call **cytokinesis**. Each of the resulting cells has the same number of chromosomes as the parent cell. At the end of mitosis, the nucleus reforms.

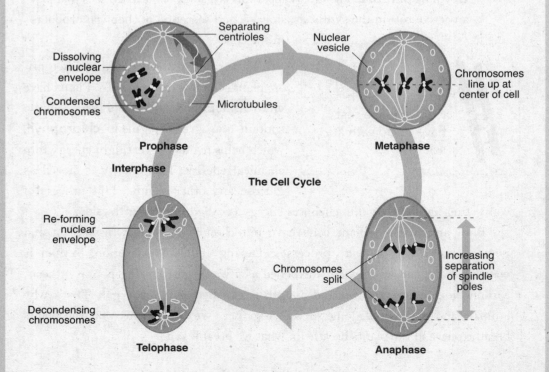

3. CELLULAR RESPIRATION

Cells get energy from a process called **cellular respiration**. In this process, the cell uses oxygen to break down sugars, releasing chemical energy. Glucose is a simple sugar that is commonly used in respiration. Glucose and oxygen are the sources for respiration. Carbon dioxide, water, and energy are the products.

4. METABOLISM

The chemical reactions that occur in the cell are known as **metabolic reactions**. The two basic reactions essential to cellular metabolism are **anabolic** and **catabolic** reactions.

Anabolism is essential to cellular growth and the storage of energy. Materials are absorbed into the cell, where complex molecules, such as proteins and fats, are formed.

Catabolism is the release of energy through the breakdown of organic materials such as glucose and other molecules. Cellular respiration is the most important catabolic reaction.

5. DNA AND GENETICS

The structure of **DNA** was discovered by James D. Watson and Francis Crick in 1953. Their famous model of the DNA molecule is a double helix, which looks like a ladder twisted into a spiral.

DNA comprises four **nucleotides,** or base pairs: **adenine**, **cytosine**, **guanine**, and **thymine**. Variation in the ordering of these pairs makes for the differences between organisms. Each individual has its own set of genes, or **genotype**.

Physical differences between organisms are known as **traits**. Each trait is determined by a gene, a section of DNA. On the GED Science test, you may see a **Punnett square**, which shows the possible genotypes that an offspring may inherit by its parents.

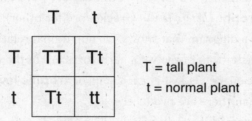

T = tall plant
t = normal plant

In a Punnett square, the genotypes of the parents are on the top row and left column. The possible genotypes of the offspring are shown in the boxes. **Dominant genes** are given capital letters. The dominant gene determines what trait will be present in the offspring. In this case, "tallness" is dominant. In the above example, both TT and Tt offspring will display the tall trait, but tt offspring will display the **recessive trait**. In humans, blue eyes are recessive. For a child to have blue eyes, she would have to receive the "blue eyes" gene from both parents.

6. EVOLUTION

Evolution is the process of change through time. In the nineteenth century, **Charles Darwin** devised a theory of evolution that was based on **natural selection** and **variation**. Darwin's theory of evolution goes like this: Genetic variation is inherited from parents and passed on through the generations. If certain genes produce traits that make an organism more suited to its environment, those traits will become more common in a population.

Different species may evolve if small groups become separated from the rest of the population. Darwin discovered this process while observing birds on different islands. Natural selection, in short, can be summarized as "only the strong survive" or "survival of the fittest."

Evolutionary biologists use tree models to represent the relationship between different organisms. A tree model shows the relationship between individuals in a population or between groups of organisms. For example, this tree model shows the relationship between fungi, plants, and animals. DNA analysis has revealed that fungi and animals are more closely related to each other than they are to plants and algae.

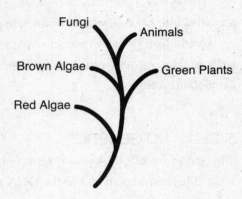

7. ECOLOGY AND ENERGY FLOW

Almost all energy on Earth comes from the sun. Green plants and algae are **producers** of energy. They trap the sun's radiant energy and use it to produce organic compounds. Some of these compounds provide chemical energy for the plants; others are used in cell growth. Because they supply their own food, plants are known as **autotrophs** (*auto* is the Greek word for self). Animals are **consumers** of energy and are known as **heterotrophs** (*hetero* is the Greek word for other).

A **food web** is a diagram that shows the nutritional relationship among species. Producers are at the bottom of the web, herbivores are in the middle, and carnivores are at the top. Some energy is lost at each step, or **trophic level**, so there are always fewer consumers than there are producers.

An **energy pyramid** is used to show the reduced energy at the top of the food chain. The population size of top-level consumers, such as carnivores, is smaller than the population size of producers. The size of a population that a particular environment can support is known as the **carrying capacity**.

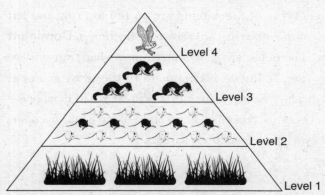

PRACTICE SET: LIFE SCIENCE I: LIFE ON OUR PLANET

Directions: Choose the <u>one best answer</u> to each question.

1. Figure A shows the normal growth curve of an organism. Figure B shows the growth curve of a similar organism of the same genus. The organism in Figure B must have some differences, because even though they are related, they do grow at different rates. Figure C is a single growth medium of an equal mixture of the organisms in figures A and B. Note that all three graphs are examples of scattergrams. The line drawn for each graph shows the closest fit for all points on each graph.

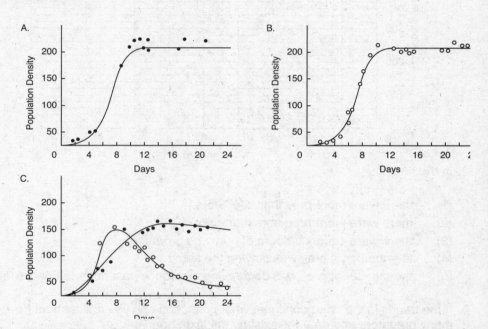

According to Figure C, which organism is more likely to survive, given more time?

(1)   Organisms A and B will survive at the same rate, after 16 days.

(2)   Organisms A and B will survive at the same rate, after 8 days.

(3)   Organism A will be more likely to survive because it is larger.

(4)   Organism A will be more likely to survive because it multiplies faster.

(5)   Organism A will probably survive because of the noted decline of organism B.

Questions 2 and 3 refer to the following passage and chart.

The chart below lists the activity of certain predators and prey in a given area. There are many ways in which predators and their prey interact. If there are no predators, then the prey will multiply in greater and greater numbers. If the predators have no limiting factors of their own (such as predators of predators), the predators will consume all of the prey and eventually go hungry.

THE

GED

INTRODUCTION

REVIEW OF
COMPREHENSION
STRATEGIES

PHYSICAL SCIENCE

LIFE SCIENCE I:
LIFE ON OUR
PLANET

LIFE SCIENCE II:
HUMAN BODY
SYSTEMS

EARTH AND SPACE
SCIENCE

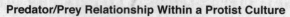

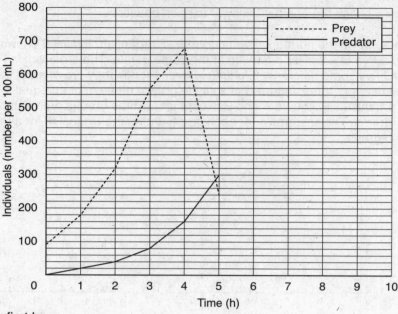

Predator/Prey Relationship Within a Protist Culture

2. In the first hour,

(1)   there were more prey than predators.
(2)   there were more predators than prey.
(3)   there were equal numbers of prey and predators.
(4)   the number of prey was staying the same.
(5)   the number of prey was decreasing due to the vast numbers of predators.

3. If the trends in the chart continue, what prediction can you make about how many predators and prey will exist by the sixth hour?

(1)   There will be more prey than predators.
(2)   There will be an equal number of predators and prey.
(3)   There will be about 300 predators and 0 prey.
(4)   There will be about 420 predators and 0 prey.
(5)   There will be about 100 predators, because the prey will not exist.

4. Plants primarily need only sunlight, carbon dioxide found in the air, and water to grow. However, plant efficiency and reproduction require certain trace elements to thrive. Vines grow on trees because their "trunks" are too weak to support tall growth. The vine uses the sturdy trunk of the tree to grow closer to the sunlight and to avoid being blocked by other leaves seeking direct sunlight. Many plants also need nitrogen to grow. But pure nitrogen must be converted into ammonia by bacteria or other means before the plants can use it.

In a plant community, the community's survival depends on the availability of which of the following elements?

(1)   nitrogen
(2)   helium
(3)   ammonia
(4)   calcium
(5)   sodium

5. The figure below is the matrix of a Punnett square, which shows the results of a pea plant with green pods (GG) crossed with a pea plant with yellow pods (gg).

What is the most likely phenotypic ratio of possible plants produced from this cross?

  (1)   1:1
  (2)   2:1
  (3)   3:1
  (4)   4:0
  (5)   4:1

Check your answers on page 234. If you missed many of the questions, review Life on Our Planet topics. If you have a good grasp of the topics, move on to the next rung.

THE
GED

LIFE SCIENCE II: HUMAN BODY SYSTEMS

A part of life science, this rung covers the form and function of the human body. Human body systems are the circulatory, skeletal, nervous, respiratory, excretory, muscular, digestive, endocrine, and reproductive systems. There are 11 topics commonly tested in the GED.

1. EPITHELIAL TISSUE

Epithelial tissue covers the outside of the body and lines the organs and cavities within the body. Sheets of tightly packed cells form the tissue.

2. DIGESTIVE SYSTEM

Like other animals, we depend on a regular supply of food from other organisms. The digestive system, which includes the mouth, esophagus, stomach, and intestines, is essential to human nutrition. It breaks down food into molecules that are small enough for the body to absorb.

3. CIRCULATORY SYSTEM

The circulatory system includes the heart, veins, arteries, and capillaries. These vessels and organs transport fluids and chemicals throughout the body. Arteries carry blood away from the heart. Veins carry blood from body tissues back to the heart.

4. RESPIRATORY SYSTEM

When we breathe, oxygen-rich air is transported to our lungs. From the lungs, oxygen is absorbed into the circulatory system and transported around the body. Oxygen is essential to converting the chemical energy in food into cellular energy.

5. IMMUNE SYSTEM

The immune system defends the body against unwelcome intruders, or pathogens, such as bacteria and viruses. White blood cells and the human lymphatic system work together to respond to these threats.

6. EXCRETORY SYSTEM

The excretory system regulates the internal environment of the body. The kidney plays an essential role in removing excess nitrogen, a toxic by-product of cellular metabolism.

7. ENDOCRINE SYSTEM

The endocrine system controls chemical communication within the body. The chemical signals used by the systems are called hormones. Although the circulatory system transports hormones throughout the body, only target cells respond to the signals. Endocrinologists, scientists who study these chemicals, have identified more than 50 hormones in the human body.

8. NERVOUS SYSTEM

Like the endocrine system, the nervous system controls communication in the body. The central nervous system consists of the brain and spinal cord. The nervous system processes sensory input, such as touch and sight, and sends messages for cells to respond to this input. The autonomic nervous system controls organs such as the heart.

The brain is responsible for regulating the conscious activities of the body, as well as many of the unconscious activities. The cerebrum is the largest part of the brain, controlling language, sensory perception, and motor control. The cerebellum coordinates muscular activity. The medulla, or brain stem, regulates automatic activities, such as the heartbeat and breathing.

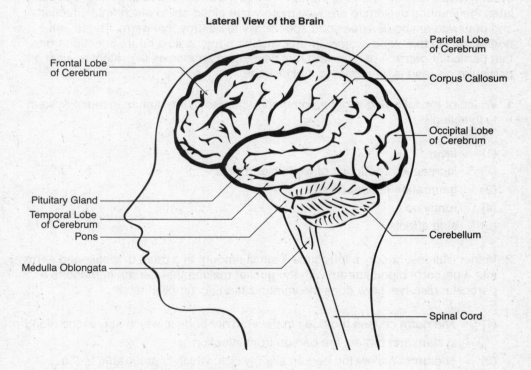

Lateral View of the Brain

Frontal Lobe of Cerebrum

Parietal Lobe of Cerebrum

Corpus Callosum

Occipital Lobe of Cerebrum

Pituitary Gland
Temporal Lobe of Cerebrum
Pons

Cerebellum

Medulla Oblongata

Spinal Cord

9. REPRODUCTIVE SYSTEM

The human reproductive system has internal and external reproductive organs. Sperm production occurs in the male gonads, or testes. Eggs are stored in the female gonads, or ovaries.

10. SKELETAL SYSTEM

The skeletal system is composed of bones, which provide support and protection for the body. Bones are also essential for locomotion.

THE
GED

CHAPTER

5

SCIENCE

THE
GED

INTRODUCTION

REVIEW OF
COMPREHENSION
STRATEGIES

PHYSICAL SCIENCE

LIFE SCIENCE I:
LIFE ON OUR
PLANET

LIFE SCIENCE II:
HUMAN BODY
SYSTEMS

EARTH AND SPACE
SCIENCE

11. MUSCULAR SYSTEM

In the muscular system, muscles contract and pull against the skeleton to move the body. Visceral and cardiac muscles are involuntary, controlled by the autonomic nervous system.

Some of the questions on human body systems involve information you may have learned through experience. Now try the practice set to assess your knowledge of human body systems, the food pyramid, and nutrition.

PRACTICE SET: LIFE SCIENCE II: HUMAN BODY SYSTEMS

Directions: Choose the one best answer to each question.

Questions 1 and 2 refer to the following passage.

When viruses or bacteria—what we generally call "germs"—invade a human body, infection occurs. The presence and activity of the germs produces unpleasant side effects, such as sore throat or pain. The body's immune system responds to the presence of invading germs in a variety of ways. Fever is one common immune response. A rise in body temperature can make conditions unfavorable to germs. Common symptoms of infection, such as a runny nose or nausea, are also immune system responses designed to protect the body. The presence of germs also stimulates the immune system to produce more white blood cells, which fight infection, and generate antibodies designed specifically to destroy that germ. These antibodies stay in the blood system, protecting the body against future infection from that particular germ. A person who has developed antibodies to protect against a particular disease is "immune" to that disease.

1. Which of the following is not a common response of the human immune system to infection?

    (1) fever
    (2) increased production of white blood cells
    (3) generation of antibodies
    (4) runny nose
    (5) side effects

2. Immunizations, or shots, introduce a small amount of a dead or weakened germ into a person's blood stream with the goal of making that person immune to a particular disease. How does the immunization accomplish this?

    (1) The germ causes the body to develop antibodies, which stay in the blood system and protect the person from infection.
    (2) The germ makes the person slightly sick, which is preferable to the extreme illness he or she would experience if not immunized.
    (3) The dead or weakened germs in the shot are modified to make them capable of fighting off other germs.
    (4) White blood cells surround the germs and create a barrier to future infection.
    (5) The immunization causes a fever, which makes conditions in the body unfavorable to germs.

Question 3 through 5 refer to the following figure and passage.

Nutrition Facts	**Nutrition Facts**	**Nutrition Facts**	**Nutrition Facts**
Serving Size 1 package Serving Per Container 1	Serving Size 1 package Serving Per Container 1	Serving Size 1 package Serving Per Container 1	Serving Size 1 package Serving Per Container 1
Amount Per Serving **Calories** 50 Calories from Fat 18	**Amount Per Serving** **Calories** 140 Calories from Fat 60	**Amount Per Serving** **Calories** 150 Calories from Fat 90	**Amount Per Serving** **Calories** 150 Calories from Fat 81
% Daily Value **Total Fat** 2g 3%	% Daily Value **Total Fat** 7g 11%	% Daily Value **Total Fat** 10g 10%	% Daily Value **Total Fat** 9g 14%
Saturated Fat 1.5g 7%	Saturated Fat 1.5g 7%	Saturated Fat 2.5g 14%	Saturated Fat 2.5g 13%
Cholesterol less than 30mg 10%	**Cholesterol** 5mg 2%	**Cholesterol** 30mg 18%	**Cholesterol** 2mg 1%
Sodium 750mg 31%	**Sodium** 170mg 7%	**Sodium** 120mg 5%	**Sodium** 24mg 1%
Total Carbohydrate 9g 10%	**Total Carbohydrate** 18g 8%	**Total Carbohydrate** 15g 5%	**Total Carbohydrate** 16g 5%
Dietary Fiber 1g 0%	Dietary Fiber 1g 4%	Dietary Fiber 1g 4%	Dietary Fiber 0g 0%
Sugars 1g	Sugars less than 1g	Sugars 0g	Sugars less than 1g
Protein 2g	**Protein** 2g	**Protein** 2g	**Protein** 2g
Vitamin A 2% • Vitamin C 0% Calcium 4% • Iron 2%	Vitamin A 0% • Vitamin C 0% Calcium 2% • Iron 2%	Vitamin A 0% • Vitamin C 10% Calcium 2% • Iron 2%	Vitamin A 0% • Vitamin C 0% Calcium 2% • Iron 0%
A	B	C	D

This figure shows informational data required on all publicly sold food products in the United States. This information must be displayed in the same way on all food containers so that the consumer can compare the contents of different brands.

3. Which of the following brands would be the wisest choice for a person who was told by her physician to cut back on salt?

   (1)   A
   (2)   B
   (3)   C
   (4)   D
   (5)   A through D

4. If you had diabetes and your doctor told you to limit your sugar consumption, which of the products shown in labels A through D should you choose to eat?

   (1)   A
   (2)   B
   (3)   C
   (4)   D
   (5)   A through D

5. According to the nutrition facts shown on the labels, what is the amount of cholesterol a person may consume during a normal day?

   (1)   5 milligrams
   (2)   30 milligrams
   (3)   less than 300 milligrams
   (4)   more than 320 milligrams
   (5)   more than 400 milligrams

Check your answers on page 235. If you answered most of the questions correctly, go on to the next rung. If you missed most of the questions, review human body systems.

THE
GED

EARTH AND SPACE SCIENCE

Earth science is the study of the geology of our planet and the reactions between the **biotic** (living) and **abiotic** (nonliving) systems. Questions on the GED test may include the structure of the earth, the changing earth, weather and climate, and the earth's resources.

Space science looks outward, beyond the atmosphere, to the solar system and the rest of the universe. There are six topics commonly tested on the GED:

1. GEOLOGIC TIMELINE

The history of the earth is often shown in a timeline from the formation of the planet, about 4.6 billion years ago, until the present day. You don't need to memorize this timeline, but it helps to be familiar with its format. There are four major eras:

a. **Precambrian**, when the earth was formed and life emerged.
b. **Paleozoic**, when life diversified into numerous complex forms. The first land plants emerged at this time.
c. **Mesozoic**, when the first mammals and birds arose and dinosaurs went extinct.
d. **Cenozoic**, the present time period when mammals became abundant and civilization began.

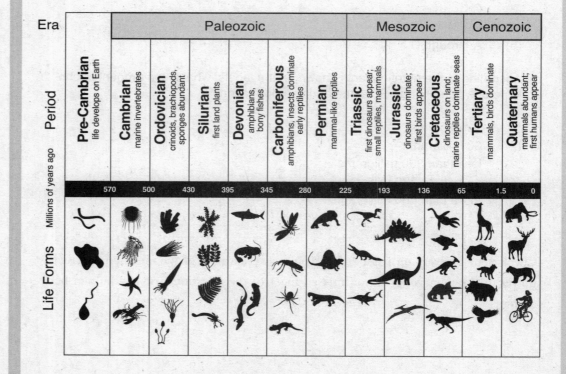

2. PLATE TECTONICS AND CONTINENTAL DRIFT

In 1915, Alfred Wegner suggested that the continents drift across the earth's surface. He proposed that all the continents were once joined together in a giant supercontinent, which he called **Pangaea**.

Earth and space science questions make up roughly **20 percent** of the GED Science test.

Wegner's idea was criticized and then ignored, in part because he did not have a mechanism to explain the movement of the continents. It wasn't until the 1960s that American geophysicist Harry Hess proposed that new crust is pushed up at midocean ridges. The new crust pushes the sea floor toward the continents. At continental margins, there are **subduction zones**, where the sea floor is pushed back into the earth's mantle. Volcanoes form along these subduction zones. Wegner's and Hess's work became part of the **theory of plate tectonics**.

Fossil evidence supports the theory that the continents were once joined together in a supercontinent. The same types of ancient land plants and animals have been found in Africa, Australia, Antarctica, and South America.

3. THE CHANGING EARTH

Large-scale motion of the continents is very slow, occurring at a pace that extends well beyond the lifespan of humans. Yet there are processes that change the earth around us in much shorter periods of time.

Volcanoes and earthquakes often occur where two tectonic plates meet. Volcanoes may occur along subduction zones, where an oceanic plate slides below a continental plate. Earthquakes can occur wherever two plates meet, with the earth moving along a fault line.

Weathering and **erosion** can also cause changes on Earth. The sun, wind, rain, ice, and even living things can break down rocks, causing weathering. Mechanical weathering occurs when rocks are broken down but remain essentially unchanged. Chemical weathering occurs when certain minerals in rocks are dissolved, for example, by the acidity of rainwater. Plants can also cause weathering; for example, tree roots can expand the cracks in rocks.

Erosion is the wearing away of soil and rock by water, wind, or glacial ice. From the Latin *erosus,* "to eat away," erosion usually takes place gradually. But human activities, such as the clear-cutting of forests, can enhance erosion, causing soils to be washed away.

4. THE WORLD'S CLIMATES

A **climate** is a region of the earth with specified weather conditions. Climate is mostly determined by the power of the sunlight an area receives and the movement of Earth through space. Because of the tilt of the earth, only the tropics receive sunlight at a 90° angle. (The tropics are located around the equator between 23.5° north and

23.5° south latitudes.) As a result, they receive the most solar energy and the least seasonal variation in sunlight of all of the earth's regions.

Precipitation, such as rain and snow, and **temperature** are also important factors in determining climate. The weather conditions on land are often influenced by the ocean. Ocean currents can carry heat from the tropics to colder areas closer to the poles. The **Gulf Stream**, for example, brings warm Caribbean temperatures north to the countries of Europe.

5. THE SOLAR SYSTEM

The solar system consists of nine planets that orbit the sun. The earth is the third planet from the sun.

The Planets at a Glance

Planet	Diameter (km)	Distance from sun (km)	Temperature	Length of Day	Length of Year	Number of Moons
Mercury	4,878	57.9 million	−180C to 430C	58.7 days	88 days	0
Venus	12,102	108.2 million	480C	243 days	224.7 days	0
Earth	12,756	149.6 million	−70C to 55C	23.93 hours	365.25 days	1
Mars	6,786	227.9 million	−120C to 25C	24.62 hours	687 days	2
Jupiter	142,984	778.3 million	−150C	9.84 hours	11.86 years	61
Saturn	120,536	1,427 million	−180C	10.23 hours	29.46 years	30
Uranus	51,118	2,871 million	−210C	17.9 hours	84 years	24
Neptune	49,528	4,497 million	−220C	19.2 hours	164.8 years	11
Pluto	2,300	5,913.5 million	−230C	6.38 days	248.5 years	1

The strength of the pull of gravity is different on each planet. Bigger planets, such as Jupiter, have greater gravitational pull than smaller planets, such as Mercury. Thus, you would weigh more on Jupiter than on Mercury. Remember, the greater the mass of an object, the stronger its gravitational pull. That is why Jupiter exerts a stronger gravitational force than Earth does.

6. THE BIG BANG THEORY

Many astronomers believe that the universe began 10 to 15 billion years ago, following an explosion at a single point. There is a lot of evidence to support the idea of a cosmic explosion. For example, American astronomer Edwin Hubble deduced that distant galaxies are moving away from the center of the universe, indicating that the effects of the explosion are still felt today. Cosmic radiation is also found throughout the universe. It is believed to be the glow left over from the explosion.

PRACTICE SET: EARTH SCIENCE

Directions: Choose the one best answer to each question.

Question 1 refers to the following passage and to Mohs Scale of Hardness.

Minerals are the building blocks of the study of geology. All rocks are composed of several minerals. Some of the physical properties of minerals are color, size, shape, and hardness. Mohs scale of hardness is shown below. The softer the mineral, the lower the number on the scale. The mineral that can scratch another is the harder mineral. A steel file has a hardness of 6.5, and glass has a hardness of 5.5. A fingernail has a hardness of about 2.

Mohs Scale of Hardness

Mineral	Hardness	Mineral	Hardness
Talc	1	Feldspar	6
Gypsum	2	Quartz	7
Calcite	3	Topaz	8
Fluorite	4	Corundum	9
Apatite	5	Diamond	10

1. Glass has a hardness of 5.5 on the Mohs scale. How can you be sure that the ring you bought is a real diamond and not glass?

   (1)   You should make a tiny scratch on the diamond with the glass. If the glass scratches the diamond, the diamond is real.
   (2)   You should make a tiny scratch on the glass with the diamond. If the diamond scratches the glass, the diamond is real.
   (3)   You should count the facets of the diamond. If the diamond has 52 facets, it is genuine.
   (4)   You should hit the diamond with a hammer on a steel surface. If the ring remains intact, the diamond is real.
   (5)   You should weigh the diamond. If the mineral is heavy, it is diamond.

2. A map projection is a flat map that represents all or part of the earth's surface. There are three types of map projections: a Mercator projection is made by wrapping a piece of paper into a tube around a globe. A polar projection is made by holding a flat piece of paper to one pole of a globe. A conic projection is made by folding a piece of paper into a cone and placing it on a globe so that the apex of the cone is directly over a pole, and the edge of the cone is parallel to the equator.

   Of the three types of map projections, which best describes a standard city map?

   (1)   Standard city maps combine polar projection and conic projection maps.
   (2)   Standard city maps are a type of conic projection map.
   (3)   Standard city maps are a type of polar projection map.
   (4)   Standard city maps are a type of Mercator projection map.
   (5)   Standard city maps are a type of globe.

THE
GED

Questions 3 and 4 refer to the following paragraph and map.

This is a map used to locate and track hurricanes during hurricane season. Latitude and longitude are always measured from the approximate center or "eye" of the hurricane. Latitude is measured east and west from the zero line, or prime meridian, which is established as going through Greenwich, England. Latitude lines are measured in degrees west of Greenwich until 180 degrees is reached on the other side of the world. This is called the International Date Line. Points east of Greenwich are also measured in degrees until the International Date Line is reached at 180 degrees east. Longitude is measured in degrees north and south of the equator, which is the zero line. The North Pole is 90 degrees north longitude.

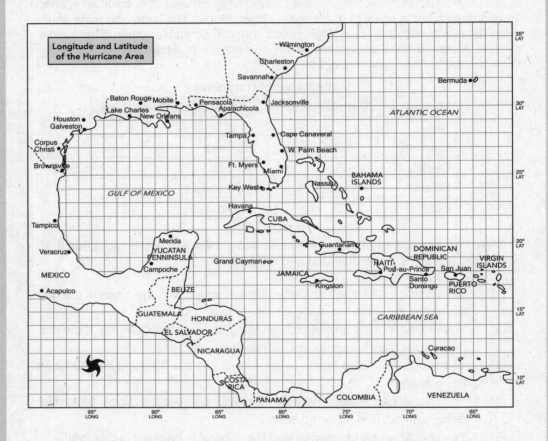

Longitude and Latitude of the Hurricane Area

3. The symbol for a Pacific hurricane is shown off the coast of southern Mexico. What is the exact location of the symbol?

(1)   11 degrees north and 95 degrees west
(2)   11 degrees west and 95 degrees north
(3)   11 degrees east and negative 95 degrees south
(4)   11 degrees south and 95 degrees east
(5)   12 degrees south and negative 95 degrees east

4. Which city is closest to the coordinates 29 degrees north and 96 degrees west?

(1)   Baton Rouge
(2)   Lake Charles
(3)   Jacksonville
(4)   Miami
(5)   Houston

Check your answers on page 236. If you answered most of the questions correctly, you can be confident that you can answer these types of questions on the Science test.

Congratulations! You have completed the ladder, and you are now well prepared to handle the different areas of science. Remember that you do not have to memorize all the facts and definitions that we have reviewed. You just want to be familiar with them so you are comfortable with the terms and definitions when you see them on test day. So, rest easy and approach the test with confidence. You're ready!

CHAPTER

5

SCIENCE

THE
GED

ANSWERS AND
EXPLANATIONS

SCIENCE EXPLANATIONS

PRACTICE SET: REVIEW COMPREHENSION STRATEGIES

1. (4)   There are more species of organisms on larger islands than on smaller islands.

Scattergrams help us see connections between two things or events. Here, the scattergram is designed to show whether there is a relationship between island size and the number of species present. Remember your scattergram technique: look for a general pattern. On this chart, there is a general rise upward to the right. This shows that as island size increases, so does the number of species. Answer (4) is correct. You might accidentally pick (3) or (5) if you read the labels on the chart incorrectly. Always make sure you know what is represented on the chart. Answers (1) and (2) don't have anything to do with connections or correlations. They are incorrect.
🄷 Life Science

2. (5)   The earth's atmosphere contains less oxygen today than it did 500 million years ago.

The correct answer is (5), because the graph slopes downward from point B, which was about a billion years ago. Answer (1) is incorrect, because the graph shows a gradual rise in atmospheric oxygen over thousands of millions of years. Answer (2) is incorrect, because points A and B are one and a half billion years apart. You can also eliminate answer (3), because the graph is heading downward, which indicates a decrease of oxygen. Answer (4) is also incorrect, because the graph shows a large rise and then a fall in the oxygen content in the earth's atmosphere.
🄷 Earth and Space Science

3. (5)   This graph does not address the reason for the rise in deaths.

Answer (5) is correct. The graph only shows data related to the number of deaths due to infectious and noninfectious diseases. The causes for the rise in deaths are a topic for a different graph. Although answers (1) through (4) may have some basis in fact, there is no evidence in the graph to support these statements.   🄷   Life Science II

CHAPTER

5

SCIENCE

THE
GED

ANSWERS AND
EXPLANATIONS

4.   (2)   They would stop orbiting the sun.

This is a basic comprehension question. You are asked to demonstrate that you understand the passage. To tackle it, first make sure you understand what the question is asking for: the result of the absence of gravity on the orbit of the planets. Scan the passage for references to "orbits" or "planets" and see what you find. If you read all the way to the end of the passage, you will see the last sentence says that the sun's gravitational pull keeps the planets in orbit. Get rid of the gravitational pull, and the planets will stop spinning around the sun. So, answer (2) is correct. There is nothing in the passage about gravity or the lack of gravity causing explosions, so (1) is incorrect. Temperature is not mentioned in the passage either, so you can eliminate answer (4). Answer (3) may be a theoretical possibility, but it isn't supported by the passage. The absence of a pull would not cause speed of any attracted object to increase, so answer (5) is also incorrect.   **Earth and Space Science**

5.   (4)   People would be able to jump much higher.

This is an application question. You need to take what you have just learned about gravity and apply it to a specific situation. As always, first make sure you know what information the question is looking for. Here, you need to figure out what would happen if the earth's mass were cut in half. Look in the passage for clues. Is there any information about mass and its relationship to gravity that might help you? Sentence three says that greater mass leads to stronger gravity. Sentence one tells us gravity is what keeps us on the ground. Let's put those facts together. If the mass of Earth were reduced, its gravitational pull would be reduced too, right? If the force that keeps us on the ground were reduced, what might happen? Let's look at the answer choices. Would we be crushed? No. Answer (1) is out. Would everything fly off the ground? No again. Gravity would be reduced, but not eliminated entirely. Eliminate answer (2). Would it be harder to throw a ball? No. In fact, with less gravity to pull the ball back to the ground, it would probably be easier, so answer (3) is wrong. Would people be able to jump higher? Yes, they would. With less gravity to pull them down, people would be able to leap higher. Answer (4) is right. Answer (5) is unrelated to the question.   **Earth and Space Science**

PRACTICE SET: PHYSICAL SCIENCE

1.   (3)   sodium and chlorine

This question tests whether you can take information from the passage and apply it to reading the chart. The question asks about combining elements. Scan the passage for information about combining elements, and you will find, in sentence three, that if elements are in columns that are far apart from each other, they are more likely to be able to combine to form a molecule. Answer (3) contains elements in columns that are far apart, so those elements will readily combine. Answers (1) and (5) are incorrect, because hydrogen, lithium, and sodium are in the same column. Elements in the same column rarely, if ever, can be made to combine. Answers (2) and (4) are incorrect, because the two elements are in adjacent columns and such elements rarely, if ever, can be made to combine.   **Atoms and Elements**

2.   (1)   The wavelength decreases.

This question tests your chart-reading skill. It's a fairly complicated chart. Take the time to sort through it carefully, and you will find that answer (1) is correct. As you move from right to left on the frequency scale, the numbers become larger. As you move from right to left on the wavelength scale, the numbers become smaller. By increasing the frequency, you decrease the wavelength. Answer (3) is incorrect, because the wavelength does change as the frequency changes. Answers (4) and (5) should be eliminated, because the height of the wave is independent of the frequency and the wavelength. In visible light, the frequency and wavelength govern the color of light, and the amplitude governs the intensity of the light.   Waves

3.   (3)   1,000 meters

According to the figure, a skyscraper can be 10^3 m tall, which equals 1,000 meters, so answer (3) is correct. Looking along the wavelength line, note that the units are meters. Answers (1), (2), (4) and (5) simply test your ability to work in the metric system and are incorrect.   Waves

4.   (5)   Bacteria and visible light waves are about the same size.

Answer (5) is correct. Answer (1) is wrong, because viruses are smaller than visible light waves. Viruses cannot be seen by conventional light microscopes, so answer (2) is wrong. The electron microscope does not use visible light to function. As seen in the figure, X-rays and gamma rays are even shorter than visible light waves, so eliminate answer (3). Bacteria are larger than viruses, but not much larger than visible light waves, making answer (4) incorrect.   Waves

5.   (2)   the visible light wave red.

This is an application, or "what-if", question. In question 2, you were asked to interpret what the chart implies about the relationship between frequency and wavelength. For this question, you must take that one step further. As frequency increases, wavelength decreases. If the frequency of an infrared ray decreased, therefore, its wavelength would increase. Look at the chart again. The ray with a frequency slightly higher than infrared is visible right light. Answer (2) is correct. If the frequency is increased, the wave becomes a red visible light wave. Answers (1) and (5) are incorrect, because the frequencies must pass through all of the spectral colors before becoming ultraviolet. Answer (3) occurs only if the frequencies are decreased, so this option should be eliminated. Answer (4) is incorrect, because the figure does not give information about TV signals, which are found on either side of the FM spectrum.   Waves

CHAPTER

5

SCIENCE

THE
GED

ANSWERS AND
EXPLANATIONS

CHAPTER

5

SCIENCE

THE
GED

ANSWERS AND
EXPLANATIONS

PRACTICE SET:
LIFE SCIENCE I: LIFE ON OUR PLANET

1.   (3)   29 centimeters

This question tests your ability to read the chart accurately and supply required information. Option (3) is correct. No branch longer than 29 centimeters had tomatoes on it. Option (1) is incorrect, because several branches measured longer than 22 centimeters. Option (2) can be eliminated. Although this branch length had the most tomatoes, it was not the longest branch. Make sure you know what the question is asking for. Option (4) is incorrect, because there is no branch measuring 30 centimeters. Option (5) is incorrect, because there were no branches measuring longer than 29 centimeters.  **Evolution**

2.   (1)   There were more prey than predators.

Answer (1) is correct. There are approximately 180 prey and 20 predators in the first hour. Answers (2) and (3) are incorrect, because the chart shows more prey than predators. The number of prey was increasing in the first hour, so answer (4) is incorrect. Answer (5) is also incorrect, because the numbers of prey and predators are rising in the first hour.  **Evolution**

3.   (4)   There will be about 420 predators and 0 prey.

Answer (4) is correct. According to the chart, there will be about 420 predators and no prey. Answer (1) is incorrect, because there will be more predators than prey. Answer (2) is incorrect, because prey and predators were about equal shortly before the fifth hour. Then the prey continued to decline, while the predators thrived. Answer (3) is incorrect, because there were 300 thriving predators in the fifth hour, even though the prey population was declining. Answer (5) is incorrect because, by extrapolation, there is no reason to suspect a sudden decline in predators . . . yet!  **Evolution**

4.   (1)   nitrogen

Answer (1) is correct: nitrogen is an essential element for plant survival. Answer (2) is incorrect, since living things have no critical need for this element. Answer (3) is incorrect, since ammonia is not an element. It is composed of the elements nitrogen and hydrogen. The chemical combination must be made by bacteria or other chemical means. Calcium is necessary for humans, but not for plants. So, answer (4) is also incorrect.  **Ecology and energy flow**

5.   (4)   4:0

The question asks for the phenotypic ratio, which refers to the outward appearance of the pea pods. All of them will be green pods even though some will be Gg and some GG. We are not interested in the genotype, so answer (4) is correct.  **DNA and genetics**

PRACTICE SET:
LIFE SCIENCE II: HUMAN BODY SYSTEMS

CHAPTER

5

SCIENCE

THE

GED

ANSWERS AND
EXPLANATIONS

1. **(5) side effects**
This question tests your ability to understand information in a passage. The question asks you to identify which choice is *not* an immune response. Read through the passage to locate mentions of immune responses. Sentence four mentions fever, so you can eliminate answer (1). Sentence six mentions runny nose as an immune response, so eliminate answer (4). Sentence seven mentions both white blood cells and antibodies, so answers (2) and (3) are out. You are left with (5), which isn't an immune response but a result of infection. ⊟ **Immune System**

2. **(1) The germ causes the body to develop antibodies, which stay in the blood system and protect the person from infection.**
You have to apply your understanding of the passage to answer this question. Review what the passage says about antibodies and immunity. If antibodies are already present in the body, ready to protect a person from a disease, then that person is immune. Antibodies form in response to the presence of a germ. We can conclude that the presence of a germ shot into the body in an immunization might also cause antibodies to develop. Answer (1) is correct. Answer (5) is somewhat attractive, because we know germs can cause fever and fever is an immune response. But fever by itself doesn't make people immune to anything, so (5) is not the best choice. Answers (2), (3), and (4) aren't supported by the passage. ⊟ **Immune System**

3. **(4) D**
You have to look for the label that shows the lowest sodium (salt) content. Answer is correct (4). ⊟ **Digestive System**

4. **(3) C**
This question requires you to know that people with diabetes avoid foods with sugar. Product C contains no sugar, and the others contain at least some sugar. Answer (3) is the best choice. ⊟ **Digestive System**

5. **(3) less than 300 milligrams**
To answer this question, you must find the amount of cholesterol and the percentage of the daily value given on each information sheet. Figures A and C state that 30 milligrams is 10% of the acceptable daily value. Thirty milligrams is 10% of 300 milligrams. The acceptable daily value would equal 300 milligrams. According to figure B, 5 milligrams is 2% of the acceptable daily value, and 250 milligrams would be another acceptable daily value. You can conclude that acceptable values may vary from 250 to 300 milligrams. Answer (3) is closest to that range. ⊟ **Digestive System**

CHAPTER

5

SCIENCE

THE
GED

ANSWERS AND
EXPLANATIONS

PRACTICE SET: EARTH AND SPACE SCIENCE

1.   (2)   You should make a tiny scratch on the glass with the diamond. If the diamond scratches the glass, the diamond is real.

Answer (2) is correct, because glass is softer than diamond and thus will be scratched by diamond. (Be careful not to do this with an expensive diamond, because the procedure will flaw the diamond if not done correctly.) Answer (1) is incorrect, because diamond will scratch glass, not the other way around. Answer (3) is also incorrect, because any stone may be faceted by a geologist to have 52 facets. Diamond is hard, but quite brittle, and will shatter when hit with a hammer, so eliminate answer (4). There is no item with which to compare the diamond, so weighing it will tell you its weight and nothing else, thus, you can rule out answer (5).

🄗 **Geologic Timeline**

2.   (4)   Standard city maps are a type of Mercator projection map.

Most of the landmass on Earth is between 60°N and 60°S, and for most purposes, the changes in accuracy as you go north and south of the equator can be corrected. The Mercator type of map best suits the creation of city maps. Answer (1) is incorrect, because all map projections belong to the three types listed. You can eliminate answer (2), because conic projections are most accurate at or near the poles, and there are not too many cities in these regions. Answer (3) is incorrect for the same reason. Polar projections are most accurate at or near the poles. Conic projections show areas, which are farther away from the poles too, a bit like looking at an area through binoculars (the polar projection) and then seeing the same area with your unaided eyes (conic projection). Answer (5) is incorrect, because a globe is not a map projection.   🄗 **The Changing Earth**

3.   (1)   11 degrees north and 95 degrees west

The hurricane is north of the equator and west of Greenwich, England, so answer (1) is correct. The map lists which numbers are the latitudes and which are the longitudes. Generally, the latitudes are listed first, and then the longitudes. The designations of north, south, east, and west must be listed, because the numbers repeat themselves above and below the equator, and right and left of the prime meridian (also called the Greenwich mean line). You can eliminate answers (3) and (5), because negative numbers are not used in specifying longitude and latitude.

🄗 **The World's Climates**

4.   (5)   Houston

Answer (5) is correct. Notice that with latitudes, the numbers increase as you go north from the equator, and then again as you go south from the equator. This is also true as you go west and east of the prime meridian. The location of the point 0 degrees north, 0 degrees west, is same point as 0 degrees south, 0 degrees east. It lies in the ocean below Liberia.   🄗 **The World's Climates**

CHAPTER

6

LANGUAGE ARTS, READING

LANGUAGE ARTS, READING

THE GED

Welcome to the Language Arts, Reading test. This test is one of the shortest on the GED, coming in at only 65 minutes. Best of all, it tests something you already know how to do: read! However, the Language Arts, Reading test measures not only how well you read but also how well you comprehend, interpret, and use what you read.

Let's get started. Here is your ladder for the Language Arts, Reading test:

Rung 1: Introduction
Rung 2: Summarizing
Rung 3: Main Ideas and Supporting Details
Rung 4: Theme and Point of View
Rung 5: Character and Motivation
Rung 6: Plot, Predictions, and Inferences
Rung 7: Figurative Language and Other Poetic Elements
Rung 8: Mood, Tone, and Style
Rung 9: Drawing Conclusions and Making Interpretations

Using the step-by-step ladder in this chapter, you can master all the skills you need to succeed on the Reading test. There are nine rungs in the ladder. Each section is designed as a single lesson. It's important to work through each rung, one at a time, to prepare yourself for all of the kinds of questions that appear on the Language Arts, Reading test. Each rung concludes with a set of practice questions. Answering these questions helps you to assess how prepared you are in each topic. If you answer most of the practice set questions correctly, you should move on to the next rung. Explanations to each practice set appear at the end of the chapter. Each rung builds on the rung before it. You can also go back and review previous lessons if you feel you need to improve in a particular area.

By the time you have reached the final rung, you will have the skills you need to interpret and draw conclusions in all the passages on the test, whether they are nonfiction, fiction, poetry, or drama.

INTRODUCTION

The Language Arts, Reading test is a one-part test that contains forty multiple-choice questions that you have 65 minutes to answer. These questions are designed to test your ability to comprehend and interpret passages of poetry, prose fiction, drama, and nonfiction. All of the information you need to answer the questions correctly is contained within the reading passages. Although it is helpful to read widely and practice your reading comprehension, you do not need to be familiar with specific works, authors, or literary themes in order to succeed on the Reading test.

QUICK OVERVIEW

Literary Texts (75% of each test)	Nonfiction Texts	Items	Time Limit
Selections may include: • poetry • drama • prose fiction before 1920 • prose fiction between 1920 and 1960 • prose fiction after 1960	Selections may include: • nonfiction prose • critical reviews of visual and performing arts • workplace and community documents	40 multiple-choice questions	65 minutes

THE PURPOSE QUESTION

The Language Arts, Reading test could seem a little tricky. Here's why: at the beginning of every reading passage on the test you will see what the test-writers call a "purpose question." That may not sound tricky, but it is a question you will never have to answer. Here's an example:

WAS IT THE BEST OF TIMES OR THE WORST OF TIMES?

It was the best of times, it was the worst of times, it was the age of wisdom, it was the age of foolishness, it was the epoch of belief, it was the epoch of incredulity, it was the season of Light, it was the season of Darkness, it was the Spring of hope, it was the winter of despair. . . (*continued*)

Four to eight multiple-choice questions will follow this passage and not one of them will ask, "Was it the best of times or the worst of times?" Strange, huh? The purpose question is given to help you focus on what is important in the reading passage and to provide a reason for reading the text. Don't let it confuse you. Think of the purpose question as a little hint.

In our example above, the purpose question tells you that you should pay attention to the description of the era that the book is describing. Is it a happy time or an unhappy time? Or is it both?

THE
GED

THE FOUR GENRES

As you saw earlier in the chart, the types of reading passages on the test fall under four main types, or "genres," of writing:

Nonfiction. Nonfiction is based on facts, real events, and real history. One of the nonfiction passages on the GED is always a business-related document, such as an excerpt from a letter, a government or legal document, or an employee or training handbook. These are the kinds of documents you may use in your everyday life. For example, you may see an excerpt on safety rules in the workplace.

Critical reviews of the visual and performing arts are another kind of nonfiction text that may be included on the Language Arts, Reading test. For example, you may be asked to read a review of a recently released movie.

Poetry. Poetry is a piece of writing characterized by combining elements of speech and song, and is written in distinctive style and rhythm. Formal poetry often uses elements such as meter, rhyme, stanza, and verse (we discuss these elements later in this chapter).

Drama. Drama passages are scenes or excerpts of plays. They may include tragedies or comedies. You may be asked to read dialogue as well as stage directions, which may provide important information about where the scene is set, how the characters are dressed or what they look like, and what actions the characters perform as they speak their lines. Remember to read *every part* of the passage.

Prose fiction. Prose fiction includes excerpts from short stories or novels that describe imaginary events and people. The writer may use a variety of techniques to tell a story or set a scene, including the use of distinctive language and writing style. The story may be told from any point of view and concern the lives of several characters. The Reading test includes prose fiction from three different eras: fiction written before 1920, fiction written between the years 1920 to 1960, and fiction written after 1960.

Each reading selection is fairly short, and many are entertaining. Each selection ranges from two hundred to four hundred words; poetry selections may be anywhere from eight to twenty-five lines. Each selection is followed by four to eight questions.

Now that you've got an idea of what the test looks like and what kinds of questions it presents, let's look at some strategies to help you read the passages and answer the questions.

Most GED questions feature nonfiction and prose fiction selections. Expect only two or three questions based on poetry and two or three on drama.

TEST-TAKING TIPS

Follow these steps as you answer each question on the Reading test:

STEP 1. READ THE PURPOSE QUESTION— USE IT TO GUIDE YOUR READING.

Remember that the question is a hint as to what to focus on in each passage. Don't let it confuse you. If the reading selection is from the book *Huckleberry Finn*, the purpose question might be, "How can a river change a boy's life?" The hint is that you need to focus on the river and the role it plays in the story.

STEP 2. READ THE TEXT FOR COMPREHENSION AND UNDERSTANDING.

As you read, ask yourself questions such as the following:

- What kind of writing is this?
- What is its purpose?
- What is taking place?
- What techniques does the author use to achieve his or her purpose?

Using Context Clues: If you run across an unfamiliar word, look at the words and phrases surrounding it for clues to its meaning. Even if you still can't figure out the precise meaning of the unfamiliar word, you can rely on these context clues to help you answer the questions.

In everyday life, you may read for pleasure and for information. They way you read a magazine, for example, is different from the way you read the instructions for hooking up your DVD player. On the GED test, you must use both strategies. First, read the text the way you would read directions to your DVD player. Then try rereading, this time focusing on how the writing makes you feel and the effect of the words.

STEP 3. READ EACH QUESTION AND ALL ANSWER CHOICES CAREFULLY.

This may sound simple, but all too often, test-takers read and fully understand the reading passage but move too quickly through the questions and miss key words that change the meaning of the question. Read carefully, and especially take note of the words *most likely*, *least likely*, *not*, *different*, *alike*, and *except*.

STEP 4. USE PROCESS OF ELIMINATION.

Here's where you can put strategies that you learned in Chapter 2, "Test-Taking Basics."

STEP 5. SKIM THE PASSAGE AS YOU ANSWER THE QUESTIONS.

Don't be afraid to skip between the passage and the question you are working on, skimming to find the best possible answer from the list of choices. Often, no mat-

CHAPTER
6

LANGUAGE
ARTS,
READING

THE
GED

CHAPTER

6

LANGUAGE
ARTS,
READING

THE
GED

ter how closely and carefully you read a selection, you simply won't remember a fact or line from the passage. If that happens, skim until you find what you need. This doesn't take too much time, and it can make a big difference.

STEP 6. CHECK YOUR ANSWER.

Sometimes, you may not be 100 percent sure that your answer is correct, so before moving on to the next reading selection, go back over your answers. An obvious point that you missed the first time may pop out the second time.

You should now have a good idea of the how the test is presented and the strategy needed to attack the Language Arts, Reading test. Let's go to the second rung of the ladder and explore the individual skills you need to conquer the test.

Tip: After you have answered all the questions on a given passage, check back over your other answers to make sure they are all correct. Sometimes, other questions on a passage help you uncover the correct answer to a different question.

SUMMARIZING

Summarizing is such a basic skill that you may not even be aware that you already practice it on a daily basis. When a friend asks what happened on your favorite television show, you give him or her a **summary**, or **synopsis**: "Letitia sang an old Motown song, and she was great. None of the other singers came close. The judges loved her and said she had the best voice they had ever heard." Or maybe you are recapping last night's basketball game: "It was a close game, but the Tarheels' best player fouled out just before overtime, and the Blue Devils won on a free throw." Perhaps you have just read a newspaper editorial and are explaining the gist of it: "The writer believes that the city should not construct a new power plant in the Garden Street neighborhood because it is so close to a public elementary school."

To summarize means to translate the major points of a passage of writing and put it into your own words. You do not, however, include your own opinions or interpretations when you summarize; you only restate what the author has written.

How do you decide what the main points of the passage are? One good strategy is to

Summarizing skills are helpful for all the reading passages on the test, including poetry, fiction, drama, and nonfiction.

Summary questions test your comprehension.

Good readers automatically summarize as they read, actively processing the reading material into usable information.

think like a news reporter. You must answer the six essential questions: Who? What? Where? Why? How? When?

Try out your summary skills on this quick practice exercise. Remember to read thoroughly and use your purpose question:

EXAMPLE

<u>Directions:</u> Read the following passage and choose the <u>one best answer</u> to the question.

<u>Question 1</u> refers to the following paragraph.

HOW DID CALAMITY JANE GET HER NAME?

It was during this campaign that I was christened Calamity Jane. It was on Goose Creek, Wyoming, where the town of Sheridan is now located. Capt. Egan was in command of the Post. We were ordered out to quell an uprising of the Indians, and were out for several days, had numerous skirmishes during which six of the soldiers were killed and several severely wounded. When on returning to the Post we were ambushed about a mile and a half from our destination. When fired upon Capt. Egan was shot. I was riding in advance and on hearing the firing turned in my saddle and saw the Captain reeling in his saddle as though about to fall. I turned my horse and galloped back with all haste to his side and got there in time to catch him as he was falling. I lifted him onto my horse in front of me and succeeded in getting him safely to the Fort. Capt. Egan on recovering, laughingly said: "I name you Calamity Jane, the heroine of the plains." I have borne that name up to the present time. (*Life and Adventures of Calamity Jane* by Marthy Cannary Burk)

Which of the following answers <u>best</u> summarizes the main points of this passage?

(1) Calamity Jane got her name in Wyoming, where Sheridan is now located.
(2) Capt. Egan was shot when fired upon.
(3) Calamity Jane got her name after rescuing the captain during an Indian skirmish.
(4) Calamity Jane would not have gotten her name if she had been wounded in the skirmish.
(5) Calamity Jane has borne her name up until the present time.

The correct answer is (3). Calamity Jane got her name after rescuing the Captain during an Indian skirmish. Answer (3) summarizes all of the main events that occur in the passage: the skirmish, the rescue of the wounded Captain, and the nicknaming of Calamity Jane. It also correctly restates how Jane got her nickname, which, by the way, answers the purpose question at the beginning of the passage. You can eliminate answers (1), (2), and (5) because these answers restate only some portions of the passage. Where Jane got her name

 Does the question ask you to summarize a passage? Look for key words in the question such as **summarize**, **restate**, **synopsis**, **main points**. A **synopsis** is the same thing as a **summary**. If a question asks you to restate what occurs in the passage or to provide a synopsis of its main points, you are being asked to summarize the passage.

CHAPTER

6

LANGUAGE
ARTS,
READING

THE
GED

is not the most important or memorable part of the passage. The fact that Capt. Egan is shot contributes to the naming of Jane, but it is not the most important part of the passage, either. Similarly, answer (5) summarizes part, but not all, of the passage. Answer (4) makes an inference; it does not summarize, so you can eliminate this answer, too.

Now that you see what is involved, try your summary skills on an actual practice set, using the following nonfiction passage:

PRACTICE SET: SUMMARIZING

<u>Directions:</u> Choose the <u>one best answer</u> to each question.

<u>Questions 1 and 2</u> refer to the following paragraphs.

WHAT IS THE PREGNANCY DISCRIMINATION ACT?

The Pregnancy Discrimination Act is an amendment to *Title VII of the Civil Rights Act of 1964*. Discrimination on the basis of pregnancy, childbirth, or related medical conditions constitutes unlawful sex discrimination under Title VII, which covers employers with 15 or more employees, including state and local governments. Title VII also applies to employment agencies and to labor organizations, as well as to the federal government. Women who are pregnant or affected by related conditions must be treated in the same manner as other applicants or employees with similar abilities or limitations.

Title VII's pregnancy-related protections include:

• Hiring
An employer cannot refuse to hire a pregnant woman because of her pregnancy, because of a pregnancy-related condition, or because of the prejudices of co-workers, clients, or customers.

• Pregnancy and Maternity Leave
An employer may not single out pregnancy-related conditions for special procedures to determine an employee's ability to work. However, if an employer requires its employees to submit a doctor's statement concerning their inability to work before granting leave or paying sick benefits, the employer may require employees affected by pregnancy-related conditions to submit such statements. If an employee is temporarily unable to perform her job due to pregnancy, the employer must treat her the same as any other temporarily disabled employee. For example, if the employer allows temporarily disabled employees to modify tasks, perform alternative assignments, or take disability leave or leave without pay, the employer also must allow an employee who is temporarily disabled due to pregnancy to do the same.

Pregnant employees must be permitted to work as long as they are able to perform their jobs. If an employee has been absent from work as a result of a pregnancy-related condition and recovers, her employer may not require her to remain on leave until the baby's birth. An employer also may not have a rule that prohibits an employee from returning to work for a predetermined length of time after childbirth. Employers must hold open a job for a pregnancy-related absence the same length of time that jobs are held open for employees on sick or disability leave.

1. Which of the following statements <u>best</u> summarizes this excerpt?

    (1)   Pregnant women have the same rights as working mothers.

    (2)   The Pregnancy Discrimination Act charges that discrimination on the basis of pregnancy, childbirth, or related medical conditions is unlawful sex discrimination.

    (3)   According to Title VII, it is unlawful for pregnant women to work.

    (4)   According to Title VII, pregnant women should remain on leave from their jobs for a period of nine months, with pay.

    (5)   The Civil Rights Act of 1964 did not originally provide protection for pregnant women.

2. Which of the following best answers a way that employers might treat a pregnant employee the same way that they would a temporarily disabled worker?

    (1)   Require the pregnant employee to remain on leave until the baby's birth.

    (2)   Prohibit the pregnant employee from working around customers.

    (3)   Excuse the pregnant employee from having to submit a doctor's note.

    (4)   Excuse the pregnant employee from collecting disability pay.

    (5)   Allow the pregnant employee to modify tasks.

You may check your answers and review the explanations on page 279. Once you're comfortable with summarizing pieces of writing, move on to the next rung.

MAIN IDEAS AND SUPPORTING DETAILS

The second-rung skill, summarizing, involved identifying and restating the major points of a passage. This rung looks at finding the main idea and supporting details. The **main idea** is the most important point or idea expressed in a paragraph or piece of writing. When you look for the main idea, you are narrowing your summary and showing that you understand the *most* important point the writer is making. **Supporting details** are sentences or additional information that further explain or help to clarify the main idea.

Main ideas can be contained anywhere in a passage: at the beginning, end, or middle of a paragraph. Nonfiction writers often state the main idea in a single sentence, which is called a **topic sentence**. Fiction writers are usually not so obvious.

Look at where the topic sentence occurs in the paragraph to see how the supporting details function. If the topic sentence is at the very beginning of a paragraph, then the supporting details follow, providing additional information to support the main idea. If the topic sentence falls at the end of the paragraph, it sums up the supporting details and information from the previous sentences of the paragraph. Typically, the main idea is a more *general* statement, and the supporting details provide *specific* information relating to the general statement.

Not all writers use traditional topic sentences. If you can't identify a strong topic sentence right away, you may have to do a bit of detective work and **infer** the **main idea** by putting together the supporting details yourself.

QUICK RECAP

Main Idea: The most important point or idea expressed in a paragraph or piece of writing.

Topic Sentence: Single sentence nonfiction writers often use to state the main idea.

Supporting Details: Sentences or additional information that further explains or clarifies the main idea.

Infer: To conclude information from several supporting details rather than from one topic sentence.

Let's put this knowledge into practice. Can you identify the main idea in the following paragraph?

EXAMPLE

Of the three writing Brontë sisters, Emily was the most peculiar, with a guarded, difficult personality that many took to be rude. Reclusive and nontalkative, she attended to her chores with a dutiful, stoic nature. Pale-complexioned with eyes that appeared gray, she dressed oddly, choosing dramatic purple fabric with lightning bolt patterns to sew her dresses. Her delights were secret and private. She loved animals: her bull mastiff Keeper was never far from her side. She could often be found baking her famous bread, meanwhile studying German or scribbling at her poems and plays. Only while roaming the moors did she become truly alive, revealing her inner, free-spirited nature, running among the streams and rocks for hours, no matter the weather or season. In fact, during the brief times she spent away from Haworth, at school in Brussels with Charlotte as a young woman, she became homesick and physically ill.

The main idea in the above paragraph is directly stated in the first sentence, which is the topic sentence: "Of the three writing Brontë sisters, Emily was the most peculiar, with a guarded, difficult personality that many took to be rude." The first sentence introduces the main idea: that Emily Brontë was the most peculiar of her sisters and had a difficult personality. The sentences in the rest of the paragraph, such as "Pale-complexioned with eyes that appeared gray, she dressed oddly, choosing dramatic purple fabric with lightning bolt patterns to sew her dresses," provide supporting details that further clarify the main idea.

Now that you see what is involved, try finding the main idea on an actual practice set, using the following nonfiction passage:

PRACTICE SET: MAIN IDEA AND SUPPORTING DETAILS

Directions:

Questions 1 through 3 refer to the following paragraphs.

Based on the following excerpt, choose the one best answer to each question.

WHAT IS THE ESSENCE OF THE CITY OF MIAMI?

The Miami on display in the Orange Bowl that Sunday afternoon would have seemed another Miami altogether, one with less weather and harder, more American surfaces, but by dinner we were slipping back into the tropical: in a virtually empty restaurant on top of a virtually empty condominium off Biscayne Boulevard, with six people at the table, one of whom was Gene Miller and one of whom was Martin Dardis, who as the chief investigator for the state attorney's office had led Carl Bernstein on through the local angles on Watergate. . . . [W]e sat and we talked and we watched a storm break over Biscayne Bay. Sheets of warm rain washed down the big windows. Lightning began to fork somewhere around Bal Harbour. Gene Miller mentioned the Alberto Duque trial, then entering its fourth week at the federal courthouse, the biggest bank fraud case ever tried in the United States. Martin Dardis mentioned the ESM Government Securities collapse, just then breaking into a fraud case maybe bigger than the Duque.

The lightning was no longer forking now but illuminating the entire sky, flashing a dead strobe white, turning the bay fluorescent and the islands black, as if in negative. I sat and I listened to Gene Miller and Martin Dardis discuss these old and new turns in the underwater narrative and I watched the lightning backlight the

islands. During the time I had spent in Miami many people had mentioned, always as something extraordinary, something I should have seen if I wanted to understand Miami, the Surrounded Islands project executed in Biscayne Bay in 1983 by the Bulgarian artist Christo. Surrounded Islands, which had involved surrounding eleven islands with two-hundred-foot petals, or skirts, of pink polypropylene fabric, had been mentioned both by people who were knowledgeable about conceptual art and by people who had not before heard and could not then recall the name of the man who had surrounded the islands. All had agreed. It seemed that the pink had shimmered in the water. It seemed that the pink had kept changing color, fading and reemerging with the movement of the water and the clouds and the sun and the night lights. It seemed that this period when the pink was in the water had for many people exactly defined, as the backlit islands and the fluorescent water and the voices at the table were that night defining for me, Miami. (Joan Didion, "Miami")

1. Which of the following answers <u>best</u> summarizes the purpose of this passage?

  (1)   Describe and define an art project in Miami.
  (2)   Convince the audience to become knowledgeable about conceptual art.
  (3)   Describe a lightning storm in Miami.
  (4)   Describe and define the nature of Miami.
  (5)   Describe connections between a fraud case and an art project in Miami.

2. Which of the following best states the central idea of this excerpt?

  (1)   The essence of Miami exists in fleeting moments, like those created by the lightning storm and the Surrounded Islands project.
  (2)   The Bulgarian artist Christo once surrounded Biscayne Bay with pink, two-hundred-foot petals.
  (3)   The ESM Government Securities collapse would maybe replace the Alberto Duque trial as the biggest fraud case tried in the United States.
  (4)   The essence of Miami can be expressed by major fraud cases, such as the Alberto Duque trial.
  (5)   The essence of Miami can be characterized by harder, more American surfaces, like the Orange Bowl.

3. Which of the following is a detail that further supports the main idea of this excerpt?

  (1)   Sheets of warm rain washed down the big windows.
  (2)   Gene Miller mentioned the Alberto Duque trial, then entering its fourth week at the federal courthouse.
  (3)   It seemed that the pink had kept changing color, fading and reemerging with the movement of the water and the clouds and the sun and the night lights.
  (4)   The Miami on display in the Orange Bowl that Sunday afternoon would have seemed another Miami altogether.
  (5)   People could not recall the name of the man who created Surrounded Islands.

You may check your answers and review the explanations on pages 279–280. In addition to summarizing, you have now learned how to identify main ideas and supporting details. Let's move to the next rung: Theme and Point of View.

THEME AND POINT OF VIEW

A **theme** is the central idea in a piece of writing: it is the meaning the writer is trying to convey or a question the author raises. A theme is *similar to* a life lesson, or a **moral**, like the kind of morals contained in fables and fairy tales. An example of a moral is found in the fable. "The Tortoise and the Hare": the moral or lesson of that story, of course, is "Slow and steady wins the race."

Unlike morals, themes do not give such explicit and direct life lessons. A theme does not instruct the reader in proper behavior. Themes are generally not stated *directly* in the writing. Often, you must infer themes.

The theme also differs from the *subject*, or topic, of a work of writing. When you look for the theme, you must decide what it is the author is saying about that subject. For example, a poem may take "love" as its subject. The theme of the poem would be the idea or meaning that the poet is trying to convey *about* the subject of love. For example, the theme could be "Love is complicated and difficult, but also wonderful and desirable."

Questions regarding theme may be worded in ways such as the following:

- Which of the following answers <u>best</u> describes the theme of this passage?
- Which of the following answers <u>best</u> expresses the central idea of this excerpt?

Let's put our understanding of theme into practice. Read the following passage and answer the following question:

EXAMPLE

<u>Directions:</u> Choose the <u>one best answer</u> to each question.

<u>Question 1</u> refers to the following passage.

<u>Background:</u> Ten years ago, Mathilde Loisel borrowed a beautiful diamond necklace from her wealthy friend Madame Forester to wear to a fancy ball. She lost the necklace, but was afraid to tell Madame Forester this. Instead, Mathilde went to a jeweler and purchased an identical necklace and returned the new necklace to her friend. It was so expensive that it took Mathilde and her husband ten years to pay the debt to the jeweler.

WHAT WOULD HAVE HAPPENED IF MATHILDE HAD TOLD THE TRUTH?

But sometimes, when her husband was at the office, she sat down by the window and she thought of that evening long ago, of that ball, where she had been so beautiful and so admired.

What would have happened if she had not lost that necklace? Who knows? Who knows? How singular life is, how changeable! What a little thing it takes to save you or to lose you.

Then, one Sunday, as she was taking a turn in the Champs Elysées, as a recreation after the labors of the week, she perceived suddenly a woman walking with a child. It was Mme. Forester, still young, still beautiful, still seductive.

Mme. Loisel felt moved. Should she speak to her? Yes, certainly. And now that she had paid up, she would tell her all. Why not?

She drew near.

"Good morning, Jeanne."

The other did not recognize her, astonished to be hailed thus familiarly by this woman of the people. She hesitated—

"But—madam—I don't know—are you not making a mistake?"

"No. I am Mathilde Loisel."

Her friend gave a cry—

"Oh!—My poor Mathilde, how you are changed."

"Yes, I have had hard days since I saw you, and many troubles,—and that because of you."

"Of me?—How so?"

"You remember that diamond necklace that you lent me to go to the ball at the Ministry?"

"Yes. And then?"

"Well, I lost it."

"How can that be?—since you brought it back to me?"

"I brought you back another just like it. And now for ten years we have been paying for it. You will understand that it was not easy for us, who had nothing. At last, it is done, and I am mighty glad."

Mme. Forester had guessed.

"You say that you bought a diamond necklace to replace mine?"

"Yes. You did not notice it, even, did you? They were exactly alike?"

And she smiled with proud and naïve joy.

Mme. Forester, much moved, took her by both hands:—

"Oh, my poor Mathilde. But mine were false. At most they were worth five hundred francs!"

(Guy de Maupassant, "The Necklace")

1. Based on what you have read in the previous passage, which of the following answers best describes the theme?

(1)   Honesty vs. lying
(2)   How singular life is, how changeable!
(3)   Beware of false jewels.
(4)   One small lie can completely change one's life.
(5)   A life of hard work ages a woman considerably.

The best answer is (4): One small lie can completely change one's life. Again, remember to use your purpose question as a clue to answering the other questions on the test. If Mathilde had been honest and confessed that she lost the necklace at the time, she would have had to spend only five hundred francs to replace it, and she would have saved herself and her husband ten years of poverty and hard work to repay the jeweler's debt.

Answer (1) is not correct because it mentions only abstract ideas, but it does not describe what the author is trying to say about those ideas. Answer (2) is a quote from the text. Although it is a good observation, it is not as specific as (4) because it does not mention that a life is changeable. Answer (3) may be good advice for Mathilde, but it misses the point, because Mathilde's real lesson is that honesty is important. Answer (5) may be true in Mathilde's case, but again, that is not the life lesson she needs to learn here; it is simply something she suffers as part of the result of telling a lie.

POINT OF VIEW

Point of view is the narrator's position in relation to the story. By selecting different points of view, the writer can choose a particular perspective on his or her story.

The narrator is the person or persons telling the story. Remember that the narrator does not necessarily represent the author, even if the text is written in the "I voice," or first person. The narrator is also not necessarily the same person as the main character of the piece (we discuss this distinction further in the next rung).

Types of Point of View

First person, or the "I voice": Single narrator, or in the case of a "we voice," multiple narrators, such as the collective voice of a community. Limited to the thoughts and experiences of the narrator telling the story. Examples: "From the moment I moved to Rockville, I knew I was different from everyone else." OR "We knew in our hearts Dr. Ortiz would make Timmy walk again."

Second person, or the "You voice": This is the least common point of view in literature. Works written in the second person are limited to the thoughts and experiences of the "you." Example: "You walk into the diner, and all eyes are upon you. Frantically, you look around for a place to hide."

Third-person close or third-person limited: Tells the narrative from a perspective that is not fully aware of the thoughts and experiences of all the characters. Generally, this perspective focuses on the experiences of a single character, usually, but not always, the main character. Example: "Emily was livid. She suspected that Marcus was lying, that he was indeed having an affair, and he didn't have the guts to tell her the truth."

Third-person omniscient: The all-knowing narrator who observes and comments on everything. Example: "All the houses on Shady Lane were dark and quiet, except one. Marcus slouched in the living room, pretending to watch television, trying to decide how to tell Emily the truth. Emily didn't care. She already suspected the truth. She was upstairs, packing her bags. She'd been ready to leave for years."

As you can see, each point of view has its particular strengths as well as its limitations. The first-person point of view is used when an author wishes to write in the character's words, to make an immediate personal connection with the audience. But beware! First-person narrators may only be telling the truth as they see it, or they may be lying to you altogether. Authors often use first-person narratives when they wish to tell a story through a slightly unreliable point of view.

When reading a first-person narrative, ask, To whom is the character speaking? Why is the character telling this story? The answers to these questions may clue you in to whether the character is telling the truth. Sometimes, the fact that the character does not know everything that is going on is what makes the story interesting, funny, or moving.

The third-person omniscient point of view is often used in stories and novels in which the author wishes to describe the inner lives of several characters. Third-person close perspective is used when an author wants to limit what the reader knows

THE
GED

about the inner lives of all the characters, but at the same time provide a point of view that may be expressed in language that is slightly different than the character's own written and spoken speech.

Let's examine the following excerpt with an eye on point of view.

EXAMPLE

Directions: Choose the one best answer to each question.

Questions 1 and 2 refer to the following passage.

WHAT IS SNOW?

At school we had air-raid drills: an ominous bell would go off and we'd file into the hall, fall to the floor, cover our heads with our coats, and imagine our hair falling out, the bones in our arms going soft. At home, Mami and my sisters and I said a rosary for world peace. I heard a new vocabulary: *nuclear bomb, radioactive fallout, bomb shelter.* Sister Zoe explained how it would happen. She drew a picture of a mushroom on the blackboard and dotted a flurry of chalkmarks for the dusty fallout that would kill us all.

The months grew cold, November, December. It was dark when I got up in the morning, frosty when I followed my breath to school. One morning as I sat at my desk daydreaming out the window, I saw dots in the air like the ones Sister Zoe had drawn—random at first, then lots and lots. I shrieked, "Bomb! Bomb!" Sister Zoe jerked around, her full black skirt ballooning as she hurried to my side. A few girls began to cry.

But then Sister Zoe's shocked look faded. "Why, Yolanda dear, that's snow!" She laughed. "Snow."

"Snow," I repeated. I looked out the window warily. All my life I had heard about the white crystals that fell out of American skies in the winter. From my desk I watched the fine powder dust the sidewalk and parked cars below. Each flake was different, Sister Zoe said, like a person, irreplaceable and beautiful. (Julia Alvarez, "Snow")

1. Which of the following best summarizes what happens in the story?

   (1)   Yolanda moves to America.
   (2)   Yolanda prays for world peace at night and goes to school during the day.
   (3)   Yolanda has been hearing so much about bombs that she mistakes snow for nuclear fallout.
   (4)   Sister Zoe and the other students laugh at Yolanda for thinking that snow is nuclear fallout.
   (5)   Yolanda must learn not to daydream in school.

2. Which best describes a reason why the author might have chosen to write the story from Yolanda's point of view?

   (1)   She is a girl.
   (2)   She is Catholic.
   (3)   She has never seen snow.
   (4)   She is living during air-raid drills.
   (5)   Both (3) and (4).

1. The best answer is (3). Yolanda has been hearing so much about bombs that she mistakes snow for nuclear fallout (summarizing). Yolanda does move to America, as it says in answer (1), but this is only part of what happens in the story, so this is not the best answer. Answer (2) also mentions only part of the story. Answer (4) is only partially correct because the story does not mention the other students laughing. Answer (5) is an opinion, not a synopsis. Answer (3), however, correctly summarizes all of the main events of the story and is therefore the best answer.

2. If Yolanda had been a boy, the story would probably not have changed a great deal, so you can eliminate answer (1). Although the fact that Yolanda is a Catholic plays into part of the story (saying the rosary at night), this does not have a major effect on the main events of the story, so answer (2) is not the best answer. Answer (3) does have an effect on the main event of the story because if Yolanda had seen snow before, she would not have mistaken it for nuclear fallout and thus there would be no story. Answer (4) also seems likely because the fact that Yolanda is living during air-raid drills makes her paranoid and worried about the possibility of being bombed in America. Answers (3) and (4) <u>both</u> affect the story's outcome, so answer (5), which combines them, is best.

When you are ready, move ahead to the fourth-rung practice set.

PRACTICE SET: THEME AND POINT OF VIEW

<u>Directions:</u> Choose the <u>one best answer</u> to each question.

<u>Questions 1 through 3</u> refer to the following passage.

WHAT HAPPENS WHEN A MAN LEAVES HIS FAMILIAR SURROUNDINGS?

When a man journeys into a far country, he must be prepared to forget many of the things he has learned, and to acquire such customs as are inherent with existence in the new land; he must abandon the old ideals and the old gods, and oftentimes he must reverse the very codes by which his conduct has hitherto been shaped. To those who have the protean faculty of adaptability, the novelty of such change may even be a source of pleasure; but to those who happen to be hardened to the ruts in which they were created, the pressure of the altered environment is unbearable, and they chafe in body and in spirit under the new restrictions which they do not understand. This chafing is bound to act and react, producing diverse evils and leading to various misfortunes. It were better for the man who cannot fit himself to the new groove to return to his own country; if he delay too long, he will surely die.

The man who turns his back upon the comforts of an elder civilization, to face the savage youth, the primordial simplicity of the North, may estimate success at an inverse ratio to the quantity and quality of his hopelessly fixed habits. He will soon discover, if he be a fit candidate, that the material habits are the less important. The exchange of such things as a dainty menu for rough fare, of the stiff leather shoe for the soft, shapeless moccasin, of the feather bed for a couch in the snow, is after all a very easy matter. But his pinch will come in learning properly to shape his mind's attitude toward all things, and especially toward his fellow man. For the courtesies of ordinary life, he must substitute unselfishness, forbearance, and tolerance. Thus, and thus only, can he gain that pearl of great price—true comradeship. He must not say 'thank you'; he must mean it without opening his mouth, and prove it by responding in kind. In short, he must substitute the deed for the word, the spirit for the letter. (Jack London, "In a Far Country")

1. Which of the following statements best expresses the theme of this excerpt?

   (1)   When a man travels to a distant land, he must be ready to forget old
          habits and ways of thinking, and adapt to the rituals of a new place.
   (2)   When a man travels to a far country, he must hold on to material habits.
   (3)   Those traveling to far countries should beware of diverse evils and various
          misfortunes.
   (4)   A man journeying to far lands must keep with him his ideals and manners.
   (5)   It is important to journey to far lands, but always return to one's own
          country.

2. According to the excerpt, what is the most difficult thing about adjusting to life in
   a vastly different place from one's own familiar surroundings?

   (1)   eating rough fare
   (2)   living in the wild
   (3)   facing diverse evils and possible misfortunes
   (4)   changing one's attitude toward one's fellow man
   (5)   facing the savage youth and the primordial simplicity of the North

3. What is most likely meant by the last sentence of this excerpt: "In short, he must
   substitute the deed for the word, the spirit for the letter"?

   (1)   One should embrace the courtesies of ordinary life.
   (2)   Actions speak louder than words.
   (3)   The pearl of great price is true comradeship.
   (4)   Men must practice unselfishness and tolerance.
   (5)   One must not get caught up in hopelessly fixed habits.

You may check your answers and review the explanations on pages 280–281. Once
you are satisfied that you understand theme and point of view, move on to the next
rung of the ladder: Character and Motivation.

CHARACTER AND MOTIVATION

CHARACTER

Characters in fiction and drama are the people in the play, story, or novel. The main character is known as the **protagonist**, and the main conflict of the story or drama centers on this character.

Remember, the protagonist is not necessarily the **narrator** of the story. The narrator is the character who tells the story. For instance, in F. Scott Fitzgerald's novel *The Great Gatsby*, Gatsby is the protagonist, but the character Nick Carraway tells the story. Nick is the narrator.

Questions regarding character may be worded in ways such as the following:

- Which of the following phrases <u>best</u> describes Lear?
- Which of the following words <u>best</u> describes the way Jake feels toward Brett?
- Which description <u>best</u> describes the relationship between Madame Bovary and Charles?

We get to know a character by observing:

- What the character says and does (dialogue and actions).
- How other characters respond to and talk about this character.
- How the author or narrator describes the character.
- What the character is thinking.

Different genres give us different types of insight into characters. When reading a play, for example, we do not get to know what a character is thinking. We only know what the character says he or she is thinking. It is also important to remember that characters, like real people, are often not reliable. A character may very likely say one thing, but mean something else altogether.

QUICK RECAP

Characters: The people in the play, story, or novel.
Protagonist: The main character in a theatrical or fictional work. The central conflict of the fiction or drama centers on the protagonist.
Narrator: The character who tells the story. The reader experiences the story through the eyes of the narrator. There can be many different narrators in a story or drama.

CHAPTER

6

LANGUAGE
ARTS,
READING

INTRODUCTION

SUMMARIZING

MAIN IDEAS AND
SUPPORTING
DETAILS

THEME AND
POINT OF VIEW

CHARACTER AND
MOTIVATION

PLOT, PREDICTIONS,
AND INFERENCES

FIGURATIVE
LANGUAGE AND
OTHER POETIC
ELEMENTS

MOOD, TONE,
AND STYLE

DRAWING
CONCLUSIONS
AND MAKING
INTERPRETATIONS

COMPARISON AND CONTRAST OF CHARACTERS

Another way to understand a character is to examine him or her in relation to the other characters in the work. Comparing means identifying and showing how two or more separate things are alike. Contrasting means highlighting the differences between two or more separate things. Comparing and contrasting are skills that can help you on the Language Arts, Reading test when you answer questions about characters in fiction and plays.

Questions regarding comparison and contrast may be worded in ways such as the following:

- In which of the following ways are Rupal and Shemeem alike?
- According to this author, what is one of the major differences between New York and Los Angeles?
- Based on the information in this passage, how does Operation Desert Storm compare to the Vietnam War?
- How does Li's situation differ from Raoul's in this excerpt?

Let's look at a passage that clearly illustrates the comparison and contrast of characters, from the Grimm tale "Snow-White and Rose-Red."

EXAMPLE

There was once a poor widow who lived in a lonely cottage. In front of the cottage was a garden wherein stood two rose-trees, one of which bore white and the other red roses. She had two children who were like the two rose-trees, and one was called Snow-white and the other Rose-red. They were as good and happy, as busy and cheerful, as ever two children in the world were, only Snow-white was more quiet and gentle than Rose-red. Rose-red liked better to run about in the meadows and fields seeking flowers and catching butterflies; but Snow-white sat at home with her mother, and helped her with her house-work, or read to her when there was nothing to do. ("Snow-White and Rose-Red," Jacob and Wilhelm Grimm)

If you were asked to compare Snow-white and Rose-red, you would look for answers that list ways in which the two characters are similar: "good and happy, busy and cheerful." If you were asked to contrast Snow-white and Rose-red, you would look for answers that list ways in which the two characters differ from one another: "Snow-white is more gentle and quiet than Rose-red"; "Rose-red liked to run outside in the fields, but Snow-white preferred to stay at home with her mother."

MOTIVATION

Motivation is the reason that characters do and say the things they do. Most of the questions about character motivation concern drama passages on the Language Arts, Reading test, but you may also be asked to answer motivation questions on fiction passages as well.

Questions regarding motivation may be worded in ways such as the following:
- Why is Mr. Franklin upset?
- Which of the following is the *most likely* reason that Haruki lied to Jun?

Answering questions about character motivation requires a bit of detective work. If you were investigating a murder case, for example, you would have to find a suspect's motive for committing the crime. You would closely examine the suspect's past whereabouts, actions, and quotes in order to determine a motive.

Similarly, when looking for clues to what motivates a character to behave a certain way, you examine what the character says and does.

Test your skills in understanding character, comparing and contrasting, and determining character motivation on the following practice set.

PRACTICE SET: CHARACTER AND MOTIVATION

Directions: Choose the one best answer to each question.

Questions 1 through 4 refer to the following passage.

Background: In the following scene from the Eugene O'Neill play *Anna Christie*, Anna has just met Marthy at "Johnny-the-Priest's," a bar near the waterfront in New York City. The two women do not know one another. The stage directions tell us that Anna is a woman of 20, and Marthy is in her 40s or 50s. When the scene begins, Marthy has just advised Anna that she may have had one too many drinks.

WHY IS ANNA AT THE NEW YORK WATERFRONT?

ANNA—[After a moment's hesitation.] Guess you're right. I got to meet someone, too. But my nerves is on edge after that rotten trip.
MARTHY—Yuh said yuh was just outa the hospital?
ANNA—Two weeks ago. [Leaning over to MARTHY confidentially.] The joint I was in out in St. Paul got raided. That was the start. The judge give all us girls thirty days. The others didn't seem to mind being in the cooler much. Some of 'em was used to it. But me, I couldn't stand it. It got my goat right—couldn't eat or sleep or nothing. I never could stand being caged up nowheres. I got good and sick and they had to send me to the hospital. It was nice there. I was sorry to leave it, honest!
MARTHY—[After a slight pause.] Did yuh say yuh got to meet someone here?
ANNA—Yes. Oh, not what you mean. It's my Old Man I got to meet. Honest! It's funny, too. I ain't seen him since I was a kid—don't even know what he looks like—yust had a letter every now and then. This was always the only address he give me to write him back. He's yanitor of some building here now—used to be a sailor.
MARTHY—[Astonished.] Janitor!
ANNA—Sure. And I was thinking maybe, seeing he ain't never done a thing for me in my life, he might be willing to stake me to a room and eats till I get rested up. [Wearily.] Gee, I sure need that rest! I'm knocked out. [Then resignedly.] But I ain't expecting much from him. Give you a kick when you're down, that's what all men do. [With sudden passion.] Men, I hate 'em—all of 'em! And I don't expect he'll turn out no better than the rest. [Then with sudden interest.] Say, do you hang out around this dump much?
MARTHY—Oh, off and on.
ANNA—Then maybe you know him—my Old Man—or at least seen him?
MARTHY—It ain't old Chris, is it?
ANNA—Old Chris?
MARTHY—Chris Christopherson, his full name is.
ANNA—[Excitedly.] Yes, that's him! Anna Christopherson—that's my real name— only out there I called myself Anna Christie. So you know him, eh?
MARTHY—[Evasively.] Seen him about for years.

THE
GED

1. Based on the dialogue in this scene, which answer best describes Anna's character?

    (1)   sensible and even-tempered
    (2)   excitable and talkative
    (3)   hesitant and evasive
    (4)   good-natured and kind
    (5)   willful and stubborn

2. Which of the following reveals the most about Anna's character?

    (1)   what she thinks
    (2)   her actions
    (3)   what other say about her
    (4)   how others react to her
    (5)   what she says

3. Which answer best describes Anna's reason for coming to the waterfront?

    (1)   to have a few drinks at Johnny-the-Priest's
    (2)   no meet up with her friend Marthy
    (3)   to find a husband because she is all alone
    (4)   to try to find her father because she has nowhere to turn
    (5)   to "get rested up"

4. Why does Anna have mixed feelings about the man she is trying to find?

    (1)   He is a sailor.
    (2)   He is a janitor.
    (3)   He has never done anything for her.
    (4)   He will probably send her back to jail.
    (5)   He knows Marthy.

Review the answers and explanations on pages 281–282. If you are satisfied with your performance, go on to the next rung. If you didn't do as well as you hoped, review the lesson before moving on.

Now, with five rungs under your belt, you are halfway to the top. Let's tackle the sixth rung, Plot, Predictions, and Inferences.

PLOT, PREDICTIONS, AND INFERENCES

Every work of fiction or drama must have **conflict** in order to build an interesting, believable story. For example, a character may be in disagreement with her mother, or a character may attempt to revolt against his government.

The **plot** is the arrangement of events through which the conflict of the story is resolved. Every plot has a beginning, middle, and end. In the beginning, the basic setting, characters, and conflicts are introduced. In the middle, the conflict continues to unfold and evolve as new events take place, and perhaps additional characters and conflicts are introduced. In the end, the major conflicts reach a climax and are generally resolved in some way.

You already know how to identify the major points of a plot because you have learned to summarize the main points and events of a piece of writing in the second rung. Some of the Language Arts, Reading questions relating to plot simply test your ability to comprehend what is taking place in an excerpt from a piece of writing.

Other plot-related questions may ask you to apply your comprehension of the passage and make an **inference**. As you know from the previous rung, making an inference is a skill you rely on when information is not directly stated or when you do not have all the necessary information and must decide or determine something based only on the information you have.

The types of inference questions on the GED test generally fall under the categories of determining **cause-and-effect** and making **predictions**.

CAUSE AND EFFECT

Cause-and-effect questions measure your ability to determine how one event in a story causes another event to occur. Cause-and-effect questions are very similar to questions on character motivation, which you just learned to answer in the rung before this one.

Questions regarding cause-and-effect may be worded in ways such as the following:

- Based on the excerpt, what causes the mill to burn down?
- Which answer *best* describes what happened as a result of Larry's visit?

Let's look at how motivation and cause-and-effect questions are closely related.

CHAPTER

LANGUAGE
ARTS,
READING

THE
GED

EXAMPLE

<u>Directions:</u> Read the following passage and answer the questions below.

<u>Questions 1 and 2</u> refer to the following paragraphs.

Background: In the following passage, Joe and Bobby are construction workers who must cut plywood wings to secure the sides of the manlift at the worksite. Frank is an elevator operator who assists them with the work. McCann is the foreman.

WHY CAN'T JOE, BOBBY, AND FRANK ALL WORK TOGETHER?

Though he was already working fast, the pieces Joe had hung weren't secured well. Bobby wished he didn't have to say anything.

"I know how much you want to get on steady, Joe," he said as kindly as he could, "but we still got a few hours today. Let's work together. If we don't work together, we're down the road together."

"This is how I work," Joe replied, though he directed his words to Frank, who had stopped the lift to watch. "When I was a kid I worked at a hotel. I carried all the luggage I could and I would still hold the elevator doors open for the people I was helping. When we got to their room I'd make sure they had clean glasses and towels and if they didn't I'd rush out to get them whatever it was without them asking. I'd get them anything they'd ask for and I did it as quickly as I could. That's because that's how I learned how to do things. That's how I was raised."

Frank nodded his head. Bobby didn't think he'd be able to say anything to him the rest of the day. Bobby and Frank went down for the other plywood rippings and the foreman, McCann, already displeased about the railing, came back up with them. He shook the plywood wing Joe had put up and said that it was no good, it wasn't how he wanted it, and then he explained again. McCann walked across the silver Robinson-decking and took the stairs back down. Joe got more than quiet. (Dagoberto Gelb, "Franklin Delano Roosevelt Was a Democrat")

1. Based on the excerpt, what happens as a result of Joe's work on the plywood rippings?

    (1)   Bobby, Joe, and Frank finish the job successfully.
    (2)   McCann reprimands Joe for his poor work.
    (3)   Joe is hired on permanently for steady work.
    (4)   Bobby feels that he can talk easily with Joe.
    (5)   Joe worked hard at a hotel when he was a kid.

2. What motivates Joe to work the way he does?

    (1)   He is hoping to get steady work at the construction site.
    (2)   He wants to win Bobby's friendship.
    (3)   He wants to win McCann's praise.
    (4)   He was raised to work quickly and hard.
    (5)   His work is no good.

Question 1. As you can see, motivation and cause and effect are very closely linked in this case. The correct answer for question 1 is (2), McCann reprimands Joe for his poor work. This is what occurs in the final paragraph as a result of Joe's work, when McCann appears displeased and shakes the plywood wing Joe has put up, saying it is no good. We can see that answer (1) is incorrect because the men do not finish the job to McCann's liking. Based on what we have read, answer (3) seems unlikely to happen. Answer (4) is also incorrect because Bobby tries twice to talk to Joe and thinks later that he probably won't be able to say anything to him the rest of the day. Answer (5) is not the correct answer: although it is true, according to the passage, that Joe worked hard at a hotel when he was a kid, this is what causes or motivates him to work the way he does. It is not the effect or end result or of Joe's work on the plywood rippings. Think of cause as "before the fact" and effects as "after the fact."

Question 2. The correct answer to question 2 is shown in the previous paragraph. It is, of course, answer (4), which explains Joe's background and sheds some insight on what motivates him as a character to do and say the things he does. It is also the cause of the main conflict in this brief excerpt. Therefore, cause and motivation function in almost identical ways in this passage. Answer (1) is incorrect because we cannot tell whether Joe wants steady work. He seems to ignore Bobby's advice and tries to work independently. He does not seem to care whether he is friends with anyone, so answer (2) cannot be the correct answer. The same holds true for answer (3), although after McCann gives Joe a talking-to in the last paragraph, Joe does seem clearly disappointed. Answer (5) is not a cause or motivation, but it is the result, or effect, of Joe's work performance.

PREDICTIONS

On the Language Arts, Reading test, you get to hone your fortune-telling skills when you make **predictions** based on the reading passages. Think of predictions as a close cousin to cause-and-effect questions. In cause-and-effect questions, you look at the text and identify how one part of the plot takes place as a result of a previous part of the plot. With prediction questions, you guess what *might* take place in the future based on the passage you have read.

Questions regarding predictions may be worded in ways such as the following:

- Based on the information in this passage, how will Nadine *probably* react to Mike on their date?
- Based on the excerpt, which of the following *best* describes what Mrs. Quimby is *most likely* to do next?

Hone your skills in assessing and analyzing plot in the following practice set.

CHAPTER

6

LANGUAGE
ARTS,
READING

THE
GED

PRACTICE SET: PLOT, PREDICTIONS, AND INFERENCES

Directions: Choose the one best answer to each question.

Questions 1 through 3 refer to the following passage.

Background: Asbury is a twenty-five-year-old man who says he is very sick and is coming home from New York to stay with his mother, Mrs. Fox, and his sister, Mary George.

WHY DOES ASBURY RETURN?

Mrs. Fox had pointed out that he was only twenty-five years old and Mary George had said that the age most people published something at was twenty-one, which made him exactly four years overdue. Mrs. Fox was not up on things like that but she suggested that he might be writing a very *long* book. Very long book, her eye, Mary George said, he would do well if he came up with so much as a poem. Mrs. Fox hoped it wasn't just going to be a poem.

She pulled the car into the side drive and a scattering of guineas exploded into the air and sailed screaming around the house. "Home again, home again, jiggity jig!" she said.

"Oh, God," Asbury groaned.

"The artist arrives at the gas chamber," Mary George said in her nasal voice.

He leaned on the door and got out, and forgetting his bags he moved toward the front of the house as if he were in a daze. His sister got out and stood by the car door, squinting at his bent unsteady figure. As she watched him go up the front steps, her mouth fell slack in her astonished face. "Why," she said, "there *is* something the matter with him. He looks a hundred years old."

"Didn't I tell you so?" her mother hissed. "Now you keep your mouth shut and let him alone."

He went into the house, pausing in the hall only long enough to see his pale broken face glare at him for an instant from the pier mirror. Holding on to the banister, he pulled himself up the steep stairs, across the landing and then up the shorter second flight and into his room, a large open airy room with a faded blue rug and white curtains freshly put up for his arrival. He looked at nothing, but fell face down on his own bed. (Flannery O'Connor, "The Enduring Chill")

1. What does Mary George learn about her brother in this excerpt?

    (1)   He is very self-centered.
    (2)   He has not yet published anything.
    (3)   He is very sarcastic toward his mother.
    (4)   He is all alone at twenty-five.
    (5)   He is actually sick.

2. What is Mary George most likely to do next, based on the excerpt?

    (1)   Regard her brother differently.
    (2)   Listen at his door to make sure he hasn't fallen.
    (3)   Ask him how his book is going.
    (4)   Tell her mother that Asbury is faking.
    (5)   Announce that she is ill.

3. Which of the following best characterizes the mother in this excerpt?

    (1)   caring; doting on her son
    (2)   absent; not aware what is happening with her son
    (3)   hopeful; pretending that everything is fine
    (4)   sarcastic; trading clever remarks with her daughter
    (5)   happy; content with herself and her family

You may check your answers and review the explanations on page 282. Ready to move on? Then proceed to the seventh rung, where we review figurative language and poetic elements.

FIGURATIVE LANGUAGE AND OTHER POETIC ELEMENTS

The Language Arts, Reading test does not ask you to uncover hidden or difficult meanings in the poems you read. You do not have to understand everything that is meant or intended in the poem. However, you do have to know something about the elements that make up a poem, such as rhyme, rhythm, and figurative language.

Figurative language is used by poets and writers to express ideas, impressions, and moods through analogy or comparison. You can expect the test to include figurative language such as symbolism and imagery, metaphor and simile, and personification.

You are not required to label examples of similes and metaphors on the GED test. However, you must be able to recognize the ways in which figurative language is used to create impressions or effects in poetry.

Figurative Language
Language that displays the imaginative and poetic use of words in such a way as to achieve some effect beyond literal meaning.

THE GED

IMAGE AND SYMBOL

An **image** is simply a mental picture or representation of an actual thing, described in such a way as to appeal to the senses of hearing, sight, taste, touch, and smell. In a literary work, an image of a hot, red sun might represent heat or summer.

If you see an image repeated more than once in a poem or other literary work, it should tell you that this image is being used as a symbol. Like an image, a **symbol** is a word or group of words that stands for itself but simultaneously represents another thought, idea, or impression.

In this excerpt from T. S. Eliot's long poem "The Waste Land," repeated images are used to suggest an overall impression:

What are the roots that clutch, what branches grow
Out of this stony rubbish? Son of man,
You cannot say, or guess, for you know only
A heap of broken images, where the sun beats,
And the dead tree gives no shelter, the cricket no relief,
And the dry stone no sound of water.

The accumulation of images such as "stony rubbish," "roots that clutch," "beating sun," "dead tree," and "dry stone" seem to represent a barren, dry, wasteland with no growth or life. You could say that these images symbolize death.

PERSONIFICATION

Personification is a kind of exaggerated figurative language in which the poet gives human qualities to animals, objects, or ideas in order to create an impression. An example of personification is, "The wind caressed their cheeks and whispered lullabies in their ears."

Of course, the wind did not literally whisper lullabies. The writer of this sentence wants to describe the wind as something motherly and gentle.

SIMILE AND METAPHOR

Similes and metaphors are the two major kinds of poetic figures of speech used on the Language Arts, Reading test. A **simile** is a comparison in which one thing is likened to another, using the words like or as. Examples are "I float like a butterfly," and "Matt is as tall as a flagpole."

A **metaphor**, however, is a representation in which one word or phrase represents something with which it is not usually associated; for example, "His smile was sunshine on a rainy day."

If the previous example had been a simile, the writer would have said, "His smile was like sunshine." In a metaphor, however, the writer says that the smile actually is sunshine, figuratively speaking.

Before going on to the poetic elements of rhyme and rhythm, let's review figurative language by reading and answering questions about the following poem.

EXAMPLE

Directions: Choose the <u>one best answer</u> to each question.

Questions 1 through 3 refer to the following passage.

WHAT IMPRESSIONS DOES THIS SPEAKER
HAVE OF THE CITY OF CHICAGO?

Chicago

Hog Butcher for the World,
Tool Maker, Stacker of Wheat,
Player with Railroads and the Nation's Freight Handler;
Stormy, husky, brawling,
City of the Big Shoulders:
They tell me you are wicked and I believe them, for I have seen your
    painted women under the gas lamps luring the farm boys.
And they tell me you are crooked and I answer: Yes, it is true I have
    seen the gunman kill and go free to kill again.
And they tell me you are brutal and my reply is: On the faces of women
    and children I have seen the marks of wanton hunger.
And having answered so I turn once more to those who sneer at this my
    city, and I give them back the sneer and say to them:
Come and show me another city with lifted head singing so proud to be
    alive and coarse and strong and cunning.
Flinging magnetic curses amid the toil of piling job on job, here is a tall
    bold slugger set vivid against the little soft cities;
Fierce as a dog with tongue lapping for action, cunning as a savage
    pitted against the wilderness,
Bareheaded,
Shoveling,
Wrecking,
Planning,
Building, breaking, rebuilding,
Under the smoke, dust all over his mouth, laughing with white teeth,
Under the terrible burden of destiny laughing as a young man laughs,
Laughing even as an ignorant fighter laughs who has never lost a battle,
Bragging and laughing that under his wrist is the pulse and under his
    ribs the heart of the people,
Laughing!
Laughing the stormy, husky, brawling laughter of Youth, half-naked,
    sweating, proud to be Hog Butcher, Tool Maker, Stacker of Wheat,
    Player with Railroads and Freight Handler to the Nation.
(Carl Sandburg, "Chicago")

1. Which of the following shows contrasting representations of Chicago that are
   used together in this poem?

   (1)   as a fierce dog and a cunning savage
   (2)   as a slugger and a little soft city
   (3)   as a young man and a burden of destiny
   (4)   as a fighter and a farm boy
   (5)   as the Nation's Freight Handler and a painted woman

THE
GED

2. What is likely meant by the lines "And they tell me you are brutal and my reply is: On the faces of women and children I have seen the marks of wanton hunger"?

(1)   Chicago is a tough city that allows its women and children to starve.
(2)   The hungry have made their marks on the women and children of Chicago.
(3)   The hungry are a brutal force in Chicago.
(4)   There are many hungry people in Chicago, and that is part of why it is so rough and proud.
(5)   The women and children live under a terrible burden of destiny.

3. What is the effect of the images of laughing in the final eight lines of the poem?

(1)   warm and funny
(2)   menacing and proud
(3)   flirtatious and dangerous
(4)   bragging, yet hard-working
(5)   cunning, yet innocent

1. Answer (1) is correct because it represents the only set of contrasting images used *together* in the poem. All of the other options combine images from very different parts of the poem and are therefore not the best answer.

2. Answer (1) is incorrect because the poet seems to have more complicated feelings about Chicago, a mixture of pride and fear, but he does not condemn the city. Answer (2) is too simple a statement, saying only that there are many hungry people in Chicago, but making no comment about this. Answer (3) can be ruled out because the hungry women and children are not described as brutal. Answer (5) suggests that the women and children live under a terrible burden of destiny, which may or may not be true, but that idea is nowhere in the two lines to which the question refers. This leaves us with Answer (4), and it is the best answer because it expresses the poet's conflicting feelings toward his city: that although people starve there, this gives the place a kind of rugged pride, roughness, and strength.

3. The idea of laughing is repeated in the poem's final eight lines. The images of laughing seem to represent a kind of doom: laughing in the face of imminent destruction, for example, as the "ignorant fighter" does who has never lost a fight. This then builds up to the prideful, stormy, husky, brawling laughter of Youth. Images of sweating, butchering, and fighting give the laughter a tough, menacing, and prideful connotation, so answer (2) is the best answer. The laughter is certainly not warm or funny, as answer (1) suggests, flirtatious as answer (3) suggests, or hard-working, cunning, or innocent, as some of the terms in answers (4) and (5) describe.

As you have just learned, figurative language is the descriptive language writers use to suggest and create ideas and impressions. Now, let's take a quick look at other language tools used specifically by poets:

OTHER POETIC ELEMENTS

Poets combine figurative language with the creative use of other poetic elements to further enhance the meaning of a poem. The elements covered here are sound effects that support the ideas and impressions suggested by figurative language. The two major kinds of sound effects are **rhythm** and **rhyme**.

Rhyme is a sound effect used in many poems, caused by the repetition of sounds at the ends of words. For example, *gory* and *story* are words that share **full rhyme**. **Partial rhyme** occurs when word endings sound similar but are not exactly alike, such as *tech* and *tuck*.

Rhythm is simply the beat or meter of a poem. Even poems that are not written in a standard form, such as a sonnet, have some kind of rhythm. The beat or rhythm of a poem is the pattern of sounds in the poem.

Rhythm in poetry is created in three main ways:

- By the use of punctuation, such as commas and periods, or by the absence of punctuation
- By a pattern of stressed syllables
- By the division of lines in a poem

Let's look at an example of how line division creates rhythm. For instance, how would the rhythm T. S. Eliot creates in the first four lines of "The Waste Land" be changed if he had divided the lines differently? T. S. Eliot's text:

April is the cruelest month, breeding
Lilacs out of the dead land, mixing
Memory and desire, stirring
Dull roots with spring rain.

Compare Eliot's original with this modified version:

April is the cruelest month,
Breeding lilacs out of the dead land,
Mixing memory and desire,
Stirring dull roots with spring rain.

The rhythm of the second example is regular and flat, whereas the rhythm of the first example is more unusual and varied, with each verse lingering and flowing into the next phrase.

The first rhythm suggests that the actions of the poem are continuous, that one action leads to the next. April breeds lilacs out of the dead land, and the appearance of the lilacs, which represent spring, inspires one to mix memory (the past) with desire (hope for the future), which is also represented by dull roots mixing with spring rain. All of these elements are contained in "April," but the first example by T.S. Eliot gives the impression that one thing leads to another.

In the second example, however, each action is separated by a comma and does not seem very connected to the action on the previous line. It sounds like three separate actions rather than one continuous movement or idea.

In the following practice set, combine your understanding of figurative language and rhyme and rhythm.

PRACTICE SET: FIGURATIVE LANGUAGE AND POETIC ELEMENTS

Directions: Choose the one best answer to each question.

Questions 1 through 3 refer to the following passage.

WHERE IS THE HEART OF A WOMAN CONTAINED?

The heart of a woman goes forth with the dawn,
As a lone bird, soft winging, so restlessly on,
Afar o'er life's turrets and vales does it roam
In the wake of those echoes the heart calls home.
The heart of a woman falls back with the night,
And enters some alien cage in its plight,
And tries to forget it has dreamed of the stars
While it breaks, breaks, breaks on the sheltering bars.
(Georgia Douglas Johnson, "The Heart of a Woman")

1. What is the heart of the woman compared to, or how is it represented, in this poem?

    (1)   the arrival of nightfall
    (2)   the sun at dawn
    (3)   a bird
    (4)   the stars
    (5)   the call of home

2. What is the effect of the repetition of the word *breaks* in the final line of the poem?

    (1)   It creates a pleasant sound for the poem's ending.
    (2)   It sounds like a bird hitting its head on a window.
    (3)   It sounds like a shooting star might sound.
    (4)   It creates a dreamlike impression.
    (5)   It hammers in the meaning of the poem.

3. Which answer best describes the meaning of the poem?

    (1)   A restless woman is a heartless woman.
    (2)   Women are strong and should be independent and free.
    (3)   Women are essentially imprisoned and, like prisoners, try to forget they dream of freedom.
    (4)   Dawn sheds new light on the heart of a woman.
    (5)   Women draw inspiration from the night and the stars to seek their freedom.

You may check your answers and review the explanations on page 283.

Let's move on now to Mood, Tone, and Style.

MOOD, TONE, AND STYLE

You have just examined some of the language and plot tools that a writer uses to create a desired effect. As you climb the seventh rung, you will define and look closely at the different types of literary effects that a writer attempts to achieve.

MOOD

The **mood** is the feeling or atmosphere created by the writer. The writer creates the mood through language and the arrangement of words and sentences. A mood may be characterized in many ways: romantic, gloomy, cheerful, fanciful, tense, sorrowful.

A mystery thriller might have a *suspenseful* mood, whereas the writer of a poem fondly describing "the good old days" might create a *nostalgic* mood. A play about the prolonged history of a country might have a *patriotic* mood.

TONE

Another effect, similar to mood, is **tone**, which is the overall attitude a writer suggests through word choices, sentence or verse rhythms, and descriptions. The tone of a piece of writing may be described as formal, informal, serious, humorous, dramatic, neutral, satirical, witty, matter-of-fact, pompous.

An essay poking fun at a political institution might have a *satirical* tone. A cover letter to a prospective employer might have a *formal* tone, whereas a letter to a good friend probably has an *informal* tone.

Questions concerning tone and mood may be worded in ways such as the following:

- Which of the following *best* describes the mood of this excerpt?
- What is the tone of this passage?
- Which of the following phrases helps to create the overall mood of this piece?

STYLE

Simply put, **style** is the sum of the many different ways a writer chooses to use language. Every writer has his or her own style. Some writers may adopt different styles when composing different types of literature.

The main characteristics of a writer's style are usually easy to recognize. Ernest Hemingway, for example, is famous for his simple, short sentences. Edgar Allan Poe is well known for creating a suspenseful and terrifying mood in many of his stories and poems.

THE
GED

Sometimes it is hard to figure out exactly what makes a writer's style his or her own. You might ask yourself some of the following questions when trying to identify or describe a writer's style:

Style Checklist

- Are the sentences long or short? Simple or complex?
  Are they fragments, or do they contain many clauses?
  Is the word order straightforward or unusual?

- Is the writing tight, clean, and efficient? Or is it long-winded or elaborate?
  Does the writer get off track, or does he or she stick to the main point or story?

- Does the writing concern the main action and plot?
  Or does it focus on descriptions?

- Does the writer make much use of dialogue or conversation?

- Does the writer use figurative language?
  Does the writer experiment with language?

- What point of view does the writer use?

- What is the tone and mood of the piece?

Compare and contrast the following short fictional excerpts. What are some of the major differences in the style of these two writers? Use the checklist.

From the oval-shaped flower-bed there rose perhaps a hundred stalks spreading into heart-shaped or tongue-shaped leaves half way up and unfurling at the tip red or blue or yellow petals marked with spots of colour raised upon the surface; and from the red, blue or yellow gloom of the throat emerged a straight bar, rough with gold dust and slightly clubbed at the end. The petals were voluminous enough to be stirred by the summer breeze, and when they moved, the red, blue and yellow lights passed one over the other, staining an inch of the brown earth beneath with a spot of the most intricate colour. (Virginia Woolf, "Kew Gardens")

Here is the checklist with possible responses base on the passage above.

Style Checklist: Virginia Woolf

- **Are the sentences long or short? Simple or complex? Are they fragments, or do they contain many clauses? Is the word order straightforward or unusual?** The sentences are extremely long and complex, with many subordinate clauses.

- **Is the writing tight, clean, and efficient? Or is it long-winded or elaborate? Does the writer get off track, or does he or she stick to the main point or story?** The writing is elaborate and seems to be inefficient; that is, the writer takes a long time describing these petals and does not seem to be getting on with the story.

- **Does the writing concern the main action and plot? Or does it focus on descriptions?** The writing seems to ignore plot, focusing entirely on describing the flowers.

- **Does the writer make much use of dialogue or conversation?** There is no dialogue in this passage.
- **Does the writer use figurative language? Does the writer experiment with language?** Yes, the writer experiments with language, layering description over description, with lots of imagery that appeals to sight (colors and descriptions) and sound ("stirred by the summer breeze"). The writer personifies the flowers ("tongue-shaped throat" and "gloom of the throat").
- **What point of view does the writer use?** The writer uses third-person point of view.
- **What is the tone and mood of the piece?** The piece is written in a slow, languid, speculative tone, creating an imaginative and impressionistic mood.

As you read the next passage, apply the same checklist in your head.

A very little boy stood upon a heap of gravel for the honor of Rum Alley. He was throwing stones at howling urchins from Devil's Row who were circling madly about the heap and pelting at him.
His infantile countenance was livid with fury. His small body was writhing in the delivery of great, crimson oaths.
"Run, Jimmie, run! Dey'll get yehs," screamed a retreating Rum Alley child.
(Stephen Crane, *Maggie: A Girl of the Streets*)

You probably noted some major differences between Stephen Crane's writing and Virginia Woolf's. Woolf's writing includes many descriptions and doesn't seem to concern plot. Crane focuses on action and dialogue. Crane also uses dialect like "Dey'll get yehs," to make the characters' speech sound realistic. Because Crane uses lots of verbs—pelting, circling, throwing, howling, writhing, screamed—we can describe his style as active and energetic style. Woolf's style in the above piece is slow and thoughtful. You may also notice that Crane's writing is more direct and straightforward. He doesn't use as many commas as Woolf. His sentences are shorter and more to the point. They are also written in conventional subject-verb order.

Now that you have examined the style of two major authors, read the following excerpt and answer some practice questions regarding style, tone, and mood.

PRACTICE SET: MOOD, TONE, AND STYLE

<u>Directions:</u> Choose the <u>one best answer</u> to each question.

<u>Questions 1 through 3</u> refer to the following passage.

WHAT IS THE APPEAL OF THE ICEBOUND HOTHOUSE?

There for most of the month of January, everything was frozen cracking silver. We'd had a "silver freeze": rain all night, a sudden drop in temperature, everything brittle, silvery, ice-encased, breakable trees cracking, streets and sidewalks paved with ice, houses like iced cakes. Fierce, burning world, untraversable, a harsh world of thorns, daggers, blades. Passing every frozen morning in this silver winter, the elegant greenhouse, tropical oasis on that desert campus, in the month of January when everything was frozen silver, I saw him weaving inside the ice-gripped glass. Under a frozen sky I moved like a cripple over the frozen land. The greenhouse was a cake of ice decorated with blooms and silver windows. I could hardly see through the panes with their white icing. Yet inside I saw glimmering colors, salmon and rose and purple and red, glimmering in the roselight lampglow. I was drawn to the glow and laureate warmth of the icebound hothouse. The vision in the frozen hothouse! Glimmering and locked in the icestorm. And through the window I saw the figure of the Nurseryman. Drunk! Worming his way under hanging baskets of showering blooms, staggering around fountains of lace-leaves, lurching through fountainous palms. An evil figure? Would he harm the growing, the blooming? This lone figure, moving among the growing blooms—he haunted me, haunts me yet. Even now. (William Goyen, "In the Icebound Hothouse")

1. Which of the following <u>best</u> characterizes the mood of this excerpt?

    (1)   cheerful and inviting
    (2)   somber and nostalgic
    (3)   mysterious and secretive
    (4)   glimmering and blooming
    (5)   harsh and untraversable

2. Which of the following <u>best</u> expresses the style of this passage?

    (1)   lush, descriptive, and suspenseful
    (2)   straightforward and direct
    (3)   energetic and conventional
    (4)   tight, clean, and efficient
    (5)   figurative and humorous

3. Based on the impressions and descriptions in the passage, which of the following <u>best</u> expresses the contrast between the outside world and the hothouse?

    (1)   The greenhouse is a cake of ice and the outside world is frozen.
    (2)   The greenhouse is more elegant than the outside world.
    (3)   The outside world is frozen and deathly, and the greenhouse is teeming with life.
    (4)   The greenhouse is tended by a nurseryman, whereas the outside world is on its own.
    (5)   The greenhouse is full of colors, but soon, the outside world will be blooming, too.

Once again, check your answers against the corrections and explanations on pages 283–284.

In our final rung, you must draw upon the skills you reviewed in *all* of the previous lessons, so if you feel you need to look back over any of the lessons, now is the time to review. Feel refreshed and ready to move on? Then onto the final rung: Drawing Conclusions and Making Interpretations.

DRAWING CONCLUSIONS AND MAKING INTERPRETATIONS

You have reached the final rung. Congratulations! You have mastered almost all of the reading skills you need to succeed on the GED test. In this section, you pull together everything you have learned so far about the Language Arts, Reading test and work on making literary interpretations. In order to make good interpretations of literary texts, you must get a few additional skills under your belt: recognizing the author's viewpoint, drawing conclusions, and applying ideas.

RECOGNIZING AUTHOR'S VIEWPOINT

When you answer questions to the nonfiction passages on the GED test, you may be asked to answer questions about the author's viewpoint. It is important to be able to tell the difference between the author's opinion or viewpoint on a particular topic and the information provided *about* that topic.

Questions about the author's viewpoint may be worded in ways such as the following:

- Based on the excerpt, which statement most closely expresses the author's feeling about this issue?
- Based on the information in this passage, with which of the following statements would the author *most likely* agree?

DRAWING CONCLUSIONS

Drawing conclusions is similar to making inferences, a skill we first reviewed in the second rung: Main Ideas and Supporting Details. When you draw conclusions, you rely on the facts and information given in the passage and then reach a decision or form an opinion or explanation.

APPLYING IDEAS

Applying ideas is the process of comprehending given information and transferring or applying your understanding to a new situation. When you read news about tax laws and use that knowledge to file your personal tax return, you are *applying information*.

THE
GED

REAL-LIFE EXAMPLE INVOLVING DRAWING CONCLUSIONS AND APPLYING IDEAS

You receive a memo at work instructing all employees to beware of opening e-mail attachments from unknown sources because they may contain viruses that may cause your computer to crash. At work the next morning, you check your e-mail and get a message from "John Doe" with the attached file "This is funny.xbq." Based on your reading of the memo and the fact that you don't know John Doe, you can draw a conclusion that the attachment likely contains a virus that might infect your computer. You apply this information to your current situation and delete the message altogether.

Before we look at making interpretations, let's practice with an example from a book review.

EXAMPLE

<u>Directions:</u> Read the following passage and choose the best answer from the choices below.

<u>Questions 1 and 2</u> concern the following excerpt.

WHY DID THIS AUTHOR WRITE A BOOK ABOUT ABANDONED PETS?

Few actions draw more public outrage than the mistreatment and neglect of animals, but it's easy for owners to abandon their pets, by either dropping them off at a shelter or simply losing them on the streets. But where the owner's responsibility ends, a shelter's responsibility begins, and most people never get a glimpse of the amount of work that goes on in animal-support sectors. Elizabeth Hess' *Lost And Found* hopes to remedy that ignorance with its troubling tales of animal abuse and compassionate rehabilitation. The book provides a simple, clear-headed document of the year Hess spent working at the Columbia-Greene Humane Society in rural New York, which cares for over 5,000 animals a year. As can be expected, Hess's heartstrings were pulled every time she walked into the shelter, and once she began to volunteer, her commitment to the livelihood of the put-upon creatures only increased. She discovered that the world of animal shelters, like any other workplace, has its own group mentality that often manifests itself in us-against-them scenarios. In this case, the "them" is animal breeders (and their "puppy mills"), deluded "collectors" (who hoard dozens of stray animals in tiny and ill-suited homes), and a constant stream of incompetent and sometimes malevolent pet owners. Hess's book isn't just pro-animal propaganda: After all, who would argue against the humane treatment of animals? Instead, it provides an educational look at the lives of the innocent dogs and cats that are carted around from owner to owner in a desperate attempt to keep them from being destroyed. Long before Hess even addresses the complex issues of euthanasia in *Lost And Found*'s final and most powerful chapter, she has made it clear that were it not for the work of the shelter's volunteers, hundreds of perfectly healthy pets would be destroyed. *Lost And Found* is a touching and informative memoir that highlights the unselfish souls willing to take responsibility for the folly of others, and ably addresses the issue of animal abandonment. (Joshua Klein, "Elizabeth Hess: Lost And Found")

1. Based on this passage, with which of the following statements would the author of this review <u>most likely</u> agree?

   (1)   Sometimes dog owners have to abandon their pets, and this is perfectly understandable.
   (2)   Elizabeth Hess's book is another case of pro-animal propaganda.
   (3)   The average person has a pretty good idea of what goes on in the animal support world.
   (4)   Elizabeth Hess's book is ignorant in its depiction of the lives of dogs and cats that are carted around from owner to owner in an attempt to keep them alive.
   (5)   If not for the work of a few unselfish volunteers, many healthy pets would be killed.

2. Based on this passage, what can you infer might be a possible solution to the problem of abandoned pets?

   (1)   breeding animals
   (2)   collecting large numbers of stray animals
   (3)   allowing anyone who wants to keep a pet to do so
   (4)   assisting those who work in animal shelters
   (5)   euthanasia

The best answer to question 1 is (5). You can deduce the answer easily by eliminating the other options, with which the author of this review clearly does not agree. The author does seem to agree with the first part of answer (1), but he does not find this "perfectly understandable" and in fact suggests that it is highly irresponsible. Answer (2) is incorrect because the author says that Hess's book goes beyond pro-animal propaganda. In fact, she educates people as to what goes on behind the scenes in the animal-support world, which contradicts answers (3) and (4). This leaves answer (5), which the author states in the sentence ". . . [S]he has made it clear that were it not for the work of the shelter's volunteers, hundreds of perfectly healthy pets would be destroyed."

The best answer to question 2 is (4). This is an application or inference question. You can easily eliminate incorrect answers like (1) and (2), which the author says in his review are actually part of the problem of abandoned animals:

She discovered that the world of animal shelters, like any other workplace, has its own group mentality that often manifests itself in us-against-them scenarios. In this case, the "them" is animal breeders (and their "puppy mills"), deluded "collectors" (who hoard dozens of stray animals in tiny and ill-suited homes), and a constant stream of incompetent and sometimes malevolent pet owners.

The last part of this sentence also proves answer (3) incorrect because allowing just anyone to keep a pet means that many incompetent and potentially malevolent people would continue to be pet owners. As for answer (5), Klein mentions that Hess includes a chapter addressing the complex issue of euthanasia, but he does not clearly state whether this is a worse option for some pets or whether pets should always be allowed to live, regardless of the situation. Either way, we do not have enough information to choose answer (5) as the correct answer.

CHAPTER

6

LANGUAGE
ARTS,
READING

INTRODUCTION

SUMMARIZING

MAIN IDEAS AND
SUPPORTING
DETAILS

THEME AND
POINT OF VIEW

CHARACTER AND
MOTIVATION

PLOT, PREDICTIONS,
AND INFERENCES

FIGURATIVE
LANGUAGE AND
OTHER POETIC
ELEMENTS

MOOD, TONE,
AND STYLE

DRAWING
CONCLUSIONS
AND MAKING
INTERPRETATIONS

MAKING INTERPRETATIONS

Making interpretations is simply forming your own ideas about the text, determining what ideas or information the author is trying to get across, and identifying the tools and elements the writer used in order to communicate his or her message.

Questions that ask you to make interpretations may be worded in ways such as the following:

- Based on the information in these paragraphs, which of the following inferences can you make about mistakes to *avoid* in a job interview?
- Based on the following passage, how would the union *most likely* carry out a protest?
- Which reason *most likely* expresses why the author chose to write the story from Ellen's point of view?
- What does Mr. Hutchinson *most likely* mean when he tells Christine, "You knew the real reason all along"?

Making interpretations may be the last and highest skill on our ladder, but it should not be difficult. After all, you have already learned everything you need to know in order to interpret the passages on the GED test. Making interpretations involves the combined use of *all* of the skills and strategies we have reviewed thus far, from summarizing and making comparisons to drawing conclusions and applying ideas. When you make interpretations, you draw on your full understanding of the reading material: you rely on all of the skills and knowledge you learned as you climbed all the previous rungs of the Language Arts, Reading ladder.

PRACTICE SET: DRAWING CONCLUSIONS AND MAKING INTERPRETATIONS

Directions: Read the following passage and choose the best answer from the choices below.

Questions 1 through 3 refer to the following passage.

WHAT'S THE BIG DEAL ABOUT *PEE-WEE'S BIG ADVENTURE*?

As a character, Pee-wee Herman doesn't fit any pattern of behavior, yet the actor has the sureness of touch to make you accept the contradictory things he does—the infantile ones and the sophisticated ones—and see them all as facets of Pee-wee. It could be said that he appeals to young audiences because he represents the confusion of a boy who refuses to grow up—that he's a Peter Pan of the shopping-mall era or the male equivalent of the young ballerinas who ward off physical maturity by becoming anorexic. But there's another element in the character: like a lot of teen-age consumers, he's hooked on American kitsch. And, with its peppermint-stripe storefronts and polka-dot décor, the movie is somewhere between a parody of kitsch and a celebration of it. Pee-wee himself plays to the audience like a cartoon version of the host of a kiddie show (the character he worked out in his club shows), and he's as manically good-natured as a TV pitchman.

Pee-wee's Big Adventure seems no more than a slapstick novelty, but Pee-wee is part of a—perhaps warped—tradition. The heavily lipsticked, masklike face recalls the god-awful stage makeup on the silent-screen comics of the twenties and also evokes Marcel Marceau in all his preciousness. Pee-wee is like a dangling marionette, with just his tippy-toes touching the floor. Whether he's twirling in pleasure because some new toy or gizmo has come into his life, or his face is lighting up because an idea just hit him, his whole body is involved. He moves with the precision and imagination of a gifted mime. (At one point, he makes a glorious dive onto a freight train.) What saves him from being cloying is that he uses his skills without trying to tell us that he's an artist. He gives everything he's got to gags such as the ones in which he breaks into a pet shop that's on fire and rescues each species—wanting to pass over the snakes, but finally, his face turned away in revulsion, carrying them out on his arms. I liked the movie's unimportance. It isn't *saying* anything. (Pauline Kael, "Pee-wee's Big Adventure")

1. Which statement <u>best</u> characterizes the reviewer's overall opinion of *Pee-wee's Big Adventure*?

    (1)   It is similar to the silent-screen movies of the 1920s.
    (2)   It makes a statement about the dangers of teen-age consumerism.
    (3)   It is refreshing because it doesn't try, or need, to say anything.
    (4)   It is a slapstick novelty flick.
    (5)   Its main actor is frustratingly contradictory.

2. Which statement best expresses the main idea of the first paragraph?

    (1)   Pee-wee Herman represents the confusion of a boy who refuses to grow up.
    (2)   Pee-wee Herman celebrates American kitsch.
    (3)   Pee-wee Herman symbolizes the American teen-age shopping mall consumer.
    (4)   The movie *Pee-wee's Big Adventure* represents a cartoon version of a kiddie show.
    (5)   Pee-wee Herman has the ability to make the audience accept the contradictory things he does as part of his character.

3. What is the overall tone of this review?

    (1)   considerate and ultimately appreciative
    (2)   gushing and ultimately praising
    (3)   wary and ultimately skeptical
    (4)   boring and ultimately overly academic
    (5)   funny and ultimately hilarious

Review your answers and the explanations on pages 284–285.

THE
GED

CHAPTER

6

LANGUAGE
ARTS,
READING

THE
GED

INTRODUCTION

SUMMARIZING

MAIN IDEAS AND
SUPPORTING
DETAILS

THEME AND
POINT OF VIEW

CHARACTER AND
MOTIVATION

PLOT, PREDICTIONS,
AND INFERENCES

FIGURATIVE
LANGUAGE AND
OTHER POETIC
ELEMENTS

MOOD, TONE,
AND STYLE

DRAWING
CONCLUSIONS
AND MAKING
INTERPRETATIONS

A FEW FINAL WORDS OF ADVICE

Congratulations. You've made it to the top of the ladder. Before you do your little victory dance, review these final words of advice:

- Review Test-Taking Tips and Strategy section on pages 241–242 and use it!
- Close reading is half the battle. Read your questions and answer options thoroughly.
- Don't get hung up on words whose precise meanings you don't know. Use context clues (see page 241) to help you guess their meaning.
- Use the purpose question (see page 239) to guide your reading and to focus on the correct answers to each question.
- Eliminate answers that are clearly wrong to help narrow down your choices.
- Skim over the passage when you are looking back for the best answer.
- After you have answered all the questions on a given passage, check over your other answers to make sure they are all correct. Sometimes, other questions on a passage help you uncover the correct answer to a different question.

Approach the Language Arts, Reading portion of the test with the confidence that you now have all the tools you need to pass the test. Good luck.

LANGUAGE ARTS, READING EXPLANATIONS

PRACTICE SET: SUMMARIZING

1. **(2)** The Pregnancy Discrimination Act charges that discrimination on the basis of pregnancy, childbirth, or related medical conditions is unlawful sex discrimination.

You can eliminate answer (1) because this excerpt does not mention working mothers. Answers (3) and (4) are untrue statements, according to the provided passage. Answer (5) is a statement that can be inferred from the text, because if there is an amendment, then obviously nothing was specified for pregnant women's rights in the original Civil Rights Act. However, an inference is not the same as summarizing. The question asked you for the statement that best summarizes the passage. Answer (2) is a complete statement that includes all of the main points of the passage and is the best correct answer. **(H) Summarizing**

2. **(5)** Allow the pregnant employee to modify tasks.

Answers (1), (2), and (3) contradict what is outlined in the passage. You may have to do a little close reading to determine that answer (4), also conflicts with what is said in the excerpt. This leaves answer (5), and indeed, the article says that " if the employer allows temporarily disabled employees to modify tasks, perform alternative assignments or take disability leave or leave without pay, the employer also must allow an employee who is temporarily disabled due to pregnancy to do the same."
(H) Restating information

PRACTICE SET: MAIN IDEA AND SUPPORTING DETAILS

1. **(4)** Describe and define the nature of Miami.

Use your purpose question on this one, because you have to infer the purpose of the passage and then summarize it. You can eliminate answer (1) because the article does more than simply define an art project. Answer (2) is incorrect because the article merely mentions that some of the residents did not know the name of the artist, but there is no attempt to encourage the reader to do anything in this article. Answer (3), like answer (1), might seem plausible because the author does describe a storm. But again, the article concerns itself with more than the storm. Answer (5) is incorrect because there is only a subtle attempt, at best, to connect the art project to the fraud case. Answer (4) is what the writer of the piece loosely tries to do in her conversation about the fraud cases, her description of the storm, and her imagination of what the Christo art project looked like and how it and the storm represent the nature or essence of Miami. **(H) Summarizing, inferring**

CHAPTER

6

LANGUAGE
ARTS,
READING

THE
GED

ANSWERS AND
EXPLANATIONS

2. (1) The essence of Miami exists in fleeting moments, like those created by the lightning storm and the Surrounded Islands project.

Again, the purpose question helps you immensely on this question. You have to do a little bit of inferring, but also look at the first and last sentences, where the main ideas are usually contained. The main idea is contained in the last sentence of the excerpt in this case: "It seemed that this period when the pink was in the water had for many people exactly defined, as the backlit islands and the fluorescent water and the voices at the table were that night defining for me, Miami." If you didn't choose answer (1) right away, let's look at why the other answers are correct. Answers (2) and (3) correctly restate some information from the excerpt, but do not mention any of the other major events of the paragraph or comment on their significance. Answer (4) claims that the essence of Miami is the fraud trials, but this ignores the entire second paragraph of the excerpt, so it cannot be the best answer. Answer (5) places too much significance on an impression briefly mentioned in the first two sentences of the piece, ignoring the remaining paragraph.  **Main ideas, summarizing, inference**

3. (3) It seemed that the pink had kept changing color, fading and reemerging with the movement of the water and the clouds and the sun and the night lights.

If you got the answer right to question 2, then this answer should be easy to find. Answer (1) is a detail supporting the impressions of the storm, so it is not the best choice. Answer (2) supports the points about the Duque trial; answer (4) is merely a sentence that helps to set the scene for the lightning storm and the author's subsequent realizations about the significance of the storm and the art installation. Answer (5) is merely a detail about the creator of the art installation. Answer (3), however, is a descriptive detail that helps illustrate *how* the art installation resembled the lightning storm that the author witnesses in this excerpt. Therefore, it supports the main idea that the essence of Miami exists in these two kinds of fleeting moments. **Restating, supporting details**

PRACTICE SET: THEME AND POINT OF VIEW

1. (1) When a man travels to a distant land, he must be ready to forget old habits and ways of thinking, and adapt to the rituals of a new place.

The correct answer is (1), which restates the first line of this excerpt. This opening line simultaneously introduces the theme and is supported by the details in the remainder of this fictional passage. Answer (2) contradicts what we learn in the excerpt because man is supposed to *forget* dependence on material habits, according to this author. Answer (3) does not cover all aspects expressed in the paragraphs. Answer (4) is not true: London writes that man must be ready to give up these ideals if necessary. We can eliminate answer (5) because the author does not place importance on returning to one's own country. **Identifying themes**

2.   (4)   changing one's attitude toward his fellow man

Answer (4) is correct, because the author suggests the most difficult thing to overcome is adapting to new ways of thinking and to different people. Answers (1) and (2) represent two of the easier things to overcome in a new place. Both eating different food and living a little less comfortably refer to material comforts rather than spiritual changes. Answer (3) represents what might happen if one cannot adjust to the challenges of answers (1), (2), and (4). Answer (5) simply gives an example of traveling to a remote place, such as the primordial simplicity of the North. **Ⓗ Inference**

3.   (2)   Actions speak louder than words.

Answer (2) is the one clear answer here because it restates the meaning of the quote in an aphorism, or well-known saying. All of the other answers refer to *other* ideas expressed within the text, but none of them explain the provided quote in the question. **Ⓗ Comprehension, application, restating**

PRACTICE SET: CHARACTER AND MOTIVATION

1.   (2)   excitable and talkative

Answer (1) is not a good answer, because we see that Anna's mood changes swiftly and that she is also drinking in the bar. Answer (2) is correct: Anna is definitely prone to excitement, and she is very chatty here, talking to Marthy, whom she does not even know. Answer (3) is incorrect because Anna does not seem to hide much, and she only hesitates once, when Marthy suggests at the opening that she not have another drink. It is Marthy who is described as being evasive. Answers (4) and (5) can be ruled out because we don't know from this passage whether Anna is kind or good natured, or willful and stubborn. **Ⓗ Character**

2.   (5)   what she says

Answer (5) is correct because in this passage, Anna does a lot of talking and doesn't hold back much. We don't know what she thinks because we can't get into her head as we might be able to in fiction, so we can rule out answer (1). Answer (2) can be eliminated because there is not a lot of action in this passage, and Anna's own speech still seems more revealing. Answers (3) and (4) do not apply, because there are only two characters in this passage. **Ⓗ Character**

3.   (4)   to try to find her father because she has nowhere to turn

Anna is at the bar drinking, but this does not seem to be her main motive for coming to the waterfront, as she tells Marthy, so answer (1) is not the best answer. Answer (2) is false because she only just met Marthy. Answer (3) is incorrect because we have no information supporting this idea. Answer (5) represents something that Anna hopes to do after she finds her father and convinces him to take her in. She tells Marthy she is looking for her father and that she is a little desperate, so answer (4) is the correct answer. **Ⓗ Motivation**

CHAPTER
6

LANGUAGE
ARTS,
READING

THE
GED

ANSWERS AND
EXPLANATIONS

CHAPTER

6

LANGUAGE
ARTS,
READING

THE
GED

ANSWERS AND
EXPLANATIONS

4.   (3)   He has never done anything for her.

Anna's father used to be a sailor, but this does not seem to be the source of her apprehension about finding him, so answer (1) is incorrect. He is also a janitor, or "yanitor," as Marthy says, but this is also not why she has mixed feelings about meeting him, which eliminates answer (2). Answer (4) is not the right answer because we have no information supporting the idea that he might send her back to jail. Answer (5) is wrong because Anna has no idea at this moment in the play that Marthy knows her father. Answer (3) is the best answer because Anna does say that her father has never done anything for her. **(H) Motivation**

PRACTICE SET: PLOT, PREDICTIONS, AND INFERENCES

1.   (5)   He is actually sick.

Mary George realizes in this passage that her brother looks very sick, indeed, so answer (5) is the correct answer. Answer (1) is not correct because we get the impression that she already thinks her brother is self-centered. Similarly, we can rule out answers (2), (3), and (4) because these are things that Mary George already believes or knows about her brother Asbury. **(H) Plot**

2.   (1)   Regard her brother differently.

Mary George will most likely regard her brother differently now that she realizes he is actually sick and not pretending or just visiting home, so answer (1) is correct. Her mother has asked her to leave him alone, so we can guess that she will not listen at his door or ask about his book. Therefore answers (2) and (3) are unlikely. Answer (4) seems unlikely because Mary George really does believe her brother is ill. Also, answer (5) is implausible because Mary George is probably so surprised by her brother's illness that she would not think to draw attention to herself in this particular situation. **(H) Prediction**

3.   (3)   hopeful; pretending that everything is fine

The mother glosses over unfortunate characteristics or events and tries to seem hopeful, believing that her son will publish a book and saying cheerful and inane things like, "Home again, home again, jiggity jig!" Therefore, answer (3) is best. You can eliminate answer (1) because although the mother is caring toward her son, this is not the prominent characteristic shown in this passage. Answer (2) is simply incorrect, as the mother is very present in her son's life whenever he allows her to be. Answer (4) is incorrect, as Mary George is the sarcastic one, and the mother is generally optimistic. Answer (5) is probably not true either, as the mother seems to wish better things for her children, who are both unsatisfied. **(H) Character**

PRACTICE SET: FIGURATIVE LANGUAGE AND OTHER POETIC ELEMENTS

1. **(3) a bird**

In the first two lines, the heart of a woman is compared in a simile, "as a lone bird," so (3) is the best answer. All of the other answers describe images or ideas contained or suggested by the poem, but none of these appear to represent the heart of a woman. **(H) Figurative language**

2. **(2) It sounds like a bird hitting its head on a window.**

If you got the first question right, answering this question probably came easily. The "breaks, breaks, breaks" does call to mind the sound of a bird striking its head on a window, trying to escape, so answer (2) is correct. The repetition of this harsh-sounding word does not make a pleasant sound, so you can rule out answer (1). The poet does not mention shooting stars, so we cannot infer that "breaks, breaks, breaks" refers to shooting stars: answer (3) is incorrect. Answer (4) suggests a dreamlike impression, which does not apply here: again, the repetition is not a fluid sound, but literally a break in the flow of the poem. Answer (5) does not explain how "breaks, breaks, breaks" hammers in the poem's meaning. **(H) Poetic elements**

3. **(3) Women are essentially imprisoned and, like prisoners, try to forget they dream of freedom.**

By synthesizing, or putting together, the images in this poem and what they represent, you can conclude that (3) is the best answer. Women in this poem are compared to caged birds. Answer (1) contradicts the idea of this poem, that restlessness is in the heart of a woman. Answer (2) represents an opinion that the speaker of this poem might share, but it is not the overall meaning expressed in this particular poem. The poem does not give us enough information to support answers (4) and (5). **(H) Theme, synthesis**

PRACTICE SET: MOOD, TONE, AND STYLE

1. **(3) mysterious and secretive**

The author of this short story creates a mysterious and secretive mood. The icebound hothouse is something the reader does not understand but, like the narrator, is drawn to because it is described as the only thing alive and colorful in a world that is otherwise frozen and silver. So answer (3) is the best correct answer. Answer (1) can be ruled out because the mood of the place is not inviting or cheerful. There is no evidence in this passage to support answer (2), which claims that the piece is nostalgic. Answers (4) and (5) contain words used in this passage but do not accurately reflect the overall mood. **(H) Mood**

CHAPTER

6

LANGUAGE
ARTS,
READING

THE
GED

ANSWERS AND
EXPLANATIONS

2.   (1)   lush, descriptive, and suspenseful

Answer (1) is correct because this answer encompasses the major characteristics of this author's style. Goyen creates a lush, heavily descriptive world, full of adjectives and images. His language is also energetic and suspenseful, luring the reader into this mysterious place. He is certainly not direct or straightforward, so you can rule out answer (2). Nor is he conventional or efficient, tight and clean, which strikes out answers (3) and (4). Although his language is figurative, this passage is not particularly funny or humorous, so answer (5) cannot be correct. **Style**

3.   (3)   The outside world is frozen and deathly, and the greenhouse is teeming with life.

The main contrast of the story is between the frozen outside world and the secret life of the greenhouse, so answer (3) is the best answer. Answer (1) is incorrect because the greenhouse, of course, is not a cake of ice—it is a hothouse. Answer (2) represents a judgment rather than an impression created by the author, so this answer is incorrect. Answer (4) does not refer to contrasts evident in the story, and we do not have enough information about the nurseryman or the conditions of the outside world to make this judgment. We also do not have enough information in this excerpt to be able to conclude that answer (5) is a good answer. **Comparison and contrast**

PRACTICE SET: DRAWING CONCLUSIONS AND MAKING INTERPRETATIONS

1.   (3)   It is refreshing because it doesn't try, or need, to say anything.

The answer to this question is conveniently contained in the last lines of the excerpt. Again, the first and last lines of passages often clue you in to the main idea and, in this case, to the author's opinion because first lines introduce and last lines generally summarize. Answers (1), (2), and (4) are all different ideas expressed by the author throughout the review, but none of them represent her *overall* opinion. Answer (5) incorrectly describes the author's opinion of the actor Pee-wee Herman and does not answer the question correctly. **Recognizing author's opinion, interpretation**

2.   (5)   Pee-wee Herman has the ability to make the audience accept the contradictory things he does as part of his character.

In this instance, look to the *first* sentence of the review. It tells you the author's main idea. You can then easily see that answers (1), (2), (3), and (4) are incorrect because they are details *supporting* the larger, main idea guiding the entire paragraph. **Main idea**

3.   (1)   considerate and ultimately appreciative

This question asks you to judge the author's overall opinion of the film as well as describe the tone she uses in her review. The author seems to consider and weigh and really think about the different aspects of the film. She is aware of some of the faults of the film but overall seems to appreciate the film for what it is, so answer (1) is correct. Answer (2) is false because the author is certainly not gushing or overly praising in her review. Similarly, answer (3) can be ruled out because the author also is not suspicious or wary in her write-up. You probably found the review somewhat interesting and engaging, so answer (4) is also incorrect. On the other hand, you probably did not laugh out loud as you were reading it, so you know that answer (5) is also not the best answer. **(H) Interpretation, tone**

CHAPTER

7

MATHEMATICS

MATHEMATICS

This chapter reviews all the math that's tested on the GED test and helps it all make sense. Soon, you'll be able to handle the GED Mathematics test. Here is your ladder for the Mathematics test:

Rung 1: Introduction
Rung 2: Whole Numbers and Basic Operations
Rung 3: Your Calculator
Rung 4: Fractions, Decimals, and Percentages
Rung 5: Measurement
Rung 6: Data Analysis
Rung 7: Algebra
Rung 8: Geometry

By using the step-by-step ladder in this chapter, you can master all the skills you need to succeed on the Mathematics test. There are eight rungs in the ladder. Each is designed as a single lesson and should take just about an hour to complete. It's important to work through each rung, one at a time, to prepare yourself for all of the kinds of questions found on the Mathematics test. Each rung builds on the one before it. The ladder begins with an introduction to the test and basic math tasks involving operations (addition, subtraction, multiplication, and division) and familiarity with symbols (<, >, %, etc.). As you move up the ladder, you practice working with more complex math concepts, including algebra and geometry. You can go back and review previous lessons if you feel you need to improve in a particular area. By the final rung, you will have the skills you need to handle the most challenging problems on the Mathematics test.

Each section concludes with a set of practice questions. Answering these questions will help you to assess how prepared you are in each topic. If you answer most of the practice set quesions correctly, you should move on to the next rung. Explanations to each practice set appear at the end of the chapter. The icon at the end of the explanation will indicate the specific skill that is being tested.

INTRODUCTION

The GED Mathematics test consists of two parts. Part I contains 25 multiple-choice questions for which you are allowed to use a calculator. The calculator is issued to you at the test site, along with printed directions on how to use it (we cover calculator use in depth on the third rung). Part II is also 25 questions, you may not use a calculator in this section.

Both parts consist of mathematical problems and real-world situations. Roughly 50 percent of the test involves working with drawings, diagrams, charts, and graphs. Approximately 20 percent of the answers are "alternate format." Alternate format means that you must come up with the answer yourself, just as you would on a regular math test. Instead of choosing an answer from a list as in a multiple-choice question, you solve the problem and enter your answers on either standard grids or coordinate grids.

The scores earned on Parts I and II are combined and reported as a single score. If you do not complete either Part I or Part II, you will have to retake both parts. You cannot retake just Part I or Part II.

Finally, a sheet of formulas is provided for your reference. You do not have to memorize how to calculate volume or circumference. You only have to be able to select the appropriate formula from the chart. We cover using this page of formulas later in this section.

QUICK OVERVIEW

Test	Items	Time Limit
Math (Part I)	25 multiple-choice or alternate format questions	45 minutes
Math (Part II)	25 multiple-choice or alternate format questions	45 minutes

The questions on both parts of the test cover four content areas:

- **Numbers and operations (20–30%)**—These questions test your ability to work with whole numbers, fractions, decimals, percentages, ratios, and proportion.
- **Measurement and data analysis (20–30%)**—These questions involve calculating length, perimeter, circumference, area, volume, and time. You must be familiar with both the U.S. and metric systems, but you do not have to memorize formulas. Data analysis refers to the ability to interpret and work within charts, tables, and graphs. It may also cover probability as well as the concepts of mean, median, and mode.
- **Algebra (20–30%)**—Algebra questions involve variables, algebraic expressions, and equations. Concepts such as percentage, ratio, and proportion can

also be used with algebra questions. Algebra questions also ask you to work with graphs: graphing points, finding the slope of lines, and locating ordered pairs. This section requires you to use the alternate format grid upon which you actually graph a point by bubbling in a coordinate on a grid.

- **Geometry (20–30%)**—Geometry questions require you to work with lines, angles, circles, triangles, and various polygons.

TEST-TAKING TIPS

Before we look at the types of questions, let's first look at the steps you should take to answer many of the multiple-choice questions on the Mathematics test:

1. **Read the question carefully and look for *key words*.** Key words help you understand the question. Watch for words and phrases such as *how many, how much, more, less, total, in all, all together, approximately, percentage, equally, average*—such words help you determine whether you must add, subtract, divide, or multiply. Pay close attention also to words like *not, if, after,* and *before*—they put a condition on the problem that affects your answer.

2. **Estimate a possible answer.** The number values in the problem can help you make a reasonable guess about the answer.

3. **Use process of elimination.** Step 2 can help you rule out some answer choices.

4. **Solve the problem and plug in your answer.** By inserting your answer choice into the problem, you can double-check the result and be more confident of your answer.

In addition to multiple-choice questions, the Mathematics test contains alternate format questions, which we cover right after this section. These questions are similar to the multiple-choice questions, but they don't have any answer choices. You must provide your own answer.

We review how to use the four steps listed above to solve each kind of multiple-choice question on the Mathematics test.

THE THREE TYPES OF MULTIPLE-CHOICE QUESTIONS

Three types of multiple-choice questions are featured on the Mathematics test:

- Basic math operations questions
- Concept questions
- "How" questions

BASIC MATH OPERATIONS

In basic math operations questions, a short word problem supplies information and asks a question. You must decide the operation or operations to perform and correctly answer the question. Here's an example:

Directions: Choose the <u>one best answer</u> to each question.

Angel paid $31 to get into the amusement park and then spent $19 to buy lunch. How much did he spend altogether?

(1) $12
(2) $28
(3) $50
(4) $68
(5) Not enough information is given.

Let's follow the steps listed on the previous page to get us through this problem.

1. **Read the question carefully and look for *key words*.** This question is typical of the word problems found on the test. You must choose the right operation and perform it correctly. After reading the question, you know that the problem asks for a total: the key word is *altogether*. This tells you that the question asks for a *total*.

2. ***Estimate* a possible answer.** You can estimate that the answer must be larger than $31, because that is the highest figure given in the question. Remember, as you are looking for how much he spent *altogether*, the answer logically must be larger than the two separate amounts.

3. **Use process of *elimination*.** Answers (1) and (2) are smaller than the amount paid just to get into the park, so they cannot be correct. Answer (4) is larger than the price of admission plus the price of lunch. Rule that out as well.

4. **Solve the problem and *plug in* your answer.** Careful addition yields $50, which is answer choice (3) and the correct answer!

Not enough information: Note that some questions, including this one, give you the option of marking "Not enough information is given." You should not be afraid to choose this option, but if you plug in your answer choice and it works, "not enough information" can safely be eliminated.

CONCEPT QUESTIONS

These test your knowledge of math concepts. They involve basic math operations, but also require you to apply another concept, such as percentages and ratios. Read the following example:

Directions: Choose the <u>one best answer</u> to each question. You may use a calculator.

There are 460 people working at the Best-Fit clothing factory. If 30% of the employees work in the jeans area, how many employees is this?

(1) 25
(2) 138
(3) 160
(4) 322
(5) 430

Let's see how our step method works to get us through this problem.

CHAPTER

7

MATHEMATICS

THE
GED

INTRODUCTION

WHOLE NUMBERS
AND BASIC
OPERATIONS

USING THE *fx*-260
CALCULATOR

FRACTIONS,
DECIMALS, AND
PERCENTAGES

MEASUREMENT

DATA ANALYSIS

ALGEBRA

GEOMETRY

1. **Read the question carefully and look for *key words*.**
   This question is typical of the *concept* questions found on the test. You must choose the correct operation and perform it accurately. After reading the question, you know that you are dealing with percentages. In this question, the percentage is given to you; you must find the corresponding actual number. The first sentence in the question gives you the total number of people. You must figure out a percentage, or part, of that total. The key word *percentage* (in this case, the symbol %) and the key words *how many* tell you this.

2. ***Estimate* a possible answer.** You can estimate that 30% is roughly $\frac{1}{3}$. It is often helpful to think of $\frac{1}{3}$ of a piece of pie or $\frac{1}{3}$ of a dollar (33 cents). You can estimate that $\frac{1}{3}$ of 460 is around 150. So, you know that the answer is probably around 150, but definitely less than 230, which is $\frac{1}{2}$ of 460, and more than 115, which is $\frac{1}{4}$ of 460.

3. **Use process of *elimination*.** Answer (1) can be eliminated because 25 is much too small to be a third of 460—it is too small to even be a tenth of 460. Answers (4) and (5) can also be eliminated: they are both much larger than our estimate of 150; in fact, they are both at least half of 460. That leaves you with two possible answer choices: (2) and (3).

4. **Solve the problem and *plug in* your answer.** With careful math, you can determine whether 138 or 160 is the correct answer. We cover percentages later in this chapter, but for now, convert 30% to its decimal (0.30) and multiply by 460. Rechecking your multiplication, you can see that answer (2) is correct.

When dealing with concept questions, you must use your existing knowledge of math concepts to work with the given information. In the example above, you needed to be familiar with the correct way to calculate percentage.

"HOW" QUESTIONS

This type of problem looks the same as any other math question, but instead of asking you for an actual answer, the questions ask you to determine *how* the problem should be solved. Let's look at an example:

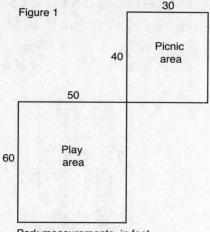

Figure 1

Park measurements, in feet.

Using Figure 1, which expression shows how to calculate the total area of the park?

(1)   50 + 60 + 40 + 30
(2)   (50 × 30) + (60 × 40)
(3)   50 × 60 × 30 × 40
(4)   100 + 120 + 60 + 80
(5)   (50 × 60) + (30 × 40)

①②③④⑤

Once again, let's use our trusty step method.

1. **Read the question carefully and look for *key words*.** This question is typical of the *how* questions on the test. Often, these questions ask you to choose the correct formula from the formula sheet provided at the beginning of the test and to input the numbers given in the problem. After reading the question, you know that the problem asks for the *total area*. This means the area of *both* of the individual squares. You will see the formula to calculate area on the formula sheet in the next section, but for now the formula is Area = Length × width.

2. ***Estimate* a possible answer.** To find the answer, you must perform *two* separate calculations, because the *two* areas must be combined to get the total area. Therefore, you can guess that parentheses are needed in the answer choice because you are working *two* functions separately and then combining them.

3. **Use process of *elimination*.** By simply eliminating answer choices that don't use parentheses, you can eliminate answers (1), (4), and (3)

4. **Solve the problem and *plug in* your answer.** Now you're down to (2) and (5). Careful examination of answer (2) shows that it multiplies the wrong numbers. Answer (5) must be correct. Unlike the other types of multiple-choice questions, you do not solve how questions for a final number. You solve them by selecting the appropriate method that would give you the correct answer. In these cases, you won't have an actual number to plug in, so simply plug in your answer choice.

THE
GED

ALTERNATE FORMAT QUESTIONS

Scattered throughout both Part I and Part II of the Mathematics test are alternate format questions. There are usually about ten of them throughout the test. These questions require you to come up with your own answer and key it in to a grid that looks like this:

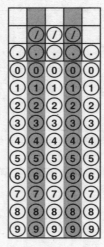

These questions are explained to you at the beginning of the Mathematics test. Here are the directions from the test:

Mixed numbers, such as $3\frac{1}{2}$, cannot be entered in the alternate format grid. Instead, represent them as decimal numbers (in this case, 3.5) or fractions (in this case, 7/2). No answer can be a negative number, such as −8.

To record your answer for an alternate format question,
• begin in any column that will allow your answer to be entered.
• write your answer in the boxes on the top row.
• in the column beneath a fraction bar or decimal point (if any) and each number in your answer, fill in the bubble representing that character.
• leave blank any unused column.

Example:
The scale on a map indicates that $\frac{1}{2}$ inch represents an actual distance of 120 miles. In inches, how far apart on the map will two towns be if the actual distance between them is 180 miles?

The answer to the above example is $\frac{3}{4}$, or 0.75, inches. The answer could be gridded using any of the methods below:

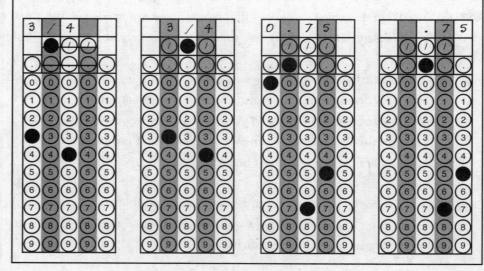

Basically, here's what you need to know:

- The computer that grades your GED test cannot read anything but ovals, so you don't have to write anything in the spaces at the top of the grid. However, it is a good idea to write your answer in those spaces so you can fill in the correct bubbles below each number or symbol.

- The grid cannot accept any number longer than four digits, any fraction or decimal that has more than three numbers, or any negative numbers. This is good news because if you come up with an answer that doesn't fit these criteria, you know that it is wrong!

- You can express your answer as a fraction or a decimal. Either answer is correct.

- You must transform all mixed numbers to fraction form. For example, if you come up with the answer $3\frac{1}{2}$, you must enter the answer as $7/2$ because 3 1/2 will be marked as wrong by the computer.

- The computer cannot read commas, and there is no corresponding oval for a comma, so leave them out of your answer.

These aren't the only alternate format questions included on the test. There are also questions that require you to grid your answers onto a graph that looks like this:

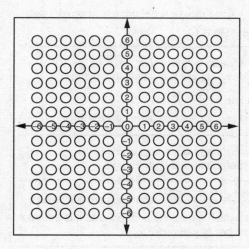

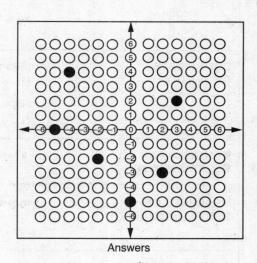

Answers

These questions deal with algebra, and the answer you are asked to provide will be a point somewhere on this graph. You simply bubble in the correct circle on the graph. We cover using these graphs in the Algebra rung.

USING THE FORMULAS PAGE

The Mathematics test-writers are on your side. At the beginning of the Mathematics test, after the directions on alternate format questions, is a page of formulas, which we show you on the following page:

If you are stuck on a question, refer to the formulas page. Simply looking at the formulas may trigger something in your memory that will help you solve the problem.

FORMULAS

AREA of a:

square	Area = side^2
rectangle	Area = length × width
parallelogram	Area = base × height
triangle	Area = $\frac{1}{2}$ × base × height
trapezoid	Area = $\frac{1}{2}$ × (base$_1$ + base$_2$) × height
circle	Area = π × radius^2; π is approximately equal to 3.14

PERIMETER of a:

square	Perimeter = 4 × side
rectangle	Perimeter = 2 × length + 2 × width
triangle	Perimeter = side$_1$ + side$_2$ + side$_3$

CIRCUMFERENCE of a circle — Circumference = π × diameter; π is approximately equal to 3.14

VOLUME of a:

cube	Volume = edge^3
rectangular container	Volume = length × width × height
square pyramid	Volume = $\frac{1}{3}$ × (base edge)^2 × height
cylinder	Volume = π × radius^2 × height; π is approximately equal to 3.14
cone	Volume = $\frac{1}{3}$ × π × radius^2 × height; π is approximately equal to 3.14

COORDINATE GEOMETRY

distance between points = $\sqrt{(x_2 - x_1)^2 + (y_2 - y_1)^2}$; (x_1, y_1) and (x_2, y_2) are two points in a plane

slope of a line = $\frac{y_2 - y_1}{x_2 - x_1}$; (x_1, y_1) and (x_2, y_2) are two points on a line

PYTHAGOREAN RELATIONSHIP

$a^2 + b^2 + c^2$; a and b are legs and c is the hypotenuse of a right triangle

MEASURES OF CENTRAL TENDENCY

mean = $\frac{x_1 + x_2 + \ldots + x_n}{n}$; where x's are the values for which a mean is desired, and n is the total number of values for x

SIMPLE INTEREST — interest = principal × rate × time

DISTANCE — distance = rate × time

TOTAL COST — total cost = (number of units) × (price per unit)

You can refer to this page at any point during either part of the Mathematics test, and you should refer to it often. Most times, it is fairly obvious when you need to use it. A question might ask you to "Find the area of a square. . ." In these cases, you simply need to look at the formulas page to see that the area of a square = side^2.

With some questions, you can work backward to find the answer. For example, if a question gives you the volume of a cube and asks you for the length of an edge, you can use the formula for the volume of a cube to find the answer.

We've looked at the three types of questions, a step-by-step strategy to use on the multiple-choice questions, and how to work with alternate format questions. You are now ready to tackle the next rung of the ladder, and the first real math review.

WHOLE NUMBERS AND BASIC OPERATIONS

Whole numbers are also known as **counting numbers**. All possible numbers that can be named are created with the **digits** 0, 1, 2, 3, 4, 5, 6, 7, 8, and 9. **Place value** describes the location of each digit and the value it is has. Although this sounds complicated, it is something you already know. You know that 345 is a smaller number than 543, even thought they both use the same digits.

hundred billions	ten billions	billions	hundred millions	ten millions	millions	hundred thousands	ten thousands	thousands	hundreds	tens	ones
									3	4	5
		,			,			,	5	4	3

One number has a 3 in the hundreds place, and the other has a 5 in the hundreds place, making it the larger number. Using the place value chart, we can break a number down into individual values.

What is the value of each digit in 45,032?

4 is in the ten thousands place	$4 \times 10{,}000 = 40{,}000$
5 is in the thousands place	$5 \times 1{,}000 = 5{,}000$
0 is in the hundreds place	$0 \times 100 = 000$
3 is in the tens place	$3 \times 10 = 30$
2 is in the ones place	$2 \times 1 = 2$

Notice that commas are used every three places, starting from the ones and working higher. When you read this number, first read the highest group of three, and then work your way to the right.

The number 45,032 is read and spelled out **forty-five thousand, thirty-two**.

ROUNDING WHOLE NUMBERS

Rounding is used to make large number calculations easier to manage. If City A has 6,908,423 people, City B has 3,512,783 people, and City C has 9,001,765 people, it would take fairly long to add up the numbers. By rounding, you can get an answer that is much easier to work with. What is the approximate total population of cities A, B, and C to the nearest million?

To round numbers, follow these steps:

City A: 6,908,423

Step 1: Circle the digit in the place that is asked for. That is, if you are asked to round to the nearest million, circle the millions place.

6 is in the millions place.
⑥908,423

Step 2: Look at the digit that is just to its right.

⑥908,423
The digit to the right is 9.

If it is 4 or less, don't change the circled digit.

If it is 5 or more, increase the circled digit by 1.

The 6 changes to 7.
⑦908,423
⑦000,000

Step 3: Change all numerals to the right of the circle to zero.

The population of City A rounded to the nearest million is 7,000,000.

Now follow the steps to round off the populations of cities B and C.

City B _____

City C _____

City B's population, rounded to the nearest million, would be 4,000,000, and City C's would be 9,000,000.

To find the total approximate population, it is easy to add 7 million, 4 million, and 9 million. 7 + 4 + 9 = 20, so the total approximate population of the three cities is 20 million people.

NUMBER OPERATIONS

Most math problems require some sort of application of these four operations: addition, subtraction, multiplication, and division.

Test yourself by trying these problems without using a calculator.

(1) 233 + 108
(2) 756 − 419
(3) 25 × 13
(4) 450 ÷ 5

Answers:
(4) 90
(3) 325
(2) 337
(1) 341

If you got the right answers, you have no problem with basic math operations and you can skip to the section on word problems (page 302). If you did not get the correct answers, continue with the next sections for a quick review of the basic math operations.

ADDING WHOLE NUMBERS

Find the answer to 191 + 235.

```
   1 9 1        1 9 1        ¹1 9 1       ¹1 9 1
 + 2 3 5      + 2 3 5      + 2 3 5      + 2 3 5
 _____      _____      _____      _____
                    6            2 6        4 2 6
```

The answer is 426.

SUBTRACTING WHOLE NUMBERS

Find the answer to 628 – 153.

```
   6 2 8        6 2 8       ⁵6̷¹2 8       ⁵6̷¹2 8
 – 1 5 3      – 1 5 3      – 1 5 3      – 1 5 3
 _____      _____      _____      _____
                    5            7 5        4 7 5
```

As in addition problems, start at the ones column. Subtract 8 – 3 = 5.

Subtract the next column. Since you cannot take 5 from 2, you need to "borrow." Subtract 1 from the next digit over (in this case, the 6) and put it in front of the 2, making it 12. Now find 12 – 5. Put down the 7.

Subtract the last column, 5 – 1. Write down the 4.

The answer is 475.

MULTIPLYING WHOLE NUMBERS

Multiply 423 × 61.

We work multiplication problems in layers. Put the larger number on the top and the smaller number on the bottom, and multiply the digits on the bottom by each one on the top, working right to left.

```
   4 2 3        4 2 3       ¹ ¹4 2 3      ¹ ¹4 2 3
 ×   6 1      ×   6 1      ×   6 1      ×   6 1
 _____      _____      _____      _____
                4 2 3        4 2 3       ¹4 2 3
                           2 5 3 8 0   + 2 5 3 8 0
                                        _____
                                        2 5 8 0 3
```

When you move on to the next row, where you multiply by the next digit of the number on the bottom, or the *multiplicand*, always put another zero *placeholder* in the far right space. Then add the column of numbers to find your answer.

The answer is 25,803.

DIVIDING WHOLE NUMBERS

Division, or *long division*, as it is shown here, is an easy process if you can remember **DMSB**. It stands for *divide*, *multiply*, *subtract* and *bring down*. When you do these steps in order, long division is simple.

THE
GED

Divide 408 ÷ 3.

D Divide 3 into the first number: 3 goes into 4 one time. Put the 1 above the 4.

M Multiply 1 × 3 = 3. Put the 3 under the 4.

S Subtract. 4 − 3 = 1. Write it down.

B Bring down the next digit. You now have a 10. Start over with DMSB by dividing the 3 into the 10.

A fun way to remember DMSB is to think, "**D**oes **M**cDowell's **S**erve **B**urgers?"

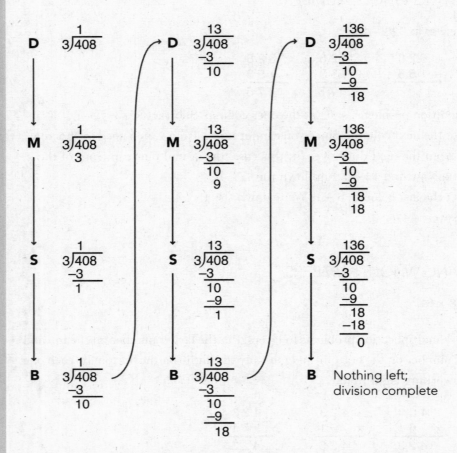

When you no longer have any numbers to bring down, you are done. Any number left after the subtraction is called the remainder.

The answer is 136.

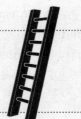

If you still have problems with these four operations, you may need more extensive tutoring or an adult math education course before you take the GED test.

ORDER OF OPERATIONS

Test your knowledge of order of operations with this problem:

$5 + 6 \times 3 = ?$

There could be two ways to work the problem:

5 + 6 = 11, and then 11 × 3 = 33, or
5 added to 6 × 3, or 5 + 18 = 23.

Each way comes up with a different answer, so it is important to follow the order of operations, a rule devised by early mathematicians about the order in which numbers are to be worked. Here is the basic **order of operations**:

First, work out all operations in parentheses as they occur from left to right.

Next, work out all multiplication and division as it occurs from left to right.

Last, work out all addition and subtraction as it occurs from left to right.

The answer to $5 + 6 \times 3$ is 23. Remember, do the multiplication first and the addition second.

You start with the original problem: $5 + 6 \times 3 = ?$

Do the multiplication: $5 + (6 \times 3) = 5 + 18 = ?$

Then do the addition: $5 + 18 = 23$

Try this math sentence:

$5 \times 4 - 2 + 6 \div 3 \times 9 = ?$

- **First**, all parentheses. There are no parentheses in this sentence. Go to the next step.
- **Next**, all multiplication and division as it occurs from left to right.

$$5 \times 4 - 2 + 6 \div 3 \times 9 = ?$$
$$2 \times 9 =$$
$$20 - 2 + 18$$

- **Last**, all addition and subtraction as it occurs from left to right.

$20 - 2 + 18 = ?$
$18 + 18 = 36$

The correct solution is 36.

Nana sewed 2 shirts and 3 sweaters every day for a week. How many total pieces of clothing did she sew?

To solve this problem, you must add the 2 shirts to the 3 sweaters before you multiply it by the seven days. Since you multiply before adding, this problem cannot be written $2 + 3 \times 7$. This is when parentheses are needed. Put parentheses around all operations that you want done first.

First, parentheses, left to right.	$(2 + 3) \times 7 = ?$
Next, all multiplication and division, left to right.	$5 \times 7 = ?$ $5 \times 7 = 35$
Last, all addition and subtraction, left to right	None

Nana sewed 35 pieces of clothing.

WORD PROBLEMS

Most math problems you encounter, both on the GED test and in life, are set up as word problems. You must determine *how* the problem should be solved. However, as we discussed in our strategy section on pages 290–293, you also need a good estimation skills. Before you calculate an answer, consider what a reasonable answer would be. Read the problem below:

Alex used 125 gallons of gasoline in his car last month. This month he used 108 gallons. What is his total for the two months?

Stop and Think: Before you look at the answers, think what a reasonable answer would be. Alex used over 100 gallons last month, and a little over 100 this month. The question asks for a total, which indicates addition. A little more than 100 plus just over 100 would be more than 200, but probably not higher than 300. Now solve the problem and look at the choices:

(1)   13
(2)   133
(3)   223
(4)   233
(5)   328

Answers (1) and (2) are clearly too low for Alex's two-month total. Answer (5) is probably too high. Choosing between answers (3) and (4) depends on adding correctly. Did you remember to carry the one and add it in? If you did, you should have gotten answer (4): 233.

While estimation is extremely helpful in deciphering word problems, it is important to determine what the problem is really asking you to do. Although the symbol + did not appear in the word problem above, it did ask for a total. Certain words and phrases can signal the operation you need to use. In this case, *total* signaled addition. Here are some more examples:

Math Symbol	Operation	Key Phrases/Situations
+	addition	**total, combined, all together, in all, sum, full amount**: these problems usually follow the pattern "some and some more."
−	subtraction	**how much less, how much/many fewer, how much/many left** (or **left over**), **difference**: these problems usually follow the pattern "some and some taken away."
×	multiplication	use the same amount many times; percentage of; fraction of
÷	division	a whole into parts; how many equal amounts of a whole

At this point, you have done a quick review of basic math. None of this should have been overly difficult. Every concept from this point forward is based on these operations.

PRACTICE SET: WHOLE NUMBERS AND BASIC OPERATIONS

The following questions test your basic math skills. Read carefully, then select the best answer to each question.

1. What is the value of the **9** in the number 291,380?

    (1)   9
    (2)   90
    (3)   900
    (4)   9,000
    (5)   90,000

Use the chart below to answer question 2.

Ted's Monthly Mileage Record	
June	1751
July	987
August	1993
September	667
October	1201

2. Rounded to the nearest thousand, how many miles did Ted drive during this five-month period?

    (1)   6,000
    (2)   6,500
    (3)   6,600
    (4)   7,000
    (5)   8,000

3.   9,238
    + 4,587

Enter your response in the alternate format grid below.

4. Elaine bought a stereo system at a total cost of $372. She uses a payment plan that divides her cost into three equal monthly payments. Which expression can be used to find the amount of one payment?

   (1)   372 + 3
   (2)   372 ÷ 2
   (3)   372 ÷ 3
   (4)   372 − 3
   (5)   None of these expressions will find the correct answer.

For problem 5, you may use your calculator.

5. Ice Palace produces 107 ice cream bars in a day. At this rate, how many ice cream bars will be produced in a week?

   (1)   114
   (2)   535
   (3)   642
   (4)   700
   (5)   749

Check your answers on page 392. How did you do? If you got most of the answers right, you should be feeling calm and confident! You are ready to take a moment to get acquainted with your calculator.

USING THE *fx*-260 CALCULATOR

The Mathematics test is divided into two parts. You are tested on all of the material covered on the rungs in the ladder on both parts. What differentiates the two sections is calculator use. You can use a calculator on Part I but not on Part II.

You can't use just any calculator. In fact, you must use the one provided to you at the testing center, a Casio *fx*-260 solar calculator, the official calculator for the GED test, and you have to be able to use it.

You will receive directions on how to use this calculator at the beginning of the Mathematics test, but we highly recommended that you practice using this guide. Not all calculators perform mathematical operations the same way. You don't want to get frustrated or lose time figuring out how to use the *fx*-260 calculator when you should be focused on the test. You can buy the Casio *fx*-260 at major mass retailers and office supply stores. They usually cost between $10 and $15 and are even cheaper online.

Here are the directions for the Casio *fx*-260 that are provided at the beginning of the Mathematics test:

CALCULATOR DIRECTIONS

To prepare the calculator for use the <u>first</u> time, press the (ON) (upper-rightmost) key. "DEG" will appear at the top-center of the screen and "0." at the right. This indicates the calculator is in the proper format for all your calculations.

To prepare the calculator for <u>another</u> question, press the (ON) or the red (AC) key. This clears any entries made previously.

To do any arithmetic, enter the expression as it is written. Press (=) (equals sign) when finished.
EXAMPLE A: 8 − 3 + 9
     First press (ON) or (AC).
     Enter the following:
     8 (−) 3 (+) 9 (=)
     The correct answer is 14.

If an expression in parentheses is to be multiplied by a number, press (×) (multiplication sign) between the number and the parenthesis sign.
EXAMPLE B: 6(8 + 5)
     First press (ON) or (AC).
     Enter the following:
     6 (×) ([(---) 8 (+) 5 (---)]) (=)
     The correct answer is 78.

To find the square root of a number,
     • enter the number
     • press (SHIFT) (upper-leftmost) key ("SHIFT" appears at the top-left of the screen);
     • press (x²) (third from the left on top row) to access its second function: square root. DO NOT press (SHIFT) and (x²) at the same time.
EXAMPLE C: √64
     First press (ON) or (AC).
     Enter the following:
     64 (SHIFT) (x²)
     The correct answer is 8.

To enter a negative number such as −8,
     • enter the number without the negative sign (enter 8);
     • press the "change sign" ((+/−)) key which is directly above the 7 key.
All arithmetic can be done with positive and/or negative numbers.
EXAMPLE D: −8 − −5
     First press (ON) or (AC).
     Enter the following.
     8 (+/−) (−) 5 (+/−) (=)
     The correct answer is −3.

In addition to these directions, the test administrator provides several practice questions before the test officially begins so you will be comfortable using the calculator.

Try out your calculator skills on the questions that follow.

CHAPTER

7

MATHEMATICS

THE
GED

INTRODUCTION

WHOLE NUMBERS AND BASIC OPERATIONS

USING THE *fx-260* **CALCULATOR**

FRACTIONS, DECIMALS, AND PERCENTAGES

MEASUREMENT

DATA ANALYSIS

ALGEBRA

GEOMETRY

PRACTICE SET: USING THE *fx*–260 CALCULATOR

The following questions test your familiarity with your calculator. Figure carefully, then select the best answer to each question. You may use a calculator on all five questions.

1. 7 ⊗ 8 ⊖ 4 ⊗ 5 ⊜

    (1)   20
    (2)   36
    (3)   140
    (4)   260
    (5)   344

2. $3\frac{1}{4}$ ⊕ $1\frac{2}{3}$ ⊜

    (1) $4\frac{3}{7}$
    (2) $4\frac{11}{12}$
    (3) $1\frac{7}{12}$
    (4) $5\frac{5}{12}$
    (5) $\frac{83}{322}$

3. Convert 6,088 meters to kilometers.
   Enter your response in the alternate format grid.

4. What is $\sqrt{5} + 9^3$, rounded to the nearest tenth?

    (1)   29.2
    (2)   32
    (3)   60.4
    (4)   731.2
    (5)   1630.1

5. What is 30% of 5,690?

    (1)   5660
    (2)   3983
    (3)   1707
    (4)   190
    (5)   170

Check your answers on pages 392–393. How did you do? If you got most of the answers right, you're comfortable using the calculator. Let's move on to problems with fractions, decimals, and percentages.

FRACTIONS, DECIMALS, AND PERCENTAGES

Although counting numbers are used for the majority of everyday math problems, they sometimes fail to express our math needs. You need gasoline for your car and find that 12 gallons is not enough, but 13 is too much. Perhaps you have eight slices of pizza to share among three friends. It is important to know whether your fever of over 100° is closer to 100° or to 101°. In all these instances, there is a need for numbers that fall between the traditional counting numbers. This is the world of fractions and decimals.

CHAPTER

7

MATHEMATICS

FRACTIONS

Fractions show parts of numbers. A fraction has a numerator (the number on top) and a denominator (the number on bottom). The numerator shows the number of parts being considered, and the denominator shows the total number of equal parts.

 The line in between the numerator and denominator is called the fraction bar. It means "divided by." So $\frac{1}{2}$ is read "1 divided by 2."

THE

GED

This shows $\frac{1}{2}$, or one-half.
Two equal parts, one is shaded.

This shows $\frac{1}{4}$ or one-quarter.
The shaded part is one-quarter of the entire square.

Now try this problem:

Ned brought home 12 eggs. Seven were broken. What fraction of the eggs was broken?

(1) $\frac{12}{12}$

(2) $\frac{12}{7}$

(3) $\frac{12}{5}$

(4) $\frac{5}{12}$

(5) $\frac{7}{12}$

 Fractions that have the same numerator and denominator or a numerator that is larger than the denominator are called **improper** fractions.

A fraction indicates:

$$\frac{\text{How many you are asking about}}{\text{How many total}}$$

The question asks for

$$\frac{\text{The number of broken eggs}}{\text{Total eggs}} = \frac{7}{12}$$

The answer is (5), $\frac{7}{12}$ of Ned's eggs were broken. Answer (1) indicates that all of the eggs were broken. Answers (2) and (3) indicate that more eggs were broken than there were to start with. Answer (4) indicates the number of eggs that were not broken.

Name the fraction illustrated in each example.

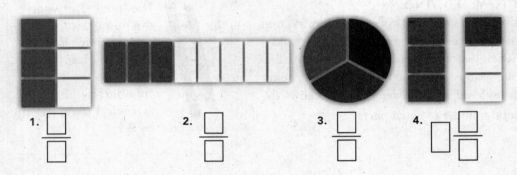

1. $\Box \over \Box$ 2. $\Box \over \Box$ 3. $\Box \over \Box$ 4. $\Box \Box \over \Box$

1. $\frac{3}{6}$ Three parts out of the six are shaded.
2. $\frac{3}{8}$ Three parts out of the eight are shaded.
3. $\frac{3}{3}$, **or 3 ÷ 3 = 1** All three parts out of the three are shaded, so $\frac{3}{3}$ is correct, although it is an improper fraction and not usually written this way. When a fraction has the same numerator and denominator, it is one whole.
4. $\frac{4}{3}$ **or 1$\frac{1}{3}$** Again, although $\frac{4}{3}$ is a correct description of the figures, it is an improper fraction because the numerator is higher than the denominator. Because neither figure is divided into sixths, $\frac{4}{6}$ is not a correct answer.

CHANGING IMPROPER FRACTIONS TO PROPER FRACTIONS

Change $\frac{4}{3}$ to a proper fraction.

You can see that $\frac{4}{3}$ is actually $\frac{3}{3} + \frac{1}{3}$. Therefore, the proper fraction is $1\frac{1}{3}$.

To convert $\frac{4}{3}$, say to yourself:

3 goes into 4 how many times?	One time.	= 1
How many left over?	$\frac{1}{3}$ is left.	= $\frac{1}{3}$
Answer:		= $1\frac{1}{3}$

Improper Fraction	Numerator	Divided by	Denominator	Proper Fraction
$\frac{4}{3}$	4	÷	3	$1\frac{1}{3}$
$\frac{95}{6}$	95	÷	6	$15\frac{5}{6}$
$\frac{3}{3}$	3	÷	3	1
$\frac{81}{9}$	81	÷	9	9

You can also change a proper fraction to an improper fraction.

Change $1\frac{1}{3}$ to an improper fraction.

Multiply the denominator by the whole number.	$1\frac{1}{3}$	$3 \times 1 = 3$
Add the numerator.	$1\frac{1}{3}$	$3 + 1 = 4$
Write that total over the denominator.	$\frac{4}{3}$	

$\frac{4}{3}$ is the improper fraction for $1\frac{1}{3}$.

Change $15\frac{5}{6}$ to an improper fraction.

Multiply the denominator by the whole number.	$15\frac{5}{6}$	$15 \times 6 = 90$
Add the numerator.	$15\frac{5}{6}$	$90 + 5 = 95$
Write that total over the denominator.	$\frac{95}{6}$	

$\frac{95}{6}$ is the improper fraction for $15\frac{5}{6}$.

EQUAL FRACTIONS

One day Carlos goes into a pizza parlor and orders a pizza. The clerk asks if he would like it cut into eight or ten pieces. "Oh, eight, please," answers Carlos. "I can't eat ten pieces!"

What makes this joke funny is that Carlos doesn't realize that the pizza is the same amount of food whether it is cut into eight slices or ten. If he can eat $\frac{8}{8}$ of a pizza, he can eat $\frac{10}{10}$ of a pizza.

In the following illustration, you can easily see the equal fractions:

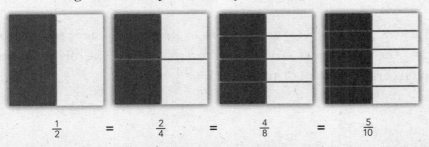

$$\frac{1}{2} \quad = \quad \frac{2}{4} \quad = \quad \frac{4}{8} \quad = \quad \frac{5}{10}$$

CHAPTER

7

MATHEMATICS

THE
GED

INTRODUCTION

WHOLE NUMBERS
AND BASIC
OPERATIONS

USING THE *fx-260*

FRACTIONS,
DECIMALS, AND
PERCENTAGES

MEASUREMENT

DATA ANALYSIS

ALGEBRA

GEOMETRY

You can also use **cross products** to determine if fractions are equal.

Are $\frac{3}{6}$ and $\frac{5}{10}$ equal fractions?

$$\frac{3}{6} \diagup\!\!\!\!\diagdown \frac{5}{10} \qquad \text{cross} \atop \text{multiply} \qquad \overset{30}{\underset{}{\frac{3}{6}}} \diagup\!\!\!\!\diagdown \overset{30}{\underset{}{\frac{5}{10}}}$$

$30 = 30$; yes, these fractions are equal.

Cross products can be used to find the larger of two fractions as well. Multiply, then compare the results. If the number on the left is larger, then the fraction on the left is the larger one. If the number on the right is larger, then the fraction on the right is larger.

Which is the larger fraction, $\frac{7}{8}$ or $\frac{5}{6}$?

$$\overset{42}{\underset{}{\frac{7}{8}}} \diagup\!\!\!\!\diagdown \overset{40}{\underset{}{\frac{5}{6}}}$$

$\frac{7}{8}$ is the larger fraction.

RATIOS AND PROPORTION

You must compare fractions when using ratios and proportions. A **ratio** is a fraction that relates one occurrence to another. For every apple, I have two oranges, so the ratio of apples to oranges is 1 to 2. **Proportion** describes the relationship between parts as the total increases or decreases. In other words, we can scale ratios up and down, but the proportion remains the same. If the ratios represent equal fractions, then they also represent equivalent proportions—just as $\frac{1}{2} = \frac{2}{4} = \frac{4}{8} = \frac{5}{10}$, 1:2 = 2:4 = 4:8 = 5:10.

RATIOS

They easiest way to see and understand ratios is to look at a real-life example.

PRACTICE

When Sunny cooks rice, she uses 1 cup of rice with 2 cups of water. What is the ratio of rice to water?

(1)   1 to 1
(2)   1 to 2
(3)   2 to 2
(4)   1 to 3
(5)   1:1

Answers (1), (3), and (5) are the same expression that show equal parts water and rice. Answer (4) shows 1 cup of water to 3 cups of rice. The correct answer is (2). The ratio of rice to water is **1 to 2**, or **1:2**, or $\frac{1}{2}$.

PRACTICE

How much water should Sunny use if she wants to cook 3 cups of rice?

  (1) $\frac{1}{2}$ cup
  (2)   1 cup
  (3)   2 cups
  (4)   4 cups
  (5)   6 cups

Use the given fraction to increase the proportion. The ratio reads, "For every 1 cup of rice, use 2 cups of water." If Sunny uses 2 cups of rice, she needs 4 cups of water.

$$\frac{1 \text{ cup rice}}{2 \text{ cups water}} = \frac{2}{4} = \frac{3}{6} = \frac{4}{8} = \frac{5}{10} \text{ rice} \atop \text{water}$$

For 3 cups of rice, Sunny should use 6 cups of water—answer (5). Answers (1), (2), and (3) are incorrect because to make 3 cups of rice, it is clear that Sunny will need more than the 2 cups of water that she needs to make 1 cup of rice. Answer (4) is only twice as much water as is needed for 1 cup of rice.

 Although ratios look like improper fractions, it is correct to leave them that way. They are written correctly.

PRACTICE

To make the color he needs, Perry mixes 3 gallons of green paint for every 2 gallons of blue paint. How many gallons of blue paint will be needed with 12 gallons of green paint?

  (1)   3 gallons
  (2)   5 gallons
  (3)   7 gallons
  (4)   8 gallons
  (5)   12 gallons

$$\frac{3 \text{ gallons of green paint}}{2 \text{ gallons of red paint}} \quad \begin{array}{c} \times \\ \times \end{array} \frac{4}{4} = \frac{12}{8}$$

The key words are *how many*. We can estimate that the amount of blue paint needed to mix with 12 gallons of green will be a multiple of 2 (the proportion of blue in the original ratio), yet smaller than 12 (the amount of green, which is larger than the amount of blue in the original ratio). The ratio of green to blue is 3:2. What is the relationship between 3 gallons and 12 gallons of green paint? Divide 12 by 3 to find that the number of gallons of green paint to be used is 4 times the number given in the ratio. So Perry should also multiply the number of gallons of blue paint by 4 to find out how many are needed to maintain the correct proportion with the green: 8 gallons of blue paint are needed. The other answers are incorrect because they are either not divisible by 2 or not smaller than 12.

You can also work backward to find an amount *per* unit, or a rate.

PRACTICE

Renee earned $96 for 6 hours of work. What was her rate per hour?

(1) $16
(2) $90
(3) $96
(4) $102
(5) $576

$$\frac{96}{6 \text{ hours}} = \frac{?}{1 \text{ hour}}$$

It makes sense that if Renee earns $96 for 6 hours, then the amount she earns per hour is less than $96. Answers (3), (4), and (5) are all too large. Answer (2) is less than $96, but if she made $90 per hour, she would have earned more than $96 in 6 hours. To solve this problem, divide the amount of money earned by the number of hours worked: $96 \div 6 = 16$. Answer (1) is correct; Renee earned $16 per hour.

It is helpful to set up your ratio using the labels in the problem so you can keep track.

PRACTICE

The gumball machine has 36 gumballs, colored yellow and red. There are 27 yellow gumballs. What is the ratio of yellow to red gumballs?

(1)   36 to 27
(2)   4:3
(3)   1:3
(4)   3:1
(5)   4

Write your labels down first so that you know exactly what information you need. A fraction indicates:

$$\frac{\text{How many you are asking about}}{\text{How many total}}$$

The question asks for

$$\frac{\text{\# of yellow gumballs}}{\text{\# of red gumballs}} = \frac{\text{This information was in the problem}}{\substack{\text{This was not stated, but can be} \\ \text{learned from the problem:} \\ \text{36 total} - \text{27 yellow gumballs}}} = \frac{27}{9} \text{ reduces to } \frac{3}{1}$$

Answers (1) and (2) are the same ratio, but they compare total gumballs to red ones. Answer (5) is not in the form of a ratio. Answer (3) has the ratio backwards. Answer (4) is correct: the ratio of yellow to red gumballs is 3 to 1, or $\frac{1}{3}$, or 3:1.

Make sure you keep your labels in order. It does not matter whether yellow or red or gumballs is the numerator or denominator, but if you put yellow on top, keep yellow on top throughout that problem. If the problem asks for yellow to red, put the numbers in that order.

PROPORTIONS

Proportions are equivalent ratios. You can use cross products (mentioned on page 310) to find proportions.

PRACTICE

Tyler can wash 9 cars in 1 hour. At this rate, how many hours will it take him to wash 36 cars?

(1) 3
(2) 4
(3) 18
(4) 36
(5) 324

Tyler can wash almost 10 cars in an hour, so to wash almost 40 would not take him more than 4 hours. With that estimate, you can eliminate answers (3), (4), and (5) immediately, so it is between answers (1) and (2). One way to solve this equation is to set the ratios up as equal ratios, then use cross products to find the missing term: 1×36 is 36, and 9 times what is 36?

$$\frac{9 \text{ cars}}{1 \text{ hour}} = \frac{36 \text{ cars}}{? \text{ hours}}$$

Since $4 \times 9 = 36$, 4 is the missing term. Answer (2) is correct: it will take Tyler 4 hours to wash 36 cars.

REDUCING FRACTIONS

Fractions are easier to work with if they are in their lowest terms. Asking for $\frac{18}{36}$ of a pound of coffee may be the same as asking for a $\frac{1}{2}$ pound, but it will be very confusing for the sales clerk! To reduce a fraction, divide both the numerator and the denominator by the same number.

PRACTICE

During the game, 15 goals were attempted. Out of those, 10 were missed. What fraction of the goals was missed?

(1) $\frac{2}{3}$
(2) $\frac{15}{10}$
(3) 10
(4) $\frac{1}{5}$
(5) $\frac{5}{15}$

Answers (2) through (5) are varying placements of numbers in the problem as numerators and denominators. Answer (3) isn't even a ratio. The ratio of missed goals to attempted goals is $\frac{10}{15}$, but this is not given as a choice. You must reduce the fraction to its lowest terms. Ask yourself: "What number, if any, will divide into both numerator and denominator?"

$$\frac{10 \div 5}{15 \div 5} = \frac{2}{3}$$

Answer (1) is correct: $\frac{2}{3}$ of the goals were missed. Answers on the GED test always are in lowest terms. This means that if you have an answer that does not meet any of the choices, it is possible that you have the correct answer but just need to reduce it further.

PRACTICE

Forty-two bags of wheat were in the warehouse. Mice chewed through 24 of them. What fraction of the bags was NOT chewed?

(1) $\frac{4}{7}$

(2)   18

(3)   2.3

(4) $\frac{1}{2}$

(5) $\frac{3}{7}$

The key words are *NOT chewed*. You must find the number of bags that were not chewed and write it over the total number of bags. The number of bags the mice *did not chew* is not given in the problem, but the problem does provide enough information to find it. The total number of bags minus the number of bags chewed equals the number of bags not chewed, or $42 - 24 = 18$. The fraction of bags not chewed is $\frac{18}{24}$. Start by dividing each number by two. You are left with $\frac{9}{21}$. This is not yet completely reduced. Divide again by 3. This makes answer (5) correct: $\frac{3}{7}$ of the bags in the warehouse were not chewed. Answer (2) is the number of bags not chewed, but the question calls for a fraction. Answer (1) is the fraction that *were* chewed.

ADDING AND SUBTRACTING FRACTIONS

$\frac{1}{5} + \frac{2}{5} =$

$\frac{7}{8} - \frac{4}{8} =$

If the denominators are the same, simply add or subtract the numerators, keeping the same denominator.

$\frac{1}{5} + \frac{2}{5} = \frac{3}{5}$

$\frac{7}{8} - \frac{4}{8} = \frac{3}{8}$

If the denominators are not the same, you must find a common, or same, denominator.

PRACTICE

In Nassir's Shoe Store, $\frac{2}{5}$ of the shoes were black, and $\frac{1}{2}$ were brown. What fraction of the shoes was black or brown?

(1) $\frac{3}{7}$

(2) $\frac{6}{10}$

(3) $\frac{9}{10}$

(4) $\frac{2}{10}$

(5) $\frac{12}{10}$

The denominators are 5 and 2. You can get a quick common denominator by multiplying them by each other. Don't forget to multiply the numerator by the same number as its denominator.

$$\frac{2}{5} \times \frac{2}{2} = \frac{4}{10}$$
$$+ \frac{1}{2} \times \frac{5}{5} = \frac{5}{10}$$
$$\overline{\frac{9}{10}}$$

Answer (1) merely adds the numerators and denominators. This is never correct. Answers (2), (4), and (5) have the denominators converted correctly, but the numerators converted incorrectly. Answer (3) is correct: $\frac{9}{10}$ of the shoes were black or brown.

PRACTICE

Tara bought $\frac{3}{4}$ of a yard of cloth. The pattern used $\frac{1}{2}$ of a yard. How much cloth will Tara have left over after she uses the pattern?

(1) $\frac{1}{2}$

(2) $\frac{2}{2}$

(3) $\frac{2}{4}$

(4) $\frac{3}{2}$

(5) $\frac{1}{4}$

$$\frac{3}{4} \times \frac{1}{1} = \frac{3}{4}$$
$$- \frac{1}{2} \times \frac{2}{2} = \frac{2}{4}$$
$$\overline{\frac{1}{4}}$$

The denominators are 4 and 2. The first number they share is 4. You could use 8 or 12, but it is easiest to use the lowest common denominator. Answers (1) and (3) represent the same amount: half. Answer (2) is straight subtraction of the numerators and denominators, which is never correct. Answer (4) is the same as $1\frac{1}{2}$, which is more than Tara started with, so this answer is also incorrect. Answer (5) is correct: $\frac{1}{4}$ of the cloth is left.

If the answer results in an improper fraction, don't forget to reduce it again.

THE

GED

PRACTICE

Nancy bought $\frac{5}{6}$ pound of coffee and $\frac{1}{2}$ pound of tea. How much did her total purchase weigh?

(1)　　$\frac{6}{8}$ pound

(2)　　$\frac{6}{6}$ pound

(3)　　$\frac{5}{12}$ pound

(4)　　$1\frac{1}{3}$ pound

(5)　　$1\frac{1}{2}$ pound

$$\begin{array}{r} \frac{5}{6} \times 1 \quad \frac{5}{6} \\ +\ \frac{1}{2} \times \frac{3}{4} \quad \frac{3}{6} \\ \hline \frac{8}{6} \end{array}$$

First, estimate the answer: $\frac{5}{6}$ is almost 1, so "almost 1" plus $\frac{1}{2}$ will be more than 1 but less than $1\frac{1}{2}$. To add $\frac{5}{6}$ and $\frac{1}{2}$, first you must put the fractions in common denominators. $\frac{1}{2}$ is the same as $\frac{3}{6}$. $\frac{5}{6} + \frac{3}{6} = \frac{8}{6}$, but this is an improper fraction, so it will not appear as a choice. Reduce: 6 goes into 8 one time, with 2 left over. This leaves the fraction $1\frac{2}{6}$, but $\frac{2}{6}$ is still not reduced. Answer (4) is correct: Nancy's total purchase was $1\frac{1}{3}$ pounds. Answer (1) is just the sum of the numerators over the sum of the denominators, which is not the right way to add fractions. Answer (2) is incorrect because $\frac{6}{6}$ is the same as 1, which your estimation should tell you is too low to be the answer. Answer (3) is the product, not the sum, of the fractions. Answer (5) is incorrect because your estimation should tell you that the answer is smaller than $1\frac{1}{2}$.

ADDING AND SUBTRACTING MIXED NUMBERS

PRACTICE

Len worked on his boat for $6\frac{1}{2}$ hours on Saturday and $7\frac{3}{8}$ hours on Sunday. How much time did he spend working on his boat over the weekend?

(1)　　$13\frac{5}{12}$ hours

(2)　　$13\frac{6}{6}$ hours

(3)　　$13\frac{7}{8}$ hours

(4)　　$1\frac{7}{8}$ hours

(5)　　14 hours

First, estimate the answer: $7\frac{3}{8}$ is almost $7\frac{1}{2}$, and $7\frac{1}{2} + 6\frac{1}{2}$ would be 14, so $7\frac{3}{8} + 6\frac{1}{2}$ will be almost 14.

Now, set the problem up.

$$6\frac{1}{2} \times \frac{4}{4} \quad \frac{4}{8}$$
$$+ 7\frac{3}{8} \times \frac{1}{1} \quad \frac{3}{8}$$
$$\overline{13 \qquad \frac{7}{8}}$$

To add the two compound fractions, add the whole numbers and add the fractions. Again, you must find the common denominator: 8 is a multiple of two, so multiply $\frac{1}{2}$ by $\frac{4}{4}$ to make it $\frac{4}{8}$, a number you can easily add to $\frac{3}{8}$. $6 + 7 = 13$, and $\frac{4}{8} + \frac{3}{8} = \frac{7}{8}$, so answer (3), 13, is correct. Answers (1) and (2) are both closer to 13 than 14, and your estimate said that the answer would be almost 14, so they are wrong. Answer (4) is a smaller amount of time than Len worked on either day, so it could not possibly be the sum of hours worked on both days. Answer (5) is exactly 14 hours, but your estimate told you the answer would be *almost*, but *not quite*, 14.

PRACTICE

How much more time did Len work on Sunday than on Saturday?

(1) $\frac{7}{8}$ hours

(2) $1\frac{1}{4}$ hours

(3) $1\frac{7}{8}$ hours

(4) $1\frac{1}{8}$ hours

(5) $\frac{1}{8}$ hours

The key words are *how much*. You can estimate the answer. As we saw in the previous question, $7\frac{3}{8}$ is almost $7\frac{1}{2}$. $7\frac{1}{2}$ minus $6\frac{1}{2}$ would be 1, so $7\frac{3}{8}$ minus $6\frac{1}{2}$ is almost 1.

Now, set the problem up and solve it.

$$\overset{6}{\cancel{7}}\frac{3}{8} \times \frac{1}{1} \quad \overset{\frac{8}{8} + \frac{3}{8} = \frac{11}{8}}{\frac{3}{8}}$$
$$- 6\frac{1}{2} \times \frac{4}{4} \quad \frac{4}{8}$$
$$\overline{\qquad\qquad \frac{7}{8}}$$

When subtracting fractions, you need to put the fractions in the same form as when adding fractions. So, $7\frac{3}{8} - 6\frac{1}{2}$ can be written as $7\frac{3}{8} - 6\frac{4}{8}$. We can't subtract $\frac{4}{8}$ from $\frac{3}{8}$, but just as in a whole-number subtraction problem, there are times when you must borrow to subtract fractions. Here, you borrow from the whole number. Remember that a whole number is any fraction that has the same numerator and denominator. You can borrow 1 from the 7 and use it as $\frac{8}{8}$. Now you can express the problem as $6\frac{11}{8} - 6\frac{4}{8}$, and it's easy to see that the answer is $\frac{7}{8}$. Answers (2) and (4) subtracted the fractions incorrectly. Answer (3) forgot to make the 7 into a 6 when borrowing. Answer (1) is correct: Len worked $\frac{7}{8}$ more hours on Sunday. Answers (2), (3), and (4) are all more than 1, and your estimation said the difference would be almost, but not quite, 1. Answer (5) is incorrect because it is closer to 0 than 1.

THE
GED

MULTIPLYING FRACTIONS

Multiplying fractions is as easy as multiplying regular numbers. Let's look at three examples.

$$\frac{1}{2} \times \frac{2}{3} = -$$

$$\frac{8}{9} \times \frac{1}{4} = -$$

$$\frac{4}{5} \times \frac{3}{7} = -$$

To multiply fractions, multiply straight across, numerators and denominators. (Don't forget to reduce those answers!)

$$\frac{1 \times 2}{2 \times 3} = \frac{2}{6} = \frac{1}{3}$$

$$\frac{8 \times 1}{9 \times 4} = \frac{8}{36} = \frac{1}{4}$$

$$\frac{4 \times 3}{5 \times 7} = \frac{12}{35}$$

MULTIPLYING FRACTIONS WITH MIXED NUMBERS

When multiplying fractions with mixed numbers, do *not* straight multiply the whole numbers. Change both fractions to improper fractions as needed, then multiply as before.

PRACTICE

Doug needs $1\frac{3}{4}$ cups of flour for a dozen cookies. If he is making $2\frac{1}{2}$ dozen cookies, how much total flour will he need?

(1) $4\frac{1}{4}$ cups

(2) $4\frac{3}{8}$ cups

(3) $3\frac{3}{8}$ cups

(4) $3\frac{1}{4}$ cups

(5) $\frac{1}{12}$ cups

$$1\frac{3}{4} \times 2\frac{1}{2} =$$

$$\frac{7}{4} \times \frac{5}{2} = \frac{35}{8} = 4\frac{3}{8} \text{ cup}$$

 Do not let the word **dozen** confuse you— it is just a unit. You could just as well think of it as "Doug needs $1\frac{3}{4}$ cups of flour for 12 cookies. Two and a half dozen is 30 cookies. How much flour will he need to make 30 cookies?"

To find the answer, multiply $1\frac{3}{4}$ and $2\frac{1}{2}$. First, convert both numbers to improper fractions: $1\frac{3}{4} = \frac{7}{4}$, and $2\frac{1}{2} = \frac{5}{2}$. Now you have $\frac{7}{4} \times \frac{5}{2}$, and you can multiply straight across to get the answer:

$$\frac{7 \times 5}{4 \times 2} = \frac{35}{8}$$

Now rewrite that as a proper fraction, and you see that Doug needs $4\frac{3}{8}$ cups of flour. Answer (1) incorrectly added the fractions. Answer (3) multiplied all numbers individually. Answer (4) is less than double the amount needed for one dozen cookies, and we know he needs more than double that amount. Answer (5) is even less than is needed to make one dozen, and we know he needs more than the amount needed for one dozen. Answer (2) is correct: Doug needs $4\frac{3}{8}$ cups of flour.

DIVIDING WITH FRACTIONS

At some point during your work in multiplication and division, you likely noticed that multiplication and division are **inverse operations**. You create the inverse of a number by switching the numerator and denominator, so the inverse of $\frac{5}{6}$ is $\frac{6}{5}$. All whole numbers are considered to have the denominator 1, so the inverse of 3 is $\frac{1}{3}$. Dividing is the same thing as multiplying by the inverse. This means that $\frac{3}{4} \div \frac{5}{6}$ is the same as $\frac{3}{4} \times \frac{6}{5}$, and $12 \div 3$ is the same as $12 \times \frac{1}{3}$. When working with fraction division, it is easiest to work with inverse multiplication.

$$\frac{2}{3} \div \frac{1}{6} = \text{—}$$

You can think of this problem as asking, "Two-thirds can be divided into how many one-sixths?" or better yet, "How many one-sixths are there in two-thirds?"

To solve this type of problem, simply invert, or turn over, the fraction you are dividing by.

$\frac{2}{3} \times \frac{1}{6} =$ **Don't forget to change to a proper fraction and reduce if necessary.** $\frac{12}{3} = 4$

This means that the fraction $\frac{2}{3}$ has **four** $\frac{1}{6}$s. You can confirm it by drawing an illustration.

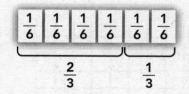

THE
GED

PRACTICE

Ferry needs $\frac{2}{3}$ of a yard of cloth to make one bear costume for the play. How many bear costumes will he be able to make using 24 yards of cloth?

(1)   1
(2)   8
(3)   14
(4)   36
(5)   48

Again, you can estimate the answer. If it takes a little less than a yard to make one costume, then the number has to be more than 24. Answers (1), (2), and (3) can be eliminated immediately, because they are all less than 24. Now set up the problem:

$$24 \div \frac{2}{3} = \frac{24}{1} \div \frac{2}{3} = \frac{24}{1} \times \frac{3}{2} = \frac{72}{2} = 36$$

To divide fractions, remember to multiply by the inverse. Answer (4) proves to be correct: Ferry can make 36 costumes.

DECIMALS

Fractions are one way of writing amounts that describe parts of numbers. Another way is using **decimals**. Decimals are the numbers on the place-value chart to the right of the ones column. They represent one whole divided into tenths, hundredths, thousandths, and so on.

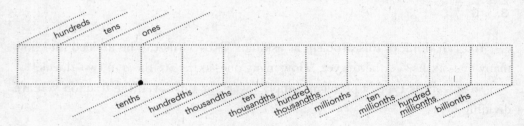

Rounding decimals is very important when you consider that money is written in decimal form! A cent is worth $\frac{1}{100}$ of a dollar, or 1 per**cent** of a dollar. Although when dealing with money, we only use the first two places to the right of the decimal—the tens and hundreds places—we could continue to the right to represent thousandths, ten-thousandths, hundred-thousandths, and so on.

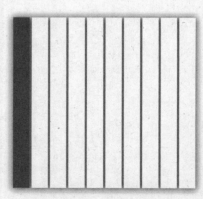

$\frac{1}{10}$, or 0.1

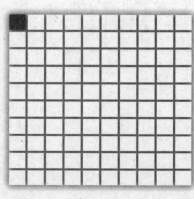

$\frac{1}{100}$, or 0.01

How do you write 6,185.207 in words?

Start with the numbers to the left of the decimal. Although it is common to say six thousand, one hundred **and** eighty-five, do not do this! Say "and" only at the decimal mark, just before you read everything to the right of it: "Six thousand, one hundred eighty-five **and** two hundred seven thousandths" is the correct way to read 6,185.207.

DECIMAL RULES OF THUMB

A zero is often written to the left of the decimal when there is no whole number. Although .36 is a correct expression of thirty-six tenths, it is better to write 0.36. This does not change the number, but helps the reader recognize that a decimal is present.

Adding zeros behind the last number after a decimal does not change the number. 3.6, 3.60, 3.600, and 3.6000 are all the same number. However, it is usually preferred that all unnecessary zeros are dropped when writing a decimal number. The GED answers do not contain these extra zeros.

To round decimals, use the same procedure as rounding whole numbers.

Round 65.792 to the nearest tenth.

$$65\,⑦92$$

Look to the right of the 7, which is the digit in the tenths place. Because 9 is larger than 5, change the 7 to an 8. Change all numbers to the right of the 8 to zeros, or just drop them.

   65.792 rounds to 65.800 or 65.8.

PRACTICE

Lily bought food for the family reunion.

Pasta $10.10
Sauce $ 5.75
Salad $ 8.02
Bread $ 9.99

She paid with a $50 and got back $11.14 in change. Was this the right amount of change?

   At first glance, it seems to be right. She did buy a lot of food, and she got back a good bit of change. However, if she had made a quick estimate of her total, she would have found this:

THE
GED

Item	Cost	Estimate
Pasta	$ 10.10	$ 10
Sauce	$ 5.75	$ 6
Salad	$ 8.02	$ 8
Bread	$ 9.99	$ 10
Total:		**$ 34**

$50 – $34 = $16. Did you notice that this was a multistep problem? In order to find out how much change Lily should have received, you had to do two operations. First, you had to add the food prices to get a total. Next, you had to subtract that amount from what she paid. Use your order of operations from page 301 to make sure you used the numbers successfully.

The change was wrong by about $5.

PRACTICE

If Lily's grocery bill is wrong by an average of $5 each week, how much will this cost her in a year?

(1) $5
(2) $10
(3) $57
(4) $100
(5) $260

Answer (1) is the amount in one week. Answer (2) is the amount in two weeks. Answer (3) added 52 weeks to $5. Being shortchanged $5 per week × 52 weeks in a year will result in overpayment of $260, or answer (5). It pays to estimate!

When comparing decimal numbers, make sure to compare like places.

Which is larger, 0.1 or 0.09?

Although 9 is a larger number than 1, in this case 0.09 is not the larger number. There are two places to the right of the decimal in 0.09, and only one place in the number 0.1. Remember, you can put any amount of zeros after the 1 to help you visualize the amounts.

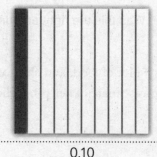

0.10

One-tenth is the same as ten hundredths.

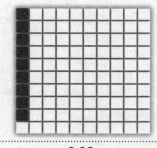

0.09

Nine-hundredths is less than ten hundredths.

THE

GED

INTRODUCTION

WHOLE NUMBERS
AND BASIC
OPERATIONS

USING THE *fx-260*

**FRACTIONS,
DECIMALS, AND
PERCENTAGES**

MEASUREMENT

DATA ANALYSIS

ALGEBRA

GEOMETRY

322

When comparing decimal numbers, make sure to take whole numbers into account.

Which is the larger number, 12.002 or 1.999?

Whole numbers ordered **before** the decimal parts are considered. Twelve is larger than one, so 12.002 is the larger number despite the .999.

A digital scale at the pharmacy weighed the medicine amounts at 1.09 g, 0.004 g, 0.096 g, and 0.108 g. Put these amounts in order from least to greatest.

Line up the numbers in columns, fill in any zeros to help you, and compare.

1.0900
0.0040
0.0960
0.1082

In order from least to greatest, the numbers are 0.004, 0.096, 0.1082, 1.09.

ADDING AND SUBTRACTING DECIMALS

Addition and subtraction with decimals uses all the same rules as whole numbers, with one important point to remember: you must always line up the decimals of the numbers you are working with.

To solve the problem 13.14 + 0.907, do not place the numbers directly under each other. They must line up in order of place value.

$$\begin{array}{r} 13.140 \\ + 0.907 \\ \hline 14.047 \end{array} \qquad \begin{array}{r} 13.14 \\ + .0907 \\ \hline \textbf{WRONG} \end{array}$$

This also holds true for subtraction. If a place is empty in the top number, simply insert a zero and continue as the rules of subtraction dictate.

What is 56.7 − 0.421?

$$\begin{array}{r} 56.7 \\ - 0.421 \end{array} \qquad \begin{array}{r} {}^{6\,9\,1}56.\cancel{7}\cancel{0}0 \\ - 0.421 \\ \hline 56.279 \end{array}$$

Fill in the answer to this problem on the alternative format grid.

PRACTICE

Buy-a-Lot Foods sells tomatoes for $1.29 per pound. If Trey buys 1.8 pounds, what will be his cost to the nearest cent?

(1) $3.09
(2) $2.32
(3) $1.29
(4) $0.51
(5) $23.32

When setting up decimal multiplication problems, it is not necessary to line up the decimals. However, you must keep track of the number of decimal places. There are two decimal places in 1.29 and one decimal place in 1.8. When you are done multiplying, move the decimal three places to the left in the answer.

```
    1.29   two decimal places
 x  1.8    one decimal place
   1032    three decimal places
 + 1290
   2.322   move 3 places
```

The cost of the tomatoes is a little over $1 per pound. If Trey bought almost two pounds, then his cost should be somewhere around $2. Answers (3), (4), and (5) are suspicious. Answer (1) adds the two numbers in the problem. The answer is 2.322, but you cannot pay that amount. The problem asks for rounding to the nearest cent. The correct answer is (2): $2.32 for the tomatoes.

PRACTICE

Brendan bought a box of watermelons for $9.98. If there were 4 melons in the box, what was the cost per watermelon to the nearest cent?

(1) $39.92
(2) $249.50
(3) $2.39
(4) $2
(5) $2.50

Set up this decimal problem as you would any other division problem. Make sure to put a decimal directly above the decimal in the problem.

```
     2.495
 4)9.980
  -8
   1 9
  -1 6
    38
   -36
    20
   -20
```

Beware of look-alike answers! You know that $100.00, $10.000, $1.0000, and $0.10000 don't represent the same thing. Keep a close eye on decimal places when taking the GED test—the answer choices often differ only in the decimal point placement.

CHAPTER 7

MATHEMATICS

THE GED

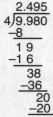

With 4 watermelons for about $10.00, answers (1) and (2) are unreasonable. The answer is 2.495, but we only use the first two decimal places when talking about money. Round to the nearest hundredth. Brendan paid $2.50 per watermelon, answer (5).

CHANGING DECIMALS TO FRACTIONS

Some questions ask you to work with fractions, while others require decimal use. You may also be asked to work back and forth between the two. Again, consider money. You know that a quarter is $\frac{1}{4}$ of a dollar, 25 cents, 25 percent, and $0.25. The following chart shows useful equivalents that you probably already know.

Decimal	Fraction	Percentage	Portion
0.10	1/10	10%	tenth
0.20	2/10 or 2/5	20%	fifth
0.25	25/100 or 1/4	25%	quarter
0.33	33/100 or 1/3	33%	third
0.50	5/10 or 1/2	50%	half
0.67	67/100 or 2/3	67%	two-thirds
0.75	75/100 or 3/4	75%	three-quarters

PRACTICE

Jenny used her calculator to find the answer to a problem. The calculator display reads 0.875, but the multiple choices are all in fractions. Which fraction is the correct answer? Change 0.875 to a fraction.

(1) $\frac{7}{8}$

(2) $2\frac{3}{4}$

(3) $8\frac{3}{4}$

(4) $87\frac{1}{2}$

(5) $875\frac{1}{10}$

Remember that the places after the decimal are tenths, hundredths, thousandths, and so on. Because 0.875 is in the thousandths place, put 875 over 1,000 and reduce.

The decimal 0.875 is equal to the fraction $\frac{875}{1000}$, which reduces by 125 to $\frac{7}{8}$, answer (1). Answers (2) through (5) are all incorrect because they are all greater than 1, and 0.875 has only a zero to the left of the decimal, so it must be smaller than 1.

 The number of places after the decimal will be equal to the number of zeros in the denominator. 0.875 has three decimal places, 1,000 has three zeros.

THE
GED

CHAPTER

7

MATHEMATICS

INTRODUCTION

WHOLE NUMBERS
AND BASIC
OPERATIONS

USING THE *fx-260*

FRACTIONS,
DECIMALS, AND
PERCENTAGES

MEASUREMENT

DATA ANALYSIS

ALGEBRA

GEOMETRY

CHANGING FRACTIONS TO DECIMALS

To change a fraction to a decimal, remember that the fraction bar reads "divided by." Although there are some special situations, all of them involve the same procedure: divide the numerator by the denominator.

Change $\frac{1}{2}$ to a decimal.

Read the fraction as "1 divided by 2." Write this division problem down.

$$
\begin{array}{r}
0.5 \\
2\overline{)1.0} \\
\underline{-0} \\
1\ 0 \\
\underline{-1\ 0} \\
0
\end{array}
$$

Put a decimal and as many zeros as is needed after the 1. The fraction $\frac{1}{2}$ equals the decimal 0.5.

PERCENTAGES

Another way to work with parts of a whole is to use percentages. You have probably seen many stores advertise items at "50% or 75% off" or heard about "rate increases of 125%." You know what this means at a basic level, but where does percentage fit in with decimals and fractions?

Percentage refers to the number of parts out of 100. Drawing A shows 100%. Drawing B shows 50%, or $\frac{50}{100}$. It is also the fraction $\frac{1}{2}$. Drawing C shows that percentages can exceed 100. It is 125%, or $1\frac{1}{4}$.

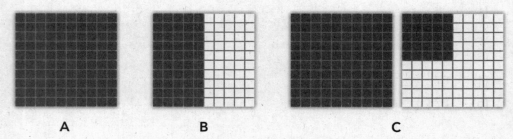

A   B   C

PERCENTAGES EXPRESSED AS DECIMALS

To change percentage to a decimal value, move the decimal two places to the left.

Name the decimal values indicated by the following percentages: 20%, 8.5%, 0.5%

20. %	8.5 %	.5 %
0.20.	0.08.5	0.00.5

20% is the equivalent of 20 hundredths, which is written 0.20.

8.5% is equal to 8 hundredths and 5 thousandths, written 0.085.

0.5% means $\frac{1}{2}$ of one percent, also described as 5 thousandths, written 0.005.

DECIMALS EXPRESSED AS PERCENTAGES

To change decimal value to percentage, move the decimal two places to the right.

Name the percentages indicated by the following decimals: 0.35, 4.5, 0.01

0.35. = 35%   4.50. = 450%   0.01. = 1%

0.35 is the same as   4.5 is the same as   0.01 is the same as 1
35 hundredths,   4 whole and   one-hundredth, written
written 35%   50 hundredths, written   1%
                               450%

FRACTIONS EXPRESSED AS PERCENTAGES

To change a fraction to a percentage, convert the fraction to a decimal and move the decimal point to the right two places. Or, multiply the fraction by $\frac{100}{1}$.

$\frac{1}{4}$ is the same as what percent?

$\frac{1}{4} = 1 \div 4 = 0.25$

$\quad$ 0.25. = 25%   or $\quad \frac{1}{4} \times \frac{100}{1} = \frac{100}{4} = 25\%$

PERCENTAGES EXPRESSED AS FRACTIONS OR MIXED NUMBERS

To change a percentage to a fraction, put the percent over 100 and reduce.

Change 45% to a fraction.

Write the percent over 100, and reduce the fraction.

$$\frac{45}{100} = \frac{45 \div 5}{100 \div 5} = \frac{9}{20}$$

45% is the same as the fraction $\frac{9}{20}$.

Change 125% to a fraction.

Write the percent over 100, and re-duce the fraction.

$$\frac{125}{100} = \frac{125 \div 25}{100 \div 25} = \frac{5}{4} = 1\frac{1}{4}$$

There is always an understood decimal point, even if it is not written: 32 is the same as 32.0

125% is the same as the fraction $1\frac{1}{4}$.

Change 62.5% to a fraction.

Write the percent over 100, and reduce the fraction.

$$\frac{62.5}{100}$$

THE
GED

Wait a minute. Now we have decimals in fractions. While it isn't wrong to describe 62.5% as 62.5 hundredths, what is another way to describe that number? It would be simpler to do away with the decimal altogether and call it "625 thousandths" and proceed as before. If you convert 62.5% to a decimal, there are three digits after the decimal point—out to the thousandths place. So, write the three digits over 1,000, and reduce the fraction.

$$\frac{62.5}{100} = \frac{625 \div 125}{1000 \div 125} = \frac{5}{8}$$

62.5% is the same as fraction $\frac{5}{8}$.

Change $41\frac{2}{3}$% to a fraction.

Write the percent over 100, and reduce the fraction.

$$\frac{41\frac{2}{3}}{100}$$

Hold on. Now we have fractions in fractions. But we can solve this using processes we've already reviewed. First, change $41\frac{2}{3}$ to an improper fraction: $41\frac{2}{3} = \frac{125}{3}$

Now, divide that by 100:

$$\frac{\frac{125}{3}}{100}$$

But we also know that when working with fraction division, it is easiest to work with inverse multiplication. So, instead of looking at it as " $\frac{125}{3}$ divided by 100," let's think of it as " $\frac{125}{3}$ times $\frac{1}{100}$."

$$\frac{\frac{125}{3}}{100} = \frac{125}{3} \div \frac{100}{1} = \frac{125}{3} \times \frac{1}{100} = \frac{125}{300} = \frac{5}{12}$$

$41\frac{2}{3}$% is the same as the fraction $\frac{5}{12}$.

FINDING PERCENTAGES

To find the answer to a percentage problem, remember that there are four terms: the **base**, the **part** of the base, the **rate**, and **100%**. They are set up as equal proportions:

$$\frac{\text{Part}}{\text{Base}} = \frac{\text{rate \%}}{100\%}$$

In a percentage problem, 100% is always the same. You are given two of the remaining three variables and asked to find the third. Here's how it works:

Of the last 250 days, 50 of them were rainy. This equals 20% rainy days.

Base: This is the entire amount. There were **250** total days.

Part: This is the portion of the base that is being focused on. There were **50** rainy days.

Rate: This is the percentage of the base—**20%** were rainy days.

100%: Percentage is based on 100%, so it is a constant.

$$\frac{50}{250} = \frac{20\%}{100\%}$$

5000   5000

The cross products are equal, so the numbers given were correct.

PRACTICE

16 is 25% of what number?

(1) 16
(2) 32
(3) 64
(4) 100
(5) 400

The problem gives you the rate and the part of the whole. It asks for the base. Fill in the blanks.

$$\frac{16}{?} = \frac{25\%}{100\%}$$

Using cross products, $16 \times 100 = 1,600$. Divide by 25 to find the missing value. Answer (3) is correct: 16 is 25 % of 64. Answer (1) is incorrect because 16 is 100% of 16. Answer (2) is incorrect because 16 is 50% of 32. Answer (4) is incorrect because 16 is 16% of 100. Answer (5) is incorrect because 16 is 4% of 400.

PRACTICE SET: FRACTIONS, DECIMALS, AND PERCENTAGES

The following questions test your abilities to work with fractions, decimals, ratios, and percentages. Read carefully, then select the best answer to each question.

1. There are 60 animals in the City Zoo that require a special diet. The other 30 animals are on a regular diet. What fraction of the animals are on a special diet?

(1) $\frac{30}{60}$
(2) $\frac{1}{2}$
(3) $\frac{30}{90}$
(4) $\frac{1}{3}$
(5) $\frac{2}{3}$

2. What is the ratio of the "special diet" animals to "regular diet" animals from question 1?

(1) 1:2
(2) 2:2
(3) 2:1
(4) 30:90
(5) 60:90

You may use your calculator on question 3.

3. Zookeepers at the City Zoo make $580 each week. If this amount is for 40 hours of work, how much per hour does a zookeeper make?

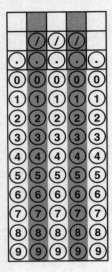

4. To make Krispy Treats, Kerry needs 1 cup of cereal for every 1/2 cup of marshmallows. How many cups of marshmallows will Kerry need if she is to use 5 cups of cereal?

(1)   5

(2) $2\frac{1}{2}$

(3) $\frac{1}{2}$

(4)   10

(5)   2

5. If you have 3 eggs left from a carton of 12 eggs, which decimal represents the portion of the eggs you have used?

(1)   0.25
(2)   0.33
(3)   0.50
(4)   0.67
(5)   0.75

THE
GED

INTRODUCTION

WHOLE NUMBERS
AND BASIC
OPERATIONS

USING THE *fx-260*

FRACTIONS,
DECIMALS, AND
PERCENTAGES

MEASUREMENT

DATA ANALYSIS

ALGEBRA

GEOMETRY

Check your answers on pages 393–394. If you got most of the answers right, way to go! You've finished the third rung of the ladder. You're ready to deal with whatever kinds of numbers you encounter—whole numbers, fractions, decimals, and even combinations. Now let's move on and practice the ways you may need to apply those numbers.

MEASUREMENT

The Guinness Book of World Records lists the highest, the fastest, the longest, and the shortest of just about anything that can be measured. Measurement is essential to our lives every day—we measure the time we sleep, the calories we eat, the miles we drive, and the money we spend. Knowing our measurement systems and how to work within them is crucial to our daily existence and, of course, to passing the GED test.

THE CUSTOMARY U.S. SYSTEM

The GED Mathematics test assumes a basic knowledge of the U.S. system of measurement. The chart below is a quick overview of the measurements (and their abbreviations) with which you should already be familiar. These conversions are *not* provided on the test.

Length

1 foot (ft) = 12 inches (in)
1 yard (yd) = 3 ft
1 mile (mi) = 5,280 ft

Weight

1 pound (lb) = 16 ounces
1 ton (t) = 2,000 lb

Volume

1 cup (c) = 8 fluid ounces (fl oz)
1 pint (pt) = 2 c
1 quart (qt) = 2 pt
1 gallon (gal) = 4 qt

Time

1 minute (min) = 60 seconds (sec)
1 hour (hr) = 60 min
1 day = 24 hr
1 week = 7 days

Knowing these basic relationships allows you to convert from the longest to the shortest or the lightest to the heaviest measurements with ease.

When solving conversion problems, set up equivalent proportions just like in the chart above. Let's look at a few sample questions.

PRACTICE

Taylor needs to record 2 hours of tape. How many minutes will this be?

    (1)   60
    (2)   90
    (3)   120
    (4)   150
    (5)   180

Your units are hours and minutes. Use the conversion of those units, which is 1 hr = 60 min, to find the answer. Multiply the number of hours (2) by the number of minutes in an hour (60) to solve.

2 hours of tape × 60 minutes per hour = 120 minutes of tape

The correct answer is (3): 2 hours is 120 minutes. Answer (1) is incorrect because 60 minutes equals only one hour. Answer (2) is incorrect because 90 minutes equals one-and-a-half hours. Answer (4) is incorrect because 150 minutes equals two-and-a-half hours. Answer (5) is incorrect because 180 minutes equals three hours.

THE
GED

PRACTICE

The diving board is $6\frac{1}{2}$ feet long. How long is this in inches?

(1)   12
(2)   36
(3)   60
(4)   78
(5)   156

Your units are feet and inches. Use the conversion of those units, which is 1 ft = 12 in, to find the answer. Multiply the number of feet $(6\frac{1}{2})$ by the number of inches in a foot (12) to solve.

$6\frac{1}{2}$ feet × 12 inches in a foot =

To continue, first we have to convert the fraction to an improper fraction to multiply:

$6\frac{1}{2}$ feet = $\frac{13}{2}$ feet × 12 inches in a foot = $\frac{156}{2}$ inches

Now, reduce to find your answer: $\frac{156}{2}$ inches = 78 inches

The diving board is 78 inches, answer (4). Answer (1) is incorrect because 12 inches is only one foot. Answer (2) is incorrect because 36 inches is just three feet. Answer (3) is incorrect because 60 inches is five feet. Answer (5) is incorrect because 156 inches is 13 feet.

Not all conversions come out even. You may express the remainder as a part of the unit, a fraction, or a decimal.

PRACTICE

If a baby weighs 104 ounces, what is her weight in pounds?

(1)   6 lbs
(2)   6 lbs 5 oz
(3)   6 lbs 8 oz
(4)   6 lbs 12 oz
(5)   7 lbs

Your units are ounces and pounds. Use the conversion of those units, which is 1 lb = 16 oz., to find the answer. Divide the number of ounces (104) by the number of ounces in a pound (16) to solve.

104 oz ÷ 16 = 6.5 lbs

To describe the baby's weight in pounds and ounces, it is 6 whole pounds and one half pound, which is the same as 6 pounds, 8 ounces.

Answer (3) is correct: the weight of the baby can be written as 6 lbs 8 oz, or $6\frac{1}{2}$ lbs, or 6.5 lbs. Answer (1) is incorrect because that would be 96 ounces. Answer (2) is incorrect because that would be 101 ounces. Answer (4) is incorrect because that would be 108 ounces. Answer (5) is incorrect because that would be 112 ounces.

OPERATIONS WITH MEASUREMENTS

When adding or subtracting measurements, you must work with the same units. You cannot add "feet" units to "inches" units.

PRACTICE

Elizabeth worked for 8 weeks on painting the walls of her kitchen and for 16 days touching up the trim. What was the total amount of time she spent?

(1) 24 days
(2) 2 weeks
(3) 10 weeks, 2 days
(4) 70 days
(5) 24 weeks

This problem asks for the total amount of time that Elizabeth worked. Although an answer could be correctly stated in either days or weeks, the GED answer uses the larger of the units, so you should, too.

First, convert all figures to common units. Your units are days and weeks. Use the conversion of those units, which is 7 days = 1 week, to find the answer. Divide the number of days by 7 to get a total number of weeks:

16 days touching up the kitchen = $\frac{16}{7}$ weeks = $2\frac{2}{7}$ weeks = 2 weeks, 2 days

Now, add the time spent painting the walls (8 weeks) to the time spent touching up (2 weeks, 2 days):

8 weeks + 2 weeks, 2 days = 10 weeks, 2 days

The total length of time spent on the kitchen was 10 weeks, 2 days: answer (3). Answers (1) and (2) both are less than the time it took to paint the walls. Answer (4) is incorrect because 70 days is exactly 10 weeks, which is less than the entire amount of time. Answer (5) is incorrect because 24 weeks is three times longer than it took to paint just the walls—much more time than the entire project took.

PRACTICE

Garrett made 3 gallons of lemonade for the picnic. There was 1 gallon, 1 quart left over. How much lemonade was consumed at the picnic?

(1) 1 gal, 1 qt
(2) 1 gal, 3 qt
(3) 2 gal, 1 qt
(4) 2 gal, $\frac{1}{2}$ qt
(5) 2 gal, 3 qt

As before, convert all figures to common units. Your units are gallons and quarts. Use the conversion of those units, which is 4 quarts = 1 gallon, to find the answer. Multiply the number of gallons by 4 to get a total number of quarts:

At the beginning of the picnic, there were 3 gallons of lemonade:

3 gallons × 4 quarts in a gallon = 12 quarts

At the end of the picnic, there was 1 gallon, 1 quart of lemonade:

1 gallon + 1 quart = (1 gallon × 4 quarts in a gallon) + 1 quart
            = 4 quarts + 1 quart
            = 5 quarts

12 quarts − 5 quarts = 7 quarts were consumed at the picnic. But how many gallons were consumed?

There are 4 quarts in a gallon, so divide the number of quarts by 4 to convert to gallons:

7 quarts = $\frac{7}{4}$ gallons = 1.75 gallons = 1 gallon, 3 quarts

The correct answer is (2): 1 gallon and 3 quarts of lemonade were consumed at the picnic. Answer (1) is only 5 quarts, which would mean 7 quarts were left over. Answers (3), (4), and (5) are all more than 2 gallons, which would mean that less than a gallon of lemonade was left over after the picnic.

Make sure to "reduce" measurements if necessary.

PRACTICE

For her birdhouse, Lizette cut 18 pieces of wood that were each 9 inches long from a single piece of wood. How long was the original piece of wood?

(1)   180 in
(2)   6 ft
(3) $6\frac{1}{2}$ ft
(4)   9 ft
(5) $13\frac{1}{2}$ ft

Although 18 × 9 inches = 162 inches, 162 would not be a choice on the GED. The GED answer would reduce it to feet and inches by dividing by 12.

162 ÷ 12 = 13.5, or $13\frac{1}{2}$ feet

The original piece of wood was $13\frac{1}{2}$ feet long, answer (5). Answer (1) is incorrect because 180 is more than 18 × 9 inches. Answer (2) is incorrect because 6 feet = 72 inches, which is less than 18 × 9 inches. Answer (3) is incorrect because $6\frac{1}{2}$ feet = 78 inches, which is less than 18 × 9 inches. Answer (4) is incorrect because 9 feet = 108 inches, which is less than 18 × 9 inches.

PRACTICE

The city needs to put a marker every 40 feet along a street. The street is $2\frac{1}{2}$ miles long. How many markers must they put out?

(1)   90 markers
(2)   300 markers
(3)   330 markers
(4)   5,280 markers
(5)   13,200 markers

INTRODUCTION

WHOLE NUMBERS
AND BASIC
OPERATIONS

USING THE *fx-260*
CALCULATOR

FRACTIONS,
DECIMALS, AND
PERCENTAGES

MEASUREMENT

DATA ANALYSIS

ALGEBRA

GEOMETRY

As we have done before, convert all figures to common units. Your units are miles and feet. Use the conversion of those units, which is 5,280 feet = 1 mile, to find the answer. Multiply the number of miles, $2\frac{1}{2}$, by 5,280 to get the total number of feet:

When dividing using measurements, it is usually easier to convert to the smaller measurement before dividing.

$$2\frac{1}{2} \times 5280 = \frac{5}{2} \times 5280 = \frac{26,400}{2} = 13,200$$

There are 13,200 feet in $2\frac{1}{2}$ miles. Now, divide by 40 to find out how many markers are needed.

$$13,200 \div 40 = 330$$

The city needs 330 markers: answer (3). Answers (1) and (2) are incorrect because neither would be enough markers to have one every 40 feet for $2\frac{1}{2}$ miles. Answer (4) is enough markers to have one every 2.5 feet. Answer (5) is enough to have one marker every foot for $2\frac{1}{2}$ miles.

THE METRIC SYSTEM

The metric system is the world's most widely used system of measurement. In fact, the United States is the only country that hasn't switched to this simple, logical, decimal system. To convert units in the United States, you have to memorize all the different relationships: 12 inches to a foot, 3 feet to a yard, 5,280 feet to a mile, 16 ounces to a pound, and so on. With the metric system, each unit is either 10 times larger or 10 times smaller than the next—and the prefixes tell you which.

The three basic units in the metric system are listed in the following chart:

Base Unit	Abbreviation	Measures
gram	g	weight
meter	m	length
liter	l	volume

The prefixes that tell you how many times bigger or smaller than the base unit your measurement is are listed in the following chart:

thousands	hundreds	tens	Basic Unit	tenths	hundredths	thousandths
1000	100	10	ones	0.1	0.01	0.001
kilo-	hecto-	deca-	(meter, gram, liter)	deci-	centi-	milli-

Most metric system conversions are a simple matter of moving the decimal right or left. The key to knowing whether the decimal must move left or right is knowing what the unit prefixes mean.

THE
GED

PRACTICE

How many kilograms are there in 2 centigrams?

To change between metric units, use the table on page 333. Put a finger on the **kilo-** box and one on the **centi-** box. Count the jumps it would take to get from the one you do know (2 centigrams) to the one you want to know (kilograms). There are five jumps, or spaces, to the **left**.

Write the number you are converting:	2 = 2.0
Now move the decimal five places to the left, adding zeros as needed:	2.0
	0.00002

2 centigrams is equal to 0.00002 kilograms.

PRACTICE

How many milliliters are there in 0.7 decaliters?

Put a finger on the **milli-** box and one on the **deca-** box. Count the jumps it would take to get to get from the one you do know (0.7 decaliters) to the one you want to know (milliliters). There are four jumps, or spaces, to the **right**.

Write the number you are converting:	0.7
Now move the decimal five places to the left, adding zeros as needed:	0.7
	7000.

There are 7,000 milliliters in 0.7 decaliters.

PRACTICE

A bridge is 750 meters long. What is its length in hectometers?

Changing meters to hectometers is just moving the decimal point two spaces to the left.

The bridge is 7.5 hectometers.

The metric system works with the same rules as decimals, so perform these calculations as any other decimal operations. You may review decimal operations on pages 320–326. As with any other units, you may add and subtract like units only. If you need to add a number of kilograms to a number of centigrams, convert one of them to the other.

With this refresher course on measurement systems, you should feel comfortable using them and converting one unit to another. Now, we can look at the most common measures of size. These calculations work the same way whether you use U.S. or metric units.

We start with "flat" measurements—those that use two dimensions. In the next section, we add a third dimension—height or depth—and measure volume.

PERIMETER

Perimeter is a measure of the outer edge of a flat figure. A flat figure has only two dimensions, like a square or circle. To find the perimeter, add the lengths of its sides.

PRACTICE

A daycare center must fence its playground. According to Figure 1, how many feet of fencing is needed?

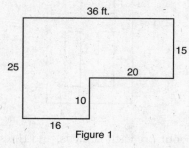

Figure 1

Because the fence goes around the outside, or perimeter, of the playground, the segments are added together.

36 + 15 + 20 + 10 + 16 + 25 = 122

It will take 122 feet of fencing to enclose the playground.

Not all segments of a figure are labeled, but you can use the given information to find how long the unlabeled segments are. For example, a square has four equal sides and four right corners. If you know the length of one side, you know the other three sides are the same length.

PRACTICE

What is the perimeter of Figure 2?

Figure 2

The perimeter of Figure 2 is 12. If one side of the square is 3, each side of the square is 3, so 3 + 3 + 3 + 3 = 12.

A rectangle has four right angles with opposite sides of equal length.

PRACTICE

Stephanie wants to put weather stripping around all four sides of the door in Figure 3. How many yards of weather stripping does she need?

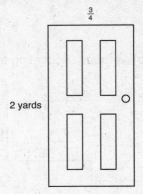

Figure 3

The long sides of the door are each 2 yards, and the short sides are $\frac{3}{4}$ yard.

Long sides:	$2 + 2 = 4$
Short sides:	$\frac{3}{4} + \frac{3}{4} = \frac{6}{4}$, or $1\frac{2}{4}$, or $1\frac{1}{2}$

$$4 + 1\frac{1}{2} = 5\frac{1}{2} \text{ yards}$$

AREAS OF SQUARES AND RECTANGLES

Area is the measure of the surface of a flat figure. Area is measured in square units. It describes the number of square units that will fit inside the figure.

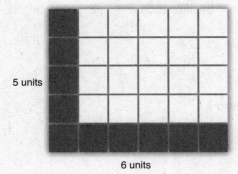

5 units × 6 units = 30 total square units.

PRACTICE

Raj's lawn is square. Using Figure 4, how many square yards of grass does he need to cover the lawn?

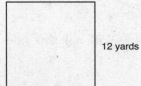

12 yards

Figure 4

One side of the square is 12 yards. Multiply 12×12 to find the amount in the square. Raj needs 144 square yards of grass.

PRACTICE

Ingrid's garage is rectangular (Figure 5). If she wants to paint the floor, how many square feet should she plan to cover?

Figure 5

Area of a rectangle is found by multiplying length times width: $18 \times 20 = 360$.

PRACTICE

What is the total amount of carpet needed, in square feet, for the office space in Figure 6?

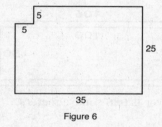

Figure 6

There are several ways to work problems like this one. We look at two different ways. Note that not all the dimensions are given. Your first move should be to find the dimensions of the missing sides. Then go on to the problem.

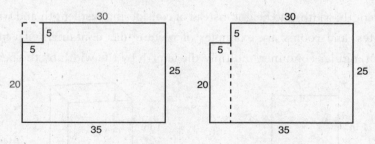

Option 1: Find out the total area of the large square and subtract the missing part.

The total area of the square is 25 × 35, or 875.
The area of the missing part is 5 × 5, or 25.
875 − 25 = 850

Option 2: Look at this figure as a combination of a square and a rectangle. Find the areas of each part and add them together.

The area of the smaller rectangle is 20 × 5, or 100.
The area of the larger rectangle is 30 × 25, or 750.
100 + 750 = 850

Either way you work it, the correct answer is 850 square feet.

THE
GED

PRACTICE

A parking lot measures 50 meters by 100 meters. A sidewalk will be added along the perimeter, and the entire area will become 56 by 106 meters. What is the area of the sidewalk **alone**?

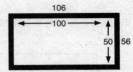

Again, there are two ways to solve this problem. You can observe that the shaded area is a series of four rectangles. Find the areas of the rectangles and add them together.

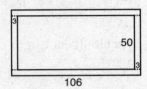

You can also determine that the area of the entire lot (the large rectangle) minus the size of the small lot (the little rectangle) will leave you the area of the sidewalk (the shaded area).

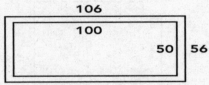

Either way, the correct answer is 936 square meters.

VOLUME

Measurements of the insides of three-dimensional objects are called **volume**. Think of how much milk fits in a milk carton. For these calculations, we must consider the three dimensions of length, width, and height instead of considering just length and width.

Boxes, crates, and rooms are examples of rectangular containers. To find the volume of a rectangular container, multiply the length by the width by the height.

Area = l × h = 1 × 1 = 1 sq. in   *Area = l × h × w = 1 × 1 × 1 = 1 cu. in*

What is the volume of the hamster cage in Figure 7?

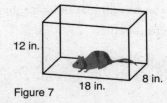

Figure 7

INTRODUCTION

WHOLE NUMBERS
AND BASIC
OPERATIONS

USING THE *fx*-260
CALCULATOR

FRACTIONS,
DECIMALS, AND
PERCENTAGES

MEASUREMENT

DATA ANALYSIS

ALGEBRA

GEOMETRY

Multiply 12 × 18 × 8 to find the volume. The hamster cage is 1,728 cubic inches.

PRACTICE SET: MEASUREMENT

The following questions test your ability to apply concepts in measurement.
Read carefully, then select the best answer to each question.
For questions 1 through 5, refer to the diagram of Jeanne's Swimming Pool.

Jeanne's Swimming Pool

1. Jeanne wishes to put a row of tile around the top edges of the pool. How many feet of tile does she need?

   (1)   24 ft
   (2)   33 ft
   (3)   48 ft
   (4)   96 ft
   (5)   135 ft

2. It took workers 60 hours to paint the inside of the pool. How many days did it take?

   (1)   1.25
   (2)   2
   (3)   2.5
   (4)   5
   (5)   5.5

3. What is the area of the bottom (the shaded part) of Jeanne's pool? Enter your answer using the grid on the right.

You may use your calculator for question 4.

4. What is the total maximum volume in cubic yards for Jeanne's pool?

   (1)   120 cu yd
   (2)   270 cu yd
   (3)   370 cu yd
   (4)   700 cu yd
   (5)   1215 cu yd

5. If Jeanne's pool holds 15,000 liters of water, how many kiloliters does it hold?

   (1)   0.0015 kl
   (2)   0.015 kl
   (3)   0.15 kl
   (4)   1.5 kl
   (5)   15 kl

Check your answers on pages 394–395. How did you do? If you got most of the answers right, you are ready to move on up the ladder.

DATA ANALYSIS

Our world constantly gives us information. Facts, figures, and numbers are communicated at dizzying speeds in lists, charts, and tables. It is our task to absorb this information, pick out the parts we need, and work with them. Here, on the sixth rung of the ladder, we explore ways to understand information.

MEAN, MEDIAN, AND MODE

Mean is another word for the **average** of a list of numbers. It is not uncommon for weather experts to refer to the "mean temperature" of a city. This is the average temperature of a city over time. Averages are used for all kinds of purposes: calculating test scores or grades, reporting prices, keeping track of weight loss, sports statistics, and literally millions of other details.

PRACTICE

Yolanda had test scores of 95, 65, 77, 83, and 90. What is her mean, or average, score?

To find the average, add up all of the data and divide by the number of scores given.

95 + 65 + 77 + 83 + 90 = 410.

There are five scores, so divide 410 by 5.

410 ÷ 5 = 82

Yolanda's average score is 82.

Median is the middle number in a list of numbers. To find median, order the information from least to greatest (or greatest to least), and find the number that occurs in the middle.

PRACTICE

Yolanda's test scores this semester were 83, 90, 65, 95, and 77. What is the median of Yolanda's scores?

Ordered from highest to lowest, the scores are 95, 90, 83, 77, and 65. The middle number is 83.

Yolanda's median score is 83.

If there is an even number of data, then there will be two middle numbers. In this situation, the median is the average of those two numbers.

PRACTICE

M	9
Tu	12
W	14
Th	10
F	28
S	23

Swim Class enrollment

What is the median number of students enrolled in swimming classes?

Lowest to highest, the numbers are 9, 10, 12, 14, 23, 28. The two middle numbers are 12 and 14. 12 + 14 = 26. 26 ÷ 2 = 13. The median number of students in the swimming classes is 13.

The **mode** of a list of numbers is the number that occurs most often. It is possible to have no mode, one mode, or several modes. Look at the chart below and find the modes for the lists of library holdings.

Library Holdings for Children's Titles in the City Libraries			
Library / Book	Walnut Creek	Round Rock	Georgetown
Nancy Drew	23	21	14
Magic Tree House	17	17	20
Little House	10	13	14
Clifford	23	20	12
Magic School Bus	14	11	20

a. What is the mode for the books at Walnut Creek? _____
b. What is the mode for the books at Round Rock? _____
c. What is the mode for the books at Georgetown? _____

At Walnut Creek, the only number that occurs more than once is 23. The mode is 23. At Round Rock, there is no number that occurs any more times than any other. There is no mode. At Georgetown, two numbers occur twice. The modes are 14 and 20.

RANGE

Range is the amount between the highest and the lowest numbers. To find the range for any list of numbers, subtract the lowest from the highest.

a. What is the range for the books at Walnut Creek? _____
b. What is the range for the books at Round Rock? _____
c. What is the range for the books at Georgetown? _____

THE
GED

At Walnut Creek, the highest minus the lowest number is 23 − 10. The range is 13. At Round Rock, the highest minus the lowest number is 21 − 11. The range is 10. At Georgetown, the highest minus the lowest number is 20 − 12. The range is 8.

PROBABILITY

Probability is the study of chance. It tells how likely or unlikely it is that an event will happen. Probability can be expressed in several ways. A weather forecaster may say, "The chance of rain tomorrow is 90%." This lets you know that rain is not only possible, but also very likely. A lottery ticket may have, in tiny print, "Odds of winning are 1 in 50 million." This is definitely a very small chance! Probability cannot determine what will happen, but only what is likely to happen.

When expressed as a percentage (such as the probability of rain), the range of probability is from 0%, meaning the event will not occur at all, to 100%, meaning the event is certain to occur. Probability also is expressed as a fraction or decimal equivalent to a percentage. "Probability of 1" means the same as 100%. "Probability of ½" means the same as 0.5 or 50%.

To find the probability of a given event, there are two important numbers: the favorable outcomes and the number of total outcomes. Expressed as a fraction, it looks like this:

$$\text{Probability} = \frac{\text{Number of events you want to happen}}{\text{Number of events possible}}$$

PRACTICE

Marie flips a coin. What is the probability that it will come up heads?

Put the number of events desired over the number of possible events. There is one head on the coin, and there are two total possibilities (heads or tails) in this situation.

$$\text{Probability} = \frac{1 \text{ "heads" possible}}{2 \text{ total possibilities}} = \frac{1}{2} = 0.5 = 50\%$$

The probability of a heads on Marie's coin toss is 1 out of 2, or 1 in 2, or 50%. In this situation, there is just as much chance that she will get a heads as that she will not.

PRACTICE

Olivia bought 10 raffle tickets at the Harvest Festival. If 500 tickets are sold, what is the probability that one of Olivia's tickets will be chosen?

$$\frac{\text{Desired outcomes}}{\text{over total outcomes}} = \frac{10 \text{ tickets are Olivia's}}{500 \text{ total possibilities}} = \frac{10}{500} = \frac{1}{50} = 0.02 = 2\%$$

Olivia has a 1 in 50 or 2%, chance of winning.

The following practice examples refer to dice, or to one die, a standard six-sided cube that has the numbers one through six represented in dots on its sides.

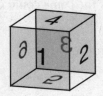

PRACTICE

1. What is the probability that Chris will get an even number with one roll?

2. Cindy needs to roll a six to win. What is her probability of winning on her next roll?

3. Clarissa will lose her turn if she rolls a 2 or a 5. What is the probability she will roll a 2 or a 5?

4. Cyril needs any number 3 or greater to be rolled. What is the probability that he will get it?

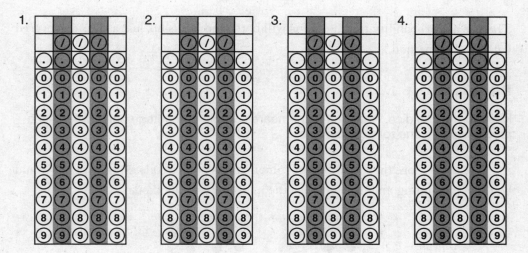

Question 1 asks for all possibilities that are even. The possibilities are a 2, a 4, and a 6. The fraction is $\frac{3}{6}$, or $\frac{1}{2}$, or 50%. Question 2 looks for one possibility only: a 6. The possibility is 1 in 6, or $\frac{1}{6}$, or 17%. Question 3 looks for two possibilities out of the six: $\frac{2}{6}$, $= \frac{1}{3}$, $= 33\%$. Question 4 includes the numbers 3, 4, 5, and 6. This is four out of six, or $\frac{4}{6}$. This reduces to $\frac{2}{3}$, which expressed as a possibility is 67%.

INDEPENDENT AND DEPENDENT PROBABILITY

If the probability of heads up when one coin is $\frac{1}{2}$, what is the probability when two coins are tossed? What would be the probability of them *both* being heads?

PRACTICE

Two quarters are tossed into the air. What is the probability that they will both land heads up?

You need the number of favorable events over the number of possible events. To find these numbers, you could make a list of the possible ways the two coins could fall.

These are the only four ways the coins could come up:

Coin 1: heads; Coin 2: heads
Coin 1: heads; Coin 2: tails
Coin 1: tails; Coin 2: heads
Coin 1: tails; Coin 2: tails

Only one of these possibilities is heads-heads. Therefore, the probability is 1 in 4, or 25%.

There are only two coins with only two different possibilities, so it was easy to make a list of the outcomes. There are times, however, when this kind of list would be so long that it would be overwhelming to attempt. Fortunately, there is second method to working this type of problem: Find the probability for each of the coins alone, then multiply them.

Coin 1: Probability of a heads is $\frac{1}{2}$. Coin 2: Probability of a heads is $\frac{1}{2}$.

$$\frac{1}{2} \times \frac{1}{2} = \frac{1}{4}$$

There is a $\frac{1}{4}$ probability that the coins will both land heads up, just as was discovered with the list method.

PRACTICE

Kirsten rolls two dice. Rounded to the nearest whole percentage point, what is the probability that she rolls double sixes?

There are more than 30 different combinations of dice rolls. Making a list would be time-consuming and difficult. Use the multiplication method.

Probability of a six is $\frac{1}{6}$ Probability of a six is $\frac{1}{6}$

Rolling them at the same time, the probability that both will land on six would be

$$\frac{1}{6} \times \frac{1}{6} = \frac{1}{36}$$

Kirsten has a $\frac{1}{36}$ chance, or 3% chance, of rolling double sixes.

PRACTICE

Reggie has a bag of marbles. Four are red, and six are blue. Without looking, Reggie pulls out a marble. Without replacing the first one, he selects a second marble. What is the probability that the marbles are <u>both</u> blue?

In the previous coin and dice problems, the outcomes were **independent**. The result of one coin or die result would not have any effect on what the second one could be. In this problem, the outcomes are **dependent**. Because Reggie's first marble draw will not be replaced, there are now fewer marbles in the bag to choose from. This has changed the numbers for the second draw. You must take this into consideration when finding the probabilities of each of the selections of marbles.

First selection: There is a 6 in 10 probability that Reggie will pull out a blue marble.

Second selection: Now that the first marble is gone, there are only nine left.

For the purposes of probability, you assume that the first selection was the one you wanted. That would mean that there are five blue marbles left. The probability for the second selection is $\frac{5}{9}$.

Multiply the two probabilities:

$$\frac{6}{10} \times \frac{5}{9} = \frac{30}{90} = \frac{1}{3}$$

There is a 1 in 3 probability that Reggie's first two marble draws will be blue.

TABLES, CHARTS, AND GRAPHS

Information is frequently given in the form of tables, charts, and graphs so that it is better organized and easier to find. The most important thing when interpreting a table or graph is to make sure that you understand what kind of information is displayed. Look at the title of the table, read all of the labels, and focus only on the information you need. Remember, the GED test gives you much more data than you need to solve the problems.

TABLES AND CHARTS

At least a few questions on the Mathematics test ask you to use information presented in charts and tables. Let's look at a mileage chart as an example of how to use a chart to find the information you need.

El Paso	Amarillo	Abilene	
443	287		Abilene
296	284	488	Albuquerque, NM
419		273	Amarillo
335	227	109	Big Spring
183	261	277	Carlsbad, NM
491	114	155	Childress
617	353	190	Dallas
424	457	247	Del Rio
478	512	392	Eagle Pass
	483	443	El Paso
238	345	263	Ft. Stockton
742	597	352	Houston
345	122	167	Lubbock
302	237	148	Midland
252	257	176	Odessa
209	330	241	Pecos
692	124	305	Perryton
289	123	287	Portola, NM
415	301	92	San Angelo
564	513	250	San Antonio

A mileage chart tells you the number of miles between cities. The names of the cities are placed across the top of the chart, and then repeated down the side. Find the name of one of cities you are interested in along the top, and the find the other along the side. Move your fingers down the column and across the row until they meet. That number is the mileage between the two cities.

PRACTICE

What is the mileage between Amarillo and Dallas?

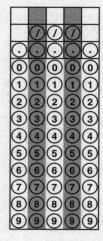

Find Amarillo on the top of the chart and Dallas on the right. Move down the Amarillo column and across the Dallas row until the two meet at 353.

The distance from Amarillo to Dallas is 353 miles.

PRACTICE

Derrick drove from Abilene to El Paso, and then from El Paso to Del Rio. What is the total number of miles he traveled?

According to the chart, the number of miles from Abilene to El Paso is 443, and from El Paso to Del Rio is 424. Add the numbers to get the total number of miles Derrick drove: 443 + 424 = 867.

Derrick drove a total of 867 miles.

FREQUENCY TABLE

The mileage chart in the examples above is only one type of chart you might encounter. Now let's look at a practice example using is a frequency table:

PRACTICE

The emergency room recorded the reason for emergency visits to determine the types of doctors needed. How many more people came in for lacerations (cuts) than for broken bones?

Burns	~~HHH~~ ~~HHH~~ ~~HHH~~ ~~HHH~~ ~~HHH~~
Lacerations	~~HHH~~ ~~HHH~~ ~~HHH~~ ~~HHH~~ ~~HHH~~ III
Broken bones	~~HHH~~ ~~HHH~~ ~~HHH~~ IIII
Food poison	II
Fever	~~HHH~~ II

ER patient complaints, July 4

Count the tally marks for the category Lacerations (30) and the category Broken Bones (19).

Subtract to find the difference: 30 − 19 = 11. The correct answer is 11.

GRAPHS

Graphs represent information as more of a picture than a list. Some information is easier to understand when presented in a graph than as raw numbers. The parts of a graph include a title, a scale, vertical and horizontal axis lines, labels, and a key.

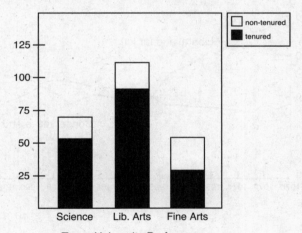

Texas University Professors

This graph is called a bar graph. The title appears at the top or bottom of the graph to tell you what is shown on the graph. The scale is the numbers that appear along the vertical and/or horizontal axes to tell you how many units a bar, line, or point represents. The vertical axis runs up and down, and the horizontal axis runs left to right. Labels appear with each bar or line to tell you what each one represents. The key is in a little box apart from the graph to tell you what each color or pattern in the graph represents. A bar scale has only one scale, and each bar is labeled. Always pay careful attention to these labels.

THE
GED

PRACTICE

About how many liberal arts professors at Texas University have tenure?

The graph key indicates that the black area represents the tenured professors. The second bar is labeled Liberal Arts, and the black part of the bar is just over the line that corresponds to 75. A good estimate, then, would be over 80 but less than 100. About 85 liberal arts professors have tenure.

A line graph has two scales. In most line graphs, the vertical axis measures a given amount, and the horizontal axis shows different points in time. The points are connected by a line, which helps to show a rising or falling trend. You can use these trends to make predictions about future events that may not be shown on the graph.

The next four practice examples refer to the following graph.

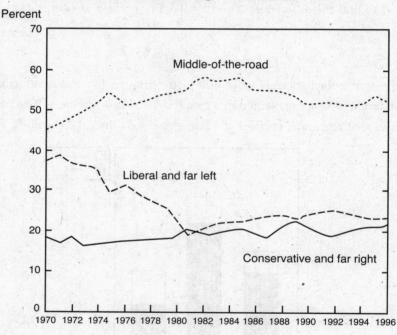

Political Views of College Freshmen, 1970–1996

PRACTICE

Overall, with what political view do most college freshmen identify?

(1)   Middle-of-the-road
(2)   Liberal/far left
(3)   Conservative/far right
(4)   Republicans
(5)   The information cannot be determined from this graph.

The line that shows the highest percentage of freshmen is the one labeled Middle-of-the-road; therefore, answer (1) is correct. Answers (2) and (3) are incorrect because the Middle-of-the-road line is higher than both the Liberal and Conservative lines over the whole span of the graph. Answer (4) is incorrect because Republican is not one of the viewpoints listed on the graph. Answer (5) is incorrect because there is enough information on the graph to answer the question.

From 1972 to 1980, what happened to the number of freshmen who identified themselves as liberal?

(1)   The number increased.
(2)   The number declined.
(3)   The number stayed the same.
(4)   The number of liberals and conservatives was equal.
(5)   The information cannot be determined from this graph.

Find the line labeled Liberal and follow it from the horizontal point 1972 to the horizontal point 1980. You can see that **overall**, or for the most part, the line goes down. This indicates a lowering of percentage, so the answer is (2): the number declined. Answer (1) is incorrect because if the number had increased the line would move upward to the right. Answer (3) is incorrect because if the number stayed the same, the line would be flat. In 1980, the number appeared to be about equal with conservatives (answer 4), but the question asks you to consider an entire time period. Answer (5) is incorrect because there is enough information on the graph to answer the question.

According to this graph, what could you expect to be the percentage of freshmen in the year 2000 who will identify themselves as conservatives?

(1)   70%
(2)   50%
(3)   40%
(4)   25%
(5)   10%

The answer is (4): 25%. This information is not actually on the graph, but one of the advantages of line graphs is that you can predict events based on what the trend seems to be at the end of the graph. The conservative line from 1992 and on had been rising steadily slightly, and the last point was about 22%. It can be inferred that the line would continue to rise slightly, so you need an answer that is just above 22%. Answers (3), (2), and (1) are all sharp increases, and answer (5) is a sharp decrease.

What percentage of freshmen identified themselves as middle-of-the-road in 1974?

(1)   15%
(2)   18%
(3)   30%
(4)   45%
(5)   54%

You are asked to find the point at which 1974 and Middle-of-the-road meet. This occurs in the middle of 50% and 60%. The best answer, then, is (5): 54%. Answers (1), (2), (3), and (4) all represent points well below 1974's level for Middle-of-the-road.

CIRCLE GRAPHS

Circle graphs are most often used to show the breakdown of a whole into parts. The circle always represents 100%, and the parts of the graph (usually shown in percentages, but sometimes as whole numbers, fractions, or decimals) add up to 100%. Circle graphs are an excellent way to show budgets.

PRACTICE

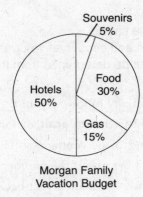

Morgan Family
Vacation Budget

What percentage of the Morgan family's vacation budget will be spent on gasoline?

Look at the section labeled Gasoline. It is marked 15%.

Hotel costs will take up what fraction of the budget?

The question asks for the label and its equivalent fraction. The parts of the graph are labeled in percentages, so you must convert the percentage to a fraction. Hotels is given 50% of the graph. To change a percentage to a fraction, put the percentage over 100: 50/100 is equal to $\frac{1}{2}$.

Hotel costs will be $250. What will be the dollar amount allotted to souvenirs?

There are a few ways to find the answer. One way to figure out how much money is set aside for souvenirs is to figure the dollar amount budgeted for the entire vacation and then find the portion of that total marked for souvenirs (5%). If hotel costs are $250, then the value of the entire graph must be $500, because the full 100% is twice as much as the amount set aside for hotels, 50%. You are left with the question, How much is 5% of $500? To figure a percentage of a number, remember from page 328:

$$\frac{\text{Part}}{\text{Base}} = \frac{\text{rate}\%}{100\%} = \frac{x}{500} = \frac{5\%}{100\%}$$

Using cross products, $5 \times 500 = 2,500$. Divide by 100 to find the missing value. The correct answer is $25.

Another way to solve the problem is with proportion. The ratio of souvenirs to hotels in percentage is 5/50, which reduces to 1/10. The Morgans will spend one-tenth of the amount they spend on hotels to buy souvenirs. So, multiply that fraction by the amount of money they will spend on hotels.

$$\$250 \times \frac{1}{10} = \frac{\$250}{10} = \$25$$

The correct answer is $25 no matter how you approach the problem. Use the method that makes the most sense to you. If you have time, finding the answer using another method is a good way to check your work.

PRACTICE SET: DATA ANALYSIS

The following questions test your comfort with tools to analyze data. Read carefully and select the best answer.

	Jan.	Feb.	Mar.	Apr.	May	June	
Sunny days	15	8	20	21	25	18	Sunny days
Average temp.	47°	50°	57°	68°	79°	81°	Average temp.
High temp.	83°	80°	83°	94°	101°	98°	High temp.
Low temp.	19°	22°	30°	32°	52°	58°	Low temp.
Rainfall	1.7	4.9	0.9	0.1	0.5	4.1	Rainfall

2003 Weather Data for Austin, TX

1. Which expression shows how to find the range of temperatures for January?

   (1)   47 − 19
   (2)   83 − 47 − 19
   (3)   83 − 19
   (4)   83 ÷ 31
   (5)   83 × 19

You may use your calculator for question 2.

2. What was the average number of sunny days for the first six months of 2003, to the nearest whole day?

   (1)   5
   (2)   6
   (3)   15
   (4)   25
   (5)   18

THE
GED

3. What is the total amount of rainfall for January through June?

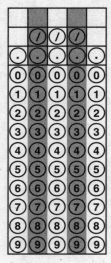

4. What was the probability of a sunny day in June of this year?

(1)   3:5
(2)   1:2
(3)   18:1
(4)   15:18
(5)   2:5

5. If a line graph were to be made of the average temperatures from January to June, which of the following graphs would be the most likely result?

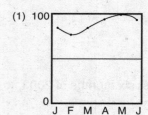

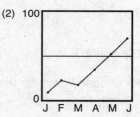

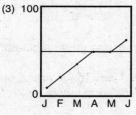

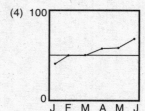

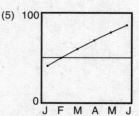

Check your answers on pages 395–396. How did you do? If you got most of the answers right, you are ready to go on to the last two rungs.

ALGEBRA

At this point, you have used many concepts that are directly related to your daily life. It is easy to see how learning to calculate taxes, plan a budget, and convert measurements is useful. But now we get to algebra. Many students regularly complain that they will probably never use math in their adult lives unless they pursue careers in science or technology. While it is true that you may never again factor a quadratic equation, the basic techniques in algebra are used for logical thinking and problem - solving. Take the following situation:

The temperature in Point Barrow, Alaska, was 10° at 6:00 in the evening. An hour later, the temperature had fallen 15 degrees. What was the temperature reading on the thermometer then?

This question asks you to demonstrate a use of **integers**, the term for the set of whole numbers, their negatives, and zero. The number line no longer begins at zero, but extends negatively and positively in both directions.

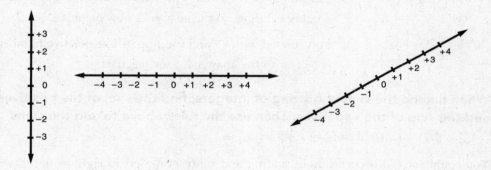

Up until this point, positive numbers have not been written with a + sign because it is understood that a number with no sign is taken to be positive. A negative number always is written with a minus (–) sign. A zero has no sign and is neither positive nor negative. When adding or subtracting positive and negative numbers, visualize the movement on the number line.

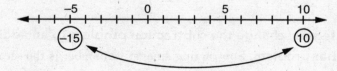

The correct answer to the temperature question is −5°.

Although you can always draw a quick number line to help you with a problem, there are times when this is not feasible. Familiarize yourself with these **rules for integers**.

INTEGER RULES OF THUMB AND TIPS

ADDING AND SUBTRACTING INTEGERS

A positive plus a positive is always a positive.

$(+3) + (+8) = (+11)$

$(+20) + (+30) = (+50)$

A negative plus a negative is always a negative.

$(-3) + (-8) = (-11)$

$(-20) + (-30) = (-50)$

A positive plus a negative, or a negative plus a positive, means to find the difference between the two and use the sign of the larger number.

$(+6) + (-2) = (+4)$	You started with 6 and went backwards 2. The positive number is larger, so the answer is still positive.
$(-9) + (+8) = (-1)$	You started with −9 and only went up +8. The larger number is negative, so the answer is still negative.
$(+6) + (-10) = (-4)$	You started with 6 and went backwards 10. The negative number is larger, so the answer is now negative.
$(-7) + (+9) = (+2)$	You started with −7 and went up 9. The positive number is larger, so the answer is now positive.

When finding the sum of a string of integers, find the sum of the positives and the sum of the negatives. Then use the rules above to add the sums.

$(+15) + (-2) + (-10) + (+8) + (+20) + (-6) =$

You could solve this correctly by adding and subtracting left to right as necessary, but it's easier to first add all the positives together and then all the negatives together. Otherwise, you have to alternate between addition and subtraction and are more likely to make a mistake.

$(+15) + (+8) + (+20) = (+43)$ $\qquad\qquad$ $(-2) + (-10) + (-6) = (-18)$

$$(+43) + (-18) = (+25)$$

The answer is +25.

To subtract integers, change the subtraction problem to an addition of a negative number problem. Subtracting a negative number is the same thing as adding a positive number, which is easier to understand.

What is $(+8) - (-10)$?

Change the subtraction sign to an addition sign, and change the sign on the number being subtracted. $\qquad$ $(+8) - (-10) = (+8) + (+10)$

Then finish the problem. $\qquad\qquad\qquad$ $(+8) + (+10) = (+18)$

What is $(-25) - (+5)$?

Change the subtraction sign to an addition sign, and $\quad$ $(-25) - (+5) = (-25) + (-5)$
change the sign on the number being subtracted.

Then finish the problem. $(-25) + (-5) = (-30)$

MULTIPLYING AND DIVIDING INTEGERS

Before you go on to multiplying and dividing integers, take a moment to notice that the next multiplication problem has no "times" sign. In algebra, parentheses can indicate not only order of operations (page 300) but also multiplication. The parentheses have to be around only one of the multiplicands.

If the signs are the same,
the answer is positive.

$$(-8)(-5) = 40$$
$$(2)(3) = 6$$
$$-4(-7) = 28$$
$$\frac{24}{8} = 3$$
$$\frac{-42}{-7} = 7$$

 Do not confuse operation parentheses with multiplication parentheses. $(7 + 7 \times 3)$ are parentheses that should be done first, but $(-9)(-3)$ is just a regular multiplication problem.

If the signs are different,
the answer is negative.

$$(5)(-6) = -30$$
$$(-2)(10) = -20$$
$$4(-9) = -36$$
$$\frac{81}{-9} = -9$$
$$\frac{-21}{7} = -3$$

You remember from page 300 that math has an order of operations. Algebraic functions have a place in the order of operations as well. We now expand the list to include the functions we are about to learn.

- **First**, all operations in parentheses are to be worked as they occur from left to right, multiplying and dividing first, then adding and subtracting. The fraction bar counts as a division symbol.
- **Second**, find all values of exponents and roots (page 363).
- **Next**, work out all multiplication and division as it occurs from left to right.
- **Last**, work out all addition and subtraction as it occurs from left to right.

PRACTICE

Find the value of the following expression: $\frac{20}{4} + (-9)(-3) - (7 + 21) =$

First, work out all operations in parentheses,
left to right, with multiplication and division $\frac{20}{4} + (-9)(-3) - (7 + 21) =$
first, and addition and subtraction second.

No other roots or exponents.

All multiplication and division. $5 + (-9)(-3) - (28) =$

All addition and subtraction. $5 + (27) - 28 = 32 - 28 = 4$

The answer is 4.

VARIABLES AND ALGEBRAIC EXPRESSIONS

You must be able to "read" algebra. Algebraic equations are written in certain ways; once you are able to read them, algebra is merely a matter of performing the same functions you have done all along. The entire idea of algebra rests on being able to work with variables, or missing numbers.

Missing numbers can be represented by any letter, but the most common is x, followed by y and z. Also, a, b, c, and n are frequently used. These are called **variables**. Read a variable by saying "a number" or "some number."

The expression...	is read this way.
$4x$	4 times a number
$(10)n$	10 times some number
$2 + x$	2 more than a number
$a + b$	a number plus another number
$y - 8$	8 less than a number
$5 - z$	5 minus a number
$\frac{1}{2}x + 3$	one half of a number, then add 3
$\frac{x}{7}$ or $x/7$	a number divided by 7

When variables are part of a math sentence, the math sentence is called an **algebraic expression**. An algebraic expression allows for many solutions.

PRACTICE

The One-Price clothing store raised its prices. Everything went up by $6. What is the new cost of the clothes?

This word problem can be expressed algebraically. Refer to the "old" price of the clothes as x. If everything goes up by $6, then 6 is added to x. The new price of clothes is $x + 6$, and the result can be called y.

$x + 6 = y$

Now that you have an expression, you can use it to find the new clothes prices.

Clothes	Old Price	(x + 6)	New Price
Shoes	$10	10 + 6	$16
Shirts	$15	15 + 6	$21
Socks	$4	4 + 6	$10
Scarves	$3	3 + 6	$9
Pants	$16	16 + 6	$22

Depending on the number, the value of the expression changes.

PRACTICE

What is the value of $(x + 2y)$ when $x = 3$ and $y = 5$?

When given the value of a variable, simply substitute the number into the expression and solve. Don't forget your order of operations!

$$(x + 2y) =$$
$$(3 + 2 \times 5) =$$
$$(3 + 10) = 13$$
$$x + 2y = 13$$

Some expressions must be **simplified**, which means that all like variables must be put together. We can add and subtract numbers expressed in terms of the same variable just as if the variable weren't there. Just as $5 + 10 = 15$, the expression $5x + 10x = 15x$.

The variables $5x + y + 2xy - x + 9y - x^2 - 9xy + 8x$ would be simplified by combining like terms:

$5x - x + 8x$ simplifies to $12x$.

Note that x^2 is not in the x group. x^2 can only combine with another x^2. The same holds true for $2xy$. It has an x, but it is not the same term. Also, each term keeps its sign, + or −.

$2xy - 9xy$ simplifies to $-7xy$.
$y + 9y$ simplifies to $10y$.

Then, put all the simplified terms together in a new, simplified equation:

$12x - 7xy + 10y - x^2$

It does not matter the order in which the terms appear: $-7xy - x^2 + 12x + 10y$ is just as correct. If your simplified answer does not match a GED answer exactly, try looking at just the terms. As long as they have the right sign and are grouped correctly, it is still correct.

SIMPLIFYING ALGEBRAIC EXPRESSIONS THAT HAVE PARENTHESES

Simplify $3x(5x - 8)$.

Do you remember the order of operations? If not, flip back to page 301 for a quick review. The order of operations says to work within parentheses first. You cannot combine either of the terms in this set of parentheses because they do not have the same variable, but you can multiply the outside term with both of the terms inside the parentheses.

$3x \ (5x - 8)$
$3x \ (5x) + 3x \ (-8)$
$15x^2 - 24x$

$3x(5x - 8)$ is equal to $15x^2 - 24x$.

EQUATIONS

ONE-STEP EQUATIONS

When you solve the problem $4 + 1$, you write it as an equation: $4 + 1 = 5$. You use the equal sign to show that what is to the left of the equal sign is mathematically the same as what is to the right. No other number besides 5 would work in this equation, but how about another expression? $4 + 1 = 2 + 3$ is also a true equation. Think of it as a scale: you can change it, but to keep it balanced, you must perform the same operations on both sides.

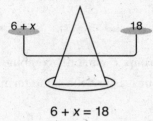

$$6 + x = 18$$

x can be only one number to keep the equation equal. You can probably guess that $x = 12$, but how would you find it if the equation were more complicated? Just keep in mind that you can do anything to an equation as long as you do the exact same thing to both sides. If you add, subtract, multiply, or divide on one side, you must do the exact same operation to the other.

The object of solving an equation is to find the ultimate value of x (or y or b or whatever variable is used). If you could get x to be the only term on one side, it would then to be equal the other side, and you would know the value of x.

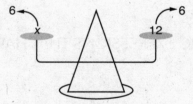

Solve $6 + x = 18$.

This expression says that some number plus 6 equals 18. If we were to take away 6 from both sides:

$6 + x - 6 = 18 - 6$

then

$x = 12$ is the solution for the equation.

When you try to solve for x, the best way is to remember inverse operations. Addition is the inverse of subtraction, and multiplication is the inverse of division. When you determine that 6 was added to x, then to get rid of the 6, do the inverse, or subtraction.

Use the inverse to solve for x.

Solve $7x = 42$.

If you put $7x$ over 7, then the 7 cancels out because $7 \div 7 = 1$. Of course, always do the same operation to both sides!

$$7x = 42 \qquad \frac{7x}{7} = \frac{42}{7} \qquad x = \frac{42}{7} \qquad x = 6$$

$x = 6$ is the solution.

USING EQUATIONS IN WORD PROBLEMS

Algebraic equations can help solve word problems. You must analyze the information carefully to set up your equation. All quantities will be in relation to the unknown amount. Above all, have in mind a quick estimate of what a reasonable answer should be for your problem.

PRACTICE

Valerie is 4 years older than Dana. If their ages are added, they get 28. How old is Valerie?

Valerie's is the age in question, so assign x there. Use what you know from the problem to create the rest of the equation.

- We decide that Valerie's age $= x$.
- Valerie is 4 years older than Dana, so $(x - 4)$ must equal Dana's age. (Dana is 4 years younger than Valerie).
- We also know that Valerie's age added to Dana's age is equal to 28. Substitute the variables in the problem.

$$
\begin{aligned}
x + (x - 4) &= 28 \\
x + x - 4 &= 28 \\
2x - 4 &= 28 \\
2x - 4 + 4 &= 28 + 4 \\
2x &= 32 \\
x &= 16
\end{aligned}
$$

Valerie is 16, and Dana is 12. This fulfills the word problem: Valerie is 4 years older than Dana, and their ages added together are 28.

PRACTICE

Three consecutive odd integers added together equal 33. What is the smallest integer?

(1)   1
(2)   9
(3)   11
(4)   13
(5)   15

THE

GED

Assign x to the smallest number. The second number is the next odd number, so it must be represented by $(x + 2)$. The last number would be $(x + 4)$. We know from the problem that the three numbers added together are 33. Therefore:

Combine like terms.	$x + (x + 2) + (x + 4) = 33$
You can combine the whole numbers and the x terms.	$3x + 6 = 33$
Subtract from both sides to get just a variable term on one side and just a whole number on the other.	$3x + 6 - 6 = 33 - 6$ $3x = 27$
Divide both sides by 3 to solve for x.	$\frac{3x}{3} = \frac{27}{3}$
The three numbers are 9, 11, and 13: answer (2).	$x = 9$

Tip: Although this is how to use algebra to solve the problem, there is another way for you to approach it in a multiple-choice test. These answers are given to you as multiple choices, so it is always possible to just use the answers to see which one is right. Use each answer, find the next two numbers, and add. Only one set will be correct. This is called **working backward**.

An important part of algebra is formulas, constant math sentences that do not change. The test gives you all of the parts of the information you need and asks you to find the missing part. To find miles per hour or distance traveled, you need the distance formula. The GED test provides a formula sheet with all the formulas you need for the test. To be ready for the test, it is more important to understand *how* the formulas work than to worry about memorizing them. For instance, you may be given a distance problem. On your formula sheet, you find that the distance formula is

distance = rate × time $d = rt$

You will be provided two of the three terms (or given the information necessary to find them) and asked to find the missing one. Put the numbers you know into the formula, and solve to find the last one.

PRACTICE

A train travels at 50 miles per hour for 2 hours. How many miles did the train travel?

Using the distance formula, $d = rt$, put in the values you are given: 50 miles per hour is the rate, and 2 hours is the time.

$d = rt$
$d = 50 \times 2$
$d = 100$ miles

The correct answer is that the train traveled 100 miles.

You also may have to use the cost formula.

Total cost = number of units × rate per unit $\qquad c = nr$

PRACTICE

The total cost of the shipment of dishwashers is $1,875. If there are 5 dishwashers, how much is each dishwasher?

Using the cost formula, $c = nr$, put in the values you are given: $1,875 is the total cost, and 5 is the number of units.

$c = nr$
$\$1875 = 5 \times r$
$\dfrac{\$1875}{5} = \dfrac{5r}{5}$
$\$375 = r$

The rate per dishwasher is $375.

EXPONENTS AND ROOTS

Exponents and roots are special ways of showing multiplication and division by the same number.

Any number multiplied by itself can be shown as an **exponent**.

$3 \times 3 = 3^2 = 9$
$5 \times 5 \times 5 = 5^3 = 125$
$4 \times 4 = 4^2 = 16$
$8 \times 8 \times 8 \times 8 \times 8 \times 8 = 8^6 = 262{,}144$
$2 \times 2 = 2^2 = 4$
$10 \times 10 \times 10 \times 10 = 10^4 = 10{,}000$

An exponent shows how many times a number is multiplied by itself. Note that 3^2 is *not* 3×2, but 3×3, and 9^3 is $9 \times 9 \times 9$, not 9×3.

Exponents are useful for writing very small or very large numbers. When discussing the planets in our solar system, most numbers expressing distance from the sun are very large. For example, the earth is 93,000,000 miles away from the sun. It would be time-consuming and unwieldy to write this number over and over again. Instead, we know that 1,000,000 is the same as $10 \times 10 \times 10 \times 10 \times 10 \times 10$, or 10^6. Therefore, you can write 93,000,000 as 93×10^6.

Exponents can be negative numbers. This results in very small numbers.

$10^1 = 10 \qquad\qquad 10^{-1} = \frac{1}{10}$
$10^2 = 100 \qquad\quad\; 10^{-2} = \frac{1}{100}$
$10^3 = 1000 \qquad\quad 10^{-3} = \frac{1}{1,000}$

SPECIAL EXPONENTS RULES

Any number with an exponent of 0 equals 1.

$2^0 = 1$ $\qquad\qquad$ $9^0 = 1$ $\qquad\qquad$ $10^0 = 1$

Any number with an exponent of 1 equals itself.

$2^1 = 2$ $\qquad\qquad$ $9^1 = 9$ $\qquad\qquad$ $10^1 = 10$

Any number raised to the power of 2 is referred to as "squared."

2 squared is 4. $\qquad\qquad$ $9^2 = 81$ $\qquad\qquad$ $10^2 = 100$

Any number raised to the power of 3 is referred to as "cubed."

2 cubed is 8. $\qquad\qquad$ $9^3 = 729$ $\qquad\qquad$ $10^3 = 1,000$

ROOTS

Roots are the opposite of raising a number to an exponent. It asks, what number was multiplied by itself to get a certain result? The most common root is the square root. The square root of a number is the number that was multiplied by itself.

You should memorize the squares and their roots up to 12.

$1^2 = 1$ $\qquad$ $4^2 = 16$ $\qquad$ $7^2 = 49$ $\qquad$ $10^2 = 100$

$2^2 = 4$ $\qquad$ $5^2 = 25$ $\qquad$ $8^2 = 64$ $\qquad$ $11^2 = 121$

$3^2 = 9$ $\qquad$ $6^2 = 36$ $\qquad$ $9^2 = 81$ $\qquad$ $12^2 = 144$

PRACTICE

What is the square root of 81?

The correct answer is 9. If 9 raised to the power of 2 is 81, then the square root of 81 is 9.

PRACTICE

What is the square root of 40? (Do not use a calculator.)

(1) 5.36
(2) 6
(3) 6.32
(4) 7
(5) 7.265

You know that the square root of 36 is 6, and the square root of 49 is 7. The square root of 40 would therefore be a number between 36 and 49. The correct answer is (3): 6.32.

PATTERNS AND FUNCTIONS

The Mathematics test includes questions that seem like puzzles or riddles. These ask you to find a pattern. Let's look at a practice example:

PRACTICE

Tony is playing a computer game. Every time Tony enters a number into the computer, the computer displays a number on the screen. The computer is following a rule, and Tony must discover what the computer's rule is. Use the chart below to discover the computer's rule.

Tony's number	Computer number
5	15
9	27
3	9
10	30
11	33

(1) Add 20.
(2) Multiply by 1.
(3) Add 10.
(4) Multiply by 3.
(5) Multiply by 8.

To find the rule, or pattern, that is being followed, look at what was done to each of the numbers and try to find a common operation. If a 5 is entered, a 15 is returned. This could mean the rule is to add 10. The most efficient solution is to assume that the first rule you think of is the one being used. Then, check the next number to confirm. If it is confirmed, keep the hypothesis; if it's not confirmed, look for another rule that will work for both one and two. It could also mean the rule is to multiply by 3. To find the correct rule, enter another number. The next number entered is 9. If the rule were add 10, the computer would have returned a 19. It returned a 27, and that fits the other rule: multiply by 3. Check all the other numbers, and multiply by 3 is the correct rule: answer (4).

A function is an algebraic pattern. It shows a chart, gives the rule, and asks for the new number.

PRACTICE

For the function $y = 9 - 2x$, what are the values needed to complete the chart?

x	−3	−2	−1	0	1	2
y	15	13		9	7	

(1) 14 and −1
(2) 11 and −5
(3) 5 and 0
(4) −1 and 6
(5) 11 and 5

If the value for x is given, substitute it into the equation. Solve for y. The only two numbers that return a true equation are in answer (5): 11 and 5.

$y = 9 - 2x$ $y = 9 - 2x$
$y = 9 - (2)(-1)$ $y = 9 - (2)(2)$
$y = 9 - (4)$ $y = 9 - (-2)$
$y = 9 + 2$ $y = 5$
$y = 11$

THE
GED

MULTIPLYING FACTORS

Multiply $(x - 2)(2x + 4)$.

When two terms are to be multiplied, use the FOIL method:

First, **O**uter, **I**nner, **L**ast.

The FOIL method makes sure that all terms were multiplied properly.

First: multiply the first terms	$(x - 2)(2x + 4)$	x times $2x$	$2x^2$
Outer: multiply the outer terms	$(x - 2)(2x + 4)$	x times 4	$4x$
Inner: multiply the inner terms	$(x - 2)(2x + 4)$	-2 times $2x$	$-4x$
Last: multiply the last terms	$(x - 2)(2x + 4)$	-2 times 4	-8

Write down all the terms, and combine like terms: $2x^2 + 4x - 4x - 8$

The answer is $2x^2 - 8$.

You might also try another method. Just set up the terms as you would any other multiplication problem. As long as you keep your terms straight, it works!

$$
\begin{array}{r}
x - 2 \\
\times\ 2x - 4 \\
\hline
4x - 8 \\
+\ 2x^2 - 4x \\
\hline
2x^2 - 0 - 8 \\
= 2x^2 - 8
\end{array}
$$

SOLVING QUADRATIC EQUATIONS

PRACTICE

What are the possible values for x if $x^2 + x - 5 = 1$?

(1) $x = -3$ and $x = 2$
(2) $x = -2$ and $x = 3$
(3) $x = -1$ and $x = 6$
(4) $x = -6$ and $x = 0$
(5) $x = -3$ and $x = -2$

To solve this problem, you can go through the process of factoring. It is easier, however, to substitute the answers in the equation and see which one fits. Only answer (1) has both answers that make the equation true.

SOLVING AND GRAPHING INEQUALITIES

In the equations we have examined so far, there has been only one possible solution for each problem. However, some equations have more than one solution. Let's look at them.

Find all the values for $x \geq 3$.

On the number line, x can be equal to 3, so put a circle around the 3. x can also be greater than 3, so shade all values to the right of the 3. Your illustration shows that x can be 3 or any value shaded, which are all numbers greater than 3. This is what the equation asks for.

Solve $3x - 3 \geq x + 5$.

Simplify so that x is the only term on one side.

$$3x - 3 \geq x + 5$$
$$2x \geq 8$$
$$x \geq 4$$

This shows that all values greater than or equal to 4 will solve the equation.

Inequalities are solved much like equations, with one important difference: **If a negative number is multiplied or divided on both sides of an inequality, the inequality sign must be reversed.**

$$-4x \leq 36 \quad = \quad \frac{-4x}{-4} \leq \frac{36}{-4} \quad = \quad x \geq -9$$

THE COORDINATE PLANE

Imagine the top of a square table. You place a checker somewhere on the table. How do you report the exact location of the checker to someone who cannot see the table? One way would be to describe the location as being a certain number of inches from the right or left edge of the table, and a certain number of inches from the top or bottom of the edge of the table. If you can visualize that, then you understand how a **coordinate plane** works.

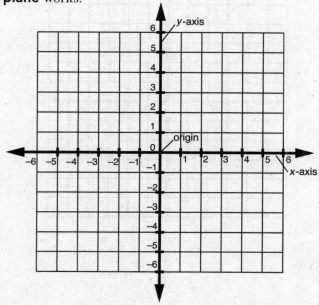

A coordinate plane uses two number lines to divide a flat space into four quadrants. The horizontal number line is called the **x-axis**. The vertical number line is called the **y-axis**. The number lines cross at each one's zero mark; therefore, the exact middle of the coordinate plane is described by **(0,0)**. As you move right along the *x*-axis, the numbers are positive and get larger, and as you move left, the numbers are negative and get smaller. As you move up along the *y*-axis, the numbers are positive and get larger, and as you move down, the numbers are negative and get smaller.

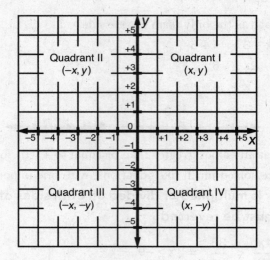

Every location in the coordinate plane is "named" by a set of two numbers, called a **point**. The numbers tell how far right, left, up, or down that point is from the exact middle, or (0,0). The point (0,0) means that there was no movement off of the *x*-axis and no movement off of the *y*-axis. To keep things constant, the numbers in a point are always written (*x*-axis, *y*-axis): first the horizontal position and them the vertical position.

Find the letter or point for the following locations.

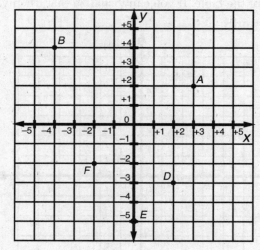

1.   Point (3,2)
2.   Point (−4,4)
3.   Point (−5,0)
4.   Letter D
5.   Letter E
6.   Letter F

You must put points on an alternate format grid for some answers. Practice plotting points A through F on the grid that follows. The answers are to the right.

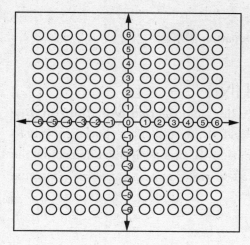

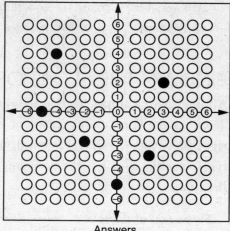

Answers

GRAPHING EQUATIONS

When you solve an equation, you find values for x and values for y. Put the solutions together as a point, (x,y), and you can now graph the equation.

Graph the equation $y = x - 6$.

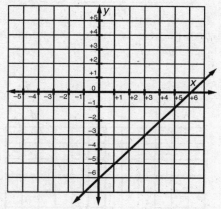

All of the values for x and y that fit the equation will be on this line, even if they are not shown on the graph. This means that the point $(27, 21)$ will be on the graph of this equation, even if this point can't be seen on this plane because $21 = 27 - 6$.

You can know a point is on a line even without having to see it, so you can answer questions about graphing without actually plotting on a graph.

PRACTICE

Which of the following points lies on the graph of the equation $y = 2x - 0$?
(1) $(-2, -4)$
(2) $(-5, -4)$
(3) $(0, 1)$
(4) $(2, 1)$
(5)   Not enough information is given.

Instead of drawing the graph, just substitute numbers to see which point solves the equation:

Answers for (1) create the equation $-4 = -4$

Answers for (2) create the equation $-4 = -10$

Answers for (3) create the equation $1 = 0$

Answers for (4) create the equation $1 = 4$

Only answer (1), $(-2,-4)$, creates a true equation.

FINDING THE SLOPE OF A LINE

All lines have a **slope**. To find the slope of a line, find the **rise over the run**. *Rise* describes the line's movement up or down, and *run* describes its movement left to right. Since the y-axis is the vertical, or up-and-down, axis, y variables determine the rise. Since the x-axis is the horizontal, or left-to-right, axis, x variables determine the run.

Slope (m) of a line $= \dfrac{\text{rise}}{\text{run}} = \dfrac{y_2 - y_1}{x_2 - x_1}$

where (x_1, y_1) and (x_2, y_2) are two points on a line.

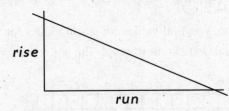

It doesn't matter which point is (x_1, y_1) or (x_2, y_2), as long as you make sure to subtract in the same order.

PRACTICE

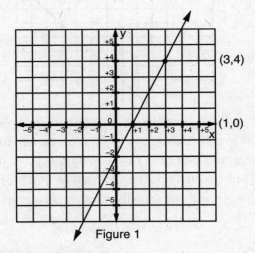

Figure 1

What is the slope of the line in Figure 1?

Find two points on the line. In this case, they are $(3,4)$ and $(1,0)$. Pick any point, and call it (x_1, y_1). Call the other point (x_2, y_2). If the graph is available, you can just count using the graph. If the graph of the line is not available, then use the formula for slope. It will be provided for you on the GED formulas sheet.

For Figure 1 we use the formula.

$$\text{slope } (m) = \frac{\text{rise}}{\text{run}} = \frac{0 - 4}{1 - 3} = \frac{-4}{-2} = 2$$

The slope of the line is 2.

FINDING THE DISTANCE BETWEEN TWO POINTS

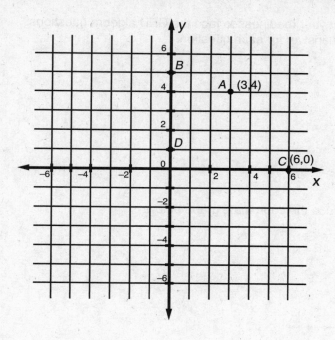

(0,1) to (0,5) = $d = 4$

(3,4) to (6,0) = $d = 5$

Find points B and D on the coordinate plane above. What is the distance between them? Finding the distance between two points on the same line is simple: subtract the small point from the larger one, subtracting x_1's from x_2's, and y_1's from y_2's.

$B(0,5)$ to $D(0,1)$: There is no movement horizontally, so the movement is vertical from 5 to 1. This is a difference of 4 units.

Subtraction of two points that are not on an axis line involves a formula.

What is the distance between points A and C?

The distance is no longer along the y-axis or x-axis, so you cannot just count the small squares. The slope must be taken into account. The distance between two points on a coordinate plane is the square root of the difference between the x coordinates squared, plus the difference between the y coordinates squared. It looks like this:

$$\sqrt{(x_2 - x_1)^2 + (y_2 - y_1)^2}$$

Use the distance formula and substitute in the given points.

$A = (3,4)$ $C = (6,0)$

distance $= \sqrt{(3 - 6)^2 + (4 - 0)^2}$

$= \sqrt{(-3)^2 + (4)^2}$

$= \sqrt{9 + 16}$

$= \sqrt{25}$

$= 5$

The correct answer is 5.

Again, it doesn't matter which point is (x_1, y_1) or (x_2, y_2) as long as you make sure to subtract in the same order.

PRACTICE SET: ALGEBRA

The following questions test your readiness to face the GED algebra questions. Calculate or select the best answer for each question.

1. Simplify $2x - y - 8x + 7x^2 + 12y$

    (1) $y - x$
    (2) $6x + 7x^2 + 12y$
    (3) $5x + 4y$
    (4) $7x^2 - 6x + 11y$
    (5) $7x^2 + 11y + 6x$

For questions 2 through 4, use the coordinate graph below.

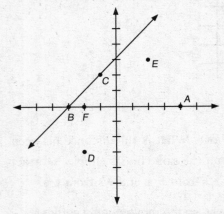

2. Which point would lie on the graph of $x^2 - 1 = y$?

    (1)   *A*
    (2)   *B*
    (3)   *C*
    (4)   *D*
    (5)   *E*

3. What is the slope of this line?

    (1)   1
    (2)   −1
    (3)   2
    (4)   −2
    (5)   The slope cannot be determined from the information given.

4. What is the distance between point *A* and point *B*?

    (1)   5
    (2)   3
    (3)   8
    (4)   2
    (5)   7

You may use your calculator for question 5.

5. Three consecutive integers add to 66. What is the largest integer?

Check your answers on page 396. How did you do? If you got most of the answers right, you are $\frac{6}{7}$, or 85.7%, of the way up the ladder! The only skill left for us to master is geometry—so let's move on to the eighth rung.

THE
GED

GEOMETRY

What do stop signs, pizza, swimming pools, and soda cans all have in common? Geometry! The stop sign is an octagon, a pizza is a circle, a swimming pool can be a rectangular solid, and soda cans are cylinders. Geometry includes two-dimensional figures, three-dimensional figures, points, lines, and angles. It calculates the area of a rug and the height of a telephone pole. It is also 25% of the GED.

For the most part, the key to geometry lies in the ability to use formulas. Remember, the formulas you need are provided on the GED formulas sheet. Familiarize yourself with terms used and the rules they follow. The rest is just substitutions and simple math.

FORMULAS OF PERIMETER

> Perimeter = addition of the lengths of all the sides.

	Polygon	**Circle** (circumference)
Shape		
Formula	add all sides	$c = \pi d$

PRACTICE

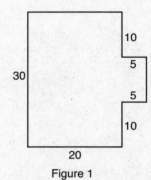

Figure 1

Which of the following expressions calculates the perimeter of Figure 1?

(1)   30 + 10 + 5 + 5 + 10 + 20
(2)   30 × 20
(3)   30 × 6
(4)   30 + 20 + 10 + 5 + 10 + 5 + 20
(5)   30 + 10 + 5 + 5 + 10 + 20 + 10

Answer (4) adds the lengths of all the sides, which tells us the figure's perimeter.

PERIMETER OF A CIRCLE

Although perimeter involves the addition of the sides of a figure, the perimeter of a circle is a special matter. Because a circle has a curved edge, it needs a special formula.

$C = \pi \times d$ Circumference = pi times diameter

The Greek letter π (pi) represents the ratio relationship of a circle's circumference to its diameter. The value of π is $\frac{22}{7}$, generally shown as 3.14, although the real number is much longer. The GED uses 3.14 for all number substitutions of pi.

Diameter (d) is the distance across the center of a circle. The distance from the edge of a circle to the center is called the **radius** (r). The radius is $\frac{1}{2}$ of the diameter; therefore, the diameter of a circle can also be expressed as $2r$.

 If you are given the radius of a circle, double it to find the diameter.

PRACTICE

Holly wants to run a line of braiding around the mirror in Figure 2. How many inches of braiding does she need?

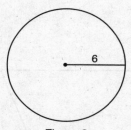

Figure 2

Use the formula for the perimeter of a circle, $C = \pi d$.

$C = \pi d = \pi 2r$
$C = (3.14)(2 \times 6)$
$C = 37.68$

The answer is 37.68. Remember that the radius is half the diameter.

FORMULAS OF AREA

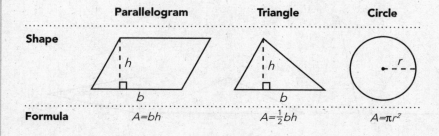

	Parallelogram	**Triangle**	**Circle**
Shape			
Formula	$A = bh$	$A = \frac{1}{2}bh$	$A = \pi r^2$

THE
GED

AREA OF A PARALLELOGRAM

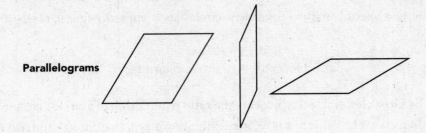

Parallelograms

$A = b \times h$ Area = base times height

In a square or a rectangle, base and height are easy to find. They form a right angle (or 90° angle) with each other. In a parallelogram with sides that are "leaning," the base and height are also lines that form a 90° angle.

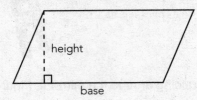

PRACTICE
What is the area of Figure 3?

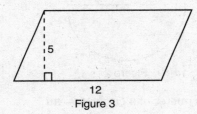

Figure 3

Finding the area of Figure 3 requires the formula for the area of a parallelogram, $A = b \times h$.

$A = b \times h$
$A = 5 \times 12$
$A = 60$

AREA OF A TRIANGLE

Triangles

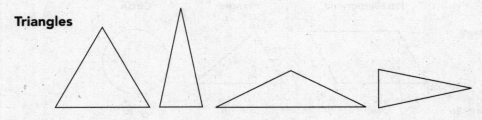

$A = \frac{1}{2} \times b \times h$

$A = \dfrac{\text{base} \times \text{height}}{2}$

PRACTICE

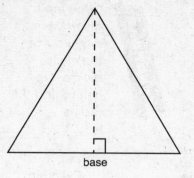 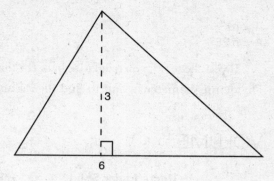

Figure 4

What is the area of Figure 4?

Use the formula for the area of a triangle, $A = \frac{1}{2} \times b \times h$.

$A = \frac{1}{2} \times b \times h$

$A = \frac{1}{2} \times 6 \times 3$

$A = 9$

AREA OF A CIRCLE

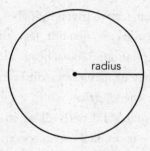

$A = \pi r^2$ Area = pi times the square of the radius

Remember that π is the value 3.14, and radius is the distance to the midpoint of the circle. To find the area of a circle, square the radius and multiply by 3.14.

PRACTICE

Figure 5

Which of the following expressions calculates the area of Figure 5?

(1) $A = \pi\,50$
(2) $A = \pi\,50^2$
(3) $A = \pi\,25$
(4) $A = \pi\,25^2$
(5) $A = \pi\,100$

The correct formula to use is $A = \pi r^2$.

$A = \pi r^2$
$A = \pi\, 25^2$

If you chose (2), you tried to square the diameter. Divide the diameter in half to find the radius.

If you are given the diameter of the circle, divide it in half to find the radius.

VOLUME

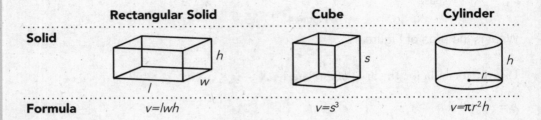

	Rectangular Solid	Cube	Cylinder
Solid			
Formula	$v = lwh$	$v = s^3$	$v = \pi r^2 h$

Volume is the measure of cubic units of space inside a three-dimensional object. The object does not necessarily have to be empty; space refers to the amount of matter that *is* or *can be* inside it. Imagine a cubic unit as a sugar cube, and you have to find out how many neatly stacked cubes it would take to fill an object.

If the dimensions of an object are given in inches, then you must find the volume in cubic inches. If the dimensions are given in feet, then you must find the volume in cubic feet. Imagine a rectangular solid like a brick: all its surfaces are flat and meet at right angles, and its edges may or may not be different lengths. To find the volume of a rectangular solid, multiply the length × width × height. For a cube, picture a sugar cube: it is a special rectangular solid with all square sides. To find the volume of a cube, you could use the same formula as for a rectangular solid, but because length, width, and height are all the same, it is easier to just think of it as the side, cubed. A cylinder is like a can, with circles at the top and bottom, and straight sides. To find the volume of a cylinder, first find the area of one of the circular ends and multiply it by the height.

PRACTICE

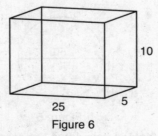

Figure 6

What is the volume of Figure 6?

Volume is found by using the formula $V = l \times w \times h$

$V = l \times w \times h$
$V = 25 \times 5 \times 10$
$V = 1250$

Which expression calculates the volume of the cube in Figure 7?

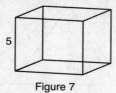

Figure 7

(1) 5×3
(2) 5×5
(3) 5^3
(4) $3 \times 3 \times 5$
(5) 5^2

The volume of a cube is calculated in the same way as the volume of a rectangular solid, $V = l \times w \times h$. Or you can just cube the side, which is the same idea.

$V = s^3$
$V = 5^3$

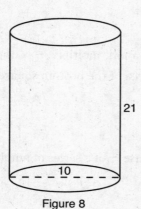

Figure 8

What is the volume of the soda can in Figure 8?

To find the volume of a soda can, multiply π by the radius squared by the height. The formula is $V = \pi r^2 h$

$V = \pi(5^2)21$
$V = \pi(25)21$

The volume of the can is $\pi 525$.

PYRAMIDS AND CONES

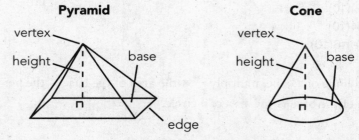

The figures that have been shown so far have all been "regular" solids; that is, they have two identical bases. A cube has the same two squares for a top and a bottom. A cylinder has the same two circles for a top and a bottom. Pyramids and cones are solids that are three-dimensional, and have a base and identical sides, but have no top.

THE
GED

PRACTICE

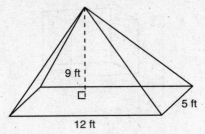

Which equation calculates the volume of the pyramid?

(1) $\dfrac{12(5)(9)}{3}$

(2) $12(5)(9)$

(3) $\dfrac{12(5)}{3}$

(4) $(12)(5) + \dfrac{9}{3}$

(5) $3(12)(5)(9)$

For the volume of a pyramid, multiply $\frac{1}{3} \times$ the area of the base $\times$ the height. Remember, the base is the area of the bottom square, or $l \times w$.

$V = \frac{1}{3} bh$

$V = \frac{1}{3} 12(5)(9)$

The answer is $\dfrac{12(5)(9)}{3}$ because $\frac{1}{3}$ of a series of numbers is the same as dividing by 3.

PRACTICE

Which equation calculates the volume of the cone?

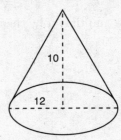

(1) $\frac{1}{3} \pi(12)(5)$

(2) $\frac{1}{3} \pi(36)(10)$

(3) $\pi(12)(10)$

(4) $\pi 144(10)$

(5) $\pi 3 + \pi 6(10)$

For the volume of a cone, multiply $\frac{1}{3} \times$ the area of the base $\times$ the height. In this case, the area of the base is the area of a circle.

$V = \frac{1}{3} bh$

Because b is πr^2, the entire formula would be

$V = \frac{1}{3} \pi r^2 h$

$V = \frac{1}{3} \pi 6^2 (10)$

THE GED

The correct answer is $V = \frac{1}{3}\pi(36)(10)$.

LINES AND ANGLES

Most of the questions about lines and angles on the Mathematics test ask you to identify types of angles, find the measurement of one angle given another, and show that you understand basic properties of lines and angles.

A line that extends from a point is called a **ray**. When two rays come from a common point, the space between them is called an **angle**, written ∠. The rays *BA* and *BC* form the ∠*1*.

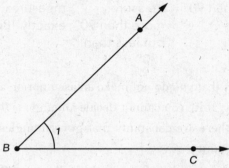

Angles are measured in degrees (°). The measure of angle *1* is 45°. You can also name this angle using the points that are in the diagram. Angle *1* can also be named ∠*ABC* or ∠*B*.

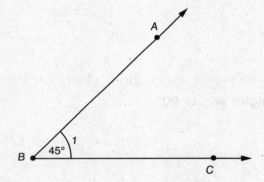

This is written $m\angle 1 = 45°$, or $m\angle ABC = 45°$.

We use a device called a protractor to measure angles. You know that a full circle contains 360°; therefore, a half circle contains 180°. The $m\angle 2$ would then be 135° because $180 - 45 = 135$.

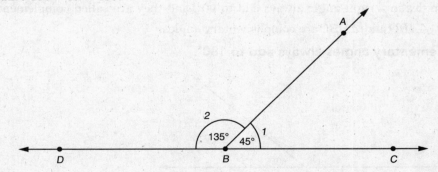

TYPES OF ANGLES

Angles fall into groups based on their number of degrees.

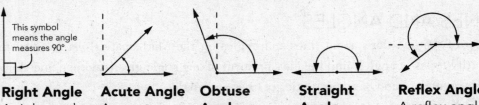

Right Angle
A right angle measures exactly 90°

Acute Angle
An acute angle measures less than 90°

Obtuse Angle
An obtuse angle measures more than 90° but less than 180°

Straight Angle
A straight angle measures exactly 180°

Reflex Angle
A reflex angle measures more than 180°

It is very important that you do not make an assumption about the measure of an angle simply by looking at it. You cannot decide an angle is 90° just because it looks like it is. Fortunately, there are constants that govern angles and allow you to find measurements with certainty.

The small square in the corner of an angle indicates 90°.

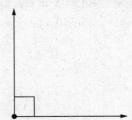

If there is a small square present in an angle, you know it is a 90° angle.

Complementary angles add to 90°.

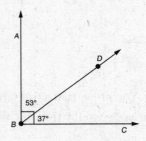

Two angles in a right angle always add to 90°, and they are called complementary angles. ∠ABD and ∠DBC are complementary angles.

Supplementary angles always add to 180°.

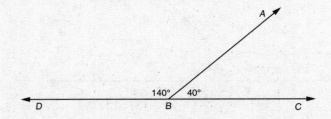

Two angles in a straight angle always add to 180°, and they are called **supplementary** angles. ∠ABD and ∠ABC are supplementary angles.

Congruent angles have the same measure.

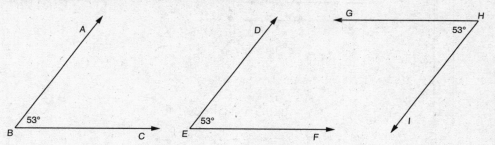

No matter which way an angle is turned, if its measure is equal to that of another angle, the equal angles are called **congruent**.

∠ABC, ∠DEF, and ∠GHI are congruent.

Vertical angles are congruent.

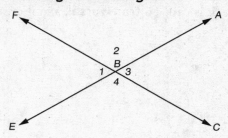

Angles formed by the intersection of two lines have two pairs of vertical angles. They are opposite each other and are congruent. ∠1 and ∠3 are congruent, and ∠2 and ∠4 are congruent.

EXAMPLE

Which two angles in the figure above are supplementary?

(1)   only ∠2
(2)   ∠2 and ∠4
(3)   ∠1 and ∠3
(4)   ∠1 and ∠2
(5)   Not enough information is given.

Supplementary angles add to 180°. There are several pairs of supplementary angles in Figure 9: ∠1 and 2, ∠2 and 3, ∠3 and 4, and ∠1 and 4. The correct answer is (4), ∠1 and 2. Although there are several pairs, this pair is the only listed as an answer choice.

Angles 1 and 2 can also be described as adjacent. They share a common vertex and one common ray. Angles 1 and 3 are nonadjacent because although they share a common vertex, they do not share a ray.

If, in the figure above, m∠1 = 45°, find the measures of the other three angles.

m∠2 _____   m∠3 _____   m∠4 _____

Answers:

m∠2 = 135°   m∠3 = 45°   m∠4 = 135°

TYPES OF LINES

Parallel lines run side by side, always at the exact same distance from each other. No matter how far you extend these lines out, they will never meet.

Perpendicular lines are two lines that cross at right angles. The measure of these angles will always each be 90°.

When a line extends over parallel lines, it is called a **transversal**, and it creates some special situations.

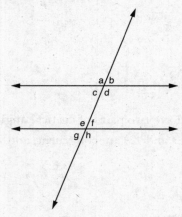

Corresponding angles: in the same position with respect to the transversal.

∠*a* and ∠*e*   ∠*b* and ∠*f*   ∠*c* and ∠*g*   ∠*d* and ∠*h*

Alternate exterior angles:

∠*a* and ∠*h*   ∠*b* and ∠*g*

Alternate interior angles:

∠*c* and ∠*f*   ∠*d* and ∠*e*

All that is needed is the measure of just one of these angles, because you can find the measure of every other angle using the relationships that you have learned.

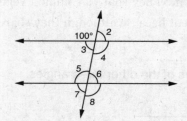

TRIANGLES AND QUADRILATERALS

Figure 10 shows triangle *ABC*, also described as Δ*ABC*.

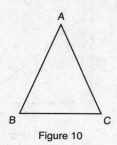

Figure 10

The vertices are *A*, *B*, and *C*.

The triangle can be named Δ*ABC*, or Δ*BCA*, or Δ*CAB*, and so on.

The three sides are $\overline{AB}$, $\overline{BC}$, and $\overline{AC}$.

Like all triangles, the sum of the measure of the interior angles will always be 180°.

SPECIAL TRIANGLES

Triangles are described by two descriptions: length of sides and measure of angles.

Length of sides: equilateral, isosceles, or scalene.

Equilateral triangle
All sides and angles are congruent; each angle measures 60°.

Isosceles triangle
Two sides and the two angles opposite these sides are congruent.

Scalene triangle
No sides and no angles are congruent.

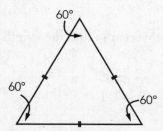

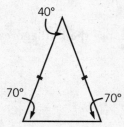

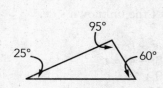

Measure of angles: right, acute, or obtuse.

Right triangle
One angle is a right angle (equal to 90°).

Acute triangle
All three angles are acute (less than 90°).

Obtuse triangle
One angle is obtuse (greater than 90°).

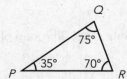

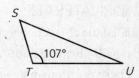

THE
GED

THE PYTHAGOREAN RELATIONSHIP

The ancient Egyptians discovered a special theorem, or rule, concerning right triangles:

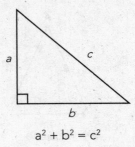

$$a^2 + b^2 = c^2$$

When two sides of a right triangle are known, the third can be found using this formula. a and b always refer to the sides next to the right angle, and c is always the **hypotenuse**, or the side opposite the right angle.

PRACTICE

If $a = 3$ and $b = 4$, what is the measure of $\overline{AC}$ on $\triangle ABC$?

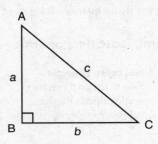

Since $\triangle ABC$ is a right triangle, use the Pythagorean theorem to find the length of the unknown side.

$$a^2 + b^2 = c^2$$
$$3^2 + 4^2 = c^2$$
$$9 + 16 = c^2$$
$$25 = c^2$$
$$\sqrt{25} = \sqrt{c^2}$$
$$5 = c$$

The measure of $\overline{AC}$ is 5.

QUADRILATERALS

A quadrilateral is a polygon with four sides. The sum of the measures of the interior angles will always be 360°.

These polygons may appear on the Mathematics test are these:

Parallelogram
opposite sides are parallel and congruent; opposite angles are of equal measure

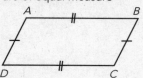

Rectangle
special parallelogram with four right angles

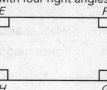

Rhombus
special parallelogram with four sides of equal length

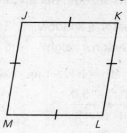

Square
special parallelogram/rhombus/rectangle with four sides of equal length and four right angles

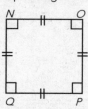

Trapezoid
only one pair of parallel sides (called bases)

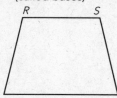

CONGRUENT FIGURES

Congruent figures are those figures that are the same shape and size. Congruent figures fit over each other perfectly, although rotating or flipping them may be necessary.

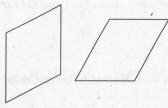

SIMILAR FIGURES

Similar figures that have the same shape, but not the same size. Their corresponding angles have the same measure, but the sides are longer or shorter. Have you ever reduced or enlarged anything on a copy machine? This is the same idea. Although everything is larger or smaller, it is in proportion to the original. Similar triangles can be useful in measuring tall objects that would be impractical to physically measure.

EXAMPLE

What is the height of the telephone pole?

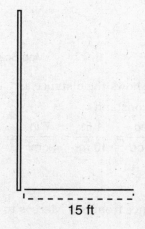

6 ft

3 ft   15 ft

THE
GED

As the pole casts a shadow, so does the person. Shadows are proportional, so the ratio of the person's height to his shadow is the same as the ratio of the pole's height to its shadow. Set up the equal ratios:

$$\frac{\text{Person's shadow}}{\text{Person's height}} = \frac{3 \text{ ft}}{6 \text{ ft}} = \frac{15 \text{ ft}}{x \text{ ft}} = \frac{\text{Pole's shadow}}{\text{Pole's height}}$$

To solve, set up cross-multiplication.

$$\frac{3 \text{ ft}}{6 \text{ ft}} = \frac{15 \text{ ft}}{x \text{ ft}}$$

$$3x = 90$$

$$\frac{3x}{3} = \frac{90}{3}$$

$$x = 30$$

The pole is 30 feet high.

We also use proportion in geometry in making and reading maps. Obviously, the diagrams on a map cannot be the actual measurements, so a map is proportionally smaller than the physical location it represents. A scale tells us what proportion was used. In this map, the key indicates that every inch is equal to 10 miles.

PRACTICE

What is the distance in miles from San Marcos to Cedar Park?

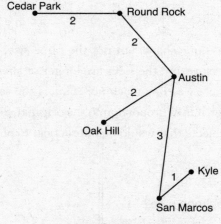

Map Scale = 1 in = 10 mi.

The map shows the distance as 7 inches, so you can set up equal ratios. Use the scale as your constant.

$$\frac{\text{Map distance}}{\text{Actual distance}} = \frac{1 \text{ in}}{10 \text{ mi}} = \frac{7 \text{ in}}{x \text{ mi}} = \frac{\text{Map San Marcos to Cedar Park}}{\text{Actual San Marcos to Cedar Park}}$$

$$7(10) = (1)x$$
$$70 = x$$

The distance from San Marcos to Cedar Park is 70 miles.

IRREGULAR FIGURES

EXAMPLE

Austin Elementary has a walking track. The school wants to plant grass in the interior of the track. Which expression shows how many square feet the grass must cover?

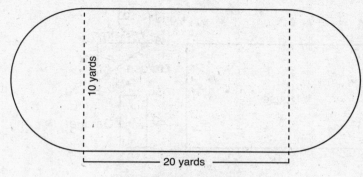

Austin Elementary walking track

(1)　　$\pi\,20^2 + 20$
(2)　　$\pi\,10^2 + 200$
(3)　　$\pi\,10^2 + 100$
(4)　　$\pi\,5^2 + 30$
(5)　　$\pi\,5^2 + 200$

   This figure is actually two figures placed together. There is one circle divided into two parts, with a half at each end. Between the circle halves is a rectangle. Find the area of the circle, find the area of the rectangle, and add the two together.

Area of a circle
$A = \pi r^2$
$A = \pi 5^2$

Area of a rectangle
$A = b \times h$
$A = 20 \times 10$
$A = 200$

   The correct answer is (5), $\pi 5^2 + 200$.

EXAMPLE

If the storage building below could be <u>completely</u> filled, what expression would be used to find how many cubic feet of space there is to fill?

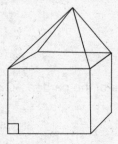

   Again, there are two figures to consider. There is a rectangular solid and a pyramid. You are asked to fill an object; therefore, you need formulas for volume.

Volume of a rectangular solid
$V = lwh$

Volume of a pyramid
$V = \frac{1}{3}$ (Area of the base)(height)

   The correct answer is $\frac{1}{3}Ah + lwh$.

PRACTICE SET: GEOMETRY

These questions test your mastery of the geometry concepts found on the Mathematics test. Consider each question carefully and indicate the best answer.

For questions 1 through 3, use the **Martin House Plan**.

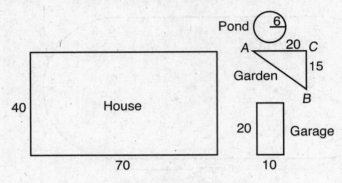

Martin House Plan

1. Which expression would be used to find the area of the Martins' pond?

    (1) π6
    (2) 36π
    (3) 12π
    (4) (3.14)(12²)
    (5) (3.14)6

2. What is the combined area of the Martins' house and garage?

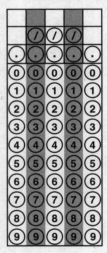

3. What is the length of the side of the garden $\overline{AC}$? (You may use a calculator.)

    (1) 15
    (2) 20
    (3) 25
    (4) 30
    (5) 35

THE
GED

INTRODUCTION

WHOLE NUMBERS
AND BASIC
OPERATIONS

USING THE fx-260
CALCULATOR

FRACTIONS,
DECIMALS, AND
PERCENTAGES

MEASUREMENT

DATA ANALYSIS

ALGEBRA

GEOMETRY

For questions 4 and 5, use the following figure.

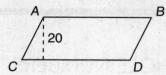

4. The area of the parallelogram ABCD is 180. What is the length of side $\overline{CD}$?

(1)   9
(2)   90
(3)   160
(4)   180
(5)   200

5. The measure of $\angle ACD = 85°$. What is the measure of $\angle BDC$?

(1)   5°
(2)   35°
(3)   50°
(4)   95°
(5)   275°

Check your answers on page 397. You now have a pretty solid math foundation and the ability to work within all the variety of situations presented on the Mathematics test.

THE
GED

CHAPTER

7

MATHEMATICS

THE
GED

ANSWERS AND
EXPLANATIONS

ANSWERS AND EXPLANATIONS

PRACTICE SET: WHOLE NUMBERS AND BASIC OPERATIONS

1. **(5) 90,000**
The 9 is in the ten thousands place, making the 9 equal in value to 90,000; the correct answer is (5). Answers (1) through (4) are incorrect because answer (1) is a 9 in the ones place, answer (2) is a 9 in the tens place, answer (3) is a 9 in the hundreds place, and answer (4) is a 9 in the thousands place. **Place Value**

2. **(4) 7,000**
Ted drove a total of 6,599 miles in the five-month period (1751 + 987 + 1993 + 667 + 1201 = 6,599). Answers (2) and (3) are rounded to the hundereds place, but the question asked you to round to the nearest thousand. Answers (1) and (5) are incorrect roundings. Answer (4), 7,000, is correct. **Rounding Whole Numbers**

3. The answer is 13825. Make sure you do not include a comma on the answer grid.

4. **(3) 372 ÷ 3**
The correct answer will divide the total cost of the stereo system by the number of payments. Answers (1) and (4) are incorrect because the wrong operation is used. The correct answer is (3), 372 ÷ 3. Answer (2) used the correct option, but is incorrect because it would only result in the total for two payments. Answer (5) is incorrect. **Dividing Whole Numbers**

5. **(5) 749**
To answer this question you should multiply the number of ice cream bars in a day by the number of days in a week (107 × 7 = 749). Ice Palace produces more than 100 bars every day, so it is clear that they will produce more than 700 a week. Answers (1) through (4) are incorrect because they are all equal to or less than 700. The correct answer is (5), 749. **Multiplying Whole Numbers**

PRACTICE SET: USING THE *fx*-260 CALCULATOR

1. **(2) 36**
This is an order of operations problem, meaning that you should perform the multiplication operations before you do the subtraction. When you perform the multiplication first, the problem becomes 56 − 20 = 36, which is answer (2). If you take the operations in the order they appear, you get answer (4), 260, which is incorrect. Answers (1), (3), and (5) are also incorrect because the arithmetic is incorrect. On the official GED calculator, the correct keystroke sequence is

7 × 8 − 4 × 5 = | 36. |, answer (2). The *fx*-260 is programmed with the order of operations, so it waits after the 4 is entered, performing 4 × 5 before completing the subtraction. ⊟ **Order of Operations**

2. (2) $4\frac{11}{12}$

Answer (1) is simply the sum of each part of the problem. Answer (3) is the difference, not the sum. Answer (4) is too large to be the sum of "a little more than three" and "almost two." Answer (5) is less than one—too small to be the sum of numbers both larger than one. Keep in mind that whenever the *fx*-260 has a fraction that is improper or is not reduced, it automatically corrects it. If you would like to reduce a fraction, just enter it using the fraction key, then press =. The display shows a properly reduced fraction. ⊟ **Adding Fractions With a Calculator**

3. 6,088 meters = 6.088 kilometers

You can use the *fx*-260 to convert from milli- to "base unit" to kilo-. You cannot convert to any of the other metric units, but this could be a helpful double-check. Enter the keystroke sequence 6088 SHIFT ENG | 6.088 ^{03} |. This sequence results in the answer 6.088. ⊟ **Decimals With a Calculator**

4. (4) 731.2

The keystroke sequence you should use is 5 SHIFT x^2 + 9 x^y 3 =. Your estimate should tell you that the square root of 5 will be between 2 and 3, and that $9^3 = 9 \times 9 \times 9$, which is 81×9, will be close to 720. Answers (1), (2), and (3) are all too small to be the correct answer, and answer (5) is too large. ⊟ **Square Roots With a Calculator**

5. (3) 1707

To find percentage, enter 5690 × 30 SHIFT =%. This results in a display of 1707, answer (3). Notice that the calculator automatically displays the answer as soon as the % key is pressed. Your estimate should tell you that the correct answer is a just under a third of a little less than 6,000, so your answer must be less than 2,000. Answers (1) and (2) are both too large to be the correct answer, and answers (4) and (5) are both too small. ⊟ **Percentages With a Calculator**

PRACTICE SET: FRACTIONS, DECIMALS AND PERCENTAGES

1. (5) $\frac{2}{3}$

Remember that fractions are **parts** over **totals**. The part in question is special diet animals, or 60. The total number of animals is 90. If you got answers (1) or (2), you did not find the total number of animals. If you got answers (3) or (4), you figured out the number of animals NOT on a special diet. If you got the correct fraction $\frac{60}{90}$, and were wondering why it was not listed as a choice, remember that fractions are reduced on the GED test: $\frac{60}{90}$ reduces to $\frac{2}{3}$, answer (5). ⊟ **Proportions**

CHAPTER

7

MATHEMATICS

THE

GED

ANSWERS AND
EXPLANATIONS

2. **(3) 2:1**

A ratio is a comparison of two numbers, usually separated by a colon. As with fractions, ratios may be reduced. The correct answer is 60:30, or 2:1, answer (3). Answers (1), (4), and (5) are incorrect because the smaller number comes first, but the number of animals on special diets is greater than the number not on special diets, so the first number in the ratio should be larger than the second. Answer (2) incorrectly indicates that the same number of animals are on special diets as are on regular diets. 🔘 **Ratios**

3. **580 ÷ 40 = 14.50**

This problem should be set up as a comparison of ratios. Start with 580 (dollars): 40 (hours), then divide both sides by 40 to find out what zookeepers earn for one hour's work. The correct answer is $14.50. Remember that the answer is correct as either 14.50 *or* 14.5. Do not include a dollar sign in your answer. 🔘 **Ratios**

4. **(2) $2\frac{1}{2}$**

Kerry is using five times more cereal than the recipe calls for. To keep the proportion balanced, she must also use five times more marshmallows ($5 \times \frac{1}{2}$), or answer (2). Your estimate should have told you that the new amount of marshmallows would be half the new amount of cereal. Answer (1) is the same as the new amount of cereal. Answer (3) is the same as the old amount of marshmallows. Answer (4) is more than the new amount of cereal. Answer (5) is only four times the old amount of marshmallows. 🔘 **Proportions**

5. **(5) 0.75**

This question asks you for the decimal form of the fraction that represents $\frac{\text{eggs used}}{\text{total eggs}}$. The number of eggs used is not given in the problem, but we can figure it out by subtracting the number of eggs remaining from the total eggs. The fraction is $\frac{12-3}{12}$ $= \frac{9}{12} = \frac{3}{4}$, and $\frac{3}{4}$ is the same as 0.75, answer (5). Answer (1) is incorrect because 0.25 is equivalent to 3 eggs used. Answer (2) is incorrect because 0.33 is equivalent to 4 eggs used. Answer (3) is incorrect because 0.50 is equivalent to 6 eggs used. Answer (4) is incorrect because 0.67 is equivalent to 8 eggs used. 🔘 **Decimals**

PRACTICE SET: MEASUREMENT

1. **(3) 48 ft.**

The top edge is a rectangle, with two sides of length 15 and two sides of length 9. Add all sides together to find perimeter. The correct answer is $15 + 15 + 9 + 9 = 48$, answer (3). Answer (1) is the sum of one long side and one short side. Answer (5) is the product of the two sides. Answers (2) and (4) are incorrect because the arithmetic is incorrect. 🔘 **Perimeter**

2. **(3) 2.5**

There are 24 hours in 1 day, so set up equal fractions and solve. $\frac{60 \text{ hours of work}}{? \text{ days of work}}$ $= \frac{24 \text{ hours}}{1 \text{ day}}$. Divide both sides by 24 to find that 60 hours equals 2.5 days. Answer (1) is incorrect because 1.25 days is only 30 hours. Answer (2) is incorrect because 2 days is only 24 hours. Answer (4) is incorrect because 5 days is 120 hours. Answer (5) is incorrect because 5.5 days is 132 hours. **Operations With Measurements**

3.　　　$A = bh$. Therefore, $A = (15)(9)$, or 135.

4.　(5)　1215 cu yd

The volume of a rectangular prism is $V = lwh$. For this problem, that is $V = (15)(9)(9)$, or answer (5), 1215 cubic yards. **Volume**

5.　(5)　15 kl

Kilo means "one thousand," so one kiloliter = 1,000 liters. A calculator is not allowed on this question, so convert liters to kiloliters by moving the decimal three places to the left. This results in answer (5), 15 kiloliters. Answers (1), (2), (3), and (4) all involve moving the decimal more than the three places that is required for this conversion. **Metric System**

PRACTICE SET: DATA ANALYSIS

1.　(3)　83 − 19

To find range, subtract the highest from the lowest number. The highest temperature in January is 83°, and the lowest is 19°. Subtracting the two extremes, 83 − 19 (answer 3) is the expression used to find the range of temperatures in January. Answers (1) and (2) do not use only the highest and lowest temperatures. Answers (4) and (5) do not use the correct operation, which is subtraction. **Using Charts**

2.　(5)　18

To find an average, add all the pieces of data and divide by the number of data. The sunny days are 15, 8, 20, 21, 25, and 18, the sum of which is 107, and 107 divided by 6 is 17.8. Since the question calls for rounding to the nearest whole day, the answer is 18, answer (5). The other answers are incorrect because they either use incorrect arithmetic or look at sunny days in a particular month rather than at the actual mean of six months. **Using Charts**

3.　　　12.2 (grid-in)

The total amount of rainfall is found by adding all of the amounts. Remember to line up decimal points before you add. The answer entered on your grid should be 12.2. **Using Charts**

4.　(1)　3:5

Probability is the number of desired events over the total number of events. There were 18 sunny days in June, out of 30 possible days. $\frac{18}{30}$ reduces to $\frac{3}{5}$. There was a 3 in 5 chance, or answer (1), of a sunny day that June. The other options are incorrect because they relate something other than the number of sunny days to the total number of days. **Using Charts**

CHAPTER

7

MATHEMATICS

THE
GED

ANSWERS AND
EXPLANATIONS

CHAPTER

7

MATHEMATICS

THE
GED

ANSWERS AND
EXPLANATIONS

5. (5)

Looking at the data for the average temperatures, the temperatures start at 47° and rise steadily. The line graphs that most readily show this are (4) and (5). The differences between the two are slight, but important. Note that in graph (4) there are two cases of identical temperatures, one occurring on the 50° line. The March temperature was not 50°, but 57°, so the graph should show a slight increase. Only graph (5) does this, and it is the most correct answer. 〈H〉 **Using Graphs**

PRACTICE SET: ALGEBRA

1. (4) $7x^2 - 6x + 11y$

Combine all like integers, x with x, y with y, and so on. Do not combine x^2 with x, however, and be very aware of positive and negative signs. The correct answer is (4): $7x^2 - 6x + 11y$. If you ended up with $11y + 7x^2 - 6x$, remember that this is still correct. It is just not a choice! Answers (1) and (3) are incorrect because neither has an x^2 variable. Answers (2) and (5) are incorrect because ignoring signs leads to incorrect arithmetic. 〈H〉 **Simplifying Expressions**

2. (5) E

Find the points indicated by the choices, and insert them into the equation. Only point E, answer (5), works. Point (2,3) inserted into the equation is $2^2 - 1 = 3$ is true because $4 - 3 = 1$. 〈H〉 **Coordinate Graphs**

3. (1) 1

The slope of the line is 1. Using the slope formula, $\frac{y_2 - y_1}{x_2 - x_1}$, use points B and C as the slope points. It does not matter which point is first and which is second. Both ways result in slopes of $\frac{2}{2}$ or $\frac{-2}{-2}$, and those are both simplified to 1, answer (1). 〈H〉 **Finding the Slope of a Line**

4. (5) 7

The two points are along one of the xy axes, so the points can be subtracted from each other: $4 - (-3) = 7$. The distance between the points is 7, or answer (5). 〈H〉 **Coordinate Graphs**

5. $x + (x + 1) + (x + 2) = 66$; $x = 21$; $x + 2 = 23$

Call the first number x. The second and third numbers would be $x + 1$ and $x + 2$. Use these three algebraic expressions to write a number sentence. $x + (x + 1) + (x + 2) = 66$. Simplify this expression to $3x + 3 = 66$, and then to $3x = 63$. $x = 21$. The numbers a 21, 22, and 23. These do indeed add to 66. Since the question asks for the largest integer, the answer is 23, entered on your grid. 〈H〉 **Algebraic Expressions**

PRACTICE SET: GEOMETRY

1. **(2) 36π**

Find the area of a circle with the formula $A = \pi r^2$. The radius is the distance to the center of the circle. The correct answer is (2): 36π. Answers (1) and (5) are incorrect because the radius, 6, is not squared. Answer (3) incorrectly doubles the radius instead of squaring it. Answer (4) uses the diameter instead of the radius. Did it throw you off that the 36 came before π? Don't let it! Multiplication can occur in any order, so it doesn't matter if π is first or second. 🅗 **Formulas of Area**

2.   **40 × 70 + 10 × 20 = 3000**

Find the area of the Martins' home by multiplying 40 by 70, which is 2800. Then add this to the area of the garage, which is 10 × 20. Add the two results: 2800 + 200 = 3000. Enter your answer on the alternate format grid. 🅗 **Formulas of Area**

3. **(3)   25**

The small square in the lower corner indicates a right angle. This is a right triangle, so use the Pythagorean theorem, $a^2 + b^2 = c^2$. The two sides are 15 and 20, so $15^2 + 20^2 = c^2$, or 225 + 400 = 625. The square root of 625 is 25, answer (3). Answers (1) and (2) are incorrect because those are the same as the given sides. Answer (4) is incorrect because of incorrect arithmetic. Answer (5) is just the sum of the two given sides rather than the square root of the sum of the squares of the sides.
🅗 **Pythagorian Theorum**

4. **(1)   9**

The area of a parallelogram is $A = bh$. You know the area and the height, so substitute to find the base: 180 = b(20). Answer (1), 9, is correct, because 180/20 = 9. Answer (2) is 180/2 instead of 180/20. Answer (3) uses the wrong operation: 180−20 instead of 180/20. Answer (4) is incorrect because the area cannot be the same as the base. Answer (5) uses the wrong operation: 180+20 rather than 180/20.
🅗 **Formulas of Area**

5. **(4)   95°**

This question requires you to remember the rules of complementary and supplementary angles. The angles ACD and BDC form complementary angles, and the two measures add to 180°. Since ∠ACD is 85°, the m∠BDC must be 180° − 85°. This results in answer (4): 95°. Answer (1) is incorrect because ∠BDC would have to be a complementary angle to ∠ACD (they would add to 90°). Answer (5) is incorrect because, combined with ∠ACD, 275° would equal 360°, or a complete circle.
🅗 **Lines and Angles**

CHAPTER

7

MATHEMATICS

THE
GED

ANSWERS AND
EXPLANATIONS

PART III

CHAPTER
8
PRACTICE TESTS

LANGUAGE ARTS, WRITING PART I

This Language Arts, Writing test is designed to measure your ability to use and evaluate standard written English. Spend no more than 75 minutes answering the fifty questions on this test. You may detach the answer sheet at the back of this book and use it to mark your responses. When you are finished, review the Answers and Explanations section on page 419 to determine whether you are ready to take the GED Language Arts, Writing test or you need additional review in specific areas.

Directions: Choose the <u>one best answer</u> to each question.

<u>Questions 1 through 9</u> refer to the following letter of application.

February 9, 2004

Ms. Ana Sasaki
Director
Greenlake Day Care Center
777 Ravenna Ave., NW
Seattle, WA 98100

Dear Ms. Sasaki:

(A)

(1) I would like to apply for the teaching position advertised in the *Seattle Times.* (2) I believe my education and work experience have enabled me to excel in the position described in the advertisement. (3) In December, I graduated from Rain City Community College with a degree in education. (4) Earning a 4.0 grade point average. (5) I, while studying at Rain City, also worked part-time as a teaching assistant at Aurora Elementary School. (6) In that position, I worked with children in kindergarten and first grade, assisting instructors with all aspects of teaching. (7) However, I also have extensive experience working with younger children, as I served as an intern at the Happy Day Preschool last Fall. (8) My experience working at Happy Day made me realize that I want to work with preschool-aged children in our career.

(B)

(9) I have enclosed my résumé completed application, and references for your perusal. (10) As my work history and interests show, I am committed to the kinds of goals Greenlake Day Care Center embraces. (11) One of my favorite activities is rock-climbing. (12) I am also an extremely hard worker, learn fast, and responsible person.

(C)

(13) I am excited about the challenges and opportunities that working at Greenlake Day Care Center would provide. (14) Thank you for your consideration, and I look forward to speaking with you soon.

Sincerely,

Patricia Toer

Patricia Toer
100 Emerald Lane
Seattle, WA 98111

---

1. Sentence 2: **I believe my education and work experience have enabled me to excel in the position described in the advertisement.**

   Which correction should be made to sentence 2?

   (1) Insert a comma after <u>education</u>.
   (2) Insert <u>and</u> after <u>excel</u>.
   (3) Change <u>have enabled</u> to <u>would enable</u>.
   (4) Change <u>described</u> to <u>describe</u>.
   (5) No correction is necessary.

2. Sentences 3 and 4: **In December, I graduated from Rain City Community College with a degree <u>in education. Earning</u> a 4.0 grade point average.**

   Which is the best way to write the underlined portion of these sentences? If the original is the best way, choose option (1).

   (1) in education. Earning
   (2) in education. Having earned
   (3) in education. I am earning
   (4) in education, had earned
   (5) in education, earning

3. Sentence 5: **I, while studying at Rain City, also worked part-time as a teaching assistant at Aurora Elementary School.**

   If you rewrote sentence 5 beginning with

   While studying at Rain City,

   the next words should be

   (1) I also worked
   (2) and also working
   (3) with working and teaching
   (4) had worked and taught
   (5) at Aurora Elementary School

4. Sentence 7: **However, I also have extensive experience working with younger children, as I served as an intern at the Happy Day Preschool last Fall.**

   Which correction should be made to sentence 7?

   (1) Remove the comma after However.
   (2) Replace as with whenever.
   (3) Insert a comma after experience.
   (4) Replace Fall with fall.
   (5) No correction is necessary.

5. Sentence 8: **My experience working at Happy Day made me realize that I want to work with preschool-aged children in our career.**

   Which correction should be made to sentence 8?

   (1) Replace Happy Day with happy Day.
   (2) Insert a comma after realize.
   (3) Replace made with maid.
   (4) Replace our with my.
   (5) No correction is necessary.

6. Sentence 9: **I have enclosed my résumé completed application, and references for your perusal.**

   Which correction should be made to sentence 9?

   (1) Remove the comma after application.
   (2) Insert a comma after résumé.
   (3) Replace your with you're.
   (4) Replace for with at.
   (5) No correction is necessary.

7. Which revision would improve the effectiveness of this letter?

   Begin a new paragraph with

   (1) sentence 3
   (2) sentence 4
   (3) sentence 6
   (4) sentence 8
   (5) sentence 11

8. Sentence 12: **I am also an extremely hard worker, learn fast, and responsible person.**

   Which is the best way to write the underlined portion of this sentence? If the original is the best way, choose option (1).

   (1) hard worker, learn fast, and responsible person.
   (2) hard worker learn fast, and responsible person.
   (3) hard worker, fast learner, and responsible person.
   (4) hard working, having learned fast, and responsible.
   (5) hard worker. I learn fast and am a responsible person.

9. Which revision would improve the effectiveness of paragraph B?

   (1) Move sentence 12 to the beginning of the paragraph.
   (2) Move sentence 10 to the end of the paragraph.
   (3) Remove sentence 10.
   (4) Remove sentence 11.
   (5) No revision is necessary.

How to Select a Cell-Phone Plan

(A)

(1) More and more people are using cellular or cell phones for business and personal communication. (2) With so many people using cell phones. (3) There are also increasing numbers of cell-phone companies offering different types of plans. (4) The options can be confusing. (5) If you are looking for a cell-phone plan, one should keep in mind the following steps.

(B)

(6) Next, you should choose the plan that offer you the most calling-time minutes for your money. (7) Cell-phone companies offer a certain amount of calling-time minutes for a basic monthly fee. (8) For example you may get 500 minutes of calling time per month for the basic monthly fee of $49 dollars. (9) The more minutes you have to make calls, the more expensive the plan will be. (10) The first thing you need to do is decide how much money you want to spend. (11) You will also pay more for a national calling plan, which allows you to call from anywhere in the united States rather than calling only from a home calling area. (12) Depending on the type of plan you choose, fees range from about $30 dollars to $200 dollars per month.

(C)

(13) You should also know that most cell-phone plans divide the number of calling-time minutes between anytime minutes and night and weekend minutes. (14) Anytime minutes, which are also called peak minutes, apply during weekdays, usually Monday through Friday from 8:00 a.m. to 8:00 p.m. (15) When comparing plans, you should choose the one that offers you the most anytime minutes for the least amount of money. (16) If you exceed the number of minutes allotted in your cell-phone plan, you can expect to pay 25 to 45 cents per minute for him. (17) If you exceed your minutes every month, your cell-phone bill will be very high, you will be paying more than you should.

10. Sentences 2 and 3: **With so many people <u>using cell phones. There are</u> also increasing numbers of cell-phone companies offering different types of plans**.

    Which is the best way to write the underlined portion of these sentences? If the original is the best way, choose option (1).

    (1) using cell phone. There are
    (2) using cell phones and are
    (3) using cell phones, there are
    (4) using cell phones. There were
    (5) use cell phones, yet there are

11. Sentence 5: **If you are looking for a cell-phone plan, one should keep in mind the following steps.**

    Which correction should be made to sentence 5?

    (1) Remove the comma after <u>plan</u>.
    (2) Replace <u>one</u> with <u>you</u>.
    (3) Change <u>are looking</u> to <u>have looked</u>.
    (4) Insert <u>and</u> after the comma.
    (5) No correction is necessary.

12. Sentence 6: **Next, you should choose the plan that offer you the most calling-time minutes for your money.**

    Which correction should be made to sentence 6?

    (1) Insert a comma after <u>plan</u>.
    (2) Change <u>choose</u> to <u>have chosen</u>.
    (3) Replace <u>your</u> with <u>you're</u>.
    (4) Change <u>offer</u> to <u>offers</u>.
    (5) No correction is necessary.

13. Sentence 8: **For example you may get 500 minutes of calling time per month for the basic monthly fee of $49 dollars.**

    Which correction should be made to sentence 8?

    (1) Remove the second <u>for</u>.
    (2) Change <u>you</u> to <u>they</u>.
    (3) Replace <u>may</u> with <u>May</u>.
    (4) Insert a comma after <u>example</u>.
    (5) No correction is necessary.

14. Which revision would improve the effectiveness of paragraph B?

    (1) Remove sentence 7.
    (2) Move sentence 10 to the beginning of the paragraph.
    (3) Move sentence 8 to the end of the paragraph.
    (4) Move sentence 12 to the beginning of the paragraph.
    (5) Replace sentence 12 with <u>Cell-phone plans are expensive</u>.

15. Sentence 11: **You will also pay more for a national calling plan, which allows you to call from anywhere in the united States rather than calling only from a home calling area.**

    Which correction should be made to sentence 11?

    (1) Change <u>will also pay</u> to <u>will also have paid</u>.
    (2) Replace <u>allows</u> with <u>allow's</u>.
    (3) Replace <u>united</u> with <u>United</u>.
    (4) Insert a comma after <u>rather</u>.
    (5) Insert <u>while</u> after <u>than</u>.

16. Which revision would improve the effectiveness of paragraph C?

    (1) Remove sentence 14.
    (2) Move sentence 15 to the end of the paragraph.
    (3) Begin a new paragraph with sentence 16.
    (4) Remove sentence 16.
    (5) Move sentence 17 to the beginning of the paragraph.

17. Sentence 16: **If you exceed the number of minutes allotted in your cell-phone plan, you can expect to pay 25 to 45 cents per minute for him.**

    Which correction should be made to sentence 16?

    (1) Replace <u>him</u> with <u>the extra minutes</u>.
    (2) Remove the comma after <u>plan</u>.
    (3) Insert a comma after <u>pay</u>.
    (4) Replace <u>cents</u> with <u>sense</u>.
    (5) Change <u>expect</u> to <u>expected</u>.

18. Sentence 17: **If you exceed your minutes every month, your cell-phone bill will be <u>very high, you will be</u> paying more than you should.**

    Which is the best way to write the underlined portion of this sentence? If the original is the best way, choose option (1).

    (1) very high, you will be
    (2) very high you will be
    (3) very high although you will be
    (4) very high, and you will be
    (5) very high. Will be

The Great Barrier Reef

(A)

(1) The Great Barrier Reef is one of the great wonders of the natural world. (2) The biggest coral reef on the planet, it is the only living thing on earth that can be seen from outer space! (3) The reef is over 1,250 miles long, stretches through the southern Pacific Ocean, and lying mostly along the eastern coast of Australia.

(B)

(4) The reef is not actually a single reef, it is made up of over 2,900 small reefs that lie right next to each other. (5) The reef also contains over 600 islands, which were once part of the mainland. (6) Thousands of types of fish and hundreds of different corals and birds live in the reef. (7) Many of these fish and the corals are brightly colored. (8) It is also home to thousands of different mollusks and strange animals like sea snakes and sea turtles. (9) These unique creatures attract thousands of human visitors each year.

(C)

(10) The reef's beauty draw people from all over the world. (11) People go to the reef to swim, snorkel, and scuba-dive. (12) Some visitors fly over the reef in airplanes or helicopters, while others like to stay on the land and watch the birds. (13) People are warned to be careful, so that future visitors can enjoy its attractions. (14) The Great Barrier Reef, like other reefs, is made of the bodies of living and dead coral. (15) It grows slowly at a rate of a few millimeters per year, and people have damaged the reef by polluting, dropping things on it, and breaking pieces off of it. (16) In 1981, the World Heritage listed the reef as a special site in order to help maintain it's amazing marine life.

19. Sentence 2: **The biggest coral reef on the planet, it is the only living thing on earth that can be seen from outer space!**

    Which correction should be made to sentence 2?

    (1) Change it is to they are.
    (2) Remove the comma.
    (3) Replace earth with Earth.
    (4) Insert a comma after earth.
    (5) No correction is necessary.

20. Sentence 3: **The reef is over 1,250 miles long, stretches through the southern Pacific Ocean, and lying mostly along the eastern coast of Australia.**

    Which correction should be made to sentence 3?

    (1) Change is to am.
    (2) Remove the second comma.
    (3) Replace the second comma with a semicolon.
    (4) Change lying to lies.
    (5) Replace eastern with Eastern.

21. Sentence 4: **The reef is not actually a single reef, it is made up of over 2,900 small reefs.**

    Which is the best way to write the underlined portion of the sentence? If the original is the best way, choose option (1).

    (1) a single reef, it is made up
    (2) a single reef, its made up
    (3) a single reef but is made up
    (4) a single reef, and is
    (5) a single reef; made up

22. Which revision would improve the effectiveness of paragraph B?

    (1) Remove sentence 7.
    (2) Insert at the beginning of the paragraph The Great Barrier Reef is a complex system supporting many animals and plants that do not exist elsewhere.
    (3) Replace sentence 9 with If you've ever seen a sea snake, you'll understand what I'm talking about.
    (4) Move sentence 8 to the beginning of the paragraph.
    (5) No revision is necessary.

23. Sentence 10: **The reef's beauty draw people from all over the world.**

Which correction should be made to sentence 10?

(1) Change <u>reef's</u> to <u>reefs'</u>.
(2) Insert a comma after <u>people</u>.
(3) Replace <u>world</u> with <u>World</u>.
(4) Remove the apostrophe in <u>reef's</u>.
(5) Change <u>draw</u> to <u>draws</u>.

24. Sentence 11: **People go to the reef to swim, snorkel, and scuba-dive.**

Which correction should be made to sentence 11?

(1) Change <u>swim</u> to <u>swum</u>.
(2) Change <u>snorkel</u> to <u>snorkeling</u>.
(3) Remove the second comma.
(4) Replace the second comma with a semicolon.
(5) No correction is necessary.

25. Sentences 12 and 13: **Some visitors fly over the reef in airplanes or helicopters, while others like to stay on the land and <u>watch the birds. People are warned</u> to be careful, so that future visitors can enjoy its attractions.**

Which is the best way to write the underlined portion of these sentences? If the original is the best way, choose option (1).

(1) watch the birds. People are warned
(2) watch the birds. However, people are warned
(3) watching the birds and warning people
(4) watch the birds. People would have warned
(5) watch the birds, with people who are warned

26. Sentence 14: **The Great Barrier Reef, like other reefs, is made of the bodies of living and dead coral.**

If you rewrote sentence 14 beginning with

<u>Like other reefs,</u>

the next words should be

(1) the Great Barrier Reef is made
(2) making and living reefs
(3) the Great Barrier Reef, made
(4) which are made of living
(5) live and dead coral is made

27. Sentence 16: **In 1981, the World Heritage listed the reef as a special site in order to help maintain it's amazing marine life.**

Which correction should be made to sentence 16?

(1) Replace <u>site</u> with <u>sight</u>.
(2) Change <u>listed</u> to <u>have listed</u>.
(3) Replace <u>it's</u> with <u>its</u>.
(4) Insert a comma after <u>reef</u>.
(5) No correction is necessary.

Questions 28 through 34 refer to the following memo.

MEMORANDUM

TO: All Employees of Cable and Cord Designs
FROM: Desmond Roush, Director of Human Resources
Re: Health Fair on May 20

(A)

   (1) On Friday May 20, the company will be holding its annual health fair. (2) From 1:00 p.m. to 5:00 p.m., vendors will be hosting various health-related activities between buildings E and F in booths on the plaza. (3) In addition to the vendors we invited last year, such as Tai Chi of Texas, we had asked new health experts such as yoga master Micaela McMann, who will lead an introductory yoga class. (4) Dr. Shawn Wu, a founder of the School of Chinese Medicine, will perform acupuncture on anyone who is interested. (5) You will also be able to measure your percentage of body fat at the booth sponsored by Hearty Heart Health Club and analyze his diet at the booth run by a nutritionist from East Side Hospital. (6) Please sea the attached schedule for a full list of vendors, events, and times. (7) A few activities such as the very popular 15-minute massage from Hyde Park Massage Therapy require advance scheduling, so please sign up for these activities before the fair. (8) The activities requiring sign-ups are marked in red on the schedule, and the sign-up sheets are posted on the wall outside of the Human Resources office on the first floor of building A.

(B)

   (9) The fair has been organized with your needs in mind. (10) We are committed to creating a healthy environment for you to work in and to accommodating your individual health needs. (11) I hope that you will be able to take time out to enjoy the activities at the fair. (12) After the fair, I will be distributing questionnaires to each of you to determine which activities was the most useful to you. (13) Nevertheless, please feel free to contact me at extension 555, if you have ideas about how to make Cable and Cord a healthier place to work.

---

28. Sentence 2: **From 1:00 p.m. to 5:00 p.m., vendors will be hosting various health-related activities between buildings E and F in booths on the plaza.**

    Which correction should be made to sentence 2?

    (1) Change <u>will be hosting</u> to <u>have hosted.</u>
    (2) Remove the comma.
    (3) Insert <u>and</u> after the comma.
    (4) Move <u>between buildings E and F</u> to the end.
    (5) No correction is necessary.

29. Sentence 3: **In addition to the vendors we invited last year, such as Tai Chi of Texas, we had asked new health experts such as yoga master Micaela McMann, who will lead an introductory yoga class.**

    Which correction should be made to sentence 3?

    (1) Remove the first comma.
    (2) Change <u>had asked</u> to <u>have asked</u>.
    (3) Replace <u>master</u> with <u>Master</u>.
    (4) Insert a comma after <u>lead</u>.
    (5) Replace <u>new</u> with <u>knew</u>.

30. Sentence 5: **You will also be able to measure your percentage of body fat at the booth sponsored by Hearty Heart Health Club and analyze his diet at the booth run by a nutritionist from East Side Hospital.**

Which is the best way to write the underlined portion of this sentence? If the original is the best way, choose option (1).

(1) Health Club and analyze his diet
(2) health club and analyze his diet
(3) Health Club. And analyze his diet
(4) Health Club, analyzing his diet
(5) Health Club and analyze your diet

31. Sentence 6: **Please sea the attached schedule for a full list of vendors, events, and times.**

Which correction should be made to sentence 6?

(1) Replace sea with see.
(2) Remove the second comma.
(3) Replace time with timing.
(4) Change and to or.
(5) No correction is necessary.

32. Which revision would improve the effectiveness of this memo?

Begin a new paragraph with

(1) sentence 2
(2) sentence 4
(3) sentence 6
(4) sentence 10
(5) sentence 12

33. Sentence 12: **After the fair, I will be distributing questionnaires to each of you to determine which activities was the most useful to you.**

Which correction should be made to sentence 12?

(1) Remove the comma.
(2) Change will be distributing to have distributed.
(3) Replace the first to with two.
(4) Replace activities with activity's.
(5) Change was to were.

34. Sentence 13: **Nevertheless, please feel free to contact me at extension 555, if you have ideas about how to make Cable and Cord a healthier place to work.**

Which correction should be made to sentence 13?

(1) Replace Nevertheless with Furthermore.
(2) Remove the first comma.
(3) Replace me with I.
(4) Insert a comma after ideas.
(5) No correction is necessary.

Questions 35 through 42 refer to the following article.

How to Remove Stains from Floors

(A)

(1) There are a variety of methods you can use to remove stains from hard-surface floors. (2) Different types of stains require different approaches for its removal. (3) To remove candle wax, for example you can use ice cubes to chill the wax in order to make it harder. (4) After the wax becomes brittle, you should use a plastic spatula to scrape the wax from the floor, and to remove coffee stains, you should soak a cloth in a solution of glycerine and water and then place the cloth over the stain for a few hours. (5) To remove ink, you can try covering the stain with a mixture of diatomaceous earth and rubbing alcohol, covering the mixture with plastic wrap, and letting the mixture stand overnight.

(B)

(6) Certain types of stains, such as those from blood or dyes, required you to use household chemicals such as rubbing alcohol, hydrogen peroxide ammonia, or chlorine bleach. (7) You should take precautions. (8) When using these chemicals. (9) It's a good idea to wear rubber gloves when handling them. (10) Diatomaceous earth, which can be found in hardware stores, is a substance derived from diatoms or algae remains. (11) You may also want to ventilate the room your working in by opening windows and doors and using a fan. (12) Ventilating the room will decrease your exposure to harmful fumes. (13) You should also remember to never mix chemicals with each other although the product gives specific directions to do so. (14) Mixing ammonia and chlorine bleach will produce a toxic gas. (15) Finally, before using chemicals, you should test their effects on a small portion of the stain. (16) If the chemical you are using is not the correct one to remove the stain, you will have only damaged a small part of the floor.

35. Sentence 2: **Different types of stains require different approaches for its removal.**

    Which correction should be made to sentence 2?

    (1) Insert a comma after <u>stains</u>.
    (2) Change <u>require</u> to <u>have required</u>.
    (3) Change <u>approaches</u> to <u>approach</u>.
    (4) Change <u>its</u> to <u>their</u>.
    (5) No correction is necessary.

36. Sentence 3: **To remove <u>candle wax, for example you can use</u> ice cubes to chill the wax in order to make it harder.**

    Which is the best way to write the underlined portion of this sentence? If the original is the best way, choose option (1).

    (1) candle wax, for example you can use
    (2) candle wax for example you can use
    (3) candle wax, for example, you can use
    (4) candle wax. For example, you can use
    (5) candle wax, for example you can have used

37. Sentence 4: **After the wax becomes brittle, you should use a plastic spatula to scrape the wax from <u>the floor, and to remove</u> coffee stains, you should soak a cloth in a solution of glycerine and water and then place the cloth over the stain for a few hours.**

    Which is the best way to write the underlined portion of this sentence? If the original is the best way, choose option (1).

    (1) the floor, and to remove
    (2) the floor and to remove
    (3) the floor, while removing
    (4) the floor, to remove
    (5) the floor. To remove

38. Sentence 6: **Certain types of stains, such as those from blood or dyes, required you to use household chemicals such as rubbing alcohol, hydrogen peroxide, ammonia, or chlorine bleach.**

    Which correction should be made to sentence 6?

    (1) Replace <u>dyes</u> with <u>dies</u>.
    (2) Change <u>required</u> to <u>require</u>.
    (3) Remove the comma after <u>alcohol</u>.
    (4) Remove the comma after <u>ammonia</u>.
    (5) Replace <u>to</u> with <u>too</u>.

39. Sentences 7 and 8: **You should <u>take precautions.</u> <u>When using</u> these chemicals.**

Which is the best way to write the underlined portion of these sentences? If the original is the best way, choose option (1).

(1) take precautions. When using
(2) taking precautions and using
(3) take precautions when using
(4) take precautions, and use
(5) take precautions; using

40. Sentence 11: **You may also want to ventilate the room your working in by opening windows and doors and using a fan.**

Which correction should be made to sentence 11?

(1) Replace <u>your</u> with <u>you're</u>.
(2) Insert a comma after <u>windows</u>.
(3) Insert a comma after <u>doors</u>.
(4) Change <u>using</u> to <u>use</u>.
(5) No correction is necessary.

41. Sentence 13: **You should also remember to never mix chemicals with each other although the product gives specific directions to do so.**

Which correction should be made to sentence 13?

(1) Change <u>remember</u> to <u>remembered</u>.
(2) Insert a comma after <u>chemicals</u>.
(3) Change <u>although</u> to <u>unless</u>.
(4) Change <u>gives</u> to <u>will give</u>.
(5) Replace <u>so</u> with <u>sew</u>.

42. Which revision would improve the effectiveness of paragraph B?

(1) Begin a new paragraph with sentence 9.
(2) Move sentence 10 to paragraph A.
(3) Move sentence 12 to the end of paragraph B.
(4) Move sentence 13 to the beginning of paragraph B.
(5) Remove sentence 15.

Democracy

(A)

(1) While delivering his famous speech the Gettysburg Address in 1863, president Abraham Lincoln employed the phrase, "a government of the people, by the people, for the people." (2) He was describing a democracy, the kind of society he thought the United States should become. (3) Derived from two Greek words, *demos* meaning "the people" and *kratos* meaning "rule," the term democracy refers to a way of governing in which the people rule itself. (4) In a democracy, the people are citizens or participating members of a city state, or nation. (5) As citizens, they can freely make decisions about policies or public rules.

(B)

(6) In a direct democracy, decisions are made directly by all the people, who gather together to decide on issues. (7) However, this type of democracy is rare. (8) It is difficult to gather everyone when the population is large, yet most countries are too big to accommodate this type of system. (9) The more common type of government is called representative democracy. (10) In this type of democracy, citizens elect representatives to speak and acting for them. (11) Representative democracy is the most common type of government in the world and is used in many countries including the United States, where citizens elect national, state, and local leaders. (12) There are several types of democracies. (13) These representatives make the decisions about policies, which effect the way people live.

(C)

(14) In a true democracy, everyone has the same rights to take part in the government. (15) All people have the right to vote for able leaders to represent them, and people have access to education so that they can make informed decisions about issues. (16) Education and participation by the people makes democracy possible.

43. Sentence 1: **While delivering his famous speech the Gettysburg Address in 1863, president Abraham Lincoln employed the phrase, "a government of the people, by the people, for the people."**

    Which correction should be made to sentence 1?

    (1) Change <u>delivering</u> to <u>delivered</u>.
    (2) Insert a comma after <u>speech</u>.
    (3) Remove the comma after <u>1863</u>.
    (4) Replace <u>president</u> with <u>President</u>.
    (5) Change <u>employed</u> to <u>have employed</u>.

44. Sentence 3: **Derived from two Greek words, *demos* meaning "the people" and *kratos* meaning "rule," the term democracy refers to a way of governing in which the people rule itself.**

    Which correction should be made to sentence 3?

    (1) Replace <u>Greek</u> with <u>greek</u>.
    (2) Change <u>refers</u> to <u>has referred</u>.
    (3) Replace <u>way</u> with <u>weigh</u>.
    (4) Change <u>governing</u> to <u>governed</u>.
    (5) Change <u>itself</u> to <u>themselves</u>.

45. Sentence 4: **In a democracy, the people are citizens or participating members of a city state, or nation.**

    Which correction should be made to sentence 4?

    (1) Remove the comma after <u>democracy</u>.
    (2) Replace <u>citizens</u> with <u>citizen's</u>.
    (3) Change <u>participating</u> to <u>participated</u>.
    (4) Insert a comma after <u>city</u>.
    (5) No correction is necessary.

46. Sentence 8: **It is difficult to gather everyone when the population <u>is large, yet most countries</u> are too big to accommodate this type of system.**

    Which is the best way to write the underlined portion of this sentence? If the original is the best way, choose option (1).

    (1) is large, yet most countries
    (2) is large yet most countries
    (3) is large, and most countries
    (4) is large, yet more countries
    (5) is large, yet most country's

47. Sentence 10: **In this type of democracy, citizens elect representatives to speak and acting for them.**

Which correction should be made to sentence 10?

(1) Remove the comma.
(2) Replace <u>representatives</u> with <u>representative's</u>.
(3) Change <u>speak</u> to <u>spoke</u>.
(4) Change <u>acting</u> to <u>act</u>.
(5) Replace <u>them</u> with <u>it</u>.

48. Sentence 13: **These representatives make the decisions about policies, which effect the way people live.**

Which correction should be made to sentence 13?

(1) Change <u>make</u> to <u>made</u>.
(2) Replace <u>policies</u> with <u>policy's</u>.
(3) Remove the comma.
(4) Replace <u>effect</u> with <u>affect</u>.
(5) No correction is necessary.

49. Which revision would improve the effectiveness of paragraph B?

Begin the paragraph with

(1) sentence 7
(2) sentence 9
(3) sentence 10
(4) sentence 11
(5) sentence 12

50. Sentence 16: **Education and participation by the people makes democracy possible.**

Which correction should be made to sentence 16?

(1) Change <u>participation</u> to <u>participating</u>.
(2) Replace <u>by</u> with <u>buy</u>.
(3) Replace <u>people</u> with <u>People</u>.
(4) Change <u>makes</u> to <u>make</u>.
(5) No correction is necessary.

LANGUAGE ARTS, WRITING PART II

Essay Directions and Topic

Look at the box on the next page. In the box are your assigned topic and the letter of that topic.

You must write on the assigned topic ONLY.

You will have 45 minutes to write on your assigned essay topic. You may return to the multiple-choice section after you complete your essay if you have time remaining in this test period. Do not return the Language Arts, Writing booklet until you finish both Parts I and II of the Language Arts, Writing Test.

Two trained readers will score your essay according to its overall effectiveness. Their evaluation will be based on the following features:

- Well-focused main points
- Clear organization
- Specific development of your ideas
- Control of sentence structure, punctuation, grammar, word choice, and spelling

REMEMBER, YOU MUST COMPLETE BOTH THE MULTIPLE-CHOICE QUESTIONS IN PART I AND THE ESSAY IN PART II TO RECEIVE A SCORE ON THE LANGUAGE ARTS, WRITING TEST. To avoid having to repeat both parts of the test, be sure to do the following:

- Do not leave the pages blank.
- Write legibly in ink so that the readers who evaluate your test will be able to read your writing.
- Write on the assigned topic. If you write on a topic other than the one assigned, you will not receive a score for the Language Arts, Writing Test.
- Write your essay on the lined pages of the separate answer sheets. Only the writing on these pages will be scored.

TOPIC A

Do you think cities are good places for people to live in?

Write an essay explaining the advantages or disadvantages of living in a city. Use your personal observations, experience, and knowledge to support your view.

Part II is a test to determine how well you can use written language to explain your ideas.

In preparing your essay, you should take the following steps:

- Read the DIRECTIONS and the TOPIC carefully.
- Plan your essay before you write. Use the scratch paper provided to make any notes. These notes will be collected but not scored.
- Before you turn in your essay, reread what you have written and make any changes that will improve your essay.

LANGUAGE ARTS, WRITING PART I ANSWERS AND EXPLANATIONS

1. **(3) Change <u>have enabled</u> to <u>would enable</u>.**

The use of the original verb tense, *have enabled*, implies that the applicant and the employer have already been working together. However, because the applicant is actually seeking employment, it is clear that she has not worked with this company before. The verb tense *would enable* effectively conveys the possibility for a beneficial future relationship for both if the applicant were to be hired. Answer (1) can be eliminated, because no comma is needed after *education*. Answer (2) can also be eliminated, because adding "and" after *excel* is not necessary. Answer (4) should be eliminated, because the verb *described* is already in the correct tense. **⊕ Verbs**

2. **(5) in education, earning**

This question requires you to identify the sentence fragment and revise it so that the resulting sentence, which combines the first sentence and the sentence fragment, is structured more effectively. Answer (2) yields two sentence fragments. Answer (3) should be ruled out, as the second sentence beginning with "I am earning" is in the wrong tense. Answer (4) is incorrect because *had earned* is in the wrong tense. **⊕ Common Sentence Errors**

3. **(1) I also worked**

In the original sentence, the words between the commas separate main sentence parts, thereby interrupting the clear flow of ideas. By moving the subordinating clause to the beginning of the sentence and following with the independent clause starting with "I also worked," the relationship of working while in school is established. Answer (2) yields a sentence that is punctuated incorrectly, because there should not be a comma between *City* and *and also working*. The other answers can also be eliminated, because placing the subordinate clause at the beginning of the sentence requires that what follows is the subject *I*. **⊕ Coordination and Subordination**

4. **(4) Replace <u>Fall</u> with <u>fall</u>.**

The names of seasons are not capitalized. The introductory word *However* requires a comma after it, so eliminate answer (1). Answer (2) is incorrect, because *as* is the proper subordinating conjunction. Answer (3) is incorrect because no comma is necessary after *experience*. **⊕ Capitalization and Spelling**

5. **(4) Replace <u>our</u> with <u>my</u>.**

The possessive pronoun preceding *career* must agree with its antecedent *I* in number. *I* is singular, so the singular possessive pronoun *my* is correct. Answer (1) can be eliminated, because proper names should be capitalized. Answer (2) is incorrect, because no comma is required before *that*. Answer (3) is incorrect because the original word *made* is appropriate. **⊕ Pronouns**

CHAPTER

8

PRACTICE
TESTS

THE

GED

LANGUAGE
ARTS,
WRITING
PART I

6.   (2)   Insert a comma after résumé.

In this list of three items, a comma must be used to separate the items in the series. Eliminate answer (1), because the final comma separating items in the series is fine. Eliminate answer (3), because the possessive *your* is correct. Answer (4) is incorrect because *for* is the right preposition. (H) Punctuation

7.   (1)   sentence 3

This question requires you to study the whole document in order to determine where an effective paragraph break should occur. A paragraph beginning with sentence 3 would summarize and highlight the applicant's accomplishments. Sentence 4 is a sentence fragment, so answer (2) can be eliminated. You can eliminate answers (3) and (4), because beginning paragraphs with those sentences would disrupt the flow of ideas. Answer (5) can be ruled out, because sentence (11) does not belong in the letter at all. (H) **Restructuring Paragraphs**

8.   (3)   hard worker, fast learner, and responsible person.

The items in the series must match in form and part of speech. Changing *learn fast* to *fast learner* makes all three items in the series nouns. Answer (2) can be eliminated because commas are required between items in a series. Answer (4) presents a series in which the items are not parallel. Answer (5) is acceptable, but it is not as efficient as the solution in answer (3). (H) **Parallel Structure**

9.   (4)   Remove sentence 11.

Sentence 11 should be removed because it contains irrelevant ideas that distract the reader from the main idea of the paragraph. Answer (1) is incorrect, because sentence 12 does not belong at the beginning of the paragraph. Answers (2) and (3) can be eliminated, because sentence 10 is important to the paragraph in its current location. (H) **Restructuring Paragraphs**

10.   (3)   using cell phones, there are

Sentence 2 is a sentence fragment. Combining sentence 2 with sentence 3 creates a complex sentence that flows smoothly. Answer (2) can be eliminated, because the verb *are* is missing a subject. Answer (4) does not correct the sentence fragment in sentence 3. Answer (5) creates a sentence in which the verb *use* is in the wrong tense. (H) **Common Sentence Errors**

11.   (2)   Replace one with you.

In the original sentence, there is a shift from the second person pronoun *you* to the third-person pronoun *one*. To correct the pronoun shift, *one* should be changed to *you*. Answer (1) can be eliminated, because the comma is necessary after the introductory subordinate clause. Answer (3) can be eliminated, because *are looking* is in the correct tense. Answer (4) is incorrect, because no conjunction is necessary after the comma. (H) **Pronouns**

12.   (4)   Change offer to offers.

The singular subject *plan* requires the singular verb form *offers*. You can rule out answer (1), because no comma is necessary before *that*. You can also rule out answer (2) because *choose* is in the correct tense. Answer (3) can be eliminated, as the possessive *your* is correct. ⊕ **Verbs**

13. (4) Insert a comma after <u>example</u>.

A comma should be used after the transition *For example*, because it introduces the main idea of the sentence. The comma separates the introductory element from the rest of the sentence. Answer (1) is wrong, because the second *for* is necessary. Answer (2) creates a pronoun shift from *you* to *they*. Answer (3) changes the correct verb *may* to the incorrect and nonsensical month *May*. ⊕ **Punctuation**

14. (2) Move sentence 10 to the beginning of the paragraph.

Moving sentence 10 to the beginning of the paragraph gives the paragraph an effective topic sentence, which introduces the paragraph's main idea. Moving sentence 10 to the beginning also provides the paragraph with a smooth transition from the previous paragraph. You can eliminate answer (1) because sentence 7 contains ideas that are important to the paragraph. In answer (3), moving sentence 8 to the end of the paragraph would be illogical. Answer (5) can be eliminated because the replacement sentence is more general and less informative than the existing sentence 12. ⊕ **Restructuring Paragraphs**

15. (3) Replace <u>united</u> with <u>United</u>.

Proper nouns naming specific persons, places, or things must be capitalized. The verb tense in the original sentence is correct, so eliminate answer (1). You can also eliminate answer (2) because the verb *allows* is correct as is. In answer (4), no comma is necessary after *rather*. Inserting "while" after *than*, as in answer (5), creates an illogical series of words. ⊕ **Capitalization and Spelling**

16. (2) Move sentence 15 to the end of the paragraph.

In the original paragraph, sentence 15 disrupts the flow of ideas among the sentences. By moving sentence 15 to the end of the paragraph, the paragraph becomes more coherent, and the sentence serves as a summarizing or concluding statement. You can eliminate answer (1) because sentence 14 contains ideas that are important to the paragraph. Removing sentence 16 in answer (4) is also a mistake because that sentence is also important to the paragraph. Moving sentence 17 to the beginning of the paragraph, as in answer (5), makes the organization of ideas less logical.
⊕ **Restructuring Paragraphs**

17. (1) Replace <u>him</u> with <u>the extra minutes</u>.

In the original sentence, *him* does not have a clear antecedent. To avoid vague pronouns in this sentence, the object should be stated clearly as in answer (1). You can eliminate answer (2) because the comma is needed after the introductory subordinating clause. Answer (4) can be eliminated because the homonym *sense* is illogical within the sentence. Answer (5) can also be eliminated because the verb *expect* is already in the correct tense. ⊕ **Pronouns**

CHAPTER
8

PRACTICE
TESTS

THE
GED

LANGUAGE
ARTS,
WRITING
PART I

CHAPTER

8

PRACTICE
TESTS

THE
GED

LANGUAGE
ARTS,
WRITING
PART I

18. **(4)** very high, and you will be

The original sentence contains a comma splice because the coordinating conjunction is missing. Answer (4) provides the correct coordinating conjunction and includes the necessary comma preceding the conjunction. Answer (2) creates a run-on sentence. Answer (3) is incorrect because the sentence it creates is missing a comma and *although* is not the correct conjunction. Answer (5) creates a sentence fragment. **H Punctuation**

19. **(3)** Replace earth with Earth.

Proper nouns naming specific persons, things, or places, such as the planet Earth, must be capitalized. You can eliminate answer (1) because *it* is the correct pronoun. You can also eliminate answer (4) because no comma is necessary after *earth*. **H Capitalization and Spelling**

20. **(4)** Change lying to lies.

All the items in the series should match in form and part of speech. Changing the verb form of *lying* to present tense *lies* makes all three verbs parallel. Answer (1) incorrectly uses *am* in the wrong verb form. Eliminate answer (3) because commas are needed between items in a series. Answer (5) is incorrect because directions should not be capitalized. **H Parallel Structure**

21. **(3)** a single reef but is made up

The original sentence contains a comma splice, as there is not a conjunction joining the two independent clauses. The conjunction that makes the most sense in this context is *but*, which implies contrast. In the revision, no comma is warranted because the sentence uses a compound verb rather than two independent clauses. In answer (2), *its* is the possessive form and the answer does not correct the comma splice. Answer (4) does not offer the right conjunction. The second part of answer (5), "made up," lacks a subject. **H Punctuation**

22. **(2)** Insert at the beginning of the paragraph The Great Barrier Reef is a complex system supporting many animals and plants that do not exist elsewhere.

This question requires you to identify that the paragraph would be improved by the insertion of a topic sentence. Answer (2) provides a topic sentence summarizing the main idea of the paragraph. Answer (3) is wrong because the replacement sentence changes the tone of the paragraph and introduces ideas that are not necessary. Answer (4), moving sentence 8 to the beginning of the paragraph, would disrupt the logical order of ideas. **H Restructuring Paragraphs**

23. **(5)** Change draw to draws.

The singular subject *beauty* requires the singular form of the verb *draws*. Rule out answer (2) because no comma is necessary after *people*. Answer (3) can be eliminated because *world* is not a proper noun and does not need to be capitalized. Answer (4) changes the correct possessive form of *reef's* (the "reef's beauty") the incorrect plural form *reefs*. (H) **Verbs**

24. (5) No correction necessary.
The original complex sentence is correct as it is. You can cross out answer (1) because "swum" is not the correct verb tense. Answers (3) and (4) can be eliminated because the commas between each item in the series are correct. Answer (2) would ruin the parallel structure of the items. (H) **Verbs**

25. (2) watch the birds. However, people are warned
Although the original sentences are grammatically correct, they are improved by the addition of the transition *However*, which shows the relationship between the ideas in the two sentences. Answer (3) introduces verbs in the wrong tenses. The second part of answer (4), *People would have warned*, is also in the incorrect tense. (H) **Coordination and Subordination**

26. (1) the Great Barrier Reef is made
In the original sentence, the phrase *like other reefs* separates the subject and the verb. In answer (1), the subject immediately follows the phrase that modifies it, eliminating confusion over what should be modified. Answers (2), (4), and (5) can be eliminated, because the subject, the Great Barrier Reef, must directly follow the introductory phrase that modifies it. Answer (3) creates a sentence in which the helping verb *is* is missing. (H) **Misplaced and Dangling Modifiers**

27. (3) Replace it's with its.
The possessive pronoun *its* should be used instead of the contraction *it's*. The antecedent for *its* is *the reef*. Answer (1) can be eliminated because *site* is the correct homonym. Answer (2) offers the wrong verb tense for *listed*. (H) **Punctuation**

28. (4) Move between buildings E and F to the end.
In the original sentence, the modifying phrase *between buildings E and F* is misplaced, as it follows *activities*. In answer (4), the modifier immediately follows *plaza*, the word it modifies. The verb *will be hosting* is already in the correct tense, so answer (1) is wrong. Answer (2) removes a necessary comma after the adverb phrase, and answer (3) adds an unnecessary conjunction after it. (H) **Misplaced and Dangling Modifiers**

29. (2) Change had asked to have asked.
The sentence requires you to change the verb tense from past perfect, which implies that the action was completed before another past action began, to the present perfect, which expresses an action that began in the past but is already completed. The commas in this sentence are used correctly, so answers (1) and (4) are wrong. You can eliminate answer (3) because *master* is not a proper noun and thus should remain uncapitalized. You can also eliminate answer (5) because *new* is the correct homonym. (H) **Verbs**

CHAPTER

8

PRACTICE
TESTS

THE
GED

LANGUAGE
ARTS,
WRITING
PART I

30. (5) Health Club and analyze your diet

The pronoun should be changed from *his* to *your* to keep it consistent with its antecedent, *You*. Answer (2) can be ruled out because the proper noun *Hearty Heart Health Club* should remain capitalized. Answer (3) creates a sentence fragment beginning with *And*. Answer (4) maintains the pronoun shift from *you* to *his*. 🄷 **Pronouns**

31. (1) Replace sea with see.

Homonyms are words that sound alike but have different spellings and meanings. The sentence requires the verb *see*, meaning "to perceive." Eliminate answer (2) because removing the second comma in the series does not improve the sentence. Answer (3) ruins the parallel structure of the items in the list. 🄷 **Capitalization and Spelling**

32. (3) sentence 6

This question requires you to study the entire memo to determine where an effective paragraph break should occur. A paragraph starting with sentence 6 would focus on the schedule of events and what employees need to do to sign up for certain activities. Rule out answer (1) because beginning a new paragraph with sentence 2 would leave sentence 1 in a paragraph by itself. Answer (2) can be eliminated because sentence 4 belongs in the first paragraph with other sentences explaining who will be at the fair. Answers (4) and (5) are incorrect because beginning a new paragraph with either of these sentences would not improve the paragraph. 🄷 **Restructuring Paragraphs**

33. (5) Change was to were.

The plural noun *activities* requires the plural form of the verb *were*. Answer (2) creates the wrong verb tense with *have distributed*. Answer (3) replaces the correct word *to* with the incorrect homonym *two*. Answer (4) replaces the correct plural form of *activities* with the incorrect possessive *activity's*. 🄷 **Verbs**

34. (1) Replace Nevertheless with Furthermore.

This sentence requires you to identify that the original conjunctive adverb provides a misleading transition. Answer (1) provides a more logical transition and establishes the correct relationship between the ideas in sentences 12 and 13. Answer (2) can be eliminated because introductory words require a comma following them. Answer (3) is wrong, because the pronoun *me* is already in the correct form. 🄷 **Punctuation**

35. (4) Change its to their.

The possessive pronoun must agree with its antecedent *types* in number, and because *types* is plural, the pronoun must be *their*. Answer (1) adds an unnecessary comma after *stains*. *Require* is in the correct verb tense, so eliminate answer (2). Answer (3) replaces the correct plural form of *approaches* to the incorrect singular form of *approach*. 🄷 **Pronouns**

36. (3) candle wax, for example, you can use

The parenthetical expression *for example* must be set off with commas on both ends. Answers (1), (2), and (5) do not set off the parenthetical expression with commas on both ends. Answer (4) creates a sentence fragment. 🄷 **Punctuation**

37.   (5)   the floor. To remove

This question requires that you identify a run-on sentence. The two main ideas are best written in separate sentences, as specified in answer (5). All the other answers maintain the run-on sentence. 🄷 **Common Sentence Errors**

38.   (2)   Change <u>required</u> to <u>require</u>.

The verb should be in the present tense to be consistent with the verb tenses in other sentences in the paragraph. Answer (1) is wrong because the original *dyes* is the appropriate word. Answer (3) removes commas that are required between items in a series. Answer (5) replaces the correct *to* with the incorrect *too.* 🄷 **Verbs**

39.   (3)   take precautions when using

This question requires you to identify that the original sentence 8 is a sentence fragment. Answer (3) offers the most logical way to combine the sentence fragment with the preceding sentence. Answer (2) changes the verbs to incorrect verb tenses. Answer (4) is incorrectly punctuated—there should be no comma between *precautions* and *and.* Answer (5) is incorrect because what follows the semicolon should be able to stand alone as a sentence. 🄷 **Common Sentence Errors**

40.   (1)   Replace <u>your</u> with <u>you're</u>.

The possessive pronoun *your* must be replaced by the contraction of *you are.* Answers (2) and (3) can be eliminated because no commas are required in those places. Answer (4) makes the words *opening* and *using* unparallel. 🄷 **Pronouns**

41.   (3)   Change <u>although</u> to <u>unless</u>.

Unless should be used as the subordinating conjunction introducing the subordinate clause, as *unless* establishes the correct relationship between the ideas in the two clauses. Answer (1) changes the verb to the wrong tense. Answer (2) is incorrect because no comma is required after *chemicals.* Answer (4) changes the verb to the wrong number. Answer (5) introduces the word *sew,* which is nonsensical in this sentence. 🄷 **Coordination and Subordination**

42.   (2)   Move sentence 10 to paragraph A.

This question requires that you identify that sentence 10 disrupts the unity of ideas in paragraph B and that it is more logical to place it in paragraph A, after sentence 5. Answer (1) is incorrect because sentence 9 should remain in the paragraph, as it follows up on ideas in sentence 8. Answer (3) is also incorrect because sentence 12 logically follows sentence 11. In answer (4), sentence 13 also logically remains where it is, following sentence 12. Answer (5) should be eliminated because sentence 15 adds important information to the paragraph. 🄷 **Restructuring Paragraphs**

43.   (4)   Replace president with President.

President directly precedes the person's name, so the title should be capitalized. Answer (1) changes the verb to an incorrect verb tense. Answer (3) can be deleted because the introductory subordinate phrase should be followed by a comma. Answer (5) changes the verb to an incorrect tense. 🄷 **Capitalization and Spelling**

CHAPTER

8

PRACTICE
TESTS

THE
GED

LANGUAGE
ARTS,
WRITING
PART I

44. **(5)** Change <u>itself</u> to <u>themselves</u>.

The pronoun needs to be changed to *themselves* to agree in number with the plural antecedent *people*. Answer (1) can be eliminated, because *Greek* is a proper noun and should be capitalized. Answer (3) replaces the correct word *way* with the incorrect *weigh*, which means "to measure or consider." ⟨H⟩ **Pronouns**

45. **(4)** Insert a comma after <u>city</u>.

In a series, each item must be separated by a comma. Answer (2) is wrong because the plural form *citizens* is correct. Answer (1) is incorrect because a comma is needed after the word "democracy." Answer (3) is incorrect because changing "participating" to "participated" changes the intended meaning of the sentence. ⟨H⟩ **Punctuation**

46. **(3)** is large, and most countries

The conjunction *and* establishes the correct relationship between the two independent clauses in this sentence. Answer (2) is incorrectly punctuated: there should be a comma between two independent clauses joined by a conjunction. Answer (4) is wrong because *more* implies comparison between two things, while the correct word, *most* implies comparison among three or more things. Answer (5) contains the incorrect possessive form of *country's*. ⟨H⟩ **Coordination and Subordination**

47. **(4)** Change <u>acting</u> to <u>act</u>.

Both verbs, *speak* and *act*, should be in the same form to maintain parallel structure. Eliminate answer (2) because the original plural form *representatives* is correct. Answer (3) changes the verb to the wrong tense. Answer (5) changes the pronoun to the incorrect singular form. ⟨H⟩ **Verbs**

48. **(4)** Replace <u>effect</u> with <u>affect</u>.

The word *affect*, which means to act upon or have an effect on someone, is the appropriate word for this sentence. Answer (1) changes the verb incorrectly to the past tense. Eliminate answer (2) because the original plural form of *policies* is correct. Answer (3) is wrong because the comma is necessary preceding *which*.
⟨H⟩ **Capitalization and Spelling**

49. **(5)** sentence 12

Answer (5) provides a topic sentence that states the main idea of this paragraph. In answer (1), sentence 7 logically follows sentence 6 and does not belong at the beginning of the paragraph. In answer (2), sentence 9 also logically follows sentence 8. Similarly, sentence 10 should follow sentence 9 in answer (3). Answer (4) is incorrect because sentence 11 builds on the preceding sentences in the paragraph and is therefore necessary. ⟨H⟩ **Restructuring Paragraphs**

50. **(4)** Change <u>makes</u> to <u>make</u>.

The compound subject *Education and participation* takes the plural form of the verb *make*. Answer (1) ruins the parallel structure of *Education and participation*. Answer (2) is wrong because *by* is the correct word. Answer (3) is incorrect because *people* is not a proper noun and should not be capitalized. ⟨H⟩ **Verbs**

LANGUAGE ARTS, WRITING PART II ANSWERS AND EXPLANATIONS

Here is a sample high-scoring essay in response to the prompt given on the test. To grade your essay yourself, return to the last rung of the Language Arts, Writing ladder. Does your essay have all of the necessary ingredients? Compare your essay to the one below. Does yours follow the same general structure as this one (think of the hamburger)? You may also ask a friend or coworker to grade your essay.

Why It Is Good to Live in Cities

In my opinion, cities are good places for people to live in. It is true that many cities are dirtier, noisier, and more crowded than small towns or rural areas. They can be difficult to negotiate, and life may be more stressful in cities than in the country. However, cities also offer a wide array of choices that make them appealing places to reside.

One of the things that cities have to offer people is a broad spectrum of jobs. Because of their dense populations, most cities support many different kinds of industries. For example, in Seattle, people work in occupations ranging from aircraft-building to software development to coffee-roasting. It is difficult to find that kind of diversity of work opportunities in smaller towns. In addition, there are usually many employers within particular industries in a city, and having several potential employers to work for is advantageous for people working in those fields.

Cities also give people more cultural options than smaller places. In most sizable cities, people have the opportunities to enjoy a range of musical performances, art and historical museums, the opera, poetry readings, and dance performances. In small towns, sometimes the only cultural options are seeing movies or visiting a gallery. I believe that having access to a wide array of cultural happenings makes life more interesting and enjoyable, and that only cities can support a rich cultural existence.

A third factor that makes cities good places to live is human diversity. In cities such as New York City, Chicago, and Los Angeles, people from many different racial and ethnic groups coexist all the time. In most cities, people also practice different kinds of religion and support different political viewpoints. This diversity makes life more vibrant and fosters the rich cultural life that I believe is crucial to a satisfying life. Urban diversity also creates more tolerance for difference, and I think that tolerance is another factor that makes cities good places to live.

In conclusion, I would like to say that cities are excellent places to live, if you are the type of person who values having a lot of choices. Cities support more work opportunities, cultural activities, and diversity of population than small towns or rural areas. Having a wide array of choices in many areas of life benefits people who seek those kinds of options. Cities have their drawbacks, and if you are a person who needs to be in the wilderness all the time, then cities are probably not for you. However, if you like the excitement and variety that cities support, then living in cities is a good choice.

SOCIAL STUDIES

This simulated GED Social Studies test is designed to measure your general knowledge of U.S. government, U.S. history, world history, economics, and geography. Spend no more than 70 minutes answering the fifty questions on this test. When you are finished, review the Answers and Explanations section on page 447 to determine whether you are ready to take the GED Social Studies test or need additional review in specific areas.

Directions: Choose the <u>one best answer</u> to each question.

<u>Questions 1 through 3</u> refer to the following paragraph and graph.

Cash or the ability to easily turn an asset into cash is called "liquidity." The Federal Reserve Bank influences the supply of money in circulation by adjusting the interest rate—the cost of borrowing money. When interest rates are high, people prefer to earn more by keeping their money in less liquid assets. The graph illustrates the relationship between interest rates and the demand for money, with zero at the origin and increasing along the *x*- and *y*-axes.

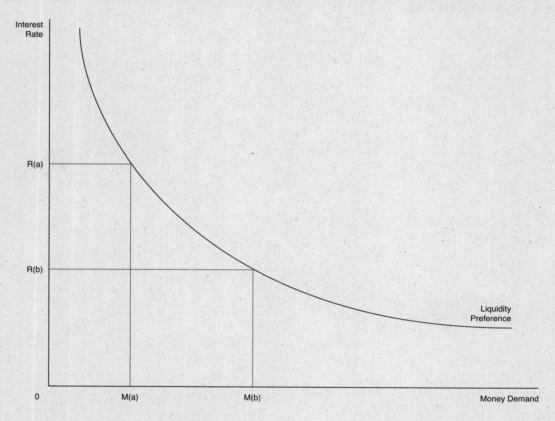

1. At interest rate R(a), what amount of money do people prefer to keep liquid?

   (1) R(b)
   (2) M(a)
   (3) M(b)
   (4) R(a)
   (5) A(m)

2. When the money supply increases, what happens to the interest rate?

   (1) It remains the same.
   (2) It falls.
   (3) It rises.
   (4) It is unrelated to the money supply.
   (5) It vanishes.

3. If the interest rate were raised to some level higher than R(a), what would you expect to happen to the demand for money?

   (1) It would be lower than M(a).
   (2) It would be between M(a) and M(b).
   (3) It would be higher than M(b).
   (4) It would remain unchanged.
   (5) It would become zero.

Question 4 refers to the following chart.

Percentage of United States Population in Urban Areas

Year	Percentage
1790	4%
1800	5%
1810	5%
1820	6%
1830	8%
1840	10%
1850	12%
1860	15%
1870	20%
1880	27%
1890	32%
1900	36%
1910	42%
1920	49%
1930	50%
1940	55%
1950	61%
1960	68%
1970	70%
1980	74%
1990	77%
2000	80%

4. Based on the chart, which describes the trend in U.S. population because 1790?

    (1) Americans are unlikely to move from their birthplace.
    (2) Agriculture remains a major source of income for Americans.
    (3) Americans have increasingly migrated toward cities.
    (4) The country's population has grown by 80%.
    (5) Americans like to travel.

Question 5 refers to the following passage.

The United States Constitution protects its citizens from their own government by guaranteeing speedy and public trials and due process of law. These protections are part of what makes the United States a free society, a society in which even the most powerful are bound by the same laws and liberties. These guarantees are part of the Bill of Rights—the basis of American personal freedoms because 1791. But the idea of laws to protect the citizenry from the absolute power of a ruler is much, much older.

In the early 13th century, King John of England—brother of Richard the Lionheart and villain of Robin Hood stories—abused his royal power so outrageously that English landowners rebelled. They wrote a pact, the "Magna Charta," to try to protect themselves and their property from the king's arbitrary rule. The king refused to accept the agreement, prompting the barons to turn against him. They marched on London and captured the city, forcing King John to reconsider his position. On June 15, 1215, John accepted the charter by affixing the royal seal, binding himself and future English monarchs to grant the liberties described in the charter to all future English free citizens. The king was no longer above the law.

Centuries later when English colonists left for the New World, they took charters guaranteeing that their rights as English citizens would remain the same even on the other side of the Atlantic. A century later, descendents of these first colonists could not bear being denied the "due process of law" promised to subjects of the English crown. They were moved to war, not for new freedoms, but for ancient ones. It is clear that the first Americans valued those cornerstones of liberty laid out nearly 600 years earlier: "No freeman shall be taken, imprisoned, . . . or in any other way destroyed . . . except by the lawful judgment of his peers, or by the law of the land. To no one will we sell, to none will we deny or delay, right or justice."

5. What title best expresses the main idea of this passage?

    (1) Absolute Power Corrupts Absolutely
    (2) English Roots of an American Principle
    (3) Foundations of a Free Society
    (4) The History of the U.S. Constitution
    (5) Understanding Due Process

PRACTICE TESTS

SOCIAL STUDIES

431

Question 6 refers to the following passage and chart.

"Drink your milk. Wash your hands. Cover your mouth." Parents have relied on the science of Louis Pasteur to guard their kids' health for more than 100 years. He proved that tiny organisms caused many diseases, and that killing those bacteria could prevent many diseases. Through his work with the invisible germs, he improved food safety, hospital care, and disease prevention, and extended the average human life dramatically.

He learned that he could kill harmful bacteria in foods with heat. The process—called pasteurization in honor of its inventor—is widely used today to make milk, juice, and honey safe. He later applied his understanding of germs to figure out how diseases could be passed from one person to another even without direct contact. His reasoning and experiments led him to develop treatments to prevent the spread of viruses like rabies. But his simplest discovery may have been his most important: the easiest way to prevent disease is to wash your hands. Before Pasteur, half of the people who were admitted to hospitals died there because doctors carried infections from sick patients to healthy ones on their hands and instruments. Today we accept that handwashing is a basic habit for good health for everyone.

There were about one billion people alive in 1800. That number doubled just 130 years later, reaching two billion in 1930, and had exploded to six billion by the end of the twentieth century. Dr. Pasteur was born in France in 1822 and died there in 1895. The chart shows how the world population has grown because the life of Louis Pasteur.

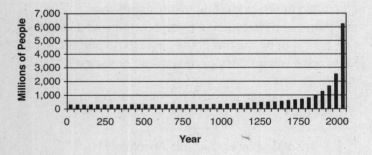

6. Louis Pasteur's biggest contribution to health care was information on how to

(1) comfort patients.
(2) educate doctors.
(3) promote nutrition.
(4) cure diseases.
(5) prevent illness.

Question 7 refers to the following passage.

In the historic *Brown v. Board of Education* decision in 1954, the U.S. Supreme Court deemed that racial segregation in public education was unconstitutional. Some opponents of civil rights tried to fight the decision on the grounds that it was an issue for the states to decide and that the federal government had overstepped its bounds by insisting that students of all races be allowed the opportunity to attend any public school.

For nearly a decade, segregationists waged a war for what they called "states' rights," claiming that the Tenth Amendment gave them the right to discriminate. In 1962, George Wallace was elected governor of Alabama with the campaign promise that he would "stand in the schoolhouse door" to prevent the federal government from forcing racial integration. In June of 1963, he did just that. A federal judge ordered the University of Alabama to allow Vivian Malone and James Hood—both African Americans—to enroll. Wallace made his symbolic stand and made a statement of objection, but ultimately stepped aside and allowed the students, escorted by the National Guard, to enter.

President Johnson put an end to the states' rights argument in 1964 by signing the Civil Rights Act into law, banning discrimination on the basis of race, color, sex, national origin, or religion in employment and education. In 1965, Vivian Malone made history as the first African American to graduate from the University of Alabama. In 1996, George Wallace said that Vivian Malone "was at the center of the fight over states' rights and conducted herself with grace, strength and, above all, courage."

7. Why did Wallace make the 1963 stand against integration?

(1) To make Vivian Malone's victory more important.
(2) To prevent Vivian Malone from getting an education.
(3) To fulfill a promise as a politician.
(4) To win national support for injustice against Alabama.
(5) To advance the cause of civil rights.

Question 8 refers to the following passage.

The framers of the U.S. Constitution designed a government that separated the responsibilities for the military, placing the responsibilities firmly in civilian hands.

Article I, Section 8 of the Constitution states that Congress shall have the power "to raise and support Armies" and "to provide and maintain a Navy."

Article II, Section 2 states, "The President shall be the Commander in Chief of the Army and Navy of the United States, and of the Militia of the several States when called into the actual Service of the United States."

By giving one branch of government the power to declare war and another branch the power to command the military, the framers planned for the president and Congress to work together to use the military.

Of the country's forty-three presidents from George Washington to George W. Bush, twenty-five served in the military. Like Ulysses S. Grant, some of the nation's greatest wartime heroes served as presidents in peacetime, and like Franklin D. Roosevelt, some wartime presidents' first military service was in the role of Commander in Chief.

8. Why did the framers of the Constitution want a civilian in control of the military?

   (1) to make sure the Commander in Chief has military experience
   (2) to make sure the president has no military ambitions
   (3) to make sure no one person commands the military
   (4) to force Congress and the president to act together on military decisions
   (5) to strengthen the president's authority over the army

Question 9 refers to the following cartoon.

Mike Keefe, Cagle Cartoons, Inc.

9. What does the artist of this cartoon assume readers know about deficits?

   (1) Future generations will have to deal with them.
   (2) Sacrifices now will pay off in the future.
   (3) Future generations will appreciate them when they grow up.
   (4) Parents need to plan for their children's future.
   (5) Future generations will benefit from them.

Questions 10 and 11 refer to the following historical document.

Bill of Rights

Amendment I: Congress shall make no law respecting an establishment of religion, or prohibiting the free exercise thereof; or abridging the freedom of speech, or of the press; or the right of the people peaceably to assemble, and to petition the government for a redress of grievances.

Amendment II: A well regulated militia, being necessary to the security of a free state, the right of the people to keep and bear arms, shall not be infringed.

Amendment III: No soldier shall, in time of peace be quartered in any house, without the consent of the owner, nor in time of war, but in a manner to be prescribed by law.

Amendment IV: The right of the people to be secure in their persons, houses, papers, and effects, against unreasonable searches and seizures, shall not be violated, and no warrants shall issue, but upon probable cause, supported by oath or affirmation, and particularly describing the place to be searched, and the persons or things to be seized.

Amendment V: No person shall be held to answer for a capital, or otherwise infamous crime, unless on a presentment or indictment of a grand jury, except in cases arising in the land or naval forces, or in the militia, when in actual service in time of war or public danger; nor shall any person be subject for the same offense to be twice put in jeopardy of life or limb; nor shall be compelled in any criminal case to be a witness against himself, nor be deprived of life, liberty, or property, without due process of law; nor shall private property be taken for public use, without just compensation.

Amendment VI: In all criminal prosecutions, the accused shall enjoy the right to a speedy and public trial, by an impartial jury of the state and district wherein the crime shall have been committed, which district shall have been previously ascertained by law, and to be informed of the nature and cause of the accusation; to be confronted with the witnesses against him; to have compulsory process for obtaining witnesses in his favor, and to have the assistance of counsel for his defense.

Amendment VII: In suits at common law, where the value in controversy shall exceed twenty dollars, the right of trial by jury shall be preserved, and no fact tried by a jury, shall be otherwise reexamined in any court of the United States, than according to the rules of the common law.

Amendment VIII: Excessive bail shall not be required, nor excessive fines imposed, nor cruel and unusual punishments inflicted.

Amendment IX: The enumeration in the Constitution, of certain rights, shall not be construed to deny or disparage others retained by the people.

Amendment X: The powers not delegated to the United States by the Constitution, nor prohibited by it to the states, are reserved to the states respectively, or to the people.

10. The first ten amendments to the U.S. Constitution are known collectively as the *Bill of Rights*. Which sentence best summarizes the purpose of these amendments?

    (1) Citizens of a democracy should be ready to serve in government.
    (2) The government may defend itself from its people.
    (3) Personal liberties should be restricted as much as possible.
    (4) The government should not restrict personal freedoms unnecessarily.
    (5) Americans are in charge of their own government.

11. When people "take the Fifth" rather than answer questions from an investigator or prosecutor, which right, guaranteed by the *Bill of Rights*, are they asserting?

    (1) the right of free speech
    (2) the right to bear arms
    (3) the right not to incriminate themselves
    (4) the right to due process
    (5) the right to not face cruel and unusual punishment

Questions 12 through 14 refer to the following paragraph and chart.

States raise money to run their governments and provide public services to their residents by collecting taxes, primarily on income, sales, and property. Every state is different in the average amount of state tax each resident pays and the proportion of the total tax that comes from each source. The chart is based on 2002 information and shows the five states with the highest and the five states with the lowest average tax per person, as well as each one's percentage of overall revenue from taxes on property, sales, and individual income.

	Rank	Tax Per Capita	Property	Sales	Individual Income
Hawaii	1	$2,748	–	47.1%	32.5%
Delaware	2	$2,693	–	–	33.0%
Connecticut	3	$2,610	–	33.7%	40.8%
Minnesota	4	$2,577	0.1%	28.9%	42.1%
Vermont	5	$2,486	31.6%	14.0%	24.4%
Oregon	46	$1,459	–	–	71.5%
S. Carolina	47	$1,400	0.2%	40.6%	34.0%
Tennessee	48	$1,345	–	60.0%	1.9%
Texas	49	$1,316	–	50.8%	–
S. Dakota	50	$1,283	–	53.6%	–

12. Of the ten states listed, which derives more of its budget from individual income taxes than any other?

(1) Delaware
(2) Minnesota
(3) Oregon
(4) Tennessee
(5) South Dakota

13. How much, on average, does each resident of South Carolina pay in state taxes every year?

(1) $47
(2) $1,400
(3) 2%
(4) 40.6%
(5) 34%

14. Which statement is supported by the information provided about state taxes?

(1) Residents of Vermont pay taxes on their property, sales, and income.
(2) South Dakota gets more of its budget from sales tax than any other state.
(3) Neither Texans nor Hawaiians have to pay state income taxes.
(4) Oregon does not collect any taxes from its residents.
(5) Tennessee has a smaller government than Connecticut.

Question 15 refers to the following paragraph and chart.

In the American system of government, power is divided among three branches of government—legislative, executive, and judicial—each with "checks" to "balance" the powers of the others. The following chart gives examples of the checks and balances.

Branch	Function	Checks and Balances
Legislative	Makes laws	Must approve nominations to the Supreme Court May impeach the president
Executive	Carries out laws	May veto laws enacted by Congress Appoints members of the Supreme Court
Judicial	Interprets laws	Can reverse laws passed by Congress Can review the president's actions

15. The "presidential pardon," the president's power to set aside any federal judgment, is an example of what kind of check on governmental power?

(1) a legislative check over executive power
(2) a legislative check over judicial power
(3) a judicial check over executive power
(4) a judicial check over legislative power
(5) an executive check over judicial power

Question 16 refers to the following chart.

Changes in the U.S. Economy by Decade

Decade	Productivity Growth	Population Growth	Labor Force Participation Growth	Median Real Income Growth
1950s	0%	1.75%	0.10%	3.70%
1960s	3.30%	1.30%	0.15%	3.40%
1970s	2.10%	1.05%	0.60%	1.00%
1980s	1.25%	1.00%	0.45%	0.45%
1990s	1.15%	0.90%	0.05%	−1.05%

16. Which statement is supported by the information provided about the U.S. economy?

    (1) Population growth has been slowing because the 1950s.
    (2) Participation in the labor force has grown because the 1950s.
    (3) Real income declined in the 1980s.
    (4) American productivity is declining.
    (5) Americans had more wealth in the 1950s than in the 1970s.

---

17. In his famous "Gettysburg Address," President Lincoln said that "government of the people, by the people, for the people shall not perish from the earth." What system of government was he describing?

    (1) monarchy
    (2) dictatorship
    (3) theocracy
    (4) democracy
    (5) autocracy

Questions 18 through 20 are based on the following passage.

In 1846, an American thinker and individualist spent a night in jail in personal protest, and inspired a new kind of revolution. Henry David Thoreau objected to slavery and refused to pay a tax that he felt supported the immoral institution. After the experience he wrote an essay called *Civil Disobedience*, arguing that people can force changes by peacefully refusing to obey unjust laws. With this philosophy, also known as passive resistance, reformers have demanded and won social and political rights with determination and dignity. Mohandas Gandhi, a British-educated Indian lawyer, used nonviolent protest to draw attention to autocratic British rule in India. He finally saw his dream of Indian independence realized in 1947, after more than thirty years of struggle.

Inspired by Gandhi, Dr. Martin Luther King, Jr. applied the principles of civil disobedience in the fight for civil rights in the United States in the 1950s and 1960s. He led a year-long boycott of the city busses in Montgomery, Alabama, which ended with the Supreme Court's decision that racial segregation was unconstitutional. Dr. King was a Southern Baptist minister who attracted support speaking passionately and eloquently about social injustices in the United States. Preaching nonviolence and tolerance, he focused global attention on the racist conditions in the American South. He was the youngest person ever awarded the Nobel Peace Prize in 1964—the same year the Civil Rights Act became law.

Gandhi and King were both imprisoned several times for their activism, though neither ever faltered in his resolve. Neither would endorse violence even in the face of attacks to their own safety. The more their opponents tried to stop them, the more the world was forced to acknowledge the righteousness of their causes. Although the twentieth century's greatest advocates for justice and peace both died in violence at the hands of assassins, their message of nonviolence and perseverance endures.

18. A central aspect of civil disobedience is that the policy being protested must be

    (1) emotional.
    (2) irrational
    (3) illegal.
    (4) unpopular.
    (5) unjust.

19. Which saying best describes passive resistance?

    (1) Turn the other cheek.
    (2) A stitch in time saves nine.
    (3) The early bird gets the worm.
    (4) There's more than one way to skin a cat.
    (5) Misery loves company.

20. How would Thoreau probably have felt about the way Gandhi and King applied his philosophy of civil disobedience?

    (1) He would have disapproved that they challenged legal authority.
    (2) He would have supported their challenges to racist policies.
    (3) He would have been outraged that his beliefs about taxes were being applied to social problems.
    (4) He would have been proud that his essay had become famous.
    (5) He would have been embarrassed by all the attention to criminals.

21. Media scholar Marshall McLuhan said of the Vietnam War: "Television brought the brutality of war into the comfort of the living room. Vietnam was lost in the living rooms of America—not on the battlefields of Vietnam." What did he believe was the problem with the war?

    (1) poor military planning
    (2) lack of public interest
    (3) unclear political objectives
    (4) lack of public support
    (5) overwhelming international protest

Question 22 is based on the following passage and table.

On June 24, 1912, President Taft signed an executive order that established proportions of the U.S. flag and provided for arrangement of the stars in six horizontal rows of eight stars each. President Eisenhower issued an executive order on January 3, 1959, stating that the flag's stars should be in seven rows of seven stars each. The most recent order on the matter came on August 21, 1959, which arranged the fifty stars in nine horizontal and eleven vertical rows. The following chart shows when the last five states were admitted to the Union.

State	Entered Union
46. Oklahoma	November 16, 1907
47. New Mexico	January 6, 1912
48. Arizona	February 14, 1912
49. Alaska	January 3, 1959
50. Hawaii	August 21, 1959

22. Based on the chart, what event prompted President Eisenhower's order of January 3, 1959?

    (1) Oklahoma became one of the United States of America.
    (2) New Mexico became one of the United States of America.
    (3) Arizona became one of the United States of America.
    (4) Alaska became one of the United States of America.
    (5) Hawaii became one of the United States of America.

Questions 23 and 24 are based on the following passage.

Russia was a loose confederation of cities until Tsar Ivan IV (the Terrible) unified the country in the mid-1500s. The unification didn't change much in the daily lives of Russians until the dawn of the 18th century, when Tsar Peter "the Great" came to power intent on "westernizing" his country. He legislated changes in customs and dress to bring Russia more in line with its European neighbors and created a world-class military to further his vision. He also created a new, modern city at Russia's western edge—St. Petersburg—and made it the capital.

He instituted his reforms and works at great cost to the Russian peasants, who were increasingly forced into servitude to survive. Peter's granddaughter-in-law, Catherine the Great, came to power in 1762 and continued to work toward making Russia a great modern country. She became less liberal and more authoritative in fear after the overthrow of the monarchy in France in 1789, creating even more hardship for her country's common classes.

Because Ivan the Terrible, the tsars demanded more and more influence over the nobles, but compensated by granting them more and more power over the serfs. The peasant class was enslaved by their poverty and powerlessness, but resentment was growing. Tsar Alexander II decided to emancipate the serfs in 1861 (before they emancipated themselves), but legal freedom did little to improve the lives of rural workers in the industrialized world. Alexander also lifted state censorship, which fostered new socialist and communist political parties and cries for revolution. They won wider civil rights after a huge labor strike in 1905, but were not content with incremental advances. The imperialist government lasted a few more years, but ended abruptly with the 1917 Bolshevik Revolution and the formation of the Soviet Union.

23. What kind of government did Russia have before the Bolshevik Revolution?

    (1) constitutional democracy
    (2) communist dictatorship
    (3) absolute monarchy
    (4) autonomous collective
    (5) fundamentalist theocracy

24. Which statement best summarizes an underlying theme of the passage?

    (1) Laborers are more interested in security than in liberty.
    (2) A free press is a danger to the government.
    (3) Loyalty results from compassion.
    (4) Modernization benefits the whole society.
    (5) Revolution grows from oppression.

Questions 25 and 26 are based on the following passage.

The third president of the United States, Thomas Jefferson, doubled the size of the nation one day with the stroke of a pen. Until then, the country was made up of the land from the Mississippi River eastward to the Atlantic Ocean. The president was negotiating to buy the port of New Orleans from France in order to expand commercial trade outlets. At war in Europe and unable to focus on French territories in North America, Napoleon Bonaparte surprised the Americans by deciding to sell all of the land west of the Mississippi River to the United States for $15 million, or about three cents an acre. The deal was known as the Louisiana Purchase. Opponents to Westward Expansion doubted that one nation could govern an entire continent and called the purchase a waste of money.

However, Jefferson was so intent on expanding the U.S.'s trade opportunities that he had secretly planned for the exploration of the territory even before the Louisiana Purchase. He believed expanding the young country's commercial prospects was key to securing its future. He requested authorization for the expedition from Congress in January 1803, and received it in February. The Louisiana Purchase treaty was signed two months later on April 30, 1803.

Jefferson chose Meriweather Lewis to lead the exploration, and directed him to find the most direct route from the Missouri River across the continent to the Pacific Ocean. The president believed the discovery of such a "Northwest Passage" would allow easy trade with the Orient. Lewis and his friend William Clark embarked on the mission, called the "Corps of Discovery," in May 1804.

Sacagawea, a member of the Shoshone tribe, and her French husband joined the expedition as guides in the first winter. She was a valued member of the team, once rescuing their records from an overturned canoe. With Sacagawea's help, they were able to foster good relations with most of the peoples they encountered. Lewis and Clark led a group of forty soldiers and civilians up the Missouri River, across the Rocky Mountains, and down the Columbia River to the Pacific Ocean, which they first saw on November 7, 1805. Although they did not discover the fabled Northwest Passage, they did open the western frontier of country that stretched across a continent.

25. What did Jefferson hope to gain with the Louisiana Purchase?

(1) possession of gold in California
(2) military advantage over Mexico
(3) valuable trade opportunities
(4) personal reputation for visionary leadership
(5) enhanced relations with France

26. What was Sacagawea's main contribution to the expedition of Lewis and Clark?

(1) She knew where to find the Northwest Passage.
(2) She safeguarded the team's documents and records.
(3) She helped the team get along with the native people.
(4) She spoke the languages of the Americans, French, and Shoshone.
(5) She was a skilled boatwoman.

Question 27 refers to the following map.

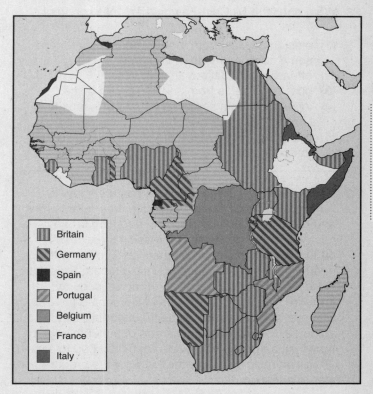

Britain
Germany
Spain
Portugal
Belgium
France
Italy

27. Based on the map of colonial influence in Africa in 1912, which European country had the smallest interest in Africa?

(1) Britain
(2) Belgium
(3) Germany
(4) Spain
(5) Portugal

A basic principle of democracy is that citizens elect representatives to act on their behalf in government. In the 1970s, people started to worry that wealthy people and corporations could influence elected officials by making huge donations to their campaigns. The Federal Election Commission was formed to limit the amount any candidate could receive from any one source. Not limited, however, was "soft money"—the amount that political parties or causes were allowed to accept. To minimize the influence of special interest groups in public policy, the McCain-Feingold Act tried a new approach: rather than restricting how political contributions are raised, it restricts how the money is spent. Republican Senator John McCain and Democratic Senator Russell Feingold cosponsored the legislation, and with the support of both major parties, passed the bill through congress. President Bush signed the act into law in 2002.

28. What does the McCain-Feingold Act try to prevent?

   (1) elected officials from feeling more obligated to some constituents than to others
   (2) offensive political advertising
   (3) poor candidates from seeking public office
   (4) individuals from speaking out about issues they care about
   (5) one political party from growing more powerful than another

29. At the beginning of the twentieth century, more Americans were moving away from their rural homes and toward industrialized jobs in booming urban centers. When the Great Depression struck in the 1930s, Americans found themselves in crisis without nearby family to provide economic support. President Roosevelt called for a system of "social security" for retired workers, which was implemented in 1937 with average one-time payments of about $24 to some 53,000 retirees. By the end of the 20th century, benefits had grown to provide almost $9,500 to almost 46 million recipients, and the future of the program was in question.

Which of the following is the most likely reason for the worry about Social Security?

   (1) The role of government is to care for its people.
   (2) The number of elderly Americans is declining.
   (3) People carefully plan for their retirement.
   (4) More people are dependent on the system.
   (5) Americans cannot rely on government programs.

Mike Keefe, Cagle Cartoons, Inc.

30. Which fact does the artist assume you know to understand the cartoon?

   (1) It is important to face challenges with a positive attitude.
   (2) Retirement planning is unreliable.
   (3) If you own a home, financial hardships are easier.
   (4) People who lose their jobs become homeless.
   (5) Favorable mortgage rates help people buy homes.

31. What is the main message of the cartoon?

   (1) Good mortgage rates will balance other financial problems.
   (2) Owning a home is important to financial security.
   (3) A strong economy requires more than just good mortgage rates.
   (4) Now is a good time to buy real estate.
   (5) The government understands the problems of average Americans.

32. Which of the following is an opinion with which the cartoonist would disagree?

   (1) The economy is in great shape.
   (2) Unemployment is a problem.
   (3) Government assistance should be increased.
   (4) People are responsible for their own misfortunes.
   (5) Housing is more important than health insurance.

Questions 33 and 34 refer to the following passage and poster.

Following America's entry into World War I in April 1917, the United States had to quickly raise a big enough military to fight the war in Europe. By the next month, the U.S. Congress approved a policy of conscription, requiring men between the ages of 21 and 30 to register for military service. On the eve of the next world war in 1940, President Roosevelt signed the Selective Training and Service Act, creating the country's first peacetime draft. Men were drafted to fill vacancies in the armed forces that could not be filled by volunteers. The draft was suspended in 1973 and the U.S. converted to an all-volunteer military. Although the draft has not been used because the Vietnam War, young men are still required to register with Selective Service in case the need to quickly boost participation in the armed forced arises again.

The famous portrait of "Uncle Sam" was painted by James Montgomery Flagg and originally published in a magazine in 1916. It was reproduced as a poster in 1917, and by 1918, four million copies had been printed as part of the public relations campaign for the war. The popular image was adapted to bolster support for World War II and remains a familiar face of American patriotism.

33. What was the function of the "I Want You" poster in the war effort?

(1) to inform men that they were required to register for military service
(2) to boost good feelings about the fact that men had to register for military service
(3) to persuade men to volunteer for the Army
(4) to build public support for building the Army in peacetime
(5) to unite public opinion against a common enemy

34. What does Uncle Sam represent?

(1) personal liberties
(2) the spread of democracy
(3) the United States of America
(4) a military career
(5) the Commander in Chief

Questions 35 through 37 refer to the following paragraph.

The Mississippi River system is the longest in North America and third longest in the world, after the Nile and Amazon. The river "system" is considered to be the combination of the Mississippi and Missouri Rivers, which together run about 3,470 miles from the headwaters in the Rocky Mountains to the Gulf of Mexico. The Mississippi and its tributaries drain most of the land between the Rocky Mountains and the Appalachians, covering about thirty states, and the Mississippi itself runs through or alongside ten states: Minnesota, Wisconsin, Iowa, Illinois, Missouri, Kentucky, Arkansas, Tennessee, Mississippi, and Louisiana. It is a meandering river with an inconstant course, sometimes shifting after a flood or earthquake. The U.S. Army Corps of Engineers maintains a system of levies to keep it in place. It was a major artery for trade until the late 1800s, but became less important to interstate commerce as railroads flourished. Thanks to Mark Twain and his stories that take place along the river, it maintains an important feature of the American cultural identity.

35. Which statement is the best summary of the paragraph?

(1) The Mississippi River is important to the United States' geography, history, and culture.
(2) The Mississippi River is the world's third-longest river.
(3) The Mississippi River is not just in the State of Mississippi.
(4) The Mississippi River is no longer important for trade.
(5) The Missouri River is as majestic as the Mississippi.

36. What would happen if the Corps of Engineers stopped its work on the river?

(1) Commercial shipping would become impossible on the river.
(2) It would separate from the Missouri.
(3) It would empty into the Gulf of Mexico.
(4) Its course would change.
(5) It would overflow.

37. What led to the river's reduced role in commerce?

(1) the attention drawn to it by the stories of Mark Twain
(2) the age of railroads
(3) the invention of the paddleboat
(4) the ever-shifting course of the river
(5) the decreased demand for U.S.-grown crops

Question 38 refers to the following chart.

Average Annual Earnings of Workers 25 to 64 Years Old by Educational Attainment (1997–1999)

Educational Attainment	Earnings
Not high school graduate	$18,900
High school graduate	$25,900
Some college	$31,200
Associate's Degree	$33,000
Bachelor's Degree	$45,400
Master's Degree	$54,500
Professional Degree	$99,300
Doctoral Degree	$81,400

Source: U.S. Census Bureau, Current Population Surveys, March 1998, 1999, and 2000.

38. Which conclusion is supported by the chart?

(1) No one makes more than $100,000 per year.
(2) If you are not going to graduate from college, there is no point in attending at all.
(3) A high-school diploma is not important to your earning potential.
(4) The more time you spend in school, the more money you will earn.
(5) On average, people with professional degrees earn more money than people with doctoral degrees.

Jeff Parker, Cagle Cartoons, Inc.

39. What is the main idea of the cartoon?

(1) Public education programs are inexpensive to operate.
(2) School funding is not a serious issue.
(3) State governments are committed to improving public education.
(4) School districts should be more resourceful to raise money.
(5) School districts aren't getting the financial support they need from their state governments.

40. How do the people at the school district feel about the package from the state government?

(1) They are happy to have some guidance about raising money.
(2) They are angry that the state wants them to earn their own revenue.
(3) They are disappointed that they're not getting pay increases.
(4) They are surprised they're not getting the revenue they expected.
(5) They are relieved that their wait is over.

41. Which fact does the artist assume you know to understand the cartoon?

(1) School districts are expected to make a profit.
(2) School districts tend to spend money foolishly.
(3) School administrators are also financial planners.
(4) Having a bake sale is a way to raise small amounts of money.
(5) School districts are charitable organizations.

42. The cartoon is intended to have an effect on the reader. Which message is most likely the one the artist wants to express?

(1) We all have to make sacrifices in tough economic times.
(2) Schools should learn how to do more with less.
(3) Schools do not have the funding they need.
(4) Citizens should donate to school fundraisers.
(5) The state has more important things to pay for than education.

43. The National Labor Relations Act became law in 1935, giving workers the right to form unions and negotiate contracts with their employers. Which of the following is the most important reason for having unions?

(1) Bargaining as a group gives workers more power than negotiating individually.
(2) Union meetings provide social support for those experiencing job-related stress.
(3) Union members can create higher standards of professional practice through competition.
(4) Unionized workers can control lawmakers by making big campaign donations.
(5) Only unionized workers may legally go on strike.

Questions 44 and 45 are based on the following passage.

When the Internet came into the public awareness in the 1990s, it brought a new way to learn, communicate, and do business. What started as a way to secure communication among government agencies in the event of an emergency grew to include research universities sharing supercomputers. It was called the Advanced Research Projects Agency Network, or ARPANET. The term "Internet" refers to the network of computers that share data. Students and scientists began communicating with each other over the network, and began inventing ways to improve the process. Hypertext was the key to viewing and navigating the information available on the Internet. The inventions of hypertext markup language (HTML) and hypertext transfer protocol (http) turned the Internet into the World Wide Web—the total collection of documents available to users by pointing and clicking online.

Sharing information became so fast, easy, and inexpensive that whole new modes of communication, research, and commerce emerged. Many people can't imagine a day without e-mailing friends and colleagues. Users can have conversations in real time and share huge files of documents and images in an instant, without the cost of postage. Information and entertainment media have evolved too. Some consumers have come to prefer getting their morning news from the computer rather than from the newsstand, so news sources now must produce online editions in addition to print. Without the cost of printing and distributing books and journals, the Internet has created a boom in self-publishing personal web pages and journals. Online shopping is bringing together buyers and sellers who may have never found each other before, while online services like banking improve customer care and convenience. Consumers are enjoying the competitive prices as well, because the Internet storefronts don't have to pay the costs of running a traditional physical shop.

By the turn of the century, personal computers were more affordable and using Internet services was easier than ever. About 360 million people had access to the Internet in 2000, and that number is expected to grow ten times by 2010. People are using the Internet to maintain relationships, participate in their own health care, and be informed members of their local and international communities. The Internet is delivering the world's great libraries to the most remote villages, and connecting people with common concerns from all corners of the globe. If knowledge is power, then the Internet is empowering the world.

44. Which best describes the purpose of ARPANET?

(1) to motivate students to innovate computer-based communication
(2) to find the best bids for government contracts
(3) to provide the means to spread information widely and quickly
(4) to provide a way for government agencies to communicate
(5) to provide a central bank of information

45. Which institution's purpose is most like one of the main uses of the Internet?

(1) hospital
(2) voting booth
(3) courtroom
(4) railroad
(5) library

Question 46 is based on the following passage.

The United States government operated a federal immigration station on Ellis Island, a small island in New York Harbor. Between 1892 and 1954, twelve million mostly European immigrants sailed past the Statue of Liberty on their way to be processed at Ellis Island and to new lives in the New World. If the person's papers were in order and they were in good health, the Ellis Island inspection process lasted a few hours. Doctors would briefly scan every immigrant for obvious health problems in what became known as "six second physicals." Of all those who came to Ellis Island to immigrate to the United States, ninety-eight percent were admitted. Those turned away usually posed a public health risk with a contagious disease or a public welfare threat with no means to support themselves. Immigration peaked in 1907 when 1.25 million people entered the U.S. through the gateway at Ellis Island. The last immigrant was processed there in November 1954.

In 1965, President Johnson declared Ellis Island part of the Statue of Liberty National Monument. It was opened to the public on a limited basis between 1976 and 1984, and underwent a major restoration starting in 1984. The Ellis Island Immigration Museum was reopened to the public in 1990. There are nearly 300 million U.S. citizens today. More than 100 million are descended from those who entered the country through the doors at Ellis Island.

46. Why was Ellis Island named a national monument?

(1) It is next to the Statue of Liberty.
(2) It is meant to honor the suffering of those who were turned away.
(3) One out of three Americans can trace their ancestors to the immigration station.
(4) The U.S. national identity is based on the importance of natural-born citizens.
(5) It is meant to honor the doctors who processed twelve million immigrants.

Questions 47 and 48 refer to the following cartoon.

Mike Lane, Cagle Cartoons, Inc.

47. What does the artist assume you understand in order to appreciate the cartoon?

(1) Polar bears actually do enjoy warm weather.
(2) Scientists think global warming will have devastating effects.
(3) Scientists think global warming will have beneficial effects.
(4) Scientists think global warming is a natural and harmless phenomenon.
(5) Global warming is a fringe theory that most serious scientists ignore.

48. The cartoon is intended to have an effect on the reader. Which message is most likely the one the artist wants to express?

(1) The U.S. government is dedicated to reversing global warming.
(2) The U.S. government is foolishly ignoring global warming.
(3) Individuals should do more to protect the environment.
(4) The cracked polar ice shelf should be repaired.
(5) The U.S. government should research the causes of global warming.

Question 49 refers to the following paragraph.

The European Union (EU) came into being on November 1, 1993. Although the Union was primarily concerned with promoting free trade in the region, it also shares foreign and defense policies. The nations of Western Europe had been gradually creating free markets because the 1950s, first opening the coal and steel trade, and later working together on nuclear energy for the region. Originally the agreements applied only to Belgium, France, Germany, Italy, Luxembourg, and the Netherlands, but has grown to include Denmark, the United Kingdom, Ireland, Greece, Spain, Portugal, Germany, Austria, Finland, and Sweden. Some countries have been denied entry into the union because they fail to meet certain standards, while others have opted not to join even though they are eligible. The 1993 Maastrich Treaty called for a central bank and a common currency. The currency, known as the euro, came into being in 1999. By March 2002, all earlier individual national currencies had been withdrawn from circulation.

49. Which of the aspects of the EU presented in the paragraph represents the highest degree of unity among the member states?

    (1) free trade in the region
    (2) a common energy source
    (3) shared foreign policy
    (4) a unified military
    (5) a single currency

Question 50 refers to the following passage and cartoon.

AIDS was first categorically identified in the United States in 1981. By 1990, the disease had spread to virtually all areas of the world. By 2003, more than 40 million people worldwide were living with the AIDS virus, more than half of whom were under the age of 25. Worldwide, more than 10,000 people contract HIV every day, with 95 percent of these new infections occurring in developing countries. The region with the fastest rising rate of new HIV infections is Eastern Europe/Central Asia, where roughly one million people were positive for HIV by the end of 2001, a quarter of which were newly infected that year.

Of people with HIV or AIDS all over the world, roughly 70 percent live in sub-Saharan Africa and 17 percent in South and Southeast Asia. The virus is the leading cause of death in Africa and the fourth cause of

death worldwide. India has an estimated 5 million to 6 million HIV cases, less than one percent in a nation of more than a billion people. But in some districts, more than 5 percent of adults have HIV—a rate comparable to Africa's. China's epidemic has spread to 31 provinces, with concentration of infection rates reaching up to 15 percent of IV drug users.

HIV and AIDS are not limited by global economics, however—about a million people in the United States and 560,000 people in Western Europe were living with HIV by the end of 2001; almost 5 percent of these infections were acquired that year. In the United States and Western Europe, the disease has become a chronic, survivable illness thanks to expensive medication.

However, the treatment appears to have slowed prevention efforts, and new infections have begun to grow again in the developed world. The Centers for Disease Control and Prevention fears a resurgence in the epidemic in the United States, with research showing an overall 5.1 percent increase in new diagnoses between 1999 and 2002. Most frustrating to doctors is that the cycle of new infections has not been broken in more than twenty years of combating the disease. Treatments are good, but they're expensive and can't keep up with the rate of new infections.

Jeff Parker, Cagle Cartoons, Inc.

50. Based on the information in the passage, which statement captures the main idea of the cartoon?

    (1) AIDS is a global crisis.
    (2) Africa should be the most concerned about stopping the spread of AIDS.
    (3) The U.S. should lead the charge to stop the spread of AIDS.
    (4) AIDS will be the end of the world.
    (5) AIDS will take care of itself.

SOCIAL STUDIES
ANSWERS AND EXPLANATIONS

CHAPTER

8

PRACTICE
TESTS

THE
GED

SOCIAL
STUDIES

1. **(2) M(a)**

Answer (2) is correct because the point on the liquidity preference curve that corresponds to interest rate R(a) on the *y*-axis corresponds to the level M(a) of demand for money. Answers (1) and (4) are wrong because they represent interest rates, not the demand for money the question asked. Answer (3) is wrong because it is the demand level that corresponds to interest rate R(b). Answer (5) is wrong because the graph does not include that variable. ⊕ **Understanding Visual Materials**

2. **(2) It falls.**

Answer (2) is correct. The graph shows that as the money supply grows, interest rates fall. Answers (1), (3), (4), and (5) are wrong because they do not describe the relationship between interest rates and the amount of money in circulation as represented by the liquidity preference curve. ⊕ **Understanding Visual Materials**

3. **(1) It would be lower than M(a).**

Answer (1) is correct because the graph shows that as interest rates rise, the demand for money falls. Answers (2), (3), (4), and (5) are wrong because they do not follow the pattern between interest rates and the amount of money in circulation as represented by the liquidity preference curve. ⊕ **Understanding Visual Materials**

4. **(3) Americans have increasingly migrated toward cities.**

Answer (3) is correct. The chart shows the percentage of the U.S. population living in urban areas has risen steadily because 1790. Answer (1) is wrong because if Americans stayed where they were born, we wouldn't expect to see such a shift in the population pattern over time. Answer (2) is wrong because if agriculture were still a major source of American income, Americans wouldn't be moving away from rural areas so dramatically. Answer (4) is wrong because the chart shows the proportion of the population living in urban areas, not population growth. Answer (5) is wrong because the chart shows where Americans live, not how they spend their time. ⊕ **Understanding Visual Materials**

5. **(2) English Roots of an American Principle**

Answer (2) is correct. The passage describes how the modern U.S. government is based on principles the colonists brought with them from England. Answer (1) is wrong because even though King John was corrupt, the legacy of the Magna Charta is more focused on rule of law than on restricting the monarchy. Answers (3), (4), and (5) are wrong because while personal freedoms, the Constitution, and the meaning of due process are mentioned in the passage, each is only touched on and could not alone be considered a main idea. ⊕ **Understanding What You Read**

CHAPTER

8

PRACTICE
TESTS

THE
GED

SOCIAL
STUDIES

6.　**(5)　prevent illness**

Answer (5) is correct because by making the food supply safer, by vaccinating against disease, and by preventing the spread of infections, Pasteur prevented illness and thereby saved lives. Answers (1), (2), (3), and (4) are wrong because while the doctor may or may not have done those things, none of them is reflected in his three biggest scientific breakthroughs. **Applying Ideas**

7.　**(3)　To fulfill a promise as a politician**

Answer (3) is correct because because Wallace obeyed the order to integrate the school and later spoke with admiration of Vivian Jones, his "stand" was motivated out of the wish to fulfill his promise that he would do so rather than out of a genuine attempt to prevent integration. Answer (1) is wrong because a governor elected on the segregationist platform would not mean to emphasize the success of integration. Answer (2) is wrong because Wallace never suggested that Vivian Jones did not have the right to an education. Answer (4) is wrong because the attention that Wallace's gesture drew Alabama was not necessarily favorable. Answer (5) is wrong because a governor elected on the segregationist platform would not mean to advance the cause of civil rights. **Understanding What You Read**

8.　**(4)　to force Congress and the president to act together on military decisions**

Answer (4) is correct because by dividing the power over the military and placing that power in the hands of elected officials, the framers wanted to make sure that the military could not be deployed unless many people agreed that it was necessary. Answer (1) is wrong because there is no requirement that the Commander in Chief have military experience. Answer (2) is wrong because while the president may want to use the military for his own glory, the Congress has ways to prevent him from doing so. Answer (3) is wrong because one person does command the military. Answer (5) is wrong because the fact that he is a civilian does not diminish the president's authority over the military. **Analyzing Relationships**

9.　**(1)　Future generations will have to deal with them.**

Answer (1) is correct because the reader must know that deficits must be paid at some point in the future to understand why the child in the cartoon considers them to be a bad gift. Answer (2) is wrong because deficits have nothing to do with sacrifices in the present. Answer (3) is wrong because future generations are more likely to resent the burden of inherited deficits. Answer (4) is wrong because deficits represent the opposite of planning for children's future. Answer (5) is wrong because inherited deficits are more likely to create hardships than benefits. **Interpreting Political Cartoons**

10.　**(4)　The government should not restrict personal freedoms unnecessarily.**

Answer (4) is correct because the *Bill of Rights* explicitly guarantees certain personal freedoms and specifies if and how they may be overridden. Answer (1) is wrong because the document says nothing about public service. Answer (2) is wrong because it says nothing about people posing a threat to the government. Answer (3) is wrong because it says just the opposite. Answer (5) is wrong because the *Bill of Rights* is not the document that describes the method of government. **Understanding What You Read**

11. (3) the right not to incriminate themselves

Answer (3) is correct because the Fifth Amendment states that no person "shall be compelled in any criminal case to be a witness against himself." Answers (1), (2), (4), and (5) are wrong because those rights relate to amendments other than the fifth.

⊕ **Comprehension/Political Science**

12. (3) Oregon

Answer (3) is correct because, at 71.5%, Oregon gets more of its budget from individual income taxes than does any other state listed. Answers (1), (2), (4), and (5) are wrong because Delaware's 33.0%, Minnesota's 42.1%, Tennessee's 1.9%, and South Dakota's 0% are all less than Oregon's 71.5% derived from individual income taxes.

⊕ **Understanding Visual Materials**

13. (2) $1,400

Answer (2) is correct because $1,400 is the amount in the Tax Per Capita column that corresponds to the South Carolina row. Answers (1), (3), (4), and (5) are wrong because those figures do not represent South Carolina's tax per capita.

⊕ **Understanding Visual Materials**

14. (1) Residents of Vermont pay taxes on their property, sales, and income.

Answer (1) is correct because it is the only one of the five choices that is true. Answer (2) is wrong because Tennessee gets more of its budget from sales tax than does South Dakota. Answer (3) is wrong because Hawaiians do have to pay state income taxes. Answer (4) is wrong because Oregonians have to pay state income taxes. Answer (5) is wrong because while Tennessee collects less tax per capita than Connecticut, the size of the state government also depends on the population, which is not given in the table. ⊕ **Understanding Visual Materials**

15. (5) an executive check over judicial power

Answer (5) is correct: the president is the head of the executive branch of the federal government, so the power to set aside a ruling of the judicial branch is an executive check over the judiciary. Answers (1), (2), (3), and (4) are wrong because they do not describe the nature of the check. ⊕ **Understanding Visual Materials**

16. (1) Population growth has been slowing because the 1950s.

Answer (1) is the only answer choice that is true: the percentage in the Population Growth column gets smaller with each new decade. Answer (2) is wrong because growth in participation in the labor force has declined because the 1970s. Answer (3) is wrong because while growth of real income declined in the 1980s, growth was still positive—indicating that real income was still higher in the 1980s than in previous decades. Answer (4) is wrong because while productivity growth is declining, growth is still positive. Answer (5) is wrong because although growth was slowing, income was still higher in the 1970s than in the 1950s.

⊕ **Understanding Visual Materials**

CHAPTER

8

PRACTICE
TESTS

THE
GED

SOCIAL
STUDIES

17. **(4)   democracy**

Answer (4) is correct because a democracy is a government by the people. Answers (1), (2), (3), and (5) are wrong because a monarchy derives its power from heredity, a dictatorship derives its authority from power, a theocracy derives its authority from religion, and an autocracy is a dictatorship. 🅗 **Evaluating Information**

18. **(5)   unjust**

Answer (5) is correct because the righteousness of one's cause is what gives the protestors the authority to disobey a law. Answers (1), (2), (3), and (4) are incorrect because policies that are emotional, irrational, illegal, or unpopular are not necessarily unjust. 🅗 **Understanding What You Read**

19. **(1)   Turn the other cheek.**

Answer (1) is correct because it describes the refusal to answer violence with violence. Answer (2) is wrong because it is about addressing minor problems before they become major problems. Answer (3) is wrong because it is about the value of hard work. Answer (4) is wrong because it says there is not just one right way. Answer (5) is wrong because it is about wallowing in misfortune rather than overcoming it. 🅗 **Evaluating Information**

20. **(2)   He would have supported their challenges to racist policies.**

Answer (2) is correct because Gandhi and King were true to Thoreau's belief that immoral policies should be abandoned. Answer (1) is wrong because Thoreau supported challenges to laws. Answer (3) is wrong because Thoreau was concerned about immoral laws in general, not specifically about taxes. Answer (4) is wrong because Thoreau was interested in justice, not fame. Answer (5) is wrong because Thoreau believed that to be right, sometimes protestors must break laws and draw attention to themselves as criminals. 🅗 **Analyzing Relationships**

21. **(4)   lack of public support**

Answer (4) is correct because "brutality of war into the comfort of the living room" indicates that once average, private citizens witnessed the brutality of war, they became uncomfortable supporting it. Answer (1) is wrong because McLuhan does not suggest that there was anything wrong with the military's plan. Answer (2) is wrong because reference to television indicates that people were watching and interested. Answer (3) is wrong because the quote does not mention political objectives. Answer (5) is wrong because the quote does not mention international opinions. 🅗 **Identifying Implications**

22. **(4)   Alaska became one of the United States of America.**

Answer (4) is correct because Eisenhower ordered the arrangement of forty-nine stars on the flag on the same day that Alaska became the forty-ninth state. The stars on the U.S. flag represent the states in the union, so answers (1), (2), (3), and (5) are wrong because the number of stars on the flag mandated by the January 3, 1959, order does not reflect there being forty-six, forty-seven, forty-eight, or fifty states in the union. 🅗 **Understanding Visual Material**

23. (3) absolute monarchy

Answer (3) is correct because Russia's tsars were monarchs who ruled based on hereditary right and absolute power. Answer (1) is wrong because a democracy is governed by elected representatives. Answer (2) is wrong because a dictator rules by force, not heredity. Answer (4) is wrong because members of a collective have a voice in their governance. Answer (5) is wrong because a theocracy makes laws to follow religious teachings. 🌐 **Understanding What You Read**

24. (5) Revolution grows from oppression.

Answer (5) is correct because the Russian peasants overthrew the tsars after centuries of oppression. Answer (1) is wrong because workers went on strike, gambling their security for liberty. Answer (2) is wrong because a free press is not a threat to a representative government but is impossible in an oppressive one. Answer (3) is wrong because although Tsar Alexander tried to win the peasants' loyalty by improving their condition, they still ultimately demanded a new government. Answer (4) is wrong because Russia's modernization did not benefit its poorest people.
🌐 **Analyzing Relationships**

25. (3) valuable trade opportunities

Answer (3) is correct because the passage sates that Jefferson wanted to expand the commercial prospects of the United States. Answers (1), (2), (4), and (5) are wrong because Jefferson's thoughts about California, Mexico, his own reputation, and France were not given as reasons for seeking the Northwest Passage.
🌐 **Understanding What You Read**

26. (3) She helped the team get along with the native people.

Answer (3) is correct because although Sacagawea helped in many ways, the role only she could fill was that of ambassador between the natives and the European-Americans. Answer (1) is wrong because they did not find the Northwest Passage. Answer (2) is wrong because she was more than the expedition's archivist. Answer (4) is wrong because she did more than translate. Answer (5) is wrong because the passage does not mention her boating skills. 🌐 **Evaluating Information**

27. (4) Spain

Answer (4) is correct because Spain is the country with the smallest representation in the map of colonial Africa. Answers (1), (2), (3), and (5) are wrong because Britain, Belgium, Germany, and Portugal all had larger colonial interests in Africa than Spain. 🌐 **Understanding Visual Material**

28. (1) elected officials from feeling more obligated to some constituents than to others.

Answer (1) is correct because the goal of reforming campaign finance is to minimize the possibility influence of a few individuals over elected officials. Answer (2) is wrong because the law does not regulate the tastefulness of political advertising. Answer (3) is wrong because a principle of democracy is that candidates from any sector of society may run for office. Answer (4) is wrong because the law does not ban

CHAPTER
8

PRACTICE
TESTS

THE
GED

SOCIAL
STUDIES

CHAPTER

8

PRACTICE
TESTS

THE
GED

SOCIAL
STUDIES

issue advertising. Answer (5) is wrong because the bi-partisan law gives no party an advantage over any other. **(H) Evaluating Information**

29. **(4)** More people are dependent on the system.
Answer (4) is correct because the number of people receiving Social Security benefits and the amounts of those benefits are growing dramatically. Answer (1) is wrong because if it were true, it would not be the cause of worry about Social Security. Answers (2), (3), and (5) are incorrect because they are not facts.
(H) Evaluating Information

30. **(5)** Favorable mortgage rates help people buy homes.
Answer (5) is correct because a good mortgage rate is apparently something the man in the cartoon is happy about. Answer (1) is wrong because the man's positive attitude does not seem rational. Answer (2) is wrong because how the man lost his retirement is not central to the cartoon. Answers (3) and (4) are wrong because they are not true. **(H) Interpreting Political Cartoons**

31. **(3)** A strong economy requires more than just good mortgage rates
Answer (3) is correct because in spite of the good mortgage rates, the family is still in terrible financial shape. Answer (1) is wrong because the family still has financial problems despite the good mortgage rate. Answer (2) is wrong because the family owns a "home" and is still financially insecure. Answer (4) is wrong because the cartoon doesn't suggest anything about whether real estate is a wise investment. Answer (5) is wrong because the cartoon does not demonstrate a realistic attitude toward the economy. **(H) Interpreting Political Cartoons**

32. **(1)** The economy is in great shape.
Answer (1) is correct because the cartoonist seems to be saying that the economy is not in good shape at all. Answer (2) is wrong because the cartoonist would agree that unemployment is a problem. Answer (3) is wrong because the cartoon suggests no opinion about government assistance. Answer (4) is wrong because the cartoon does not suggest anything about the responsibility for the man's problems. Answer (5) is wrong because the cartoon does not suggest that one aspect of financial security is more important than another. **(H) Interpreting Political Cartoons**

33. **(2)** to boost good feelings about the fact that men had to register for military service
Answer (2) is correct. Because men had no choice about whether to register for military service, the poster tries to ensure that they fulfill their duty with a positive attitude. Answer (1) is wrong because the poster contains no information about military obligations. Answer (3) is wrong because there was no choice about whether to register. Answer (4) is wrong because when the poster was part of the war effort, the country was not at peace. Answer (5) is wrong because the poster does not mention an enemy. **(H) Understanding Visual Material**

34. (3) the United States of America

Answer (3) is correct because the poster represents men being called into the service of their country. Answers (1), (2), (4), and (5) are wrong because Uncle Sam does not stand for any one aspect of the United States, but for the sum of American values and institutions. 🅗 **Understanding Visual Material**

35. (1) The Mississippi River is important to the United States' geography, history, and culture.

Answer (1) is correct because the paragraph touches on several important aspects of the Mississippi River. Answers (2), (3), and (4) are wrong because they are each just single facts presented in the paragraph. Answer (5) is wrong because it is an irrelevant opinion that does not appear in the piece.
🅗 **Understanding What You Read**

36. (4) Its course would change.

Answer (4) is correct because the paragraph states that the Corps of Engineers works to keep the course of the river in place. Answers (1) and (2) are wrong because they are not true. Answers (3) and (5) are wrong because the river already floods and empties into the Gulf of Mexico. 🅗 **Understanding What You Read**

37. (2) the age of railroads

Answer (2) is correct because the paragraph says that railroads took traffic away from the river. Answer (1) is wrong because Twain's writings enhanced the river's image but did not affect commerce. Answers (3), (4), and (5) are wrong because they are not the issues to which the paragraph attributes reduced commerce.
🅗 **Understanding What You Read**

38. (5) On average, people with professional degrees earn more money than people with doctoral degrees.

Answer (5) is correct: people with professional degrees earn more money on average than people with doctoral degrees. Answer (1) is wrong because the chart shows averages, so it is impossible to say that no individual makes $100,000. Answer (2) is wrong because the chart shows that those who attend some college but don't graduate tend to earn more than those who don't attend college at all. Answer (3) is wrong because the chart shows that high school graduates earn more on average than those who do not graduate from high school. Answer (4) is wrong: it takes longer to earn a doctoral degree than a professional degree, but people with professional degrees earn more money on average than people with doctoral degrees.
🅗 **Understanding Visual Material**

39. (5) School districts aren't getting the financial support they need from their state governments.

Answer (5) is correct because the cartoon portrays a school district not receiving adequate financial support from state government. Answer (1) is wrong because the cartoon suggests that the district needs more money than it has. Answer (2) is wrong

CHAPTER

8

PRACTICE
TESTS

THE

GED

SOCIAL
STUDIES

because if school funding weren't important, the cartoonist would not have been moved to highlight the issue in a political cartoon. Answer (3) is wrong because the cartoon suggests just the opposite. Answer (4) is wrong because the cartoon is sympathetic to the administrators, suggesting that they need more support from the government. **Interpreting Political Cartoons**

40. **(4)** They are surprised they're not getting the revenue they expected.
Answer (4) is correct because the first panel shows that the administrators expect revenue and the second panel shows wide-eyed surprise. Answers (1), (2), (3), and (5) are wrong because nothing in their reactions shows happiness, anger, disappointment, or relief. **Interpreting Political Cartoons**

41. **(4)** Having a bake sale is a way to raise small amounts of money.
Answer (4) is correct because the reader needs to recognize that a bake sale is a method of fundraising to understand the implication that the state government will not be providing funds. Answers (1), (2), (3), and (5) are wrong because they are not true, so they would not contribute to the reader's understanding of the cartoon.
Interpreting Political Cartoons

42. **(3)** Schools do not have the funding they need.
Answer (3) is correct because the cartoon makes the reader consider the problem of funding public education. Answer (1) is wrong because the artist does not seem to suggest that the schools should be making sacrifices. Answer (2) is wrong because the artist does not seem to think that schools should have to do more with less. Answer (4) is wrong because the cartoon suggests that education should be supported by state government. Answer (5) is wrong because the cartoon prompts the reader to wonder what could be more important than education.
Interpreting Political Cartoons

43. **(1)** Bargaining as a group gives the workers more power than negotiating individually.
Answer (1) is correct because bargaining as a group balances power between labor and management and leads to the greatest advances for workers. Answer (2) is wrong because social support is possible without unionization. Answer (3) is wrong because it is a union's function to increase labor's wages, not reduce them. Answers (4) and (5) are wrong because they are not true. **Analyzing Relationships**

44. **(4)** to provide a way for government agencies to communicate
Answer (4) is correct because the passage states explicitly that ARPANET's purpose was to provide a way for government agencies to communicate. Answer (1) is wrong because innovations in communication were effects of ARPANET, but not its purpose. Answer (2) is wrong because it is not the purpose of ARPANET stated in the passage. Answer (3) is wrong because fast, easy dissemination of information was an effect of ARPANET, but not its purpose. Answer (5) is wrong because a bank of information was an effect of ARPANET, but the bank is not centralized, nor was it ARPANET's original purpose. **Understanding What You Read**

45. (5) library

Answer (5) is correct because the Internet is a way to access a broad spectrum of information, as is a library. Answers (1), (2), (3), and (4) are wrong because health care, voting, justice, and travel must be accomplished in person rather than online.

🎧 Applying Ideas

46. (3) One out of three Americans can trace their ancestors to the immigration station.

Answer (3) is correct because it demonstrates the importance of Ellis Island to the history of a huge number of Americans. Answer (1) is wrong because something must be significant in its own right to become a national monument. Answer (2) is wrong because not many immigrants suffered or were turned away. Answer (4) is wrong because it is not true. Answer (5) is wrong because the legacy of Ellis Island is in the immigrants who were processed there, not the doctors who worked there.

🎧 Evaluating Information

47. (2) Scientists think global warming will have devastating effects.

Answer (2) is correct because readers won't worry about global warming if they don't believe that it is a bad thing. Answers (1), (3), (4), and (5) are wrong because they are not true, so the artist wouldn't expect the reader to believe those things.

🎧 Interpreting Political Cartoons

48. (2) The U.S. government is foolishly ignoring global warming.

Answer (2) is correct because the purpose of the cartoon is to convince the reader that action should be taken to address global warming. Answer (1) is wrong because the artist does not seem to believe that the U.S. government takes global warming seriously. Answer (3) is wrong because the cartoon seems to say that the government should be doing more. Answer (4) is wrong because nothing indicates that it is possible to do anything about a cracked polar ice shelf. Answer (5) is wrong because the cartoon suggests that the research is in and that it is time to act.

🎧 Interpreting Political Cartoons

49. (5) a single currency

Answer (5) is correct because the common currency is the only aspect of the EU mentioned in the paragraph that member nations gave up an individual, national institution for. Answer (1) is wrong because free trade reflects fairness and openness, but not unity. Answer (2) is wrong because is it not true: working together on one energy project does not mean that all European countries share an energy source. Answer (3) is wrong because shared policy outlines how the nations should behave toward each other but does not force those countries to act as one. Answer (4) is wrong because the countries of the EU do not share a common military, and the paragraph does not mention the EU's armed forces.

🎧 Understanding What You Read

CHAPTER

8

PRACTICE
TESTS

THE
GED

SOCIAL
STUDIES

50. (1)   AIDS is a global crisis.

Answer (1) is correct because the cartoon shows AIDS as a bomb with a lit fuse, poised to destroy the entire planet. Answer (2) is wrong because the cartoon shows all areas of the globe will suffer the same fate from AIDS. Answer (3) is wrong because the cartoon does not suggest any solution to or responsibility for the problem. Answers (4) and (5) are wrong because the point of the cartoon is to raise awareness and spur action; the artist must believe there is hope in the fight against AIDS—if we recognize it as the global threat that he portrays.

H **Interpreting Political Cartoons**

SCIENCE

This Science test covers basic science concepts. You are asked to interpret and apply both scientific knowledge from your everyday life and information provided on the test itself. Spend no more than 80 minutes answering the following fifty questions. When you are finished, review the Answer and Explanations section on page 470 to determine whether you are ready to take the GED Science test or need additional review in specific areas.

Question 1 refers to the information below.

1 IA																	18 VIIIA
1 H	2 IIA											13 IIIA	14 IVA	15 VA	16 VIA	17 VIIA	2 He
3 Li	4 Be											5 B	6 C	7 N	8 O	9 F	10 Ne
11 Na	12 Mg	3	4	5	6	transition metals 7	8	9	10	11	12	13 Al	14 Si	15 P	16 S	17 Cl	18 Ar
19 K	20 Ca	21 Sc	22 Ti	23 V	24 Cr	25 Mn	26 Fe	27 Co	28 Ni	29 Cu	30 Zn	31 Ga	32 Ge	33 As	34 Se	35 Br	36 Kr
37 Rb	38 Sr	39 Y	40 Zr	41 Nb	42 Mo	43 Tc	44 Ru	45 Rh	46 Pd	47 Ag	48 Cd	49 In	50 Sn	51 Sb	52 Te	53 I	54 Xe
55 Cs	56 Ba	57 La	72 Hf	73 Ta	74 W	75 Re	76 Os	77 Ir	78 Pt	79 Au	80 Hg	81 Tl	82 Pb	83 Bi	84 Po	85 At	86 Rn
87 Fr	88 Ra	89 Ac	104 Rf	105 Db	106 Sg	107 Bh	108 Hs	109 Mt	110 Uun	111 Uuu	112 Uub				halogens	noble gases	

alkali metals   alkaline earth metals

lanthanides	58 Ce	59 Pr	60 Nd	61 Pm	62 Sm	63 Eu	64 Gd	65 Tb	66 Dy	67 Ho	68 Er	69 Tm	70 Yb	71 Lu
actinides	90 Th	91 Pa	92 U	93 Np	94 Pu	95 Am	96 Cm	97 Bk	98 Cf	99 Es	100 Fm	101 Md	102 No	103 Lr

1. There are two cubes of metal on a table. Each weighs exactly 10 grams. One cube is solid zinc (Zn) and the other is solid aluminum (Al). Use the periodic table above to determine which of the following statements is true:

(1) The aluminum cube is larger.
(2) The zinc cube is larger.
(3) Both cubes are the same size.
(4) The aluminum cube is heavier.
(5) The zinc cube is heavier.

Questions 2 through 4 refer to the information below.

	Mercury ☿	Venus ♀	Earth ⊕	Moon ☽	Mars ♂	Jupiter ♃	Saturn ♄	Uranus ♅	Neptune ♆	Pluto ♇	Sun ✸
Average Distance from the Sun in light years	3M 13S	6M 1S	8M 19S	1.3S (from Earth)	12M 40S	43M 17S	1H 19M 21S	2H 39M 35S	4H 10M 24S	5H 28M 4S	4.3Y (To nearest star)
...in Astronomical Units	.387	.723	1.0	0.0026 (from Earth)	1.523	5.203	9.539	19.184	30.107	39.47	275,000 (To nearest star)
Length of Year (revolution)	87.97D	224.7D	365.26D	27.32D (to orbit Earth)	1.88Y	11.86Y	29.46Y	84.01Y	164.76Y	247.99Y	220,000,000 (years to orbit Galaxy)
Length of Day (rotation)	58D 15H 36M	243D 0H 14M (retrograde)	23H 56M 4S	27D 7H 43M	24H 37M 48S	9H 55M 30S	10H 39M 22S	17H 14M (retrograde)	16H 7M	6D 9H 18M	3M13S
Equatorial Diameter (Earth=1)	0.382	0.949	1.0	0.2725	0.532	11.209**	9.449**	4.007**	3.883**	0.18	109
Surface Gravity (Earth=1)	0.38	0.91	1.0	0.17	0.38	2.53	1.07	0.91	1.14	0.077	27.9
Temperature Extremes High, °C	425	463	58	127	17	20,000*	12,000*	6,000*	6,000*	-218	15,000,000*
Low, °C	-173	462	-88	-173	-143	438**	407**	346**	347**	-228	4,000**
Atmosphere Principal Gases	N/A	CO_2	N_2, O_2	None	CO_2	H_2, He	H_2, He	H_2, He	H_2, He	CH_4, ?	H_2, He
# Of Known Satellites	0	0	1	0	2	16? Plus Rings	18? Plus Rings	15? Plus Rings	8? Plus Rings	1	9 Planets

2. What planet has an equatorial diameter closest to that of Earth?

   (1) Pluto
   (2) Mars
   (3) Venus
   (4) Mercury
   (5) Neptune

3. If a calendar similar to the standard Earth calendar were to be developed for Mars, one Mars year would consist of how many months made of up of how many days?

   (1) 12 months with about 32 days each
   (2) 1.88 months with about 30 days each
   (3) 23 months with about 30 days each
   (4) 40 months with about 32 days each
   (5) 6 months with 15 days each

4. How long, in light minutes and seconds, would it take to send a command to a robot on Mars and receive a confirmation of the command?

   (1) 8 minutes, 19 seconds
   (2) 16 minutes, 38 seconds
   (3) 4 minutes, 21 seconds
   (4) 8 minutes, 42 seconds
   (5) 32 minutes 32 seconds

5. Spectators watching the demolition of a building from a distance of a few blocks see the smoke and dust rise and the building begin to fall before hearing the boom of the explosion that caused it. What is the <u>best</u> explanation for this?

    (1) Light waves travel faster than sound waves.
    (2) The spectators are preoccupied by the spectacle of the demolition.
    (3) The noise of the explosion is contained within the falling building.
    (4) The spectators are hard of hearing.
    (5) The explosion occurred slowly.

6. Which of the following is the most important consideration when storing acids?

    (1) proper labeling
    (2) cost of the acid
    (3) shape of the acid container
    (4) name of the purchaser
    (5) volume of the container

7. According to the theory of natural selection, an organism whose needs and abilities are most closely matched to the resources available in its environment stands the best chance of surviving and passing its genes on to its offspring. According to the theory of natural selection, what is the <u>most likely</u> fate of a species that is unable to adapt to a changing environment?

    (1) It will become extinct.
    (2) It will thrive.
    (3) It will change color.
    (4) It will change the environment.
    (5) It will slowly gain weight.

8. The familiar states of matter are solid, liquid, and gas. As the temperature of a substance increases, its molecules spread apart and move more quickly. As the temperature decreases, molecules pack themselves densely together and move more slowly. As a rule, any type of matter is denser and occupies less space in a solid state than it does in a liquid state. Which type of matter provides an exception to this rule?

    (1) nitrogen
    (2) lava
    (3) water
    (4) gold
    (5) mercury

<u>Question 9</u> refers to the information below.

Group A	Group B			
	Amines	Ammonia	Caustics	Ketones
Vinyl acetate	X	X		
Nitric acid	X	X	X	X
Sulfuric acid	X	X	X	X
Organic acid	X	X	X	

9. Which pair of chemicals <u>cannot</u> be safely stored together?

    (1) vinyl acetate and caustics
    (2) organic acids and ketones
    (3) vinyl acetate and ketones
    (4) organic acid and ammonia
    (5) They all can be stored together safely.

Questions 10 through 12 refer to the information below.

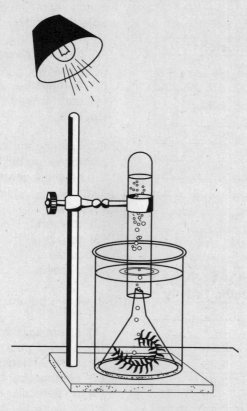

The diagram above shows *Elodia*, a common aquarium plant, under a funnel in a beaker of water being illuminated by a light. The bubbles escaping from the funnel into the test tube are evidence than the plant is producing oxygen.

10. Which of the following <u>best</u> explains why *Elodia* produces oxygen?·

    (1) The funnel shape channels oxygen into the test tube.
    (2) Water pressure is greatest at the bottom of the beaker.
    (3) Water pressure squeezes oxygen from the plant.
    (4) Water pressure is least at the bottom of the beaker.
    (5) The light makes the process of photosynthesis possible.·

11. By doubling the number of *Elodia* under the funnel, you could do which of the following?

    (1) continue to produce about the same amount of oxygen
    (2) nearly double the amount of oxygen produced
    (3) cut the amount of oxygen produced by half
    (4) kill the *Elodia* by starvation
    (5) kill the *Elodia* by overcrowding

12. Temperature is a significant limiting factor in biochemical processes. Within certain bounds, the higher the temperature, the faster biological reactions will take place. The lower the temperature, the slower biological reactions take place.

    If the temperature of the liquid in the *Elodia* experiment falls from 28 degrees C to 14 degrees C, what would be the effect on the oxygen production by the *Elodia*?

    (1) Oxygen production would increase.
    (2) Oxygen production would decrease.
    (3) Oxygen production would remain the same.
    (4) Oxygen production would cease entirely.
    (5) The *Elodia* would begin to produce carbon dioxide.

Questions 13 through 16 refer to the two charts below.

Chart 1

Mohs Scale of Hardness of Some Gemstones	
10	Diamond
9	Corundum
8	Topaz
7	Quartz
6	Zircon
5	Lapis
4	Flourite
3	Calcite
2	Amber
1	Talc (not a gemstone)

Chart 2

Examples of Hard Gemstones on Mohs Scale		
Mohs Scale	Gemstone	Specific Gravity
10.0	Diamond	3.52
5.0	Paste	3.74
7.0	Quartz	2.65
6.5	Rutile	4.25
9.0	Sapphire	3.99
8.0	Topaz	3.56
7.5	Zircon	4.69
8.5	Zirconia	5.7

13. According to chart 1, which of the following can scratch a piece of zircon?

    (1) topaz
    (2) lapis
    (3) calcite
    (4) talc
    (5) amber

14. Considering both charts 1 and 2, how is paste (often used to simulate diamond) most easily distinguished from diamond?

    (1) specific gravity
    (2) density
    (3) hardness
    (4) carat weight
    (5) size

15. Considering the information in chart 2 and assuming all stones are the same size, which of the following is the heaviest gemstone?

    (1) quartz
    (2) diamond
    (3) topaz
    (4) paste
    (5) zirconia

16. In what order are the entries in chart 2 listed?

    (1) scientific order of importance
    (2) order of cost per carat
    (3) order of density
    (4) alphabetical order
    (5) no particular order

Questions 17 through 19 refer to the following chart.

Effect of Single Daily Doses on Intragastric pH

Time	Placebo	20 mg	40 mg	80 mg
		Median pH on day 7		
6 a.m. – 8 a.m. (24 hours)	1.3	2.9	3.8	3.9
8 a.m. – 10 p.m. (Daytime)	1.6	3.2	4.4	4.8
10 p.m. – 8 a.m. (Nighttime)	1.2	2.1	3.0	2.6

The pH scale is a way of measuring the relative strength of an acid or base. The scale runs from 1 to 14, with 1 being a very strong acid, 7 being neutral, and 14 being a very strong base. This chart details the effects of a particular substance on stomach acid. A placebo is a substance with no experimental effect.

17. Based on the information in the chart above, which of the following can be inferred to be the overall normal pH level of stomach acid?

    (1) about 1.3
    (2) about 2.9
    (3) about 4.4
    (4) about 2.1
    (5) about 3.8

18. Which of the following would be the best type of graph for displaying the information contained in the chart above?

    (1) line graph, because the information is continuous
    (2) some line and some bar graphs, because the information is not continuous
    (3) all bar graphs, because the information is not continuous
    (4) a pie chart, because it is easier to read
    (5) line graphs, because the information is not continuous

19. Based on the information in the chart, can you conclude that the substance being tested reduces the acidity of stomach acid?

    (1) Yes.
    (2) No.
    (3) The data are inconclusive.
    (4) The data are not significant.
    (5) The data are not valid.

Questions 20 through 25 refer to the following chart.

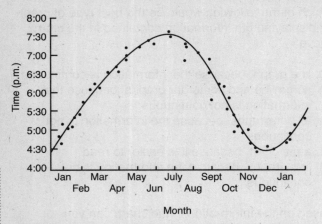

Chart 3: Variation in the time of day flying squirrels become active.

20. According to the chart, during what time of year are flying squirrels active latest in the day?

    (1) summer
    (2) fall
    (3) winter
    (4) spring
    (5) December

21. According to the chart, during which month are flying squirrels <u>most</u> active?

    (1) January
    (2) July
    (3) December
    (4) can't tell from the information given
    (5) March

22. Why would the information in the chart <u>not</u> best be demonstrated by a bar graph?

    (1) There is not enough information there.
    (2) The information is continuous.
    (3) The information is not continuous.
    (4) There is too much information there.
    (5) Bar graphs are known to be inaccurate.

23. You are walking in the woods on an evening in July in an area inhabited by flying squirrels. According to the chart, why would you probably not see any squirrels?

    (1) It is 6:00 p.m., too early for them to be active.
    (2) It is 6:00 a.m., too early for them to be active.
    (3) It is 4:30 p.m., too late for them to be active.
    (4) It is 4:30 a.m., too early for them to be active.
    (5) It is 4:30 a.m., too late for them to be active.

24. The ecliptic plane is the plane traced by the Earth's orbit around the Sun. Most objects in the solar system orbit in roughly this plane and in the same direction around the Sun as the Earth. There are exceptions. Many comets move in the opposite direction. In general, objects in our solar system appear from Earth to be moving from east to west.

    While stargazing at night, you see a relatively bright object move slowly across the sky from north to south. What is the object <u>most likely</u> to be?

    (1) a satellite
    (2) a star
    (3) a planet
    (4) a moon
    (5) a comet

25. Actual movement of body parts is principally accomplished by use of the muscular system and what other system?

    (1) circulatory system
    (2) endocrine system
    (3) reproductive system
    (4) lymphatic system
    (5) skeletal system

Questions 26 through 27 refer to the following diagram.

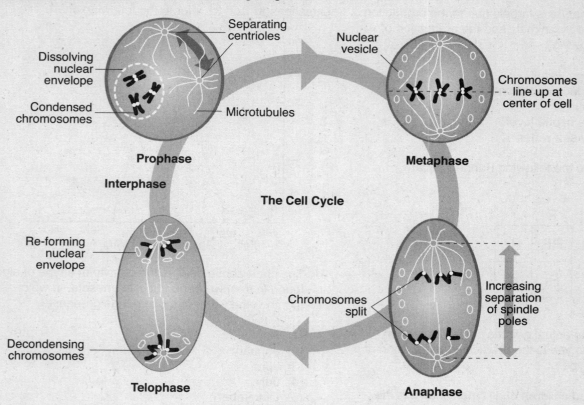

The Cell Cycle

Mitosis is the process by which a single cell duplicates and divides itself into two identical cells. Some types of cells, like skin cells, undergo mitosis frequently. Other types of cells, like nerve cells, rarely, if ever, undergo mitosis. In cells that do undergo duplication and division, the process of mitosis makes up about 5% of the life cycle of the cell.

26. In which phase do cells spend most of their time?

(1) prophase
(2) metaphase
(3) anaphase
(4) interphase
(5) telophase

27. A cell has twelve chromosomes during interphase. After mitosis, how many chromosomes will each daughter cell have?

(1) 6 chromosomes
(2) 12 chromosomes
(3) 24 chromosomes
(4) 48 chromosomes
(5) 50 chromosomes

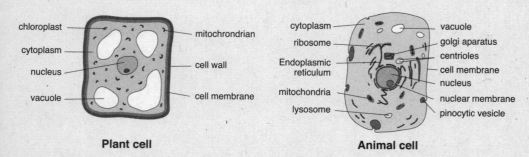

Plant cell

Animal cell

28. Which of the following are found in plant cells but not in animal cells?

(1) a nucleus
(2) mitochondria
(3) ribosomes
(4) cell walls
(5) vacuoles

465

29. The balance of nature is largely due to the production of carbon dioxide by animals and the production of which of the following?

(1) oxygen by sea water
(2) nitrogen by decomposition
(3) oxygen by plants
(4) ozone by the ozone layer
(5) hydrogen by sea water

Question 30 refers to the following Punnett square.

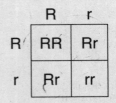

30. A genotype is the actual genetic constitution of an organism. Phenotype is the physical manifestation of a particular genotype.

If the parents had children of all types shown in the Punnett square, how many phenotypes would be demonstrated?

(1) one
(2) two
(3) three
(4) four
(5) eight

Questions 31 and 32 refer to the following chart.

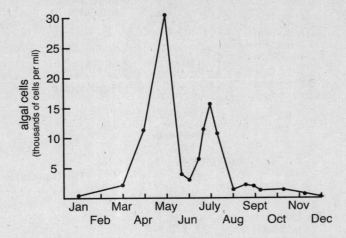

31. The chart above depicts the density of a type of algae found in freshwater ponds in Minnesota. In which month is the water in those ponds greenest?

(1) April
(2) January
(3) June
(4) July
(5) December

32. If you were growing the algae for profit, which of the following would be the best time to clean your ponds for the next growing season?

(1) summer
(2) fall
(3) winter
(4) spring
(5) July

33. Relative humidity is the amount of water vapor in the air divided by the amount of water vapor the air can hold. Relative humidity is generally expressed as a percentage. When air temperature increases, the amount of water vapor the air can hold also increases.

The relative humidity in a room is 50%. You raise the temperature by 10 degrees F. Assuming all other factors remain the same, what will happen to the relative humidity?

(1) It will increase.
(2) It will decrease.
(3) It will stay the same.
(4) It depends on the barometric pressure.
(5) It will cause fog.

34. Dew point is the temperature to which air must be cooled for saturation to occur. When the air temperature reaches the dew point, what is the approximate relative humidity?

(1) boiling
(2) 50%
(3) 100%
(4) freezing
(5) 0%

35. Which part(s) of Earth is/are included in the biosphere?

(1) the lithosphere, or solid portion of the earth
(2) the hydrosphere, or liquid portion of the earth
(3) the atmosphere, or gaseous portion of the earth
(4) the lithosphere and hydrosphere only
(5) the lithosphere, hydrosphere, and atmosphere

36. Which of the following is the most accurate model of the earth?

(1) a standard wall map
(2) a satellite projection viewed on a television screen
(3) an atlas
(4) a globe
(5) a marble

37. Where is a mercator projection map (the kind of map used in standard wall maps) of the earth most accurate?

(1) at the North Pole
(2) at the South Pole
(3) at the equator
(4) at the Tropic of Cancer
(5) at the Tropic of Capricorn

38. Which of the following would be the smallest particle to which carbon dioxide can be broken down and still be carbon dioxide?

(1) proton
(2) molecule
(3) atom
(4) element
(5) ion

39. Symbiosis is a close relationship between members of two different species. The type of symbiosis in which both species benefit is called mutualism. Which of the following is an example of a mutualistic relationship?

(1) Fleas attach themselves to a person's skin and suck their blood.
(2) Remora fish attach themselves to sharks and eat scraps of food left over after the shark feeds.
(3) The crocodile bird removes harmful parasites and leeches and eats food scraps from between the teeth of the Nile crocodile.
(4) Mistletoe attaches itself to a tree and draws its nourishment from the branches of the tree.
(5) A tapeworm infests a cow's intestinal tract, drawing nutrients from the cow's partially digested food.

40. Diabetes is a disease that occurs when the body is not able to use sugar as it should. In a healthy person, the body changes carbohydrates into glucose, a form of sugar used by the body's tissues. A hormone called insulin, produced by pancreas, is necessary for the glucose to be taken up by the tissues. Type 2 diabetes, the most common type, occurs when the pancreas is not able to make enough insulin or the body's cells ignore the insulin. Which of the following is likely to be a symptom of untreated type 2 diabetes?

(1) skin rash
(2) fatigue
(3) loss of hair
(4) bad breath
(5) ringing in the ears

41. If you had a question about barometric pressure, which of the following scientists would be the best to ask?

(1) a meteorologist
(2) a physician
(3) an astrophysicist
(4) a geologist
(5) a biologist

42. Galileo, a scientist from the 1500s, theorized that all objects, regardless of mass, will fall at the same rate as long as there is no force opposing the falling objects. He has because been proven correct. However, we can observe that if a tennis ball and a feather are dropped from a roof at the same time, the tennis ball will hit the ground much sooner. What is the likeliest explanation for this?

(1) The tennis ball is bigger.
(2) Air resistance prevents the feather from falling as quickly as the ball.
(3) The tennis ball is heavier.
(4) Feathers are meant for flying.
(5) Tennis balls did not exist in Galileo's day.

43. An ecosystem is a web of interactions and relationships between the plants and animals in a given area. An energy pyramid is a type of diagram used to show the transfer of energy from one organism to another within an ecosystem. The base of the pyramid represents the plant or animal that is most widely available. The tip of the pyramid represents the plant or organism population that is smallest. If you had to create an energy pyramid to depict the relationship between mice, grain, weasels, and owls in a given ecosystem, which would you place at the bottom of the pyramid?

(1) owls
(2) weasels
(3) mice
(4) grain
(5) weasels and mice together

44. Heat affects the density of the gases in our air. The hotter the air, the less dense it is.

If the fire heating the air inside a hot air balloon in midair was extinguished, what would be the result?

(1) The air inside the balloon would ignite.
(2) The balloon would rise.
(3) There would be no effect on the balloon.
(4) The balloon would spin out of control.
(5) The balloon would begin to fall toward the ground.

Questions 45 and 46 refer to the following chart.

Speed of sound through various substances, in m/s	
CO_2	259
Air	331
Helium	965
Ethanol	1,207
Distilled H_2O	1,498
Sea water	1,531
Lead	1,200
Glass	5,170
Granite	6,000

45. Based on the information in the chart, which of the following is a correct inference?

(1) The denser the substance, the faster sound travels through it.
(2) The less dense the substance, the faster sound travels through it.
(3) Density is not involved in the speed of sound.
(4) Liquids conduct sound better than solids.
(5) Gases conduct sound better than liquids.

46. If a sound were transmitted and received in two seconds in sea water, what would be the approximate distance of the object from the transmitter?

(1) 3,062 meters
(2) 1,531 meters
(3) 1498 seconds
(4) 765 meter/seconds
(5) 6,122 meters

47. Newton's third law of motion states that if one object exerts a force on a second object, then the second object will exert an equal and opposite force on the first object. You want to achieve greater distance while jumping out of a canoe floating in a calm lake. Which of the following will be <u>most effective</u> in helping you achieve that goal?

(1) Be alone in the canoe.
(2) Hold onto something heavy while you jump.
(3) Jump sideways from the center of the canoe.
(4) Have something heavy in the canoe with you.
(5) Leap as high as you can.

48. The speed of sound waves depends on the density of the medium through which they are transmitted. The denser the medium, the faster the sound waves travel. Through which of the following media would sound travel <u>fastest</u>?

(1) a vacuum
(2) outer space
(3) solids
(4) liquids
(5) gases

49. The radios of two astronauts standing on the moon's surface have stopped functioning. Which of the following must the astronauts do in order to communicate most effectively?

(1) yell loudly
(2) replace the batteries
(3) touch helmets and speak
(4) face each other
(5) be in sunlight

50. An influenza virus has become epidemic in San Francisco. During the epidemic, which of the following would be the <u>most effective</u> action citizens could take to prevent the spread of the disease?

(1) Get vaccinated.
(2) Stay indoors and gargle with salt water.
(3) Cover their mouths and noses when coughing or sneezing, and wash their hands frequently.
(4) Take vitamin C.
(5) Read the newspaper daily.

CHAPTER

8

PRACTICE
TESTS

THE
GED

SCIENCE

SCIENCE ANSWERS AND EXPLANATIONS

1. **(1)   The aluminum cube is larger.**

Aluminum is less dense than the others, thus larger. Answers (2) and (3) are incorrect because zinc is denser than aluminum. Weight is not a factor in this question, making (4) and (5) incorrect also. Use the periodic table supplied to verify your answer.  **Physical Science**

2. **(3)   Venus**

The supplied chart shows that Venus is closest to Earth in diameter. Check to ensure that you are looking at the diameter and not the rotation of the planet.  **Earth and Space Science**

3. **(3)   23 months with about 30 days each**

It takes Mars about twice as long as Earth to travel around the sun. Remember that the question asks you to base the calendar on our Earth calendar. Answer (1) is nearly an Earth calendar, so it cannot be correct. Answer (2) is far too short. Answers (4) and (5) assume that you did not read the question carefully.  **Earth and Space Science**

4. **(4)   8 minutes, 42 seconds**

The distance being considered is Earth to Mars. Subtract the Earth-Sun distance from the Earth-Mars distance in light-minutes to get 4 minutes and 21 seconds. That makes answer (3) tempting, but it is still wrong. Remember that the question asks for confirmation of the message, so you must double that time, so answer (4) is correct. Answers (1) and (2) assume that your math is faulty. Answer (5) has no basis.  **Earth and Space Science**

5. **(1)   Light waves travel faster than sound waves.**

Answer (1) is correct. You are able to see the demolition occur because seeing involves perceiving reflected light, and light travels 186,000 miles per second. Sound, however, travels only about 1,100 feet per second, depending on air temperature, which is considerably slower than the speed of light. You can often see loud events before hearing them. The question gives no information about the spectators' physical or mental condition, and these factors would have no effect on the sound of the explosion anyway, so (2) and (4) are wrong. Explosions cannot happen "slowly," so (5) is wrong. Answer choice (3) seems tempting, but the sound of an explosive charge large enough to demolish a building could not be dampened by the debris of the falling building.  **Physical Science**

6. **(1)   proper labeling**

Proper labeling, answer (1), is essential for safe science. Cost, shape of container, volume, and name of the purchaser are not real safety concerns.  **Physical Science**

7. **(1)** **It will become extinct.**

Answer (1) is correct. According to the theory of natural selection, only organisms that can adapt to suit their environments will thrive. Those that cannot adapt will die. Answer (2) is the least likely fate of an organism unable to adapt to its environment. Answer (3), changing color, is a common adaptation, but it does not accurately answer the question. Answers (4) and (5) are not involved in natural selection. **Life Science I: Life on Our Planet**

8. **(3)** **water**

Answer (3) is correct. You have probably noticed that ice floats in water. This is because ice, the solid form of water, is less dense that water in its liquid state. This is also why water poured into an ice tray expands when frozen. This is an unusual property. All of the other types of matter listed are denser in solid form than in liquid form. **Physical Science**

9. **(4)** **organic acids and ammonia**

An X at the intersection of two chemicals indicates incompatibility. Answers (1), (2), and (3) are combinations that meet at blank spaces. If you read the chart carefully, you can see that only answer (4) is correct. **Physical Science**

10. **(5)** **The light makes the process of photosynthesis possible.**

With few exceptions, living things need light to grow. This is one of the fundamental concepts of biology. Green plants need light to convert carbon dioxide and water into carbohydrates through a process called photosynthesis. Oxygen is a byproduct of photosynthesis. All of the answer choices focus on a particular aspect of the environment of the *Elodia*, but the only factor that plays a role in photosynthesis is light. Answer (5) is correct. **Life Science I: Life on Our Planet**

11. **(2)** **nearly double the amount of oxygen produced**

By doubling the number of plants, you eliminate other possible limiting factors of oxygen production. More plants will produce more oxygen. Answers 1 and 3 assume that you do not understand the process of oxygen production by water plants, and answers 4 and 5 assume that you are confusing ecology and a biological process. **Life Science I: Life on Our Planet**

12. **(2)** **Oxygen production would decrease.**

We know that a change in temperature will cause a change in the biological process in question—in this case, the production of oxygen by the *Elodia*. Right away, we can eliminate answer (3) as a possibility. Answer (5) is also highly unlikely: The biological process will speed up or slow down, but not change entirely. Read the question carefully, and you see that the temperature is going down, so oxygen production will slow down, but probably not cease altogether, which means answers (1) and (4) are wrong, and answer (2) is right. **Life Science I: Life on Our Planet**

CHAPTER

8

PRACTICE
TESTS

THE
GED

SCIENCE

13. **(1) topaz**

Topaz (8) is harder than zircon (6). A careful reading of the chart shows answers (2), (3), (4), and (5) are all softer than zircon and therefore cannot scratch zircon. **Earth and Space Science**

14. **(3) hardness**

Hardness is relatively easy to establish if the tested items are more than two scale units apart. Specific gravity and density are not easy to determine. Carat weight and size are not involved in gemological identification. **Earth and Space Science**

15. **(5) zirconia**

Zirconia has the greatest specific gravity (5.7) of all the items on the list. Specific gravity, density, and weight are all related. Objects of the same size will increase in weight as the specific gravity of each substance increases. **Physical Science**

16. **(4) alphabetical order**

Understanding the differences between the Mohs scale and specific gravity leads to the conclusion that the order is alphabetical. There is no "scientific order of importance," because the importance varies according to the experiments being conducted, so answer (1) is incorrect. Cost is not given, so you cannot determine if this is the ordering factor; eliminate answer (2). Answers (3) and (5) assume that you do not understand the question. **Physical Science**

17. **(1) about 1.3**

A placebo has no experimental effect on the subject, so the pH of normal gastric contents, according to the chart, is 1.3. Answers (2) through (5) are results of graph-reading errors. If you find yourself having trouble interpreting graphs, review the material on graphs and charts in Chapter 4. **Life Science I: Life on Our Planet**

18. **(1) line graph, because the information is continuous**

Graph interpretation requires knowledge of appropriate graphing. Because the effects of certain drugs degrade over time, a line graph, with one line for each treatment, is best. Answer (1) is correct. Understanding how to interpret graphs and charts is extremely important on the GED test. Refer to the section on graphs and charts in Chapter 4 for review. A mixture of graphs, suggested in answer (2), is confusing and inappropriate. Answers (3) and (4) are wrong because they do not suit the type of information that needs to be shown. Answer (5) will catch you if you don't read the entire question carefully. Line graphs require continuous—not discontinuous—information. **Life Science II: Human Body Systems**

19. **(1) Yes.**

The data support the claim, so the answer is yes. All the other answers are various ways of saying no, so they are incorrect.
Life Science II: Human Body Systems

20. (1) summer

The apex of the graph indicates the latest time of squirrel activity, which is in the summer. Answers (2), (3), (4), and (5) are not in the summer. Remember that the graph shows time of activity, not amount of activity, for flying squirrels.

H Life Science I: Life on Our Planet

21. (4) can't tell from the information given

This graph depicts only time of activity, not amount of activity. Always be sure of what the graph is designed to show. Remember that the graph shows time of activity for these squirrels, and not amount of activity. You cannot answer this question with the chart provided, so only answer (4) can be correct.

H Life Science I: Life on Our Planet

22. (2) The information is continuous.

This is another question testing your understanding of graphs and their functions. Bar graphs are suited to showing information that is discontinuous. The information in the chart is continuous over time, so a bar graph isn't the best choice. Answer (2) is correct and, conversely, answer (3) is wrong. Bar graphs are very useful and accurate, so answer (5) is wrong. Bar graphs can be used to demonstrate large and small amounts of information, so answers (1) and (4) are incorrect.

H Life Science I: Life on Our Planet

23. (1) It is 6:00 p.m., which is too early for them to be active.

You must read both the question and the answer choices carefully to get this right. According to the chart, squirrels become active at about 7:30 p.m. in July. The a.m. and p.m. times are mixed with "too early" and "too late" to confuse you. Take your time, and you can see that only answer (1) is correct.

H Life Science I: Life on Our Planet

24. (1) a satellite

No stars or planets move across our sky from north to south. Some comets move across the Earth's sky from west to east. Some minor planets appear at a high inclination, meaning they appear in our sky to move from northeast to southwest. Only man-made objects, such as satellites, can travel north to south around the Earth in what is called circumpolar orbit. **H Earth and Space Science**

25. (5) skeletal system

Muscles attached to bones (the skeletal system) allow for most voluntary movement in the body. Make sure you review the functions of all biological systems. Systems listed in answers (1) through (4) are not associated with movement.

H Life Science II: Human Body Systems

26. (4) interphase

Interphase is the time during which the cell does what it is supposed to do other than multiply. All answers choices are phases of mitosis. A cell spends only a small portion of its life span undergoing mitosis. **H Life Science I: Life on Our Planet**

CHAPTER

8

PRACTICE
TESTS

**THE
GED**

SCIENCE

27. (2) 12 chromosomes

A daughter cell is a complete, genetic copy of the original cell. If cells changed the number of their chromosomes, the whole scheme of replication would not work. Answers (1), (3), and (4) are multiples of the correct answer, so they might have distracted you. Answer (5) is there to allow for a wild guess.

Life Science I: Life on Our Planet

28. (4) cell walls

Plant cells have cell walls. Animal cells have cell membranes. Cell walls are more rigid and protective of the cell. The other items listed are common to both plant and animal cells. **Life Science I: Life on Our Planet**

29. (3) oxygen by plants

Plants produce oxygen and use carbon dioxide. Animal cells produce carbon dioxide and use oxygen, for the most part. The interchange of carbon dioxide and oxygen keeps life on Earth going. Sea water does contain both oxygen and hydrogen, but it doesn't "produce" oxygen or hydrogen. Answer (2) is not involved in the overall balance of nature, and neither is answer (4). **Life Science I: Life on Our Planet**

30. (3) three

Answers (1) and (4) check to see if you have understood the difference between phenotype and genotype. Answers (2) and (5) bear no relation to the chart and can be eliminated immediately. Answer (3) is correct.

Life Science I: Life on Our Planet

31. (1) April

The line graph demonstrates most algae present in April. This point is the highest point of plant production. The growth of algae is continuous, so a line graph is most appropriate here. **Life Science I: Life on Our Planet**

32. (3) winter

According to the graph, algae exist in lowest numbers during winter, making regrowth faster and more profitable. Answers (1), (2), (4), and (5) would make cleaning the tanks much more difficult and decrease the profit margin by shutting down production in the growing phase. **Life Science I: Life on Our Planet**

33. (2) It will decrease.

The higher the temperature, the more water vapor can be contained in a room or container. This question can be confusing unless you take a few moments to sort out the various factors. It is also a math question in disguise. Relative humidity is "water vapor present" divided by "capacity for holding water vapor." If the capacity for holding water vapor increases, as it does when the temperature goes up, the relative humidity percentage goes down. Answer (2) is correct. **Physical Science**

34. (3) 100%

The air must be fully saturated for water to start settling on the ground as dew. When the air is fully saturated, the relative humidity is 100%, which is answer (3). Confusion over the meaning of "saturation" and the definition of "dew point" and "relative humidity" might cause you to select the wrong answer here. Carefully read the questions and all information given, bearing in mind that the questions may test unstated information that is simply implied by passages, charts, or diagrams provided. ⏣ **Physical Science**

35. (5) the lithosphere, hydrosphere, and atmosphere

Bio means "life." The biosphere is where all the life is happening on Earth—on land, in the air, and in the water. The biosphere includes solid ground, air, and water. Answers (1) through (4) do not include all three "spheres."
⏣ **Life Science I: Life on Our Planet**

36. (4) globe

A globe is a three-dimensional representation of the earth, which, as you know, is a three-dimensional object. This makes (4) the best choice. Although a marble is round, it has no other features of the earth, so (5) is wrong. Answers (1) and (3), a wall map and an atlas, distort the earth by design. You simply cannot depict a three-dimensional object on a flat surface without some distortion. It is not clear whether answer (2) is an earth model, so it should be eliminated.
⏣ **Earth and Space Science**

37. (3) at the equator

Think of the map of the world you have seen because childhood. All the boxes formed by the latitude and longitude lines were small near the equator but very big and tall near the north and south poles. Greenland and Canada looked unbelievably huge, didn't they? This is actually a distortion caused by the difficulties of showing the "round" earth on a flat surface. This map of the world you are used to is called a mercator projection. It is most accurate near the equator and least accurate at the poles. Answer (3) is correct. ⏣ **Earth and Space Science**

38. (2) molecule

Answer (2) is correct. A molecule is the smallest piece into which matter can be broken down and still retain its properties. Carbon dioxide is made up of carbon and oxygen: two elements. An element is a substance that cannot be broken down into simpler substances. If you broke carbon dioxide down into carbon and oxygen, it would cease to be carbon dioxide, so (4) is wrong. Atoms make up molecules, but if you broke down a molecule into atoms, it would no longer retain its properties, so (3) is wrong. Protons are parts of atoms. Answer (1) is wrong. Answer (5), ion, has to do with electricity. ⏣ **Physical Science**

39. (3) The crocodile bird removes harmful parasites and leeches, and eats food scraps from between the teeth of the Nile crocodile

Answer (3) is correct because both the crocodile and the crocodile bird benefit from the relationship. Answers (1), (4), and (5) are examples of parasitism. In these cases,

CHAPTER

8

PRACTICE
TESTS

THE
GED

SCIENCE

one of the species is harmed by the relationship, usually because the other species deprives it of nourishment. Answer (2) is an example of commensalism, where one species benefits, in this case the remora, and the other, the shark, is unaffected. **Life Science I: Life on Our Planet**

40. **(2)   fatigue**
Answer (2) is correct. If your body is unable to use glucose, it won't have enough energy to perform routine tasks. This will lead you to feel tired. Answers (1), (3), (4), and (5) are not typical diabetes symptoms and have little to do with the body's use of glucose. **Life Science II: Human Body Systems**

41. **(1)   a meteorologist**
Meteorology is the scientific study of weather phenomena, so answer (1) is correct. A physician, answer (2), is a medical doctor. Astrophysicists, (3), study the chemical and physical properties of planets and stars. Geologists study the earth. Biologists study living organisms. **Earth and Space Science**

42. **(2)   Air resistance prevents the feather from falling as quickly as the ball**
Air resistance is a force opposing the fall of the objects. The shape of the feather makes it prone to resistance from the air. Answer (2) is correct. The weight and size of the tennis ball have nothing to do with how fast it will fall, so answers (1) and (3) are incorrect. Feathers do come from birds, but it is the birds that do the flying, not the feathers. Eliminate answer (4). Answer (5) is true, but not relevant. Rubber tennis balls were unknown to Galileo, but his theory still holds true. **Physical Science**

43. **(4)   grain**
Answer (4) is correct. Plants are at the bottom of most food pyramids. The higher one searches on a food pyramid, the less mass of consumers one finds. There are more producers than there are consumers. Although answers (1), (2), and (3) are part of the pyramid, they are near the top of the pyramid, and are consumers. Answer (5) is incorrect because weasels typically eat mice, and would not share the same position on an energy pyramid diagram. **Life Science I: Life on Our Planet**

44. **(5)   The balloon would begin to fall toward the ground**
Answer (5) is correct. Hot air balloons fly because the air inside the balloon is heated and therefore less dense than the air around the balloon. The less dense air floats within the denser air. If the fire heating the air was put out, the air would begin to cool and the balloon would move more and more rapidly toward the ground. Answer (4) is incorrect because the balloon would only rise if the air inside it got hotter. Heat causes the balloon to rise in the first place, the cooling of the air must have some effect, so answer (3) is incorrect. The remaining answer choices are not supported by the information given. **Physical Science**

45. **(1)   The denser the substance, the faster sound travels through it.**
Density is a variable of the speed of sound through an object. Sound moves faster in media which are more concentrated, or denser. Answer (1) is correct.
Physical Science

46. (2) 1,531 meters

It takes two seconds for the sound to travel to the object and back to the receiver: one second there, one second back. This is another math question in disguise. If you are careless in your calculations or set up the problem incorrectly, you might come up with answer (1), (3), (4), or (5). Math is an important part of science, so don't be surprised by math "word problems" that pop up on the Science test. **(H) Physical Science**

47. (4) Have something heavy in the canoe with you.

Answer (4) is correct. Increasing the mass of the launch pad increases the available inertia for the jumper. The best distance can be achieved from a stationary object, like a dock. The more dock-like you can make the canoe, the better. Inertia is a fairly complicated concept, so the remaining answer choices may all seem tempting. We all have plenty of experience with inertia, however. Imagine yourself in this situation, and the answer becomes clear. Remember, the question asks for the "most effective" tactic. Leaping high is important, but it won't help you as much as stabilizing the canoe will. **(H) Physical Science**

48. (3) solids

Solids transmit sound faster than gases or liquids do because the molecules are closer together. Reread the answer to question 45, which is based on the same concept. **(H) Physical Science**

49. (3) touch helmets and speak

Sound needs a medium through which to travel. If the astronauts touch helmets, the sound of their voices can travel through the helmets. Sound cannot travel in a vacuum, and outer space is a vacuum. Answers (1), (2), (4), and (5) do not involve the principle of conduction and sound transmission. **(H) Earth and Space Science**

50. (3) Cover their mouths and noses when coughing or sneezing, and wash their hands frequently.

Viruses are often airborne. Wearing masks during flu season is a habit in Japan. You were no doubt taught to cover your mouth when you sneeze or cough. This is good medical advice. Viruses also live on surfaces such as doorknobs and counters, and can easily find their way onto people's hands. Washing your hands frequently decreases the chances you will introduce a virus into your own body or spread it to others. Answer (3) is correct. Getting a vaccine after the outbreak of an epidemic would not be likely to protect you. Vaccines typically take several weeks to give you immunity to a disease, so answer (1) is incorrect. Saltwater gargles may help a sore throat, but they don't prevent diseases, so answer (2) is also wrong. Taking vitamin C is a popular preventative measure against colds and flu, but it is not the most effective step a citizen could take to prevent the spread of the flu, so answer (4) is wrong. Staying informed during an epidemic is important, but in itself, reading the newspaper does not prevent the spread of disease, so answer (5) is also incorrect. **(H) Human Body Systems**

LANGUAGE ARTS, READING

This Language Arts, Reading test is designed to measure your ability to understand and interpret fiction, nonfiction, poetry, and drama. Spend no more than 65 minutes answering the forty questions on this test. When you are finished, review the Answers and Explanations section on page 493 to determine whether you are ready to take the GED Language Arts, Reading test or need additional review in specific areas.

Directions: Choose the <u>one best answer</u> to each question.

Questions 1 through 5 refer to the following excerpt from a novel.

HOW CAN RALPH MAKE HIS SISTER HAPPY?

Once Grandpa had said that Molly was "a deep one" and Ralph almost thought this was true. He had said it because she insisted that she had learned Braille in kindergarten, and though people would
(5) explain to her that what she was thinking of was the beads on a frame that you moved about to learn to count, she replied, "I said I learned Braille and I mean it."

"Will you listen to my poem?" she said
(10) pleadingly.

"How long is it?" Ralph did not care for poetry.

"It's real little." And then, without waiting for him to say "All right" she went on. "It's called 'Gravel,'" she said, and this is it:
(15)　　　Gravel, gravel on the ground,
　　　Lying there so safe and sound,
　　　Why is it you look so dead?
　　　Is it because you have no head?"

"Say it again," said Ralph, puzzled now. And
(20) when she had repeated it, he said, "It doesn't make any sense. Gravel doesn't have a head."

"That's what I said. 'Is it because you have no *head*?'"

"Well, I don't know what you're talking about."
(25) "You're merely jealous because you can't write poems yourself," said Molly, close to tears. She took her handkerchief out of the pocket of her middy and snuffled into it and beginning to cry, she said, "Now you've gone and made me had another nosebleed."
(30) He did not even open his eyes. He knew that she didn't have a nosebleed and he was so tired of her poems that he was just not going to make any effort to understand that one or to praise it. But neither did he want her to have a mad on him because that
(35) would spoil Grandpa's arrival and so he said, "Why don't you go write it down on a piece of paper and then maybe I can get the drift of it?" It was true that he never could hear things as well as he could see them and until just this year he had always thought that the song was "O Beautiful for Spacious Guys."

"I will! I will!" cried Molly and she ran to the house, chanting her poem.

Jean Stafford, *The Mountain Lion*

1. Which of the following descriptions does <u>not</u> characterize Molly?

   (1) Molly is "a deep one."
   (2) Molly is sensitive to others' opinions.
   (3) Molly admits when she is wrong.
   (4) Molly says she learned Braille in kindergarten.
   (5) Molly wants her brother to like her poem.

2. Which of the following descriptions best characterize Ralph?

   (1) Ralph enjoys taunting his sister.
   (2) Ralph is indifferent toward his family.
   (3) Ralph is a great reader of poetry and literature.
   (4) Ralph possesses excellent hearing.
   (5) Ralph likes things to make sense.

3. What is the main conflict in this passage?

   (1) Grandpa is late to arrive.
   (2) Molly has a nosebleed.
   (3) Ralph is tired.
   (4) Ralph does not want to upset his sister.
   (5) Ralph does not care for poetry.

4. How does Ralph get Molly to stop crying?

   (1) He praises Molly's poem.
   (2) He tries to understand the meaning of Molly's poem.
   (3) He offers to sing Molly a song.
   (4) He tells Molly to write down the poem.
   (5) He offers Molly his handkerchief.

5. Based on the passage, how do you think Ralph will <u>most likely</u> approach his sister in the future?

   (1) He will ask Molly not to show him any more poems.
   (2) He will begin to write his own poems and ask Molly to read them.
   (3) He will continue to humor his sister.
   (4) He will make fun of his sister's poem in front of Grandpa.
   (5) He will cause her to have more nosebleeds.

WHO IS THIS DANCER?

Applauding youths laughed with young prostitutes
And watched her perfect, half-clothed body sway;
Her voice was like the sound of blended flutes
Blown by black players upon a picnic day.
(5)   She sang and danced on gracefully and calm,
The light gauze hanging loose about her form;
To me she seemed a proudly-swaying palm
Grown lovelier for passing through a storm.
Upon her swarthy neck black, shiny curls
(10) Profusely fell; and, tossing coins in praise,
The wine-flushed, bold-eyed boys, and even the girls,
Devoured her with their eager, passionate gaze;
But, looking at her falsely-smiling face
I knew her self was not in that strange place.

The Harlem Dancer, Claude McKay

6. Where can you infer is "that strange place" in which the dancer is dancing?

(1) a park
(2) an island
(3) an opera house
(4) a church
(5) a bar

7. Which words *best* hint at where the poem is set?

(1) applauding youths, young prostitutes
(2) the sound of blended flutes
(3) a picnic day
(4) the wine-flushed, bold-eyed boys
(5) both answers 1 and 4

8. Which of the following statements best describes the audience's reaction to the dancer?

(1) indifferent toward the dancer
(2) angry at the dancer
(3) entranced by the dancer
(4) shocked by the dancer
(5) embarrassed by the dancer

9. Which of the following statements best describes what the poet means by comparing the dancer to a palm "grown lovelier for passing through a storm"?

(1) Light gauze hangs loosely around her body.
(2) The dancer has received many coins from the audience.
(3) The dancer is graceful and calm.
(4) Practice and dedication have made the dancer successful and attractive.
(5) Enduring difficult experiences in life has made the dancer strong and beautiful.

10. What adjective best describes the dancer's emotional state at the end of the poem?

(1) detached
(2) happy
(3) passionate
(4) hurt
(5) wine-flushed

11. Which of these earlier lines from the poem contains a hint about the emotional state of the dancer in the last line?

(1) "And watched her perfect, half-clothed body sway"
(2) "Her voice was like the sound of blended flutes"
(3) "Grown lovelier for passing through a storm"
(4) "The wine-flushed, bold-eyed boys, and even the girls"
(5) "Devoured her with their eager, passionate gaze"

12. What is something we know about the dancer from the poem?

(1) She is a prostitute.
(2) She is a young mother.
(3) She has black, curly hair.
(4) She is tall, like a palm.
(5) She is always surrounded by people.

13. Which statement best describes the main idea of the poem?

(1) The audience is attracted to the physical movement of the dancer, but her mind and true self are elsewhere.
(2) The dancer is dreaming of a picnic day.
(3) The audience does not know that the dancer is a prostitute.
(4) The dancer only pretends to be mysterious.
(5) The audience does not know what to make of the dancer.

This is part of a play about a murder that seems to have taken place in unusual circumstances. The part you will read takes place in the home of the murdered man. In this passage, the county attorney questions a man named Hale, one of the first people to speak to Mrs. Wright after her husband's death.

WHO KILLED MRS. WRIGHT'S HUSBAND?

COUNTY ATTORNEY: I think I'd rather have you go into that upstairs, where you can point it all out. Just go on now with the rest of the story.

HALE: Well, my first thought was to get that rope off.
(5)   It looked . . . (*stops, his face twitches*) . . . but Harry, he went up to him, and he said, 'No, he's dead all right, and we'd better not touch anything.' So we went back down stairs. She was still sitting that same way. 'Has anybody been notified?' I asked. 'No', says she
(10) unconcerned. 'Who did this, Mrs Wright?' said Harry. He said it business-like—and she stopped pleatin' of her apron. 'I don't know', she says. 'You don't *know*?' says Harry. 'No', says she. 'Weren't you sleepin' in the bed with him?' says Harry. 'Yes', says she, 'but I
(15) was on the inside'. 'Somebody slipped a rope round his neck and strangled him and you didn't wake up?' says Harry. 'I didn't wake up', she said after him. We must 'a looked as if we didn't see how that could be, for after a minute she said, 'I sleep sound'. Harry was
(20) going to ask her more questions but I said maybe we ought to let her tell her story first to the coroner, or the sheriff, so Harry went fast as he could to Rivers' place, where there's a telephone.

COUNTY ATTORNEY: And what did Mrs Wright do
(25) when she knew that you had gone for the coroner?

HALE: She moved from that chair to this one over here (*pointing to a small chair in the corner*) and just sat there with her hands held together and looking down. I got a feeling that I ought to make
(30) some conversation, so I said I had come in to see if John wanted to put in a telephone, and at that she started to laugh, and then she stopped and looked at me—scared, (*the* COUNTY ATTORNEY, *who has had his notebook out, makes a note*) I dunno, maybe
(35) it wasn't scared. I wouldn't like to say it was. Soon Harry got back, and then Dr Lloyd came, and you, Mr Peters, and so I guess that's all I know that you don't.

COUNTY ATTORNEY: (*looking around*) I guess we'll go upstairs first—and then out to the barn and
(40) around there, (*to the* SHERIFF) You're convinced that there was nothing important here—nothing that would point to any motive.

SHERIFF: Nothing here but kitchen things.

Trifles, Susan Glaspell

14. Which of the following statements *best* describes the plot in the preceding passage?

    (1) Mr. Wright asked Hale to put in a phone.
    (2) Mrs. Wright did not want Hale to put in a phone.
    (3) Mr. Wright was strangled to death last year.
    (4) The county attorney and sheriff are investigating Mr. Wright's very recent death.
    (5) Mrs. Wright says she did not wake up when her husband died.

15. Which statement or statements best describe the sheriff's assessment of the situation at hand?

    (1) The sheriff did not find any important evidence.
    (2) The sheriff agrees that they should look for clues in the basement.
    (3) The sheriff agrees that they should look for clues elsewhere.
    (4) Both 1 and 2 are correct.
    (5) Both 1 and 3 are correct.

16. Based on the passage, what can be inferred about Harry?

    (1) Harry probably killed Mr. Wright.
    (2) Harry is bolder and more confrontational than Hale.
    (3) Harry is extremely gullible.
    (4) Harry is not much of a man of action.
    (5) Harry used to work as a coroner.

17. What is Mrs. Wright's alibi during the time her husband was killed?

    (1) She was sleeping soundly.
    (2) She was sitting downstairs.
    (3) She was pleating her apron.
    (4) She had gone to Rivers' place to use the telephone.
    (5) She was in the barn.

18. Based on Hale's account of his meeting with Mrs. Wright, what can you infer about Mrs. Wright's emotional state?

    (1) amused by the murder
    (2) scared because she is guilty
    (3) scared and unconcerned
    (4) in a state of mournful grief
    (5) angry at her husband's murderer

19. Based on the excerpt, what is the most likely outcome for Mrs. Wright?

    (1) Mrs. Wright will no longer be considered a suspect in the death of her husband.
    (2) She will commit suicide.
    (3) She will continue to be a suspect in the case, and the investigators will look for more clues.
    (4) Mrs. Wright will refuse to bury her husband's body.
    (5) She will forge her husband's will.

20. In speaking with the county attorney, what does Hale's motive appear to be?

    (1) to fully answer the county attorney's questions
    (2) to divert any suspicion away from himself
    (3) to implicate Mrs. Wright in the murder
    (4) to make conversation with the county attorney
    (5) to make light of the situation

Questions 21 through 26 refer to the following document.

WHAT IS THE UNITED STATES REFUGEE PROGRAM AND WHO BENEFITS?

Every year millions of people around the world are displaced by war, famine, civil unrest, and political unrest. Others are forced to flee

(5) their countries in order escape the risk of death and torture at the hands of persecutors. In mid-1998, the United Nations High Commissioner for Refugees estimated the world's population of refugees and asylum seekers to be 13

(10) million. The United States works with other governmental, international, and private organizations to provide food, health care, and shelter to millions of refugees throughout the world.

(15) Resettlement in third countries, including the United States, is considered for refugees in urgent need of protection, refugees for whom other durable solutions are not feasible, and refugees able to join close family members.

(20) In seeking durable solutions for refugees, the United States gives priority to the safe, voluntary return of refugees to their homelands. This policy, recognized in the Refugee Act of 1980, is also the preference of the United

(25) Nations High Commissioner for Refugees (UNHCR). If safe, voluntary repatriation is not feasible, other durable solutions are sought including resettlement in countries of asylum within the region and resettlement in third

(30) countries.

In addition, the United States considers persons for admission into the United States as refugees of special humanitarian concern. People who meet the definition of a refugee

(35) and who are otherwise admissible to the United States may be resettled in the United States if they have not been firmly resettled in a third country. (Many grounds of inadmissibility may be waived for refugees.) Generally, refugees

(40) are people who are outside their homeland and have been persecuted in their homeland or have a well-founded fear of persecution there on account of race, religion, nationality, membership in a particular social group, or

(45) political opinion.

Asylum and refugee statuses are closely related; however, they differ depending on where a person applies for the status. If an applicant is already in the United States, he or

(50) she may apply for asylum status. If a person is not in the United States, he or she may be eligible to apply for refugee status.

21. According to this document, which of the following persons would most likely be classified as a refugee?

(1) a man in the United States who has been persecuted in his homeland
(2) a woman who has lost her job in her homeland and wants to move to the United States
(3) a man who is outside his homeland and does not have a well-founded fear of persecution there
(4) a woman who is not yet in the United States and has been persecuted in her homeland on account of her political opinion
(5) a man who is not yet in the United States but has been firmly resettled in another country

22. What groups does the United States work with to provide food, health care, and shelter to refugees?

(1) persecutors
(2) governmental organizations
(3) international and private organizations
(4) both 2 and 3
(5) both 1 and 2

23. According to this article, what policy is the *priority* of the United States in providing solutions for refugees?

(1) voluntary return of refugees to their homeland
(2) unlimited supply of food, health care, and shelter in the United States
(3) refugee status in the United States
(4) refugee status in a third country other than the United States
(5) separation from their family members

24. According to the information given in this article, under what condition might a person apply for asylum status rather than refugee status?

(1) The applicant is living in his or her homeland.
(2) The applicant is living in the United States.
(3) The applicant is living in a third country that is *not* the United States.
(4) Both 1 and 2 are correct.
(5) Both 1 and 3 are correct.

25. Which of the following statements does *not* describe a problem that refugees may face?

(1) risk of death and torture in their homeland
(2) being separated from close family members
(3) being protected and safe in their homeland
(4) being persecuted on account of their religion or race
(5) being displaced by war, famine, civil unrest, and political unrest

26. What is the purpose of this article?

(1) to describe the United States High Commissioner for Refugees
(2) to explain how the United States refugee program works and who benefits from it
(3) to work with other governmental, international, and private organizations
(4) to find durable solutions for refugees.
(5) to inspire refugees and asylum seekers

Questions 27 through 32 refer to the following excerpt from an autobiography.

WHAT WILL BECOME OF THE TWO BUNDLES?

When my mother died, leaving me a small child vulnerable to all the world, my father took me and placed me in the care of the same woman he paid to wash his clothes. It is
(5) possible he emphasized to her the difference between the two bundles: one was his child, not his only child, but the only child he had with the only woman he had married so far; the other was his soiled clothes. He would have handled
(10) one more gently than the other, he would have given more careful instructions for the care of one over the other, he would have expected better care for one than the other but which one I do not know, because he was a very vain man,
(15) his appearance was very important to him. That I was a burden to him, I know; that his soiled clothes were a burden to him, I know; that he did not know how to take care of me by myself, or how to clean his clothes by himself, I know.

(20) He had lived in a very small house with my mother. He was poor, but it was not because he was good; he had not done enough bad things yet to get rich. This house was on a hill and he had walked down the hill balancing in one hand
(25) his child, in the other his clothes, and he had given them, bundle and child, to a woman. She was not a relative of my mother's; her name was Eunice Paul, and she had six children already, the last one was still a baby. That was
(30) why she still had some milk in her breast to give to me, but in my mouth it tasted sour and I would not drink it. She lived in a house that was far from other houses, and from it there was a broad view of the sea and the mountains,
(35) and when I was irritable and unable to console myself, she would prop me up on pieces of old cloth and place me in the shade of a tree, and at the sight of that sea and those mountains, so unpitying, I would exhaust myself in tears.

Jamaica Kincaid, *The Autobiography of My Mother*

27. Which of the following is a <u>false</u> statement about the two bundles mentioned in this passage?

    (1) One bundle contains soiled clothes.
    (2) One bundle is to be handled more gently than the other.
    (3) Both bundles are a burden to the father.
    (4) The father gives more careful instructions for the care of one bundle over the other.
    (5) One bundle contains the father's only child.

28. How is the father in this story characterized?

    (1) wealthy
    (2) noble and well-respected
    (3) concerned with his looks
    (4) easily irritated
    (5) generous

29. Who is Eunice Paul in relation to the father?

    (1) his laundress
    (2) his mistress
    (3) his wife's relative
    (4) one of six children
    (5) his only child

30. Why does the father give the child to Eunice Paul?

    (1) She has too many children of her own.
    (2) She has a view of the mountains and the sea.
    (3) She can nurse and feed the child.
    (4) He wants to take care of the child by himself.
    (5) She can teach the child to do laundry.

31. Which of the following best describes the tone of this passage?

    (1) suspenseful
    (2) serious
    (3) romantic
    (4) humorous
    (5) adventurous

32. Based on this passage, what is the <u>most likely</u> outcome for the narrator?

    (1) She will accept Eunice Paul as her new mother.
    (2) She will have a good relationship with her father.
    (3) She will take comfort in her new surroundings.
    (4) She will have conflicted feelings about her childhood.
    (5) She will move to the city and become famous.

Questions 33 through 37 refers to the following passage.

The Facts About Young Worker Safety and Health

Through part-time employment, school-to-work programs, apprenticeships, and internships,
(5) teens are a vital and an increasing part of our labor force. For adolescents, employment can be a valuable experience: in addition to its financial benefits, work gives adolescents the opportunity to learn important job skills, explore
(10) future careers, and, in some cases, enhance their academic education.

But employment also can have negative consequences for young workers. Far too often, working teens suffer injuries that can have
(15) devastating effects on their physical well-being. And working too many hours can jeopardize an adolescent's academic and social development.

Although increased prevention efforts are needed to reduce occupational injuries among
(20) all workers, young workers warrant special attention for the following reasons:

Most teens in the United States work.

In 1996, approximately 42% of 16- and 17-year-old teens were in the labor force at any single
(25) time. An estimated 80% of youths are employed at some point before they leave high school.

Teens aged 16 and 17 worked an average of 21 hours per week, 23 weeks of the year in 1988.
(30) Teens typically work at part-time, temporary, or low-paying jobs, often after already putting in a day of work at school. Twenty hours of employment per week during the school year combined with a full class schedule adds up to
(35) a 50-hour workweek, not including homework or extracurricular activities.

Teens work predominantly in retail and service industries. Typical places of employment include restaurants, grocery
(40) stores, department stores, gas stations, and offices.

Thousands of U.S. teens are injured or killed on the job every year.

No single data source provides a
(45) comprehensive picture of teen injuries, but the following findings indicate the scope of the problem:

Many working teens get injured.

The National Institute for Occupational Safety
(50) and Health (NIOSH) estimates that in the United States, 200,000 teens aged 14 to 17 are injured on the job every year. Among the most common injuries suffered by working teens are lacerations, contusions, abrasions, sprains and
(55) strains, burns, and fractures or dislocations. Not surprisingly, most injuries occur in the workplaces that employ the most teens—retail shops, restaurants, and grocery stores. What may be surprising is the fact that teens are
(60) injured at a higher rate than are adult workers, even though youths are prohibited from holding the most dangerous types of jobs, such as mining, manufacturing, and construction.

33. According to this article, what is one of the benefits of part-time employment for teenagers?

(1) It can jeopardize their academic and social development.
(2) Twenty hours of employment combined with a full class schedule adds up to a fifty-hour work week.
(3) It can cause them to miss school.
(4) Teens are a vital and increasing part of our labor force.
(5) Part-time employment allows teens to explore future careers.

34. From the choices below, based on the article, where would a teen be most likely to work?

(1) a hardware store
(2) a construction site
(3) a coal mine
(4) a chemical manufacturer
(5) a rock quarry

35. Which statement is not true according to the information provided in the article?

(1) An estimated 200,000 teens aged 14 to 17 are injured on the job every year in the United States.
(2) Most injuries by working teenagers in the United States occur at construction sites.
(3) In 1988, youth aged 16 and 17 worked an average of 21 hours per week, 23 weeks of the year.
(4) Teenagers are a vital part of the workforce.
(5) Increased prevention efforts are needed to reduce occupational injuries among all workers.

36. Which of the following statements suggests the most likely reason why many working teens are injured on the job?

(1) Teens often go to work after putting in a full day at school.
(2) Teens hold the most dangerous kinds of jobs.
(3) Teens are highly experienced workers.
(4) Among the most common injuries suffered by teens are lacerations and abrasions.
(5) Work gives adolescents the opportunity to learn valuable job skills.

37. Which phrase or phrases best describes the purpose of this article?

(1) to inform the reader about job opportunities for young people
(2) to inform the reader about a growing problem with young worker safety
(3) to alert the reader to workplace dangers in the mining industry
(4) to alert the reader to the need for increased prevention efforts among young workers
(5) both 2 and 4

Questions 38 through 40 refer to the following excerpt from a novel.

In the following passage, a husband and wife meet up one afternoon by chance, after not having seen each other for several years.

YOU WILL NEVER UNDERSTAND ME

"Where are you living now?"

"With the gentleman here, Dmitry Ivanitch, as a huntsman. I furnish his table with game, but he keeps me . . . more for his pleasure than

(5) anything."

"That's not proper work you're doing, Yegor Vlassitch. . . . For other people it's a pastime, but with you it's like a trade . . . like real work."

"You don't understand, you silly," said Yegor,

(10) gazing gloomily at the sky. "You have never understood, and as long as you live you will never understand what sort of man I am. . . . You think of me as a foolish man, gone to the bad, but to anyone who understands I am the

(15) best shot there is in the whole district. The gentry feel that, and they have even printed things about me in a magazine. There isn't a man to be compared with me as a sportsman.

. . . And it is not because I am pampered and

(20) proud that I look down upon your village work. From my childhood, you know, I have never had any calling apart from guns and dogs. If they took away my gun, I used to go out with the fishing-hook, if they took the hook I caught

(25) things with my hands. And I went in for horse-dealing too, I used to go to the fairs when I had the money, and you know that if a peasant goes in for being a sportsman, or a horse-dealer, it's good-bye to the plough. Once the spirit of

(30) freedom has taken a man you will never root it out of him. In the same way, if a gentleman goes in for being an actor or for any other art, he will never make an official or a landowner. You are a woman, and you do not understand,

(35) but one must understand that."

The Huntsman, Anton Chekhov

38. What does Yegor compare *himself* to?

(1) a fishing-hook
(2) a gentleman who becomes an actor
(3) a horse-dealer who misses his plough
(4) a village worker
(5) a foolish man gone to the bad

39. Which of the following best describes the main conflict between Yegor and the woman in this passage?

(1) Yegor wants to be a landowner, and the woman thinks this is a bad idea.
(2) The woman is jealous of the work that Yegor does.
(3) Yegor is envious of the woman's village work.
(4) Yegor thinks the woman cannot understand why he lives the way he does.
(5) The woman does not believe Yegor is the best shot in the district.

40. What does Yegor mean when he says that "once the spirit of freedom has taken a man you will never root it out of him"?

(1) Once a man has gone hunting, he will most likely enjoy fishing.
(2) Once a man is an actor, he will also make it as an official.
(3) Once a man has experienced something new and tantalizing, he cannot live life otherwise.
(4) Once a man has become a sportsman, he will miss the plough.
(5) Once a man has become pampered, he will respect those who still live in the village.

LANGUAGE ARTS, READING TEST ANSWERS AND EXPLANATIONS

1. **(3) Molly admits when she is wrong.**

Answer (3) is correct because Molly does not readily admit when she is wrong; for example, she insists that she learned Braille even though she was proven wrong. Answers (1), (2), (4), and (5) all represent true statements about Molly's character that are revealed in the passage. **H Character and Motivation**

2. **(5) Ralph likes things to make sense.**

Answer (5) is correct because Ralph is described as someone who does not care about poetry, as being "puzzled" and feeling so tired he cannot even attempt to understand one of Molly's poems. Answer (1) is incorrect because Ralph does not seem to enjoy upsetting Molly, and he does not seem sure how to tease her without offending her. Answer (2) is not the best answer because he does not want to spoil Grandpa's arrival and because he seems to have some regard for Molly's feelings. Answer (3) is incorrect because Ralph does not care for poetry. Answer (4) is incorrect because Ralph misheard "America the Beautiful" and admits things are easier to understand when he can see them. **H Character and Motivation**

3. **(4) Ralph does not want to upset his sister.**

Answer (4) is correct. Answers (1), (2), (3), and (5) all represent smaller conflicts within the story—Ralph is tired, Molly claims to have a nosebleed, Grandpa is coming to visit, and Ralph does not care for poetry—but they are part of the larger conflict at hand: for the preceding reasons, Ralph does not wish to upset his sister. **H Main Ideas and Supporting Details**

4. **(4) He tells Molly to write down the poem.**

Answer (4) is correct. Ralph does ask Molly to copy down the poem so he can see it. In the passage, he is too tired to try to understand her poem, so (2) is incorrect, and he does not praise it, so (1) is incorrect. Ralph neither offers to sing a song nor offers his sister his handkerchief, so answers (3) and (5) are also incorrect. **H Main Ideas and Supporting Details**

5. **(3) He will continue to humor his sister**

Answer (3) is the most likely scenario: Ralph humored his sister in this passage, and it seemed to work, so most likely he will continue to humor her rather than ask her not to show him any more poems (1) or make fun of her poetry in front of their grandfather. Ralph does not care for poetry, so writing his own poems (2) is unlikely. He does not want to cause his sister to have any more nosebleeds, whether they are real or pretended, so (5) is also unlikely. **H Drawing Conclusions and Making Interpretations**

CHAPTER

8

PRACTICE
TESTS

THE
GED

LANGUAGE
ARTS,
READING

6.   (5)   a bar

Answer (5) is correct. Because it is populated by "applauding youths," we can guess it is a place where public performances are held. "Young prostitutes" hints at a more adult location, such as a bar, and "wine-flushed, bold-eyed boys" also suggests a bar.
🅗 **Plot, Predictions, and Inferences**

7.   (5)   both answers 1 and 4

Answer (5) gives the best clues about the poem's setting. The phrases "applauding youths," "young prostitutes" and "wine-flushed, bold-eyed boys" support our conclusion in question 6 that the setting is a bar. Answers (2) and (3) are examples of metaphorical language used in the poem to describe the dancer's voice; they do not describe the setting of the poem.
🅗 **Figurative Language and Other Poetic Elements**

8.   (3)   entranced by the dancer

Answer (3) is correct. The audience—"even the girls"—eagerly and passionately gaze at the dancer. There is no evidence in the poem to support answers (1), (2), (4), or (5). 🅗 **Main Ideas and Supporting Details**

9.   (5)   Enduring difficult experiences in life has made the dancer strong and
             beautiful.

Answer (5) is correct. Answers (1), (2), and (3) merely describe statements about the dancer. Answer (4) is incorrect because nothing in the poem suggests the dancer has grown beautiful and successful due to practice. A palm suggests loveliness and fragility as well as strength and flexibility, and a storm suggests difficulty. In this comparison, the dancer is like the palm, and the storm represents a life of hardship.
🅗 **Figurative Language and Other Poetic Elements**

10.   (1)   detached

Answer (1), detached, is correct. The dancer only pretends to smile, and it becomes apparent to the speaker in the poem that her true self is elsewhere. There is no evidence in the poem to support answers (2) or (4). Answers (3) and (5) refer to the audience, not the dancer. 🅗 **Summarizing**

11.   (3)   "Grown lovelier for passing through a storm"

Answer (3) is correct. It hints at a difficult experience that sets the dancer apart from the blissful, passionate audience in the bar. Answer (1) refers to the dancer's outward appearance, not her emotional state. Answer (2) merely praises her voice. Answers (4) and (5) are incorrect because they refer to the audience.
🅗 **Main Ideas and Supporting Details**

12.   (3)   She has black, curly hair.

Answer (3) is correct because the poem mentions her "black, shiny curls." Answer (1) is incorrect because it is unknown whether the dancer, like some of the women in the audience, is also a prostitute. Answer (2) is not supported by any information in the poem. Answer (4) is incorrect because even though the dancer is compared to a palm, her height is not mentioned in the poem. Answer (5) is unsupported; it is clear only in this particular situation that the dancer is surrounded by people.

⊕ Character and Motivation

13. (1) The audience is attracted to the physical movement of the dancer, but her mind and true self are elsewhere

Answer (1) is correct. There is no information in the poem that clearly supports any of the other answers. Throughout the poem, it is evident that the dancer and her physical beauty entrance the audience; in the last lines, it is revealed that her mind—and true self—are elsewhere.

⊕ Drawing Conclusions and Making Interpretations

14. (4) The county attorney and sheriff are investigating Mr. Wright's very recent death.

Answer (4) is correct. The attorney is interrogating Hale, and the sheriff is looking for evidence. Answer (1) is incorrect because it is unknown whether Mr. Wright did ask Hale to put in a phone. Answer (2) is incorrect because there is no information about Mrs. Wright's feelings toward owning a phone. At the time of this passage, Mr. Wright was recently strangled, so eliminate answer (3). Answer (5), although it mentions something that does occur in the play, does not *best* describe the events of the play. ⊕ **Plot, Predictions, and Inferences**

15. (5) Both 1 and 3 are correct.

Answer (5) is correct because the sheriff has yet to uncover any useful evidence, but he agrees with the attorney to look upstairs and in the barn. There is no mention of looking in the basement, so answers (2) and (4) are incorrect. ⊕ **Summarizing**

16. (2) Harry is bolder and more confrontational than Hale.

Answer (2) is correct. According to Hale, Harry asks Mrs. Wright all the questions, especially the more pointed questions, and it is Harry who runs off to the coroner to get the investigation moving. There is no evidence that Harry was a coroner, so answer (5) is incorrect. It is clear that Harry is a man of action, so answer (4) is also incorrect. There is no evidence that Harry killed Mr. Wright, so answer (1) is incorrect. Harry repeatedly and disbelievingly questions Mrs. Wright, so it is unlikely that he is gullible, making answer (3) also incorrect.

⊕ Drawing Conclusions and Making Interpretations

17. (1) She was sleeping soundly.

Answer (1) is correct, because Mrs. Wright insists she was asleep when the murder must have occurred. ⊕ **Plot, Predictions, and Inferences**

18. (3) scared and unconcerned

Answer (3) is correct. Mrs. Wright is described by Hale as both scared and unconcerned. She only laughs when Hale lightly jokes about the phone, so it cannot be assumed she is amused by the murder. Hale does not openly suggest that Mrs. Wright is guilty, so answer (2) is also incorrect. Answer (4) is incorrect, because

CHAPTER

8

PRACTICE
TESTS

THE

GED

LANGUAGE
ARTS,
READING

Mrs. Wright does not appear to be openly mourning her husband's death, and answer (5) is incorrect because she does not express anger toward the killer. 🔵 **Drawing Conclusions and Making Interpretations**

19. (3) She will continue to be a suspect in the case, and the investigators will look for more clues.

Answer (3) is correct because it is unlikely that the investigators will no longer suspect Mrs. Wright. Therefore, answer (1) is incorrect. There is no evidence to support a theory that she will commit suicide or refuse to bury Mr. Wright, and there is no mention of his will, so answers (2), (4), and (5) are also incorrect. 🔵 **Drawing Conclusions and Making Interpretations**

20. (1) to fully answer the county attorney's questions

Answer (1) is correct. Hale appears to willingly and thoroughly answer the attorney's questions. Although at times he seems to implicate Mrs. Wright, he does not even indirectly accuse her of murder. His answers to the attorney are largely straightforward, so (2), (3), (4), and (5) are all incorrect. 🔵 **Character and Motivation**

21. (4) a woman who is not yet in the United States and has been persecuted in her homeland on account of her political opinion

Answer (4) is correct. It describes a woman who fits two of the criteria for classifying refugees. She is outside her homeland, and she has been persecuted for her political beliefs. Answer (1) is incorrect because persons who are already in the United States are more likely to receive asylum rather than refugee status. Answer (2) is incorrect because it is only evident that the woman lost her job. We do not know the reason she lost it. Otherwise, she would need to show proof of persecution or a well-founded fear of persecution in order to apply for refugee status. Answer (3) is incorrect because the man does not have a well-founded fear of persecution. Answer (5) is incorrect because the man has already been successfully resettled in another country, and it is unlikely the United States government would grant him refugee status. 🔵 **Drawing Conclusions and Making Interpretations**

22. (4) both 2 and 3

Answer (4) is the best correct answer. The article states that the United States "works with other governmental, international, and private organizations to provide food, health care, and shelter to millions of refugees throughout the world." Answer (1) is incorrect because persecutors are those people who caused refugees to flee their homelands; because (1) is incorrect, answer (5) cannot be correct either. Answers (2) and (3) are partially correct, but each answer alone describes only *some* of the groups that the United States works with to assist refugees. 🔵 **Summarizing**

23. (1) voluntary return of refugees to their homeland

Answer (1) is correct. Although the article discusses many different solutions for refugees, this is the one *priority* policy according to the Refugee Act of 1980, which is mentioned in this article. Although the article says that the United States works with organizations to provide food, health care, and shelter to refugees, this is considered assistance, not a "durable" solution, and therefore is not the policy preferred by the government. Answers (3) and (4) are incorrect because these are not the priority policies favored by the government. There is no support given for answer (5). **(H) Summarizing**

24. **(2) The applicant is living in the United States.**
Answer (2) is correct. The article states "If an applicant is already in the United States, he or she may apply for asylum status." Applicants who are not in the United States may be eligible to apply for refugee status. Therefore, answers (1), (2), (4), and (5) are incorrect because they describe situations in which a person would apply for refugee status. **(H) Main Ideas and Supporting Details**

25. **(3) being protected and safe in their homeland**
Answer (3) is correct. Answers (1), (2), (4), and (5) all describe different risks, threats, and problems that many refugees throughout the world face. Answer (3) describes an ideal situation rather than a problem or condition that would cause someone to flee his or her homeland and seek refuge in another country.
(H) Drawing Conclusions and Making Interpretations

26. **(2) to explain how the United States refugee program works and who benefits from it**
Answer (2) is the correct and best answer because the article attempts to both explain the United States' refugee program and describe who benefits from it. Answer (1) is incorrect because although the article mentions the United Nations High Commissioner for Refugees, this is not the main idea of the article. Answers (3) and (4) are incorrect because they describe what the United States government attempts to do rather than what the article attempts to do. Answer (5) is incorrect because the goal of the article is to inform, not to inspire.
(H) Drawing Conclusions and Making Interpretations

27. **(5) One bundle contains the father's only child.**
Answers (1), (2), (3), and (4) are all true statements according to the passage, but (5) is the only false statement and therefore is the correct answer to the question. The passage states that one bundle was "*not* his only child." **(H) Summarizing**

28. **(3) concerned with his looks**
The father is described as being a "very vain" man. The narrator says that he was poor, so (1) cannot be correct. There is no evidence to support answers (2), (4), and (5) in the passage. **(H) Character and Motivation**

29. **(1) his laundress**
Answer (1) is correct because the narrator states that her father "placed me in the care of the same woman he paid to wash his clothes." There is no evidence to support answers (2), (4), or (5). The narrator says that Eunice Paul is not "a relative of my mother's," so answer (3) cannot be correct. **(H) Summarizing**

CHAPTER

8

PRACTICE
TESTS

THE
GED

LANGUAGE
ARTS,
READING

30. **(3) She can nurse and feed the child**

Answer (3) is correct. Eunice Paul "still had some milk in her breast," so she was able to nurse and feed the narrator. Answer (1) is a personal judgment, not a reason. Answer (2) is a true statement, according to the passage, but there is no evidence to suggest that this is the reason the father gives his daughter to Eunice Paul. Answer (4) is incorrect because the father does not know how to take care of the child by himself. There is no evidence to support answer (5). 🅗 **Character and Motivation**

31. **(2) serious**

Answer (2) is correct. The pace of the passage is slow, and there is no sense of information being withheld, so answer (1) cannot be correct. The passage does not contain any love or romantic elements, or characteristics of adventure or comedy, so answers (3), (4), and (5) are incorrect. 🅗 **Mood, Tone, and Style**

32. **(4) She will have conflicted feelings about her childhood.**

Answer (4) is correct because the narrator describes herself as a baby as "irritable" and "unable to console" herself, as well as being "in tears." Answer (1) is incorrect because the narrator refuses to drink Eunice Paul's milk as a child. Answer (2) is incorrect because the narrator describes herself as a "burden" to her father. Answer (3) is incorrect because the narrator cries at the sight of her new surroundings. There is no evidence in this excerpt to support answer (5).
🅗 **Drawing Conclusions and Making Interpretations**

33. **(5) Part-time employment allows teens to explore future careers.**

Answer (5) is correct. It is one of the reasons listed in the article that employment can be a "valuable experience." Answers (1) and (3) describe two of the negative aspects of employment for teens. Answer (2) is not a benefit but simply a statement about the average length of time per week that teens work. Answer (4) is also not a benefit but a statement about the role of teens in the workforce. 🅗 **Summarizing**

34. **(1) a hardware store**

Answer (1) is correct because it is a specific type of retail shop. According to the article, the "workplaces that employ the most teens" include retail shops, restaurants, and grocery stores. Answers (2), (3), (4), and (5) are incorrect because they are dangerous jobs that youths are *prohibited* from holding: mining, manufacturing, and construction. 🅗 **Summarizing**

35. **(2) Most injuries by working teenagers in the United States occur at construction sites.**

Answer (2) is correct. It represents a statement that is false according to the information provided in this article. While answers (1), (2), (4), and (5) all quote statements made in the article, answer (2) suggests that most injuries among teens occur at construction sites. Because the article says that teens are prohibited from working construction jobs, this statement cannot be true. 🅗 **Summarizing**

36. **(1) Teens often go to work after putting in a full day at school.**

Answer (1) is correct. We can infer that teens may be tired after going to school all day and then going to work, where they may be fatigued and less attentive. Answer (2) is incorrect because teens are prohibited from holding the most dangerous jobs. Answer (3) is incorrect because teens are young and therefore not highly experienced. Answer (4) is not a reason but a statement about the kinds of injuries received by teens. Answer (5) describes a benefit of part-time employment for teens, not a reason they are injured. **ⓗ Drawing Conclusions and Making Interpretations**

37. **(5) both 2 and 4**

Answer (5) is correct because it includes both (2) and (4), which inform the reader about the problem of young worker safety and also alert the reader to needs for increased prevention among young workers. Answer (1) is incorrect because the article does not discuss job opportunities. Answer (3) is incorrect because the article does not focus on the mining industry. **ⓗ Main Ideas and Supporting Details**

38. **(2) a gentleman who becomes an actor**

Answer (2) is correct because Yegor describes himself as being like the gentleman who becomes an actor and afterward cannot make it as a landowner or official. Answers (1) is incorrect because Yegor mentions using a fishing-hook but does not compare himself to the hook. Answer (3) is incorrect because Yegor compares himself to a horse-dealer who cannot go back to the plough, not as one who misses the plough. Answer (4) is incorrect because this is what Yegor calls the woman. Answer (5) is incorrect because this is what Yegor imagines the woman thinks of him.
ⓗ Figurative Language and Other Poetic Elements

39. **(4) Yegor thinks the woman cannot understand why he lives the way he does.**

Answer (4) is correct. The woman does not understand why Yegor chooses to live and work as he does. Answer (1) is incorrect because Yegor does not express a desire to be a landowner. Answer (2) is incorrect because the woman does not express jealousy over Yegor's work but instead says it is "not proper work" he is doing. Answer (3) is incorrect because Yegor looks down upon the woman's "village work." Answer (5) does not state the main idea of the story. **ⓗ Plot, Predictions, and Inferences**

40. **(3) Once a man has experienced something new and tantalizing, he cannot live life otherwise.**

Answer (3) describes the meaning behind Yegor's quote. Answer (1) is irrelevant to the idea that man experiences freedom and can never imagine life without it. Answers (2), (4), and (5) all directly contradict what Yegor says to the woman in his speech. **ⓗ Drawing Conclusions and Making Interpretations**

MATHEMATICS

Part I

Directions

This Mathematics test is designed to measure your general mathematics skills. The exam consists of multiple-choice questions as well as student-produced responses. Multiple-choice questions have five answer choices, only one of which is the correct answer. Most student-produced responses are placed in a grid like the one shown on page 502. Be sure to grid your answers according to the directions on that page.

Spend no more than 45 minutes answering the twenty-five questions on this part of the test. You may detach the appropriate answer sheet at the back of this book and use it to mark your responses.

Calculators may be used on Part I of the Mathematics test. You may not use a calculator on Part II.

Some questions provide sufficient information needed to solve the problems. Other questions do not. If not enough information is provided to solve a problem definitively, choose the answer choice marked "Not enough information is given."

Various formulas can be found at the beginning of each part of the Math exam. These formulas may be useful in solving some problems. Not every formula given is needed on the exam.

When you are finished, review the Answers and Explanations section on page 515 to determine whether you are ready to take the Mathematics test or need additional review in specific areas.

Directions for Answering Student-Produced Responses

These questions require you to fill in the answer on a grid like the one shown below:

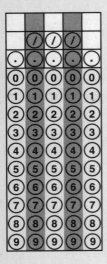

Here are the steps you must remember when filling in an answer:

1. Start writing your answer in any column that will allow your answer to be entered correctly.
2. Write your answer on the space provided above the grid.
3. In the column beneath your written answer, darken in the appropriate circle (number, fraction bar, or decimal point) that corresponds to the written answer above.
4. Always darken in the circles completely.
5. Never darken more than one circle in any column.
6. Leave all unused columns blank.

Answers that are simple fractions may be entered as either fractions or decimals. For example, the fraction 1/5 (0.20 in decimal form) may be gridded in the following ways:

  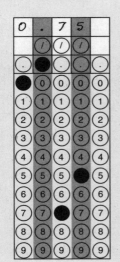 

Additional Points to Remember

1. There are no negative signs to be used. All answers are positive.
2. Mixed numbers like 3 1/5 may not be entered into the grid in fraction form. They must be converted to decimal form such as 3.2 or 3.20.
3. There may be more than one correct answer for a problem. Grid in only one of the correct answers.

FORMULAS

AREA of a:

square	Area = side^2
rectangle	Area = length × width
parallelogram	Area = base × height
triangle	Area = $\frac{1}{2}$ × base × height
trapezoid	Area = $\frac{1}{2}$ × (base$_1$ + base$_2$) × height
circle	Area = π × radius^2; π is approximately equal to 3.14

PERIMETER of a:

square	Perimeter = 4 × side
rectangle	Perimeter = 2 × length + 2 × width
triangle	Perimeter = side$_1$ + side$_2$ + side$_3$

CIRCUMFERENCE of a circle　　Circumference = π × diameter; π is approximately equal to 3.14

VOLUME of a:

cube	Volume = edge^3
rectangular container	Volume = length × width × height
square pyramid	Volume = $\frac{1}{3}$ × (base edge)^2 × height
cylinder	Volume = π × radius^2 × height; π is approximately equal to 3.14
cone	Volume = $\frac{1}{3}$ × π × radius^2 × height; π is approximately equal to 3.14

COORDINATE GEOMETRY

distance between points = $\sqrt{(x_2 - x_1)^2 + (y_2 - y_1)^2}$; (x_1, y_1) and (x_2, y_2) are two points in a plane

slope of a line = $\frac{y_2 - y_1}{x_2 - x_1}$; (x_1, y_1) and (x_2, y_2) are two points on a line

PYTHAGOREAN RELATIONSHIP

$a^2 + b^2 + c^2$; a and b are legs and c is the hypotenuse of a right triangle

MEASURES OF CENTRAL TENDENCY

mean = $\dfrac{x_1 + x_2 + \ldots + x_n}{n}$; where x's are the values for which a mean is desired, and n is the total number of values for x

SIMPLE INTEREST　　interest = principal × rate × time

DISTANCE　　distance = rate × time

TOTAL COST　　total cost = (number of units) × (price per unit)

Directions: You have 45 minutes to answer the twenty-five questions that follow. You may use you calculator on this section.

1. In four years, Jenna's age will be half her brother's. If Jenna's brother will be 16 at that time, what is Jenna's age now?

   (1) 1
   (2) 2
   (3) 4
   (4) 6
   (5) 8

Question 2 refers to the following chart.

Cleaning Supplies	
Item	**Cost per case**
Light bulbs	$11.98
Cleaning solution	$17.48
Trash bags	$15.98

2. Fredrick oversees the maintenance of an office building. The chart above shows the cost of cleaning supplies per case. Fredrick orders two cases of light bulbs and half a case of trash bags. Which expression shows how to find the cost of the order?

   (1) $(11.98 \times 2) + (15.98 \div 2)$
   (2) $(11.98 \div 2) + (15.98 \times 2)$
   (3) $(11.98 \times 2) + (15.98 \times 2)$
   (4) $(11.98 + 15.98) \times 2$
   (5) $2(11.98 + 15.98) \div 2$

3. Find the missing number in this series: 1, 4, 9, 16, 25, 36, _____, 64. Enter your answer on the alternate format grid.

Question 4 refers to the following diagram.

4. When plotted on the grid below, which two points will complete the corners of a square?

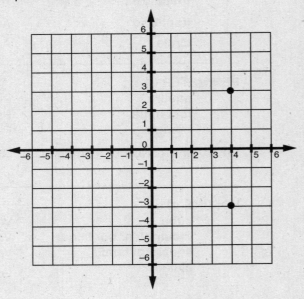

Plot your answers on the coordinate plane grid on your answer sheet.

Question 5 refers to the following diagram.

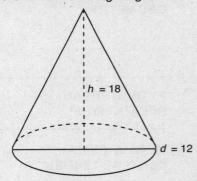

5. Which expression calculates the volume of the cone?

   (1) $(3.14 \times 6^2 \times 18) \div 3$
   (2) $(3.14 \times 12^2 \times 18) \div 3$
   (3) $3.14 \times 36 \times 18$
   (4) $3.14 \times 144 \times 18$
   (5) $(3.14 \times 6 \times 18) \div 3$

6. Which of the following is true if $3x + 4 < x + 12$?

   (1) $x > 4$
   (2) $x < 4$
   (3) $x = 7$
   (4) $x > 10$
   (5) $x > 12$

Question 7 refers to the following diagram.

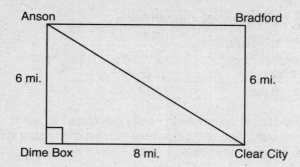

7. Terry drove from Anson to Clear City, and then to Bradford. How many miles did she drive in all?

    (1) 10
    (2) 16
    (3) 18
    (4) 20
    (5) 36

8. Six babies in the hospital nursery weighed 6 lb, 12 oz; 5 lb, 12 oz; 7 lb, 8 oz; 9 lb, 2 oz; 5 lb, 4 oz; and 9 lb, 9 oz. What is the <u>approximate</u> range (to the nearest pound) for the births?

    (1) 5
    (2) 6
    (3) 7
    (4) 8
    (5) 9

9. What are the two factors of $x^2 - 5x - 6$?
    (1) $(x + 1)(x - 6)$
    (2) $(x + 2)(x - 3)$
    (3) $(x - 1)(x + 6)$
    (4) $(x - 3)(x - 3)$
    (5) $(x - 1)(x - 6)$

10. This Wednesday, Darlene's ice cream stand sold $3\frac{1}{2}$ gallons of chocolate ice cream and $4\frac{7}{8}$ gallons of vanilla. What was the total amount of ice cream sold?

    (1) 1.375 gallons
    (2) 7.80 gallons
    (3) 7.9 gallons
    (4) 8.2 gallons
    (5) 8.375 gallons

Question 11 refers to the following diagram.

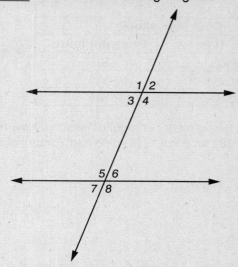

11. The measure of $\angle 1$ is 127°. Which of the following statements is true?

    (1) $m\angle 4$, $m\angle 7$, and $m\angle 8$ are congruent.
    (2) The $m\angle 2$ and $m\angle 3$ are also 127°.
    (3) The $m\angle 5$ and $m\angle 8$ are also 127°.
    (4) The $m\angle 1 + m\angle 4 = 180°$.
    (5) The $m\angle 2 + m\angle 6 < 90°$.

12. In the equation $y^2 - y = 0$, which pair of numbers are possible values for y?

    (1) −2 and −1
    (2) −2 and 0
    (3) −1 and −2
    (4) 1 and 0
    (5) 2 and −1

13. A farmer wishes to divide his land into pastures of equal acreage. If he has 15 acres and wants each pasture to be $\frac{3}{4}$ acre, how many pastures will he have?

    (1) 11
    (2) $14\frac{1}{4}$
    (3) $15\frac{3}{4}$
    (4) 20
    (5) 180

14. Emily pays $36 for cable each month. What is the total cost, in dollars, of her cable service in a one-year period? Disregard the dollar sign when you enter your answer on the alternate format grid.

Questions 15 and 16 refer to the following chart.

Cost of Lessons	
Lesson Type	Price per hour
Piano	$16
Voice	$25
Guitar	$19

15. Darla is taking piano, and guitar lessons. How much will she pay for 8 hours of voice and 7 hours of piano?

    (1) $41
    (2) $60
    (3) $303
    (4) $312
    (5) $328

16. Darla later took 12 hours of guitar lessons. If she paid $150 toward the guitar bill, how much does she still owe?

    (1) $42
    (2) $78
    (3) $138
    (4) $228
    (5) $378

17. A farmer flips a quarter twice. What is the probability that the quarter will come up heads both times?

    (1) $\frac{1}{2}$
    (2) $\frac{1}{4}$
    (3) $\frac{3}{4}$
    (4) $\frac{2}{4}$
    (5) $\frac{2}{2}$

18. The scenic route is $28\frac{1}{4}$ miles long. If Dan has already driven 11.90 miles of it, how much further does he have to go? Show your answer on the alternate format grid.

Questions 19 and 20 refer to the following chart.

Dave's Hourly Commission	
9:00 a.m.	$38.13
10:00 a.m.	$46.94
1:00 p.m.	$25.82
2:00 p.m.	$13.05

19. Dave is paid commission each hour based on work completed. Approximately how much did he make on this day before noon?

    (1) $40
    (2) $75
    (3) $85
    (4) $110
    (5) $124

20. Dave's car payment is $199. After the morning's work, how much will he still need to earn during the afternoon to make his car payment?

    (1) $75.06
    (2) $85.07
    (3) $88.11
    (4) $113.93
    (5) $123.94

21. Which operation shows the conversion of 20 kilometers to meters?

    (1) 20 × 1,000
    (2) 20 ÷ 100
    (3) 20 ÷ 1,000
    (4) 20 × 100
    (5) 20 + 1,000

22. A business bought 12 computer systems at a total cost of $5,388, not including taxes. The systems are identical in format and price. What is the cost of each system *after an 8% tax is added*?

    (1) $35.92
    (2) $431.00
    (3) $449.00
    (4) $484.92
    (5) $5,819.04

23. Of the 48 soccer goals Emily attempted this season, she made 75%. How many goal attempts were unsuccessful?

(1) 12
(2) 24
(3) 36
(4) 60
(5) 123

Question 24 refers to the following chart.

Movie Palace Attendance		
Movie	**Friday**	**Saturday**
Renegade	369	378
A Hamster's Life	404	303
Twin Bridges	218	326

24. One of the movies at the Movie Palace dropped in attendance this weekend from Friday to Saturday. What percentage did it drop?

(1) 9%
(2) 25%
(3) 101%
(4) 108%
(5) 120%

25. Eric's aquarium measures 24 inches long, 10 inches wide, and 12 inches high. How many <u>cubic inches</u> of water will completely fill it? Enter your answer on the alternate format grid.

Part II

Directions

This simulated Mathematics test is designed to measure your general mathematics skills. The exam consists of multiple-choice questions as well as student-produced responses. Multiple-choice questions have five answer choices, only one of which is the correct answer. Most student-produced responses are placed in a grid like the one shown on page 509. Be sure to grid your answers according to the directions on that page.

Spend no more than 45 minutes answering the twenty-five questions on this part of the test. You may detach the appropriate answer sheet at the back of this book and use it to mark your responses.

Calculators may NOT be used on Part II of the Mathematics test.

Some questions provide sufficient information needed to solve the problems. Other questions do not. If not enough information is provided to solve a problem definitively, choose the answer choice marked "Not enough information is given."

Various formulas can be found at the beginning of each part of the Math exam. These formulas may be useful in solving some problems. Not every formula given is needed on the exam.

When you are finished, review the Answers and Explanations section on page 519 to determine whether you are ready to take the Mathematics test or need additional review in specific areas.

Directions for Answering Student-Produced Responses

These questions require you to fill in the answer on a grid like the one shown below:

Here are the steps you must remember when gridding in an answer:

1. Start writing your answer in any column that will allow your answer to be entered correctly.
2. Write your answer on the space provided above the grid.
3. In the column beneath your written answer, darken in the appropriate circle (number, fraction bar, or decimal point) that corresponds to the written answer above.
4. Always darken in the circles completely.
5. Never darken more than one circle in any column.
6. Leave all unused columns blank.

Answers that are simple fractions may be entered as either fractions or decimals. For example, the fraction 1/5 (0.20 in decimal form) may be gridded in the following ways:

Additional Points to Remember

1. There are no negative signs to be used. All answers are positive.
2. Mixed numbers like 3 1/5 may not be entered into the grid in fraction form. They must be converted to decimal form such as 3.2 or 3.20.
3. There may be more than one correct answer for a problem. Grid in only one of the correct answers.

FORMULAS

AREA of a:

square	Area = side^2
rectangle	Area = length × width
parallelogram	Area = base × height
triangle	Area = $\frac{1}{2}$ × base × height
trapezoid	Area = $\frac{1}{2}$ × (base$_1$ + base$_2$) × height
circle	Area = π × radius^2; π is approximately equal to 3.14

PERIMETER of a:

square	Perimeter = 4 × side
rectangle	Perimeter = 2 × length + 2 × width
triangle	Perimeter = side$_1$ + side$_2$ + side$_3$

CIRCUMFERENCE of a circle   Circumference = π × diameter; π is approximately equal to 3.14

VOLUME of a:

cube	Volume = edge^3
rectangular container	Volume = length × width × height
square pyramid	Volume = $\frac{1}{3}$ × (base edge)^2 × height
cylinder	Volume = π × radius^2 × height; π is approximately equal to 3.14
cone	Volume = $\frac{1}{3}$ × π × radius^2 × height; π is approximately equal to 3.14

COORDINATE GEOMETRY

distance between points = $\sqrt{(x_2 - x_1)^2 + (y_2 - y_1)^2}$; (x_1, y_1) and (x_2, y_2) are two points in a plane

slope of a line = $\dfrac{y_2 - y_1}{x_2 - x_1}$; (x_1, y_1) and (x_2, y_2) are two points on a line

PYTHAGOREAN RELATIONSHIP

$a^2 + b^2 + c^2$; a and b are legs and c is the hypotenuse of a right triangle

MEASURES OF CENTRAL TENDENCY

mean = $\dfrac{x_1 + x_2 + \ldots + x_n}{n}$; where x's are the values for which a mean is desired, and n is the total number of values for x

SIMPLE INTEREST   interest = principal × rate × time

DISTANCE   distance = rate × time

TOTAL COST   total cost = (number of units) × (price per unit)

Part II

Directions: You have 45 minutes to answer the twenty-five questions that follow. You may NOT use you calculator on this section.

26. Tina, Andrea, and two other friends plan to share apartment expenses equally. The total apartment bills are $824 each month. Which operation shows the amount each person will pay for her share?

    (1) 824 ÷ 4
    (2) 4 × 824
    (3) 4 + 824
    (4) 824 − 4
    (5) 4 ÷ 824

Question 27 refers to the following chart.

Bonus Chart	
Bonus Level	Sales
Level 1	$130–430
Level 2	$431–503
Level 3	$504–598
Level 4	$599–630

27. Ronny works at a company that pays bonuses based on weekly sales. What will Ronny's bonus level be this week if he has sales of $530?

    (1) Level 1
    (2) Level 2
    (3) Level 3
    (4) Level 4
    (5) He will earn no bonus this week.

28. Andrew's Appleworks purchased 9,600 tons of apples. Sixty percent of that purchase was turned into applesauce. How many tons of apples were used for applesauce production?

    (1) 3840
    (2) 5760
    (3) 6900
    (4) 9540
    (5) 9660

29. River City has 25,876 stop signs. Last year, 3,390 of them had to be replaced. About how many stop signs did NOT have to be replaced?

    (1) 13,000
    (2) 21,000
    (3) 23,000
    (4) 29,000
    (5) 30,000

Question 30 refers to the following diagram.

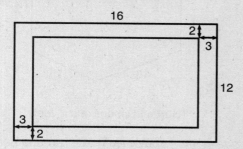

30. What is the area of the interior rectangle in the figure above?

    (1) 80
    (2) 112
    (3) 130
    (4) 192
    (5) 272

31. The proposed highway around the city will be $23\frac{3}{8}$ miles when completed. If $10\frac{1}{2}$ miles are already finished, how many miles are left to build?

    (1) $12\frac{7}{8}$
    (2) $13\frac{1}{8}$
    (3) $13\frac{2}{6}$
    (4) $33\frac{4}{10}$
    (5) $33\frac{7}{8}$

32. For the function, $y = 2x - 6$, what numbers are needed to complete the equation?

    (1) $x = 0$ and $y = -4$
    (2) $x = -4$ and $y = -6$
    (3) $x = -4$ and $y = -8$
    (4) $x = -2$ and $y = -10$
    (5) $x = -6$ and $y = 10$

33. Jim's Smokehouse cooked 251 pounds of beef on Saturday and 379 pounds of beef on Sunday. How many pounds of beef were cooked that weekend? Enter your answer on the alternate format grid.

Question 34 refers to the following diagram.

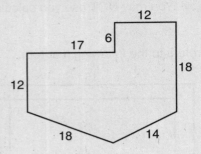

Garden Dimensions in feet.

34. Aimee wants to put a tile border around her garden. How many feet of tile will she need? Enter your answer on the alternate format grid.

35. Lakecreek Elementary had 25% of its 420 students absent due to the flu. Of the remaining students, 20% did not feel well. Which operation shows the number of students who did not feel well but were present at school?

(1) 420 × 0.75 − 0.20
(2) 420 × 0.25 × 0.20
(3) 420 ÷ 0.25 ÷ 0.20
(4) 420 × 0.75 × 0.20
(5) Not enough information is given

Questions 36 and 37 refer to the following chart.

Students in Risinger's Government Class	
Period 1	26
Period 2	18
Period 3	21
Period 5	30
Period 6	38
Period 8	47

36. What is the median number of students in Mr. Risinger's classes?

(1) 21
(2) 26
(3) 28
(4) 29
(5) 35

37. Calculate the average (mean) number of students in Mr. Risinger's classes. Enter your answer on the alternate format grid.

38. A rectangular parking lot measures 36 yards by 42 yards. Grass and trees take up 150 square yards in the lot. The rest is concrete. What operation shows the amount of concrete in square yards?

(1) (36 × 42) − 150
(2) (36 × 42) ÷ 150
(3) (36 × 42) + 150
(4) 150 − (36 + 42)
(5) (36 ÷ 150) + (42 ÷ 150)

39. Brittany bought a prepaid long-distance calling card that had 390 minutes on it. What is this amount in hours?

(1) 3 hours
(2) 4 hours
(3) $6\frac{1}{2}$ hours
(4) $8\frac{1}{2}$ hours
(5) 9 hours

Question 40 refers to the following diagram.

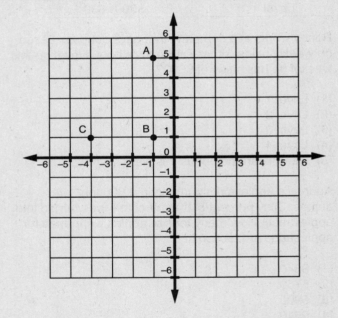

40. What is the linear distance between point A and point C?

(1) 3
(2) 4
(3) 5
(4) 9
(5) 25

41. Six cookies are in a cookie jar. Half of them have chocolate chips. Adam removes a cookie from the jar at random, without looking. Then, without replacing the first cookie, he removes a second. What is the probability that both cookies had chocolate chips?

(1) 20%
(2) 22%
(3) 50%
(4) 75%
(5) 80%

42. The measure of angle ABC is 27°. Which of the following statements is true about ∠ABC?

(1) ∠ABC is a right angle.
(2) ∠ABC is an obtuse angle.
(3) ∠ABC is an acute angle.
(4) ∠ABC is a reflex angle.
(5) Not enough information is given.

Question 43 refers to the following chart.

Students in After-School Classes at Deepwood Elementary			
	Cooking	Science	Art	Music
Monday		15		27
Tuesday	8	10	7	
Wednesday		11	14	
Thursday	10			45

43. How many <u>more</u> students are enrolled in music classes than in cooking and art classes combined? Enter your answer on the alternate format grid.

44. A nurse needs to set up a 1200-milliliter IV drip. How many liters will this be?

(1) 0.012 L
(2) 0.1200 L
(3) 1.200 L
(4) 12 L
(5) 120 L

45. Carolyn sells newspapers two days a week, for a weekly total of $196. Which operation shows how much she could make if she sold papers five days a week?

(1) $\frac{196}{2} \times 5$
(2) $196 \div 5$
(3) $\frac{2 \times 196}{5}$
(4) $2 \times 196 \times 5$
(5) $(196 \div 2) \div 5$

Question 46 refers to the following graph.

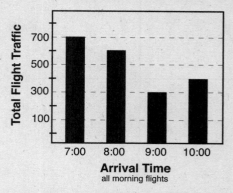

Flights into International Airport

46. What percentage of morning flights at International Airport arrived at 10:00?

(1) 10%
(2) 16%
(3) 20%
(4) 40%
(5) 80%

47. From its normal level, a lake rose 3 feet during the spring thaw, dropped 8 feet during the summer drought, and rose 6 feet during the fall rains. What is the lake's current condition?

(1) 5 feet above normal
(2) 2 feet above normal
(3) 1 foot above normal
(4) normal level
(5) −3 feet below normal

48. Which expression simplifies to $-2y + 3x$?

(1) $-10y + 10x - 7x + 8y$
(2) $x - 1x - 1x + 4y$
(3) $-2y + 2y - 1x - 2x$
(4) $2y - 4x + 1y + 6y$
(5) $-2x + 3y - 2x + 3y$

49. Three odd consecutive integers add to 69. What is the smallest integer? Enter your answer on the alternate format grid.

Question 50 refers to the following diagram.

Grocery Spinner

50. At the supermarket, shoppers spin the wheel
shown above to win free groceries. Every section
of the Grocery Spinner is of equal size. Using this
information, what is the probability that a shopper will
win a free pizza with only one spin?

(1) 3 in 10
(2) 1 in 4
(3) 2 in 12
(4) 3 in 4
(5) 4 in 12

MATHEMATICS PART I
ANSWERS AND EXPLANATIONS

CHAPTER

8

PRACTICE
TESTS

THE
GED

MATHEMATICS
PART I

1.　(3)　4

The proper algebraic equation must be set up and then solved. Make Jenna's current age the variable j. In four years, $(j + 4)$, Jenna will be half as old as her brother, who will be 16. This means $(j + 4) = \frac{16}{2}$. You divide 16 by 2 because Jenna will be half as old as her brother. Working the equation to solve for j, you find that $j = 4$, answer choice (3). ⊕ **Algebra**

2.　(1)　(11.98 x 2) + (15.98 ÷ 2)

The total of two light bulb cases is added to half of the price of a case of trash bags. Answer (2) uses half a case of light bulbs, and two cases of trash bags. Answers (3) and (4) use two cases of everything. Answer (5) buys two cases, and then divides by two cases. ⊕ **Measurement and Data Analysis**

3.　49 (grid in)

This pattern is a progression of squared numbers. $1^2 = 1$, $2^2 = 4$, $3^2 = 9$, and so forth. The number right before the blank is 36, or 6^2. The next number must be 7^2, which would make it 49. ⊕ **Algebra**

4.　The points (−2,3) and (−2,−3)

In a square, all sides are of equal length. The distance between the two points that you do know, (4,3) and (4,−3), is 6. You find this by subtracting the y-coordinates 3 and −3 so that $3 − (−3) = 3 + 3 = 6$. In a square, all four sides meet at rights angles, which means you must move six spaces directly to the left of each of the known points in order to find the unknown points. For the top point, the y-coordinate stays the same, but $4 − 6 = −2$, so the new x-coordinate is −2. The new point is at (−2,3). The y-coordinate stays the same for the bottom point as well, and $4 − 6 = −2$ again, so the last point is at (−2,−3). ⊕ **Geometry**

5.　(1)　$(3.14 \times 6^2 \times 18) \div 3$

The formula for a cone can be found in the formula chart at the beginning of the section. Answers (2) and (4) use diameter instead of the radius. Answer (3) does not divide by 3. Answer (5) does not square the radius. ⊕ **Geometry**

6.　(2)　$x < 4$

You solve the inequality in the following manner:

$3x + 4 < x + 12$

$3x + 4 − 4 < x + 12 − 4$

$3x < x + 8$

$3x − x < x − x + 8$

$2x < 8$

$\frac{2x}{2} < \frac{8}{2}$

$x < 4$. This is answer choice (2). ⊕ **Algebra**

CHAPTER

8

PRACTICE
TESTS

THE
GED

MATHEMATICS
PART I

7. (2) 16

The distance from Anson to Clear City (10 miles) is found using the Pythagorean theorem. This route is the hypotenuse of a right triangle with the other sides of length 6 miles and 8 miles respectively. Once you find the distance of the first leg, you must add the distance from Clear City to Bradford (6 miles). This gives you 16 miles total. Answer (1) finds only the distance between Anson and Clear City. Answer (5) is the hypotenuse. 🅗 **Geometry**

8. (1) 5

First, the pound amounts are rounded to the nearest pound. Those numbers are arranged from least to greatest. To find range, the least is subtracted from the greatest. The smallest baby is about 5 pounds, (5 lb, 4 oz), while the largest is close to 10 (9 lb, 9 oz). This gives you a range of $10 - 5 = 5$, answer (1). Answers (2), (3), (4), and (5) are amounts of pounds in rounded form. 🅗 **Measurement and Data Analysis**

9. (1) (x + 1) (x − 6)

You must use the FOIL method (First, Outside, Inside, Last) on the answer choices to find which one yields the expression. Answer (1) is correct: $x^2 - 5x - 6$. Answer (2) results in $x^2 - 1x - 6$. Answer (3) is $x^2 + 5x - 6$. Answer (4) is $x^2 - 6x - 9$. Answer (5) is $x^2 - 7x + 6$. 🅗 **Algebra**

10. (5) 8.375 gallons

The numbers are added to find a total.

(3.5 gallons) + (4.875 gallons) = 8.375

Using your calculator makes it very easy to convert these fractions into decimals. Answer (1) subtracts. Answers (2) and (3) incorrectly convert the improper fraction. 🅗 **Numbers and Operations**

11. (3) The mL5 and mL8 are also 127°.

∠5 and ∠8 are corresponding angles to ∠1, so they are all equal. In answer (1), m∠7 is not congruent. m∠2 and ∠3 are supplementary, not congruent, so answer (2) can be eliminated. Answer (4) is wrong because m∠1 + m∠4 would be 254°. m∠2 and ∠6 is 106°, which is not less than 90°, so answer (5) is wrong. 🅗 **Geometry**

12. (4) 1 and 0

There are five possible numbers you must plug into the equation: −2, −1, 0, 1, and 2. After trying each one, you should be able to look down and possibly eliminate some answer choices. For instance, once you try −2 and find that it does not work in the equation $y^2 - y = 0$, you can rule out choices (1), (2), and (3). From here, if you plug in $y = 0$ and discover that it does work in $y^2 - y = 0$, the answer must be (4). 🅗 **Algebra**

13. (4) 20

To find the number of different pastures, you must divide the total amount of acreage, 15, by the size of each pasture ($\frac{3}{4}$ acre). If you covert $\frac{3}{4}$ acre into the decimal 0.75, you can then punch into your calculator 15/0.75 = 20, answer (4). 🅗 **Numbers and Operations**

14. $ 432 (grid-in)

$36 is multiplied by 12 (the number of months in one year) to get $432.

⬡ **Whole Numbers and Basic Operations**

15. (4) $312

The cost for voice lessons is multiplied by 8, and the cost for piano lessons is multiplied by 7. These totals are added together. This gives the equation:

(8 hours voice)($25 an hour) + (7 hours piano)($16 an hour) =

$(8)(25) + (7)(16) =$

$200 + 112 = 312$

Answer (1) adds only the given numbers for piano and voice. Answers (2), (3), and (5) add the totals incorrectly. ⬡**Whole Numbers and Basic Operations**

16. (2) $78

The cost for guitar lessons is multiplied by 12, then $150 is subtracted from that total to find the amount that Darla still owes.

(12 hours guitar)($19 an hour) − (amount already paid) = what she stills owes

$(12)(19) − 150 =$ what she stills owes

$228 − 150 =$ what she stills owes

$78 =$ what she stills owes, answer (2).

Answer (4) is the total bill. Answer (5) adds another $150. Answers (1) and (3) subtract incorrectly. ⬡ **Whole Numbers and Basic Operations**

17. (2) $\frac{1}{4}$

Each event is expressed as a fraction, with the number of desired possibilities placed above the total number of possibilities. The fractions are then multiplied. On the first coin toss, the odds of the quarter landing on heads are $\frac{1}{2}$ (2 is the lower number, because there are two total possibilities, head or tails). The second coin toss has the same probability, $\frac{1}{2}$. Multiplying $\frac{1}{2}$ and $\frac{1}{2}$ yields $\frac{1}{4}$, which is answer choice (2).

⬡ **Fractions, Decimals, and Percentages**

18. 16.35 (grid in)

You want to avoid mixed numbers on alternate format questions, because you can't grid them in. Therefore, a good idea is to convert the mixed number $28\frac{1}{4}$ into the decimal 28.25. Dan has already driven 11.90, so to find the remaining miles, you subtract $28.25 − 11.90 = 16.35$.

⬡ **Beyond Counting Numbers: Fractions, Decimals, and Percentages**

19. (3) $85

First round the two payments for the hours before noon: $38.13 becomes $40, and $46.94 becomes $45. Adding these two estimates gives you $85, answer (3). Even if you had rounded $46.94 to $50, this choice is still the closest. Answers (4) and (5) total the entire day. ⬡ **Fractions, Decimals, and Percentages**

CHAPTER

8

PRACTICE
TESTS

THE
GED

MATHEMATICS
PART I

20. (4) $113.93

Here you must be more precise, but you do have a calculator. The morning's work is $38.13 + $46.94 = $85.07. Dave's car payment is $199, so he still needs to earn $199 − $85.07 = $113.93.

Answer (2) is the amount he has earned, while answer (5) forgets to borrow.

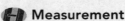 **Fractions, Decimals, and Percentages**

21. (1) 20 × 1,000

Conversion of kilometers to meters requires multiplying by 1,000. Answers (2), (3), and (5) use other operations, and answer (4) converts to decameters.

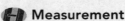 **Measurement**

22. (4) $484.92

The price of each system is identical, so you can divide the price of all computer systems by 12 to find the cost of a single system.

$5,388 ÷ 12 = $449. This is the cost of a single system.

Now multiply $449 by 0.08 to find the tax:

($449)(0.08) = $35.92

Add this number to the amount of a single system.

$449 + $35.92 = $484.92. This is the correct amount.

Answer (1) figures only the amount of tax. Answer (5) figures the amount of all 12 systems. 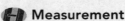 **Fractions, Decimals, and Percentages**

23. (1) 12

Multiply 48 by 0.75 to find the number of successful goals. This number, 36, is subtracted from 48 to find the number of unsuccessful goals. The answer is 48 − 36 = 12. You could also realize that if 75% of all attempted goals were successful, then 25% were unsuccessful, so (48)(0.25) would equal the number of unsuccessful goals. Of course, (48)(0.25) yields the answer 12 as well.

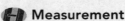 **Fractions, Decimals, and Percentages**

24. (2) 25%

In this multistep problem, you must first determine which movie experienced a decline in attendance from Friday to Saturday. The movie *A Hamster's Life* dipped from 404 to 303 viewers, so it's the movie in question. The difference in viewers is 404 − 303 = 101. Answer (3) might look appealing at this point, but the question asks for the *percentage* change, so you must determine what percent of 404 is 101. $\frac{101}{404} = \frac{1}{4}$, or 25%. This is answer (2).   **Fractions, Decimals, and Percentages**

25. 2880 (grid in)

To find the cubic volume of a rectangular solid like an aquarium, you multiply all the dimensions together.

(length)(width)(height) = total cubic inches

(24)(10)(12) = total cubic inches

2880 = total cubic inches

 Measurement

MATHEMATICS PART II
ANSWERS AND EXPLANATIONS

CHAPTER

8

PRACTICE
TESTS

THE
GED

MATHEMATICS
PART II

26. **(1)   824 ÷ 4**

With the first choice, the cost of the bill is divided equally among 4 people. The answer must be smaller than 824, so answers (2) and (3) are wrong.
(H) Whole Numbers and Basic Operations

27. **(3)   Level 3**

The number 530 falls within the range 504 to 598. This occurs under Level 3 on the table. **(H) Data Analysis**

28. **(2)   5,760**

This is a straightforward computation made a little more difficult without a calculator. To determine the amount of apples used for applesauce, multiply 9,600 tons by 60%: $(9600)(0.60) = 5,760$, answer (2). Answer (1) is the amount of apples not turned into applesauce. **(H) Fractions, Decimals, and Percentages**

29. **(3)   23,000**

The question underlines the word <u>about</u>, so you can round the numbers in the question to make computation easier: 25, 876 rounds to 26, 000 and 3, 390 rounds to 3, 000. The problem asks for the stop signs *not* replaced, these rounded numbers are then subtracted. $26,000 − 3,000 = 23,000$, answer (3). Answers (2) and (4) use incorrect rounding. Answer (5) uses addition instead of subtraction.
(H) Whole Numbers and Basic Operations

30. **(1)   80**

The area of a rectangle can be found using the formula (length)(width) = area. To find the length and width of the interior rectangle, you have to use the numbers given to you in the figure. These show that the length of the interior rectangle can be found by starting with the length of the outer rectangle, 16, and subtracting 3 twice. (There is a margin of 3 on both sides of the length, just as there is a margin of 2 on both sides of the width.)
Length of interior rectangle = $16 − 3 − 3 = 10$
Width of interior rectangle = $12 − 2 − 2 = 8$
You can now plug these values into the area formula:
(length)(width) = area
$(10)(8)$ = area
80 = area of the interior rectangle
(H) Geometry

31. **(1) $12\frac{7}{8}$**

The number of miles completed is subtracted from the total miles in order to find the number of miles left to build. The answer choices are in mixed fraction form, but it is easier to subtract decimals from each other. You can either convert the mixed

CHAPTER

8

PRACTICE
TESTS

THE
GED

MATHEMATICS
PART II

numbers into improper fractions and then subtract, or you can change them into decimals, do the computation, and then convert them back to mixed number form.

(total miles needed) − (miles already built) = miles left to build

$23.375 − 10.5 =$ miles left to build

$12.875 =$ miles left to build

You don't actually have to convert this decimal back into a mixed number, because there is only one answer choice that starts with the number 12, choice (1). Answers (2) and (3) forget to borrow. Answers (4) and (5) add the numbers.

 **Fractions, Decimals, and Percentages**

32. **(4)** $x = -2$ and $y = -10$

There's nothing fancy you can do here except try the answer choices. Keep plugging in the different values for x and y until you find a combination that yields a true solution. Using $x = -2$ and $y = -10$, you get

$y = 2x - 6$

$-10 = (2)(-2) - 6$

$-10 = -4 - 6$

$-10 = -10$

Answer (4) is the only choice in which the two values work.  **Algebra**

33. **630 (grid in)**

The question asks for the total amount of beef cooked on that weekend, so you must add the values for Saturday and Sunday together. $251 + 379 = 630$ is the answer.

 **Whole Numbers and Basic Operations**

34. **97 (grid in)**

Questions that ask for the perimeter of a geometric figure often require the use of a perimeter formula. However, in this case the garden is not a single geometric form, so no formula can be employed. Instead, you must simply move around the perimeter of the figure and add up all the different numbers in order to find the amount of tile that Aimee would need.

Starting at the top left corner of the figure, this gives you the equation:

$17 + 6 + 12 + 18 + 14 + 18 + 12 =$ perimeter

97 feet $=$ perimeter

 **Geometry**

35. **(4)** $420 × 0.75 × 0.20$

If 25% of the students are absent, then 75% (100 % − 25%) of the students must be at school. Considering the Lakecreek Elementary has 420 students, the number of students present would be found with the equation $(420)(0.75)$. You could determine what this value is if you had to, but the problem does not call for it. However, 20% of these students do not feel well, so the question now becomes, "What is 20% of $(420)(0.75)$?" $(420)(0.75)(0.20)$ is the same as $420 × 0.75 × 0.20$, the answer.

 **Fractions, Decimals, and Percentages**

36. (3) 28

The first step is to arrange the data from least to greatest. The middle number (or average of the two middle numbers in the case of two middle numbers) is the median. Students: 26, 18, 21, 30, 38, 47

Students arranged from least to greatest: 18, 21, 26, 30, 38, 47

The two middle values are 26 and 30. The average of these two numbers is 28, so answer (3) is the median value. Answer (1) would be used in determining range. Answers (2) and (4) are close to the middle, but they are not an average. **Data Analysis**

37. 30 (grid in)

To find the average (mean), you add up all the values and then divide this total by the number of values used. Mr. Risinger has six classes, so you add up all the students to find the total number of students in all classes, and then divide this number by 6 (the number of classes).

$(26 + 18 + 21 + 30 + 38 + 47)/6 = $ mean

$(180)/6 = $ mean

$30 = $ mean

Data Analysis

38. (1) (36 × 42) − 150

To find the area enclosed in concrete, you must find the total area and then subtract the amount covered by grass and trees. The total area is found by multiplying the dimensions together, so (36×42) must be part of the correct answer. Therefore, answers (4) and (5) must be incorrect. The amount covered by grass and trees, 150, is then subtracted. This is answer (1). **Geometry**

39. (3) $6\frac{1}{2}$ hours

This is a basic conversion problem. There are 60 minutes in every hour, so 390 minutes should be divided by 60 to yield $6\frac{1}{2}$ hours. **Measurement**

40. (3) 5

The linear distance from A to C can be found using the Pythagorean theorem. You can draw in the sides of the triangle with points A, B, and C to see the right triangle. The distance of AB is 4. (This is found by subtracting the y-coordinate value of B from the y-coordinate value for A: $5 - 1 = 4$.) The length of BC is found in a similar manner. In that case, the x-coordinates are subtracted:

$-4 - (-1) = -4 + 1 = -3$. Because distances cannot be negative, this value is simply 3. You now have a right triangle with sides 3 and 4. Placing these values into the Pythagorean theorem,

$a^2 + b^2 = c^2$

$(3)^2 + (4)^2 = c^2$

$9 + 16 = c^2$

$25 = c^2$

$5 = c$

The distance between A and C is the length of the hypotenuse, 5. **Geometry**

CHAPTER

8

PRACTICE
TESTS

THE
GED

MATHEMATICS
PART II

41. (1) 20%

Each event is expressed as a fraction, with the number of desired possibilities placed above the total number of possibilities. The fractions are then multiplied. The first time a cookie is drawn, there is a $\frac{3}{6}$ probability of its being chocolate chip. The second time, the probability is $\frac{2}{5}$, because there are two chocolate chip cookies left out of the five remaining cookies.

$\frac{3}{6} \times \frac{2}{5} = \frac{6}{30}$.

$\frac{6}{30}$ is also $\frac{1}{5}$, and that equals 20%.

Answer (3) assumes the cookies have an equal chance. Answers (4) and (5) do not include subtraction. **⊕ Fractions, Decimals, and Percentages**

42. (3) ∠ABC is an acute angle.

This is a definitional problem. If you know the names of the different angles, this one will not be much trouble. All angles less than 90° are acute angles, so the answer is (3). Answer (1) would be an angle equal to 90°. Answer (2) is any angle over 90° but less than 180°. Answer (4) would be an angle greater than 90° but less than 360°. **⊕ Geometry**

43.   33 (grid-in)

The chart provides the numbers you need.

Total music students = 27 (Monday) + 45 (Thursday) = 72

Total cooking students = 8 (Tuesday) + 10 (Thursday) = 18

Total art students = 7 + 14 = 21

Cooking and art students combined = 18 + 21 = 39

You need to find how many <u>more</u> are in music than in cooking and art combined, so $72 - 39 = 33$ students. **⊕ Whole Numbers and Basic Operations**

44. (3) 1.200 L

Conversion from milliliters to liters requires dividing by 1,000, or remembering that there are 1,000 milliliters in a liter. Therefore, 1,200 milliliters is 1.200 liters. Answers (1) and (2) are too small, and answers (4) and (5) are too large. **⊕ Measurement**

45. (1) $\dfrac{196}{2} \times 5$

Dividing 196 by 2 shows the total for one day. Multiplying that result by 5 shows the amount for 5 days. Only answer (1) divides and then multiplies. **⊕ Fractions, Decimals, and Percentages**

46. (3) 20%

Divide the total number of morning flights by the number of flights at 10:00. Total morning flights can be found by adding up the four bar graphs.

(7:00 flights) + (8:00 flights) + (9:00 flights) + (10:00 flights) = total morning flights

700 + 600 + 300 + 400 = total morning flights

2,000 = total morning flights

Flights at 10:00 are 400. To find the percentage of flights at 10:00, place 400 over 2,000.

This equals $\frac{1}{5}$. Expressed as a percentage, $\frac{1}{5} = 20\%$, because $\frac{1}{5} = \frac{20}{100}$, and percent means "by 100." 🌐 **Fractions, Decimals, and Percentages**

47. (3) **1 foot above normal**

Using a number line can help on this problem. Start at 0, and then add and subtract as indicated. First add 3, then subtract 8, and finally add 6.

$0 + 3 - 8 + 6 = 1$

This gives you answer (3).

Answer (1) subtracts 3 from 5. Answer (2) forgets to count zero as a level.

🌐 **Whole Numbers and Basic Operations**

48. (1) **−10y + 10x − 7x + 8y**

You might want to tackle this problem one variable at a time. This can save you some seconds and still lead you to the right answer. Start with either variable. For this example, begin with x. The goal is to find an expression that, after adding or subtracting, yields $3x$. Answers (1) and (3) do this, but answers (2), (4), and (5) do not, so they can be ruled out. You now only have to check two answer choices to find the correct y value. Answer (3) gives an incorrect value with no y, while answer (1) yields the correct $-2y$. 🌐 **Algebra**

49. **21 (grid-in)**

You can set up an algebraic expression to solve this problem. Numbers that are consecutive and odd increase by 2, so three in a row would look like this:

$x, \ x + 2, \ x + 4$

Added together, these three numbers equal 69, so:

$(x) + (x + 2) + (x + 4) = 69$

$3x + 6 = 69$

$3x + 6 - 6 = 69 - 6$

$3x = 63$

$\frac{3x}{3} = \frac{63}{3}$

$x = 21$

🌐 **Algebra**

50. (2) **1 in 4**

The number of desired possibilities is placed above the total number of possibilities. There are three "free pizzas" and 12 possible spaces on which to land: $\frac{3}{12}$ can be reduced to $\frac{1}{4}$, so the possibility is 1 in 4 that the spinner will land on free pizza. Answers (1) and (5) incorrectly count the possibilities in the denominator. Answers (3) and (4) incorrectly count the numerator possibilities.

🌐 **Fractions, Decimals, and Percent**

CHAPTER
8

PRACTICE TESTS

THE
GED

MATHEMATICS
PART II

ANSWER SHEETS

Language Arts, Writing Part I

1 ① ② ③ ④ ⑤   11 ① ② ③ ④ ⑤   21 ① ② ③ ④ ⑤   31 ① ② ③ ④ ⑤   41 ① ② ③ ④ ⑤

2 ① ② ③ ④ ⑤   12 ① ② ③ ④ ⑤   22 ① ② ③ ④ ⑤   32 ① ② ③ ④ ⑤   42 ① ② ③ ④ ⑤

3 ① ② ③ ④ ⑤   13 ① ② ③ ④ ⑤   23 ① ② ③ ④ ⑤   33 ① ② ③ ④ ⑤   43 ① ② ③ ④ ⑤

4 ① ② ③ ④ ⑤   14 ① ② ③ ④ ⑤   24 ① ② ③ ④ ⑤   34 ① ② ③ ④ ⑤   44 ① ② ③ ④ ⑤

5 ① ② ③ ④ ⑤   15 ① ② ③ ④ ⑤   25 ① ② ③ ④ ⑤   35 ① ② ③ ④ ⑤   45 ① ② ③ ④ ⑤

6 ① ② ③ ④ ⑤   16 ① ② ③ ④ ⑤   26 ① ② ③ ④ ⑤   36 ① ② ③ ④ ⑤   46 ① ② ③ ④ ⑤

7 ① ② ③ ④ ⑤   17 ① ② ③ ④ ⑤   27 ① ② ③ ④ ⑤   37 ① ② ③ ④ ⑤   47 ① ② ③ ④ ⑤

8 ① ② ③ ④ ⑤   18 ① ② ③ ④ ⑤   28 ① ② ③ ④ ⑤   38 ① ② ③ ④ ⑤   48 ① ② ③ ④ ⑤

9 ① ② ③ ④ ⑤   19 ① ② ③ ④ ⑤   29 ① ② ③ ④ ⑤   39 ① ② ③ ④ ⑤   49 ① ② ③ ④ ⑤

10 ① ② ③ ④ ⑤   20 ① ② ③ ④ ⑤   30 ① ② ③ ④ ⑤   40 ① ② ③ ④ ⑤   50 ① ② ③ ④ ⑤

```
┌─────────────────────────────────────────────────────────────────────┐
│                              TOPIC A                                   │
│                                                                       │
│   Do you think cities are good places for people to live in?          │
│                                                                       │
│   Write an essay explaining the advantages or disadvantages of living │
│   in a city. Use your personal observations, experience, and          │
│   knowledge to support your view.                                      │
│                                                                       │
└─────────────────────────────────────────────────────────────────────┘
```

Part II is a test to determine how well you can use written language to explain your ideas.

In preparing your essay, you should take the following steps:

- Read the DIRECTIONS and the TOPIC carefully.
- Plan your essay before you write. Use the scratch paper provided to make any notes. These notes will be collected but not scored.
- Before you turn in your essay, reread what you have written and make any changes that will improve your essay.

_____

_____

_____

_____

_____

_____

_____

_____

_____

_____

_____

_____

_____

_____

Social Studies

1 ① ② ③ ④ ⑤   11 ① ② ③ ④ ⑤   21 ① ② ③ ④ ⑤   31 ① ② ③ ④ ⑤   41 ① ② ③ ④ ⑤

2 ① ② ③ ④ ⑤   12 ① ② ③ ④ ⑤   22 ① ② ③ ④ ⑤   32 ① ② ③ ④ ⑤   42 ① ② ③ ④ ⑤

3 ① ② ③ ④ ⑤   13 ① ② ③ ④ ⑤   23 ① ② ③ ④ ⑤   33 ① ② ③ ④ ⑤   43 ① ② ③ ④ ⑤

4 ① ② ③ ④ ⑤   14 ① ② ③ ④ ⑤   24 ① ② ③ ④ ⑤   34 ① ② ③ ④ ⑤   44 ① ② ③ ④ ⑤

5 ① ② ③ ④ ⑤   15 ① ② ③ ④ ⑤   25 ① ② ③ ④ ⑤   35 ① ② ③ ④ ⑤   45 ① ② ③ ④ ⑤

6 ① ② ③ ④ ⑤   16 ① ② ③ ④ ⑤   26 ① ② ③ ④ ⑤   36 ① ② ③ ④ ⑤   46 ① ② ③ ④ ⑤

7 ① ② ③ ④ ⑤   17 ① ② ③ ④ ⑤   27 ① ② ③ ④ ⑤   37 ① ② ③ ④ ⑤   47 ① ② ③ ④ ⑤

8 ① ② ③ ④ ⑤   18 ① ② ③ ④ ⑤   28 ① ② ③ ④ ⑤   38 ① ② ③ ④ ⑤   48 ① ② ③ ④ ⑤

9 ① ② ③ ④ ⑤   19 ① ② ③ ④ ⑤   29 ① ② ③ ④ ⑤   39 ① ② ③ ④ ⑤   49 ① ② ③ ④ ⑤

10 ① ② ③ ④ ⑤   20 ① ② ③ ④ ⑤   30 ① ② ③ ④ ⑤   40 ① ② ③ ④ ⑤   50 ① ② ③ ④ ⑤

Science

1 ① ② ③ ④ ⑤   11 ① ② ③ ④ ⑤   21 ① ② ③ ④ ⑤   31 ① ② ③ ④ ⑤   41 ① ② ③ ④ ⑤

2 ① ② ③ ④ ⑤   12 ① ② ③ ④ ⑤   22 ① ② ③ ④ ⑤   32 ① ② ③ ④ ⑤   42 ① ② ③ ④ ⑤

3 ① ② ③ ④ ⑤   13 ① ② ③ ④ ⑤   23 ① ② ③ ④ ⑤   33 ① ② ③ ④ ⑤   43 ① ② ③ ④ ⑤

4 ① ② ③ ④ ⑤   14 ① ② ③ ④ ⑤   24 ① ② ③ ④ ⑤   34 ① ② ③ ④ ⑤   44 ① ② ③ ④ ⑤

5 ① ② ③ ④ ⑤   15 ① ② ③ ④ ⑤   25 ① ② ③ ④ ⑤   35 ① ② ③ ④ ⑤   45 ① ② ③ ④ ⑤

6 ① ② ③ ④ ⑤   16 ① ② ③ ④ ⑤   26 ① ② ③ ④ ⑤   36 ① ② ③ ④ ⑤   46 ① ② ③ ④ ⑤

7 ① ② ③ ④ ⑤   17 ① ② ③ ④ ⑤   27 ① ② ③ ④ ⑤   37 ① ② ③ ④ ⑤   47 ① ② ③ ④ ⑤

8 ① ② ③ ④ ⑤   18 ① ② ③ ④ ⑤   28 ① ② ③ ④ ⑤   38 ① ② ③ ④ ⑤   48 ① ② ③ ④ ⑤

9 ① ② ③ ④ ⑤   19 ① ② ③ ④ ⑤   29 ① ② ③ ④ ⑤   39 ① ② ③ ④ ⑤   49 ① ② ③ ④ ⑤

10 ① ② ③ ④ ⑤   20 ① ② ③ ④ ⑤   30 ① ② ③ ④ ⑤   40 ① ② ③ ④ ⑤   50 ① ② ③ ④ ⑤

Language Arts, Reading

1 ① ② ③ ④ ⑤	11 ① ② ③ ④ ⑤	21 ① ② ③ ④ ⑤	31 ① ② ③ ④ ⑤
2 ① ② ③ ④ ⑤	12 ① ② ③ ④ ⑤	22 ① ② ③ ④ ⑤	32 ① ② ③ ④ ⑤
3 ① ② ③ ④ ⑤	13 ① ② ③ ④ ⑤	23 ① ② ③ ④ ⑤	33 ① ② ③ ④ ⑤
4 ① ② ③ ④ ⑤	14 ① ② ③ ④ ⑤	24 ① ② ③ ④ ⑤	34 ① ② ③ ④ ⑤
5 ① ② ③ ④ ⑤	15 ① ② ③ ④ ⑤	25 ① ② ③ ④ ⑤	35 ① ② ③ ④ ⑤
6 ① ② ③ ④ ⑤	16 ① ② ③ ④ ⑤	26 ① ② ③ ④ ⑤	36 ① ② ③ ④ ⑤
7 ① ② ③ ④ ⑤	17 ① ② ③ ④ ⑤	27 ① ② ③ ④ ⑤	37 ① ② ③ ④ ⑤
8 ① ② ③ ④ ⑤	18 ① ② ③ ④ ⑤	28 ① ② ③ ④ ⑤	38 ① ② ③ ④ ⑤
9 ① ② ③ ④ ⑤	19 ① ② ③ ④ ⑤	29 ① ② ③ ④ ⑤	39 ① ② ③ ④ ⑤
10 ① ② ③ ④ ⑤	20 ① ② ③ ④ ⑤	30 ① ② ③ ④ ⑤	40 ① ② ③ ④ ⑤

Math, Part I

1 ① ② ③ ④ ⑤

2 ① ② ③ ④ ⑤

3

4

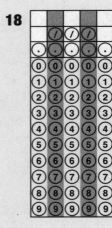

5 ① ② ③ ④ ⑤

6 ① ② ③ ④ ⑤

7 ① ② ③ ④ ⑤

8 ① ② ③ ④ ⑤

9 ① ② ③ ④ ⑤

10 ① ② ③ ④ ⑤

11 ① ② ③ ④ ⑤

12 ① ② ③ ④ ⑤

13 ① ② ③ ④ ⑤

14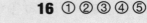

15 ① ② ③ ④ ⑤

16 ① ② ③ ④ ⑤

17 ① ② ③ ④ ⑤

18

19 ① ② ③ ④ ⑤

20 ① ② ③ ④ ⑤

21 ① ② ③ ④ ⑤

22 ① ② ③ ④ ⑤

23 ① ② ③ ④ ⑤

24 ① ② ③ ④ ⑤

25

Math, Part II

26 ① ② ③ ④ ⑤

27 ① ② ③ ④ ⑤

28 ① ② ③ ④ ⑤

29 ① ② ③ ④ ⑤

30 ① ② ③ ④ ⑤

31 ① ② ③ ④ ⑤

32 ① ② ③ ④ ⑤

33

	/	/	/	
.	.	.	.	.
0	0	0	0	0
1	1	1	1	1
2	2	2	2	2
3	3	3	3	3
4	4	4	4	4
5	5	5	5	5
6	6	6	6	6
7	7	7	7	7
8	8	8	8	8
9	9	9	9	9

34

	/	/	/	
.	.	.	.	.
0	0	0	0	0
1	1	1	1	1
2	2	2	2	2
3	3	3	3	3
4	4	4	4	4
5	5	5	5	5
6	6	6	6	6
7	7	7	7	7
8	8	8	8	8
9	9	9	9	9

35 ① ② ③ ④ ⑤

36 ① ② ③ ④ ⑤

37

	/	/	/	
.	.	.	.	.
0	0	0	0	0
1	1	1	1	1
2	2	2	2	2
3	3	3	3	3
4	4	4	4	4
5	5	5	5	5
6	6	6	6	6
7	7	7	7	7
8	8	8	8	8
9	9	9	9	9

38 ① ② ③ ④ ⑤

39 ① ② ③ ④ ⑤

40 ① ② ③ ④ ⑤

41 ① ② ③ ④ ⑤

42 ① ② ③ ④ ⑤

43

	/	/	/	
.	.	.	.	.
0	0	0	0	0
1	1	1	1	1
2	2	2	2	2
3	3	3	3	3
4	4	4	4	4
5	5	5	5	5
6	6	6	6	6
7	7	7	7	7
8	8	8	8	8
9	9	9	9	9

44 ① ② ③ ④ ⑤

45 ① ② ③ ④ ⑤

46 ① ② ③ ④ ⑤

47 ① ② ③ ④ ⑤

48 ① ② ③ ④ ⑤

49

	/	/	/	
.	.	.	.	.
0	0	0	0	0
1	1	1	1	1
2	2	2	2	2
3	3	3	3	3
4	4	4	4	4
5	5	5	5	5
6	6	6	6	6
7	7	7	7	7
8	8	8	8	8
9	9	9	9	9

50 ① ② ③ ④ ⑤